JUSTIFICATION

JUSTIFICATION

UNDERSTANDING THE
CLASSIC REFORMED DOCTRINE

J. V. FESKO

PUBLISHING
P.O. BOX 817 • PHILLIPSBURG • NEW JERSEY 08865-0817

Page design and typesetting by Lakeside Design Plus

Printed in the United States of America

Library of Congress Cataloging-in-Publication Data
Fesko, J. V., 1970–
    Justification : understanding the classic Reformed doctrine / J.V. Fesko.
        p. cm.
    Includes bibliographical references and index.
    ISBN-13: 978-1-59638-086-8 (pbk.)
    1. Justification (Christian theology) 2. Reformed Church—Doctrines. I. Title.
    BT764.3.F46 2008
    234'.7—dc22

                                                          2008005079

In memory of
John Juan Valero
(1947–69)

Dedicated to
John Valero Fesko Jr.
(2007–)

CONTENTS

PREFACE

This work is the culmination of five years of research that began in the summer of 2002. Though, in one sense, the work goes back even further. When I was in seminary in 1995 the Evangelicals and Catholics Together controversy was in full swing, and I was somewhat surprised to see debate surrounding *sola fide* surface once again in church history. In studying the sixteenth-century Reformation, I somewhat naively thought that since the doctrine of justification by faith alone was nailed down, the church would not see much debate over this subject in the future. It was several years later that I was discussing doctrinal trends with a colleague who was disenchanted with the theological debate of the day, the length of the days of creation. He told me that he had approached a number of students who were from a conservative Reformed seminary and listened to their debates over the various positions. My colleague asked these students if they had heard about the New Perspective on Paul. They blankly stared at him, revealing that they did not have the foggiest idea. He said that he could not help but think that in debating the length of the days of the creation the Reformed church was fiddling while Rome, or perhaps more fittingly Geneva, was burning. At the time I had read only one or two small monographs on the subject but decided that I should investigate the matter more thoroughly.

Initially, I had planned only on researching the New Perspective and writing several essays to crystalize my thoughts. The more I read, the more I was drawn in, and the more I wrote. Not only did I believe it was necessary to address many points brought forward by the New Perspective, but I thought it would be helpful to flesh out the historic Reformed doctrine of justification in light of the recent challenges and questions. I also wanted to address a number of issues that were scattered about in comments in chapters in books or in academic journals. Namely, I wanted to apply the insights of biblical theology to the doctrine of justification for a full-orbed systematic-theological treatment of the subject. I additionally wanted to investigate the claims of the Roman Catholic and Eastern Orthodox churches, especially in view of the recent ecumenical efforts in the broader church.

One of the most helpful things for the writing of this book was serving on the committee of my denomination, the Orthodox Presbyterian Church, that was established to critique the teachings of the New Perspective on Paul and the Federal Vision. There were many fruitful and at times lively discussions that took place around my dining-room table that proved helpful in sorting out some of the issues in my own mind. I am grateful to the men on that committee who helped me sharpen my own thinking in many different ways. In addition to this venue, I also used the present material in a series of Sunday School lectures for the adults at my church. I am thankful for the nine months of attentive listening that I received. I also used this material as the basis for a systematics elective on the doctrine of justification that I taught at Reformed Theological Seminary–Atlanta in the fall of 2006. My thanks to John Sowell for letting me teach the course and to those students who helped me iron out some of the wrinkles in the work.

I am grateful to the many colleagues and friends who helped me by reading portions of the manuscript during various stages and offering feedback and critique: Greg Beale, Jay Collier, Brent Ferry, Dick Gaffin, James Grant, Mike Horton, John Muether, Danny Olinger, Greg Reynolds, John Sowell, Jonathan Stuckert, and Lane Tipton. I am especially indebted to those friends and colleagues who were willing to read the whole manuscript and offer helpful critique: Dave VanDrunen, Bryan Estelle, Scott Clark, and Wally King. Special thanks to Marvin Padgett and the editorial staff at P&R Publishing who worked diligently to see this manuscript to publication.

Much thanks are due to my congregation, Geneva OPC, in Woodstock, Georgia, and especially to my session, Wally King and Bud Winslow. I am appreciative of their encouragement for me to pursue this project and for the book allowance that the congregation gives me, which has made doing research profoundly easier. Grace Mullen and Em Sirinides helped me find an unpublished lecture by Cornelius Van Til in the Westminster Theological Seminary library, and also assisted me when I was on campus doing research in the falls of 2005 and 2006.

I owe a great deal of thanks to my family, my parents, in-laws, and brother and sister-in-law for their prayers and encouragement. I am, however, profoundly beholden to my wife, Anneke, who at present carries our first child, who has encouraged me at more times and in more ways than I can count. I am appreciative of her willingness to let me tiptoe off in the wee hours of the morning when I would be awakened by percolating thoughts. Thank you, Wife, for your love, care, and encouragement.

It is to the memory of my uncle and namesake, John Juan Valero, that I dedicate this book. He died on the field of battle in a hamlet in South Vietnam. He has been and always will be one of my heroes, and not simply because of his posthumous Bronze Star with a "Combat V" and Purple Heart that hang in my home. It is also to my son, John Valero Fesko Jr., that I dedicate this book. My son, I pray that by God's sovereign grace you will one day embrace the wonderful gospel of Jesus Christ and begin to plumb the depths of what it means to be justified by grace alone through faith alone in Christ alone. I pray that not only you, but that many others with the help of this work will sound out the depths of God's love in Christ. *SDG.*

ABBREVIATIONS

General Abbreviations

c.	*circa*, about
cf.	*confer*, compare
e.g.	*exempli gratia*, for example
EOC	Eastern Orthodox Church
i.e.	*id est*, that is
LXX	Septuagint
MMT	*Misqat ma'ase ha-torah*
MT	Masoretic text (of the Old Testament)
NT	New Testament
OPC	Orthodox Presbyterian Church
OT	Old Testament
PCA	Presbyterian Church in America
RCC	Roman Catholic Church
s.v.	*sub verbo*, under the word
v., vv.	verse, verses
vol.	volume

Abbreviations for Translations

*	Author's own translation
ASV	Authorized Standard Version

ESV	English Standard Version
KJV	King James Version
NAB	New American Bible
NASB	New American Standard Bible
NIV	New International Version
NKJV	New King James Version
NLT	New Living Translation
NRSV	New Revised Standard Version
RSV	Revised Standard Version
Vul	Vulgate

Abbreviations for Periodicals, Reference Works, and Commentary Series

AB	Anchor Bible
ANE 2	James B. Pritchard. *The Ancient Near East*. Vol. 2. Princeton: Princeton University Press, 1958
ANF	Ante-Nicene Fathers
AOTC	Apollos Old Testament Commentary
BAGD	W. Bauer, W. F. Arndt, F. W. Gingrich, and F. W. Danker. *A Greek-English Lexicon of the New Testament and Other Early Christian Literature*. 2nd ed. Chicago: University of Chicago Press, 1979
BAR	*Biblical Archaeology Review*
BBR	*Bulletin of Biblical Research*
BDB	F. Brown, S. R. Driver, and C. A. Briggs. *A Hebrew and English Lexicon of the Old Testament*. Oxford: Oxford University Press, 1907
BECNT	Baker Exegetical Commentary on the New Testament
Bib	*Biblica*
BJRL	*Bulletin of the John Rylands University Library of Manchester*
BNTC	Black's New Testament Commentaries
BRev	*Bible Review*
BSac	*Bibliotheca Sacra*
CBQ	*Catholic Biblical Quarterly*
CH	*Church History*

CNTC	Calvin's New Testament Commentaries
CTJ	*Calvin Theological Journal*
CTQ	*Concordia Theological Quarterly*
CTS	Calvin Translation Society
EBC	Expositor's Bible Commentary
ExpTim	*Expository Times*
HBT	*Horizons in Biblical Theology*
HTR	*Harvard Theological Review*
ICC	International Critical Commentary
IJST	*International Journal of Systematic Theology*
ITQ	*Irish Theological Quarterly*
JAAR	*Journal of the American Academy of Religion*
JBL	*Journal of Biblical Literature*
JETS	*Journal of the Evangelical Theological Society*
JPSTC	Jewish Publication Society Torah Commentary
JQR	*Jewish Quarterly Review*
JRE	*Journal of Religious Ethics*
JSNT	*Journal for the Study of the New Testament*
JTS	*Journal of Theological Studies*
LC	Larger Catechism
LCC	Library of Christian Classics
LQ	*Lutheran Quarterly*
LSJ	H. G. Liddell, R. Scott, and H. S. Jones. *A Greek-English Lexicon*. Rev. ed. Oxford: Clarendon, 1996
LW	Luther's Works
MAJT	*Mid-America Journal of Theology*
NCB	New Century Bible
NIB	The New Interpreter's Bible
NICNT	New International Commentary on the New Testament
NICOT	New International Commentary on the Old Testament
NIDNTT	*New International Dictionary of New Testament Theology*. 4 vols. Edited by Colin Brown. Grand Rapids: Zondervan, 1986
NIDOTTE	*New International Dictionary of Old Testament Theology and Exegesis*. 5 vols. Edited by Willem A. VanGemeren. Grand Rapids: Zondervan, 1997

NIGTC	New International Greek Testament Commentary
NIVAC	NIV Application Commentary
NovT	*Novum Testamentum*
NPNF[1/2]	Nicene and Post-Nicene Fathers, First and Second Series
NSBT	New Studies in Biblical Theology
NTC	New Testament Commentary
NTS	*New Testament Studies*
OTL	Old Testament Library
PNTC	Pillar New Testament Commentary
PR	*Presbyterian Review*
ProEccl	*Pro ecclesia*
RevQ	*Revue de Qumran*
RRJ	*Revival and Reformation Journal*
RTR	*Reformed Theological Review*
SC	Shorter Catechism
SEÅ	*Svensk exegetisk årsbok*
SJT	*Scottish Journal of Theology*
StPatr	*Studia Patristica*
SVTQ	*St. Vladimir's Theological Quarterly*
TDNT	*Theological Dictionary of the New Testament.* 10 vols. Edited by Gerhard Kittel. Grand Rapids: Eerdmans, 1964–76
TDOT	*Theological Dictionary of the Old Testament.* 15 vols. Edited by G. Johannes Botterweck. Grand Rapids: Eerdmans, 1974–
Them	*Themelios*
TNTC	Tyndale New Testament Commentary
TOTC	Tyndale Old Testament Commentary
TWOT	*Theological Wordbook of the Old Testament.* 2 vols. Edited by R. Laird Harris et al. Chicago: Moody, 1980
TynBul	*Tyndale Bulletin*
WBC	Word Biblical Commentary
WCF	Westminster Confession of Faith
WTJ	*Westminster Theological Journal*
ZNW	*Zeitschrift für die neutestamentliche Wissenschaft*
ZTK	*Zeitschrift für Theologie und Kirche*

INTRODUCTION

The doctrine of justification has always been a point of contention for the covenant community, which is especially evident in Paul's letter to the Galatian church. If a church planted by the apostle Paul could quickly depart from the gospel, which has at its root the doctrine of justification, then it is no wonder that the church has witnessed no small uproar over this doctrine throughout the years. Whether in the Augustine-Pelagius debates in the patristic era, the disputes that sparked and fueled the Reformation with Martin Luther's ninety-five theses, the contentions over the center of Paul's theology in the nineteenth century, or the current debates surrounding justification and the New Perspective on Paul, the doctrine of justification has always been a subject of contention.[1] While there has

1. See Augustine, *Four Anti-Pelagian Writings*, ed. Thomas P. Halton et al., trans. John A. Mourant and William J. Collinge, Fathers of the Church (Washington: Catholic University of America Press, 1992); Pelagius, *Pelagius's Commentary on St Paul's Epistle to the Romans*, ed. and trans. Theodore de Bruyn (Oxford: Oxford University Press, 1993); B. B. Warfield, "Augustine and the Pelagian Controversy," in *The Works of B. B. Warfield*, ed. E. D. Warfield et al., 10 vols. (1930; Grand Rapids: Baker, 1981), 4:289–412; W. S. Babcock, "Augustine and Paul: The case of Romans 9," *StPatr* 16/2 (1985): 474–79; John Calvin, *Institutes of the Christian Religion*, ed. John T. McNeill, trans. Ford Lewis Battles, LCC 20–21 (Philadelphia: Westminster, 1960), 3.11.1ff.; Alister McGrath, *Iustitia Dei*, 2 vols. (1986; Cambridge: Cambridge University Press, 1995), 2:1–97; F. C. Baur, *Paul the Apostle of Jesus Christ* (1873; Peabody, MA: Hendrickson, 2003); Albert Schweitzer, *The Mysticism of Paul the Apostle*, trans. William Montgomery (1931; Baltimore: Johns Hopkins University Press, 1998); N. T. Wright, *What St. Paul Really Said* (Grand Rapids: Eerdmans, 1997); Stephen Westerholm, "The New Perspective at Twenty-Five," in *Justification and Variegated Nomism*, ed. D. A. Carson, Peter T. O'Brien, and Mark A. Seifrid (Grand Rapids: Baker, 2004), 2:1–38; David E. Aune, "Recent Readings of Paul Related to Justification by Faith," in *Rereading Paul Together*, ed. David E. Aune (Grand Rapids: Baker, 2006), 188–246; R. Scott

certainly been no shortage of monographs on the subject from both Protestant and Roman Catholic theologians, there is much to commend a fresh exploration of the doctrine in the light of past and recent debate.[2]

It is certainly fair to say that there is nothing new under the sun (Eccl. 1:9), and in this regard, we may say that the same issues continue to swirl about; at the same time it is also fair to say that different issues surface in different ages. In earlier centuries, debate largely focused upon the *ordo salutis*, or the order of salvation. In current debates, many questions have arisen regarding not only the *ordo salutis* but also how justification relates to the *historia salutis*, or redemptive history. Additionally, given that in recent years we have witnessed the discovery of many new documents from the first century, we have more information about the first-century context in which the New Testament (NT) arose. Given these factors, it seems that a fresh restatement of the classic Reformed doctrine of justification is in order.

Recent monographs on the doctrine of justification have largely focused upon the *ordo salutis*.[3] While this is a necessary connection to explain, as much of the debate surrounding justification concerns the relationship of the doctrine to good works, at the same time a more thorough treatment of the doctrine is needed. As we will see, while the doctrine of justification should not be the central dogma of one's theological system, it is nevertheless helpful not only to explicate the doctrine but to also explain how the one doctrine relates to the rest of the loci of systematic theology. For example, what theological presuppositions must be explored? There are matters, therefore, that concern prolegomena. How does justification

---

Clark, "How We Got Here: The Roots of the Current Controversy over Justification," in *Covenant, Justification, and Pastoral Ministry*, ed. R. Scott Clark (Phillipsburg, NJ: P&R, 2007), 3–24; J. V. Fesko (contributor), *Justification* (Willow Grove, PA: Committee on Christian Education for the OPC, 2007); *Report of Ad Interim Study Committee on Federal Vision, New Perspective, and Auburn Avenue Theology* (Atlanta: Presbyterian Church of America, 2007); *Doctrinal Testimony regarding Recent Errors* (Dyer, IN: Mid-America Reformed Seminary, 2007).

2. E.g., James Buchanan, *The Doctrine of Justification* (1867; Edinburgh: Banner of Truth, 1991); Eberhard Jüngel, *Justification*, trans. Jeffrey F. Cayzer (Edinburgh: T & T Clark, 2001); Hans Küng, *Justification* (1964; Louisville: Westminster John Knox, 2004); Anthony N. S. Lane, *Justification by Faith in Catholic-Protestant Dialogue* (Edinburgh: T & T Clark, 2002); John Piper, *Counted Righteous in Christ* (Wheaton, IL: Crossway, 2002); Albrecht Ritschl, *The Christian Doctrine of Justification and Reconciliation* (1902; Eugene, OR: Wipf & Stock, 2004); Mark A. Seifrid, *Christ, Our Righteousness* (Downers Grove, IL: InterVarsity, 2000); R. C. Sproul, *Faith Alone* (Grand Rapids: Baker, 1995); Robert Traill, *Justification Vindicated* (1692; Edinburgh: Banner of Truth, 2002).

3. So Buchanan, *Justification*; Sproul, *Faith Alone*; Piper, *Counted Righteous*.

relate to protology, that is, man as he was initially created, and Christology, the person and work of Christ? Related to the question of the first and last Adams is the greater question of the structure of redemptive history. Few make an effort to place justification in the *historia salutis*, or relate it to biblical theology. If Paul's soteriology is his eschatology, then this of course must have an impact upon one's understanding of redemptive history, salvation, and eschatology.[4] In this regard, we will, as Geerhardus Vos long ago maintained, employ biblical theology to serve the queen of the theological disciplines, systematic theology, to obtain a better understanding of the doctrine of justification.[5]

Other important questions surround not the grand picture of redemptive history but the narrower question of the first-century historical context. What issues, for example, did Paul face that caused him to set forth his doctrine of justification in his epistles to Galatia and Rome? Understanding justification in its historical context, however, has become a much more challenging task, as many common assumptions have been challenged by those holding to the New Perspective on Paul. Not only have many common assumptions about first-century Judaism been questioned, but many of the traditional elements of the doctrine of justification have been recast in the light of the supposed new evidence from the first century. Moreover, scholars have noted that the fields of systematic theology and biblical studies are often separated by a wide gulf. David Aune comments, "Systematic theologians are rarely acquainted with recent trends in biblical scholarship, and many biblical scholars are functionally illiterate when it comes to systematic theology."[6] In an effort, therefore, to close the gap between systematic theology and biblical studies, we will explore and interact primarily with the writings of N. T. Wright, as his work has been the most influential in the Reformed community. We will therefore enter into dialogue with Wright on matters pertaining to the historical context, the doctrine of justification proper, and the related doctrine of imputation. It is not only important, though, to interact with the latest scholarship on the doctrine of justification, but also to relate it to key elements of the *ordo salutis*.

4. See Geerhardus Vos, *The Pauline Eschatology* (1930; Phillipsburg, NJ: P&R, 1994), 1–41.

5. Geerhardus Vos, "The Idea of Biblical Theology as a Science and as a Theological Discipline," in *Redemptive History and Biblical Interpretation*, ed. Richard B. Gaffin Jr. (Phillipsburg, NJ: P&R, 1980), 3–24, esp. 23–24.

6. Aune, "Recent Readings of Paul," 242.

What are the connections of justification to the believer's union with Christ, sanctification, and the final judgment? Not only does one's understanding of justification impact these doctrines, but so too one's ecclesiology. What type of impact does one's understanding of justification have for the doctrine of the church and issues such as the nature of the church, questions concerning corporate justification, missions, pastoral counseling, and the sacrament of baptism? There are also questions surrounding justification and ecumenism. Historically, it has been the doctrine of justification, among many other issues, that has separated Protestant from both the Roman Catholic and Eastern Orthodox churches. Yet in recent years there has been a flurry of ecumenical effort at moving forward toward reunification. Are the battles between East and West, Protestant and Catholic, over? Some would say yes.[7] We will explore these issues, namely the question of justification and ecumenism.

This essay is a restatement of the classic Reformed doctrine of justification by grace alone through faith alone in Christ alone; justification is based upon the imputed righteousness of Jesus Christ, which is the sole ground and basis for the believer's declaration of righteousness both in the present and at the final judgment. Some will perhaps ask, If this is a classic restatement of the Reformed doctrine of justification, then what need is there for yet another monograph on the subject? While this essay is a restatement of the classic Reformed view, it is unique in that it does so with an eye to history, doctrinal issues including both the *ordo* and *historia salutis*, and the future, particularly the ecumenical future vis-à-vis the Roman Catholic and Eastern Orthodox churches.

Before we proceed, one should note a few things regarding the nature of this essay. First, we must understand the relationship between the Scriptures and doctrinal confessions, especially the Westminster Standards. Some will undoubtedly balk at appeals to a confession of faith; the assumption is likely that appeal is no longer to the Scriptures but rather to dogmatic formulation, or church tradition. While confessions have certainly been used in such a manner, this is not the case in this essay. Rather, appeal will be made to Scripture to substantiate that the historic Reformed confessional formulations on justification are still sound and that

---

7. So Mark A. Noll and Carolyn Nystrom, *Is the Reformation Over?* (Grand Rapids: Baker, 2005).

they reflect the teaching of Scripture. At the same time, however, reference ultimately to confessional standards does not represent an appeal to the formula but to the exegetical tradition that stands behind the formula.[8]

Second, if one examines this essay by perusing the table of contents, it is perhaps easy to mistake this work for a system of justification. This is a hasty conclusion. Rather, this essay explores the doctrine of justification by relating it to multiple aspects, such as historical theology, the *ordo* and *historia salutis*, and other loci of systematic theology. While this work certainly touches on many facets of soteriology, it is not intended to be an essay on the locus of soteriology but rather the narrower issue of one part of the *ordo salutis*, namely justification by faith alone. Relating the doctrine of justification to the other doctrines and loci with which it is connected is an effort to acknowledge the organic nature of systematic theology.

Third, at present there is debate in the Reformed community over the so-called Federal Vision, or Auburn Avenue theology. For the most part, this is a difficult movement to trace, as those associated with it disseminate much of their work through the internet rather than through traditional publishing. What one might write today is possibly retracted or modified days later. In addition to this, much of their thought on the doctrine of justification is not original but derivative, either adopting or modifying the work of others for their own formulations. We will therefore explore and interact with some of the sources to which Federal Vision advocates appeal. Moreover, others have ably critiqued the Federal Vision, and we do not want to revisit the same ground.[9] Keeping these three caveats in mind, we can move forward and begin where any study of doctrine must, with its historical development.

---

8. See Richard A. Muller, *Post-Reformation Reformed Dogmatics*, 4 vols. (Grand Rapids: Baker, 2003), 2:63–223. Contra Paul A. Rainbow, *The Way of Salvation* (Carlisle: Paternoster, 2005), 5; N. T. Wright, "The Letter to the Galatians: Exegesis and Theology," in *Between Two Horizons*, ed. Joel B. Green and Max Turner (Grand Rapids: Eerdmans, 2002), 206, 213, 215–17; John R. Franke, *The Character of Theology* (Grand Rapids: Baker, 2005), 43. Cf. Vos, "The Idea of Biblical Theology," 23–24; B. B. Warfield, "The Task and Method of Systematic Theology," in *The Works of B. B. Warfield*, ed. E. D. Warfield et al., 10 vols. (1932; Grand Rapids: Baker, 1981), 9:91–108.

9. See E. Calvin Beisner, ed., *The Auburn Avenue Theology* (Fort Lauderdale: Knox Theological Seminary, 2004); Steve Wilkins and Duane Garner, *The Federal Vision* (Monroe, LA: Athanasius Press, 2004); Guy P. Waters, *The Federal Vision and Covenant Theology* (Phillipsburg, NJ: P&R, 2006), esp. 59–95; also see the denominational reports of the PCA, OPC, United Reformed Churches, Bible Presbyterian Churches, and the Reformed Church in the US, as well as the *Doctrinal Testimony* of Mid-America Reformed Seminary.

1

JUSTIFICATION IN CHURCH HISTORY

Robert Traill (1642–1716), who wrote about controversies in his own day, gives an excellent summary of the key issues surrounding the doctrine of justification: "The subject of the controversy is the justifying grace of God in Jesus Christ. Owned it is by both sides: and both fear it is abused, either by turning it into wantonness, hence the noise of Antinomianism, or by corrupting it with the mixture of works, hence the fears on the other side, of Arminianism."[1] Traill identifies the two sides of the spectrum, on the one hand, antinomianism, and on the other, Arminianism, neonomianism, or legalism. The doctrine of justification was neither supposed to be a license to sin, something the apostle Paul countered in his own missionary journeys (Rom. 6:1–2), nor was it supposed to be a new starting point that wiped the slate clean with Jesus as a new Moses giving a new law where salvation was based upon a combination of God's grace and one's good works, which again was something that Paul faced (Rom. 3:20; Gal. 2:16).

1. Robert Traill, *Justification Vindicated* (1692; Edinburgh: Banner of Truth, 2002), 5.

Between the two poles of antinomianism and neonomianism Traill identifies a third position, "Luther gave the stroke, and plucked down the foundation, and all by opening one vein, long hid before, wherein lies the touchtone of all truth and doctrine, as the only principal origin of our salvation, which is, our free justification, by faith only, in Christ the Son of God."[2] While perhaps guilty of overgeneralization, it is nevertheless fair to say that the history of the doctrine of justification has moved between these poles with the orthodox position lying in the middle, between the Scylla of antinomianism and the Charybdis of neonomianism. It is necessary to survey briefly the history of the doctrine of justification so that one may see its development to establish that justification exists between the poles of antinomianism and neonomianism. A brief survey cannot do justice to the subject of the history of the doctrine, as it has been the subject of a number of monographs; nevertheless it is helpful to reconnoiter the terrain to familiarize ourselves with the major trends and players in the development of this doctrine.[3] We will therefore survey the history of the development of justification, summarizing the characteristics that dominate each period's expression of the doctrine and identifying key issues that must be addressed in the exegetical and theological exposition.

The Patristic Era (100–600)

Early Church Fathers

The patristic era lacks a precise formulation of the doctrine of salvation, and more specifically a doctrine of justification. Louis Berkhof (1873–1957) explains that the church fathers' "representations are naturally indefinite, imperfect, and incomplete, and sometimes even erroneous and self-contradictory."[4] In the writings of the church fathers, one can find a number of significant statements that show that some had a basic concept

---

2. Ibid., 32.

3. See, e.g., Albrecht Ritschl, *A Critical History of the Christian Doctrine of Justification and Reconciliation*, trans. John S. Black (Edinburgh: Edmonston and Douglas, 1872); Alister E. McGrath, *Iustitia Dei*, 2 vols. (1986; Cambridge: Cambridge University Press, 1995).

4. Louis Berkhof, *The History of Christian Doctrines* (1937; Edinburgh: Banner of Truth, 1991), 203. For an excellent essay on the doctrine of justification, one that proved quite helpful for many of the patristic citations in this section, see Nick Needham, "Justification in the Early Church Fathers," in *Justification in Perspective*, ed. Bruce L. McCormack (Grand Rapids: Baker, 2006), 25–54.

of justification by faith. In John Chrysostom's (c. 347–407) sermons on Romans, he gives a definition of justification when he answers the question "What does the word justified mean?" Chrysostom answers, "That, if there could be a trial and an examination of the things He had done for the Jews, and of what had been done on their part towards Him, the victory would be with God, and all the right on His side."[5] Chrysostom clearly recognizes that "justify" is a forensic or law-court term. One can find similar statements in the writings of Clement of Rome (d. c. 98), Justin Martyr (100–165), and Hippolytus (d. 235).[6] In addition to the recognition of the meaning of "justify," we also find scattered throughout patristic literature the term placed in antithesis with the term "condemn." For example, Gregory of Nazianzus (329–89) writes: "For where sin abounded Grace did much more abound; and if a taste condemned us, how much more does the Passion of Christ justify us?"[7]

In terms of several of the constituent elements of the doctrine of justification, one can also find the ideas that justification is the forgiveness of sins, involves the imputation of righteousness, and that it is by faith alone. In Chrysostom's homilies on Romans, we find the following where he equates the forgiveness of sins with justification: "If any then were to gainsay, they do the same as if a person who after committing great sins was unable to defend himself in court, but was condemned and going to be punished, and then being by the royal pardon forgiven, should have the effrontery after his forgiveness to boast and say that he had done no sin."[8] We see that "royal pardon" and "forgiven" are synonymous with justification.[9] We also find Justin Martyr affirming the idea of the imputation of righteousness in justification: "For the goodness and loving-kindness of God, and His boundless riches, hold righteous and sinless the man who, as Ezekiel tells, repents of sins; and reckon sinful, unrighteous, and impious the man who falls away from piety and righteousness to unrighteousness and ungodliness."[10]

5. John Chrysostom, *Homilies on Romans* 6, in NPNF[1] 6:372.

6. See Clement of Rome, *First Epistle to the Corinthians*, 16, in ANF, 1:9; Justin Martyr, *First Apology*, 51, in ANF, 1:180; Hippolytus, *Refutation of All Heresies* 7.22, in ANF, 5:114.

7. Gregory of Nazianzus, *Orations* 38.4, in NPNF[2] 7:346; see also Tertullian, *Of Patience* 7, in ANF 3:711; Athanasius, *To the Bishops of Egypt*, §19, in NPNF[2] 4:233.

8. Chrysostom, *Homilies on Romans* 7, in NPNF[1] 11:378–79.

9. Needham, "Justification in the Early Church Fathers," 31.

10. Justin Martyr, *Dialogue with Trypho* 47, in ANF, 1:218–19; see other references in Needham, "Justification in the Early Church Fathers," 32–36.

In addition to this, we can also find some church fathers teaching, at least substantively, justification by faith alone, though at times even the very phrase does appear in some places. Origen (c. 185–c. 254), commenting upon Luke 23:43, writes:

> A man is justified by faith. The works of the law can make no contribution to this. Where there is no faith which might justify the believer, even if there are works of the law these are not based on the foundation of faith. Even if they are good in themselves they cannot justify the one who does them, because faith is lacking, and faith is the mark of those who are justified by God.[11]

Similarly, one finds an equally clear affirmation of the centrality of faith in justification in the Western church from the pen of Clement of Rome who writes: "And we, too, not justified by ourselves, nor by our own wisdom, or understanding, or godliness, or works which we have wrought in holiness of heart; but by that faith through which, from the beginning, Almighty God has justified all men."[12] Though Origen and Clement do not say "faith alone," it appears that is what they intend. One can find similar statements in the writings of Tertullian (160–220), Irenaeus (c. 115–90), and Eusebius (c. 275–339).[13]

In his well-documented essay, Nick Needham comes to the conclusion that in the Fathers of the first four centuries there is a major strand of justification teaching where the meaning is forensic, a not-guilty verdict, an acquittal, a declaration of righteousness, a non-imputation of sin, and an imputation of righteousness.[14] Similarly, Louis Berkhof observes that among the early church fathers, Irenaeus and Origen in the East and Tertullian, Cyprian (200–258), and Ambrose (c. 339–97) in the West all placed strong emphasis upon the centrality of faith in salvation to the exclusion of works.[15] This is not to say, however, that every patristic expression was equally as clear on the centrality of faith.

11. Quoted in Thomas Oden, *The Justification Reader* (Grand Rapids: Eerdmans, 2002), 45.
12. Clement, *First Epistle 32*, in ANF, 1:13.
13. Tertullian, *Against Marcion* 5.3, in ANF, 3:433–35; Irenaeus, *Against Heresies* 4.16.2, in ANF, 1:481; Eusebius, *Church History* 1.4, in NPNF[2] 1:88; see Needham, "Justification in the Early Church Fathers," 33.
14. Needham, "Justification in the Early Church Fathers," 36.
15. Berkhof, *History of Christian Doctrines*, 204. See also Oden, *Justification Reader*, 44–47.

In this vein one sees the coordination of faith and works as co-instrumental in one's salvation, which is no more evident than in the development of the doctrine of baptism.[16] It was Tertullian, for example, who though he placed a strong emphasis upon faith, nevertheless argued that in baptism sins were washed away. Contrasting pagan washing rituals with Christian baptism, Tertullian argues, "Not that *in* the waters we obtain the Holy Spirit; but in the water, under (the witness of) the angel, we are cleansed, and prepared *for* the Holy Spirit."[17] As this idea of baptism gained acceptance, many early church fathers understood baptism to bring the forgiveness of sins as well as remove the guilt of original sin.[18] This is an idea that would persist through the Middle Ages and up to the present within the Roman Catholic Church (RCC).

In addition to this, it seems as though the relationship between the two testaments, or more specifically the relationship between Moses and Christ, or law and grace, had not been thoroughly established as it would later be in the Reformation. Thomas Oden makes the claim that one can find anticipations of Luther's doctrine of justification in the church fathers. Yet at times there are some questions surrounding his methodology. For example, Oden marshals only one patristic citation for the doctrine of imputation from Clement of Alexandria (c. 150–c. 215). The citation, however, is somewhat questionable, as Clement does emphasize the priority of faith, perhaps even *sola fide*, but merely quotes Romans 4:3, which is not necessarily an explicit expression of the idea of imputation on Clement's part.[19] Similarly, concerning the law-gospel hermeneutic one finds views at odds with the Reformation understanding.[20]

In the Epistle of Barnabas (c. 70–138), we read that God has abolished the old order of Moses so that "the new law of our Lord Jesus Christ, which is without the yoke of necessity, might have a human oblation."[21] Likewise, Justin Martyr spoke of the gospel as a "new law," and Tertul-

16. Berkhof, *History of Christian Doctrines*, 204–5.
17. Tertullian, *On Baptism* 5–6, in ANF, 3:671–72; see also Jaroslav Pelikan, *The Christian Tradition*, 5 vols. (Chicago: University of Chicago Press, 1971), 1:164–65.
18. Berkhof, *History of Christian Doctrines*, 205.
19. Oden, *Justification Reader*, 92; Clement of Alexandria, *Stromata* 5.1, in ANF, 2:444–46.
20. T. F. Torrance, *The Doctrine of Grace in the Apostolic Fathers* (Grand Rapids: Eerdmans, 1959).
21. Epistle of Barnabas, 2, in ANF, 1:138. For an excellent essay on the law-gospel hermeneutic, one from which a number of citations were drawn for this section, see R. Scott Clark,

lian employed the same old law–new law categories: "And so there is incumbent on us a necessity binding us, since we have premised that a new law was predicted by the prophets, and that not such as had been already given to their fathers at the time when He led them forth from the land of Egypt, to show and prove, on the one hand, that that old law had ceased, and on the other that the promised new law is now in operation."[22] Given this confusion of law and gospel, it is fair to say that for some church fathers it would be difficult to affirm a Reformation doctrine of justification because of the differing hermeneutical presuppositions. As Scott Clark observes:

> This is not an indictment of the fathers. To criticize the fathers for failing to use Luther's (or Calvin's) language is rather like criticizing Aquinas for not using Einstein's physics. The conceptual framework within which most early postapostolic Christians read the Scriptures made it difficult for them to see the forensic nature of justification. They tended to think in realistic terms rather than forensic categories. Because Christians were frequently marginalized and criticized as immoral and impious, the fathers placed great stress on piety and morality. They did not, however, always ground their parenesis in the gospel in the same way Paul did.[23]

It was during the Pelagius-Augustine debate, however, where matters pertaining to soteriology, or more specifically justification, were defined with greater precision.

The Augustine-Pelagius Debate

If the early patristic period was marked by a confusion regarding the relationship between faith and works in salvation, the debate between Augustine (354–430) and Pelagius (d. 425) brought greater clarity. One should note, though, that Augustine never addressed the topic of justification in a precise way, and he never devoted a treatise, sermon, or letter to the subject.[24] Nevertheless, it is helpful to see what contribution

---

"Letter and Spirit: Law and Gospel in Reformed Preaching," in *Covenant, Justification, and Pastoral Ministry*, ed. R. Scott Clark (Phillipsburg, NJ: P&R, 2006), 331–64.

22. Tertullian, *An Answer to the Jews* 6, in ANF, 3:157; Clark, "Letter and Spirit," 335.

23. Clark, "Letter and Spirit," 334.

24. David F. Wright, "Justification in Augustine," in *Justification in Perspective*, 55. For a general survey of the debate, see B. B. Warfield, "Augustine and the Pelagian Controversy," in

Augustine brings to the development of the doctrine, as Augustine plays a significant role in the sixteenth-century debates on justification.

Pelagius denied the doctrine of original sin and argued that sin was passed, not ontologically or forensically, but by imitation. Commenting on Romans 5:12, Pelagius writes: "By example or by pattern. . . . As long as they sin the same way, they likewise die."[25] This means, of course, that one could by his works merit his justification. While God's grace was helpful, it was not absolutely necessary. Augustine, on the other hand, held to a strong doctrine of original sin, which made the grace of God absolutely necessary and antecedent to the believer's good works. Augustine writes: "Grace is therefore of him who calls, and the consequent good works of him who receives grace. Good works do not produce grace but are produced by grace. Fire is not hot in order that it may burn, but because it burns. A wheel does not run nicely in order that it may be round, but because it is round."[26] Given the necessary priority of the grace of God, Augustine's formulation of justification placed a strong emphasis upon the necessity of faith to the exclusion of works.

Augustine understood that when the Scripture speaks of the "righteousness of God" (Rom. 1:17), it refers not to the righteousness by which God himself is righteous but that by which he justifies sinners.[27] This means that for Augustine, the sinner's justification is a free gift from God given through faith: "In a word, not by the law of works, but by the law of faith; not by the letter, but by the spirit; not by the merits of deeds, but by free grace."[28] So then, faith received great emphasis in Augustine's understanding of justification, though it should also be noted that his view of justification was more holistic. Justification was not merely a forensic declaration of righteousness but also the transformation of the sinner.[29] Historically some have sought to explain Augustine's views on justification by appeal to the translation of Hebrew and Greek terms into Latin.

The Works of B. B. Warfield, ed. Ethelbert Warfield et al., 10 vols. (1930; Grand Rapids: Baker, 1981), 10:289–412.

25. Pelagius, *Pelagius's Commentary on St Paul's Epistle to the Romans*, trans. Theodore de Bruyn (Oxford: Oxford University Press, 1998), ad loc., 92.

26. Augustine, *To Simplician—On Various Questions*, in *Augustine: Earlier Writings*, ed. John Baillie et al., trans. John H. S. Burleigh, LCC 6 (London: SCM Press, 1953), 1.2.3 (p. 388).

27. Augustine, *On the Spirit and the Letter* 11, in NPNF[1] 5:87.

28. Ibid., 22, in NPNF[1] 5:93.

29. Berkhof, *History of Christian Doctrines*, 207.

Alister McGrath explains that the initial transmission of a scriptural Hebrew or Greek concept into Latin affected the development of the doctrine of justification. He notes, for example, that *dikaioun* ("to justify") was translated by the Latin term *iustificare* ("to make righteous").[30] In other words, in the translation from Greek to Latin, the forensic nature of the verb was lost and replaced by a transformative term. "Viewed theologically," writes McGrath, "this transition resulted in a shift of emphasis from *iustitia coram Deo* to *iustitia in hominibus*. This shift of emphasis and reference from God to man is inevitably accompanied by an anthropocentricity in the discussion of justification which is quite absent from the biblical material."[31] Yet one has to wonder whether he can pin the development of the doctrine in Augustine, or in the Middle Ages, on the translation of the verb alone.

There are two factors that one should consider in this matter. First, there is the common assumption that Augustine rarely if ever used the Greek NT. Some often assume that Augustine used only the Vulgate.[32] There is evidence, however, that demonstrates that Augustine used and interacted with the Greek text. Gerald Bonner explains that Augustine was known to verify his biblical references against the Greek originals; he was not satisfied with the Latin text alone. As evidence, Bonner cites a letter written by Augustine in 414 where he compared readings of Romans 5:14 in a number of different codices.[33] Hence, it seems that one cannot say that Augustine was ignorant of the Greek NT.[34]

Second, one must take into account the greater scope of Augustine's thought, particularly his realism, which seems a more likely source for his confusion of justification and sanctification.[35] The apostle Paul worked exclusively in legal or forensic categories in his doctrine of justification, whereas Augustine did not strictly do the same. Augustine understood original sin and its transmission in realistic categories, in that sin is trans-

---

30. McGrath, *Iustitia Dei*, 1.16.
31. Ibid., 1:15–16.
32. So Adolf von Harnack, *The History of Dogma*, ed. T. K. Cheyne and A. B. Bruce, trans. James Millar, 5 vols. (London: Williams and Norgate, 1898), 5:215; see also John M. Rist, "Augustine on Free Will and Predestination," *JTS* 20/2 (1969): 430–31.
33. Gerald Bonner, "Les origines africaines de la doctrine augustinienne sur la chute et le péché originel," in *God's Decree and Destiny* (London: Variorum Reprints, 1987), 109.
34. Wright, "Justification in Augustine," 56–66.
35. Clark, "Letter and Spirit," 334.

mitted through natural descent. Conversely, the grace of God is infused in the sinner to counteract the effects of original sin.[36] Augustine also understood Romans 5:12 in realistic terms and, as noted above, was insistent upon reading the passage, in spite of his knowledge of the Greek codices, as a locative, *in quo omnes peccaverunt* ("in whom all sinned").[37] It seems like a reasonable possibility that his philosophical presuppositions rather than his knowledge of Greek grammar could have driven his exegesis. Moreover, in baptism, the church washes away original sin:

> For by this grace He engrafts into His body even baptized infants, who certainly have not yet become able to imitate anyone. As therefore He, in whom all are made alive, besides offering Himself as an example of righteousness to those who imitate Him, gives also to those who believe on Him the hidden grace of His Spirit, which He secretly infuses even into infants.[38]

Given these theological and philosophical commitments, it seems impossible that Augustine could construct a purely forensic understanding of justification. If we briefly look forward to the Reformation, the Reformers rejected this ontological conception of sin and grace, and returned to a forensic understanding. They looked at the sinner's legal relationship to the first and last Adams. Just as the sin of Adam is imputed to those in Adam, so too the righteousness of Christ is imputed to those who are in him. This ontological versus legal understanding of justification colors the development of the doctrine not only through the Middle Ages but well into the present day. In fact, as we will see in the chapter on the RCC, it is something that still separates Protestants from Catholics, and one might add the Eastern Orthodox Church.

Semi-Pelagianism and Later Augustinianism

If Augustine stressed man's inability to justify himself and the absolute necessity of the grace of God, and Pelagius stressed man's ability to justify himself by his own works apart from the grace of God, various theologians determined that a via media was the appropriate way to resolve the conflict. Semi-Pelagianism arose from certain theologians such as

---

36. Augustine, *On Forgiveness of Sins and Baptism*, 1.20, in NPNF[1] 5:22.

37. See Augustine, *Epistolae quas scripsit reliquo tempore (ab anno 411 ad 430)*, in *Patrologia Latina*, ed. J.-P. Migne (Paris, 1841), cols. 683–84.

38. Augustine, *On Forgiveness of Sins and Baptism* 1.10, in NPNF[1] 5:18–19.

John Cassian (c. 360–c. 430), who was uneasy with Augustine's views on predestination, grace, and human free will. Semi-Pelagians argued that man was unable to perform saving good works without the assistance of divine grace. It seems that once again the popular coordination of faith and works was brought forward in semi-Pelagianism.[39] Nevertheless, the church condemned Pelagianism at the Council of Ephesus (431) and again at the Synod of Orange (529), which also rejected semi-Pelagianism. Canon five of the Synod of Orange states:

> If anyone says that not only the increase of faith but also its beginning and the very desire for faith, by which we believe in him who justifies the ungodly and come to the regeneration of holy baptism—if anyone says that this belongs to us by nature and not by a gift of grace, that is, by the inspiration of the Holy Spirit amending our will and turning it from unbelief to faith and from godlessness to godliness, it is proof that he is opposed to the teaching of the apostles.[40]

So, then, the church embraced Augustine's understanding of justification, though this does not mean that the great African theologian had defined the relationship between justification and sanctification or how justification related to baptism. Moreover, the inheritors of Augustine's theological legacy did not reproduce his views with the same emphases.

Berkhof describes the elements in Augustine's soteriology that gained greater attention by subsequent theologians:

1. Participation in the grace of God is sometimes made dependent on the church and its sacraments.
2. Regeneration could be lost.
3. The doctrine of justification by faith is represented in a way that can hardly be reconciled with the doctrine of free grace.

Because Augustine did not distinguish between justification and sanctification, faith appropriated not only the forgiveness of sins but also regeneration, which enabled man to perform good works that merit eternal

---

39. Berkhof, *History of Christian Doctrines*, 207–8.
40. "The Doctrinal Chapters of the Synod of Orange," in *Creeds and Confessions of Faith in the Christian Tradition*, ed. Jaroslav Pelikan and Valerie Hotchkiss, 3 vols. (New Haven: Yale University Press, 2003), 1:693.

life. Berkhof summarizes Augustine's view by saying, "Faith justifies, not because it appropriates the righteousness of Jesus Christ, but because it works by love."[41] It is these elements that later theologians would emphasize which would bring about the resurgence, despite the rejection of the Synod of Orange, of semi-Pelagianism in the Middle Ages.

Summary

We have seen how in the patristic era there is an emphasis upon the necessity of faith in one's justification and the foundational antecedent grace of God. These are important scriptural elements of the doctrine of justification. However, we also see that elements of the *ordo salutis* were not properly distinguished and that justification and sanctification were confounded, which is especially evident in the coordination of baptism and justification as well as in the patristic realistic understanding of sin and grace. If we set up the poles of antinomianism and neonomianism, we may say that the doctrine of justification oscillated between right of center and the neonomian pole. Also, an important element of a proper biblical understanding of justification that is almost absent at this point is the doctrine of imputation. Nevertheless, the doctrine of imputation does not hinge ultimately on whether it finds expression in the early church but in Scripture.

The Middle Ages (600–1500)

Thomas Aquinas

Unfortunately, because Augustine did not distinguish between justification and sanctification, confusion of the two distinct elements of the *ordo salutis* was only intensified in the Middle Ages. A common teaching of the Middle Ages was that justification was effected by the infusion of sanctifying grace into the soul by God. It was not conceived of in legal terms of the imputation of Christ's righteousness to the believer but rather in ontological-realistic terms. Thomas Aquinas (1225–74), for example, argues that justification is the remission of sins, the infusion of grace, and the turning of the will to God.[42]

---

41. Berkhof, *History of Christian Doctrines*, 208; see also McGrath, *Iustitia Dei*, 1:30.

42. Thomas Aquinas, *Summa Theologica*, 5 vols. (Westminster, MD: Christian Classics, 1946–47), Ia2ae q. 113 a. 2.

Once again, as Augustine before him, Thomas therefore understood justification as the process of being made just.[43] In this regard, Thomas was deeply influenced by neo-Platonism, which is evident in his doctrine of participation in the divine essence. Thomas writes:

> Nothing can act beyond its species, since the cause must always be more powerful than its effect. Now the gift of grace surpasses every capability of created nature, since it is nothing short of a partaking of the Divine Nature. And thus it is impossible that any creature should cause grace. For it is as necessary that God alone should deify, bestowing a partaking of the Divine Nature by a participated likeness, as it is impossible that anything save fire should enkindle.[44]

We see that Thomas here affirms a doctrine of divinization, or theosis, in that man is deified by the infusion of grace so he can be justified. For Thomas, therefore, justification is sanctification.[45] Thomas's understanding of justification was not, however, the only one during the Middle Ages.

John Duns Scotus

Theologians such as John Duns Scotus (1265–1308) employed the covenant concept to ensure the reliability of God's twin powers, the *potentia Dei absoluta et ordinata*, the absolute and ordained power of God. In the creation God imposed upon himself an obligation in the form of a *pactum*, or covenant.[46] Within this *pactum* God would grant a *dispositio ad gratiam* to mankind. Then God would grant saving grace to the person who met the minimum requirements of justification. All man would have to do is *facere quod in se est*, "to do what is in one's self." Richard Muller explains that man could respond to God on the basis of universal grace, not with a truly meritorious act but with one that corresponded

---

43. McGrath, *Iustitia Dei*, 1:47.

44. Aquinas, *Summa*, Ia2ae q. 112 a. 1.

45. R. Scott Clark, "*Iustitia Imputata Aliena*: Alien or Proper to Luther's Doctrine of Justification?" *CTQ* 71 (2007): 269–310; see Aquinas, *Summa*, Ia2ae 68–70. Concerning Ia2ae 68–70 the editor of the critical edition writes that this portion of the *Summa* "presents the ultimate and most exquisite refinements of its theory of divinization of man by grace through the action of the Holy Spirit" (*Summa Theologiae* Ia2ae 68–70, vol. 24, ed. Edward D. O'Connor, C.S.C. [Cambridge: Cambridge University Press, 2006], xiii).

46. Alister E. McGrath, *The Intellectual Origins of the European Reformation* (Grand Rapids: Baker, 1987), 81.

to true merit that flowed from the minimal good that was in him, or *meritum de congruo*, congruent merit. On the basis, then, of the *pactum* God would respond with the grace of justification; hence the medieval phrase, *Facientibus quod in se est, Deus non denegat gratiam*, "To those who do what is in them, God will not deny grace."[47] While justification was covenantally conceived, which was an improvement over a purely ontological conception of God's relationship to man, the maxim of *facere quod in se est* represented a return to the theology of Pelagianism.

Broader Theological Developments

In the theology of Aquinas and Duns Scotus as well as other medieval theologians, such as Gabriel Biel (c. 1420–95), we still see semi-Pelagian and even Pelagian constructs in their doctrines of justification.[48] However, we should also note that broader theological developments did pave the way for the Reformation. In the theology of Aquinas, and those committed to realism, the idea that universals have an existence separate from specific concrete entities, which drew upon the philosophy of Plato (c. 427–c. 348 B.C.) and is also known as the *via antiqua* (the "old way"), there was a greater emphasis upon seeing justification strictly in ontological terms.[49] With the turn from ontology to discussions on the will of God in the theology of those committed to nominalism, the idea that universals do not have real existence but are merely names applied to qualities found within certain individual objects and that is also known as the *via moderna* (the "modern way"), for example, in the theology of Biel and William of Ockham (c. 1288–c. 1348), we see the development of the intellectual framework in which the doctrine of justification could be considered in something other than in terms of ontology.[50] In other words, it seems that nominalism opened the door to a consideration of the forensic nature of justification, and more specifically, the doctrine of imputation. This development, combined with the renaissance of Augustinianism in the fourteenth century, such as in the theology of

47. Richard A. Muller, *Dictionary of Latin and Greek Theological Terms* (Grand Rapids: Baker, 1987), 113.
48. McGrath, *Intellectual Origins*, 81–82; Heiko A. Oberman, *The Harvest of Medieval Theology* (1963; Grand Rapids: Baker, 2000), 146–84, esp. 175–78.
49. See Millard J. Erickson, *Concise Dictionary of Christian Theology* (Grand Rapids: Baker, 1994), 140, s.v. *"realism."*
50. Ibid., 116, s.v. *"nominalism."*

Thomas Bradwardine (c. 1290–1349) and Gregory of Rimini (c. 1300–58), contributed to the intellectual development that made the Reformation possible.[51]

McGrath notes six things that one finds in late medieval Augustinian theology that likely contributed to the theology of the Reformation:

1. A strict epistemological nominalism.
2. A voluntarist, as opposed to intellectualist, understanding of the *ratio meriti* ("reckoning of merit"). Voluntarism emphasizes the role of the will contrasted with that of reason or intellect.[52]
3. The extensive use of the writings of Augustine, particularly his anti-Pelagian works.
4. A strongly pessimistic view of original sin, with the fall being identified as a watershed in the economy of salvation.
5. A strong emphasis upon the priority of God in justification, linked to a doctrine of special grace.
6. A radical doctrine of absolute double predestination.[53]

With these intellectual developments in mind, we can move forward to consider the doctrine of justification in the Reformation and post-Reformation periods. It is against this backdrop that one sees the Reformation begin to give a more precise expression and definition of the doctrine of justification.

Summary

In the Middle Ages we see the confusion of justification and sanctification, undoubtedly fueled by realistic ontological assumptions. Additionally, given the role of church tradition at this point in development of the doctrine, there were also the mixed emphases of the church fathers such

51. Thomas Bradwardine, *De Causa Dei, Contra Pelagium et De Virtute Causarum, ad suos Mertonenses* (London, 1618); idem, "The Cause of God against the Pelagians," in *Forerunners of the Reformation*, ed. Heiko Oberman, trans. Paul L. Nyhus (London: Lutterworth, 1967); Heiko Oberman, *Archbishop Thomas Bradwardine, A Fourteenth Century Augustinian* (Utrecht: Kemink & Zoon, 1957). Also see Gregory of Rimini, *Super Primum et Secundum Sententiae* (1522; St. Bonaventure, NY: Franciscan Institute, 1955); Gordon Leff, *Gregory of Rimini* (Manchester: Manchester University Press, 1961).

52. Erickson, *Dictionary*, 180, s.v. *"voluntarism."*

53. McGrath, *Intellectual Origins*, 104; Heiko A. Oberman, *The Dawn of the Reformation* (1986; Grand Rapids: Eerdmans, 1992), 107.

as the old law–new law confusion that also influenced the theological discourse at the time. We may note, though, that if the resolution of the Augustine-Pelagius debate brought justification closer to right of center in the conciliar declarations of Ephesus and Orange, in the Middle Ages the doctrine drifted heavily toward the neonomian pole, though there were of course notable exceptions to this trend in such Augustinians as Bradwardine and Gregory of Rimini. There was, however, the important coordination of the doctrine of the covenant, or *pactum*, with justification, such as in the theology of Duns Scotus, which was a positive introduction of the *historia salutis*, which would be more fully developed in the Reformation and post-Reformation periods.

The Reformation and Post-Reformation (1517–1700)

The Reformation (1517–65): Luther and Calvin

With the cry of the Renaissance, *ad fontes*, "to the sources," the theologians of the Reformation studied the Scriptures in the original languages. From their study of the Scriptures, the Reformers concluded that "to justify" meant "to declare righteous," not "to make righteous." It was, of course, Martin Luther (1483–1546) and John Calvin (1509–64) who made a significant impact upon the church's understanding of justification. Luther argued that sinners cannot be righteous through their own good works, but that it is only faith in Christ that justifies the ungodly. The unrighteous are justified by faith, therefore, and it is the righteousness of Christ that is imputed to the believer. It is in the writings of Luther and Calvin where the doctrine of imputation comes to the foreground.

In the winter of 1515–16, early in his career, Luther commented on Romans 3:28, "*For we hold*, recognize and affirm, we conclude from what is said *that a man is justified*, reckoned righteous before God, whether Greek or Jew, *by faith, apart from works of the law*, without the help and necessity of the works of the Law."[54] Luther's exegetical spade work eventually was codified in early Reformation confessions such as the Augsburg Confession (1530), which explains that justification is by faith alone:

> Men cannot be justified before God by their own strength, merits, or works but are freely justified for Christ's sake through faith when they believe

54. Martin Luther, *Lectures on Romans*, LW 25 (St. Louis: Concordia, 1974), 33.

that they are received into favor and that their sins are forgiven through faith, when we believe that Christ suffered for us and that for his sake our sin is forgiven and righteousness and eternal life are given to us.[55]

The Reformed wing of the Reformation gave similar expression to its understanding of justification.

Calvin defines justification as "the acceptance with which God receives us into his favor as righteous men. And we say that it consists in the remission of sins and the imputation of Christ's righteousness."[56] Calvin largely appealed to three central texts to support his definition (Rom. 4:6–7; 5:19; 2 Cor. 5:18–21). Unlike Augustine, however, both Luther and Calvin made the important distinction, but not separation, between justification and sanctification. Luther, for example, saw the need for the law in the life of the believer after his conversion, which was informative for good works and sanctification. In Luther's 1535 commentary on Galatians, which reflects his mature thought on the doctrine of justification, Luther writes:

> The matter of the Law must be considered carefully, both as to what and as to how we ought to think about the Law; otherwise we shall either reject it altogether, after the fashion of the fanatical spirits who prompted the peasants' revolt a decade ago by saying that the freedom of the Gospel absolves men from all laws, or we shall attribute to the Law the power to justify. Both groups sin against the Law: those on the right, who want to be justified through the Law, and those on the left, who want to be altogether free of the Law. Therefore we must travel the royal road, so that we neither reject the Law altogether nor attribute more to it than we should.[57]

In the end, Luther saw a need for the law in the life of the believer so that it could guide him in his good works. Moreover, one easily sees Luther rightly recognize the two extremes of antinomianism and neonomianism.

Luther saw a necessary connection between justification and sanctification which was manifest in the importance he placed on the law:

55. Augsburg Confession 4, in Pelikan and Hotchkiss, *Creeds*, 2:60.

56. John Calvin, *Institutes of the Christian Religion*, trans. Ford Lewis Battles, ed. John T. McNeill, LCC 20–21 (Philadelphia: Westminster, 1960), 3.11.2.

57. Luther, *Lectures on Galatians*, LW 26 (St. Louis: Concordia, 1963), 343. Regarding the development in Luther's thought see Carl Trueman, "Simul peccator et justus: Martin Luther and Justification," in *Justification in Perspective*, ed. Bruce L. McCormack (Grand Rapids: Baker, 2006), 73–98, esp. 74.

Here, then, we have the Ten Commandments, a summary of divine teaching on what we are to do to make our whole life pleasing to God. They are the true fountain from which all good works must spring, the true channel through which all good works must flow. Apart from these Ten Commandments no action or life can be good or pleasing to God, no matter how great or precious it may be in the eyes of the world.[58]

So, then, Luther believed that good works were necessary for salvation, as the fruit of one's justification, not as the ground of justification. To this same end, Calvin gave expression to his famous analogy: "The sun, by its heat, quickens and fructifies the earth, by its beams brightens and illumines it. Here is a mutual and indivisible connection. Yet reason itself forbids us to transfer the peculiar qualities of the one to the other."[59] Calvin's point is the same as Luther's, though from a different angle. Justification and sanctification are necessary elements of salvation, though they are different, and one does not want to confuse the two.[60]

In this way we can see that Calvin and Luther, as well as other Reformers, could appropriate that which they believed was scriptural but at the same time depart from the church fathers when they believed they were in error. Calvin, for example, dissects Augustine's thought on justification and traces it as it comes through the Middle Ages through Peter Lombard (c. 1095–1160):

It is clear from their own writings that in using the term "grace" they are deluded. For Lombard explains that justification is given to us through Christ in two ways. First, he says, Christ's death justifies us, while love is aroused through it in our hearts and makes us righteous. Second, because through the same love, sin is extinguished by which the devil held

---

58. Martin Luther, "Large Catechism," in *The Book of Concord*, ed. Robert Kolb and Timothy J. Wengert (Minneapolis: Fortress, 2000), 428. Luther also says: "Therefore it is not without reason that the Old Testament command was to write the Ten Commandments on every wall and corner, and even on garments. Not that we are to have them there only for display, as the Jews did, but we are to keep them incessantly before our eyes and constantly in our memory and to practice them in all our works and ways. Each of us is to make them a matter of daily practice in all circumstances, in all activities and dealings, as if they were written everywhere we look, even wherever we go or wherever we stand. Thus, both for ourselves at home and abroad among our neighbors, we will find occasion enough to practice the Ten Commandments, and no one need search far for them" ("Large Catechism," 431).

59. Calvin, *Institutes*, 3.11.6.

60. J. V. Fesko, "Calvin on Justification and Recent Misinterpretations of His View," *MAJT* 16 (2005), 83–114.

us captive, so that he no longer has the wherewithal to condemn us. You see how he views God's grace especially in justification, in so far as we are directed through the grace of the Holy Spirit to good works. Obviously, he intended to follow Augustine's opinion, but he follows it at a distance and even departs considerably from the right imitation of it. For when Augustine says anything clearly, Lombard obscures it, and if there was anything slightly contaminated in Augustine, he corrupts it. The schools have gone continually from bad to worse until, in headlong ruin, they have plunged into a sort of Pelagianism. For that matter, Augustine's view, or at any rate his manner of stating it, we must not entirely accept. For even though he admirably deprives man of all credit for righteousness and transfers it to God's grace, he still subsumes grace under sanctification, by which we are reborn in newness of life through the Spirit.[61]

Here we see quite clearly that Calvin interacted with patristic and medieval theology, which of course illustrates the organic nature of the Reformation to earlier church history.[62] In this sense, the Reformation is certainly a continuation of theological development that began in the earliest days of the church. However, this does not mean that the Reformers adopted medieval or patristic thought wholesale. Rather, they critically adopted those trends and positions they believed were faithful to Scripture.

In addition to the critical use of patristic and medieval theology, we also see the refinement of the law-gospel hermeneutic during the Reformation and post-Reformation periods. Both Lutheran and Reformed theologians employed the law-gospel hermeneutic, namely recognizing those portions of Scripture that brought moral demands upon the believer in contrast with those that offered promised redemption. Hence, Lutherans believe that "everything that condemns sin is and belongs to the proclamation of the law."[63] By contrast, the gospel is "the kind of teaching that reveals what the human being, who has not kept the law and has been condemned by it, should believe: that Christ atoned and

---

61. Calvin, *Institutes*, 3.11.15.

62. On Calvin's use of patristic theology, see Anthony N. S. Lane, *John Calvin: Student of the Church Fathers* (Grand Rapids: Baker, 1999). And, more broadly, for the use of the patristics in Reformation theology, see Irena Backus, *The Reception of the Church Fathers in the West*, 2 vols. (Leiden: Brill, 2001), 2:537–700. Likewise, we see Luther, for example, who interacted with medieval theology and was familiar with both the *via antiqua* and *via moderna*, yet carved his own path in his own theology (see Oberman, *Dawn of the Reformation*, 120; idem, *The Reformation* [Grand Rapids: Eerdmans, 1994], 18–21).

63. Formula of Concord 5.3–4 in *The Book of Concord*, ed. Kolb and Wengert, 500.

paid for all sins and apart from any human merit has obtained and won for people the forgiveness of sins."[64]

In the writings of Zacharias Ursinus (1534–83), one of the chief authors of the Heidelberg Catechism, which is the authoritative catechism for the Dutch and German Reformed tradition, the use of the law-gospel hermeneutic is employed in terms of the covenants of nature and grace, which finds its parallel in Westminster's covenants of works and grace:

> The law contains the natural covenant, established by God with humanity in creation, that is, it is known by humanity by nature, it requires our perfect obedience to God, and it promises eternal life to those who keep it and threatens eternal punishment to those who do not. The gospel, however, contains the covenant of grace, that is, although it exists, it is not known at all by nature; it shows us the fulfillment in Christ of the righteousness that the law requires and the restoration in us of that righteousness by Christ's Spirit; and it promises eternal life freely because of Christ to those who believe in him.[65]

In fact, Ursinus elsewhere states, "The doctrine of the church is the entire and uncorrupted doctrine of the law and gospel concerning the truth of God, together with his will, works, and worship."[66] Ursinus was not alone in this observation.

Theodore Beza (1519–1605), Calvin's successor at Geneva, wrote, "Ignorance of this distinction between Law and Gospel is one of the principal sources of the abuses which corrupted and still corrupt Christianity."[67] Calvin could likewise observe that the medieval Roman Catholic theologians confused the categories of law and gospel or promise

> by saying that works of their own intrinsic goodness are of no avail for meriting salvation but by reason of the covenant, because the Lord of his own liberality esteemed them so highly. Meanwhile they did not observe how far those works, which they meant to be meritorious, were from

64. Formula of Concord 5.5 in *Book of Concord*, 500.
65. Larger Catechism 36, in *An Introduction to the Heidelberg Catechism*, ed. and trans. Lyle D. Bierma et al. (Grand Rapids: Baker, 2005), 168–69.
66. Zacharias Ursinus, *Commentary on the Heidelberg Catechism* (1852; Phillipsburg, NJ: P&R, n.d.), 1.
67. Theodore Beza, *The Christian Faith*, trans. James Clark (Lewes, UK: Focus Christian Ministries, 1992), 41–43.

fulfilling the condition of the promises unless preceded by justification resting on faith alone, and by forgiveness of sins, through which even good works must be cleansed of spots.[68]

Continental Reformed theologians were not alone in affirming the law-gospel hermeneutic, as one can find similar statements in the writings of British theologians such as William Perkins (1558–1602).[69] From this we conclude, "As far as the law-gospel distinction is concerned, it is as integral to Reformed theology (embedded in federalism) as it is to Lutheranism."[70]

The Counter-Reformation (1546)

As one can well imagine, the RCC did not sit idly by as large contingents of the church broke away. The RCC gathered together at Trent (1545–65) to respond to the doctrinal positions of the Protestant Reformers, both in the Lutheran and Reformed wings. Despite the Protestant expositions of the doctrine of justification, the Tridentine response to the Reformation represents the codification of a confused understanding of Augustine, which was perpetuated in the Middle Ages—a failure to distinguish properly between justification and sanctification fueled by an ontological understanding of justification. Trent made its authoritative declaration on the doctrine of justification in the sixth session, held on 13 January 1547. Trent in part agreed with the Reformers over the final, efficient, and meritorious causes of justification, the glory of God and Christ, the work of the Holy Spirit, and the work of Christ, respectively. Though one should note that the Reformers would argue that even though Trent acknowledged the work of Christ as the meritorious cause of justification, a conclusion with which they would agree, because the RCC did not maintain the sole instrumentality of faith, in the end it corrupted the meritorious cause with the works of the believer. This divergence between the RCC and the Reformation becomes evident

68. Calvin, *Institutes*, 3.17.3.

69. Expounding upon the application of Scripture in preaching, Perkins writes: "The basic principle in application is to know whether the passage is a statement of the law or of the gospel" (*The Art of Prophesying* [1606; Edinburgh: Banner of Truth, 1996], 54–56).

70. Michael Horton, "Law, Gospel, and Covenant: Reassessing Some Emerging Antitheses," *WTJ* 64/2 (2002):287.

when one explores what Trent has to say regarding the instrumental and formal causes of justification.

Chapter 7 of the decrees of Trent states that the sacrament of baptism, along with faith, is the instrumental cause of one's justification. This stands in contrast to the *sola fide* of the Reformation, that faith *alone* is the instrument of justification. One also sees the fusion of justification and sanctification when Trent states:

> The one formal cause is the justness of God: not that by which he himself is just, but that by which he makes us just and endowed with which we are renewed in the spirit of our mind, and are not merely considered to be just but we are truly named and are just, each one of us receiving individually his own justness according to the measure which the Holy Spirit apportions to each one as he wills, and in view of each one's dispositions and cooperation. For though no one can be just unless the merits of the passion of our Lord Jesus Christ are communicated to him; nevertheless, in the justification of a sinner this in fact takes place when, by the merit of the same most holy passion, the love of God is poured out by the agency of the Holy Spirit in the hearts of those who are being justified, and abides in them. Consequently, in the process of justification, together with the forgiveness of sins a person receives, through Jesus Christ into whom he is grafted, all these infused at the same time: faith, hope, and charity.[71]

It is evident that for the RCC, justification was a process rather than a legal declaration, as it was for the Protestant Reformers. One could not be declared righteous in the sight of God until he actually was righteous; hence the RCC believed that one required the infused rather than imputed righteousness of Christ. Or, as Trent states: "They grow and increase in that very justness they have received through the grace of Christ, by faith united to good works."[72]

It is important to note, though, that the RCC neither simply rejected Protestant understandings of justification, nor raised objections to a caricature of Reformed views. It seems quite clear from the Tridentine proclamations that the RCC understood the Protestant position and unambiguously condemned it. For example, in the "Canons concerning

---

71. "Dogmatic Decrees of the Council of Trent," session 6, ch. 7, in Pelikan and Hotchkiss, *Creeds*, 2:829–30.

72. Ibid., session 6, ch. 10, in Pelikan and Hotchkiss, *Creeds*, 2:831.

Justification," Trent condemns *sola fide*: "If anyone says that the sinner is justified by faith alone, meaning thereby that no other cooperation is required for him to obtain the grace of justification, and that in no sense is it necessary for him to make preparation and be disposed by a movement of his own will: let him be anathema."[73] In two successive statements, Trent also condemned *solus Christus* as well as the doctrine of imputation: "If anyone says people are justified either solely by the attribution of Christ's justice, or by the forgiveness of sins alone, to the exclusion of the grace and charity which is poured forth in their hearts by the Holy Spirit and abides in them . . . let him be anathema." In the following canon Trent states: "If anyone says that the faith which justifies is nothing else but trust in the divine mercy, which pardons sins because of Christ; or that it is that trust alone by which we are justified: let him be anathema."[74] Though there are many other points that one could raise, it is perhaps the final canon that seals the Roman Catholic rejection of the Reformation: "If anyone says that this Catholic doctrine concerning justification, set out in this present decree by the holy council, detracts in any way from the glory of God or the merits of Jesus Christ our Lord, and does not rather make clear the truth of our faith, and the glory alike of God and of Jesus Christ: let him be anathema."[75]

Post-Reformation (1565–1700)

In the period leading up to the end and following the Reformation the doctrine of justification was codified in confessions and catechisms in both Great Britain and continental Europe. The codifications of Protestant doctrine were largely shaped by the polemic debates with the RCC, and consequently there was an emphasis upon *sola fide, sola gratia*, and imputed versus infused righteousness. That is, justification was a onetime forensic declaration, not a process that also included sanctification. The French Reformed Confession of Faith (1559), for example, states: "We are made partakers of this justification by faith alone." Moreover, it states that justification not only is "the remission of our sins," but also rests in "the obedience of Jesus Christ, which is imputed to us."[76] The Belgic

---

73. Ibid., session 6, canon 9, in Pelikan and Hotchkiss, *Creeds*, 2:837.
74. Ibid., canons 11–12, in Pelikan and Hotchkiss, *Creeds*, 2:837.
75. Ibid., canon 33, in Pelikan and Hotchkiss, *Creeds*, 2:839.
76. French Reformed Confession of Faith 18, 20, in Pelikan and Hotchkiss, *Creeds*, 2:380.

Confession (1561) likewise lays emphasis upon the primacy of faith as the sole instrument of justification, which appropriates the obedience of Christ: "Faith is only the instrument by which we embrace Christ, our righteousness. But Jesus Christ is our righteousness in making available to us all his merits and all the holy works he has done for us and in our place."[77]

One finds similar affirmations in the authoritative Lutheran interpretation of the Augsburg Confession, the Formula of Concord (1577), which states: "God forgives us our sins purely by his grace, without any preceding, present, or subsequent work, merit, or worthiness, and reckons to us the righteousness of Christ's obedience, on account of which righteousness we are accepted by God." There is a similar emphasis upon the exclusivity of faith apart from works in justification: "Faith is the only means and instrument whereby we accept Christ and in Christ obtain the 'righteousness which avails before God,' and . . . for Christ's sake such faith is reckoned for righteousness."[78] In the post-Reformation period the doctrine of justification reached the pinnacle of expression in the Westminster Confession of Faith and Catechisms.

It is in the Westminster Confession and Catechisms (1647–48) where, at least for the Reformed wing of the Reformation, the doctrine of justification received some specific definition and elaboration. There are several reasons for its precision and scope. First, by this point in the history of doctrine the Westminster divines had the advantage of over one hundred years of renewed exegesis in the original languages of Scripture. Second, they also had the advantage of over one hundred years of polemics within the Reformed community, with the Lutheran and radical wings of the Reformation, and of course with the RCC through the Counter-Reformation. Third, there was greater attention not only to the definition and delineation of the *ordo salutis*, or the application of redemption to the individual, but also to the *historia salutis*, namely the historical context in which God's plan of redemption unfolded. Additionally, especially in the Reformed tradition great emphasis was placed upon the idea of covenant once again.

77. Belgic Confession 22, in Pelikan and Hotchkiss, *Creeds*, 2:416.
78. Formula of Concord 3.2–3, in Pelikan and Hotchkiss, *Creeds*, 2:176.

28

The Westminster divines set the *ordo salutis* in the context of the theological constructs of the covenants of works and grace, which explain the two-age structure of the *historia salutis,* or in Pauline terms, the eons of the first and last Adams (WCF 7.1–3; cf. Rom. 5:12–21; 1 Cor. 15:20–28, 40–49). In the prefall covenant, Adam serves as the federal head of mankind, and it was through his obedience to the command of God that he could have secured eternal life. After the fall, in the covenant of grace it is only the work of Christ that can secure eternal life for the one who places his faith in Christ. It is within this covenantal context that the Westminster Confession states:

> Those whom God effectually calls he also freely justifies; not by infusing righteousness into them, but by pardoning their sins, and by accounting and accepting their persons as righteous: not for anything wrought in them, or done by them, but for Christ's sake alone: nor by imputing faith itself, the act of believing, or any other evangelical obedience, to them as their righteousness; but by imputing the obedience and satisfaction of Christ unto them, they receiving and resting on Him and His righteousness, by faith: which faith they have not of themselves; it is the gift of God. (WCF 11.1; cf. LC 70; SC 33)

Shortly after the composition of the Westminster Standards, the carefully balanced definitions were challenged, as evidenced by the introduction above in the work of Robert Traill, by both antinomianism and neonomianism.

Beyond the post-Reformation confessions and catechisms, we should take note of the works of two Reformed theologians during the period of high orthodoxy (1630/40–1700), namely those of John Owen (1616–83) and Francis Turretin (1623–87). Turretin was known for his *Institutes of Elenctic Theology,* in which he presented a thorough exposition of the Reformed faith. In his work he explains issues such as the forensic nature of justification, the meritorious cause of justification, imputed versus infused righteousness, as well as the imputation of the active obedience of Christ. Beyond these points, he also explores the justification of faith, that good works demonstrate or give evidence of the believer's faith, and the relationship between justification and sanctification.[79] In the process of setting his doctrine of justification, he interacted with Arminian, Roman Catholic, and Socinian understandings of the doctrine.

Owen was one of the most well known theologians of the seventeenth century. That he defended the doctrine of justification in various ways is evident on a number of fronts. Owen was one of the chief architects behind the Savoy Declaration (1658), which was a modified version of the Westminster Confession for congregationalists. In the Savoy article on justification, Owen expanded it to give explicit reference to the imputation of both the active and passive obedience of Christ.[80] In addition to this Owen wrote two polemical works in which he set forth the doctrine of justification, *Of the Death of Christ, and of Justification* (1650) and *The Doctrine of Justification by Faith* (1677).[81] In the former, Owen wrote in response to Richard Baxter's (1615–91) understanding of justification, one that was neonomian in nature; and the latter was a full-blown treatise on the doctrine, which was in effect an extended refutation of Baxter.[82]

That Baxter's views were neonomian are clearly evident in the following quote where he explains aspects of his doctrine of justification:

And that the law of grace being that which we are to be judged by, we shall at the last judgment also be judged (and so justified) thus far by or according to our sincere love, obedience, or evangelical works, as the condition of the law or covenant of free grace, which justifies and glorifies freely all that are thus evangelically qualified, by and for the merits, perfect righteousness and sacrifice of Christ, which procured the covenant or free gift of universal conditional justification and adoption, before and without any works or conditions done by man whatsoever. Reader, forgive me this

---

79. Francis Turretin, *Institutes of Elenctic Theology*, trans. George Musgrave Giger, ed. James T. Dennison Jr., 3 vols. (Phillipsburg, NJ: P&R, 1992–97), 16.1–17.1.

80. See Carl Trueman, "John Owen on Justification," in *Justified in Christ*, ed. K. Scott Oliphint (Fearn, Scotland: Christian Focus, 2007), 83; see also Pelikan and Hotchkiss, *Creeds*, 3:115–16. There is a case to be made that the WCF taken together with the LC and SC is not deficient on the question of the imputation of the active obedience of Christ (see WCF 11.1; LC 39, 48, 55; SC 25, 27; Jeffrey K. Jue, "The Active Obedience of Christ and the Theology of the Westminster Standards: A Historical Investigation," in *Justified in Christ*, ed. Oliphint, 99–130).

81. See John Owen, *The Works of John Owen*, 16 vols., ed. William H. Goold (1850–53; Edinburgh: Banner of Truth, 1991), 5.1–400; 12.591–616.

82. R. Scott Clark, "How We Got Here: The Roots of the Current Controversy over Justification," in *Covenant, Justification, and Pastoral Ministry*, ed. Clark, 15.

troublesome oft repeating of the state of the controversy; I meddle with no other. If this be justification by works, I am for it.[83]

Here we see Baxter mix the believer's works and Christ's righteousness in his understanding of justification. C. Fitzsimons Alison notes three points concerning this statement. First, free justification consists only in the procurement of the new covenant by Christ's sacrifice, "before and without any works or conditions done by man whatsoever." Second, Baxter plainly refuses, despite abundant criticism over a period of twenty-five years, to abandon his chief contention that the believer's faith is "imputed" and accepted for righteousness under the more lenient terms of the new covenant on account of the merits of Christ's righteousness; one should not forget that Baxter's definition of faith includes evangelical obedience. And, third, his use of the term "justification" is ambiguous and confusing, but was nonetheless characteristic of his teaching for some forty years.[84]

Summary

In the Reformation and post-Reformation periods, Protestant theologians of both the Lutheran and Reformed wings were able to keep the doctrine of justification in between the poles of antinomianism and neonomianism. There were attempts to move justification to right of center toward neonomianism by the Counter-Reformation as well as attempts to use the Reformation understanding of justification as a license to sin,

83. Richard Baxter, *A Treatise of Justifying Righteousness* (London, 1676), 163.
84. C. Fitzsimons Alison, *The Rise of Moralism* (1966; Vancouver: Regent College Publishing, 2003), 154–64, esp. 159. For a more positive assessment of Baxter's doctrine of justification, see J. I. Packer, *The Redemption and Restoration of Man in the Thought of Richard Baxter* (1954; Vancouver: Regent College Publishing, 2003), 237–65, esp. 261–63; Hans Boersma, *A Hot Peppercorn: Richard Baxter's Doctrine of Justification in Its Seventeenth-Century Context of Controversy* (1993; Vancouver: Regent College Publishing, 2004), 257–327. However, one should note the problematic nature of Baxter's theology as a whole, in that he was not, as some might think, indebted only to the Scriptures for his views. Rather, he was a very well read theologian, one very familiar with a number of medieval works. He was not only influenced by medieval theology but also used natural theology to construct his doctrine of justification (see Clark, "How We Got Here," 15 n. 27; J. I. Packer, "The Doctrine of Justification among the Puritans," in *Puritan Papers*, ed. J. I. Packer [Phillipsburg, NJ: P&R, 2005], 5:158–59; Carl Trueman, "A Small Step towards Rationalism: The Impact of the Metaphysics of Tommaso Campanella on the Theology of Richard Baxter," in *Protestant Scholasticism*, ed. Carl Trueman and R. Scott Clark [Carlisle: Paternoster, 1999], 181–95, esp. 185 n. 13; idem, *The Claims of Truth* [Carlisle: Paternoster, 1998], 200–206).

or antinomianism, as with Calvin's interaction against the libertines or Luther's with the Peasants' Revolt. Expositions of the Decalogue and its importance for the believer from both wings of the Reformation evidence the desire to keep justification away from antinomianism. The Reformers took great pains to distinguish but not separate justification and sanctification, emphasize the centrality of faith and grace, give exegesis to support the doctrine of imputation, and seat justification as a part of the *ordo salutis* within the covenant of grace, the *historia salutis*. Though there were undoubtedly some differences between the Reformation and patristic expressions, the Reformers saw their work in continuity with the best of the patristic theologians at specific points.[85] Beyond the Reformation, there were also neonomian tendencies in some Reformed theologians, such as Baxter. Nevertheless, others such as Owen countered these attempts to confuse justification and sanctification.

The Eighteenth and Nineteenth Centuries

Marrow Controversy (1718–23)

One of the famous eighteenth-century debates that surrounded the doctrine of justification was the Marrow Controversy. The debate erupted in Scotland surrounding the republication of a book entitled *The Marrow of Modern Divinity*. The book was likely written by Edward Fisher, a seventeenth-century theologian, and was published in two parts in 1645 and 1649. The book is a series of dialogues on the doctrine of the atonement and the dangers of antinomianism and neonomianism. At the time of its publication, the book was recommended by two prominent Westminster divines, Joseph Caryl (1602–73) and Jeremiah Burroughs (1599–1646). Moreover, the author claimed to derive his work from the teachings of a number of prominent Reformed theologians including John Ball (1585–1640), Theodore Beza, Heinrich Bullinger (1504–75), John Diodati (1576–1649), Thomas Goodwin (1600–80), Thomas Hooker (1586–1647), John Lightfoot (1602–75), Martin Luther, Peter Martyr Vermigli (1499–1562), Wolfgang Musculus (1497–1563), William Perkins, Amandus Polanus (1561–1610), Robert Rollock (1555–99), and Zacharias Ursinus, to name

---

85. See, e.g., John Calvin, "Reply to Letter by Cardinal Sadolet," in *Selected Works of John Calvin*, ed. Henry Beveridge and Jule Bonnet (1844; Grand Rapids: Baker, 1983), 1:25–71.

a few.[86] When the book was originally published, there was no uproar. The same cannot be said when it was republished in Scotland.

In Scotland in 1718 the book was republished because an English Puritan soldier brought the book with him into Scotland, and it eventually fell into the hands of Thomas Boston (1676–1732). Boston was so pleased with the work that he and a colleague had the work republished. The book displeased a number of ministers who apparently held neonomian views and therefore condemned the book for its supposed advocacy of antinomianism. A careful reading of the book will reveal that it did not advocate antinomianism, but rather set forth *sola fide*. Like Calvin before, Fisher was careful to distinguish but not separate justification and sanctification and recognize that sinful man is justified by faith alone to the exclusion of his works:

> Therefore, whensoever, or wheresoever, any doubt of question arises of salvation, or our justification before God, there the law and all good works must be utterly excluded and stand apart, that grace may appear free, and that the promise and faith may stand alone: which faith alone, without law or works, brings thee in particular to the justification and salvation, through the mere promise and free grace of God in Christ; so that I say, in the action and office of justification, both law and works are to be utterly excluded and exempted as things which have nothing to do in that behalf. The reason is this: for seeing that all our redemption springs out from the body of the Son of God crucified, then is there nothing that can stand us in stead, but that only wherewith the body of Christ is apprehended. Now, forasmuch as neither the law nor works, but faith only, is the thing which apprehends the body and passion of Christ, therefore faith only is that matter which justifies a man before God, through the strength of that object Jesus Christ, which it apprehends.[87]

Despite the book's careful delineation between justification and sanctification the Assembly of the Church of Scotland condemned it as antinomian. Nevertheless, there were a number of ministers, including Thomas Boston, who came to the book's defense, noting that it simply contained doctrinal truths couched in scriptural language and in phrases taken

86. Edward Fisher, *The Marrow of Modern Divinity* (1645, 1649; New York: Westminster, n.d.), 21.
87. Ibid., 341.

from Reformed confessions and catechisms. The Assembly eventually rebuked those who defended the book, but no further action was taken and the controversy eventually dissipated.[88]

Jonathan Edwards

When we turn to eighteenth-century colonial America, it is the theology of Jonathan Edwards (1703–58) that comes to the fore, as some have called him one of the finest minds ever to appear in human history.[89] Moreover, he is one identified as a champion of Reformed orthodoxy. Yet at the same time, there is a cloud that hangs over Edwards's doctrine of justification. In broad strokes, Edwards affirms all of the tenets of a classical view of the doctrine of justification by faith alone. He was well read in the Scriptures, but also was familiar with a wide range of Reformed theologians, including the likes of John Calvin, William Perkins (1558–1603), Stephen Charnock (1628–80), John Owen, Samuel Rutherford (1600–61), Thomas Boston (1676–1732), Francis Turretin, and Petrus van Mastricht (1630–1706). It is especially the latter two, Turretin and van Mastricht, for whom Edwards had a great deal of respect.[90]

Given his knowledge and familiarity with the Reformed tradition, one finds that Edwards affirms that justification is the forgiveness of sins, the imputation of the righteousness of Christ to the believer, and that it is by faith alone. In his discourse on the doctrine of justification, Edwards explains: "A person is said to be *justified*, when he is approved of God as free from the guilt of sin and its deserved punishment, and as having that righteousness belonging to him that entitles to the reward of life."[91] Edwards defended the doctrine of imputation and the obedience of Christ as the ground of the believer's justification. So, then, at least in these broad strokes, Edwards can be placed in the general trajectory of

88. For a history of the Marrow controversy see *Schaff-Herzog Encyclopedia of Religious Knowledge*, ed. Samuel Macauley Jackson et al., 13 vols. (New York: Funk and Wagnalls, 1910), 7:206; David C. Lachman, *The Marrow Controversy* (Edinburgh: Rutherford House, 1988); A. T. B. McGowan, *The Federal Theology of Thomas Boston* (Carlisle: Paternoster, 1997), 123–44.

89. John H. Gerstner, *The Rational Biblical Theology of Jonathan Edwards*, 3 vols. (Powhatan, VA: Berea Publications, 1991), 1:1.

90. See B. B. Warfield, "Edwards and the New England Theology," in *Works*, ed. Ethelbert D. Warfield et al., 10 vols. (1932; Grand Rapids: Baker, 1982), 9:529.

91. Jonathan Edwards, "Justification by Faith Alone," in *The Works of Jonathan Edwards*, ed. Edward Hickman, 2 vols. (1834; Edinburgh: Banner of Truth, 1992), 1:622.

Reformed orthodoxy because not only does he have these typical features in his doctrine, but he bases it upon the traditional bi-covenantal (works and grace) federal theology.[92]

When one delves into some of the specifics, however, one finds several items that are not part of mainstream Reformed theology. For example, Edwards came under criticism from Charles Hodge (1797–1878) for at times advocating the mediate imputation of Adam's sin.[93] Beyond this, one finds important qualifications in the finer points of his understanding of *solus Christus*. Concerning the obedience of Christ, Edwards argues that while his obedience is primary, there is a place for the believer's inherent holiness. Christ's righteousness "mainly" serves as the ground for the believer's justification.[94] He goes on to explain: "Here perhaps it may be said, that a title to salvation is not directly given as the reward of our obedience; for that is not by any thing of ours, but only by Christ's satisfaction and righteousness; but yet an interest in that satisfaction and righteousness is given as a reward for our obedience."[95] Here we see that Christ's work is the primary ground of justification, but that there is also some room, albeit secondary, for the reward of the believer's good works.[96]

Elsewhere Edwards explains in what way faith and works participate in the believer's justification. In Edwards's explanation of James 2, he writes:

> For if we take works as acts or expressions of faith, they are not excluded; so a man is not justified by faith only, but also by works; i.e., he is not justified only by faith as a principle in the heart, or in its first and more

92. So McGrath, *Iustitia Dei*, 2:119–20; also Samuel T. Logan Jr., "The Doctrine of Justification in the Theology of Jonathan Edwards," *WTJ* 46 (1984): 26–52; Jeffrey C. Waddington, "Jonathan Edwards's 'Ambiguous and Somewhat Precarious' Doctrine of Justification?" *WTJ* 66/2 (2004): 357–72; Gerstner, *Edwards*, 3:191–223.

93. See Charles Hodge, *Systematic Theology*, 3 vols. (Grand Rapids: Eerdmans, 1993), 2:207–14; D. G. Hart and John R. Muether, *Seeking a Better Country* (Phillipsburg, NJ: P&R, 2007), 116.

94. Edwards, "Justification," 1:639.

95. Ibid., 1:640.

96. George Hunsinger, "Dispositional Soteriology: Jonathan Edwards on Justification by Faith Alone," *WTJ* 66/1 (2004): 110–11; for a condensed version of this article see idem, "An American Tragedy: Jonathan Edwards on Justification," *Modern Reformation* 13/4 (2004): 18–21. For an older analysis that comes to similar conclusions see Thomas A. Schafer, "Jonathan Edwards and Justification by Faith," *CH* 20 (1951): 55–67.

immanent acts, but also by the effective acts of it in life, which are the expressions of the life of faith, as the operations and actions of the body are the life of that.[97]

This construction appears to contravene *sola fide* as it is traditionally understood by confusing faith and works, and specifically undermines the doctrine of imputation, as Turretin observes, "What is inherent is opposed to what is imputed."[98] Reformed theologians typically argue that works are evidence of faith, but not that they participate in any way in the believer's justification.

This divergence is further evident when Edwards explains that faith is not completed until it is manifest in the believer's good works. Edwards writes in Miscellany no. 996: "Our act of accepting of and closing with Christ is completed by doing it practically, as well as in heart, and the condition of justification is fulfilled and finished." Edwards bases his understanding in his concept of regeneration:

> The work of regeneration is of the whole man: we put off the old man and put on the new man, and the work of sanctification, when complete, is of the whole man. And so the act of closing with Christ is, when complete, not only accepting of Christ with the whole soul, but with the whole man, and by giving up all to Christ, and offering our bodies as well as souls a living sacrifice.

On the basis of this assumption, Edwards argues: "Indeed, as soon as we had done it in our hearts, the first moment our hearts had consented, we should be entitled in some sense; but we should not look on fulfillment of the condition as being all respect, till we had also actually done it."[99] One can immediately see from this construction that Edwards does not want to hinge justification entirely upon the believer's good works, as he readily admits that the believer is by faith alone "entitled in some sense" to a justified status. But at the same time, he does not want to say that the believer is justified until his faith is manifest by his good works. How can Edwards come to these conclusions?

97. Edwards, "Justification," 1.652.
98. Turretin, *Institutes*, 16.3.16.
99. Jonathan Edwards, "How We Are Justified by Works" (1743), in *Works of Jonathan Edwards On-line*, ed. Harry S. Stout, Kenneth P. Minkema, and Caleb J. D. Maskell, at www.edwards.yale.edu. All subsequent miscellanies are taken from this source.

We do not have the space to give a full-orbed explanation, but we may observe at least two important points that feature in Edwards's theology, points that one finds in various expressions that deviate from *sola fide*. First, Edwards seems to parallel Roman Catholic soteriology when he explains that in a person's conversion, he is given a disposition, what Roman Catholic theologians would call a *habitus*, a spiritual capacity or inclination.[100] Under this rubric, Edwards can write: " 'Tis the disposition and principle is the thing God looks at. Supposing a man dies suddenly and not in the actual exercise of faith, 'tis his disposition that saves him; for if it were possible that the disposition was destroyed, the man would be damned and all the former acts of faith would signify nothing" (Misc. 27b).[101]

This statement is striking, and runs contrary to the typical Reformed understanding of justification in that Edwards seems to define faith not as trust in Christ, but rather in terms of what faith produces. Edwards, for example, says that faith is a "habit and principle in the heart," which is different from how the Larger Catechism defines it: assenting to the truth, receiving and resting upon Christ and his righteousness (LC 72).[102] Additionally, "Faith justifies a sinner in the sight of God, not because of those other graces which do always accompany it, or of good works that are the fruits of it" (LC 73). In contrast to the Reformed tradition that argues that works are evidentiary, for Edwards, works contribute in a secondary way to a person's justification.[103]

Second, Edwards evidently understood union with Christ solely in legal and not personal terms. Edwards wrote that he did "not now pretend to determine what sort this union is," nor did he believe it was necessary to explain the nature of the believer's mystical union with Christ.[104] Never-

---

100. Muller, *Dictionary*, 134, s.v. *"habitus."*

101. One can see the tension produced by this type of construction when Edwards speaks of a present and future justification: "A sinner, in his first justification, is forever justified and freed from all obligation to eternal punishment." However, he can also write: "Although the sinner is actually and finally justified on the first acts of faith, yet the perseverance of faith even then, comes into consideration, as one thing on which the fitness of acceptance to life depends. . . . God in the act of final justification which he passes at the sinner's conversion, has respect to perseverance in faith, and future acts of faith, as being virtually implied in the first act, is further manifest by this" ("Justification," 1:641).

102. Edwards, "Justification," 1:641; see also Maarten Wisse, "Habitus Fidei: An Essay on the History of a Concept," *SJT* 56 (2003): 172–89, esp. 185 n. 45; also Hunsinger, "Dispositional Soteriology," 109.

103. Hunsinger, "Dispositional Soteriology," 118–19.

104. Edwards, "Justification," 1:624.

theless, it appears as though he believed that the union was purely legal: "There is a legal union between Christ and true Christians; so that . . . one, in some respects, is accepted for the other by the Supreme Judge."[105] This formulation is somewhat different from how Calvin, for example, understood it. Calvin believed that it was both legal and a personal communion, or mutual indwelling, and therefore the believer's righteousness in Christ was not just virtual but real.[106] The believer's actual or inherent righteousness does not have to bear any weight in making the believer acceptable before God in Calvin's understanding, but in Edwards's strictly legal union there is no actual righteousness present, which therefore requires that the believer provide it.[107] This is not to say that the believer brings his own works apart from the indwelling of Christ. However, one should note that Edwards departs from the classic Reformed doctrine of justification when he writes: "What is *real* in the union between Christ and his people, is the foundation of what is *legal*; that is, it is something really in them, and between them, uniting them, that is the ground of the suitableness of their being accounted as one by the Judge."[108]

At this point Edwards reverses the historic Reformed understanding of justification by grounding it in the transformative work of the Spirit rather than the imputation of Christ's righteousness. It seems that Edwards's doctrine of justification is affected by his Platonist understanding of creation, namely that God never ceases creating and that it is a continual process, thereby confounding the doctrines of creation and providence. Hodge criticized Edwards at this point for the logical consequences of the continual creative activity of God: "There can be no free agency, no sin, no responsibility, no individual existence. The universe is only the self-manifestation of God. This doctrine, in its consequences, is essentially pantheistic."[109] This understanding of creation and its organic connection to all other doctrines, including justification, gives us the likely reason for the tensions in Edwards's understanding of justification—it is both definitive declaration in the present, but must also be grounded in the

---

105. Ibid., 1:625.
106. See Calvin, *Institutes*, 3.11.10.
107. Hunsinger, "Dispositional Soteriology," 112–13; Waddington, "Doctrine of Justification," 361 n. 10.
108. Edwards, "Justification," 1.626; see also Schafer, "Edwards and Justification," 58.
109. Hodge, *Systematic Theology*, 2:220; see also Michael S. Horton, *Covenant and Salvation: Union with Christ* (Louisville: Westminster John Knox, 2007), ch. 12.

transformative work of Christ in the believer. While Edwards does much to echo the historic Reformed faith, his construction has as much in common with the medieval Roman Catholic understandings of the doctrine. Moreover, we should note that many theologians interested in Eastern Orthodox views of soteriology have found Edwards to be a helpful bridge between the historic Reformed faith and Eastern views.[110]

It does not seem possible to argue that Edwards's construction is within the confines of Reformed orthodoxy; it is difficult to maintain that he holds a view that represents the historic understanding of *sola fide* as it is expressed in the Reformed confessions and creeds, which define Reformed theology and practice.[111] In some ways, Edwards's doctrine even anticipates current debates surrounding the relationship between justification and good works. Nevertheless, given the statements that one finds on the role of good works in justification, one thing is certain: at minimum, a cloud of ambiguity hangs over Edwards's doctrine of justification.[112]

Johann Gabler and Friedrich Schleiermacher

Far from colonial America on the continent of Europe the Enlightenment began to dawn over the theological landscape. The starting point for theological inquiry was no longer Scripture but human reason, which challenged the conception and place of biblical authority. This trend developed largely from the work of Immanuel Kant (1724–1804), who argued that there are two realms, the noumenal and phenomenal. According to Kant's understanding, human reason was limited to what is given in sense perception, that which is phenomenal. Hence, man cannot say much about God because he is in the noumenal realm; he is not accessible by means of sense perception.[113] According to this line of thinking, it was no longer possible to affirm the *Deus dixit*, "God says," of Scripture. There are two

---

110. See Michael J. McClymond, "Salvation as Divinization: Jonathan Edwards, Gregory Palamas and the Theological Uses of Neoplatonism," in *Jonathan Edwards: Philosophical Theologian*, ed. Paul Helm and Oliver D. Crisp (Aldershot: Ashgate, 2003), 139–60; also Pelikan, *Christian Tradition*, 5:161–62.

111. Waddington, "Doctrine of Justification," 359–60 n. 8; Heinrich Heppe, *Reformed Dogmatics* (London: George Allen & Unwin, 1950), 563.

112. Schafer, "Edwards and Justification," 57. See also the analysis in R. Scott Clark, *Recovering the Reformed Confession* (Phillipsburg, NJ: P&R, 2008), ch. 3.

113. See Robert E. Butts, "Noumenal/phenomenal," in *A Companion to Metaphysics*, ed. Jaegwon Kim and Ernest Sosa (Oxford: Blackwell, 1995), 362.

notable theologians in whom one can see Enlightenment rationalism take effect, namely Johann P. Gabler and Friedrich D. E. Schleiermacher.

Johann P. Gabler (1753–1826) first suggested the separation of biblical from dogmatic, or systematic, theology in his inaugural address at the University of Altdorf on 30 March 1787, which was entitled *De justo discrimine theologiae biblicae et dogmaticae regundisque recte utriusque finibus*, or "On the proper distinction between biblical and dogmatic theology and the specific objectives of each." Gabler was distressed over the preponderance and proliferation of theological opinions, divisions, and contention in his day. He argued that the theological chaos in his day arose "from an inappropriate combination of the simplicity and ease of biblical theology with the subtlety and difficulty of dogmatic theology."[114] In defining and distinguishing between biblical and dogmatic theology Gabler argued that the former was of historical origin whereas the latter was of didactic origin. The former arose from the Bible, and the latter from the opinion of theologians of the church.[115] Gabler wanted to strip away built-up philosophical and theological layers that had accumulated over the centuries and distill the pristine and eternal religion of the Scriptures. The manner that he proposed for arriving at the distilled religion is found in his methodology of situating each biblical text in its historical setting. Gabler writes:

> We must carefully collect and classify each of the ideas of each patriarch— Moses, David, and Solomon, and of each prophet with special attention to Isaiah, Jeremiah, Ezekiel, Daniel, Hosea, Zechariah, Haggai, Malachi, and the rest; and for many reasons we ought to include the apocryphal books for this same purpose; also we should include the ideas from the epoch of the New Testament, those of Jesus, Paul, Peter, John, and James. Above all, this process is completed in two ways: the one is in the legitimate interpretation of passages pertinent to this procedure; the other is in the careful comparison of the ideas of all the sacred authors among themselves.[116]

114. Johann P. Gabler, "An Oration on the Proper Distinction between Biblical and Dogmatic Theology and the Specific Objectives of Each," in *The Flowering of Old Testament Theology*, ed. Ben C. Ollenburger, Elmer A. Martens, and Gerhard F. Hasel (Winona Lake, IN: Eisenbrauns, 1992), 493.
115. Ibid., 495–96.
116. Ibid., 498.

Here we see, then, the historical nature of Gabler's approach. Nonetheless, we should note another key feature of Gabler's methodology.

Gabler was of the opinion that the authors of the various parts of Scripture were divinely inspired and armed with divine authority. It was the biblical-theological task, however, to discern "whether all the opinions of the Apostles, of every type and sort altogether, are truly divine, or rather whether some of them, which have no bearing on salvation, were left to their own ingenuity."[117] In other words, we see that Gabler believed that the biblical theologian had to evaluate the Scriptures and determine what belonged to divine revelation, that which spoke of the eternal universal religion, and that which belonged to the opinion, time, or culture of the biblical writer: "We must investigate what in the sayings of the Apostle is truly divine, and what perchance merely human."[118]

Another element that we see emerge in Gabler's understanding of the relationship between the testaments is the inherent superiority of the New Testament (NT) over the OT:

> All the sacred writers are holy men and are armed with divine authority; but not all attest to the same form of religion; some are doctors of the Old Testament of the same elements that Paul himself designated with the name "basic elements" [*stoicheia*]; others are of the newer and better Christian testament. And so the sacred authors, however much we must cherish them with equal reverence because of the divine authority that has been imprinted on their writings, cannot all be considered in the same category if we are referring to their use in dogmatics.[119]

In this statement, we find important contours of Gabler's understanding of biblical and dogmatic theology. Once again we should note that Gabler believed the Bible to be divinely inspired, but it was the interpreter's task to determine where the divinely inspired message lay in the text. Moreover, it is important to see that he calls the NT the "newer and better *Christian* testament," which means that he saw the OT as inherently sub-Christian.

117. Ibid., 501.
118. Ibid., 500.
119. Ibid., 497.

For the task of biblical theology, one would collect, classify, and historically situate particular texts; however, all of the collected data are not necessarily of value for dogmatic theology. Particular data are of use for dogmatics only if part of the universal and eternal religion. In other words, there is no unified organic, historically unfolding divine revelation, but rather only punctuated moments in history where the principles of the divine eternal religion are revealed, and even then, the principles must be distilled to be of any use for dogmatics. As Gabler writes, "For only from these methods can those . . . undoubted universal ideas be singled out, those ideas which alone are useful in dogmatic theology . . . a dogmatic theology adapted to our own times."[120] With Gabler's lecture, we begin to see a clear effort to divorce systematic from biblical theology, which continues to color contemporary expositions of the doctrine in our own day.

Friedrich Schleiermacher (1768–1834) reacted in a way similar to Gabler in his own construction of theology. If the noumenal realm was closed off to reason, then he would construct his theology entirely in the phenomenal realm. Schleiermacher believed that theology could be constructed only on the basis of a proper understanding of religion. As Paul Tillich (1886–1965) explains, for Schleiermacher "religion is not theoretical knowledge; it is not moral action; religion is feeling, feeling of absolute dependence." Schleiermacher therefore rejected historic orthodoxy, what he called supernaturalism, but he also rejected Kant's program, which he believed was rationalistic.[121] Instead, Schleiermacher cut a middle path for his theological program, one that centered upon the believer's feeling of absolute dependence on God. One can see this man-centered approach to theology in the following statement:

> Religion does not strive to bring those who believe and feel under a single belief and a single feeling. It strives, to be sure, to open the eyes of those who are not yet capable of intuiting the universe, for every one who sees is a new priest, a new mediator, a new mouthpiece; but for just this reason it avoids with aversion the barren uniformity that would again destroy the divine abundance.[122]

120. Ibid., 501.
121. Paul Tillich, *A History of Christian Thought*, ed., Carl E. Braaten (New York: Simon & Schuster, n.d.), 392.
122. Friedrich Schleiermacher, *On Religion*, trans. Richard Crouter (Cambridge: Cambridge University Press, 1988), 108.

One can also see the man-centered nature in his massive theological work, *The Christian Faith*, though its English title is misleading. The German title is *Glaubenslehre*, literally, "the doctrine of faith." He did not title it *Theology*, which is the study of God; rather, his work is a description of the Christian experience as it exists in the church.[123]

As one can well imagine, this had a great impact upon Schleiermacher's understanding of the doctrine of justification. If one reads what Schleiermacher has to say on justification, he might come to the conclusion that his doctrine is somewhat orthodox, as the chapter is even replete with references to historic Reformed confessions and catechisms, as well as Calvin's *Institutes*.[124] However, given his presuppositions about the nature of doctrine, justification is entirely about the human experience of divine dependence, and not at all about a forensic act of God. In this respect, one can see not only from Gabler, but also from Schleiermacher, that in the late eighteenth and early nineteenth century, doctrine was loosed from its moorings of the authoritative Word of God and set adrift upon the sea of autonomous human reason. Though there were notable exceptions to this general trend, for example, in the work of J. B. Lightfoot (1828–89), Charles Hodge (1797–1878), and James Buchanan (1804–70), the systematic theological expression of justification was often separated from acknowledgment of the divine and revealed nature of the Scriptures.[125] Also, with the development of the study of the history of religions, the Christian faith became one among many religions, and therefore the Bible was merely one among many ancient books. It is against this backdrop that we may turn to the writings of F. C. Baur.[126]

---

123. Tillich, *History*, 398–99; Friedrich Schleiermacher, *The Christian Faith*, trans. H. R. Mackintosh and J. S. Stewart (1830; London: T & T Clark, 2006).

124. Schleiermacher, *Christian Faith*, 496, 500, 503.

125. One may note the work of J. B. Lightfoot at Cambridge University who engaged the history of religions school (see "St. Paul and the Three," in *Paul's Epistle to the Galatians* [Peabody, MA: Hendrickson, 1999], 292–374). Also of note, representing the Princetonian tradition of the period, see Hodge, *Systematic Theology*, 3:114–212. From the Scottish church in the nineteenth century there was also James Buchanan, *The Doctrine of Justification* (1867; Edinburgh: Banner of Truth, 1991).

126. What follows is largely drawn from S. J. Hafemann, "Paul and His Interpreters," in *Dictionary of Paul and His Letters*, ed. Gerald F. Hawthorne, Ralph P. Martin, and Daniel G. Reid (Downers Grove, IL: InterVarsity, 1993), 666–79; and Guy P. Waters, *Justification and the New Perspectives on Paul* (Phillipsburg, NJ: P&R, 2004), 1–13.

Baur and the Tübingen School

F. C. Baur (1792–1860) was a professor of NT at the University of Tübingen from 1826 until his death in 1860. Baur began his work synthesizing his exegesis with the dialecticism of G. W. F. Hegel (1770–1831), arguing that there was a conflict between Gentile Christianity represented by Paul and Apollos, which was marked by being free of the law and Hellenism, and Jewish Christianity, represented by Peter, which was marked by the law and a Jewish understanding of Jesus.[127] It was in the midst of this conflict that Paul developed his doctrine of justification, which, argues Baur, is at the center of Paul's theology. Additionally, Baur concludes that only Romans, Galatians, and the Corinthian correspondence are authentically Pauline because only these letters evidence the Jewish-Gentile conflict. Baur argues that this conflict context shaped the entire discussion of justification throughout church history up through the Reformation.

Baur's basic understanding of justification is that Paul wanted to sever justification from its Jewish characteristics, namely that it was still bound to the law. It is out of the conflict between Jewish and Hellenistic Christianity that Paul was able to universalize the Christian faith by detaching it from the law.[128] According to Herman Ridderbos (1909–2007), for Baur the center of Paul's thought lies in his doctrine of justification by faith alone and the Spirit, where he "takes this in the Hegelian sense as the infinite and absolute in opposition to the finite (the flesh)."[129] Baur, for example, writes: "It is now a relation of spirit to spirit, in which the spirit, as the principle of the subjective consciousness, is drawn into union with the spirit of God, as the spirit of Christ which is its objective basis."[130]

Classic Liberalism

Moving beyond Baur one finds further development in the doctrine of justification under the influence of the history of religions school.[131]

---

127. F. C. Baur, "The Christ-Party in the Corinthian Church, the Conflict between Petrine and Pauline Christianity in the Early Church, the Apostle Peter in Rome," *Tübinger Zeitschrift für Theologie* 4 (1831): 61–206; see also Herman Ridderbos, *Paul: An Outline of His Theology*, trans. John Richard De Witt (1975; Grand Rapids: Eerdmans, 1992), 16.

128. Ridderbos, *Paul*, 16.

129. Ibid.; see also F. C. Baur, *Paul the Apostle of Jesus Christ* (1873; Peabody, MA: Hendrickson, 2003), 135–68.

130. Baur, *Paul*, 161–62.

131. See, e.g., Wilhelm Bousset, *Kyrios Christos*, trans. John E. Steely (Nashville: Abingdon, 1970), 153–210; and Richard Reitsenstein, *Hellenistic Mystery-Religions*, trans. John E. Steely (Pittsburgh: Pickwick Press, 1978), 320–32.

Scholars debated the question of whether Paul's theology was influenced by Greek or Jewish thought. There was also the belief that there were two competing centers in Paul's thought: the forensic, justification by faith alone, and the mystical or relational, union with Christ.[132] The history of religions school believed that Paul was influenced by the Hellenistic thought and therefore searched for parallels in Hellenistic mystery religions. As a result, scholars from this school of thought constructed a theological portrait of Paul that was severed from historic Christianity and its cardinal doctrines.[133] According to the history of religions school, Paul was simply setting forth themes present in many other Hellenistic religions: victory, resurrection, and immortality of the deity that was to be worshiped.[134] Additionally, the history of religions school believed that the mystical, or union with Christ, was of greater foundational importance than justification. One who was diametrically opposed to the history of religions project was Albert Schweitzer.

Albert Schweitzer (1875–1965), like the history of religions school, argued that union with Christ was central to Paul's thinking, but that it was characterized by eschatology.[135] Schweitzer believed, however, that for Paul, justification was an incidental doctrine. Schweitzer famously writes: "The doctrine of righteousness by faith is therefore a subsidiary crater, which has formed within the rim of the main crater—the mystical doctrine of redemption through the being-in-Christ."[136] Additionally, Schweitzer argued that in Paul's understanding of justification "there is no logical route from the righteousness by faith to a theory of ethics"; in other words, that Paul's doctrine of justification naturally leads to antinomianism.[137]

Summary

In the eighteenth and nineteenth centuries there were many sweeping changes that took place that challenged the proper understanding of the doctrine of justification. With the onset of rationalism, theologians tried to

132. Ridderbos, *Paul*, 17–18.
133. Waters, *Justification*, 9.
134. Ridderbos, *Paul*, 23.
135. Albert Schweitzer, *The Mysticism of Paul the Apostle*, trans. William Montgomery (1931; Baltimore: Johns Hopkins University Press, 1998), 138–40.
136. Ibid., 225.
137. Ibid.

strip the Scriptures of their divine authority and construct man-centered systems of theology. In the case of Schleiermacher, however, his system is more properly understood as a system of anthropology, or better yet, psychology. There was also a tendency to search for the center of Paul's thought, some placing justification there and others union with Christ. Here in the eighteenth and nineteenth centuries are the seeds of a debate that continues into the present, namely the supposed antithesis between the forensic and mystical categories.

It should be noted that an underlying presupposition undergirding doctrinal development at this stage in church history was a low view of Scripture, one that truncated the Pauline corpus as well as pitted Scripture against itself, namely the supposed battle between the so-called Petrine and Pauline understandings of justification. Schweitzer's observation of the eschatological character of Paul's soteriology, however, is an important and positive development, one that colors future development of the understanding of justification in a positive manner. At this point, though, we may observe that during the eighteenth and nineteenth centuries justification was once again moving right of center toward neonomianism and eventually surfaced in popular movements such as the Social Gospel. There was, of course, also the claim of Schweitzer that Paul's doctrine of justification led to antinomianism. There appears to be little effort during this period to locate justification in the *historia salutis*, though one can argue that Schweitzer moved the debate in that direction with his emphasis upon eschatology. It is also in the eighteenth century where we see dogmatic, or systematic, theology pitted against biblical theology, a trend that continues in our own day.

Justification in the Twentieth Century to the Present

Karl Barth

In the twentieth century, one of the most influential theologians has been Karl Barth (1886–1968). Along with Emil Brunner (1889–1966), Barth was one of the chief representatives of neoorthodoxy. Barth rejected the theology of classic liberalism, especially the theology of the likes of Schleiermacher. At the same time, however, Barth did not want to return to the theology of Protestant orthodoxy, namely the Reformed and Lutheran scholastic theology of the seventeenth century. Barth cut his own path and hence is known for *neo-* or "new orthodoxy." So in one sense, one can say that Barth represents a rebirth of Protestant orthodoxy, something that is evident from his exhaustive quotations and citations from sixteenth- and seventeenth-century Protestant theology. On the other hand, Barth certainly did not fear departing from the classically held views, and this is certainly the case with his doctrine of justification. There are three elements of which we should take note concerning Barth's doctrine.

First, Barth rejected the classical Protestant law-gospel hermeneutic, whether in the Reformed understanding of the Scriptures in terms of the covenants of works and grace, or in the Lutheran division of the Scriptures into law and gospel. Barth inverted the traditional law-gospel hermeneutic and offered his gospel-law understanding.[138] As Clark explains, "There are not, considered hermeneutically, two words in Scripture—'do' and 'done for you'—but only one word: grace, which takes different historical forms (Moses and Christ). Of course, for Barth, 'grace' means the universal electing favor of God."[139]

This brings us to a second point, namely Barth's doctrine of election. In Barth's understanding of election, there is no selection and rejection of individuals. Rather, Jesus is both the elected and rejected man.[140] Election is of course manifest in justification. If all men are both elected and rejected in Christ, then it stands to reason that all men are therefore justified in Christ.[141] With Barth's doctrine of election, it seems like a logical conclusion that all of history, including the manifestation of man's justification, is rendered superfluous.

Third, if Barth rejected the law-gospel hermeneutic in favor of a gospel-law understanding, then it should be no surprise that he also rejected the covenant of works. In an extensive footnote, Barth traced the development of the history of bi-covenantal theology, that of the covenants of works and grace, in the Reformed tradition. Given Barth's

138. See Karl Barth, *Community, State, and Church* (1960; Eugene, OR: Wipf & Stock, 2004), 71–100; Thomas Coates, "The Barthian Inversion: Gospel and Law," *Concordia Theological Monthly* 26 (1955): 481–91; Jesse Couenhoven, "Law and Gospel, or the Law of the Gospel? Karl Barth's Political Theology Compared with Luther and Calvin," *JRE* 30 (2002): 181–205.

139. Clark, "Letter and Spirit," 351.

140. Karl Barth, *Church Dogmatics*, ed. G. W. Bromiley and T. F. Torrance, 13 vols. (Edinburgh: T & T Clark, 1936–62), 4.1:516.

141. Stanley J. Grenz and Roger E. Olson, *Twentieth Century Theology* (Downers Grove, IL: InterVarsity, 1992), 74–77.

christomonism, namely that God is solely and exclusively revealed in Christ, and not at all in nature, and his doctrine of election, that all men are elected and rejected in Christ, Barth believed that the covenant of works was a foreign imposition upon the Scriptures. Moreover, Barth believed that it was unthinkable that the members of the Trinity would make a legal agreement to redeem man. Barth therefore considered the *pactum salutis* "mythology."[142] For these reasons, then, Barth rejected the covenant of works and instead believed:

> In this free act of the election of grace there is already present, and presumed, and assumed into unity with His own existence as God, the existence of the man whom He intends and loves from the very first and in whom He intends and loves all other men, of the man in whom He wills to bind Himself with all other men and all other men with Himself. . . . He in whom the covenant of grace is fulfilled and revealed in history is also its eternal basis.[143]

Given Barth's christomonistic approach, he therefore collapses all of God's dealings with man, even those in preredemptive history, into one covenant, a covenant of grace.

One can see how Barth's understanding of justification is thereby colored by his christomonistic mono-covenantal approach. Rejecting the covenant of works, and more generally the works principle, undermines the relationship between justification and obedience, whether the obedience of the first Adam or the obedience of the last Adam as the ground of the believer's justification. To reject the works principle, or covenant of works, moves one's doctrine of justification closer to Roman Catholic theology rather than historic Protestant expressions, which reflect the traditional law-gospel contrast.[144]

Bultmann and Käsemann

In twentieth-century biblical studies it is the work of Rudolf Bultmann (1884–1976) that stands in the foreground. In a sense, one might argue that Bultmann rejected the trends of the NT guild at the

142. Barth, *Church Dogmatics*, 4.1:65.
143. Ibid., 4.1:66.
144. See Meredith G. Kline, "Gospel until the Law: Rom. 5:13–14 and the Old Covenant," *JETS* 34/4 (1991): 433–46, esp. 435.

time, the influences of the history of religions school, and explained Paul's understanding of justification in terms of traditional Lutheranism—justification was central to Paul and was to be understood in forensic terms. This is not to say, however, that Bultmann was an unreconstructed Lutheran in his understanding of justification. As many know, Bultmann was highly influenced by the existentialist philosophy of Martin Heidegger (1889–1976). Bultmann believed that the individual was central in justification, which is evident when he writes that "man's death has its cause in the fact that man in his striving to live out of his own resources loses his self," but on the other hand, "life arises out of surrendering one's self to God, thereby gaining one's self."[145] Bultmann argued that justification was granted, therefore, to the individual and that it was a forensic and eschatological concept. He also believed that it was received by God's grace and not by the works of the law.[146]

Bultmann allowed his radically individualistic understanding of justification to swallow up redemptive history; his existentialist *ordo* engulfed the *historia salutis*.[147] The individual stood in the presence of God apart from covenant or a covenant community. Though certainly of a different stripe, one may say that Bultmann's theology was something of a return to the ontological theology of Aquinas and the *via antiqua*, which conceived of man's relationship to God in ontological terms.

On the other side of the spectrum, however, one finds the work of Ernst Käsemann (1906–98). Käsemann opposed Bultmann's individualistic understanding and argued that justification needed to be understood in a corporate manner. Käsemann argued that God's righteousness was not primarily a gift given to the individual as much as it was a cosmic and creative power under which the individual was brought to live as part of a corporate body.[148] Käsemann, for example, defined the *dikaiosynē theou* of Romans 1:17, not as something that God imputes to the believer by faith but as his covenant faithfulness.[149]

---

145. Rudolf Bultmann, *Theology of the New Testament: Complete in One Volume*, trans. Kendrick Grobel (New York: Charles Scribner's Sons, 1951–55), 1:270.

146. Ibid., 1:279–80.

147. Hafemann, "Paul and His Interpreters," 676.

148. Ibid.

149. Ernst Käsemann, "The Righteousness of God in Paul," *ZTK* 58 (1961): 367–78; also idem, *New Testament Questions of Today* (Minneapolis: Fortress, 1969), 168–82.

Käsemann's emphases would be further developed by scholars of the New Perspective on Paul.

The New Perspective on Paul: Stendahl, Sanders, Wright, and Dunn

In any discipline there are always dissenting voices to commonly held assumptions, and the same can be said for NT studies and its assessment of first-century Judaism. Certainly from the earliest days, it has been almost axiomatic that first-century Judaism was a religion of works-righteousness, or legalism. There were those such as Claude G. Montefiore (1858–1938) and George Foot Moore (1851–1931), however, who in the earlier part of the twentieth century began to make strides in correcting what had essentially become a caricature of first-century Judaism.[150] The work of Montefiore and Moore was later followed by W. D. Davies's work *Paul and Rabbinic Judaism*, which was a revised version of his dissertation written under C. H. Dodd (1884–1973) and David Daube (1909–99) at Cambridge University.[151] This book had a positive assessment of the Judaism of Paul, and influenced a generation of Pauline scholars to begin a concerted effort to read Paul and the rest of the NT in the context of Judaism.[152] In the years that followed there would be others who would seek to reevaluate first-century Judaism.

Krister Stendahl, in a lecture delivered to the American Psychological Association in 1961, complained that the interpretation of Paul in the twentieth century had been unduly influenced by the interpretive legacy of Luther: "The Reformers' interpretation of Paul rests on an analogism when Pauline statements about Faith and Works, Law and Gospel, Jews and Gentiles are read in the framework of late medieval piety. The Law, the Torah, with its specific requirements of circumcision and food restric-

---

150. See Claude G. Montefiore, "Rabbinic Judaism and the Epistles of St. Paul," *JQR* 13/2 (1900–1901): 161–217; George Foot Moore, "Christian Writers on Judaism," *HTR* 14/3 (1921), 197–254.

151. W. D. Davies, *Paul and Rabbinic Judaism* (London: SPCK, 1948).

152. David E. Aune, "Recent Readings of Paul Relating to Justification by Faith," in *Rereading Paul Together*, ed. David E. Aune (Grand Rapids: Baker, 2006), 189–96; see also Cornelis Venema, *The Gospel of Free Acceptance in Christ* (Edinburgh: Banner of Truth, 2006), 94–96; Stephen Westerholm, *Perspectives Old and New on Paul* (Grand Rapids: Eerdmans, 2004), 118–28.

tions becomes a general principle of 'legalism' in religious matters."[153] Stendahl's overall criticism was that NT scholars had read Paul in terms of the individual's struggle with sin as Luther had supposedly read him in the sixteenth century.[154] According to Stendahl, Luther read the anachronistic medieval question of merit back into Paul's epistles to Rome and Galatia rather than read him in his first-century context. Stendahl's criticism did not go unheard.

E. P. Sanders in his watershed work *Paul and Palestinian Judaism* set out to destroy the general Christian view of Judaism as a religion of legalism, or works-righteousness. Sanders wrote to refute the common opinion that Jews were interested in earning their salvation through their obedience to the law. Sanders researched the literature of second-temple Judaism and concluded that it was a religion of grace. Sanders coined the term "covenantal nomism" to describe first-century Judaism: "the view that one's place in God's plan is established on the basis of the covenant and that the covenant requires as the proper response of man his obedience to its commandments, while providing means of atonement for transgression."[155] Regarding the specific nature of the law and its function within Judaism Sanders identifies eight characteristics:

1. God has chosen Israel.
2. He has given Israel the law, which implies
3. God's promise to maintain the election and
4. The requirements to obey.
5. God rewards obedience and punishes transgression.
6. The law provides for means of atonement, which results in
7. Maintenance or re-establishment of the covenantal relationship.
8. All those who are maintained in the covenant by obedience, atonement, and God's mercy belong to the group that will be saved.[156]

---

153. Krister Stendahl, "The Apostle Paul and the Introspective Conscience of the West," *HTR* 56 (1963): 199–215; also idem, *Paul among Jews and Gentiles* (Minneapolis: Fortress, 1976), 85–86.
154. Stendahl, *Paul*, 82.
155. E. P. Sanders, *Paul and Palestinian Judaism* (Minneapolis: Fortress, 1977), 75.
156. Ibid., 422.

Sanders's thesis is that Judaism is based upon election and covenant, in other words, the grace of God. In the minds of many NT scholars, Sanders's reevaluation of Judaism was the needed illumination upon Paul's context to evaluate better the historical-contextual setting of his epistles. Sanders's work sets the stage for the work of N. T. Wright.

Shortly after the work of Stendahl and Sanders, N. T. Wright joined the chorus of those objecting to a Lutheranized Paul. Wright argued that Lutheran interpreters such as Gerhard Ebeling (1912–2001) had to divorce the doctrine of justification from history in order to preserve the Lutheran distinctives of a theology of the Word and the *theologia crucis*, the theology of the cross.[157] Wright also argued, "The tradition of Pauline interpretation has manufactured a false Paul by manufacturing a false Judaism for him to oppose." Again, like Stendahl, Wright argues that the portrait of the Jews as legalistic was first manufactured in the sixteenth century by Luther in his battle against Rome.[158] Wright therefore concludes: "We have, in short, as a result of a projection of reformation and modern ideas into the world of Paul, an apostle of faith, or at least of imagination, who reveals more about his inventors than about the Paul of history."[159] Wright goes on to argue, "The categories with which we are to understand Paul, and for that matter the whole New Testament, are not the thin, tired and anachronistic ones of Lutheran polemic. They are the ones given to us by the Paul of history himself."[160] Wright was not alone in his observations, as another key player would join the chorus of dissent.

James Dunn, drawing upon Stendahl's ground-breaking essay, believes like Wright before him, that Paul had been read in terms of Luther's battle with Roman Catholicism. In the light of Sanders's work, particularly his research in the literature of the second temple, interpreters finally were able to "see Paul properly within his own context, to hear Paul in terms of his own time, to let Paul be himself."[161] It is Dunn who coined the term "the New Perspective on Paul."

157. N. T. Wright, "The Paul of History and the Apostle of Faith," *TynBul* 29 (1978): 73; cf. Gerhard Ebeling, *Word and Faith* (London: SCM Press, 1963), 34–36, 54–56.

158. Wright, "Paul of History," 78–79.

159. Ibid., 81.

160. Ibid., 87.

161. James D. G. Dunn, "The New Perspective on Paul," *BJRL* 65 (1983): 95–122; idem, *Jesus, Paul, and the Law* (Louisville: Westminster John Knox, 1990), 185–86.

Recent Ecumenical Trends: Kärkkäinen, Braaten, and Jenson

When we turn to the ecumenical scene in the late twentieth and early twenty-first century, we find a number of authors all but scuttling the doctrine of justification. Some theologians who have a great interest in ecumenism, especially those interested in repairing the breach between the Eastern and Western churches, have done much work to show that the doctrine of justification is compatible, even interchangeable, with the Eastern Orthodox doctrine of theosis, or divinization. Carl Braaten and Robert Jenson co-edited a volume that offers a rereading of Martin Luther's early thought on the doctrine of justification, that which antedates significantly his mature thought on the subject; they argue that the German Reformer's doctrine of justification is compatible with theosis. Braaten and Jenson present a Luther versus the Lutherans thesis and try to make the case that it was later Lutheranism that placed a heavy emphasis on forensic categories such as imputation.[162] Along similar lines, and working on a selective reading of the early Luther, Veli-Matti Kärkkäinen collapses justification and sanctification into his doctrine of salvation, and then argues that this holistic doctrine is compatible with theosis.[163]

Summary

Thus far we may summarize the twentieth century up to the present as an initial acceptance and subsequent rejection of the philosophically influenced exegesis of previous generations and a greater desire to explore the doctrine of justification within its immediate first-century context, which is an improvement over the history of religions school, the classic liberalism of the eighteenth and nineteenth centuries, and the existentialist reading of Bultmann. It is important, as Sanders, Dunn, and Wright have argued, to understand Paul within his historical context. New Perspective explanations, however, suffer from allowing first-

---

162. Carl E. Braaten and Robert W. Jenson, eds., *Union with Christ* (Grand Rapids: Eerdmans, 1998); see also Tuomo Mannermaa, *Christ Present in Faith* (Minneapolis: Fortress, 2005); Robert W. Jenson, *Systematic Theology*, 2 vols. (Oxford: Oxford University Press, 1999), 2:290–301. For an exchange of essays related to the Finnish interpretation of Luther and the compatibility of justification and theosis between Paul Metzger, Mark Seifrid, Carl Trueman, and Robert Jenson, see *WTJ* 65 (2003): 201–50.

163. Veli-Matti Kärkkäinen, *One with God: Salvation as Deification and Justification* (Collegeville, MN: Liturgical Press, 2004), 107.

century history to swallow the *historia salutis*. Moreover, for all of their effort to understand Paul and set aside the polemics of the sixteenth and seventeenth centuries between the Reformation and RCC, many contemporary scholars fail to recognize the established poles of antinomianism and neonomianism and that nothing new has been brought to the table in two thousand years in this regard. Or some in the current period, such as Wright and Dunn, unknowingly echo a RCC understanding of justification as their own explanations of Paul's doctrine, moving right of center toward neonomianism with concepts such as future justification on the basis of the believer's good works. The movement toward neonomianism is certainly evident in Sanders's covenantal nomism: one enters the covenant by grace but maintains his position by works. Covenantal nomism, if one pardons the anachronism, is semi-Pelagian and compatible with, if not strikingly similar to, Roman Catholic soteriology. The period is also marked by a nominal understanding of the history of the development of the doctrine of justification and even a desire to bring about ecumenism at the expense of accurate historical theology and sound exegesis.

Summary and Conclusion

We have seen that the history of the development of the doctrine of justification has been an oscillation between the two poles of antinomianism and neonomianism. Key concepts that emerge that pertain to the *ordo salutis* for which one must account in his formulation of the doctrine are faith, works, the nature of the communication of righteousness, whether it is infused or imputed, or ontological or forensic, and whether such categories are even proper. There is also the important task of relating justification to the rest of the *ordo salutis*. In other words, is justification at the center of Paul's soteriology, or is it a subsidiary crater to the greater and more important doctrine of union with Christ? Central to an understanding of justification is also the doctrine's relationship to both its historical, that is, the first-century, and redemptive-historical contexts. Was Paul reacting against Judaistic legalism? In what way is justification related to the sweep of the unfolding plan of God's redemption? Or, stated in another way, one must employ systematic and biblical theology in the effort to set forth the doctrine of justification by faith alone. In deciding

54

these issues one must beware of the Scylla and Charybdis of antinomian-ism and neonomianism. One should avoid errors in either direction but at the same time be willing to appropriate insights from any period and quarter of the development of the doctrine of justification so that, in the end, one is closer to a more accurate understanding of the message of Scripture. It is therefore to the subject of prolegomena that we now turn and begin the positive exposition of the doctrine of justification.

2

JUSTIFICATION
AND PROLEGOMENA

In any study of doctrine it is necessary for one to establish presuppositions, which in the discipline of systematic theology has been treated under prolegomena. One does not want to set forth an entire prolegomena, as this is far beyond the scope of this volume. Nevertheless, there are several issues that are related to the doctrine of justification that require attention before proceeding with our study. First, in recent literature on justification one finds the claim that justification is but one way the New Testament (NT) conceptualizes our redemption. The question must be asked, Is Paul's explanation of justification one of many different but nonetheless equal metaphors? A second issue that confronts our investigation is the question of whether justification is at the center of Paul's theology. Does it serve as Paul's and therefore the NT's central dogma? Or is it, as Albert Schweitzer once opined, a subsidiary crater alongside Paul's doctrine of union with Christ? Third, there is the question of the relationship between justification and the rest of the *ordo salutis*. In Lutheran dogmatics, for example, there are some who give justification absolute priority even over effectual calling and regeneration. In many Reformation and post-Reformation Reformed theologies, on the other hand, union with Christ is said to underlie the entire *ordo salutis*. How can one be united to Christ before one's justification? It is, then, these three issues, the nature of theological language, the question of whether justification is central for Paul's theology, and the place of justification in the *ordo salutis*, that we will cover in this chapter on prolegomena. It is to the first issue, the nature of theological language, to which we now turn.

The Nature of Theological Language

Historic Understanding

In theological treatments of the doctrine of justification prior to the nineteenth century, most believed that Paul's language of justification reflected the reality that the believer was pronounced righteous in God's sight and that this declaration would be made manifest on the day of judgment. Charles Hodge (1797–1878), for example, begins his chapter on justification by quoting the definition in the Westminster Shorter Catechism, which defines justification as "an act of God's free grace, wherein he pardons all our sins, and accepts us as righteous in his sight, only for the righteousness of Christ imputed to us, and received by faith alone" (q. 33).[1] It is immediately evident from this statement that justification is not conceived of as one of many different ways, or one metaphor among many, by which to describe one's salvation. That justification is not one among many metaphors of redemption is evident when the catechism states that justification "is an act of God." But since the nineteenth century and the rise of critical scholarship, different understandings of Paul's language about justification have arisen.

Competing Conceptions of Redemption: Wrede and Schweitzer

Wilhelm Wrede (1859–1906) argued that for Paul the doctrine of justification was merely a polemic weapon he employed against the Judaizers by which he set out to prove both the necessity of divorcing Christianity from Jewish national customs, such as circumcision, and the superiority

---

1. Charles Hodge, *Systematic Theology*, 3 vols. (Grand Rapids: Eerdmans, 1993), 3:114.

of the Christian faith.[2] In fact, in a rejection of the Reformation understanding of the centrality of justification for Paul, Wrede could write: "The Reformation has accustomed us to look upon this as the central point of Pauline doctrine; but it is not so. In fact the whole Pauline religion can be expounded without a word being said about this doctrine, unless it be in the part devoted to the Law."[3] Wrede argued that the doctrine of justification had largely disappeared in his day because the polemical context that necessitated its propagation had vanished as well.[4] Implicit in Wrede's argument is the idea that justification is not a necessary element of Paul's theology or the sinner's redemption.

In the thought of Albert Schweitzer (1875–1965) one finds similar opinions regarding the doctrine of justification. Schweitzer makes the claim that for Paul there are two independent conceptions of the forgiveness of sins. According to the first conception, God forgives sins on the basis of the atoning death of Christ. The second conception, argues Schweitzer, sees the forgiveness of sins through the death and resurrection of Christ. Schweitzer argues that the first view is the traditional, what we can label the law-court, or forensic view. The second is labeled as that of mystical union.[5] In other words, Schweitzer believed that there were two competing models of redemption in Paul's thought, the forensic and the mystical. Schweitzer's understanding of Paul's supposed two models led him to make his famous statement that "the doctrine of righteousness by faith is therefore a subsidiary crater, which has formed within the rim of the main crater—the mystical doctrine of redemption through the being-in-Christ."[6] In fact, Schweitzer argued that the church had adopted the forensic model of redemption almost to the exclusion of the mystical.[7] This same line of argumentation, though in a much more refined form, finds expression in a broad cross-section of contemporary theologians.

2. Wilhelm Wrede, *Paul*, trans. Edward Lummis (Boston: American Unitarian Association, 1908), 127.
3. Ibid., 123.
4. Ibid., 173.
5. Albert Schweitzer, *The Mysticism of Paul the Apostle*, trans. William Montgomery (1931; Baltimore: Johns Hopkins University Press, 1998), 223.
6. Ibid., 225.
7. Ibid., 387.

Justification One of Many Metaphors

There are a host of contemporary theologians who argue that justification is but one way to express our redemption in Christ. Wolfhart Pannenberg (1928–) makes the claim that "God's saving work in Jesus Christ is the central theme of all the NT writings. The doctrine of justification is just one of many ways of expounding the theme."[8] Veli-Matti Kärkkäinen states that though one does find the terminology of the "imputation of righteousness" in the NT, it "is a derivative concept and merely one way to illustrate dimensions of salvation."[9] N. T. Wright argues in his Romans commentary: "Paul develops the bookkeeping metaphor in the direction of employment and wage-earning. This is the only time he uses this metaphorical field in all his discussions of justification, and we should not allow this unique and brief sidelight to become the dominant note, as it has in much post-Reformation discussion."[10] Likewise, Stanley Grenz (1950–2005) argues in order to understand the Spirit's activity in the application of the work of Christ one may "draw from a legal metaphor," namely justification.[11] It is perhaps James Dunn who gives one of the more full-orbed statements regarding the use of metaphor in the language of redemption:

> Paul uses a rich and varied range of metaphors in his attempt to spell out the significance of Christ's death. We have highlighted the most important ones—representation, sacrifice, curse, redemption, reconciliation, conquest of the powers. It is important to recognize their character as metaphors: the significance of Christ's death could be adequately expressed only in imagery and metaphor. As with all metaphors, the metaphor is not the thing itself but a means of expressing its meaning. It would be unwise, then, to translate these metaphors as literal facts, as though, for example, Christ's death were literally a sacrifice provided by God (as priest?) in the cosmos, conceived as a temple.

8. Wolfhart Pannenberg, *Systematic Theology*, trans. Geoffrey Bromiley, 3 vols. (Grand Rapids: Eerdmans, 1998), 3:213.
9. Veli-Matti Kärkkäinen, *One with God: Salvation as Deification and Justification* (Collegeville, MN: Liturgical Press, 2004), 122.
10. N. T. Wright, *Romans*, NIB 10 (Nashville: Abingdon, 2004), 491.
11. Stanley Grenz, *Theology for the Community of God* (Nashville: Broadman & Holman, 1994), 567.

In fact, Dunn goes as far as to claim that "no one metaphor is adequate to unfold the full significance of Christ's death."[12]

Another line of argumentation that some theologians pursue in connection with metaphor and justification is the idea that in most Western theology, following Augustine (354–430) through Anselm (1033–1109) and up to Martin Luther (1483–1546), theologians have latched on to the legal metaphor. Given the cultural context and influence of Roman law, and the legal training of many prominent theologians of the Western tradition, such as Tertullian (160–220), Luther, or John Calvin (1509–64), it was only natural that the theology of the West would be dominated by the legal metaphor. Though Grenz places the onus more broadly upon the shoulders of Western theology as a whole, others such as Clark Pinnock place the blame for the supposed erroneous overemphasis upon the legal metaphor squarely on Luther's shoulders. Pinnock writes, "Union with God was not the central category for the Reformers. As a monk Luther feared God's judgment and sought acquittal in Jesus Christ. Since then Protestants have made justification a principal article of faith. This means that the legal dimension has dominated our thinking about salvation."[13]

Metaphor, Ecumenism, and Justification

If these theologians are correct in their assertion that Paul, and the rest of Scripture for that matter, uses many different metaphors to communicate the nature of our redemption, then there are a host of implications for one's doctrine of justification. The implications are most easily identified in the context of ecumenism. If, for example, the forensic language of justification is but one way to image our redemption, then it is not the only way to do so, and, as Wrede once claimed, Paul's doctrine of justification was only a product of his historical context. In our own historical context, we may choose to emphasize other metaphors. So, then, the forensic view of justification in the Western church is equally as valid as the metaphor of union with Christ. The two views are not mutually exclusive but are instead simply different noncompetitive or complementary metaphors.

12. James D. G. Dunn, *The Theology of Paul the Apostle* (Grand Rapids: Eerdmans, 1998), 231.

13. Clark H. Pinnock, *Flame of Love* (Downers Grove, IL: InterVarsity, 1996), 155; Grenz, *Theology for the Community*, 567.

If this is the true state of affairs, then if the West has an emphasis upon the forensic and the East upon theosis, deification, which many theologians argue is equivalent to union with Christ, then a reunification of the Western and Eastern churches is far more likely.[14] It is not that one is right and the other wrong, but rather that both articulate equally valid metaphors that the Bible uses to give expression to our redemption. In this regard, Dunn goes as far as to say that "it would be unwise, therefore, to make one of these images normative and to fit all the rest into it, even the predominant metaphor of sacrifice."[15] Are these assertions correct? Is the Bible's language about justification one of many metaphors? Quite simply, no. One cannot argue that justification is only a metaphor.[16]

Critique of Justification as Metaphor

Metaphor, "an implied comparison, the transfer of a descriptive term to an object to which it is not literally applicable," is certainly found throughout the pages of the Scriptures.[17] When Christ called Herod Antipas a fox (Luke 13:32), we see a use of metaphor. The use of metaphor as a grammatical category of interpretation is not the specific question at hand. Rather, it is the issue of "metaphorical theology." As some have explained it, such as Sallie McFague, theological metaphors refer to real-

14. See Carl E. Braaten and Robert W. Jenson, eds., *Union with Christ* (Grand Rapids: Eerdmans, 1998), viii; Tuomo Mannermaa, *Christ Present in Faith* (Minneapolis: Fortress, 2005), 87; Kärkkäinen, *One with God*, ix. A number of other scholars from Roman Catholic and Lutheran backgrounds make a similar claim (see Margaret O'Gara, "The Significance of the Joint Declaration on the Doctrine of Justification and the Next Steps in Ecumenical Dialogue," and Michael Root, "Continuing the Conversation: Deeper Agreement on Justification as Criterion and on the Christian as *simul iustus et peccator*," in Wayne C. Stumme, ed., *The Gospel of Justification in Christ* [Grand Rapids: Eerdmans, 2006], 29, 53, 58–59).

15. Dunn, *Theology of Paul*, 231. One finds similar conclusions in a number of works. See Joseph A. Fitzmyer, "Justification by Faith in Pauline Thought: A Catholic View," in *Rereading Paul Together*, ed. David E. Aune (Grand Rapids: Baker, 2006), 82; idem, *Paul and His Theology* (1967; Upper Saddle River, NJ: Prentice Hall, 1989), 59; N. T. Wright, "The Letter to the Galatians: Exegesis and Theology," in *Between Two Horizons*, ed. Joel B. Green and Max Turner (Grand Rapids: Eerdmans, 2002), 218; Kevin J. Vanhoozer, *The Drama of Doctrine* (Louisville: Westminster John Knox, 2005), 385; John R. Franke, *The Character of Theology* (Grand Rapids: Baker, 2005), 130.

16. So Guy P. Waters, *Justification and the New Perspectives on Paul* (Phillipsburg, NJ: P&R, 2004), 192. This is an important point, as justification as metaphor has seemingly been uncritically accepted by some (see Brian Vickers, *Jesus' Blood and Righteousness: Paul's Theology of Imputation* [Wheaton, IL: Crossway, 2006], 72, 202, 225).

17. F. B. Huey Jr. and Bruce Corley, *A Student's Dictionary for Biblical and Theological Studies* (Grand Rapids: Zondervan, 1983), 124, s.v. "*metaphor.*"

ity, in this case our redemption, but they do not refer to this reality in a positivistic or ultimate fashion. The idea behind metaphorical truth is that the metaphor is appropriate for a given situation but not binding. In each given situation the metaphors give way to new and more contextually significant metaphors.[18] Historically, Reformed theology has acknowledged something similar to McFague's metaphorical theology, though this is not to say that there is exact consonance. In fact, there are some significant differences.

Archetypal and ectypal theology

Traditionally Reformed theology has recognized that theological language about God is not univocal but ultimately analogical. Reformed theologians did not develop the terminology but harvested it from medieval theology.[19] Reformed theologians of the seventeenth century employed the pair of terms *theologia archetypa* and *theologia ectypa* to explain the difference between God's knowledge and our knowledge. *Theologia archetypa* (archetypal theology) is the infinite knowledge of God known to God alone; it is both infinite and simple, seeing that the divine essence is identical with all of the divine attributes. *Theologia ectypa* (ectypal theology), on the other hand, is all true but finite knowledge of God that he reveals in the Word; it is a copy or reflection of the archetype or pattern.[20] Employing these concepts, Francis Turretin (1623–87) explains:

> When God is set forth as the object of theology, he is not to be regarded simply as God in himself (for thus he is incomprehensible [*akatalēptos*] to us), but as revealed and as he has been pleased to manifest himself to us in his word, so that divine revelation is the formal relation which comes to be considered in this object. Nor is he to be considered exclusively under the relation of deity (according to the opinion of Thomas Aquinas and many scholastics after him, for in this manner the knowledge of him could not be saving but deadly to sinners), but as he is our God (i.e., covenanted in Christ as he has revealed himself to us in his word not only as the object

18. See Sallie McFague, *Metaphorical Theology* (Philadelphia: Fortress, 1984), 39–41; Grant R. Osbourne, *The Hermeneutical Spiral* (Downers Grove, IL: InterVarsity, 1991), 105–6, 429 nn. 25–26.

19. See, e.g., Thomas Aquinas, *Summa contra Gentiles*, trans. Anton C. Pegis, 4 vols. (1955; London: University of Notre Dame Press, 1975), 1:30–48, 139–47.

20. Richard A. Muller, *Dictionary of Latin and Greek Theological Terms* (Grand Rapids: Baker, 1987), 299–300, s.v. "*theologia archetypa*" and "*theologia ectypa*."

of knowledge but of worship). True religion (which theology teaches) consists of these two things.[21]

At this point we see Turretin root the knowledge of God, not in ontology—note Turretin's rejection of Aquinas's view—but in revelation.[22] Turretin goes on to explain, "Theology treats God and his infinite perfections, not as knowing them in an infinite but in a finite manner; nor absolutely as much as they can be known in themselves, but as much as he has been pleased to reveal them."[23] Hence it is important to recognize the analogical nature of our theological language about God. Historically, Reformed theology has not resorted to logical positivism or rationalism but rather has recognized the Creator-creature distinction.[24] Not only have Reformed theologians historically spoken of *theologia nostra* (our theology) and *theologia Dei* (God's theology), but have even distinguished eschatologically between our theology as we journey as pilgrims in the state of grace, *theologia viatorum* (theology of the pilgrims), and our knowledge of God in the state of glory, *theologia beatorum* (theology of the blessed).[25] So it is true, one may say that theological language about God is analogical, but that is not the same thing as saying that all theological language is metaphorical. Analogy is a comparison between two things that takes into account both the similarities and dissimilarities in the things compared. Metaphor, on the other hand, is when a word ordinarily used to denote one thing is used to denote another. Man, for example, is an analogy of God—he is created in God's image—man is analogous to God in his role as vice-regent over the earth. Man rules analogously over the earth as God rules over the cosmos.

Incarnational theology

It is one thing to acknowledge that *theologia nostra* is analogical so that when one reads of the "hand of God," for example, we have an analogy, an anthropomorphism to be precise, that gives us an idea of what God

---

21. Francis Turretin, *Institutes of Elenctic Theology*, trans. George Musgrave Giger, ed. James T. Dennsion Jr., 3 vols. (Phillipsburg, NJ: P&R, 1992–97), 1.5.4.
22. Cf. Aquinas, *Summa Theologica*, Ia qq. 12–13.
23. Turretin, *Institutes*, 1.5.7.
24. Contra Vanhoozer, *Drama of Doctrine*, 266–67.
25. Michael S. Horton, *Lord and Servant* (Louisville: Westminster John Knox, 2005), 17; see also Muller, *Dictionary*, 300, 303, 304, s.v. "*theologia beatorum*," "*theologia viatorum*," "*theologia nostra*."

is like. We know that God does not have a body because of the explicit statement in Scripture that "God is spirit" (John 4:24). Recognizing the analogical nature of our language about God, therefore, is of the utmost importance. When it comes to God's self-revelation in Christ, we must recognize that we are in the realm of incarnational theology. Christ, of course, explained to his disciples, "Whoever has seen me has seen the Father" (John 14:9). Christ is not a metaphor but is Yahweh in the flesh who came to tabernacle in the midst of his people (John 1:14). Christ is enfleshed analogy; the Creator becomes a creature, or to use the language of systematic theology, Christ, the archetype, becomes the ectype through the incarnation. Taking theology (proper) as it is realized in Christology, then, has a world of implications for our soteriology, especially the doctrine of justification.[26]

Christ not only reveals God the Father, but his life, death, and resurrection are also paradigmatic for soteriology. That Christ is the paradigm for salvation is evident in numerous places throughout the NT. Paul, for example, explains that the resurrection of Christ is exemplary of the resurrection of believers (Rom. 6:1–4). There is nothing metaphorical about Christ's resurrection—there is a one-to-one correspondence between Christ's resurrection and the church's resurrection.[27] Christ was raised bodily as believers will be: "As was the man of dust, so also are those who are of the dust, and as is the man of heaven, so also are those who are of heaven. Just as we have borne the image of the man of dust, we shall also bear the image of the man of heaven" (1 Cor. 15:48–49).

Similarly, Christ's pattern of humiliation and exaltation is the model for the church, his body, as Paul makes clear in several places (Rom. 5:1–5; 8:16–18; Phil. 2:5–11; Col. 1:24). That Christ is the model is especially evident in Christ's own justification, or declaration of righteousness (Rom. 1:3–4; 1 Tim. 3:16). Scholars have long noted that Christ's resurrection was his justification.[28] Geerhardus Vos explains that "Christ's resurrection was the *de facto* declaration of God in regard to his being just. His

---

26. Jürgen Moltmann, *The Way of Jesus Christ*, trans. Margaret Kohl (Minneapolis: Fortress, 1993), 46–47. See also Geerhardus Vos, *Grace and Glory* (1922; Edinburgh: Banner of Truth, 1994), 161–62.

27. Moltmann, *Way of Jesus*, 241.

28. Ibid., 77–78; also Markus Barth, *Acquittal by Resurrection* (New York: Holt, Rinehart, and Winston, 1964), 51–52.

quickening bears in itself the testimony of his justification."[29] There is nothing metaphorical about the resurrection of Christ. It was an event that occurred on the plane of history and is a prophetic declaration of the church's own resurrection on the final day. As Moltmann observes, "The raised body of Christ therefore acts as an embodied promise for the whole creation. It is the prototype of the glorified body."[30]

Because soteriology, and more specifically justification, is inextricably bound with Christology in the concrete reality of the incarnation, one cannot make the claim that justification is but one metaphor among many other legitimate images of redemption. One can easily see the problems with construing justification as a metaphor when it is compared with its theological antonym, condemnation. Reformed theologians have long noted that justification is a forensic declaration. Turretin, for example, states, "The word *htsdyq*, to which the Greek *dikaioun* answers and the Latin *justificare*, is used in two ways in the Scriptures—properly and improperly. Properly the verb is forensic, put for 'to absolve' anyone in a trial or 'to hold' and to declare 'just'; as opposed to the verb 'to condemn' and 'to accuse' (Ex. 23:7; Deut. 25:1; Prov. 17:15; Luke 18:14; Rom. 3–5)."[31] This is not a unique conclusion but has been affirmed from a broad cross-section of theologians, both Protestant and Roman Catholic.[32] If justification is only a metaphor, then one has to conclude that its counterpart, condemnation, is also a metaphor. This conclusion, however, runs against the grain of Scripture, to say the least.

There was nothing metaphorical about Christ's condemnation by the Pharisees and his subsequent justification by his resurrection (Rom. 4:25; 1 Cor. 15:17; 1 Tim. 3:16). Likewise, there is nothing metaphorical about the condemnation that lies over the unbeliever (Rom. 1:18–32). For the one who places his faith in Christ and is justified, the condemnation is removed—he is transferred from the kingdom of Satan to the kingdom of Christ, and therefore Paul can say, "There is therefore now no condemnation for those who are in Christ Jesus" (Rom. 8:1). Or, glossed in parallel fashion, "There is therefore now justification for those who are in Christ

29. Geerhardus Vos, *Pauline Eschatology* (1930; Phillipsburg, NJ: P&R, 1994), 151.
30. Moltmann, *Way of Jesus*, 258.
31. Turretin, *Institutes*, 16.1.4.
32. Pannenberg, *Systematic Theology*, 3:223; Hans Küng, *Justification* (1964; Louisville: Westminster John Knox, 2004), 209; Joseph Fitzmyer, *Romans*, AB 33 (New York: Doubleday, 1993), 116–17.

Jesus." Prior to the believer's justification, he is at enmity with God; after his justification, he is at peace with God (Rom. 5:1). If atonement and justification are merely metaphors that compete with other images such as union with Christ, then one must come to the conclusion that sin is also a metaphor: propitiation is God's metaphorical way of dealing with a metaphorical problem. The glaring problem is, of course, that sin and death are not metaphorical, and neither is the wrath of God, which Christ placates by his crucifixion, which is a propitiation (Rom. 3:25; Heb. 2:17; 1 John 2:2; 4:10).[33] To place justification, or any other element of the *ordo salutis* for that matter, into the category of metaphor does violence to the message of Scripture and destroys the gospel.

Summary

In the language of justification, therefore, we must conclude that justification is indeed an act of God, his declaration that a person is righteous in his sight. To come to this conclusion is not to resort to rationalism or logical positivism but simply to look to one's Christology and the paradigmatic nature of Christ's life, death, and resurrection, and to recognize the reality of sin and death. These conclusions, however, lead us into our next issue of prolegomena, namely the question of the center of Paul's theology. If justification is not one of many metaphors but a real aspect of our redemption, does this recognition therefore make the doctrine the center of Paul's theology? It is to this question that we now turn.

Justification and the Center of Paul's Theology

Ever since the Reformation and Luther's myriad of famous statements regarding the importance of justification, there have been both positive and negative responses. Some have responded with general agreement, others total rejection, and still yet others with a positive response that has gone far beyond Luther's own intentions. We should first briefly survey the variety of responses before we answer the question of whether justification is the central dogma for the apostle Paul.

33. Jürgen Moltmann, *The Spirit of Life*, trans. Margaret Kohl (Minneapolis: Fortress, 1992), 124; D. A. Carson, "Atonement in Romans 3:21–26: God Presented Him as a Propitiation," in *The Glory of the Atonement*, ed. Charles E. Hill and Frank A. James (Downers Grove, IL: InterVarsity, 2004), 119–39.

Let us turn then to explore some of Luther's statements regarding the importance of justification.

Luther on the Centrality of Justification

In Luther's Smalcald Articles (1537) we find some of the German Reformer's most famous statements regarding the importance and centrality of the doctrine of justification. Luther writes concerning the doctrine of justification, "Nothing in this article can be conceded or given up, even if heaven and earth or whatever is transitory passed away." He goes on to write, "On this article stands all that we teach and practice against the pope, the devil, and the world. Therefore we must be quite certain and have no doubt about it. Otherwise everything is lost, and the pope and the devil and whatever opposes us will gain victory and be proved right."[34] Given Luther's prominence and fountainhead status within the Lutheran church, it is only natural that Lutheran theologians would give the doctrine of justification a prominent place in their dogmatics. One can survey a broad cross-section of Lutheran theologians to see that justification has been accorded a chief place in their theology.

Lutherans on the centrality of justification

In the *Loci Communes* (1543) of Philip Melanchthon (1497–1560) we read that justification "contains the sum and substance of the Gospel. It shows the benefit of Christ in the proper sense, it offers a firm comfort to pious minds, it teaches the true worship of God, true invocation, and it especially distinguishes the church of God from other people—the Jews, Mohammedans, and the Pelagians."[35] Likewise, we see similar statements from one of the chief architects of the Formula of Concord (1577), Martin Chemnitz (1522–86), when the confession states that justification is the doctrine "upon which the salvation of our souls depends," and in his *Loci Theologici* he agrees with Melanchthon that it is the "sum and substance of the Gospel."[36]

34. Martin Luther, "Smalcald Articles" 1.2, in Robert Kolb and Timothy J. Wengert, eds., *The Book of Concord* (Minneapolis: Fortress, 2000), 301.

35. Philip Melanchthon, *Loci Communes* (*1543*), trans. J. A. O. Preus (St. Louis: Concordia, 1992), § 8.

36. Formula of Concord, Solid Declaration 3.58 in Kolb and Wengert, *Book of Concord*; Martin Chemnitz, *Loci Theologici*, trans. J. A. O. Preus, 2 vols. (1591; St. Louis: Concordia, 1989), 12.3.7.

Reformed theologians and the centrality of justification

Agreement with Luther during the sixteenth and seventeenth century was not restricted to the Lutheran church alone but also found voices of accord in the Reformed wing of the Reformation. Calvin, for example, stated concerning the doctrine of justification that it "is the main hinge on which religion turns, so that we devote the greater attention and care to it. Unless you first of all grasp what your relationship to God is, and the nature of his judgment concerning you, you have neither a foundation on which to establish your salvation nor one on which to build piety toward God."[37] Similarly, we see Turretin give assent to Luther's maxim when he writes:

> This must be handled with the greater care and accuracy as this saving doctrine is of the greatest importance in religion. It is called by Luther "the article of a standing and a falling church" (*Articulus stantis, et cadentis Ecclesiae*). By other Christians, it is termed the characteristic and basis of Christianity—not without reason—the principal rampart of the Christian religion. This being adulterated or subverted, it is impossible to retain purity of doctrine in other places.[38]

It is easy to find similar statements in the writings of other seventeenth-century Reformed theologians such as Wilhelmus à Brakel (1635–1711) or the *Leiden Synopsis*, written by Johannes Polyander (1568–1646), Antonius Walaeus (1573–1639), and Antonius Thysius (1565–1640).[39] One may classify this agreement with Luther as acceptance of the centrality and importance of the doctrine of justification. Since Luther, however, there have been responses both positive and negative.

37. John Calvin, *Institutes of the Christian Religion*, ed. John T. McNeill, trans. Ford Lewis Battles, LCC 20–21 (Philadelphia: Westminster, 1960), 3.11.1.

38. Turretin, *Institutes*, 16.1.1. One should note that while Turretin attributes the famous Latin phrase "articulus stantis, et cadentis Ecclesiae" to Luther, it was a Reformed theologian, Johann Heinrich Alsted (1588–1638), who coined the phrase (see J. H. Alsted, *Theologia Scholastica Didactica* [Hanover, 1618], 711, as cited in Alister E. McGrath, *Iustitia Dei*, 2 vols. [1986; Cambridge: Cambridge University Press, 1994], 2:193, n. 3; many thanks to my friend Scott Clark for drawing my attention to this reference).

39. See Wilhelmus à Brakel, *The Christian's Reasonable Service*, trans. Bartel Elshout, 4 vols. (Ligonier, PA: Soli Deo Gloria, 1992), 2:341; Heinrich Heppe, *Reformed Dogmatics*, ed. Ernst Bizer, trans. G. T. Thomson (London: George Allen & Unwin, 1950), 543.

Contemporary Reception, Rejection, and Modification

Christ as the central dogma

In the nineteenth century much of the critical scholarship blamed the Reformation for skewing the interpretation of Paul. As we saw above, scholars such as Wrede and Schweitzer believed that justification was incidental to Paul and that union with Christ was at the center of his theology.[40] Since the nineteenth century there have been some who have rejected the centrality of justification. Karl Barth (1886–1968) famously opined that "the *articulus stantis et cadentis ecclesiae* is not the doctrine of justification as such, but its basis and culmination: the confession of Jesus Christ, in whom are hid all the treasures of wisdom and knowledge."[41] Another voice of rejection has come from Roman Catholic theologian Hans Küng (1928–), who argues that "justification is not the central dogma of Christianity," and that the "central *dogma* of *Christ*ianity is the mystery of *Christ*, the mystery in which is revealed the mystery of the triune God as well as the mystery of the total creation, which was created good, fell, was redeemed, and is to be consummated."[42]

Union with Christ as central

Others coming from a broad cross-section of the church have also argued that justification is not the center of Paul's theology. Richard B. Gaffin (1936–) argues that for Paul one finds "a *central theme* which governs the whole: the unity of the resurrection of Christ and the resurrection of believers."[43] In other words, for Gaffin, union with Christ is a central concern for Paul, more so than justification. Though this is not to say that Gaffin agrees en toto with Schweitzer, as Schweitzer sees justification and union with Christ as two competing conceptions of salvation, whereas Gaffin argues that union with Christ and justification are integrally related, but that union with Christ is foundational to justification.[44]

40. See above, nn. 2–7.
41. Karl Barth, *Church Dogmatics* 4.1, *The Doctrine of Reconciliation*, trans. G. W. Bromiley (1956; Edinburgh: T & T Clark, 1988), 527.
42. Küng, *Justification*, 123.
43. Richard B. Gaffin Jr., *Resurrection and Redemption* (1978; Phillipsburg, NJ: P&R, 1987), 33.
44. Ibid., 132.

On a related but different note, Anthony N. S. Lane argues that justification cannot be the central dogma of the Christian faith but that, ultimately, the true test of Christian theology is the doctrine of Scripture.[45] To this cloud of witnesses we may also add the new Finnish interpretation of Luther, based upon a reading of Luther's earlier works, which claims that, for the German Reformer, justification was not central but that union with Christ was his foundational category. In fact, the Finnish school, headed by Tuomo Mannermaa, argues that Lutheranism, embodied in the Formula of Concord (1577), misinterpreted Luther. In other words, the Finnish school posits a Luther versus Lutheranism on the centrality of justification by faith.[46] On the other side of the equation, there are some who have taken Luther's point in the extreme opposite direction.

Justification as the methodological norm

There have been some Lutheran theologians, such as Francis Pieper (1852–1931), who have affirmed that "in Lutheran theology the article of justification is the central chief article by which the Christian doctrine and the Christian Church stands or falls (*articulus stantis et cadentis ecclesiae*); it is the apex of all Christian teaching." Moreover, Pieper insists that "justification by faith in the crucified Christ is the central article not only in Paul's theology, as some of the modern theologians will admit, but also in 'the teaching of Jesus.'" To this end, Pieper argues that "in Scripture all doctrines serve the doctrine of justification."[47]

Other theologians coming out of the Lutheran tradition such as Eberhard Jüngel (1934–) have argued that justification is the hermeneutical category that determines all of our thinking, speaking, and acting.[48] Similarly, Carl Braaten (1929–) argues that justification must be the "evangelical criterion," which according to Braaten means that it discerns "what is true and false, good and bad, in the substance of the Catholic tradition." Braaten goes on to write, "I do not believe that we can renew the

45. Anthony N. S. Lane, *Justification by Faith in Catholic-Protestant Dialogue* (Edinburgh: T & T Clark, 2002), 148.
46. See Braaten and Jenson, *Union with Christ*, 38–39. Several scholars have relied upon the work of Mannermaa and pit Luther against Lutheranism at this point (see Pannenberg, *Systematic Theology*, 3:215–18; Kärkkäinen, *One with God*, 119; Robert W. Jenson, *Systematic Theology*, 2 vols. [New York: Oxford University Press, 1997], 2:293–98).
47. Francis Pieper, *Christian Dogmatics*, 4 vols. (St. Louis: Concordia, 1951), 2:512–13.
48. Eberhard Jüngel, *Justification*, trans. Jeffrey F. Cayzer (Edinburgh: T & T Clark, 2001), 47–50; see also idem, "On the Doctrine of Justification," *IJST* 1/1 (1999): 24–52, esp. 51–52.

traditions of Christianity without using the article of justification as a methodological norm. It is essential to our evangelical catholic identity, and not merely one among biblical images or metaphors whose day is past."[49] While these statements seem to go a bit beyond what Luther intended, there are still yet others who take the doctrine of justification as the foundation to one's system of doctrine even further.

Justification as central dogma

One finds in the theology of Oswald Bayer the claim that justification has principal significance in one's theological system: "It touches on every theme. Justification concerns not merely one's own history, not only world history, but also natural history. It has to do with everything. Hence sanctification is not something that follows justification. Instead, its theme is also none other than justification."[50] Bayer believes that justification is the basis and boundary of all theology.[51]

Along these lines Gerhard O. Forde (1927–2005) argues that the doctrine of sanctification is a dangerous idea, as it is a siren to one's crucified sin nature. Therefore, he understands justification to be "the art of getting used to the unconditional justification wrought by the grace of God for Jesus' sake."[52] So for Forde, justification is so all-encompassing that it virtually swallows up the *ordo salutis*. Others have taken the doctrine of justification and burdened it with concepts and philosophical baggage that appear far from the mind of Luther, or the apostle Paul for that matter.

Paul Tillich (1886–1965), who was arguably more of a philosopher than a theologian, though some have argued that he was both, saw the main task of theology as correlating the Christian message to the existential questions of the day.[53] Given Tillich's methodological commitments, one finds him redefining key biblical categories. Sin, for example, is not

---

49. Carl E. Braaten, *Justification* (Minneapolis: Fortress, 1990), 8.

50. Oswald Bayer, *Living by Faith: Justification and Sanctification*, trans. Geoffrey Bromiley (Grand Rapids: Eerdmans, 2003), xii.

51. Oswald Bayer, "Justification as the Basis and Boundary of Theology," *LQ* 15 (2001): 273–92.

52. Gerhard O. Forde, "The Lutheran View," in *Christian Spirituality*, ed. Donald L. Alexander (Downers Grove, IL: InterVarsity, 1988), 13–15.

53. Paul Tillich, *Systematic Theology*, 3 vols. (1957; Chicago: University of Chicago Press, 1977), 2:13–16; see also 1:3–68; John P. Newport, *Paul Tillich* (Peabody, MA: Hendrickson, 1984), 87.

a transgression of God's law but is existential doubt. Tillich explains, "How is the faith through which justification comes to us related to the situation of radical doubt? Radical doubt is existential doubt concerning the meaning of life itself." Tillich takes Paul and Luther's emphasis upon justification and freights it with the existentialist question of doubt: "Paul's question, How do I become liberated from the law? and Luther's question, How do I find a merciful God? are replaced in our period by the question, How do I find meaning in a meaningless world?"[54] Radically redefined, then, justification was, for Tillich, the central doctrine of the Reformation, the article by which Protestantism stands or falls; he calls it the first and basic expression of the Protestant principle itself. Tillich writes, "It is only for unavoidable reasons of expediency a particular doctrine and should, at the same time, be regarded as the principle which permeates every single assertion of the theological system."[55]

The Place of Justification

Bound up in the history of the place of justification in the theological system are several important issues that should be addressed. The issues must be sorted and distinguished, as it appears that some theologians have misunderstood the place of justification in Paul's theology and its place within a system of doctrine. There are five issues that seem to swirl about this question: (1) the place of justification within Paul's thought; (2) the place of justification within one's theological system; (3) whether the Reformers correctly interpreted Paul on this issue; (4) the question of whether justification is a central dogma; and (5) whether justification is still the article by which the church stands or falls. Critical to addressing these issues is the term "central dogma," as defining this term is key for determining whether justification is a central dogma for Paul and the Reformers.

Defining central dogma

It is one thing to affirm that justification is central to Paul and the Reformers, and entirely another to say that it is a central dogma, which is a *terminus technicus* loaded with much philosophical freight. Christian Wolf (1679–1754) had a great influence over some eighteenth-century

54. Tillich, *Systematic Theology*, 3:227.
55. Ibid., 3:23–25.

Reformed theologians who argued that a system of thought needed to have a "principle of sufficient reason" upon which the entire system could be built.[56] This means that from one principle, an entire system of thought could be logically deduced. One finds an excellent explanation of this type of understanding of systematic theology from Otto Weber (1902–66). Weber explains:

> We understand by "system" the totality of an intellectual structure which is based upon a fundamental concept (a "principle") and which develops it logically and methodologically. The presupposition is, accordingly, that the "principle" contains potentially the one and total content which is then explained in greater detail in the systematic exposition. This means in turn that in its exposition the system cannot contain elements which are not already given in the "principle." The "principle" is, therefore, the intellectual condensation of an all-embracing totality.[57]

One can certainly see these characteristics in the affirmations of some such as Jüngel, Forde, Bayer, and Tillich and make the argument that they have a system of justification. It must be noted, though, that such a method of doing systematic theology is foreign to the sixteenth- and seventeenth-century theologians of both wings of the Reformation, Lutheran and Reformed.

Theologians of the Reformation and post-Reformation periods constructed their theology in terms of the locus method of doing theology. As Richard Muller explains,

> Not only do the theological systems of the sixteenth and seventeenth centuries attempt to survey all points of Christian doctrine rather than to gather into a cohesive whole only those doctrines which relate to particular dogmatic premises; moreover, the locus-method and the arrangement of *loci* into a historical series—adopted virtually by all of the theological systems of the sixteenth and seventeenth centuries—precludes the purely deductive patterning implied by the central dogma thesis.[58]

---

56. Richard A. Muller, *After Calvin* (Oxford: Oxford University Press, 2003), 94.

57. Otto Weber, *Foundations of Dogmatics*, trans. Darrell L. Guder, 2 vols. (Grand Rapids: Eerdmans, 1981), 1:51.

58. Muller, *After Calvin*, 94–95; for similar comments regarding Lutheranism see Barth, *Church Dogmatics*, 4.1:522.

Muller notes that the theology of Wolfian rationalists of the eighteenth century saw natural revelation as the *principium cognoscendi externum* (external cognitive foundation) and therefore believed that the *principium cognoscendi internum* (internal cognitive foundation) of theology was reason. By way of antithetical contrast, the theologians of the sixteenth and seventeenth centuries saw the *principium cognoscendi externum* as God and Scripture, and the *principium cognoscendi internum* as faith.[59] This definition and historical understanding of what constitutes a *central dogma* is important for several reasons in our quest to place the doctrine of justification in the Reformers and especially Paul.

Rejecting the central dogma theory

First, given the philosophical bent and foundation of the central dogma theory, one may safely rule out the idea that the doctrine of justification is a central dogma for the Reformers. It is a historically anachronistic method of doing theology, one foreign to the theology of the sixteenth and seventeenth centuries. Second, if the central dogma theory was a development of eighteenth-century rationalism and therefore foreign to the Reformers, then we may also safely conclude that justification is not the central dogma for the apostle Paul, as eighteenth-century Wolfian rationalism is as foreign to Paul as to Luther and Calvin. Third, if Paul's theology is in some way to be normative for our own theology, and especially our understanding of justification, then we may safely dismiss the systematic understandings of justification of Jüngel, Forde, Bayer, and Tillich. That is, we are not necessarily completely dismissing what they have to say concerning the doctrine of justification, though Tillich's redefinition of so many biblical categories makes much of what he has to say irrelevant in searching for the Pauline understanding, but we may dismiss what they have to say about the systemic implications of the doctrine. This study is ultimately concerned with setting forth the doctrine of justification as it is found in the Scriptures, not creating a monistic system of justification.

Given these conclusions, what then are we to make of the other issues that are still left, such as the place of justification in Paul's theology, in the theology of the Reformers, the Reformers' interpretation of Paul, and

59. See Richard A. Muller, *Post-Reformation Reformed Dogmatics*, 4 vols. (Grand Rapids: Baker, 2003), 1:123–32.

whether the doctrine of justification is the article by which the church stands or falls? The answer comes in moving away from the problem-laden central dogma theory.

The place of justification

In the central dogma theory there is the quest for the one principle that explains the whole, from which the entire system is deduced. Given, however, the nature of *theologia nostra*, is it possible to identify the one principle that unlocks the whole? Such a quest seems to controvert the nature of the theological enterprise as it is bound up in archetypal and ectypal theology. If there is one principle that unlocks the whole system of Christian doctrine, then it seems that such a principle would lie within the realm of archetypal theology, not the finite ectype. Therefore, it seems more reasonable to say that there are central emphases in Scripture, or especially in Paul, as we look to place the doctrine of justification in his thought and within our theological system.

To acknowledge that there are central emphases in Paul rather than one ideological or doctrinal center alleviates the interpreter of the burden of identifying the one central doctrine to the exclusion of all others. In the attempt to identify the one central doctrine, one inevitably produces conflict with the rest of Paul's doctrines. Trying to determine the absolute center of Paul's thought is like trying to identify the most important organ in the human body. The brain cannot function without the heart, the heart cannot function without the lungs, and the body cannot live without the kidneys. While one may say that there are important organs, it is all of the organs that together comprise the living body. This analogy is not new as it was employed by the apostle Paul himself in explaining the unity of the body of Christ despite its being constituted by the variegated dispensation of spiritual gifts (1 Cor. 12).

Furthermore, this is the way Reformed theologians have understood the structure of systematic theology, whether in the loci method of the sixteenth and seventeenth centuries, reflected in the Reformed confessions, or the systematic theology of one like B. B. Warfield (1851–1921). Warfield saw systematic theology in terms of an organic whole: every part was necessarily interconnected and vital, but not in the Weberian or Wolfian sense of system.[60] One may therefore conclude that there are central doctrines rather than one central dogma for Paul.

One must return to the *principia* of the Reformed theology of the sixteenth and seventeenth centuries, reaffirm the twin foci of God and Scripture as the *principium cognoscendi externum*, and with Turretin highlight that God and Scripture are supremely revealed in Christ and covenant. As David VanDrunen rightly argues, there is a need for an architectonic structure that undergirds the various threads of revealed truth, and historically for Reformed theology that structure has come in the covenants. The doctrine of the covenant, argues VanDrunen, can center one's theological system, though this does not mean that the covenant is the center, or principle from which the whole is deduced, in the Wolfian or Weberian sense.[61] In this regard Vos explains:

> The importance of this aspect of revelation has found its clearest expression in the idea of the covenant as the form of God's progressive self-communication to Israel. God has not revealed Himself in a school, but in the covenant; and the covenant as a communion of life is all-comprehensive, embracing all the conditions and interests of those contracting it.[62]

Vos's statement correlates well with Turretin's earlier point that God reveals himself in Christ and covenant. The centrality of covenant, however, is not something that one finds only in Reformed dogmatics but in the theology of Paul himself as well.

One certainly finds great emphasis upon covenant in Paul, evidenced in the two-age structure of redemptive history, that of the first and last Adams (Rom. 5:12–21; 1 Cor. 15:45), which in the Reformed tradition has historically been designated by the covenants of works and grace (see WCF 7). It is within the context of the covenants that redemption in

---

60. See B. B. Warfield, "The Task and Method of Systematic Theology," in *The Works of B. B. Warfield*, ed. Ethelbert D. Warfield et al., 10 vols. (Grand Rapids: Baker, 1981), 9:91–105.

61. David VanDrunen, "A System of Theology? The Centrality of Covenant for Westminster Systematics," in David VanDrunen, ed., *The Pattern of Sound Doctrine* (Phillipsburg, NJ: P&R, 2004), 209.

62. Geerhardus Vos, "The Idea of Biblical Theology as a Science and as a Theological Discipline," in Richard B. Gaffin Jr., ed., *Redemptive History and Biblical Interpretation* (Phillipsburg, NJ: P&R, 1980), 10. Meredith Kline employs the doctrine of the covenants in the same manner (see *Kingdom Prologue* [Overland Park, KS: Two Age Press, 2000], 1; VanDrunen, "A System of Theology?" 209–10 n. 22).

Christ is revealed, an emphasis that has been broadly affirmed. Wright, for example, though disagreeing with historic Reformed covenant theology, nevertheless argues that "covenant theology is one of the main clues, usually neglected, for understanding Paul."[63] It is within the context of the covenants, the new covenant more specifically, that one finds Paul explaining the central doctrines of redemption, the entire *ordo salutis*. Even though one must center his system in Christ and covenant, one can make the case that justification is *primus inter pares*, or first among equals. Does such a construction represent a misinterpretation of Paul by placing such an emphasis upon the doctrine of justification?

Justification as primus inter pares

There is an argument to be made that justification is *primus inter pares*, the Reformers were correct in their interpretation of Paul, and, yes, justification is the article by which the church stands or falls. To substantiate these claims, we must first see that many seem to fail to account for the historical context of the Reformation and consequently read more into the Reformers' statements than is warranted. Lane, for example, places the statements of the Reformers on the same level as those of contemporary theologians such as Jüngel and then objects that the doctrine of justification is the sole test for all other doctrines and practices. He counters, "There is little doubt that for the overwhelming majority of Evangelicals the supreme and final criterion is not justification by faith nor any other single doctrine, but scripture."[64] Can one legitimately argue that Jüngel is an unreconstructed Lutheran in the style of the Reformer himself?

It seems that some fail to account for the historical occasion of the Reformers' writings, which were not like the systems of theology we find from the pens of Turretin, Pieper, Hodge, or Louis Berkhof (1873–1957), let alone those of Braaten or Tillich.[65] Rather, given the compromised status of the doctrine of justification in the sixteenth-century Roman Catholic Church, it is only natural that the Reformers would place such weight upon the doctrine. For example, unlike Lane, who misunderstands the claims of the Reformers concerning the importance of justification,

63. N. T. Wright, *The Climax of the Covenant* (Minneapolis: Fortress, 1993), xi, 17.
64. Lane, *Justification by Faith*, 148.
65. See Root, "Continuing the Conversation," 49–50.

we find the more nuanced analysis of J. I. Packer. Packer explains that for the Reformers "the authority of Scripture was the *formal* principle of that theology, determining its method and providing its touchstone of truth; justification by faith was its *material* principle, determining its substance."[66] Moreover, when one considers the place of justification within Paul's thought, it is only natural that the Reformers would echo the apostle's emphasis.

The Reformers rightly placed a great deal of emphasis upon the doctrine of justification and called it the article by which the church stands or falls because it is at the heart of the proclamation of the gospel. While justification may be one of several central themes for Paul, when one asks, "What must I do to be saved?" as the Philippian jailer did (Acts 16:30), or "What must I do to inherit eternal life?" as the rich young ruler did (Luke 18:18; cf. Matt. 19:16; Mark 10:17), it is not union with Christ, sanctification, predestination, or all of the other elements of the *ordo salutis* that come to the fore, but the doctrine of justification by faith alone. One finds this very emphasis in Paul's letters to Galatia and Rome. If union with Christ were more central than justification by faith, as Schweitzer contends, then why when the Galatians brought forward their own works of the law did Paul not respond with a call for them to look to their union with Christ?

Paul set forth the doctrine of justification by faith alone. To this end, D. A. Carson rightly explains:

Evangelicals have often spoken of justification as a central doctrine, or at least a central focus in Pauline theology. The category of centrality is slippery, and so it deserves some reflection from the evangelical side. Justification is surely not central to, say, Pauline thought, if centrality is determined by the number of references to *dik-* forms across the Pauline corpus. On such a basis it would not even be central to Romans: "God" would beat it hands down. Nor is it clear that justification is the great unifying principle of Paul's thought, even in Romans and Galatians: The category "great unifying principle" is scarcely less slippery than "central." One might reasonably argue that the unifying worldview behind these epistles is an eschatological awareness of the

---

66. J. I. Packer, "Introductory Essay," in James Buchanan, *The Doctrine of Justification* (1867; Edinburgh: Banner of Truth, 1991), vii.

78

dawning of the age to come, and that the supremely important center for Paul is Christ himself.[67]

Carson's observations parallel those we have already made thus far, even in centering Paul's thought in Christ and covenant, understanding the new covenant as the dawn of the eschaton.[68] Nevertheless, Carson can still say, "But justification is surely central for Paul in this sense: It marks the entry point into this holistic salvation, the event by which rebels are accepted back to their Maker on the basis of a sacrifice he himself provided."[69]

It is in the sense that Carson explains the centrality of justification, not only for Paul, but also for the Reformation, as the entry point to this holistic salvation that one can affirm with the Reformers that the doctrine of justification is the article by which the church stands or falls. Granted, this raises some issues and questions concerning the relationship of justification to the rest of the *ordo salutis*, but suffice it to say that justification is a chief concern to Paul and therefore must also be for any theologian who attempts to interpret him.[70] Moltmann observes,

> Only justifying faith corresponds to the Christ crucified "for us," for it is only through justifying faith that the liberating power of Christ's resurrection is experienced. That is why christology and the doctrine of justification are inextricably bound up with one another theologically. This was the insight of the Reformers, and in arriving at it they were going back to Paul himself.[71]

For these reasons, then, we can conclude that the doctrine of justification is at the center of Paul's thought along with many other important doctrines, though it is *primus inter pares* because it is the entry point to our holistic redemption.

67. D. A. Carson, "Reflections on Salvation and Justification in the New Testament," *JETS* 40/4 (1997): 602–3.

68. See Richard B. Gaffin Jr., "Biblical Theology and the Westminster Standards," *WTJ* 65/2 (2003): 167; also Herman Ridderbos, *Paul*, trans. John Richard DeWitt (1975; Grand Rapids: Eerdmans, 1992), 14, 45, 63.

69. Carson, "Justification in the New Testament," 603.

70. So Moltmann, *Spirit of Life*, 144; M. A. Seifrid, *Justification by Faith* (Leiden: E. J. Brill, 1992), 270.

71. Jürgen Moltmann, *The Way of Jesus Christ*, trans. Margaret Kohl (Minneapolis: Fortress, 1993), 184.

In this regard, the Reformers interpreted Paul correctly. We may therefore agree with Barth when he writes, "There never was and there never can be any true Christian Church without the doctrine of justification. In this sense it is indeed the *articulus stantis et cadentis ecclesiae*."[72] Likewise, Alister McGrath rightly states that the doctrine of justification by faith alone

> constitutes the real centre of the theological system of the Christian church, encapsulating the direct and normative consequences of the historical revelation of God to mankind in Jesus Christ. There never was, and there never can be, any true Christian church without the doctrine of justification, for the community of faith cannot exist without proclaiming, in word and sacrament, the truth of what God has done for man in Christ.[73]

Similarly, J. T. Mueller explains that the doctrine of justification is the central doctrine of the Christian church, though not in terms of a central dogma, because "those who deny the Scriptural doctrine of justification by faith deny the entire Christian religion; for they are compelled to teach the paganistic way of salvation by works, by which the Gospel of Christ is annulled."[74] So, then, we have located the place of the doctrine of justification within both Paul and the theology of the Reformers. Our placement, though, of justification as the *primus inter pares* undoubtedly raises the final question with which we must deal, namely the relationship between justification and the rest of the *ordo salutis*.

Justification and the *Ordo Salutis*

We have thus far determined that justification is an act of God, not merely one metaphor among other equally valid images of redemption, and that it has a central place in Paul's soteriology. In giving justification a central place, that is, as the entry point to our redemption, how does this conclusion relate to the rest of the *ordo salutis*: predestination, regeneration, effectual calling, faith, justification, adoption, sanctification, and glorification? In dealing with the question of the relationship between the doctrine of justification and the *ordo salutis* one finds sev-

72. Barth, *Church Dogmatics*, 4.1:523.
73. McGrath, *Iustitia Dei*, 1:1.
74. J. T. Mueller, *Christian Dogmatics* (1934; St. Louis: Concordia, 1955), 371.

eral answers.[75] There are some who question the legitimacy of the entire concept of the *ordo salutis*, and therefore reject the need for it. Others place justification at the head of the *ordo*, even over regeneration and faith. Still yet others recognize that there seems to be an inherent tension in the traditional Reformed *ordo salutis*, as the Westminster Confession places union with Christ temporally prior to one's justification. How can one be united to Christ prior to his justification? In the other wing of the Reformation, Lutheran theologians typically argue that union with Christ is a consequence of one's justification and therefore cannot be temporally prior. Let us first explore the various formulations of justification vis-à-vis the *ordo salutis* and then set forth the understanding with which our investigation will proceed.

Rejection of the Ordo Salutis

Historically, Reformed dogmatics has been comfortable with the use of the concept of the *ordo salutis*, as theologians have seen the need to distinguish the elements of soteriology. For example, many have taken Paul's famous golden chain in Romans 8:30 and noted that there appears to be an order to it, "Those whom he predestined he also called, and those whom he called he also justified, and those whom he justified he also glorified."[76] There have been, however, those who have criticized the concept of the *ordo salutis*, both in its use in systematic theology and the claim that one can find it in Paul's theology. Some, such as G. C. Berkouwer (1903–96), have been critical of the idea of finding an *ordo* in Romans 8:30.[77] Weber, building upon Barth's work, also rejected the

---

75. Weber traces the term and concept of the *ordo salutis* to the work of Franz Buddeus, *Institutiones theologiae dogmaticae* (1724), 1.1.32, 43; and Jakobus Carpov, *Theologia revelata dogmatica* (1739), 2.1.3, 659 (*Dogmatics*, 2:336 n. 68). Though he also notes that Otto Ritschl (1885–1976) traced the concept to Heinrich Bullinger (1504–75) in his *De gratia et justificante* 6 (1554) (ibid., 69). Cf. Pannenberg who relies upon Reinhold Seeberg, who also traces the origin to Buddeus (*Systematic Theology*, 3:228–29).

76. Historically, though before the development of the term, one finds a schematized *ordo salutis* in the works of William Perkins (1558–1602) and Theodore Beza (1519–1605). See William Perkins, *A Golden Chain: or the Description of Theology, Containing the order of the causes of Salvation and Damnation, according to God's Word. A View whereof is to be seen in the Table annexed*, in *Works of that famous and worthy minister of Christ W. Perkins*, vol. 1 (London, 1612); Theodore Beza, *A Brief Declaration of the Chief Points of Christian Religion Set Forth in a Table* (London, n.d.); see also Muller, *Post-Reformation Reformed Dogmatics*, 1:113, 128.

77. G. C. Berkouwer, *Faith and Justification*, trans. Lewis B. Smedes (1954; Grand Rapids: Eerdmans, 1977), 29–33.

idea of the *ordo salutis*, arguing that historically theologians saw the *ordo* as a temporal sequence of events, yet he claimed that Paul's use of aorist verbs in Romans 8:29–30 shows that the events of Paul's *ordo* are already concluded and therefore cannot refer to a temporal sequence.[78]

Herman Ridderbos outright rejects the idea of the *ordo salutis* in Paul: "In Paul's preaching there is no such thing as a systematic development of the *ordo salutis*, a detailed doctrine of the anthropological application of salvation. The cause for this is not only that the character of Paul's doctrine is not 'systematic' in the scientific sense of the word, but above all that his viewpoint is a different one."[79]

One finds the theological outworking of rejecting the *ordo salutis* in Kärk-käinen, who, as we saw above, argues that justification is but one window into the biblical imagery of salvation.[80] On the basis of this understanding of justification, he can therefore write, "Sanctification and inner change form an integral part of the doctrine of justification and cannot be distinguished from each other."[81] In fact, he goes as far as to say, "Justification means both forgiveness of sins (forensic justification; favor) and inner renewal and change. In other words, justification and sanctification form one theological entity." He also concludes, "Justification is union with Christ."[82]

There are similar conclusions from those who claim to be Reformed but nevertheless implicitly reject the *ordo salutis*. John Franke, for example, writes: "A nonfoundational and contextual account of justification views its task as an ongoing participatory process involving convictional communities rather than something to be accomplished objectively in a once-for-all fashion."[83] Like Kärkkäinen, Franke turns justification into a process, melding it with sanctification. These rejections of the *ordo salutis* certainly raise the question of the legitimacy of such a construction at all, a question to which we will shortly turn.

Justification Controlling the Whole Ordo Salutis

There are some theologians such as Braaten who argue that justification must be accorded the chief place in the *ordo salutis*, not simply the

78. Weber, *Foundations of Dogmatics*, 2:336–37; Barth, *Church Dogmatics*, 4.1:502.
79. Ridderbos, *Paul*, 206.
80. Kärkkäinen, *One with God*, 122.
81. Ibid., 121.
82. Ibid., 107.
83. Franke, *Character of Theology*, 195.

primus inter pares, as we saw above, but more along the lines of a central dogma. In most typical Reformed and Lutheran understandings of the *ordo salutis*, one finds regeneration and faith preceding justification. Braaten argues, however, that the Lutheran orthodox understanding of faith, which consists of the *notitia-assensus-fiducia* sequence, "is pure intellectualizing Pelagianism."[84] Braaten argues:

> When regeneration is placed logically and causally prior to justification, the focus of interest shifts from God's unmotivated decision to justify the ungodly to the restoration of their human capacity to apply themselves to grace, to repent and believe, and thereupon to be justified. The priority of regeneration over justification removes the article of justification by faith alone from the center to a marginal role in the doctrine of salvation.[85]

Instead of adopting the typical Lutheran orthodox *ordo salutis*, Braaten argues that "justification is objectively prior to faith" and that "faith is subjectively the result of the creative impact upon the sinner of God's acceptance. Therefore, it may be said that faith justifies in the sense that it is becoming aware of that forgiving love by which it was first engendered."[86] Braaten also claims that the Reformers, Luther and Calvin, placed justification prior to regeneration in their understanding of redemption.[87] Hence we may say that rather than place justification after regeneration and faith, as many Reformed and Lutheran theologians do, he would place justification first in the *ordo salutis*.[88] Now, while Braaten wants to place justification at the head of the *ordo salutis*, there are others who come from the Reformed tradition who would not follow Braaten's *ordo* but

84. Braaten, *Justification*, 30.
85. Ibid., 22.
86. Ibid., 26.
87. Ibid., 49.
88. Braaten specifically mentions the *ordo salutis* of David Hollaz (1648–1713), who has the following: effectual calling, illumination, conversion, regeneration, justification, mystical union, renovation, perseverance, and glorification (Braaten, *Justification*, 32–33; Heinrich Schmid, *The Doctrinal Theology of the Evangelical Lutheran Church*, trans. Charles A. Hay and Henry E. Jacobs [Philadelphia: Lutheran Publication Society, 1899], 444; McGrath, *Iustitia Dei*, 2:48–49). Berkhof notes that Abraham Kuyper (1837–1920) also placed justification first in his *ordo salutis* (Louis Berkhof, *Systematic Theology: New Combined Edition* [1932–38; Grand Rapids: Eerdmans, 1996], 418; see also Herman Hoeksema, *Reformed Dogmatics* [Grand Rapids: Reformed Free Publishing Association, 1966], 450).

nonetheless note the tensions between the forensic and transformative in the *ordo salutis*.

Tensions within the Ordo Salutis

Within the Reformed tradition there has been very little written on the nature of the *ordo salutis*, though there have nevertheless been some key contributions to the discussion. A. A. Hodge asks the question, "In the application of redemption to the individual sinner, which, in the order of nature, precedes and conditions the other—justification or regeneration?"[89] Hodge observes that the Reformers place regeneration and faith prior to justification.[90] Yet Hodge also observes that redemption involves union with Christ. The benefits of the believer's union with Christ are: "(a) a change of state or relation, called justification; and (b) a change of subjective moral character, commenced in regeneration and completed through sanctification." The problem that Hodge detects is as follows:

> The satisfaction and merit of Christ are the antecedent cause of regeneration; and yet, nevertheless, the participation of the believer in the satisfaction and merit of Christ (*i.e.*, his justification) is conditioned upon his faith, which in turn is conditioned upon his regeneration. He must have part in Christ so far forth as to be regenerated in order to have part in him so far forth as to be justified.[91]

Gaffin further amplifies the horns of the dilemma upon which Hodge has apparently become stuck. Gaffin writes, "If at the point of inception this union is prior (and therefore involves the possession in the inner man of all that Christ is as resurrected), what need is there for the other acts? Conversely, if the other acts are in some sense prior, is not union improperly subordinated and its biblical significance severely attenuated, to say the least?"[92]

For those in the Lutheran tradition, there has not typically been a dilemma as one finds in Hodge and Gaffin because Lutherans apparently see union with Christ not prior to justification but rather as a consequence

---

89. A. A. Hodge, "The Ordo Salutis: Or, Relation in the Order of Nature of Holy Character and Divine Favor," *PR* 54 (1878): 304.
90. Ibid., 305.
91. Ibid., 313.
92. Gaffin, *Resurrection and Redemption*, 138–39.

of it.[93] Mueller writes, for example, that "justification effects the *mystical union* (*unio mystica*), by which the Holy Trinity, in particular the Holy Spirit, dwells in the believer." Mueller adds that union with Christ "is the result of justification, not the cause of it."[94] Pieper also argues that union with Christ is the result of justification and that "to make it the basis of justification means to mix sanctification into justification."[95] In the positive formulation, then, of the relationship of justification and the *ordo salutis*, one must seek to formulate it in such a way as to minimize or even eliminate this apparent tension. Keeping this issue in view, as well as the other two that we have explored, we now turn to a positive formulation of justification and the *ordo salutis*.

Positive Formulation: Justification and the Ordo Salutis

The necessity of the ordo salutis

In making a positive formulation of the relationship between justification and the *ordo salutis*, we must, first, establish the legitimacy of the *ordo salutis* in the Scriptures and especially in Paul's theology, and, second, develop the relationship between justification and the rest of the *ordo salutis*, especially union with Christ. Proceeding then to our first issue, it is important that one recognize the legitimacy of the *ordo salutis* in the pages of Scripture. Throughout the Scriptures we see certain aspects of redemption given priority over other aspects. We read in John's Gospel that one cannot see the kingdom of God unless he is first born again (John 3:3). We also see that Paul, on the one hand, can say that one is justified by faith apart from works but, on the other hand, he can also say that the believer must walk in the newness of life and has been created for good works (cf. Rom. 3:28; 6:1–4; Eph. 2:8–10; 1 John 3:9–10). Likewise, in the preaching of Christ and the apostles, one finds that a person cannot be redeemed, which involves the person's justification, unless he first repents and believes in Christ, which is an expression of one's faith (Mark 1:14–15; 6:12; Rom. 4:5). In fact, one cannot receive the righteousness of Christ in justification apart from faith.[96]

93. See Schmid, *Doctrinal Theology*, 441.
94. Mueller, *Christian Dogmatics*, 320.
95. Pieper, *Christian Dogmatics*, 2:410.
96. Berkhof, *Systematic Theology*, 417.

Given these different statements throughout the Bible, there are at least two options from which one can choose: (a) the Bible has no coherent systematic understanding of the truths of the gospel, and therefore these are either incoherent contradictions or perhaps multiple metaphors from which one can choose; or (b) there is a way in which these different truths about the gospel cohere, and it is a matter of relating the different doctrines to one another that are represented by the various statements. Though some have claimed that the Bible contains contradictions, this being the claim of Heikki Räisänen, who argues that Paul is contradictory in his understanding of faith and works in justification, one must recognize that the Scriptures are God-breathed and therefore inerrant and without contradiction (2 Tim. 3:16–17; 2 Peter 3:15–16).[97] Moreover, we have already seen the weaknesses inherent in looking to resolve matters through metaphorical theology. This leaves us with the task of relating the various elements of our redemption. This is of the utmost importance. In fact, one can say that without the *ordo salutis* the gospel is lost.

Reformed theologians have long observed the dangers in confounding the constituent elements of redemption. Turretin observed that his opponents converted justification, which was a forensic act, into a physical or moral process, or that which takes place before God and that which takes place in us.[98] Likewise, John Murray (1898–1975) observes that "if justification is confused with regeneration or sanctification, then the door is opened for the perversion of the gospel at its centre."[99] In other words, if it does not matter where the believer's good works enter the process of salvation, then what difference does it make whether the believer's good works come before his faith and are in some way preparatory for the grace of justification? Such confusion over the proper place of works, however, negates the grace of God in justification and the necessity of Christ's work. Without an *ordo salutis* chaos ensues and the gospel is lost. Hence, the concept of the *ordo salutis* is necessary for the preservation of the gospel but also because one finds a basic *ordo* in Paul.

97. See Heikki Räisänen, *Paul and the Law* (Minneapolis: Fortress, 1983), 199–202.
98. Turretin, *Institutes*, 17.2.24.
99. John Murray, *Redemption Accomplished and Applied* (Grand Rapids: Eerdmans, 1955), 121.

Ordo salutis *in Romans 8:29–30*

Theologians have been criticized for appealing to Romans 8:29–30 as the basis of arguing for an *ordo salutis* because, among other reasons, Paul makes no mention of sanctification. If he intended to outline an *ordo*, why would he leave out such an important category? We must continually remind ourselves that there is a necessary difference between the language of Scripture and that of systematic theology. Granted, Paul does not use the language of systematic theology; nevertheless the terminology of systematic theology is necessary as we interact with the history of the interpretation of Paul, and the Scriptures, as everyone employs biblical language and debate surfaces about what the biblical language means. It is with the language and terminology of systematic theology that we are able to understand what someone affirms or denies about what the Bible says.

Given this understanding, one may recognize that there is an *ordo* in what Paul states: predestination, calling, justification, and glorification.[100] Predestination, for example, is not at the same time as glorification (cf. Eph. 1:4; Rom. 8:17). To confound predestination and glorification would completely eliminate the need for the incarnation and history for that matter. It is necessary, therefore, to recognize an *ordo* in Paul's theology. What of the absence of sanctification in Paul's *ordo*? Keeping in mind that the terminology of systematics is often different from that of the Bible, we may note that: (1) Paul's *ordo* is not full-orbed but an occasional statement; and (2) it is likely that because Paul's understanding of redemption is largely governed by the already–not yet, we may say that sanctification is the "already" of glorification.[101] Given the presence, then, of an *ordo salutis* in Paul, how are we to relate justification to the *ordo* and especially union with Christ?

The unity of the ordo salutis

We must recognize that while there are some temporal elements of the *ordo salutis*, such as predestination being temporally prior to glorifica-

---

100. So Murray, *Redemption Accomplished*, 84.
101. See Douglas Moo, *Epistle to the Romans*, NICNT (Grand Rapids: Eerdmans, 1996), 531–32; C. E. B. Cranfield, *Romans*, 2 vols., ICC (1975; Edinburgh: T & T Clark, 2001), 1:433; C. K. Barrett, *Romans*, BNTC (1957; Peabody, MA: Hendrickson, 1991), 159; similarly Herman Witsius, *Economy of the Covenants between God and Man*, trans. William Crookshank, 2 vols. (1822; Phillipsburg, NJ: P&R, 1990), 3.8.9.

tion, the *ordo* is primarily a logical explanation of the *applicatio salutis*, in other words, how the real concrete relationships between the distinct acts of the application of redemption relate to one another.[102] While one may distinguish logically between justification and sanctification, this is not meant to imply that the two parts of our greater redemption can somehow be separated and that one might be justified but not sanctified. Additionally, we must observe that justification and sanctification likely begin at the same moment as one's regeneration and first expression of faith.

The logical prioritization of the *ordo salutis* is much like the similar understanding of the eternal decree. Though theologians have historically understood the decree to be one, based upon God's simplicity, at the same time they have seen the need to explain the unitary decree in terms of a sequence of decrees. The sequence of decrees was not intended to imply an order or sequence in the mind of God, but to recognize certain priorities and how the various elements of the decree related to one another. Likewise, we must recognize that the *applicatio salutis* is a unitary complex, in other words, a holistic redemption with various interrelated and necessary parts which must be logically related to one another.

Justification and union with Christ in the ordo salutis

The historic Reformed position on the relationship of the *ordo salutis* with the *unio mystica*, in contrast to typical Lutheran understandings, is that union with Christ undergirds the entire *ordo salutis*. The Larger Catechism, for example, states: "The communion in grace which the members of the invisible church have with Christ, is their partaking of the virtue of his mediation, in their justification, adoption, sanctification, and whatever else, in this life, manifests their union with him" (q. 69). Notice that the whole *ordo salutis* manifests the believer's union with Christ. In contrast to Lutheranism, which apparently sees union with Christ as an effect of justification, union with Christ is manifest in each stage of the *ordo salutis*. Figures 1 and 2 help demonstrate the differences between the Lutheran and Reformed conceptions of the *ordo salutis*,

---

102. Sinclair Ferguson, *The Holy Spirit* (Downers Grove, IL: InterVarsity, 1996), 97; see also Berkhof, *Systematic Theology*, 415–16. Contra Wright who seems to think that the *ordo* is merely a chronological sequence of events (see N. T. Wright, "New Perspectives on Paul," in *Justification in Perspective*, ed. Bruce L. McCormack [Grand Rapids: Baker, 2006], 255).

and more specifically the relationship between justification and union with Christ.

Fig. 1. Lutheran *ordo*

Election Regeneration Calling Faith Justification Union Adoption Sanctification Glorification

Fig. 2. Reformed *ordo*

Election Regeneration Calling Faith Justification Adoption Sanctification Glorification
—————————————————————————— Union with Christ ——————————————————————————

Though the *unio mystica* undergirds the entire *ordo salutis*, this does not therefore mean that we may swallow justification into an undifferentiated *applicatio salutis*. The *applicatio salutis* requires the *ordo salutis*, as we saw above; otherwise one could legitimately say it makes no difference where the believer's works sit within the *ordo*; whether before or after one's justification, speaking logically of course, would make no difference. Yet one can hardly square such an affirmation against the message of Scripture. Moreover, we must realize that while the *applicatio salutis* is one, this does not therefore mean that the *unio mystica* can be given logical priority over the entire *ordo salutis*.

As we will see in greater detail in the chapter on justification and the believer's union with Christ, we must recognize that the *unio mystica* is grounded upon the forensic, not vice versa.[103] To support this claim, one must consider at least two points. First, the indwelling of the Holy Spirit in the act of regeneration, though logically prior to justification in the *ordo salutis*, does not create a tension as Hodge and Gaffin find. The indwelling of the Holy Spirit beginning with regeneration occurs with a view to Christ's work and its appropriation in justification through faith. In this regard, Turretin can write that justification takes place "in this life in the moment of effectual calling, by which the sinner is transferred from a state of sin to a state of grace and is united to Christ, his head, by faith."[104] Likewise, Sinclair Ferguson writes, "Only when we are justified by grace through faith, and the covenantal purpose of God is actualized

103. Similarly, Michael S. Horton, *Covenant and Salvation: Union with Christ* (Louisville: Westminster John Knox, 2007).
104. Turretin, *Institutes*, 16.9.8.

in us, can we speak of being united to Christ."[105] One finds a similar pattern in the *historia salutis*.

Though the Holy Spirit was the agent of regeneration in the Old Testament (OT), one does not find the complete outpouring of the Holy Spirit upon the church until Pentecost, after the completion of the legal-forensic, fulfilling the requirements of the law, being punished according to the demands of the law, and being raised reversing the condemnation of the law, through Christ's life, death, and resurrection. This seems to be Paul's point in Galatians 3:13–14: "Christ redeemed us from the curse of the law by becoming a curse for us—for it is written, 'Cursed is everyone who is hanged on a tree'— so that in Christ Jesus the blessing of Abraham might come to the Gentiles, so that [*hina*] we might receive the promised Spirit through faith." One should note how the outpouring of the Spirit hinges (see Paul's use of the *hina* clause) upon the legal-forensic work of Christ.[106] Apart from the legal-forensic, there would have been no outpouring of the Spirit, no Pentecost. The salvation of OT saints and their indwelling by the Holy Spirit preceded the work of Christ; nevertheless, their indwelling proleptically looked toward and was founded upon the work of Christ (Heb. 9:15).

To give priority to justification in the *ordo salutis* makes clear the distinction but not separation between the objective, the legal-forensic, and the subjective, the transformative. There can be no subjective, or transformative work of the Spirit, apart from the objective, the work of Christ. Paul makes the point clear when he tells the Corinthians that if Christ is not raised, then they are still in their sins (1 Cor. 15:17). Therefore, the transformative is founded upon the forensic; union with Christ, though undergirding the whole *ordo salutis*, is grounded upon justification.[107]

Second, given that the *ordo salutis* is governed by the structure of redemptive history, the *historia salutis*, specifically the already–not yet, we must recognize that there are already–not yet aspects of the *unio mystica*. Though the believer's union with Christ begins with his regeneration, this does not mean that his union with Christ does not grow

---

105. Ferguson, *Holy Spirit*, 111.
106. F. F. Bruce, *The Epistle to the Galatians*, NIGTC (Grand Rapids: Eerdmans, 1982), 167–68.
107. See Hoeksema, *Reformed Dogmatics*, 450.

and mature. Calvin, for example, explains that the Lord's Supper "is a help whereby we may be engrafted into Christ's body, or engrafted, may grow more and more together with him, until he perfectly joins us with him in the heavenly life."[108] Because the believer enters the age to come by the resurrection of his inner man, but still remains in the present evil age because his outer man has yet to be raised with Christ, the believer inevitably struggles with sin.[109]

Justification covers not only the believer's past sins but also his present and future sins, which means that though the believer might struggle with indwelling sin, his union with Christ is not in jeopardy because his justification is based upon the imputed righteousness of Jesus Christ. Concerning Calvin's understanding of the already–not yet of union with Christ, one author writes, "While the *unio* of justification is in a sense total, the *unio* of sanctification is always partial and growing."[110] For these two reasons, then, we must recognize the priority of justification in the *ordo salutis*, even though the entire *ordo* is undergirded by the *unio mystica*.[111] Justification and union with Christ, therefore, as it relates to the *ordo* and *applicatio salutis*, are not in tension but are instead complementary aspects of our redemption. To this end, Herman Witsius (1636–1708) writes: "Faith justifies, as it is the bond of our strictest union with Christ, by which all things that are Christ's become also ours."[112] Or, again, with the Westminster Larger Catechism (q. 69), justification manifests our union with Christ; stated yet another way, justification is the legal aspect of our union with Christ. We may now turn and summarize our findings thus far.

Summary and Conclusion

We have surveyed three issues of how justification relates to prolegomena: the nature of theological language, the question of the place of justification in Paul's theology, and the related question of the relationship between justification and the rest of the *ordo salutis*. We have seen that justification is not one among many metaphors for our redemption, but is

108. Calvin, *Institutes*, 4.17.33.
109. Dunn, *Theology of Paul*, 474–75.
110. Dennis E. Tamburello, *Union with Christ* (Louisville: Westminster John Knox, 1994), 101.
111. Murray, *Redemption Accomplished*, 161.
112. Witsius, *Economy of the Covenants*, 3.8.51.

an act of God grounded in the incarnation, crucifixion, and resurrection of Christ. The work of Christ is no metaphor; therefore neither is our justification. We have also determined that we may legitimately say that justification is at the center of Paul's thought but not that it is a central dogma. Rather, it is the entry point to our redemption, and therefore central to our redemption and to the gospel. For this reason justification is most certainly the article by which the church stands or falls. We have also seen the relationship between justification and the rest of the *ordo salutis*. Justification is not at the head of *ordo salutis*, but is one aspect of the unitary *applicatio salutis* undergirded by the believer's union with Christ. Nevertheless, we must maintain that the *unio mystica* is logically founded upon the believer's justification.

We will see how these issues of prolegomena develop in the subsequent chapters throughout this volume. We must, however, first explore the structure of redemptive history, or the *historia salutis*. While justification is part of the *ordo salutis*, one does not want to abstract it from its place in redemptive history. One must recognize that the *ordo salutis* is inherently eschatological, seeing that it is bound up with the eschatological Adam. It is to explore the structure, then, of redemptive history that we must now turn.

3

THE STRUCTURE
OF REDEMPTIVE HISTORY

Whenever we consider any doctrine within the loci of systematic theology, we must locate the doctrine within the scope of redemptive history. To restate this principle in technical terms, we must properly locate the *ordo salutis* within the *historia salutis*. This is particularly significant because in the distant and recent past, theologians have often divorced the *ordo* from the *historia salutis*, which has the effect of creating a detached metaphysical system of redemption, one that is not necessarily rooted in history or reality. It was Rudolf Bultmann, for example, who argued that the historicity of the resurrection of Christ was inconsequential for the supposed message of the NT.[1] Locating the *ordo salutis*, and more specifically the doctrine of justification, within the plane of redemptive history is important for two reasons: (1) It recognizes the Scripture's insistence upon the reality and historicity of the events that surround our redemption; and (2) it also causes us to

1. See, e.g., Rudolf Bultmann, "New Testament and Mythology: The Problem of Demythologizing the New Testament Proclamation," in *New Testament & Mythology and Other Basic Writings*, ed. Schubert M. Ogden (Minneapolis: Fortress, 1984), 1–45.

recognize the eschatological nature of our redemption. In other words, when one considers the doctrine of justification, he must recognize that it is inextricably linked with the doctrines of Christology, the life, death, and resurrection of Christ, pneumatology, and eschatology. We must therefore turn to consider the structure of redemptive history so we can locate the place of the *ordo* within the *historia salutis*. Let us first turn to consider the nature of eschatology.

The Nature of Eschatology

The Scope

Eschatology is often conceived in terms of the web of doctrines that surround the second coming of Christ. This is true, for example, of much popular evangelical thought, as eschatology is often one of the last subjects treated in evangelical systematic theologies, and it is especially true of dispensational theology.[2] Eschatology, however, does not merely deal with the period of time immediately prior to the return of Christ but is far more encompassing. The all-encompassing scope of eschatology is evident when we find passages in both the OT and NT that speak of the "last days."

The Shiloh Prophecy (Gen. 49:8–12)

The first place this phrase appears is in Jacob's deathbed address to his sons: "Then Jacob called his sons and said, 'Gather yourselves together, that I may tell you what shall happen to you in days to come'" (Gen. 49:1). We should note that the LXX translates the Hebrew phrase *be'aharit hayyamim* as *eschatōn tōn hēmerōn*, the "last days." This phrase is not simply a chronological reference, namely that at some point in the future certain events will transpire. Rather, it is a phrase that points to an eschatological period. This conclusion is evident when we consider the substance of what Jacob tells his sons.

Jacob issues various prophecies of blessing and curse upon his sons, but the most significant statements come in his prophecy about Judah: "The scepter shall not depart from Judah, nor the ruler's staff from between his feet, until tribute comes to him; and to him shall be the obedience of the peoples" (Gen. 49:10). Now, to be sure, this statement is highly debated

2. Charles C. Ryrie, *Dispensationalism Today* (Chicago: Moody, 1965), 16–19.

and has been variously interpreted.[3] Nevertheless, within the context of the prophecy regarding Judah, Jacob begins by saying that Judah's brothers will praise him, and that he will conquer his enemies (Gen. 49:8). This is not simply a prophecy that Judah's brothers will worship him, but that his brothers, representing the eleven tribes of Israel, will bow down to him. In other words, the tribe of Judah will gain preeminence among the twelve. Moreover, Judah will also conquer his enemies. We may generalize verse 8: those inside the covenant community will worship Judah, and those outside will be conquered. Is it any wonder, given the dominance of Judah, that Jacob likens him to a lion (Gen. 49:9)? We see the significance of verses 8–9 expanded in verse 10a: "The scepter shall not depart from Judah, nor the ruler's staff from between his feet." Jacob says that the scepter will not depart from between Judah's feet; the scepter is a symbol of Judah's sovereign rule. In other words, the right of ruling the tribes of Israel will never depart from Judah or his descendants. It is in verse 10b, however, that scholars disagree over the meaning.

Several translations are unsure of its exact meaning and therefore transliterate the Hebrew of verse 10b, the scepter shall not depart from Judah "until Shiloh come" (KJV, NASB). There are others who argue that the scepter will not depart from between Judah's feet until "tribute comes to him" (ESV, NRSV; NAB).[4] Yet there is a more satisfying translation: "The scepter will not depart from Judah, nor the ruler's staff from between his feet, until he comes to whom it belongs and the obedience of the nations is his" (NIV, NLT). In other words, the scepter, that is, the symbol of authority, will not depart from Judah's feet, which is a euphemism for Judah's genitals (cf. Judg. 3:24; 1 Sam. 24:3; Isa. 7:20).[5] This reference to Judah's loins means that the scepter will be turned over to one of Judah's descendants; hence, "until he comes to whom it," that is, the scepter, "belongs." In this regard Geerhardus Vos explains:

> The "blessing of Jacob," Genesis 49, contains an approach to this point of view in what it predicts concerning Judah, vs. 10. The "Shiloh," that is "the One to whom Judah's scepter and ruler's staff belong" appears

---

3. For the interpretive variants see Nahum Sarna, *Genesis*, JPSTC (Philadelphia: JPS, 1989), 336–37; Gerhard von Rad, *Genesis*, OTL (Philadelphia: Westminster, 1972), 425; Gordon J. Wenham, *Genesis 16–50*, WBC 2 (Dallas: Word, 1994), 476–78.

4. So Sarna, *Genesis*, 336; Wenham, *Genesis*, 478.

5. Wenham, *Genesis*, 477.

here as the ultimate embodiment and virtually as the eternalizer of Judah's preeminence among the tribes. In other words, the One later called the Messiah is a Consummator in more than purely a chronological sense.[6]

Confirmation of this interpretation comes from the book of Revelation when we see Christ described as "the Lion of the tribe of Judah" who "has conquered" (Rev. 5:5).[7] We should also note that the lion of Judah rules over eschatological Israel, what Revelation describes as the 144,000, twelve thousand people from each of the twelve tribes of Israel (Rev. 7:4–8). The prophecy of Jacob takes on even greater significance when we consider the description of the effects of the rule of the lion of Judah.

Jacob describes the effects of the Messiah's reign in the following terms: "Binding his foal to the vine and his donkey's colt to the choice vine, he has washed his garments in wine and his vesture in the blood of grapes" (Gen. 49:11). Now, ordinarily no OT Israelite would leave a donkey tied to a grape vine because the beast of burden would begin to consume the precious fruit.[8] Yet there will be an abundance of grapes, indicated by the fact that the Messiah's garments will be covered in the "blood of grapes." Additionally we see that the Messiah would be marked by great beauty: "His eyes are darker than wine, and his teeth whiter than milk" (Gen. 49:12). Dark eyes, according to Scripture, are a mark of beauty (1 Sam. 16:12). White teeth are a mark of beauty; even in our own day this is true. When we consider these elements of the prophecy, we find fulfilment of them in several other places in Scripture. Christ rode into

---

6. Geerhardus Vos, *The Pauline Eschatology* (1930; Phillipsburg, NJ: P&R, 1994), 2. Vos presents the exegetical argumentation to support this conclusion: "My choice among the many and greatly varying interpretations is this. I resolve the word Shiloh, after leaving off the vowels, into the three characters *sh-l-oh*. Then *sh-* is taken as the abbreviated form of the relative *asher*; *-l-*, I take as the preposition *lamedh*; the *-oh* at the end of the word is the suffix of the third-person singular bearing the possessive sense of 'his.' Taken all together, this yields the rendering 'he to whom'" (Geerhardus Vos, *The Eschatology of the Old Testament*, ed. James T. Dennison Jr. [Phillipsburg, NJ: P&R, 2001], 99). Vos cites a parallel passage from Ezekiel as evidence to support his interpretation: "A ruin, ruin, ruin I will make it. This also shall not be, until he comes, the one to whom judgment belongs ['*asher-lo*], and I will give it to him" (Ezek. 21:27). See also von Rad, *Genesis*, 425; Bruce K. Waltke, *Genesis* (Grand Rapids: Zondervan, 2001), 608.

7. Vos, *Eschatology of the Old Testament*, 101; also G. K. Beale, *The Book of Revelation*, NIGTC (Grand Rapids: Eerdmans, 1999), 349.

8. Von Rad, *Genesis*, 425.

Jerusalem on the foal of a donkey (Matt. 21:4–5; Zech. 9:9), and the prophet Amos foretold of a time when Israel would be blessed with an abundance of wine:

> "Behold, the days are coming," declares the LORD, "when the plowman shall overtake the reaper and the treader of grapes him who sows the seed; the mountains shall drip sweet wine, and all the hills shall flow with it. I will restore the fortunes of my people Israel, and they shall rebuild the ruined cities and inhabit them; they shall plant vineyards and drink their wine, and they shall make gardens and eat their fruit. I will plant them on their land, and they shall never again be uprooted out of the land that I have given them," says the LORD your God. (Amos 9:13–15; cf. Lev. 26:5; Ps. 72:16; Isa. 25:6; Joel 2:24)[9]

For these reasons, and rightly so, Vos states that Genesis 49:11–12 is "descriptive of the eschatological state."[10]

The Last Days

Now before we proceed, we should summarize what we have observed thus far. Jacob's prophecy about the coming Messiah and his description of the days surrounding his advent occur "in the last days" (Gen. 49:1c; LXX). The "last days" formula is not an uncommon one but appears throughout the Scriptures. The phrase, and others similar to it, occur some twenty-seven times in the NT and only sometimes refer to the time immediately prior to the end of history. In fact in many places the phrase "last days" is used to describe the end times as beginning already in the first century. In the OT the "last days" are associated with a future time when

1. There will be a tribulation for Israel consisting in
   a. Great oppression (Ezek. 38:14–17),

9. Wenham, *Genesis*, 479; also Douglas Stuart, *Hosea-Jonah*, WBC 31 (Dallas: Word, 1987), 398–99.

10. Vos, *Eschatology of the Old Testament*, 102. Gunkel makes the trenchant observation that "most moderns are of the opinion that the (writing) 'prophets' first created Israel's eschatology, and, consequently, strike this verse because it contradicts this basic conviction. The author does not share this conviction. He believes, rather, that one can only understand the prophets if one assumes that they were already aware of an eschatology they adopted, resisted, transformed" (Herman Gunkel, *Genesis*, trans. Mark E. Biddle [Macon, GA: Mercer University Press, 1997], 457).

b. Persecution, false teaching, deception, and apostasy (Dan. 10:14–21; 11:27; 12:1–10).
2. After the tribulation
a. Israel will seek the Lord (Hos. 3:4–5);
b. They will be delivered (Ezek. 38:14–16; Dan. 11:40–12:2).
3. This deliverance and judgment will occur because the Messiah will finally conquer the nations (Gen. 49:1, 8–12; Num. 24:14–19; Isa. 2:2–4; Mic. 4:1–3; Dan. 2:28–45; 10:14–12:10).
4. God will establish a kingdom on the earth and rule over it (Isa. 2:2–4; Mic. 4:1–3; Dan. 2:28–45) together with a Davidic king (Hos. 3:4–5).[11]

It is important, then, that we note that the "last days" is a phrase that is used to denote the eschatological age.

At the same time, we see that the eschaton is inextricably linked with Christology, as is plainly evident in Genesis 49:10–12. Parenthetically, we may also note that the patriarchs were looking, not generally for Yahweh, but for the Messiah to deliver them and usher in the eschatological age (Gen. 18:18; 22:18; cf. Gal. 3:8, 16; John 8:56). We also see that the last days contain both favorable and unfavorable events, blessing and curses, joy and tribulation. These contrasting states hint at the already–not yet aspect of the eschatological age, but we will address this subject in greater detail below. Keeping the christological nature of the eschaton in mind, let us move forward to examine the connection that Paul makes between the protological and eschatological so we can see the structure of redemptive history, namely the way in which the beginning relates to the end.

The Structure of Redemptive History

The juxtaposition of the protological and the eschatological is evident in numerous places throughout the NT but especially in Romans 5:12–21 and 1 Corinthians 15:20–28, 45–48. In these three passages Paul places Adam and Christ in parallel, comparing their respective work and the results thereof.

11. G. K. Beale, "The New Testament and New Creation," in *Biblical Theology*, ed. Scott J. Hafemann (Downers Grove, IL: InterVarsity, 2002), 160.

Romans 5:12–21

In Romans 5:12–21 we see that because of Adam's sin, death entered the world. "So death spread to all men because all sinned" (Rom. 5:12). Paul contrasts Adam and Christ in the following manner: "Therefore, as one trespass led to condemnation for all men, so one act of righteousness leads to justification and life for all men" (Rom. 5:18). When we coordinate Romans 5:12–21 with the messianic prophecy of Genesis 49:10–12, we begin to see the structure of redemptive history emerge. In Romans 5:12–21 the structure is certainly evident; the dominance of Adam and Christ and the actions of each are determinative for the historical epochs they represent. We also see the coordination of the protological, eschatological, christological, and soteriological clearly emerge in 1 Corinthians 15.

1 Corinthians 15

In 1 Corinthians 15:20–28 we see Paul place Adam and Christ in parallel once again: "For as in Adam all die, so also in Christ shall all be made alive" (v. 22). Yet in this context we also see soteriology emerge in connection with the eschatological, as Paul deals with the subject of the resurrection, which is also clearly an eschatological event (Dan. 12:1–4). These connections become stronger in verses 45–48: "Thus it is written, 'The first man Adam became a living being'; the last Adam became a life-giving Spirit" (v. 45*). Here Paul quotes Genesis 2:7, referring to the creation of Adam, the first man. He also, however, calls Christ *ho eschatos Adam*. Concerning this appellation Vos observes:

> Most significant of all, however, is the designation of Christ as the "eschatos Adam," vs. 45, where "last" is entirely steeped in eschatological meaning, for this "last Adam" is the fountain-head of the resurrection, vss. 22, 23, a "quickening Spirit," "of heaven" and "heavenly," vss. 47–49, all this referring to the final celestial state and the conditions pertaining thereto, such as the peculiar kind of (bodily) image to be borne by believers after their resurrection.[12]

We see that Adam and Christ, then, are the fountainheads for death and life: "The first man was from the earth, a man of dust; the second man

12. Vos, *Pauline Eschatology*, 10.

is from heaven. As was the man of dust, so also are those who are of the dust, and as is the man of heaven, so also are those who are of heaven" (1 Cor. 15:47–48). However, we must not forget that Christ comes in the last days, or the eschaton, which means that Christ is the fountainhead of the eschatological age. We should also note, as does Vos, and rightly so, that Christ is "a life-giving Spirit." This is not merely a metaphorical or mystical phrase used to describe Christ's work but one that coordinates Christ's eschatological work with the Holy Spirit. We can see the coordination of the work of Christ and the Holy Spirit in several places throughout the Scriptures.

The Holy Spirit in 1 Corinthians 15:45

We begin with the creation, reading in Genesis 1:1–2 that the Spirit of God was hovering over the waters of creation, *weruach 'elohim merahepet 'al-pene hammayim*; and when we coordinate this with later NT passages, we see that the one who created the cosmos was Christ (John 1:1–18; Col. 1:16). We may say, then, that the Holy Spirit was the instrumental means of Christ's creation.

We continue to see a close synchronization of the work of the Holy Spirit and new creation at subsequent points in the OT: the re-creation of the earth after the flood, as God sent a *ruach* over the waters, which caused them to subside (Gen. 8:1; cf. 1:2); Noah sent a dove over the waters, the NT symbol for the Holy Spirit (Gen. 8:8; cf. John 1:32);[13] God superintended the creation of Israel, hovering (*yerahep*) over them like an eagle (Deut. 32:11), avian imagery as in Genesis 1:2. We also know the Holy Spirit was present at Israel's creation as well, as they emerged from the waters of the Red Sea (Hag. 2:5; Isa. 63:11); Christ, the one who ushers in the new creation, emerges from the waters of baptism accompanied by the Holy Spirit in the form of a dove (John 1:32).[14] Indeed, these water-Spirit-creation connections stand behind Christ's statement to Nicodemus: "Jesus answered, 'Truly, truly, I say to you, unless one is born of water and the Spirit, he cannot enter the kingdom of God" (John 3:5). So, then, in the creation, no less than in the new eschatological cre-

13. Warren Austin Gage, *The Gospel of Genesis* (1984; Eugene, OR: Wipf & Stock, 2001), 10–11.

14. Meredith G. Kline, *Images of the Spirit* (1980; Eugene, OR: Wipf & Stock, 1998), 19; Geerhardus Vos, *Biblical Theology* (1948; Edinburgh: Banner of Truth, 1996), 322.

ation, the work of the Holy Spirit is manifest and necessary. Returning to 1 Corinthians 15:45, the Holy Spirit's connection to new creation is why Paul says that Christ became "a life-giving Spirit."

To be sure, one should not mistake the close connection between the work of Christ and the Holy Spirit in the eschaton as a confusion of the ontological Trinity. Rather, we must see the connection and close coordination of the work of Christ and the Spirit as an aspect of the economic Trinity. Recall that Christ promised his disciples and the church that he would send the Holy Spirit after his ascension: "But when the Helper comes, whom I will send to you from the Father, the Spirit of truth, who proceeds from the Father, he will bear witness about me" (John 15:26). Parenthetically, we may note that the Father also sends the Spirit, which reminds us of the trinitarian nature of redemption. Nevertheless, Christ sends the Holy Spirit. We see the connection between Christ and the Holy Spirit when Paul, for example, states that "anyone who does not have the Spirit of Christ does not belong to him" (Rom. 8:9; cf. Acts 2:33; Phil. 1:19; 1 Peter 1:11).[15] Now why is there such a close identification of the work of Christ and the Holy Spirit as it relates to eschatology and soteriology?

As we previously noted, throughout the OT both the creation and types of the new eschatological creation, Noah and the flood, Israel and the Red Sea, involve the work of the Holy Spirit. In this regard, then, we must note that the Holy Spirit is the instrumental means of the creation as well as the new eschatological creation. This is especially evident when we see that the Holy Spirit was the empowering agent of Christ's resurrection, the first act of the new creation: "If the Spirit of him who raised Jesus from the dead dwells in you, he who raised Christ Jesus from the dead will also give life to your mortal bodies through his Spirit who dwells in you" (Rom. 8:11). In light of Paul's statement, we can say that not only is the Spirit the instrumental cause of the resurrection-act, but he is also the permanent basis of the resurrection-state, the power of the eschatological age (Heb. 6:5).[16] We see the conjunction of the Holy Spirit with the eschatological especially at Pentecost, the fulfilment of Joel's

---

15. James D. G. Dunn, *Romans 1–8*, WBC 38a (Dallas: Word, 1988), 443–44.

16. Geerhardus Vos, "The Eschatological Aspect of the Pauline Conception of the Spirit," in *Redemptive History and Biblical Interpretation*, ed. Richard B. Gaffin Jr. (Phillipsburg, NJ: P&R, 1980), 102.

OT prophecy of the outpouring of the Spirit: "And it shall come to pass afterward, that I will pour out my Spirit on all flesh" (Joel 2:28). What is interesting is that when Peter quotes Joel's prophecy, he uses the *eschatais hēmerais* formula: "And in the last days it shall be, God declares, that I will pour out my Spirit on all flesh" (Acts 2:17).[17]

Summary

Returning to 1 Corinthians 15:45–47 we see, then, that Adam is the fountainhead of the first creation, but by his disobedience he has forfeited his dominion to the powers of sin and death. Christ, on the other hand, is the fountainhead of the eschatological creation, which is marked by life, obedience, and righteousness.[18] The Scriptures call these two creations, those of Adam and Christ, this present evil age (Gal. 1:4) and the age to come (Matt. 12:32; Eph. 1:21; Heb. 6:5). This present evil age is marked by the flesh and sin: "The works of the flesh are evident: sexual immorality, impurity, sensuality, idolatry, sorcery, enmity, strife, jealousy, fits of anger, rivalries, dissensions, divisions, envy, drunkenness, orgies, and things like these. I warn you, as I warned you before, that those who do such things will not inherit the kingdom of God" (Gal. 5:19–21). By contrast, the age to come is marked by the Holy Spirit and his fruit: "But the fruit of the Spirit is love, joy, peace, patience, kindness, goodness, faithfulness, gentleness, self-control; against such things there is no law" (Gal. 5:22–23; cf. Isa. 45:8).

A person is either in Adam, and dominated by the flesh, or in Christ, and dominated by the Spirit. Paul describes those who are in Adam as *psychikos anthrōpos*, "natural man," and those in Christ as those who are *pneumatikos*, or spiritual (1 Cor. 2:14–15).[19] Indeed, those who are in Christ are not only dominated by the Holy Spirit but are "new creation"; by this, Paul does not intend to say that believers united to Christ wipe the slate clean and start anew, however true this idea may be. Rather, it is his intention to say that those who are united to Christ are part of the eschatological new creation, not simply a new creation (2 Cor. 5:17; cf.

---

17. Richard N. Longenecker, *Acts*, EBC (Grand Rapids: Zondervan, 1995), 71–72.
18. Vos, *Pauline Eschatology*, 60–61.
19. Richard B. Gaffin Jr., *Resurrection and Redemption* (1978; Phillipsburg, NJ: P&R, 1987), 108–9.

Isa. 65:17; 66:22).[20] There is one last matter regarding the structure of redemptive history that we must note, namely the already–not yet.

Already–Not Yet

We have seen thus far that the last days begin, not with the period immediately preceding the return of Christ and the final judgment, but with his first advent, with his life, death, and resurrection. Christ's first advent happens not at the end of history but in the middle of it. This means that the old creation does not end, giving way to the new. Rather, the epochs of Adam and Christ overlap, as shown in figures 3 and 4.[21]

Fig. 3. Common scheme

This age or world | The age or world to come

Fig. 4. Already–not yet

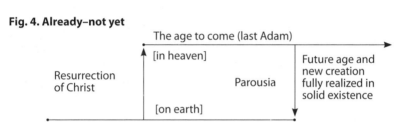

The age to come (last Adam)

[in heaven]

Resurrection of Christ

Parousia

Future age and new creation fully realized in solid existence

[on earth]

This age or world (Adam)

The overlap between the ages explains why the last days are both a period of blessing and curse, joy and tribulation. The already–not yet is manifest in such areas as the regeneration of the individual who is buried with Christ in baptism and raised with him to walk in the newness of life (Rom. 6:4); the believer is raised with Christ and seated with him in the heavenly places (Eph. 2:6; Col. 3:1). Yet, at the same time, the believer's body has yet to enter the new creation: "You, however, are not in the flesh but in the Spirit, if in fact the Spirit of God dwells in you. Anyone who does not have the Spirit of Christ does not belong to him. But if Christ is in you, although the body is dead because of sin, the Spirit is life because of righteousness" (Rom. 8:9–10). Thomas Schreiner explains that in Romans 8:9–10

20. Scott J. Hafemann, *2 Corinthians*, NIVAC (Grand Rapids: Zondervan, 2000), 243–44.

21. These figures are adapted from a diagram in Vos, *Pauline Eschatology*, 38 n. 45.

the eschatological tension of Pauline theology manifests itself here. The Spirit indwells believers and they are no longer slaves of sin, yet they still die because of sin. Sin is no longer the master over believers, but this does not mean that sin is nonexistent. The physical body of believers (which includes the whole person) indicates that Christians are still part of the old age, even though they possess the new-age gift of the Spirit. Full redemption will come at the day of resurrection when all sin and weakness will be left behind.[22]

Paul expresses this tension most famously in 2 Corinthians 4:16*: "Though our outer man is wasting away, our inner man is being renewed day by day." The inner man has been raised with Christ, whereas the outer man must await the resurrection of the dead. This is not to foist a Greek-philosophical spirit-body dualism on Paul; we must note that Paul uses the holistic terms of *exō* and *esō anthrōpos*, outer and inner man. The already–not yet, therefore, has implications not only for the *historia* but also the *ordo salutis*.[23] We will explore the already–not yet tension as it pertains especially to matters surrounding justification in the chapters to follow; nevertheless it is helpful first to outline briefly these implications.

Implications for the Doctrine of Justification

Let us summarize all of the data we have surveyed thus far and briefly state the implications for our understanding of the doctrine of justification. First, the eschaton, the age to come, dawns with the complex of events surrounding the first advent of Christ and the outpouring of the Holy Spirit at Pentecost. In terms of the loci of systematic theology, this means that Christology, pneumatology, and eschatology are inextricably intertwined. Additionally, given that redemption accomplished is primarily christological, and that the application of redemption is primarily pneumatological, both of which are eschatological, the *ordo salutis* is inherently eschatological. The *ordo salutis* must not be explained in isolation from the *historia salutis*; one must not fail to see its eschatological character.

22. Thomas Schreiner, *Romans*, BECNT (Grand Rapids: Baker, 1998), 414.
23. See Beale, "New Testament and New Creation," 164–73.

Second, if the *ordo salutis* is inherently eschatological, as it is the application of the work of the last Adam through the outpouring of the eschatological Spirit, this means that justification is eschatological.[24] For the one united to Christ by faith, this means he passes through the eschatological wrath of God the Father, not on the last day, but in Christ's crucifixion; Christ bears the wrath of the final judgment on behalf of those who look to him in faith. The believer is judged in Christ in the present, but that judgment is eschatological and final. Additionally, when the believer is declared righteous through faith alone in Christ alone, that declaration is final; it is eschatological and irreversible. Just as the wrath of the final judgment comes into the present in the crucifixion of Christ, so too the eschatological declaration of righteousness, the believer's justification, is a present reality.

Third, given the already–not yet nature of redemptive history, we may also say that the *ordo salutis* bears the same character. The believer's permanent and irreversible eschatological status in his justification does not mean that he is totally free from sin. Quite literally, the believer exists torn between the epochs of the first and last Adams. Though the believer is raised according to his inner man, he has yet to be raised according to his outer man (2 Cor. 4:16–5:4). In other words, justification is part of the eschatological "already," and glorification, the final stage of the *ordo salutis*, is part of the "not yet." The believer's sanctification straddles the already–not yet, in that the eschatological Spirit progressively conforms the believer to the image of the last Adam (1 Cor. 15:45–49), which is a part of the eschatological "already," but the abiding remnants of sin in the believer will not totally be expunged until the resurrection of the outer man, which is part of the eschatological "not yet." This means that even though the believer can and does produce good works, given the presence of sin in the believer, his good works are incapable of undergoing the scrutiny required for divine judgment. It is the already–not yet of the believer's sanctification that necessitates justification by faith alone in Christ alone and the imputation of the righteousness, the perfect obedience, of the last Adam. It is primarily these three points, the eschatological character of soteriology, justification, and the already–not yet of

---

24. Contra Chris VanLandingham, *Judgment and Justification in Early Judaism and the Apostle Paul* (Peabody, MA: Hendrickson, 2006), 17.

sanctification, that one must keep in the forefront of any exploration of the doctrine of justification.

Conclusion

Given the two-age structure of redemptive history, then, we must examine the doctrine of justification as it relates to the broader issues of soteriology, the *ordo salutis*, and always relate them to Christology, pneumatology, and eschatology, the *historia salutis*. In other words, we must recognize that justification is eschatological; it is not merely an anticipation of the final judgment, but rather is the verdict of the final judgment brought forward into the present. We will see how this understanding of justification materializes in the subsequent chapters. We must first proceed, however, to explore in greater detail the covenant of works and the labors of the first Adam. The covenant of works is necessary for a proper understanding of justification. It was in preredemptive history where man was able, by his works and obedience, to secure eternal life. The first Adam was to be either justified, declared righteous, or condemned at the conclusion of his probation.

4

JUSTIFICATION
AND THE COVENANT OF WORKS

Foundational to any understanding of the doctrine of justification is the work of Jesus Christ, his life, death, and resurrection and its application in justification, or redemption accomplished and applied. One cannot begin, however, with the work of Christ. Paul calls Christ the eschatological Adam (1 Cor. 15:45); additionally, Paul states that Adam is a type of the one to come (Rom. 5:14).[1] The connection between the two Adams therefore means that one must begin with the work of the first Adam before one can appreciate and understand the work of the last Adam. For this reason the Westminster Confession begins with the work of Adam in its chapter on God's covenants with man. The divines write: "The first covenant made with man was a covenant of works, wherein life was promised to Adam; and in him to his posterity, upon condition of perfect and personal obedience" (7.2).

1. This chapter is drawn in part from J. V. Fesko, *Last Things First* (Fearn, Scotland: Mentor, 2007), 77–114.

We begin, therefore, with the covenant of works. Wilhelmus à Brakel writes concerning the importance of the covenant of works:

Acquaintance with this covenant is of the greatest importance, for whoever errs here or denies the existence of the covenant of works, will not understand the covenant of grace, and will readily err concerning the mediatorship of the Lord Jesus. Such a person will very readily deny that Christ by His active obedience has merited a right to eternal life for the elect.[2]

This chapter therefore will demonstrate that Adam was in a covenantal relationship with God and that this relationship is properly called a covenant of works. The chapter will proceed along the following lines: it will (1) define what constitutes a covenant and give examples of OT covenants; (2) examine the evidence found within Genesis 1–3 and the rest of Scripture to demonstrate the existence of a covenant in the garden; (3) determine what work Adam was required to perform in this covenant; (4) answer objections to these conclusions; and (5) draw some important connections concerning Adam's covenant with God and the doctrine of justification.

Covenant Defined

Definition

In the OT, the Hebrew term used to denote a covenant is *berith*. What exactly is a *berith*? A generic definition of a *berith* is a treaty, alliance, or agreement between men or man and God, and it is typically translated in the OT by the term "covenant."[3] One finds confirmation of this definition,

2. Wilhelmus à Brakel, *The Christian's Reasonable Service*, trans. Bartel Elshout, vol. 1 (Ligonier, PA: Soli Deo Gloria, 1992), 355. For standard expositions of the covenant of works see Heinrich Heppe, *Reformed Dogmatics*, trans. G. T. Thomson, ed. Ernst Bizer (London: George Allen & Unwin, 1950), 281–300; Charles Hodge, *Systematic Theology*, 3 vols. (Grand Rapids: Baker, 1991), 2:117–22; Louis Berkhof, *Systematic Theology: New Combined Edition* (1932–38; Grand Rapids: Eerdmans, 1996), 211–18; Herman Bavinck, *Reformed Dogmatics*, trans. John Vriend, ed. John Bolt, 3 vols. (Grand Rapids: Baker, 2003–6), 2:563–71. For a more recent defense of the doctrine, see Bryan Estelle, "The Covenant of Works in Moses and Paul," in *Covenant, Justification, and Pastoral Ministry*, ed. R. Scott Clark (Phillipsburg, NJ: P&R, 2007), 89–136. One should also note that both the covenants of works and grace presuppose the covenant of redemption, or *pactum salutis* (see R. Scott Clark and David VanDrunen, "The Covenant before the Covenants," in *Covenant, Justification*, 167–96).

3. BDB, s.v. "*berith*," 136.

for example, in the following synonymous parallelism: "Your covenant with death will be annulled, and your agreement with Sheol will not stand" (Isa. 28:18). Given the ancient Near Eastern cultural background, and more specifically the Hittite vassal-treaty (second millennium B.C.), there are some similarities between the covenants of the ancient Near East and the covenant in the book of Deuteronomy. There are typically six elements in Hittite-vassal treaties:

1. Titular introductions of the treaty participants, such as the title of the suzerain, or covenant lord, and his vassal, or servant
2. A historical prologue rehearsing past relationships
3. Stipulations to the treaty
4. A clause requiring the treaty's regular reading and its preservation in a temple
5. Blessings and curses for either keeping or breaking the treaty
6. A list of those who witness the treaty

This is not to say, however, that there is identical consonance between the treaties of the ancient Near East and the Bible, Deuteronomy in particular.[4]

One can see, nevertheless, some of these characteristics in a small excerpt from the Hittite treaty between Suppiluliumas and Aziras of Amurru: "These are the words of the Sun Suppiluliumas, the great king, the king of the Hatti land, the valiant, the favorite of the Storm-god. I, the Sun, made you my vassal. And if you, Aziras, 'protect' the king of the Hatti land, your master, the king of the Hatti land, your master, will 'protect' you in the same way."[5] While much of the content of the biblical covenants is unique, there is, nevertheless, enough similarity between the ancient Near Eastern and the OT covenants that "the analogy of the treaties helps make the general point that Yahweh is Israel's suzerain and that the covenantal relationship demands for its preservation a certain commitment from the people."[6] What about the covenants of the OT?

4. Gordon J. McConville, "*berith*," in *NIDOTTE*, 1:747.
5. *ANE* 2, 42.
6. McConville, "*berith*," 747.

OT Covenants

There are two major types of covenants that are found in the OT: those between human parties and those between God and his people. There are several types between human parties:[7]

1. Friendship: such as David's covenant with Jonathan (1 Sam. 18:3; 20:8).
2. Parity: between rulers or powerful individuals such as Abraham's covenant with Abimelech (Gen. 21:27; see also 26:28; 31:44; 1 Kings 5:12; 15:19; 2 Kings 11:4).
3. Suzerain and vassal: a more powerful party sets the terms such as Joshua's treaty with the Gibeonites (Josh. 9:15; see also 1 Sam. 11:1; Ezek. 17:13–18; Jer. 34:8).
4. Marriage: permanent union between a man and woman (Mal. 2:14; Ezek. 16:8).

The covenants between God and his people fall into the general category of suzerain-vassal. God is clearly, in any covenant, the more powerful party. Nevertheless, this does not mean that all of God's covenants with his people take on the exact same form. Some covenants are clearly unilateral, wholly depending upon God to execute and carry them out. Other covenants are bilateral in nature, and require a response on the part of God's people.[8] Within the Bible one finds several important major covenants:

1. *Noahic*: the covenant between God and Noah, but more broadly between God and the creation (Gen. 9:8–17). This covenant falls in the unilateral category, as it essentially consists of God's prom-

---

7. Ibid., 748.
8. Ibid., 748–50. This is not to deny the sovereignty of God in his redemptive activities toward man. The bilateral aspects of a covenant do not admit synergism but recognize the importance of human responsibility. For a historical and theological treatment of these aspects of a covenant see Richard A. Muller, *Dictionary of Latin and Greek Theological Terms* (Grand Rapids: Baker, 1987), 120, 122, s.v. *"foedus monopleuron"* and *"foedus dipleuron"*; Lyle D. Bierma, "Federal Theology in the Sixteenth Century: Two Traditions?" *WTJ* 45 (1983): 304–21; J. Wayne Baker, *Heinrich Bullinger and the Covenant* (Athens: Ohio University Press, 1980). There is also a balance between the uni- and bilateral elements in salvation in confessional documents such as the WCF (3, 9).

ise. God also has an accompanying sign of the covenant, the rainbow (Gen. 9:13).

2. *Abrahamic*: the covenant between God and Abraham (Gen. 15:18; 17:2), which also includes Abraham's posterity, land, and a continuing relationship with God, with the ultimate goal of the blessing of the nations. Though emphasis lies upon the unilateral administration of this covenant, the bilateral element is present in the expected response (Gen. 17:1, 9–14). This covenant also has a sign, circumcision (Gen. 17:9–14).

3. *Mosaic*: the covenant between God and Israel on the occasion of their deliverance from Egypt (Ex. 19–24). Once again, while there are clearly unilateral elements in this covenant in that only God could deliver Israel, there is a greater emphasis upon the bilateral elements, keeping the covenant (Ex. 19:5). This covenant is accompanied by the Decalogue (Ex. 20:2–17) and the book of the covenant (Ex. 21–23), which constitutes the covenant stipulations, a covenant ratification (Ex. 24:3–8), a covenant meal (Ex. 24:9–11), the construction of the tabernacle (Ex. 25–27), the consecration of the Aaronic priesthood (Ex. 28–29), and the ritual regulations of Leviticus. The most developed form of the Mosaic covenant appears in Deuteronomy, which bears strong resemblances to Hittite treaties.[9] This covenant builds upon the Abrahamic covenant, in that circumcision is still required of its male participants, but God gives the Israelites an additional sign of the covenant, the Sabbath (Ex. 31:13).

4. *Davidic*: the covenant between God and King David (2 Sam. 7:8–17). This covenant is a unilateral covenant because it contains no explicit conditions and is exclusively based upon the promise of God. It is described as a "covenant of salt" (2 Chron. 13:5), which conveys the idea of permanence (see Lev. 2:13; and esp. Num. 18:19). This covenant is rooted in the Mosaic and Abrahamic covenants.

9. Meredith G. Kline, *The Structure of Biblical Authority* (Eugene, OR: Wipf & Stock, 1989), 37.

While the description of the above-listed covenants is not exhaustive, it nonetheless gives a framework out of which one may examine Genesis 1–3 and demonstrate that Adam was in a covenantal context.[10]

Covenant in Genesis 1–3

Genesis 1–3

In Genesis 1–3 there are places within the narrative that give evidence of the covenantal context in which Adam serves and knows God. One must, therefore, begin with a survey of those elements. One must also explore other important biblical passages to substantiate the claim that Adam was in a covenantal relationship with God. So, then, what about the creation narrative is covenantal? When we examine the initial creative acts of God, at first glance there does not appear to be evidence of any covenantal activity. For example, the text seems to report plainly the creation of day and night: "God called the light Day, and the darkness he called Night" (Gen. 1:5). God merely gives day and night their names. Yet it may surprise some that this is covenantal activity even though Genesis 1 does not identify it as such.

Considering the creation of day and night from the prophet Jeremiah, the investigator gains a great deal of relevant information. Jeremiah states, "If you can break my covenant with the day and my covenant with the night, so that day and night will not come at their appointed time, then also my covenant with David my servant may be broken, so that he shall not have a son to reign on his throne, and my covenant with the Levitical priests my ministers" (Jer. 33:20–21). Nowhere in Genesis 1 does the reader have an indication that God has established a covenant with the day and night, yet Jeremiah clearly states this is the case. When God creates, it is covenantal. This is not the only way in which the covenantal aspects of God's creative activity surface in the opening verses of Genesis.

The creative imagery of Genesis 1, particularly of the Spirit of God hovering over the chaotic waters (Gen. 1:2), reappears in other contexts that are clearly covenantal. In this regard, Meredith Kline writes:

10. For a more in-depth treatment of OT covenants see Michael S. Horton, *God of Promise: Introducing Covenant Theology* (Grand Rapids: Baker, 2006).

Special interest attaches to the appearance of the Glory-Spirit in a witness role in historical episodes or visionary scenes of re-creation that are repetitive of the original creation as described in Genesis 1:2. For besides confirming our identification of the Glory-Presence in Genesis 1:2, such evidence of the presence of God as a divine witness in Genesis 1:2 is an index of the covenantal cast of the whole creation narrative. Here we can simply suggest some of the data. In the exodus re-creation, the Glory-cloud, described by Moses by means of the imagery of Genesis 1:2, as we have seen, stood as pillar witness to the covenant that defined the legal nature of this redemptive action of God. At the beginning of the new creation, at the baptism of Jesus, the Spirit descending over the waters in avian form, as in Genesis 1:2, was a divine testimony to the Son, the Son who was given as God's covenant to the people. At the consummation of the new covenant with its new exodus-creation, the Glory-figure, apocalyptically revealed in Revelation 10:1ff., is seen clothed with a cloud, rainbow haloed, with the face like the sun and feet like pillars of fire, standing astride creation with his hand raised in oath to heaven, swearing by him who on the seventh day finished his creating of the heaven, the earth, the sea, and all their hosts that in the days of the seventh trumpet the mystery of God will be finished. In the interpretive light of such redemptive reproductions of the Genesis 1:2 scene, we see that the Spirit at the beginning overarched creation as a divine witness to the Covenant of Creation, as a sign that creation existed under the aegis of his covenant lordship.[11]

In these other covenantal contexts, the Holy Spirit is present as a witness to God's covenantal activity: the exodus, baptism of Christ, and the consummation. It stands to reason, then, that Kline's contention is correct—the Holy Spirit functioned in the same way at the beginning of the creation in Genesis 1:2. He was a witness to God's covenantal lordship. Gordon Spykman explains: "The covenant is rooted in God's work of creation. God covenanted his world into existence. Covenantal relationships are given in, with, and for all created reality. From the beginning creation is unthinkable apart from its covenantal relationship of dependence and responsiveness *coram Deo*."[12] It is clear, then, God's creative activity is covenantal. There is more evidence that one should consider from Genesis 2–3.

11. Meredith G. Kline, *Images of the Spirit* (Eugene, OR: Wipf & Stock, 1998), 19.
12. Gordon J. Spykman, *Reformational Theology* (Grand Rapids: Eerdmans, 1992), 260.

In Genesis 2–3 there are several elements that demonstrate Adam's covenant relationship with God. First, when God created Adam and placed him in the garden, the primeval temple, he issued a command that contains both blessing and curse (Gen. 2:16–17). This parallels the commands given in the Mosaic covenant not only in verbal form but also with the appended blessings and curses (Ex. 20:2–17; cf. Gen. 2:16–17) (fig. 5).[13]

Fig. 5. Parallel commands

Genesis 2:17	Hebrew	Exodus 20:13–15	Hebrew
You shall not eat.	*Lo'to'kal*	You shall not murder.	*Lo'tirtsah*
		You shall not commit adultery.	*Lo'tin'ap*
		You shall not steal.	*Lo'tignob*

A second feature seen in Genesis 1–3 is the use of the trees of life and knowledge. How do these respective trees function within the narrative? They closely parallel the signs of the Abrahamic, Noahic, and Mosaic covenants, circumcision (Gen. 17:9–14), the rainbow (Gen. 9:13–16), and the Sabbath (Ex. 31:13). A sign of the covenant typically functions as a visual reminder of the covenant between God and his servant. The two trees have a sacramental function similar to those sacramental signs of God's redemptive covenants, visible signs of God's invisible redemptive grace.

While the two trees are not signs of grace, as Adam has yet to sin, they do function sacramentally by serving as visual reminders of God's stated blessing and curse, the promise of life or death. Seeing the trees of life and knowledge as sacramental is not a new observation; it is found, for example, in John Calvin:

The term "sacrament" . . . embraces generally all those signs which God has ever enjoined upon men to render them more certain and confident of the truth of his promises. He sometimes willed to present these in natural things, at other times set them forth in miracles. Here are some examples of the first kind. One is when he gave Adam and Eve the tree of life as a guarantee of immortality, that they might assure themselves of it

13. Claus Westermann, *Genesis 1–11*, trans. John J. Scullion (Minneapolis: Fortress, 1994), 223; Nahum Sarna, *Genesis*, JPSTC (Philadelphia: JPS, 1989), 21; Martin Luther, *Lectures on Genesis*, ed. Jaroslav Pelikan, LW 1 (St. Louis: Concordia, 1958), 107–8.

as long as they should eat of its fruit. Another, when he set the rainbow for Noah and his descendants, as a token that he would not destroy the earth with a flood. These, Adam and Noah regarded as sacraments. Not that the tree provided them with an immortality which it could not give to itself; nor that the rainbow (which is but a reflection of the sun's rays upon the clouds opposite) could be effective in holding back the waters; but because they had a mark engraved upon them by God's Word, so that they were proofs and seals of his covenants.[14]

While the evidence of God's command and the sacramental function of the trees is possible proof of a covenant, when one fans out into the rest of Scripture he finds further corroboration that Adam and Eve were indeed in covenant with God. Spykman comments regarding these elements:

Though the word "covenant" (*berith*) does not appear in the creation account (Genesis 1, 2), the basic elements of classic covenant making are clearly present. They are evident in (a) the preamble with its prologue, introducing the Sovereign in his relationship to the second party, (b) the promises and obligations which define the community established by the covenantal pact, and (c) the blessing-and-curse formula, with its stated condition for fidelity and its stated penalty for infidelity.[15]

In other words, besides what has already been brought forth in the second and third items (b and c), Spykman identifies yet another element of which one should take notice, item (a), the preamble. The Israelite in covenant with God at Sinai, the time during which Genesis was compiled and written, would hear the familiar echo of Genesis 1 in Exodus 20:2. Moreover, he would take note of items (b) and (c), the promises and obligations and the blessing-and-curse formula, as well as the sacramental trees, and he would see the parallels with his own covenantal context. It seems far more likely that he would draw the conclusion that Adam was in covenant with God rather than not. One finds confirmation of this conclusion in early Jewish thought.

Early Jewish writings place Adam in covenant with God. For example, in the Testament of Moses one reads of what supposedly happened after

14. John Calvin, *Institutes of the Christian Religion*, ed. John T. McNeill, trans. Ford Lewis Battles, LCC 20–21 (Philadelphia: Westminster, 1960), 4.14.18.
15. Spykman, *Reformational Theology*, 260.

the fall: "And the Lord, coming into paradise, set his throne, and called with a dreadful voice, saying, Adam, where are you and why are you hidden from my face? Shall the house be hidden from him that built it? And he says, Since you have forsaken my covenant, I have brought upon your body seventy strokes."[16] There is also a parallel in the OT Apocrypha: "The Lord created human beings out of earth. . . . He bestowed knowledge upon them, and allotted to them the law of life. He established with them an eternal covenant, and revealed to them his decrees" (Sir. 17:1, 11–12). One sees, then, that the idea that Adam was in covenant with God has ancient pedigree, long before Augustine (354–430) or the sixteenth-century Reformers brought forth their explanations. There are further considerations from God's covenantal dealings with Noah that bear upon the idea of a covenant between Adam and God.

Genesis 6:18

The term "covenant" is first used in God's dealings with Noah: "But I will establish my covenant with you" (Gen. 6:18a). By way of contrast, when God initiates his covenant with Abraham one finds different nomenclature than what is found in Genesis 6:18. Instead of the term *qum*, which in the hiphil stem means "establish," one finds the term *karath*, "the LORD *made* a covenant with Abram" (Gen. 15:18). Literally translated the term *karath* means "to cut"; hence God "cut" a covenant with Abraham. The term *karath* reappears at the initiation of subsequent covenants such as between Abraham and Abimelech (Gen. 21:27, 32; cf. 26:28; 31:44), God and Israel at Sinai (Ex. 34:10), and in the prohibition to initiate a covenant with the Gentile inhabitants of the promised land (Ex. 23:32; cf. Gen. 17:2). What is the significance of the different nomenclature in Genesis 6:18 and 15:18?

Genesis 6:18 does not refer to the initiation of a new covenant but rather the continuation of an already existing covenant. The use of the term *qum* suggests the reestablishment of something already in place.[17] In fact, William Dumbrell argues that Genesis 6:18 "refers to a divine relationship established by the fact of creation itself." For this reason, there is the "absence of standard terminology of covenant initiation from

16. ANF, 8:565.
17. McConville, "*berith*," 748.

the early Genesis narratives."[18] This has important implications for God's subsequent covenantal dealings with Noah in Genesis 9. When God makes his covenant with Noah in Genesis 9, there are clear connections between verses 1–2 and the dominion mandate of Genesis 1:28. The Noahic covenant is rooted in creation and, as Dumbrell notes, "any theology of covenant must begin with Genesis 1:1."[19] If this analysis of Genesis 6:18 is correct, then it means that God established a covenant with Adam and that the covenant concept does not arise *de novo* in God's dealings with Noah. There is another important piece of evidence that confirms that man was in covenant with God in the garden.

Hosea 6:7

Within the history of biblical interpretation there are some verses that have received much attention with little to no consensus achieved by their interpreters. Hosea 6:7 is just such a verse: *wehemmah ke'adam 'aberu berith,* "But like men [or Adam] they transgressed the covenant." There is disagreement over exactly how the term *ke'adam* should be translated. There are those who believe it should be rendered as "like man" (LXX, NKJV, KJV). On the other hand, there are those who believe it should be translated as "like Adam" (Vul, RSV, NRSV, NASB, ASV, ESV, NIV). The implications of translation are significant. If the correct translation of the verse in question is "like Adam," then there is a clear and explicit affirmation of the existence of a covenant between Adam and God. Which of the two possible translations is preferable?[20]

There are those who argue that Hosea 6:7 should be translated, "But like men they transgressed the covenant." Calvin, for example, argues that Hosea states that the Israelites have "showed themselves to be men in violating the covenant."[21] Calvin argues that the intended comparison is between the faithfulness of God and the faithlessness of the sinful Isra-

---

18. W. J. Dumbrell, *Covenant and Creation* (Carlisle: Paternoster, 1984), 32; see esp. 25–32.

19. Ibid., 42.

20. These are not the only two options. There are those who hold that it should be translated, "they have treated my covenant as if it was dirt" (Douglas Stuart, *Hosea-Jonah*, WBC 31 [Dallas: Word Books, 1987], 111). There are others who believe that this is a reference to the city of Adam (Josh. 3:16) (Francis I. Anderson and David Noel Freedman, *Hosea*, AB 24 [New York: Doubleday, 1980], 439). See also Thomas McComiskey, *Hosea*, The Minor Prophets 1, ed. Thomas McComiskey (Grand Rapids: Baker, 1992), 95.

21. John Calvin, *Hosea*, CTS 13 (Grand Rapids: Baker, 1993), 235.

elites—they have acted like sinful men. Regarding the possibility of the alternate translation "like Adam," Calvin rather brusquely comments: "I do not stop to refute this comment; for we see that it is in itself vapid."[22] Yet, as B. B. Warfield notes, if the comparison is to men in general, it lacks the needed specificity with the bare use of the term "men." Warfield writes that "the simple 'men' must be made in some way to bear a pregnant sense—either as mere men, as opposed to God, or as common men as opposed to the noble or the priestly, or as heathen as opposed to the Israelites—to none of which does it seem naturally to lend itself here—before a significance equal to the demands of its context is given it."[23] The most natural reading of the verse is a comparison between Adam, God's son (Luke 3:38), and Israel, who is also God's son (Ex. 4:22–23).

Warfield draws upon the parallels between Adam and Israel when he favorably quotes another author who writes:

> God in his great goodness had planted Adam in Paradise, but Adam violated the commandment which prohibited his eating of the tree of knowledge, and thereby transgressed the covenant of his God. Loss of fellowship with God and expulsion from Eden were the penal consequences that immediately followed. Israel like Adam had been settled by God in Palestine, the glory of all lands; but ungrateful for God's great bounty and gracious gift, they broke the covenant of their God, the condition of which, as in the case of the Adamic covenant, was obedience.[24]

Based upon Warfield's argument, it seems that "like Adam" is the more natural and powerful comparison and that Hosea 6:7 may be cited in support of the idea that Adam was in a covenantal relationship with God.[25] One finds corroborating evidence with the similar use of *ke'adam* in Job 31:33: "If I have covered my transgressions as Adam" (NKJV, NASB, ASV, KJV). Warfield acknowledges that he is not the only one to come to this conclusion and that other luminaries such as Martin Luther, Francis Turretin, Wilhelmus à Brakel, Herman Witsius, Franz Delitzsch, A. A. Hodge,

22. Ibid.
23. B. B. Warfield, "Hosea 6:7: Adam or Man?" in *Collected Shorter Writings*, ed. John E. Meeter, 2 vols. (1970; Phillipsburg, NJ: P&R, 2001), 1:127.
24. Ibid., 128–29.
25. So McComiskey, *Hosea*, 95. This is the view of rabbinic interpreters (see Lamentations Rabbah Pro. 4).

Herman Bavinck, and Geerhardus Vos hold the same view.[26] One may also add that the American revisions of the Westminster Confession of Faith (1789) cite this passage in support of the covenant of works. While this is not proof that this interpretation is correct, one may affirm with Warfield, "If we should err, we should err in a great and goodly company."[27] Moving forward, then, one may proceed to examine a key NT passage that demonstrates that Adam was in a covenantal relationship with God in the garden.

Romans 5:12–19

In the NT the apostle Paul sets up a clear parallel between the first and last Adams (1 Cor. 15:45). There is no doubt regarding Christ as the mediator of the new covenant (Matt. 26:28; Heb. 9:15; 12:24). There is a key connection between Adam and Christ when Paul identifies Adam as a *typos* or "a type of the one who was to come" (Rom. 5:14). N. T. Wright states that Paul does not use *typos* in a general sense; he uses it in a technical sense. The thought is that Paul uses the term *typos* to convey the idea of a die or stamp that leaves an impression on wax. In other words, "Adam prefigured the Messiah in certain respects."[28] C. E. B. Cranfield notes more specifically that when *typos* is used in its technical sense, it is a "person or thing prefiguring (according to God's design) a person or thing pertaining to the time of eschatological fulfillment. Adam, in his universal effectiveness for ruin, is the type which—in God's design—prefigures Christ in His universal effectiveness for salvation."[29]

---

26. Francis Turretin, *Institutes of Elenctic Theology*, trans. George Musgrave Giger, ed. James T. Dennison Jr., 3 vols. (Phillipsburg, NJ: P&R, 1992–97), 8.3.8; Brakel, *Christian's Reasonable Service*, 1:363–65; Herman Witsius, *Economy of the Covenants between God and Man*, trans. William Crookshank, 2 vols. (1822; Phillipsburg, NJ: P&R, 1990), 2.15–3.8; C. F. Keil and Franz Delitzsch, *Commentary on the Old Testament*, 10 vols. (1866–91; Peabody, MA: Hendrickson, 1996), 10:66; A. A. Hodge, *Outlines of Theology* (1860; Edinburgh: Banner of Truth, 1991), 310; Herman Bavinck, *In the Beginning*, trans. John Vriend, ed. John Bolt (Grand Rapids: Baker, 1999), 199; Geerhardus Vos, *Biblical Theology* (1948; Edinburgh: Banner of Truth, 1996), 34. For a historical survey of the interpretation of Hosea 6:7 within the Reformed tradition see Richard A. Muller, *Post-Reformation Reformed Dogmatics*, 4 vols. (Grand Rapids: Baker, 1993), 2:456–63.

27. Warfield, "Adam or Man?" 129.

28. N. T. Wright, *Romans* NIB 10 (Nashville: Abingdon, 2003), 527.

29. C. E. B. Cranfield, *Romans*, 2 vols., ICC (1975; Edinburgh: T & T Clark, 2001), 1:283; see also Leonhard Goppelt, *Typos*, trans. Donald H. Madvig (1939; Grand Rapids: Eerdmans, 1982), 129–30.

It is important to realize that Paul's comparison between Adam and Christ, therefore, is not coincidental or convenient but predetermined by God himself.[30] Is one to conclude that Christ as the antitype merited salvation within a covenantal context, but that Adam, the type, was not in such a context? It is not impossible to assume this conclusion, but it certainly runs against the grain of Scripture if one eliminates a covenantal context for Adam. Luther, approvingly quoting Augustine, writes that "just as Adam has become a cause of death to those who are born of him, even though they have not eaten of the tree, the death brought on by the eating, so also Christ was made a provider of righteousness for those who belong to Him, even though they are entirely lacking in righteousness."[31] Now, in what context does Augustine elsewhere place Adam?

Augustine places Adam in the context of a covenant. Augustine writes in his *City of God* concerning Romans 5:12 that "even the infants, not personally in their own life, but according to the common origin of the human race, have all broken God's covenant in that one in whom all have sinned." Augustine is not unaware, however, that neither Romans 5:12, nor Genesis 1–3, explicitly state that Adam was in the context of a covenant. He goes on to write: "There are many things called God's covenants besides those two great ones, the old and the new, which any one who pleases may read and know. For the first covenant, which was made with the first man, is just this: 'In the day you eat thereof, you shall surely die.'"[32] On the basis of the parallel between Christ and Adam, the technical use of *typos*, and the covenantal context in which Christ as the last Adam brings redemption, one may conclude that Adam was also in a covenantal context.

In fact, Douglas Moo comments that the "similarity between Adam's relationship to his 'descendants' and Christ's to his underlies all of vv. 15–21."[33] Romans 5:12–21 not only tells of the existence of a covenant between God and Adam in protology, it helps the reader understand the pattern in eschatology with the work of the last Adam. Charles Hodge notes that as

30. For other views see James D. G. Dunn, *Romans 1–8*, WBC 38a (Dallas: Word, 1988), 277–79.

31. Augustine, *Contra Julianum* 1.6.22, as cited in Martin Luther, *Lectures on Romans*, trans. Jacob A. O. Preus, LW 25 (St. Louis: Concordia, 1974), 305.

32. Augustine, *City of God*, 16.27, trans. Marcus Dodds, in NPNF[1] 2:3266.

33. Douglas Moo, *Epistle to the Romans*, NICNT (Grand Rapids: Eerdmans, 1996), 334.

Adam was the head and representative of his race, whose destiny was suspended on his conduct, so Christ is the head and representative of his people. As the sin of the one was the ground of our condemnation, so the righteousness of the other is the ground of our justification. This relation between Adam and the Messiah was recognized by the Jews, who called their expected deliverer, *ha'adam ha'aharon, the last Adam*, as Paul also calls him in 1 Corinthians 15:45, *ho eschatos Adam*. Adam was the type *tou mellontos*, either of the *Adam* who was to come, or simply *of the one to come*. The Old Testament system was preparatory and prophetic. The people under its influence were looking forward to the accomplishment of the promises made to their father. The Messianic period on which their hopes were fixed was called "the world or age to come," and the Messiah himself was *ho erchomenos, ho mellōn, the one coming.*[34]

In addition to establishing Adam's covenantal relationship with God, the connection with Christ as the last Adam also begins to demonstrate other key links between protology, Christology, soteriology, and eschatology. As James Dunn notes, "Christ is the eschatological counterpart of primeval Adam."[35] Several conclusions concerning the covenant of works are in order at this point before the investigation proceeds.

Summary

Various examples and types of covenants within Scripture have thus been given. Narrowing the scope of the investigation to the question of whether Adam was in a covenantal relationship with God, we have surveyed several key elements within Genesis 1–3 and the greater scope of Scripture. A key element that the investigation has identified is that when God created, he did not create apart from a theological context. Indeed, God created the world and administers his kingdom covenantally. Though Genesis 1 does not report the covenant nature of God's creative activity, Jeremiah 33:20–22 certainly sheds light upon the fact that he created in terms of a covenant. The prologue of Genesis 1, God's command to Adam, the blessing and curse attached to it, and the sacramental trees of life and knowledge are further indicators that Adam was in covenant with God. These elements parallel those found in subsequent covenants in Scripture. We then examined Genesis 6:18, Hosea 6:7, and Romans

---

34. Charles Hodge, *Romans* (1835; Edinburgh: Banner of Truth, 1989), 162.
35. Dunn, *Romans* 1–8, 277; see also Estelle, "Covenant of Works," 116–24.

5:12–19 (esp. v. 14) to demonstrate that God confirmed with Noah an already existing covenant, a covenant that he had made with Adam. Any one of these factors by itself would not constitute irrefutable evidence, but all of them together lead to the conclusion that Adam was in a covenantal context with God.

One should also note that while the term "covenant" does not occur in Genesis 1–3, the rest of Scripture confirms its existence. The implied existence of the covenant is much like the implied existence of the covenantal relationship between Adam and Eve. The author, for example, refers to the woman as Adam's "wife" (Gen. 2:24), and he refers to the man as the woman's "husband" (Gen. 3:6). There is no mention of a marriage or ceremony, though the reader may nonetheless say that Adam and Eve were in a covenantal relationship, one that Scripture characterizes as the marriage bond (Mal. 2:14). The question to which one must now turn is, What was the nature of the covenant? What was Adam required to do in his covenantal relationship with God?

The Work of the Covenant

The Dominion Mandate

Now that Adam's covenantal relationship with God has been established, one must determine what duties or responsibilities Adam was required to fulfil. Unlike unilateral covenants that God makes, such as those with the day and night or with the postflood creation, God's other covenants are bilateral and require a response on the part of the one with whom God has covenanted. The clearest statement of man's covenant responsibilities is found in what many call the dominion mandate: "Be fruitful and multiply and fill the earth and subdue it and have dominion over the fish of the sea and over the birds of the heavens and over every living thing that moves on the earth" (Gen. 1:28). Adam was given several tasks in this command from God: (1) fill the earth with the image of God through procreation; (2) subdue the earth; and (3) have dominion over the creation, that is, exercise authority over it. Not only was Adam supposed to carry out this work of expansion, but there was also an end to Adam's labors represented in the Sabbath rest. Adam was given a period of probation in the garden, and had he passed the probation and eaten from the tree of life, he would have passed the days of his life carrying

122

on his work of expansion until he completed the work. At this point, one may give Adam's work the title of "expansion," and so one must ask, Why was Adam given this expansion task? What precisely was Adam supposed to expand?

The Dominion Mandate in Its Garden-temple Context

It is important to pay close attention to minute details in Genesis 1–3. There are several elements in Genesis 1–3 that provide important information concerning the intended goal of Adam's covenantal work. First, Adam was not merely a farmer but first and foremost a priest. As Gordon Wenham notes, "Adam should be regarded as an archetypal Levite."[36] Second, the garden of Eden is not a farm but the first temple, the place in which Adam must perform his priestly labor. Third, recall that Adam was created in the image of the triune Lord and was given vice-regency over the creation. Just as God rules over the cosmos, so too Adam must rule over the earth under God's authority (Gen. 1:26; Ps. 8). Fourth, there was a difference between the conditions inside and outside the garden. Genesis 2:5 states that "no bush of the field was yet in the land," a reference to field vegetation fit only for animal grazing. On the other hand, "no small plant of the field had yet sprung up," a reference to agriculture grown with irrigation and human effort for consumption as food.[37] This division between field vegetation and cultivated agriculture means that there was a noticeable boundary between the garden and the outside world.

God sent rain and created man to grow food (Gen. 2:6–7), and therefore in the immediate area of the garden there was order.[38] Outside the garden, however, there was less order, because man was not cultivating the ground. Inside the garden there was order maintained by Adam, whereas outside the garden there was disorder. This is not to say that God created chaos outside the garden, but that in the same way that God

---

36. Gordon J. Wenham, "Sanctuary Symbolism in the Garden of Eden Story," in *I Studied Inscriptions from Before the Flood*, ed. Richard S. Hess and David Toshio Tsumura (Winona Lake, IN: Eisenbrauns, 1994), 401.

37. See Gordon J. Wenham, *Genesis 1–15*, WBC 1 (Dallas: Word, 1987), 58; Derek Kidner, *Genesis*, TOTC (Downers Grove, IL: InterVarsity, 1967), 59; Westermann, *Genesis 1–11*, 199; see also Umberto Cassuto, *A Commentary on the Book of Genesis*, Part One, trans. Israel Abrahams (Jerusalem: Magnes Press, 1998), 101–2.

38. See Meredith G. Kline, "Because It Had Not Rained," *WTJ* 20/2 (1958): 146–57; and Mark D. Futato, "Because It Had Rained," *WTJ* 60/1 (1998): 1–21.

brought order to the initial chaos of Genesis 1:1, so too Adam was to expand the garden-order throughout the world. That Adam was to extend the garden to the ends of the earth is evident in the dominion mandate itself; Adam was to "subdue" the earth (Gen. 1:28). These factors give an interpretive key and trajectory that help set Adam's covenantal work in the proper context.

Adam's covenantal work is not merely that of farming for six days and then resting on the seventh. Rather, God covenanted with Adam to: (1) multiply the image of God through procreation; (2) fill the earth with the image of God and expand the garden-temple to fill the earth—to bring the garden-order to the earth where there was no order—to subdue the earth; and (3) expand his vice-regency throughout the whole earth by having men, made in God's image, rule over the entire creation. Along these lines John Walton comments:

> If people were going to fill the earth, we must conclude that they were not intended to stay in the garden in a static situation. Yet moving out of the garden would appear a hardship since the land outside the garden was not as hospitable as that inside the garden (otherwise the garden would not be distinguishable). Perhaps, then, we should surmise that people were gradually supposed to extend the garden as they went about subduing and ruling. Extending the garden would extend the food supply as well as extend sacred space (since that is what the garden represented). In this regard it is possible to conclude that the inclusion of where the rivers went (2:11–14) is intended to indicate some of the resources that would eventually be at humankind's disposal as they worked their way out from the garden. Gold, spices, and precious stones all found their most common functions within sacred space, and these could be procured for that purpose as the garden was expanded.[39]

Walton is not alone in this observation, as it was first made by Karl Barth some fifty years earlier:

> That the closed sanctuary with its trees has a symbolic or sacramental character is now revealed by the fact that the water which nourishes it does not take the form of a sea fed by a subterranean source and with subterranean exits, but that a whole river bursts forth which Eden is not

39. John H. Walton, *Genesis*, NIVAC (Grand Rapids: Zondervan, 2001), 186–87.

to keep to itself but to take its own share and then to pass on to surrounding districts, and which is sufficiently powerful to divide into four parts—obviously indicating the four quarters of the compass—and to bring to these four quarters and therefore to the whole earth what it had brought to Eden.[40]

This sets Adam's covenantal work on an entirely different trajectory than one typically finds. Adam's mandate is not merely to labor but to expand the garden-temple throughout the earth, fill the earth with the image of God, and subdue it by spreading the glory of God to the ends of the earth. This is what constitutes Adam's covenant responsibilities. Adam, however, was not tasked with this work indefinitely. There was a terminus to his covenantal labors.

The Goal of Adam's Covenant of Works: the Sabbath Rest

God's own work of six days and a seventh day of rest indicate that Adam was to emulate this pattern in his own work. How long this work would have taken is unknown. How long Adam's probation would have lasted is also unknown. Little is known about Adam's exact relationship to the tree of life. Had Adam refused the temptation of the serpent, would he then have eaten from the tree of life and been enabled to carry out his work unhindered by the *posse peccare*, the power to sin, the possibility of abandoning his covenant with God? To this question, there is no firm answer. One may nevertheless recognize that Adam's state in the garden was never intended to be a permanent one. Adam had the responsibility of fulfilling his covenantal obligations, after which he would have entered into a permanent Sabbath rest. The probation would have ended, death would no longer have been a possibility, *posse non mori*, and Adam would have rested from his duties as vice-regent over the creation once the earth was filled with the image and glory of God.

In this regard Samuel Rutherford, one of the Scottish advisors at the Westminster Assembly explains: "The performing of the condition of the covenant of works does justify Adam by law works, so as he is no

---

40. Karl Barth, *Church Dogmatics*, vol. 3.1, *The Doctrine of Creation*, trans. J. W. Edwards (1958; Edinburgh: T & T Clark, 1998), 255. Similar ideas emerge from the Qumran community where they speak of the rivers of Eden that cause the boughs of an everlasting plant to grow and cover the whole earth (1QH 14 [10] 14 [6], ln. 17ff.; also 1QH 18 [14]).

sinner, has fulfilled the law, has right to life eternal."[41] In other words, because there was no sin in the world, Adam could have secured eternal life through his obedience to the commands of God, the commands to refrain from eating from the tree and to fill the earth and subdue it.

In this regard Rowland Ward notes, "We can say there was an eschatology before there was sin, that is, a glorious destiny was in view of which the tree of life in Genesis 2 was also a token. Creation at the beginning was not like it will be in the end, when it will be richer and more enduring."[42] Stating it more technically, Geerhardus Vos writes: "The so-called 'Covenant of Works' was nothing but an embodiment of the Sabbatical principle. Had its probation been successful, then the sacramental Sabbath would have passed over into the reality it typified, and the entire subsequent course of the history of the race would have been radically different."[43] These conclusions, however, regarding Adam's labor and more specifically the covenant of works have not gone unchallenged.

Critics of the Covenant of Works

The affirmation of the covenant of works first existed in the earliest days of the church with Augustine's explanation of Genesis 2:16–17, but was somewhat dormant throughout the Middle Ages. It was in the post-Reformation period that the doctrine of the covenant of works became normative in Reformed theology.[44] In the Westminster Confession (1646) the doctrine was codified (WCF 7.2). Despite the ascendancy and acceptance of the covenant of works in Reformed theology, the covenant of works has not been without its critics.[45] In recent years one of the most notable critics has been John Murray. Murray writes concerning the covenant of works:

41. Samuel Rutherford, *The Covenant of Life Opened* (Edinburgh, 1655), 155. One should also note the same position in the Westminster Confession, which states, "Life was promised to Adam . . . upon condition of perfect and personal obedience" (WCF 7.2).

42. Rowland S. Ward, *God & Adam* (Wantirna: New Melbourne Press, 2003), 23.

43. Vos, *Biblical Theology*, 140.

44. See J. V. Fesko, *Diversity within the Reformed Tradition* (Greenville, SC: Reformed Academic Press, 2003), 222–35.

45. For a good historical survey of the covenant of works, and the doctrine of the covenant in general, see Geerhardus Vos, "The Doctrine of the Covenant in Reformed Theology," in *Redemptive History and Biblical Interpretation*, ed. Richard B. Gaffin Jr. (Phillipsburg, NJ: P&R, 1980), 234–70.

There are two observations. (1) The term is not felicitous, for the reason that the elements of grace entering into the administration are not properly provided for by the term "works." (2) It is not designated a covenant in Scripture. Hosea 6:7 may be interpreted otherwise and does not provide the basis for such a construction of the Adamic economy. Besides, Scripture always uses the term "covenant," when applied to God's administration to men, in reference to a provision that is redemptive or closely related to redemptive design. Covenant in Scripture denotes the oath-bound confirmation of promise and involves a security which the Adamic economy did not bestow.[46]

One should examine Murray's argument point by point to demonstrate that he is incorrect in his rejection of the covenant of works. Within Murray's statement there are three major claims: (1) that because of the elements of grace present in Adam's probation in the garden, the term "works" is not a proper label; (2) that Scripture does not designate Adam's state in the garden under the term "covenant"; and (3) Scripture always uses the term "covenant" in reference to God's redemptive dealings with man.

The Term "Works" Is an Inappropriate Label

It is important first to acknowledge what characterizes Murray's conception of the term "covenant." Murray writes that in order for one to comprehend the essence of a covenant, one must turn to God's postdiluvian dealings with Noah.[47] Murray explains that the Noahic covenant is "intensely and pervasively monergistic. Nothing exhibits this more clearly than the fact that the sign attached to attest and seal the divine faithfulness and the irrevocability of God's promise is one produced by conditions over which God alone has control and in connection with which there is rigid exclusion of human co-operation."[48]

One must recognize that Murray understands God's covenantal dealings with man in a unilateral fashion. In this connection Murray does not agree with the typical analysis and definitions of a covenant; he writes:

It is quite apparent that in this covenant we must not take our point of departure from the idea of compact, or contract, or agreement in any

---

46. John Murray, *Collected Writings of John Murray*, 4 vols. (1977; Edinburgh: Banner of Truth, 1996), 2:49.
47. John Murray, *The Covenant of Grace* (London: Tyndale, 1954), 12.
48. Ibid., 12–13.

respect whatsoever. It is not contractual in its origin, or in its constitution, or in its operation, or in its outcome. Its fulfillment or continuance is not in the least degree contingent even upon reciprocal obligation or appreciation on the part of its beneficiaries.[49]

Notice how Murray has defined a covenant. He has substantively defined a covenant as a sovereign administration of God's grace and promise, an administration that is unilateral in nature.[50] Given this definition, one has the reason why Murray rejects the term "works" in connection with Adam's prefall condition.

Murray believes that God's dealings with Adam were not on the basis of justice but of grace. Along these lines Murray writes:

> In connection with the promise of life it does not appear justifiable to appeal, as frequently has been done, to the principle enunciated in certain texts (cf. Lev. 18:5; Rom. 10:5; Gal. 3:12, "This do and thou shalt live"). The principle asserted in these texts is the principle of equity that righteousness is always followed by the corresponding award. From the promise of the Adamic administration we must dissociate all notions of meritorious reward. The promise of confirmed integrity and blessedness was one annexed to an obedience that Adam owed and, therefore, was a promise of grace. All that Adam could have claimed on the basis of equity was justification and life as long as he perfectly obeyed, but not confirmation so as to insure indefectibility. Adam could claim the fulfillment of the promise if he stood the probation, but only on the basis of God's faithfulness, not on the basis of justice.[51]

The belief that Adam stood by God's grace in his relationship with God is key to Murray's conception of man's state in the garden. Because Adam stood by grace, he could not pass the probation on the basis of justice.

Considering Murray's argument, there are several weaknesses that negate his first point. First, Murray argues that Adam's place in the garden was founded upon grace rather than justice. Murray does not take into consideration the teaching of Scripture on the relationship between grace and works. Murray contends that Adam's presence in the garden was

---

49. Ibid., 14–15.
50. Jeong Koo Jeon, *Covenant Theology* (New York: University Press of America, 1999), 186–87.
51. Murray, *Collected Writings*, 2:55–56.

conditioned upon his obedience: "The condition was obedience. Obedience was focused in compliance with the prohibition respecting the tree of the knowledge of good and evil."[52] This means that Adam's presence in the garden was based upon a mixture of grace and merit—he had to be obedient but the results of his obedience would have been rewarded on the basis of grace rather than justice. Yet what does Scripture say regarding the relationship between grace and works: "If it is by grace, it is no longer on the basis of works; otherwise grace would no longer be grace" (Rom. 11:6). Contrary to Murray, Paul places grace and works in complete antithesis. Adam stands in the garden by either works or grace but not both.[53]

There is another consideration in Murray's argumentation that is defective on this point. Why is it not possible that Adam's obedience would have been judged by God's justice rather than grace? Sin has not yet entered the stage of history. If one carefully defines the nature of merit, or the reward for a performed work, then he can legitimately maintain that Adam had the possibility to merit a permanent place in the garden. One must define merit in terms of: (1) fulfilment of the stipulations of a divinely sanctioned covenant; and (2) measurement of merit in terms of that covenant. God therefore offers Adam life or death based upon his obedience or disobedience, the terms of the covenant agreement. God does not deal with Adam as if he were his equal but in terms of the covenantal agreement. One may properly call Adam's state in the garden as one secured or lost by his own obedience or work.[54]

Latent in the idea that Adam could not merit his place in the garden is the Roman Catholic idea of condign and congruent merit.[55] Though

52. Ibid., 2:51.

53. Elsewhere Murray acknowledges this very point but does not make the connection to Adam's state in the garden: "If grace is conditioned in any way by human performance or by the will of man impelling to action then grace ceases to be grace" (John Murray, *The Epistle to the Romans*, NICNT [Grand Rapids: Eerdmans, 1968], 70).

54. If one states that Adam's reward of eternal life is disproportionate with the required obedience, then the same must hold true for the punishment—it too must be disproportionate with Adam's disobedience. One must reject the idea that the reward is disproportionate with the work of obedience. Rather, both eternal life and death are the reward and punishment for Adam's obedience or disobedience *ex pacto* (see Turretin, *Institutes*, 8.3.15–17; Meredith Kline, *Kingdom Prologue* [Overland Park, KS: Two Age Press, 2000], 107–17).

55. Lee Irons, "Redefining Merit: An Examination of Medieval Presuppositions in Covenant Theology," in *Creator, Redeemer, Consummator*, ed. Howard Griffith and John R. Muether (Greenville, SC: Reformed Academic Press, 2000), 268.

Murray does not state his understanding of Adam's state in the garden in these terms, it is fair to say that he believed that Adam's work was congruent merit, not condign. In other words, Adam required God's grace. Murray bases his understanding of the covenant of grace upon John Calvin's views.[56] Murray appropriates Calvin's views, however, without giving critical attention to Calvin's own understanding of Christ's merit. Calvin was influenced by the medieval nominalism of John Duns Scotus (c. 1266–1308).[57] Calvin's nominalism is most evident when he argues that Christ did not merit the salvation of the church on the basis of justice but grace. Calvin writes:

> In discussing Christ's merit, we do not consider the beginning of merit to be in him, but we go back to God's ordinance, the first cause. For God solely of his own good pleasure appointed him Mediator to obtain salvation for us. . . . Apart from God's good pleasure Christ could not merit anything; but did so because he had been appointed to appease God's wrath with his sacrifice, and to blot out our transgressions with his obedience. To sum up: inasmuch as Christ's merit depends upon God's grace alone, which has ordained this manner of salvation for us, it is just as properly opposed to all human righteousness as God's grace is.[58]

The nominalist influence is clear—Christ's merit is worth only what value God assigns it. Christ's work, according to Calvin, is based in the Father's grace, not justice. To use a simple analogy, Calvin argues that Christ's merit is based, not upon a gold standard, but upon whatever value the government assigns it. Or, God graded Christ's work on a curve. This understanding of Christ's merit, however, conflicts with Romans 11:6. Calvin's view was popular though it did not go unchecked.

Despite the popularity of Calvin's views on the covenant and the value of Christ's work, his views were opposed by John Owen. Owen originally held to Calvin's position on the merit of Christ.[59] The problem that Owen

---

56. Murray, *Collected Writings*, 4:218–19.

57. See François Wendel, *Calvin*, trans. Philip Mairet (1950; Grand Rapids: Baker, 1997), 228, 127–29.

58. Calvin, *Institutes*, 2.17.1.

59. See Carl R. Trueman, "John Owen's *Dissertation on Divine Justice*: An Exercise in Christocentric Scholasticism," *CTJ* 33/1 (1998): 87–103; John Owen, *Dissertation on Divine Justice*, in *Works*, ed. William H. Goold, 16 vols. (1850–53; Edinburgh: Banner of Truth, 1993), 10:482–624.

eventually discerned, however, was that if there was no inherent value in the work of Christ, then his merit, or obedience, was not absolutely necessary. If Christ's merit was not judged based upon justice and absolute necessity, then God could have redeemed man by another means. Owen writes that Christ's merit is "intimately connected with many, the most important articles of the Christian doctrine, concerning the attributes of God, the satisfaction of Christ, and the nature of sin, and of our obedience, and that it strikes its roots deep through almost the whole of theology, or the acknowledging of truth which is according to godliness."[60] A simple answer to this question comes to us from Christ's prayer in the garden of Gethsemane. If there was another way and God could have let the cup pass, then he would have been cruel to send his Son when it was not necessary (Matt. 26:39). We can take this understanding of merit and flesh out the connections to the work of Christ in greater detail.

One point that Murray does not address in his criticism of the covenant of works is the parallel between Adam and Christ (Rom. 5:12–19).[61] As argued earlier, Adam is a type of Christ (Rom. 5:14). If Murray is correct, and Adam was judged on the basis of grace instead of justice, then the work of the last Adam is based not in terms of justice but grace. In this regard Kline notes: "If meritorious works could not be predicated of Jesus Christ as second Adam, then obviously there would be no meritorious achievement to be imputed to his people as the ground of their justification-approbation."[62] Kline bases his point on Paul's statement: "For as by the one man's disobedience the many were made sinners, so by the one man's obedience the many will be made righteous" (Rom. 5:19). The parallelism between the two Adams demands that we see justice as the ground of both. If the first Adam could not earn eternal life on the condition of obedience, then neither could the last.[63] Kline is not the only one to make this crucial observation. Others have also made the same connection, though the words of Hodge suffice:

---

60. Owen, *Dissertation*, 487.
61. Though Murray has orthodox conclusions in his interpretation of Romans 5:12–19 (see *Romans*, 178–210), he analyzes the Adam and Christ connection in abstraction from the covenantal idea. Murray also does not deal with Romans 5:12–19 in his analysis of Adam's state in the garden (*Collected Writings*, 2:47–59). My colleague, Richard Gaffin, in conversation over this question called Murray "a non-covenantal federalist," an apt description.
62. Kline, *Kingdom Prologue*, 108.
63. Irons, "Redefining Merit," 268.

Perfect obedience was the condition of the covenant originally made with Adam. Had he retained his integrity he would have merited the promised blessing. For to him that works the reward is not of grace but of debt. In the same sense the work of Christ is the condition of the covenant of redemption. It was the meritorious ground, laying a foundation in justice for the fulfillment of the promises made to Him by the Father.[64]

The Term "Covenant" Does Not Appear in Connection with Adam

There are also weaknesses with Murray's second criticism. Murray argues that the term "covenant" does not appear in connection with Adam's state in the garden. Additionally, he also states that Hosea 6:7 need not be translated in a way to support the existence of the covenant of works. There are two considerations that negate Murray's propositions. First, the absence of a term in connection with a doctrine does not necessarily negate the doctrine. Stated more technically, the formal absence of a term does not mean that it is materially nonexistent in a passage. Murray, for example, has no problem in calling God's redemptive dealings with man after the fall the "covenant of grace," yet this term exists nowhere in Scripture. Murray correctly analyzes the substance of God's covenant with fallen man and concludes that it is one of grace. Similarly, when one looks at the creation of day and night in Genesis 1, there is no indication from the immediate context that God made a covenant; yet when comparing Genesis 1:5 with Jeremiah 33:20 one finds that there is a covenantal relationship between God and the creation. And in examining the creation of the first man and woman, the narrative states they are husband and wife, yet later Scripture identifies the marriage relationship as covenantal (Mal. 2:14). Second, Murray offers no alternative interpretation on which to base his dismissal of Hosea 6:7. In the absence of any argumentation, it appears that Murray rejects Hosea 6:7 on dogmatic rather than exegetical grounds.

Covenants Are Always Redemptive

We come now to the last of Murray's objections. Murray contends that "Scripture always uses the term covenant, when applied to God's administration to men, in reference to a provision that is redemptive or closely

64. Hodge, *Systematic Theology*, 2:364–65.

related to redemptive design."[65] But is this the case? Are God's covenants with man exclusively redemptive in nature? If Murray is correct, then, yes, Adam could not be in a covenant in the garden—there is no need for redemption prior to the fall. Murray's proposition is predicated on his idea that the essence of a covenant is embodied in the Noahic covenant. Murray takes a redemptive covenant and presumes that this is the only type of covenant. If sufficient evidence can be gathered to demonstrate that God created Adam in a covenantal context, Murray would be required to abandon his definition of covenant. Sufficient evidence has been brought to the table to demonstrate that God's relationship with the creation and Adam was covenantal. Foremost is the nomenclature of covenant ratification rather than initiation in the Noahic covenant (cf. Gen. 6:18; 15:18).[66]

Summary

While we respect and admire the theology of Murray at many points, his desire to reject the doctrine of the covenant of works is unscriptural. Murray's own self-avowed desire to revise, recast, and reconstruct Reformed theology concerning the covenant of works must be rejected.[67] While we do not want to adhere to the traditional interpretation merely for the sake of tradition, it is unwise to abandon the tradition without sufficient exegetical consideration and thought given to the theological implications. As Spykman writes:

> This covenantal deconstruction of Genesis 1–3 appears, moreover, to undermine Paul's teaching concerning the "two Adams" in Romans 5. . . . It also disrupts the close biblical connection between creation and redemption by reducing the idea of covenant to an exclusively salvific reality. One is then hard-pressed to avoid a dualist worldview, structured along nature-creation/grace-covenant lines. This Genesis approach also lends support to the current tendency to find in the early Genesis record

65. Murray, *Collected Writings*, 2:49. This nature-creation and covenant-grace dualism is precisely the type of construction that some suggest; see Tim J. R. Trumper, "Covenant Theology and Constructive Calvinism," *WTJ* 64/2 (2002): 387–404; idem, Review of *The Federal Theology of Thomas Boston* by A. T. B. McGowan, *WTJ* 62/1, (2000): 153–57, esp. 156–57.

66. See Estelle, "Covenant of Works," 96–97.

67. See Murray, *Covenant*, 5; cf. Jeon, *Covenant Theology*, 186; J. V. Fesko, "The Legacy of Old School Confession Subscription in the OPC," *JETS* 46/4 (2003): 673–98.

increasingly few matters of substantial importance for the faith-life and theology of the Christian community (for example, aversion to the idea of creation out of nothing, creation order, Sabbath, and now covenant). It seriously interrupts the flow of covenant-kingdom continuity as a unifying theme running throughout biblical revelation. Contrastingly, therefore, Scripture still warrants the conclusion that God's "new beginnings" with Noah, Abraham, Moses, and David represent successive renewals of the single covenant, reclaimed after the fall, but given originally and once for all time with creation.[68]

Covenantal deconstruction of Genesis 1–3 is unacceptable. It has been demonstrated that given the evidence of Genesis 1–3's covenant elements (Gen. 6:18; Jer. 33:20; Hos. 6:7), one may safely conclude that Adam, contrary to Murray's criticisms, was in relationship to God within a context of a covenant of works. This brings us to the fifth part of our exploration of the covenant of works, namely, the connections to the doctrine of justification.

The Covenant of Works and Justification

As we saw at the beginning of the chapter it is important that we comprehend the nature of the covenant of works. Adam was given the possibility *ex pacto* to obtain the eschatological rest of the seventh day by his obedience. In a prefall world, therefore, Adam would be justified by his works. Some might object to using the term "justification" in connection with Adam, as there are inherently redemptive connotations associated with the term. If, however, to be justified is to be declared righteous, contrasted with condemnation as the declaration of a person's wickedness, then Adam's justification is based upon the completion of the agreed work of the covenant.

That Adam's covenant work was to be marked by obedience sets an important element upon the table for consideration in one's doctrine of justification. It means that an important aspect of the redemptive work of the last Adam must include obedience in his covenant work—fulfilling the failed work of the first Adam on behalf of the people of God. As G. C. Berkouwer notes, "The obedience of the crucified Christ—this is

---

68. Spykman, *Reformational Theology*, 261.

the *alpha* and *omega* of our justification. He covers our disobedience with His obedience, our unrighteousness with His righteousness."[69] In technical terms, this means that an important element of Christ's work as it concerns justification is not only his passive obedience, his obedience throughout his life connected with his *passio* and ultimately his crucifixion, but also his active obedience, his fulfilment of the law. This brings up a second issue, namely the imputation of Christ's obedience to those who look to him by faith.

That Adam forfeited the right to obtain the eschatological blessing by his obedience, requiring the work of the last Adam, explains why Paul excludes the works of the law as a ground for our justification: "Yet we know that a person is not justified by works of the law but through faith in Jesus Christ, so we also have believed in Christ Jesus, in order to be justified by faith in Christ and not by works of the law, because by works of the law no one will be justified" (Gal. 2:16). Now, while in this context Paul addresses the subject of the works of Torah, that is, those who sought to be justified on the basis of their obedience to the law of the Mosaic covenant, yet the principle of excluding works, or obedience, of any kind is rooted in Adam's failure in the garden. In the world of Adam before the fall, one could be justified by works, but in the eschatological world of the last Adam, one can be justified only by faith.

One thing that is clear from Adam's state in the garden-temple is that he did not represent himself alone—he was the federal head of mankind. Paul succinctly states that all men sinned because Adam sinned: "Therefore, just as sin came into the world through one man, and death through sin, and so death spread to all men because all sinned" (Rom. 5:12). Paul's statement is clear—the universal reign of death is due to the one sin of Adam.[70] There is a parallel between the two federal heads, the first and last Adams: just as Adam's disobedience and guilt are imputed to those whom he represents, so too Christ's obedience, or righteousness, is imputed to those whom he represents. This means that one of the key elements of the doctrine of justification is the concept of imputation.

69. G. C. Berkouwer, *Faith and Justification*, trans. Lewis B. Smedes (Grand Rapids: Eerdmans, 1954), 45.
70. John Murray, *The Imputation of Adam's Sin* (Philadelphia: P&R, 1959), 19.

Conclusion

In the survey of the covenant of works this chapter has demonstrated that God gave Adam the responsibility of filling the earth with his image, extending the temple beyond the garden, subduing the earth by extending the order of the garden throughout the rest of the world, and extending God's rule through Adam's vice-regency. This was the work of Adam's covenant. That Adam's state in the garden was conditioned by work and his obedience is most evident by the presence of the Sabbath, a period of rest. If he was to rest on the seventh day, then the other six days were to be marked by labor, and his continuing labors of fulfilling the dominion mandate were of course contingent upon his obedience. As is clear from the above explanation of the covenant of works, Adam was a type, a foreshadow, of the one to come, the last Adam. It is to the work of the eschatological Adam that we now turn to see the foundational nature of Christ's active and passive obedience for the doctrine of justification.

5

JUSTIFICATION
AND THE WORK OF CHRIST

In the last chapter we saw the failed covenantal work of the first Adam. Adam was supposed to do the work of the covenant, fill the earth with the image of God, extend the garden-temple to the ends of the earth, and exercise dominion.[1] His vice-regency was to be upheld not only by his labor but ultimately by his obedience—his obedience not only to the dominion mandate but also to the prohibition of eating from the tree of the knowledge of good and evil. Adam was supposed to go about the labor of the dominion mandate for six days and then rest on the seventh, a foretaste of the eschatological rest of God's eternal seventh day, anticipating the conclusion of his own labors. The presence of the labor of the covenant and the prospect of the eschatological rest of the Sabbath day mean that Adam's entrance into that rest was on the basis of his obedience. When Adam fell, however, he created a twofold problem.

1. This chapter is drawn in part from J. V. Fesko, *Last Things First* (Fearn, Scotland: Mentor, 2007), 145–82.

First, he brought sin and death into the world by his one act of disobedience, which required the shedding of blood in sacrifice to make atonement for sin (Heb. 9:22). Second, there is still the unfinished work of the covenant, the work of the dominion mandate undergirded by obedience to God's commands, completing that labor and entering the eschatological rest of the seventh day. It is this twofold problem that requires resolution, and this is the work of the second or last Adam, Jesus Christ, who comes to remedy the failed work of the first Adam.

We must therefore explore the nature of the work of Christ as it is connected to this twofold problem, which requires us first to see that Christ completes the labor of the dominion mandate, and second to see the nature of Christ's obedience. That is, to see that the active and passive obedience of Christ are the foundation of the sinner's justification. In other words, if fallen mankind can no longer be justified by their obedience, as with the first Adam, they are in need of the last Adam not only to remedy the broken covenant of works but also to fulfil it on their behalf. Along these lines the Westminster Confession states concerning the broken covenant of works:

> Man, by his fall, having made himself incapable of life by that covenant, the Lord was pleased to make a second, commonly called the covenant of grace; wherein he freely offers unto sinners life and salvation by Jesus Christ; requiring of them faith in him, that they may be saved, and promising to give unto all those that are ordained unto eternal life his Holy Spirit, to make them willing, and able to believe. (WCF 7.3)[2]

The substance of the covenant of grace is the work of Christ, his life, death, and resurrection, which fulfils the broken covenant of works for those who look to him by faith. It is on the basis of Christ's work, then, that those who are in the last Adam are justified. We must therefore turn to see the completed work of the last Adam and see how it relates to the work of the first and to the doctrine of justification.

---

2. For standard expositions of the covenant of grace see Heinrich Heppe, *Reformed Dogmatics*, ed. Ernst Bizer, trans. G. T. Thomson (London: George Allen & Unwin, 1950), 371–409; Louis Berkhof, *Systematic Theology: New Combined Edition* (1932–38; Grand Rapids: Eerdmans, 1996), 262–304; Herman Bavinck, *Reformed Dogmatics*, trans. John Vriend, ed. John Bolt, 3 vols. (Grand Rapids: Baker, 2003–6), 3:193–232.

The Completed Dominion Mandate

The completed work of Christ is not typically a subject of much debate, though it does prove helpful to see the completed work of the last Adam against the backdrop of the failed work of the first. It is important to recognize that God did not change Adam's vocation but instead sent one who would faithfully fulfil that vocation.[3] That Christ takes up and obediently completes the work of the first Adam is evident throughout the pages of the NT. In 1 Corinthians 15 we see clear connections between the two Adams, though it is ultimately in the book of Revelation where we see the picture of the completed work of Christ. First, we turn to 1 Corinthians 15.

1 Corinthians 15:20–28

In verses 20–28 the creation of Adam and his subsequent fall lie just below the surface (Gen. 1:26–28; 3:17–19). This is evident when Paul writes: "For as by a man came death, by a man has come also the resurrection of the dead. For as in Adam all die, so also in Christ shall all be made alive" (vv. 21–22). Clearly, Paul establishes a parallel between the death brought by the first Adam and the resurrection from death brought by the last Adam. Moreover, as in Romans 5:12–21, there is a clear line of demarcation between the imputed guilt of Adam and its consequent, death, and the imputed righteousness of Christ and its consequent, eternal life. There is a further connection between Adam and Christ when Paul quotes Psalm 8:6 in connection with the resurrection of Christ: "For 'God has put all things in subjection under his feet.' But when it says, 'all things are put in subjection,' it is plain that he is excepted who put all things in subjection under him" (v. 27). Paul draws upon the dominion mandate of Genesis 1:26–27; God placed all things under Adam's feet, yet man abandoned his divine vocation (cf. Ps. 8).

God's intended goal for the creation has not changed. The mandate remained the same throughout redemptive history and awaited the arrival of the last Adam, who would take up the abandoned work of the first Adam. Along these lines N. T. Wright observes:

3. N. T. Wright, *The Resurrection of the Son of God* (Minneapolis: Fortress, 2003), 324.

Just as, when Israel failed to be the light-bearing people for the world, the covenant God did not rewrite the vocation but rather sent the Messiah to act in Israel's place . . . so now the failure of humankind ("Adam") to be the creator's wise, image-bearing steward over creation has not led the creator to rewrite the vocation, but rather to send the Messiah as the truly human being.

Unlike the first Adam, the last Adam rules the world in obedience to God the Father (Pss. 2, 72, 89).[4] In view of verse 23 and the implications of the resurrection of Christ, there are important connections to the last Adam and the new adamic humanity: "But each in his own order: Christ the firstfruits, then at his coming those who belong to Christ." Paul states that Christ is the firstfruits of the resurrection harvest (cf. Ex. 23:16, 19) and that the rest of the harvest will occur at the parousia of Christ. The implication is that the new creation will arise out of the old with the resurrection of the new adamic humanity who bear the image of the last Adam and fulfil God's intended purpose for the creation—spreading the image of God unto the ends of the earth (Rom. 8:29; Phil. 2:6–11; 3:20–21).[5]

1 Corinthians 15:35–49

The key to a proper comprehension of verses 35–49 lies in protology, Genesis 1–2. Paul expressly makes this connection when he writes: "Just as we have borne the image of the man of dust, we shall also bear the image of the man of heaven" (v. 49). In this passage one finds the major themes of Genesis 1–2. In verses 36–38 Paul speaks of seeds and plants, day three of the creation week; in verse 39 he writes of the bodies of man, fish, and birds, days five and six; and in verse 41 he writes of the astral bodies, the sun, moon, and stars, day four. Paul implicitly speaks of the work of the Holy Spirit in connection with the new adamic humanity. Just as the Holy Spirit was present at the creation hovering like a bird over the chaotic waters (Gen. 1:2), symbolically represented in Noah's dove (Gen. 8:8–11), present in the pillar of cloud in the exodus like a bird

4. Wright, *Resurrection*, 334, 336; see also Geerhardus Vos, *Biblical Theology* (1948; Edinburgh: Banner of Truth, 1996), 386; Thomas Schreiner, *Paul: Apostle of God's Glory in Christ* (Downers Grove, IL: InterVarsity, 2001), 175–76; James D. G. Dunn, *The Theology of Paul the Apostle* (Grand Rapids: Eerdmans, 1998), 241.

5. Wright, *Resurrection*, 337; also Herman Ridderbos, *Paul: An Outline of His Theology*, trans. John Richard De Witt (1975; Grand Rapids: Eerdmans, 1992), 225.

(Deut. 32:11; Ex. 13:21–22; Hag. 2:5; Isa. 63:11), and present in the form of a dove at the inauguration of the ministry of the last Adam as he too emerged from the waters (Luke 3:22), so too the Holy Spirit in conjunction with the new Adam is the one who gives life to this new humanity: "Thus it is written, 'The first man Adam became a living being'; the last Adam became a life-giving Spirit" (1 Cor. 15:45; cf. Gen. 2:7; Rom. 1:4).[6] The first creation is tied to the first Adam, and the new heavens and earth and its birth are tied to the resurrection of the last Adam. As Richard Gaffin points out, "All soteric experience involves existence in the new creation age, inaugurated by his resurrection."[7]

One may summarize the protological and christological connections in 1 Corinthians 15 with the comments of James Dunn:

> Christ is the last Adam, prototype of God's new human creation, in accord with the original blueprint. On the other hand, he is on the side of God, co-regent with God, co-lifegiver with the Spirit. And in between he is God's Son, whose sonship is shared with those who believe in him, the elder brother of a new family, firstborn from the dead. Yet he is also Son of God in power. And he is Lord, whose lordship both completes the intended dominion of Adam and exercises divine prerogatives.[8]

The life, death, and resurrection of Christ find their type in the failed work of the first Adam. We see the connections, then, between the first and last Adams here in chapter 15, though it is not until the book of Revelation that we see images of the completed work of Christ emerge.

Revelation and the Completed Work of Christ

A description of the global extent of the results of Christ's work is found in the book of Revelation: "And they sang a new song, saying, 'Worthy are you to take the scroll and to open its seals, for you were slain, and by your blood you ransomed people for God from every tribe and language

---

6. Wright, *Resurrection*, 341–42. This is not to say that Paul sees Christ and the Holy Spirit as one and the same, but that the two persons work in conjunction to produce the new adamic humanity (contra Dunn, *Paul*, 261–62; cf. Gordon D. Fee, *God's Empowering Presence* [Peabody, MA: Hendrickson, 1994], 266–67; C. K. Barrett, *The First Epistle to the Corinthians*, BNTC [1968; Peabody, MA: Hendrickson, 1996], 374).

7. Richard B. Gaffin Jr., *Resurrection and Redemption* (1978; Phillipsburg, NJ: P&R, 1987), 138.

8. Dunn, *Paul*, 265.

and people and nation'" (Rev. 5:9; 7:9). G. K. Beale explains that the new song "associates Christ's redemptive work with the beginning of a new creation." He draws this conclusion based on two factors: (1) this verse is within the context where God's creation is specifically mentioned in Revelation 4:11; and (2) the hymns of Revelation 5:12–13 are explicitly paralleled with the hymn of 4:11 and God's work of creation. The "myriads of myriads and thousands of thousands" (Rev. 5:11) of image bearers sing: "'Worthy is the Lamb who was slain, to receive power and wealth and wisdom and might and honor and glory and blessing!' And I heard every creature in heaven and on earth and under the earth and in the sea, and all that is in them, saying, 'To him who sits on the throne and to the Lamb be blessing and honor and glory and might forever and ever!'" (Rev. 5:12–13).[9] Similar images are found in other parts of Scripture.

In looking at the results of the consummated kingdom in the Psalms one reads that Christ will "have dominion from sea to sea, and from the River to the ends of the earth!" (Ps. 72:8).[10] Likewise the prophet Isaiah writes concerning Israel as God's servant, a reality that finds its ultimate significance in the work of Christ: "It is too light a thing that you should be my servant to raise up the tribes of Jacob and to bring back the preserved of Israel; I will make you as a light for the nations, that my salvation may reach to the end of the earth" (Isa. 49:6; cf. John 8:12).[11] Clearly, Christ will fulfil the dominion mandate—he will produce offspring that bear his image, the image of God, and fill the new creation to the ends of the earth. The last Adam will extend the temple to the ends of the earth as well, the second aspect of the dominion mandate.

Inherent in the original dominion mandate is the idea of extending the temple to the ends of the earth. That the last Adam will accomplish this goal emerges quite clearly once in the book of Revelation:

> Then I saw a new heaven and a new earth, for the first heaven and the first earth had passed away, and the sea was no more. And I saw the holy city, new Jerusalem, coming down out of heaven from God, prepared as a bride adorned for her husband. And I heard a loud voice from the throne saying, "Behold, the dwelling place of God is with man. He will dwell with

9. G. K. Beale, *The Book of Revelation*, NIGTC (Grand Rapids: Eerdmans, 1999), 358.
10. Derek Kidner, *Psalms 1–72*, TOTC (Downers Grove, IL: InterVarsity, 1973), 256.
11. E. J. Young, *The Book of Isaiah*, vol. 3 (1972; Grand Rapids: Eerdmans, 1997), 273–74.

them, and they will be his people, and God himself will be with them as their God." (Rev. 21:1–3)

Here multifaceted protological imagery reappears at the conclusion of redemptive history. A new heavens and earth surface, for the first heaven and earth, the domain of the first Adam, have been superseded by the domain of the eschatological Adam.[12] In the first heavens and earth the creation of the sun, moon, and stars were primarily for the marking of time (Gen. 1:4–19). In the new heavens and earth, however, there is "no need of sun or moon to shine on it, for the glory of God gives it light, and its lamp is the Lamb" (Rev. 21:23; cf. Isa. 60:19; Ezek. 43:2–5).[13] Just as God brought to the first Adam his bride, so too the bride of the last Adam, the last Eve, the church, appears. What is different, however, is that unlike the garden-temple where God was separated from his image bearers, God now has his temple in and among the new adamic humanity (1 Cor. 6:19; Eph. 2:19–22; 1 Peter 2:5; Rev. 21:22); the temple is actually God dwelling in the midst of the new adamic humanity both spatially and spiritually.[14] The great extent of the eschatological temple is represented in its symbolic size and proportions.

The holy city, new Jerusalem, the eschatological temple, is 12,000 cubic stadia in length, breadth, and height—a perfect cube. One *stadion* is approximately 607 feet; therefore the temple is approximately 1,400

12. It is important to note the Qumran understanding of eschatology and the connection to Genesis. The Qumran community read Genesis, not in terms of science, but in terms of eschatology. For example: "For God has chosen them for an everlasting Covenant and all the glory of Adam shall be theirs" (1QS 4); and "Thou wilt cast away all their sins. Thou wilt cause them to inherit all the glory of Adam and abundance of days" (1QH 4 [17], Hymn 1 [23]); and "To the penitents of the desert who, saved, shall live for a thousand generations and to whom all the glory of Adam shall belong, as also to their seed for ever" (4Q171 3). This same hope and connection between protology, soteriology, and eschatology is present in early Jewish thought. One can contrast the following statement, that of Adam immediately after the fall, "What is this thou hast done to me, because I have been deprived of the glory with which I was clothed?" (*Apocalypse of Moses*, ANF, 8:567), with the eschatological hope of Adam and Eve: "For it will not happen to thee now, but at the last times. Then shall arise all flesh from Adam even to that great day, as many as shall be a holy people; then shall be given to them all the delight of paradise, and God shall be in the midst of them" (ibid., 566). One finds similar imagery in intertestamental Judaism (see 4 Esdras 7:122–25; Dunn, *Paul*, 93 n. 69).
13. Beale, *Revelation*, 1039–48.
14. Ibid., 1046. In this vein it is interesting to note that the Qumran community looked for this same reality: "He has commanded that a Sanctuary of men be built for Himself, that there they may send up, like the smoke of incense, the works of the Law" (4Q174).

miles long, high, and wide (Rev. 21:16; see NLT). The walls that surround the massive eschatological temple are 144 cubits in thickness, or
approximately 216 feet thick (Rev. 21:17; see NLT). On the dimensions
of the eschatological temple Beale explains: "Surprisingly, the size of the
city is apparently the approximated size of the then known Hellenistic
world. This suggests further that the temple-city represents not merely
the glorified saints of Israel but the redeemed from all nations, who are
considered to be true, spiritual Israelites."[15] The last Adam accomplishes
the dominion mandate by extending the temple, which is also the people
of God, to the ends of the earth.[16] These protological echoes are not the
only elements that reappear at the consummation of the completed work
of the last Adam.

Once again, embedded protological elements resurface in the closing
chapters of John's Apocalypse.[17] The eschatological temple is situated on
a "high mountain" (Rev. 21:10), like the garden-temple and subsequent
worship sites in the OT (Ezek. 28:14, 16; Ex. 3:1; Ps. 48:1–2). As the river
of Eden flowed out to water the garden (Gen. 2:10), so too a pure river
of water of life flows out of the eschatological temple (Rev. 22:1). Likewise, the tree of life (Gen. 2:9) reappears in the eschatological temple:
"on either side of the river, the tree of life with its twelve kinds of fruit,
yielding its fruit each month. The leaves of the tree were for the healing
of the nations" (Rev. 22:2).[18] The precious stones and metals that adorned
the garden-temple, the tabernacle, and Solomon's temple also appear in
the eschatological temple (cf. Rev. 21:18–20; Gen. 2:10–14; Ezek. 28:13;
Ex. 25:11, 17, 24, 29, 36; 28:7–10).[19]

---

15. Ibid., 1074.

16. There are protological and eschatological connections once again in the Qumran
community: "I shall accept them and they shall be my people and I shall be for them for ever.
I will dwell with them for ever and ever and will sanctify my [sa]nctuary by my glory. I will
cause my glory to rest on it until the day of creation on which I shall create my sanctuary,
establishing it for myself for all time according to the covenant which I have made with Jacob
in Bethel" (2QT = 2Q19, 20 19, ln. 7–10). See also G. K. Beale, "Garden Temple," *Kerux* 18/2
(2003): 28.

17. Rabbinic interpretation also makes connections between protology and eschatology.
The righteous are so placed in the garden of Eden as to be able to see the wicked in Gehenna
(see Leviticus Rabbah 32.1; cf. Num. 13:2).

18. Rabbinic interpretation saw the righteous eating from the tree of life in the eschaton
(see Exodus Rabbah 25.8).

19. Beale, *Revelation*, 1103–11. Scripture casts the eschaton in terms of protology (see
Ezek. 36:35; also Beale, "Garden Temple," 38).

The inhabitants of the eschatological temple also perform the same priestly functions as Adam in the garden-temple. Adam was instructed to work and keep the garden (Gen. 2:15). As has been previously explained, this is priestly language (Num. 3:7–8; cf. 4:23–24, 26). Likewise, the new adamic humanity serves God in the eschatological temple, though they serve him having been redeemed from the curse of Genesis 3:15: "And there shall be no more curse, but the throne of God and of the lamb shall be in it, and his servants shall serve him" (Rev. 22:3, NKJV).[20] Once again the servants of God shall see the face of God (Rev. 22:4) as Adam and Eve once beheld his face (Gen. 3:8, MT). There is a significant difference, however, between the dress of the first priest, Adam, and that of the new humanity. Adam and Eve were naked when they served God in the garden-temple (Gen. 2:25). The new adamic humanity, however, will never appear naked before God. Instead, they are clothed in the righteousness of Christ as a permanent reminder and source of praise for the work of the last Adam (Rev. 3:18; 19:8).

It is essential that one see the completed work of Christ in Revelation in terms of the failed work of the first Adam. Beale notes this connection in an excellent summary:

The Garden of Eden was the first temple . . . not only was Adam to "guard" this sanctuary but he was to subdue the earth, according to Gen. 1:28: "And God blessed them . . . 'Be fruitful and multiply, and fill the earth, and subdue it; and rule over the fish of the sea and over the birds of the sky, and over every living thing that creeps on the surface.'" As Adam was to begin to rule over and subdue the earth, it is plausible to suggest that he was to extend the geographical boundaries of the garden until Eden extended throughout and covered the whole earth. This meant the presence of God, which was initially limited to Eden, was to be extended throughout the whole earth. What Adam failed to do, Revelation pictures Christ as finally having done. The Edenic imagery beginning in Rev. 22:1 reflects an intention to show that the building of the temple, which began in Genesis 2, will be completed in Christ and his people and will encompass the whole new creation.[21]

20. Beale, *Revelation*, 1112; also Meredith Kline, *Kingdom Prologue* (Overland Park, KS: Two Age Press, 2000), 48–49.
21. Beale, *Revelation*, 1111.

So, then, it is important that we see the connections between the work of the first and last Adams, the proton and the eschaton. It is the work of each Adam that fills in the two ages of redemptive history, this present evil age and the age to come. It is essential, however, not only to recognize the redemptive historical place of each Adam, but also to see that it is the obedience of the last Adam that undergirds not only his own work but also the redemption, and therefore justification, of the new adamic humanity. It is to the obedience of Christ that we now turn.

The Obedience of Christ as the Foundation of Justification

In exploring the obedience of the last Adam, we must first establish its twofold nature, the need for the remedy of sin and the positive fulfilment of the law. This twofold obedience has historically gone under the terms of Christ's *active* and *passive* obedience. There have been theologians throughout church history who have rejected this distinction for a number of reasons. Let us first, therefore, explore the distinction as it has been historically understood, hear the objections to it, and then establish the validity by answering objections to the passive and active obedience of Christ as the ground for justification.

Historic Understanding

In the history of the development of the doctrine of Christ there have been various objections leveled against dividing his obedience into active and passive categories. The classic Protestant use of the distinction is that Christ's active obedience is his fulfilment of the requirements of the law on behalf of the elect. Christ's passive obedience, on the other hand, is his suffering the penalty and curse of the law on behalf of the elect. Christ suffers on the cross and makes payment for the debt of sin, and it is Christ's active obedience, or his righteousness, that is imputed to the believer (Col. 2:13–14). John Calvin, commenting on Romans 5:19, states that "to declare that by him alone we are accounted righteous, what else is this but to lodge our righteousness in Christ's obedience, because the obedience of Christ is reckoned to us as if it were our own?"[22] Calvin is

---

22. John Calvin, *Institutes of the Christian Religion*, ed. John T. McNeill, trans. Ford Lewis Battles, LCC 20–21 (Philadelphia: Westminster, 1960), 3.11.23; see also 3.11.5, 8. See also idem, *2 Corinthians and Timothy, Titus and Philemon*, trans. T. A. Smail, ed. David W. Torrance and T. F. Torrance, CNTC (Grand Rapids: Eerdmans, 1960), 78; idem, *Romans and*

insistent that the ground of the believer's justification is the obedience of Christ. This insistence upon the obedience of Christ continues in the literature of other second-generation Reformers.

In the Heidelberg Catechism (1563) we find the question "How are you righteous before God?" The catechism responds, "God, without any merit of my own, out of pure grace, grants me the benefits of the perfect expiation of Christ, imputing to me the righteousness and holiness as if I had never committed a single sin or had ever been sinful, having fulfilled myself all the obedience which Christ has carried out for me" (q. 60).[23] As with Calvin, justification hinges upon the obedience of Christ, though the ideas of the active, the positive fulfilment of the law, and the passive, the penalty for violating the law, are present in this question.[24]

The same emphasis upon the active and passive obedience of Christ appears both in the theological literature and in the confessions of early and high orthodoxy. The Canons of Dort (1618–19) reject the Arminian idea that God withdrew the requirement of perfect obedience to the law, implying that perfect obedience to the law, which Christ performed, was required for salvation and more specifically for one's justification.[25] Likewise the Westminster Larger Catechism (1647) states that God accounts believers righteous in his sight, "not for any thing wrought in them, or done by them, but only for the perfect obedience and full satisfaction of Christ, by God imputed to them, and received by faith alone" (q. 70). Francis Turretin and John Owen both affirm the necessity of the imputation

---

Thessalonians, trans. Ross Mackenzie, ed. David W. Torrance and T. F. Torrance, CNTC (Grand Rapids: Eerdmans, 1960), 118.

23. See Heidelberg Catechism in Jaroslav Pelikan and Valerie Hotchkiss, eds., *Creeds and Confessions of Faith in the Christian Tradition*, 3 vols. (New Haven: Yale University Press, 2003), 2:440. In the catechism's use the term, "merit" means nothing more than obedience and does not invoke such theological questions as the condign and congruent merit common in Roman Catholic theology. See, e.g., Heidelberg Catechism 21, 60, 63, 84, 86; Belgic Confession 22, 23, 24, 25; WCF 16.5, 17.2; LC 55, 174, 193. I must acknowledge the excellent work of my friend Scott Clark, whose chapter on the active obedience of Christ, which I read in prepublication form, was a tremendous help to me in my research (see R. Scott Clark, ed., *Covenant, Justification, and Pastoral Ministry* [Phillipsburg, NJ: P&R, 2007], 229–65). For an important essay regarding active obedience and the Westminster Confession, see Jeffrey K. Jue, "The Active Obedience of Christ and the Theology of the Westminster Standards: A Historical Investigation," in *Justified in Christ: God's Plan for Us in Justification*, ed. K. Scott Oliphint (Fearn, Scotland: Mentor, 2007), 99–130.

24. See Zacharias Ursinus, *The Commentary of Zacharias Ursinus on the Heidelberg Catechism*, trans. G. W. Williard (1852; Phillipsburg, NJ: P&R, n.d.), 327–28.

25. See Canons of Dort, "Rejection of Errors" 4, in Pelikan and Hotchkiss, *Creeds*, 2:582.

of Christ's active and passive obedience to the believer in justification.[26] Not all have agreed, however, that the believer requires both the active and passive obedience of Christ.

Objections to the Distinction

From the days of the Reformation, there have been some who have argued that justification requires only the forgiveness of sins, hence the believer needs only the passive obedience of Christ. One such theologian is Johannes Piscator, who argued that when Paul defines justification, such as in Acts 13:38–39, he has in mind only the forgiveness of sin: that "the apostle in this place defines justification by forgiveness of sins only, is manifest, partly by the consequence of sentences, whereof one is added to another, as explaining the same partly by the very phrase, *to be justified from sins*: which is no other thing, than to be absolved from sins committed, and by consequence, to obtain forgiveness of sins."[27] According to Piscator, then, justification does not involve the imputation of Christ's active obedience to the believer. Piscator bases his position on his exegesis of Paul and what the apostle means by the term "justification."

More recently, others such as Emil Brunner reject the distinction because they see it bifurcating the obedience of Christ. Reacting to the position of Lutheran theologian Heinrich Schmid, who argued that only passive obedience of Christ had atoning value, Brunner argued that such a distinction was "intolerably pedantic" and was "a complete misunderstanding." On the basis of Philippians 2:8, "becoming obedient to the point of death, even death on a cross," Brunner argues that this statement is "the shortest summary of the whole life of Jesus. He actively fulfilled the Law, because He fulfilled its meaning, which is *agape*."[28]

In a similar vein, more recently Robert Reymond rejects the terms "active" and "passive" because the latter implies inaction on Christ's part:

---

26. Francis Turretin, *Institutes of Elenctic Theology*, trans. George Musgrave Giger, ed. James T. Dennison Jr., 3 vols. (Phillipsburg, NJ: P&R, 1992–97), 14.13.1; John Owen, *The Doctrine of Justification by Faith*, in *The Works of John Owen*, ed. William H. Goold, 16 vols. (1850–53; Edinburgh: Banner of Truth, 1998), 5:254.

27. Johannes Piscator, *A Learned and Profitable Treatise on Man's Justification* (London, 1599), 20.

28. Emil Brunner, *The Christian Doctrine of Creation and Redemption*, trans. Olive Wyon, vol. 2, *Dogmatics* (Philadelphia: Westminster, 1952), 282. Cf. Heinrich Schmid, *The Doctrinal Theology of the Evangelical Lutheran Church*, trans. Charles A. Hay and Henry E. Jacobs (Philadelphia: Lutheran Publication Society, 1889), 354–57.

"Nothing that he did did he do passively, that is resignedly without full desire and willingness on his part." To be sure, Reymond still employs the categories that fall under the active and passive obedience of Christ, but chooses instead the terms "preceptive" and "penal," the former referring to Christ's full obedience to the law, and the latter to his willing obedience in bearing the penalty of the law.[29]

Still yet others, such as Mark Seifrid, reject the traditional distinction for several reasons. First, because Paul never speaks of Christ's righteousness as imputed to believers, as is common in Protestant dogmatics. Instead, Paul speaks of the faith of Abraham as righteousness (Rom. 4:3). Second, Seifrid argues that typical Protestant understandings of justification separate and fragment the work of Christ so that the believer receives Christ in a rationed way, through justification, sanctification, and glorification, never by the idea of faith taking hold of the comprehensive act of God in Christ. Third, separating the obedience of Christ into active and passive categories obscures the eschatological nature of the cross as the prolepsis of the final judgment and the entrance of the age to come. And, fourth, by this separation theologians bruise or damage the nerve between justification and obedience. In other words, if Christ's obedience is imputed to the believer, then what need is there for personal obedience and holiness?[30]

We may summarize the objections to the traditional categories of the active and passive obedience of Christ in the following manner:

1. Justification involves only the forgiveness of sins, not the imputation of Christ's obedience to the believer;
2. The obedience of Christ cannot be separated;
3. The term "passive" implies inactivity on the part of Christ;
4. Paul does not write that Christ's righteousness has been imputed to the believer;
5. The separation of the obedience of Christ obscures the eschatological nature of Christ's crucifixion; and

29. Robert L. Reymond, *A New Systematic Theology of the Christian Faith* (Nashville: Thomas Nelson, 1998), 631.

30. Mark A. Seifrid, *Christ, Our Righteousness*, NSBT 9 (Downers Grove, IL: InterVarsity, 2000), 174–75.

6. The concept of the imputed active obedience of Christ damages the connection between justification and sanctification, or the need for personal obedience and holiness.

We must address each of these objections and in the process set forth the legitimacy of the doctrine of imputation of the active and passive obedience of Christ.

Answering Objections

Justification Is Not Merely the Forgiveness of Sins

The first objection hinges upon the idea that man's justification entails only the forgiveness of sins. This objection would stand if man required only the absence of sin. Certainly Adam in the garden had an absence of sin. Not only did he have an absence of sin, however, but a positive status of righteousness, for God declared that man was very good (Gen. 1:31).[31] That God called the creation and man "good" is important, as it is not merely a divine approbation but also testimony of the positive righteousness that man possessed. God pronounced his judgment upon both the creation and man, which means that the goodness of the creation and that of man, while similar, have different meanings. The creation, of course, was good because it reflected the eternal power and nature of God but also because it was not under the curse as a result of the fall (Rom. 1:20; 8:20). As the divine judgment pertains to man, however, because man was made in the image of God, man was also good in the sense that he was upright or righteous (Gen. 1:27–28; Ps. 11:7). We see the correlation, for example, of goodness and righteousness when the psalmist writes, "Good and upright is the LORD" (Ps. 25:8), or when we read the synonymous parallelism "So you will walk in the way of the good and keep to the paths of the righteous" (Prov. 2:20). This means that Adam possessed positive righteousness, not merely the absence of sin. Adam's position in the garden, however, was not static. Adam's righteousness had to be tested.

Given the nature of the dominion mandate, Adam had to extend the garden-temple to the ends of the earth. The only way to accomplish this

---

31. J. Gresham Machen, *God Transcendent* (1949; Edinburgh: Banner of Truth, 1982), 182.

work was by his constant obedience to both the mandate and the prohibition of eating from the tree of knowledge. When we consider the nature of the demands of the law, any demand that God places upon man being under the category of law, we see that perfect obedience to the whole law is required (Deut. 27:26), and to break the law at one point is to break the whole law (James 2:10). That perfect obedience to the entirety of the law is required is evident in Paul's quotation of Deuteronomy 27:26: "Cursed be anyone who does not confirm the words of this law by doing them." When Paul quotes this verse in Galatians, he inserts a word not found in the Hebrew text: "Cursed be everyone who does not abide by *all* things written in the Book of the Law, and do them" (Gal. 3:10; cf. 5:3).[32] This is why being under the law, whether the law in the garden-temple or that delivered to Israel upon Sinai, required perfect obedience: "It is not the hearers of the law who are righteous before God, but the doers of the law who will be justified" (Rom. 2:13).

There are some who might object, however, by saying that it is illegitimate to cite passages from the Torah and their subsequent Pauline interpretation and apply the conclusions to Adam's state in the garden.[33] That one may make the connection between the Torah requirements for obedience and Adam's prefall state in the garden is evident from the parallels that Paul draws between Adam's and Israel's respective positions in preredemptive and redemptive history. That Adam was under a state of law in the garden, for example, is confirmed when Paul writes, "Yet death reigned from Adam to Moses, even over those whose sinning was not like the transgression of Adam" (Rom. 5:14). Paul states that death reigned from Adam to Moses, or from the garden to the giving of the law at Sinai, even over those whose sins were not like Adam's, disobedience to the divinely revealed command of God. Paul sees Adam's state in the garden as parallel to Israel's reception of the law at Sinai. In other words, Adam transgressed the directly revealed law of God as Israel did at Sinai.[34]

---

32. Richard N. Longenecker, *Galatians*, WBC 41 (Dallas: Word, 1990), 117–18.

33. On this general point, see Norman Shepherd, *The Call of Grace: How the Covenant Illuminates Salvation and Evangelism* (Phillipsburg, NJ: P&R, 2000), 25–41.

34. For similar conclusions see John Murray, *Epistle to the Romans*, NICNT (Grand Rapids: Eerdmans, 1968), 189–90; C. E. B. Cranfield, *Romans*, 2 vols., ICC (1975; Edinburgh: T & T Clark, 2001), 1:283; Douglas Moo, *Epistles to the Romans*, NICNT (Grand Rapids: Eerdmans, 1996), 331–33; N. T. Wright, *Romans*, NIB 10 (Nashville: Abingdon, 2003), 527.

Given these data, we may say that God therefore initially judged Adam after his creation and declared him righteous; nevertheless he also set before him the work of the covenant. Upon the completion of that work, God would have once again declared him righteous. He would have been righteous by both, negatively, abstaining from the fruit of the tree of knowledge, and positively, fulfilling the requirements of the dominion mandate. It is evident, then, that man requires both the absence of sin and the presence of righteousness, or obedience to the law, to be declared just by God. That man requires both the absence of sin and presence of righteousness is evident when Paul states that "Abraham believed God, and it was counted to him as righteousness" (Rom. 4:3). That God declared Abraham righteous does not mean that he merely absolved his sins, but that in the eyes of God Abraham was viewed as having fulfilled the requirements of the law. This righteousness status, however, was *elogisthē*, "counted" (KJV) "reckoned" (NASB), "credited" (NIV), or "imputed," to Abraham.

In other words, obedience to the law, or righteousness, was imputed to Abraham by faith. One reason why the objection that justification is merely the forgiveness of sins does not hold up to scrutiny is that it looks at justification merely in terms of redemption. Piscator, for example, fails to see the priority of eschatology over soteriology. In other words, that prior to the fall there was an eschatology and that Adam could have obtained the eschatological rest of God by his obedience. In the proton there is the need for positive righteousness. This point is supported by the nature of the eschaton, in that the age to come is marked by positive righteousness, something the age of the first Adam has not known since the fall.

The Unity of the Obedience of Christ

The second objection is that to label Christ's obedience under the categories of active and passive separates the unified work of Christ. Yet, historically, theologians who employ these terms do so only to distinguish aspects of the unified work of Christ.[35] As Charles Hodge notes:

35. John Murray, *Redemption Accomplished and Applied* (Grand Rapids: Eerdmans, 1955), 21.

152

The active and passive obedience of Christ, however, are only different phases or aspects of the same thing. He obeyed in suffering. His highest acts of obedience were rendered in the garden, and upon the cross. Hence this distinction is not so presented in Scripture as though the obedience of Christ answered one purpose, and his sufferings another and a distinct purpose.[36]

The work of Christ is an integrated whole with various aspects, a unitary complex. For example, Paul preached the crucified Christ (1 Cor. 1:23), but this is not to say that there was no need for the fulfilment of the law during Christ's life (Luke 2:21–22; Matt. 3:15; 5:17–18; Gal. 4:4–5), nor does it mean that the resurrection of Christ is not a vital part of redemption, especially justification (Rom. 4:25). So, then, when we consider the obedience of Christ, it "includes all He did in satisfying the demands of the law."[37] Nevertheless, it is helpful to understand the aspects of Christ's obedience in that his active obedience was required for the fulfilment of the positive requirements of the law and his passive obedience was required to pay the penalty for the broken law. The active and passive obedience of Christ, therefore, is a distinction but in no way intends to separate the unified obedience of Christ.

The Propriety of the Terms

In the history of theology, medieval theologians divided Christ's obedience into two phases, the *obedientia activa*, the period from Christ's birth to his passion, and the *obedientia passiva*, the period when Christ accepted passively, without any resistance, the suffering and the cross. Medieval theologians such as Anselm argued that the passive obedience of Christ brought the remission of sin for God's people, but his active obedience was merely that which qualified Christ for the office of mediator.[38] The Protestant Reformers rejected this construction of the active and passive obedience of Christ. Instead, they believed that both the active and passive obedience constituted the integrated saving work

---

36. Charles Hodge, *Systematic Theology*, 3 vols. (Grand Rapids: Eerdmans, 1993), 3:143. For a more recent treatment of the subject, see Cornelis P. Venema, *The Gospel of Free Acceptance in Christ* (Edinburgh: Banner of Truth, 2006), 246–49.

37. Hodge, *Systematic Theology*, 3:143.

38. Anselm, *Why God Became Man* 9, in *Anselm of Canterbury: The Major Works*, ed. Brian Davies and G. R. Evans (Oxford: Oxford University Press, 1998), 276.

of Christ and were imputed to the believer by faith in his justification. In this light, then, the heirs of the Reformation argued that the obedience of Christ is both an *actio passiva*, a passive action, which refers to Christ's subjection to the law, and a *passio activa*, an active passion, which is the real obedience of Christ's life and death.[39]

In the light of the Protestant appropriation of the traditional distinction, it is therefore necessary to define Christ's passive suffering, not in terms of passivity or inactivity, but in terms of his *passio*, his suffering.[40] Additionally, Christ's suffering did not begin at his crucifixion but began the moment of his incarnation and is especially evident in his ministry as he ate and drank with the poor, outcasts, sinners, and when he met resistance, persecution, and ridicule from the religious leaders and his own family, and it culminated in his crucifixion. In this regard Jürgen Moltmann affirms that Christ's suffering was "no unwilling fortuitous suffering; it is a *passio activa*."[41]

The Imputation of Christ's Righteousness

The fourth objection is that Paul does not state that Christ's righteousness is imputed to the believer. This objection fails to take into account the nature of systematic theology. Systematic theology typically requires terms that are theological constructs, terms often drawn from Scripture but given a more precise meaning to express the doctrines of the Bible.[42] One of the most common theological constructs that theologians employ is the term, "Trinity." The term occurs nowhere in the Scriptures, yet it is universally employed to give expression to the idea that God is one in essence and three in person. The same may be said of the righteousness of Christ. The closest approximation of this phrase occurs in 1 Corinthians 1:30: "He is the source of your life in Christ

39. See Richard A. Muller, *Dictionary of Latin and Greek Theological Terms* (Grand Rapids: Baker, 1987), 205–6, s.v. *"obedientia Christi."*

40. See Leo F. Stelten, *Dictionary of Ecclesiastical Latin* (Peabody, MA: Hendrickson, 1995), 187, s.v. *"passio."*

41. Jürgen Moltmann, *Trinity and Kingdom*, trans. Margaret Kohl (Minneapolis: Fortress, 1993), 75; see also Murray, *Redemption*, 20–21; Robert Letham, *The Work of Christ* (Downers Grove, IL: InterVarsity, 1993), 117; G. C. Berkouwer, *The Work of Christ*, trans. Cornelius Lambregtse (Grand Rapids: Eerdmans, 1965), 323–24.

42. See D. A. Carson, "The Vindication of Imputation: On Fields of Discourse and Semantic Fields," in *Justification*, ed. Mark Husbands and Daniel J. Treier (Downers Grove, IL: InterVarsity, 2004), 46–80.

Jesus, whom God made our wisdom and our righteousness and sanctification and redemption." Nevertheless, to say therefore that Christ's righteousness is not imputed to the believer in his justification fails to account for the nature of theological terminology. Formally, the term may be absent, but is it present materially or substantively? Yes, it is present. Commenting on 2 Corinthians 5:21, D. A. Carson explains: "True, the text does not explicitly *say* that God imputes our sins to Christ, but as long as we perceive that Jesus dies in our place, and bears our curse, and was made 'sin' for us, it is extraordinarily difficult to avoid the notion of the imputation of our sins to him."[43]

Paul contrasts the disobedience of the first Adam with the obedience of the last Adam in Romans 5:12–21, and it is here in this famous passage where Paul stresses imputation both of Adam's guilt and of Christ's righteousness. Paul explains that "one trespass led to condemnation for all men," which was the sin of Adam. By contrast, "one act of righteousness leads to justification and life for all men" (Rom. 5:18), which is the work of Christ. There are some who try to confine the "one act" to Christ's crucifixion. But as we have seen above, it is impossible to isolate the crucifixion from the life and resurrection of Christ in connection with justification, or any other aspect of the *ordo salutis* for that matter. When Paul, therefore, contrasts the "one trespass" with the "one act of righteousness" the comparison is to the disobedience of Adam and the obedience, active and passive, of Christ. As John Murray explains:

> The righteousness of Christ is regarded in its compact unity in parallelism with the one trespass, and there is good reason for speaking of it as the one righteous act because, as the one trespass is the trespass of the one, so the one righteousness is the righteousness of the one and the unity of the person and of his accomplishment must always be assumed.[44]

It is the whole obedience of Christ, then, that is the ground of the believer's justification. And, as Paul states in Romans 4:3 and 4:22, faith is counted as righteousness, not because faith is the ground but rather the instrumental means by which the righteousness of Christ, or his obedi-

43. Ibid., 69.
44. Murray, *Romans*, 202; see also Cranfield, *Romans*, 1:290–91; Moo, *Romans*, 344.

ence, is imputed to the believer. Christ's righteousness is synonymous with his obedience.

That Christ's whole obedience is the ground of justification is key to our understanding this doctrine. Adam was to be justified by his works, by his obedience, but by falling into sin, the way of justification by works was closed to all but one, the last Adam. It is Adam's failed obedience to the law that lies behind Paul's statements such as "For God has done what the law, weakened by the flesh, could not do. By sending his own Son in the likeness of sinful flesh and for sin, he condemned sin in the flesh, in order that the righteous requirement of the law might be fulfilled in us, who walk not according to the flesh but according to the Spirit" (Rom. 8:3–4). Paul also writes, "Christ redeemed us from the curse of the law by becoming a curse for us" (Gal. 3:13).

Commenting on these two passages Peter van Mastricht states that we can hardly understand them if we deny the covenant of works, or the backdrop of the failed obedience of the first Adam.[45] Or, as Zacharias Ursinus explains the difference between the law and gospel:

> The law contains the natural covenant, established by God with humanity in creation, that is, it is known by humanity by nature, it requires our perfect obedience to God, and it promises eternal life to those who keep it and threatens eternal punishment to those who do not. The gospel, however, contains the covenant of grace, that is, although it exists, it is not known at all by nature; it shows us the fulfillment in Christ of the righteousness that the law requires and the restoration in us of that righteousness by Christ's Spirit; and it promises eternal life freely because of Christ to those who believe in him.[46]

Just as Adam could have secured eschatological blessing for himself and his offspring but failed, Christ was obedient to the point of death, death on a cross, and therefore God highly exalted him and gave him the name that is above every name (Phil. 2:8–9). Christ obtains the eschatological blessing for himself and his people by his obedience. It is crucial here

---

45. Peter van Mastricht, *Theoretico-practica Theologia* (Amsterdam, 1725), 3.12.23, cited in Heppe, *Reformed Dogmatics*, 289–90; see also Michael S. Horton, *Lord and Servant* (Louisville: Westminster John Knox, 2005), 128–33.

46. Larger Catechism 36, in *An Introduction to the Heidelberg Catechism: Sources, History, and Theology*, ed. and trans. Lyle D. Bierma et al. (Grand Rapids: Baker, 2005), 168–69.

that we understand the significance of the failed work of the first Adam and the faithful obedience of the last Adam.

If one does not account for the failed obedience of the first Adam, which completely closes off the path to justification by works for fallen man, then he will likely reintroduce works into postfall justification. Justification will not be by faith alone in Christ alone, grounded upon the obedience of Christ, but instead will be a combination of faith and obedience, or works. Justification by faith alone hinges on the recognition that Adam in preredemptive history and Christ in redemptive history are the only two individuals for whom justification by works, or obedience, is legitimate. It is Christ's obedience, therefore, that is the ground for our justification by faith alone. That Christ's obedience is foundational raises two related issues that should be addressed, namely whether faith and grace played a role in Christ's work as mediator.

The faith or obedience of Christ?

There is no question that Christ's work, his imputed obedience, is the outpouring of God's grace upon his people. The question that has often swirled about Christ's work as mediator is whether Christ himself required faith and the grace of God. First, we may turn to the question of whether Christ had faith. There are those, such as Norman Shepherd, who argue that the faith of Christ was integral to his work as mediator. Concerning the fulfilment of the covenant promise to Abraham, Shepherd writes that "all of this is made possible through the covenantal righteousness of Jesus Christ. His was a living, active, and obedient faith that took him all the way to the cross. This faith was credited to him as righteousness."[47] While this statement is laced with biblical language and for that reason seems to ring true, one must wonder whether it is appropriately applied to the work of Christ.

The language is inappropriately applied to Christ. Nowhere does the NT state that Christ's faith was credited to him as righteousness. When Paul puts forth an example of faith, it is Abraham, not Christ (Rom. 4:3). In fact, the NT does not speak of the faith of Christ. Instead, the NT is replete with references to Christ doing the will of the Father or his obedience, not faith (Matt. 3:15; 5:18–19; John 4:34; 6:38–40; 17:3–6;

---

47. Shepherd, *Call of Grace*, 19; see similar comments by Letham, *Work of Christ*, 117–18.

Rom. 5:12–21; Gal. 4:4–5). That Christ saves his people by his works or obedience is the reason Paul sees faith and works in stark antithesis (Rom. 2:13; Gal. 3:10; cf. Deut. 27:26). There are some, however, who claim that there is strong exegetical evidence for the idea that the NT speaks of Christ's faith as the ground of salvation.

Recently much has been made of verses such as Galatians 3:22: "But the Scripture imprisoned everything under sin, so that the promise by faith in Jesus Christ might be given to those who believe." Richard Hays argues that Galatians 3:22, *hina hē epangelia ek pisteōs Iēsou Christou dothē tois pisteuousin*, should be translated as, "in order that the promise by the faith of Christ might be given to those who believe." The question is, should the genitive phrase *pisteōs Iēsou Christou* be translated as "faith in Christ" (objective genitive) or "faith of Christ" (subjective genitive)?[48] Hays argues for the subjective genitive throughout his monograph and that *pistis*, "faith," is "the power or quality which enables Christ to carry out his mission of deliverance."[49] When it comes to passages such as Romans 4:3, where Paul speaks of Abraham's faith, Hays argues that they are to be read in terms of type and antitype. Abraham is a typological foreshadowing of Christ, "a representative figure whose faithfulness secures blessing and salvation vicariously for others." Therefore, "Christians are justified/redeemed not by virtue of their own faith but because they participate in Jesus Christ, who enacted the obedience of faith on their behalf."[50] If Hays is correct, then Shepherd is correct to speak of Christ's faith as the basis of the believer's justification.

Yet Hays's case for reading *pisteōs Iēsou Christou* as a subjective genitive, "the faith of Jesus," has exegetical problems. There is not sufficient space to elaborate the evidence; nevertheless, Moisés Silva has given four significant reasons as to why Hays's reading is improbable:

1. The early Greek fathers, whose mother tongue was Greek, when commenting on Galatians 2:16, which has the same use of the

---

48. Richard B. Hays, *The Faith of Jesus Christ: The Narrative Substructure of Galatians 3:1–4:11* (1983; Grand Rapids: Eerdmans, 2002), 148. N. T. Wright agrees with Hays's position; see "The Letter to the Galatians: Exegesis and Theology," in *Between Two Horizons*, ed. Joel B. Green and Max Turner (Grand Rapids: Eerdmans, 2002), 218. See also Douglas Harink, *Paul among the Postliberals* (Grand Rapids: Brazos, 2003), 26–30, 40–45.

49. Hays, *Faith of Jesus*, 122.

50. Ibid., 166.

genitive *pisteōs Iēsou Christou*, universally read it as an objective genitive, "faith in Jesus."

2. In the more than 240 occurrences of *pisteuō*, "I believe," the vast majority of them mean "to believe in" or "trust." In other words, the NT has a great emphasis upon human faith, and it is unlikely that the noun *pistis* would be used in any other manner apart from clear evidence within the context.

3. Paul's uses of the noun *pistis* and the verb *pisteuō* refer to the Christian's act of believing or the Christian's faith rather than a quality or attribute of Christ. In fact, Silva notes, "we cannot find one *unambiguous* reference to the *pistis* that belongs to Christ."

4. In Galatians 2–3 Paul never speaks of Christ believing or being faithful.[51]

Presenting these four reasons, Silva concludes that Hays's case for reading *pisteōs Iēsou Christou* as a subjective genitive is an "unlikely scenario, to put it mildly." In fact, Silva states that if Hays is correct, then "we may forgive every known expositor of Galatians 2–3 during the first nineteen centuries of the Christian church for failing to point out that the phrase refers to an attribute of Christ."[52] On this evidence, it is fair to conclude that the NT does not speak of the faith of Christ but rather of his obedience as the ground of justification.

Why is it necessary to ground justification in Christ's obedience? There are some who might ask, Is not Christ's faith the source of his obedience? If this is so, then why not say that our justification is grounded in Christ's faith? It is legitimate to conclude that Christ had faith, a general trust in his Father and his will. However, in terms of justification by faith, to say that Christ was justified by his faith rather than his obedience confuses important scriptural and theological concepts. In the Scriptures as well

---

51. Moisés Silva, "Faith versus Works of Law in Galatians," in *Justification and Variegated Nomism*, vol. 2, *The Paradoxes of Paul*, ed. D. A. Carson, Peter T. O'Brien, and Mark A. Seifrid (Grand Rapids: Baker, 2004), 228–32. See also John Reumann, "Justification by Faith in Pauline Thought," in *Rereading Paul Together*, ed. David E. Aune (Grand Rapids: Baker, 2006), 124; James D. G. Dunn, "Once More, *Pistis Christou*," in *Pauline Theology*, ed. E. Elizabeth Johnson and David M. Hay (Atlanta: Scholars Press, 1997), 4:61–81.

52. Silva, "Faith versus Works," 233. See also C. E. B. Cranfield, *On Romans and Other New Testament Essays* (Edinburgh: T & T Clark, 1998), 95–97.

as in Reformed theology, saving faith is extraspective in character—the sinner looks outside himself to Christ and is saved by his faith in him. When the Westminster Larger Catechism, for example, defines justifying faith, it states that it "receives and rests upon Christ and his righteousness" (q. 72). In other words, the believer looks to the work of another, to Jesus, to be saved. To say that Christ is justified by faith would mean that Christ is looking to the work of another. While Christ does look to his Father in faith, his Father does not save him.

Christ does not receive and rest upon his Father and his righteousness to the exclusion of his own obedience. Rather, it is Christ's obedience to his Father's will that secures his claim to righteousness and therefore the claim to the title of "spotless lamb," and of course to his resurrection from the dead. The Father did not save his Son from death but rather justified his Son by his resurrection. Christ's resurrection was his justification, the declaration that Christ was righteous, or obedient, and therefore death had no claim upon him (Rom. 1:3–4; 1 Tim. 3:16). There is a related question to which we must attend, namely, If Christ's obedience is the ground of our justification, then is his obedience grounded in the grace of God?

Is the obedience of Christ grounded in grace?

In determining whether Christ's obedience was grounded in the grace of God, we must first ask whether Adam's obedience was so grounded. As we saw in the last chapter, grace and works, or justification by works, are completely antithetical: "But if it is by grace, it is no longer on the basis of works; otherwise grace would no longer be grace" (Rom. 11:6; see also 4:4–5). Adam was to secure eschatological blessing by his obedience both to the prohibition of eating from the tree of knowledge and to the dominion mandate. Adam's work would have been judged by God *ex pacto* on the basis of justice, not grace. As Michael Horton explains,

> It is therefore premature to insert into the creation covenant an element of divine graciousness, strictly speaking. To be sure, God's decision and act to create constitute a "voluntary condescension" (WCF 7.1), as is his entrance into a covenantal relationship with creatures. Nevertheless, if "grace" is to retain its force as divine clemency toward those who deserve condemnation, we should speak of divine freedom, love, wisdom, goodness, justice, and righteousness as the governing characteristics of creation.

Grace and mercy are shown to covenant-breakers and reflect the divine commitment to restore that which is fallen.

It is upon this basis that Horton explains, "It is within this framework, then, that Reformed theology understood the active obedience of Jesus Christ, emphasizing the significance of his humanity in achieving redemption for his covenant heirs."[53] Christ, then, by his obedience, apart from the grace of God, secures eschatological blessing for his bride, the church.

There are some, however, who bring forward Philippians 2:7–9 in objecting to the conclusion that Christ did not require the grace of God: "And being found in human form, he humbled himself by becoming obedient to the point of death, even death on a cross. Therefore God has highly exalted him and bestowed on him the name that is above every name." Note particularly the phrase "God . . . bestowed," *echarisato*, which means "to grant" or "to give," though the word has at its root the term "grace" or *charis*. Some commentators have argued, therefore, that Christ's reward for his obedience was given to him purely by the grace of God.[54] A chief concern that lies behind the conclusion that Christ received his reward by the grace of God is that in a passage where Paul presents Christ as our example, if we say Christ earned his reward, we appear to undermine salvation by grace. Yet we must note that the correspondence is between Christ's experience and the believer's sanctification, not his justification.[55] Moreover, when we take a closer look at the conclusion that Paul's use of the term *charizomai* means that God gave Christ his reward by grace, we find there is a weakness in this argument.

We must beware of the root fallacy when defining words, that is, defining a word by its etymological root rather than by how it is used within a given context.[56] Paul uses the same term in another place, where it need not be translated by its root "grace." Paul in his appeal to Caesar told Festus that the Jews could not retain custody of him because he had done no wrong: "No one can give me up [*charisasthai*] to them" (Acts 25:11). Here

53. Horton, *Lord and Servant*, 132–33.

54. See John Calvin, *Galatians, Ephesians, Philippians, and Colossians*, trans. T. H. L. Parker, ed. David W. Torrance and T. F. Torrance, CNTC (Grand Rapids: Eerdmans, 1960), 249–51; Karl Barth, *Epistles to the Philippians* (1947; Louisville: Westminster John Knox, 2002), 66.

55. Moisés Silva, *Philippians*, BECNT (1992; Grand Rapids: Baker, 2005), 109.

56. See D. A. Carson, *Exegetical Fallacies* (1984; Grand Rapids: Baker, 1993), 26–32.

it would seem a bit odd for Paul to say, "No one can give me by grace to the Jews." If Paul were guilty, then the Jews would rightly be entitled to hold him in custody; there was no need for grace. Defining *charizomai* by its context rather than its etymological root, we may conclude that God gave to Christ, as a reward for his obedience, the name that is above every name.[57] Geerhardus Vos has an excellent summary of these issues:

> Paul here uses the verb *echarisato* to describe the bestowal by God upon Christ of the name above every name. *Echarisato* means that God bestowed it as a gracious gift, not, of course, in the specific sense of the word "grace," implying that there was any unworthiness in Christ which God had to overlook, but in the more general sense implying that this was an act in which the graciousness, the kindness of God manifested itself.[58]

Christ's obedience and reward, therefore, are grounded in God's justice, not grace. This conclusion is especially evident in the grammar of verses 7–10.

In verses 7–10 we read the following: "And being found in human form, he humbled himself by becoming obedient to the point of death, even death on a cross. Therefore God has highly exalted him and bestowed on him the name that is above every name, so that at the name of Jesus every knee should bow, in heaven and on earth and under the earth." It is specifically "therefore" (*dio*), which is at the beginning of verse 9, that is of importance. Paul links the obedience of Christ to this exaltation by the use of *dio*. This is significant, as *dio* is an inferential conjunction, which is used to draw a conclusion from a just-stated truth or to indicate a result from what has just preceded.[59] *Dio* is the "strongest inferential conjunction."[60] If we distill Paul's statements in verses 8–10, we find that he is saying: obedience therefore exaltation, which Vos characterizes as an "objective causal connection." Vos

---

57. Herman Witsius, *The Economy of the Covenants between God and Man*, trans. William Crookshank, 2 vols. (1822; Phillipsburg, NJ: P&R, 1990), 2.3.33–34.

58. Geerhardus Vos, "'Legalism' in Paul's Doctrine of Justification," in Vos, *Redemptive History and Biblical Interpretation*, ed. Richard B. Gaffin Jr. (Phillipsburg, NJ: P&R, 1980), 398–99.

59. David Alan Black, *It's Still Greek to Me* (Grand Rapids: Baker, 1998), 131; see also Daniel B. Wallace, *Greek Grammar beyond the Basics* (Grand Rapids: Zondervan, 1996), 673.

60. H. E. Dana and Julius R. Mantey, *A Manual Grammar of the Greek New Testament* (1927; New York: Macmillan, 1955), 245.

succinctly explains, "Christ by His perfect obedience was just before God, and on the ground of his being just received eternal life."[61]

The Active and Passive Obedience and Eschatology

The fifth objection is that the distinction of the active and passive obedience of Christ obscures the eschatological nature of Christ's crucifixion. Seifrid argues that "the further distinction which some Protestants made between the imputation of Christ's active righteousness (in fulfilling the law) and his passive obedience (in dying on the cross) is unnecessary and misleading" and that it represents "a failure to grasp that Christ's work represents the prolepsis of the final judgment and the entrance of the age to come."[62] Perhaps Seifrid has a point if one operates under the common medieval dissection of the obedience of Christ. To say with Anselm, for example, that one receives only the passive obedience of Christ in justification most certainly severs the work of Christ from eschatology. One has to wonder, however, whether Seifrid's objection is valid when one considers the following.

First, as noted above, the active and passive obedience of Christ are merely aspects of the unified complex of Christ's work; one cannot separate Christ's active and passive obedience. Second, considering the structure of redemptive history, the *historia salutis*, the two ages headed by the two Adams, Christ's work as mediator of the new covenant is wholly eschatological—Christ is the eschatological Adam (1 Cor. 15:45). Christ's work, however, is rooted in the proton, in the covenant of works, which required, negatively, abstinence from the tree of knowledge and, positively, fulfilment of the dominion mandate. As Christ fulfils the broken covenant of works through his active and passive obedience, believers are brought into the new creation and spared from the eschatological wrath that Christ bore on their behalf on the cross. It is a non sequitur, therefore, to argue that recognizing the active-passive distinction somehow de-eschatologizes the cross.

The Active Obedience of Christ and Sanctification

The sixth and last objection is that the imputation of the active obedience, or righteousness, of Christ makes the believer's own obedience to the law

---

61. Vos, "Legalism," 398; see also David VanDrunen, "To Obey Is Better than Sacrifice: A Defense of the Active Obedience of Christ in the Light of Recent Criticism," in *By Faith Alone*, ed. Gary L. W. Johnson and Guy P. Waters (Wheaton, IL: Crossway, 2006), 145–46.
62. Seifrid, *Christ, Our Righteousness*, 175.

unnecessary and leads to antinomianism. This argument, however, is ad hominem and fails to note that Paul faced the same objection in presenting the doctrine of justification: "What shall we say then? Are we to continue in sin that grace may abound? By no means! How can we who died to sin still live in it?" (Rom. 6:1–2). There will always be those who twist the truth, which was something Paul and James both faced (James 2). But abuse of the truth does not negate it. Moreover, when one considers justification in the context of the *ordo salutis*, one must remember that while the obedience of Christ is imputed in justification, underlying the entire *ordo* is union with Christ, which is applied by the power of the age to come, the Holy Spirit. We will explore the relationship between justification, sanctification, and union with Christ in subsequent chapters, but for now, Murray's comments about Christ's obedience are apropos: "It is obedience that finds its permanent efficacy and virtue in him. And we become the beneficiaries of it, indeed the partakers of it, by union with him."[63]

Conclusion

In our survey of the work of Christ we have seen that it is Jesus, the last Adam, who takes up the failed work of the first. Unlike the first Adam, who surrendered his vice-regency to Satan, sin, and death, and brought condemnation for all men, Jesus, the last Adam, by his obedience, not only fulfils the work that Adam was supposed to do, but he also redeems the elect out from under the fallen kingdom of the first Adam.[64] Christ's active and passive obedience, aspects of the same complex of Christ's unitary work, are imputed to the believer by faith.

Before we turn to the subject of justification by faith, we must first set the doctrine in its historical setting. We have placed justification in the *historia salutis* and filled in the structure of redemptive history with the work of the two Adams, but we must now turn to the historical setting in which we find Paul setting forth his doctrine of justification. What beliefs about the law did Paul encounter in Galatia, Rome, and Ephesus that caused him to explain the relationship between the law and justification? It is to that question that we now turn.

63. Murray, *Redemption*, 24.
64. Similarly, Brian Vickers, *Jesus' Blood and Righteousness: Paul's Theology of Imputation* (Wheaton, IL: Crossway, 2006), 198.

6

JUSTIFICATION IN ITS HISTORICAL CONTEXT

Before one can proceed to examine the doctrine of justification, it is important to explore the historical context in which Paul unfolds it.[1] We have already established the redemptive-historical context in which we find the doctrine but must set it in its historical context. In other words, What first-century issue caused Paul to set forth the doctrine of justification by faith alone? The most prominent answer to this question is Paul's need to refute those who would bring the "works of the law" to the fore in their justification. In generations past, most were in agreement that "works of the law" referred to works-righteousness, or the idea that one could merit or earn his salvation, more specifically his justification, by obedience to the law. In recent years, however, this common exegetical conclusion has been challenged. It is necessary, therefore, to determine what Paul means when he rejects "works of the law" as the basis for one's justification. By determining the meaning of this important phrase, we will

1. This chapter is a modified version of J. V. Fesko, "N. T. Wright and the Works of the Law," *Faith & Mission* 22/1 (2004): 64–83.

be able to understand the historical setting of Paul's doctrine of justification. We must therefore turn to the recent developments in the field of NT studies. It is here, as specified at the beginning of this volume, that we will primarily interact with the writings of N. T. Wright.

Background: Stendahl, Sanders, and Dunn

Krister Stendahl: The Introspective Conscience

Krister Stendahl complained that Paul's interpreters were reading him, not in the light of his immediate first-century context, but through the interpretive lens of Martin Luther: "The Reformers' interpretation of Paul rests on an analogism when Pauline statements about Faith and Works, Law and Gospel, Jews and Gentiles are read in the framework of late medieval piety. The Law, the Torah, with its specific requirements of circumcision and food restrictions becomes a general principle of 'legalism' in religious matters."[2] Stendahl's overall argument was that NT scholars have read Paul on the law in terms of the individual's struggle with sin, as has one of Paul's most famous interpreters, Luther.[3] Luther read the medieval question of merit back into Paul in Romans and Galatians rather than read him within his first-century context. Stendahl struck a chord that resonated with not a few scholars, most notably E. P. Sanders.

E. P. Sanders: Covenantal Nomism

In his watershed work *Paul and Palestinian Judaism*, Sanders set out to destroy the general Christian view of Judaism as a religion of legalistic works-righteousness. He wrote to destroy the common opinion that the Jews were interested in earning their salvation through their obedience to the law. Sanders researched the literature of the second temple and concluded that Judaism was not a works-righteousness-based religion but one of grace, which he termed "covenantal nomism": "The view that one's place in God's plan is established on the basis of the covenant and that the covenant requires as the proper response of man his obedience to its commandments, while providing means of atonement for transgres-

2. Krister Stendahl, "Paul and the Introspective Conscience of the West," in Stendahl, *Paul among the Jews and Gentiles* (Minneapolis: Fortress, 1976), 85–86.
3. Ibid., 82.

sion."[4] Regarding the specific nature of the law and its function within Judaism Sanders argues:

1. God has chosen Israel.
2. Israel has been given the law, and the law implies both
3. God's promise to maintain the election and
4. The requirement to obey.
5. God rewards obedience and punishes transgression.
6. The law provides for means of atonement, and atonement results in
7. Maintenance or reestablishment of the covenantal relationship.
8. All those who are maintained in the covenant by obedience, atonement, and God's mercy belong to the group which will be saved.[5]

Sanders's thesis is that Judaism is based upon election and covenant, in other words, the grace of God. In the minds of many NT scholars, this reevaluation of Judaism was the needed illumination upon Paul's context to evaluate better his teaching on the law.

In Sanders's study, he determined that while Judaism was marked by covenantal nomism, Paul, on the other hand, rejected this pattern. Sanders argues that "what is wrong with Judaism is not that Jews seek to save themselves and become self-righteous about it, but that their seeking is not directed toward the right goal." What is the right goal? According to Sanders's reading of Paul, it is righteousness, not through the law but through Christ:

> It is thus not first of all against the *means* of being properly religious which are appropriate to Judaism that Paul polemicizes ("by works of law"), but against the prior fundamentals of Judaism: the election, the covenant and the law; and it is because these are wrong that the means appropriate to "righteousness according to the law" (Torah observance and repentance) are held to be wrong or are not mentioned. In short, *this is what Paul finds wrong in Judaism: it is not Christianity.*[6]

4. E. P. Sanders, *Paul and Palestinian Judaism* (Minneapolis: Fortress, 1977), 75.
5. Ibid., 422.
6. Ibid., 550–52.

Sanders evaluates Paul's teaching and concludes that the covenantal no-mism of Judaism is not aimed at incorporation into Christ, though it is not a works-righteousness religion, as it is based in God's grace. Sanders's revolutionary conclusions did not go unnoticed.

James D. G. Dunn: The New Perspective

There were some in the field of NT studies who believed that Sanders's approach was a step in the right direction. James Dunn, drawing upon Stendahl's ground-breaking essay, believed that Paul's teaching on justi-fication by faith was being read, not in the light of the first century, but in terms of Luther's battle with the Roman Catholic system of merit. In the light of Sanders's work, particularly his research in the literature of the second temple, interpreters finally were able "to see Paul properly within his own context, to hear Paul in terms of his own time, to let Paul be himself."[7]

While Dunn was pleased with the new vista of first-century Juda-ism opened by Sanders, he was displeased with his evaluation of Paul's relationship to Judaism. Dunn, contra Sanders, believes that Paul was in agreement with the covenantal nomism of Judaism:

> "Works of law," "works of the law" are nowhere understood here, either by his Jewish interlocutors or by Paul himself, as works which *earn* God's favor, as merit-amassing observances. They are rather seen as *badges*: they are simply what membership of the covenant people involves, what mark out the Jews as God's people; given by God for precisely that reason, they serve to demonstrate covenant status.

This means that the works of the law are not good works in general, and that therefore the traditional Reformation exegesis of Paul at this point is incorrect.[8] Paul's point, according to Dunn, is that "from being *one* iden-tity marker for the Jewish Christian alongside the other identity markers (circumcision, food laws, sabbath), faith in Jesus as Christ becomes the primary identity marker which renders the others superfluous."[9] The Jew-ish identity markers are no longer the badges that identify God's people;

---

7. James D. G. Dunn, *Jesus, Paul, and the Law* (Louisville: Westminster John Knox, 1990), 85–86.
8. Ibid., 194.
9. Ibid., 196.

rather, faith is the new badge. We see, then, a line of development from Stendahl to Sanders to Dunn. This brief overview of the development of Paul's phrase *erga nomou* sets the stage for our examination of Wright's views on the subject.

Wright on the Works of the Law

Throughout Wright's body of work he has given basic approval for the work of Sanders and Dunn regarding their analysis of first-century Judaism, covenantal nomism, and the interpretation of the phrase "the works of the law." This is not to say that Wright agrees at every point with Sanders and Dunn, which gives us reason to examine his own analysis surrounding the works of the law.[10]

Covenantal Nomism

First, concerning first-century Judaism and its supposed penchant for legalism, Wright rejects the common view. Wright argues that first-century Jews believed that entrance to the covenant was by birth or proselyte initiation. For males, entrance to the covenant was sealed in circumcision, and status in the covenant was maintained through fidelity to the chief covenant document, the Torah:

> As Sanders has argued extensively, membership in the covenant is *demonstrated*, rather than *earned*, by possession of Torah and the attempt to keep it. When the age to come dawns, those who have remained faithful to the covenant will be vindicated; this does not mean "those who have kept the Torah completely," since the sacrificial system existed precisely to enable Israelites who knew themselves to be sinful to maintain their membership none the less. And the attempt to keep Torah, whether more or less successful, was normally and regularly understood as response, not as human initiative.[11]

It is important that we see Wright's basic agreement with Sanders. Wright believes that the Jews saw their entrance into the covenant on

10. Wright has complained that his critics often assume the New Perspective is a monolith (see N. T. Wright, "New Perspectives on Paul," 10th Edinburgh Dogmatics Conference, Rutherford House, 25–28 August 2003, 3–4).

11. N. T. Wright, *The New Testament and the People of God* (Minneapolis: Fortress, 1992), 334. Wright disagrees with Sanders regarding matters concerning ritual purity and its connection to political and revolutionary action (see *People of God*, 181–203).

the basis of God's grace and their obedience to the Torah was merely response to the divine initiative, not an attempt to merit entrance into the covenant. Wright's agreement with Sanders is clearer in his popular work, *What Saint Paul Really Said*:

> Judaism in Paul's day was not, as has regularly been supposed, a religion of legalistic works-righteousness. If we imagine that it was, and that Paul was attacking it as if it was, we will do great violence to it and to him. Most Protestant exegetes had read Paul and Judaism as if Judaism was a form of the old heresy Pelagianism, according to which humans must pull themselves up by their moral bootstraps and thereby earn justification, righteousness, and salvation. No, said Sanders. Keeping the law within Judaism always functioned within a covenantal scheme. God took the initiative, when he made a covenant with Judaism; God's grace thus precedes everything that people (specifically, Jews) do in response. The Jew keeps the law out of gratitude, as the proper response to grace—not, in other words, in order to *get* into the covenant people, but to *stay* in. Being "in" in the first place was God's gift. This scheme Sanders famously labeled as "covenantal nomism" (from the Greek *nomos*, law). Keeping the Jewish law was the human response to God's covenantal initiative.[12]

It is evident that Wright agrees with Sanders and that he lays the culpability for the misinterpretation of Paul at the feet of Protestant theologians who are more interested in dogmatic schemes than a proper analysis of the first-century context in which we find Paul.[13] We thus see Wright's essential agreement with Sanders's covenantal nomism and the overall picture of first-century Judaism. Wright is also in accord with Dunn regarding the meaning of the phrase "the works of the law."[14]

---

12. N. T. Wright, *What Saint Paul Really Said* (Grand Rapids: Eerdmans, 1997), 18–19; more recently, idem, "New Perspectives on Paul," in *Justification in Perspective*, ed. Bruce L. McCormack (Grand Rapids: Baker, 2006), 246–47.

13. N. T. Wright, *Jesus and the Victory of God* (Minneapolis: Fortress, 1996), 380.

14. Dunn has conceded, "'The works of the law' does, of course, refer to all or whatever the law requires, covenantal nomism as a whole" (James D. G. Dunn, *The Theology of Paul the Apostle* [Grand Rapids: Eerdmans, 1998], 358). Yet, despite this concession, one that would seemingly undermine his case, Dunn has not modified his overall position regarding the relationship between works of the law and justification (see David E. Aune, "Recent Readings of Paul Relating to Justification by Faith," in *Rereading Paul Together*, ed. David E. Aune [Grand Rapids: Baker, 2006], 210). Wright, by contrast, still seems to adhere to Dunn's original position (N. T. Wright, *Paul: In Fresh Perspective* [Minneapolis: Fortress, 2005], 54–55).

Works of the Law

Concerning the contested phrase Wright believes that one must first recognize the function of the Torah. Given the constant presence of the Gentile nations, the Jews, according to Wright, looked to the Torah to distinguish between those who were within and without the covenant. The "Torah provided three badges in particular which marked the Jew out from the pagan: circumcision, sabbath, and the kosher laws, which regulated what food could be eaten, how it was to be killed and cooked, and with whom one might share it. In and through all this ran the theme of Jewish 'separateness.'"[15] The law, then, is inextricably linked with Jewish identity. It is through these works of the law, circumcision, Sabbath, and food laws, that the common Jew at the street level distinguished himself from the Gentiles.[16] They did not use these works or badges, however, as the ground upon which to gain entrance to the covenant but merely to identify who was already in the covenant by God's grace.

When we combine Wright's understanding of covenantal nomism with the nature of the works of the law, namely their status as boundary markers, this yields different data regarding the nature of the conflict between Jesus and the Pharisees and Paul and the Judaizers:

> The "works of Torah" were not a legalist's ladder, up which one climbed to earn the divine favor, but were the badges that one wore as the marks of identity, of belonging to the chosen people in the present, and hence the all-important signs, to oneself and one's neighbors, that one belonged to the company who would be vindicated when the covenant god acted to redeem his people. They were the present signs of future vindication. This was how "the works of Torah" functioned within the belief, and the hope, of Jews and particularly of Pharisees.[17]

What does this conclusion mean, then, regarding Paul's conflict with the Judaizers at Galatia? Paul's conflict with the Judaizers at Galatia was not over works-righteousness but over the question of whether a person has to become a Jew in order to belong to the people of God. Did a Gentile have to be circumcised, observe the Sabbath, and keep kosher food

---

15. Wright, *People of God*, 237.
16. Wright, *Victory of God*, 384, 388; see also idem, *Climax of the Covenant* (Minneapolis: Fortress, 1993), 240.
17. Wright, *People of God*, 238.

laws in order to belong to the covenant people of God? Paul's answer to this question, according to Wright, was no. Like a flag quietly being run down its pole, the Jewish identity markers or badges were being replaced.[18] In Christ's ministry he was reconstituting Israel around himself and changing its identity markers. Drawing upon Habakkuk 2:4, Wright argues that in times of crisis the Jews were marked, not by the works of the law or covenant badges, but by their faith. Faith in Jesus replaces the badges of Jewish identity. No longer are the people of God marked out by circumcision, Sabbath, and kosher food laws but by faith in the Christ. What this means is that the conflict at Galatia was not over salvation or works-righteousness but over admitting the Gentiles to the covenant community without the attendant identity badges.[19] Wright explains that for Paul the question was "whether Jewish Christians were allowed to eat with Gentile Christians," and that "all who believe in Jesus Christ belong at the same table, no matter what their cultural or racial differences."[20] With this basic overview of Wright's interpretation of the works of the law, we may turn to critical analysis of his arguments.

Contrary to Wright, the traditional, or old perspective on Paul, is correct in its analysis of the contested phrase. This can be demonstrated by recognizing that legalism was indeed a problem within first-century Judaism and that it was a problem that Paul faced. This setting casts a different light upon the meaning of the works of the law. Before we can proceed, however, it is necessary to define legalism, as it is a key concept that will be used throughout the rest of our study. Legalism is both the attempt to earn righteousness by obedience to the law and human pride in the accomplished obedience.[21] Legalism can take on, if one pardons the anachronism, either a Pelagian or semi-Pelagian form. In other words, a person can think he can merit God's favor apart from his grace, or he can, with God's grace, add his own obedience to his efforts to seek God's favor. This is an important point, as some interpreters use the phrase *sola*

---

18. Ibid., 241, 259–60.
19. Wright, *Victory of God*, 381.
20. Wright, *Saint Paul*, 158–59.
21. T. R. Schreiner, "Works of the Law," in *Dictionary of Paul and His Letters*, ed. G. F. Hawthorne et al. (Downers Grove, IL: InterVarsity, 1993), 978; similarly, Aune, "Recent Readings of Paul," 189.

gratia, grace alone, but then freight it with semi-Pelagian constructs.[22] Keeping these things in mind, we can now turn to Paul's use of the contested phrase in Galatians.

Works of the Law in Paul

Galatians

When we come to the contested phrase, the works of the law, we must first see how Wright interprets Galatians 3:10–14. Paul writes: "For all who rely on works of the law are under a curse; for it is written, 'Cursed be everyone who does not abide by all things written in the Book of the Law, and do them'" (Gal. 3:10). First, Wright rejects the common explanations of this passage.[23] Wright argues that no Jew who failed to keep the law needed to languish under the threat of exclusion from the covenant or eternal damnation. Presupposing the framework of covenantal nomism, Wright states: "Remedies were close at hand, prescribed by God's grace within the Torah itself."[24]

So, then, what does Paul mean when he says that the law has a curse hanging over the head of the one who does not abide by it? Wright argues that one must read this passage, and others like it (Rom. 3:20), against the backdrop of the covenant theology of the OT. He states that the passage Paul quotes, Deuteronomy 27:26, comes from the greater context of chapters 27–30. He argues that the pattern in Deuteronomy 27–30

---

22. See, e.g., Kent L. Yinger, *Paul, Judaism, and Judgment according to Deeds* (Cambridge: Cambridge University Press, 1999), 285. Also, James Dunn, despite his attempts to affirm *sola fide,* nevertheless adheres to a semi-Pelagian construct in his doctrine of justification. His semi-Pelagianism is especially evident in his claim that justification is twofold, initial and final (James D. G. Dunn, *The New Perspective on Paul* [Tübingen: Mohr Siebeck, 2005], 63–72). While Dunn attempts to demonstrate his familiarity with the historic Reformed faith by citing the Westminster Confession, as well as his basic knowledge of Luther and Calvin, he never stops to ask whether his own views reflect these historic expressions (*New Perspective,* 17–22). Why do no historic Reformed confessions or catechisms have the category of "final justification"? Why do Roman Catholic documents such as the Decrees of Trent speak of an initial and final justification? The simple answer is that not only did Reformed theologians want to distinguish their own views from those of Roman Catholicism, but also they did not find the teaching in the Scriptures, or in Paul more specifically. One should compare Dunn's statements and his claims to adhere to *sola fide* and *sola gratia* to those made by Arminians (cf. Roger E. Olson, *Arminian Theology* [Downers Grove, IL: InterVarsity, 2006], 200–220, with Dunn, *New Perspective,* 72–80).

23. Wright, *Climax,* 145.

24. Ibid.

is not focused upon individual sin necessitating repentance, sacrifice, and atonement. Rather, chapters 27–30 are focused upon national sin: a pattern of exile, restoration, judgment, followed by God's mercy. "What is envisaged," argues Wright, "is not so much the question of what happens *when this or that individual sins*, but the question of what happens when *the nation as a whole fails* to keep *the Torah as a whole*."[25] What does Wright's interpretive grid mean, then, for Galatians 3:10 and the works of the law?

He argues that all who embrace the Torah are thereby embracing Israel's national way of life, manifest in its distinctive badges (circumcision, food laws, and Sabbath), or the works of the law. Israel has suffered the curse that the Torah held out for her if she violated the covenant. Therefore, everyone who embraces the Torah, and its badges, is under this curse. How is the curse overcome? Jesus overcomes it on the Roman cross, which symbolized the continuing subjugation of the people of God and brought their curse-induced exile to an end (Gal. 3:13).[26] God in Christ inaugurates the new covenant and casts aside the old covenant badges and makes use of a new badge, faith. Paul therefore is not dealing with the subject of earning one's salvation but the

> question of how you *define the people of God*: are they to be defined by the badges of Jewish race, or in some other way? Circumcision is not a "moral" issue; it does not have to do with moral effort, or earning salvation by good deeds. Nor can we simply treat it as a religious ritual, then designate ritual as crypto-Pelagian good works, and so smuggle Pelagius into Galatia as the arch-opponent after all.[27]

According to Wright, then, Paul deals with the subject of who belongs to the family of Abraham and what marks them: the Jewish covenant badges, the signs of an old covenant indicative that Israel was under the curse of exile for national disobedience, or the sign of faith, the mark of

---

25. Ibid., 146.

26. Ibid., 146–47, 151.

27. Wright, *Saint Paul*, 120–21. Wright adamantly contends that the issues in Galatia were sociological, and that Paul's concerns are not about soteriology, though there are implications for soteriology (idem, "The Letter to the Galatians: Exegesis and Theology," in *Between Two Horizons*, ed. Joel B. Green and Max Turner [Grand Rapids: Eerdmans, 2002], 234–36). Wright seems often to background what is in the foreground of Paul's arguments, and foregrounds what is in the background.

trust in Jesus who bore Israel's covenant curse. Despite Wright's attempts, there are problems with his offered interpretation.

Wright is able to offer his interpretation of Galatians 3:10–14 only by isolating it from the overall context. What one must take into account is not only verses 10–14 and the use of Deuteronomy 27:26, but also Paul's ensuing explanation, namely the typology of Hagar and Sarah in chapter 4, as it is the climax and capstone of his argument.[28] First, one must note that God gave Abraham the promise of the covenant (Gen. 12, 15). We should also keep in mind that Paul calls this promise the gospel (Gal. 3:8). Second, connected to the covenant was the promise of an heir, Isaac. Third, Paul recounts Abraham and Sarah's attempt to lay hold of the covenant promise through Sarah's plan for Abraham to impregnate Hagar: "But the son of the slave was born according to the flesh, while the son of the free woman was born through promise" (Gal. 4:23). Paul cannot mean that only Ishmael was born through sexual intercourse because Isaac was born by the same instrumental means; otherwise the promise that Abraham would have his very own son to be his heir would be empty (Gen. 15:4).[29] The contrast is between Abraham and Sarah's sinful efforts to lay hold of the promises of the covenant and God's bestowing the blessings upon them through the Spirit, a contrast in final causality.[30]

In other words, the contrast is between sinful human effort, or works-righteousness, and grace.[31] This is what Paul means when he says that Hagar, who corresponds to Mount Sinai, the Torah, and first-century Jerusalem, gives birth to children of slavery because its inhabitants try to lay hold of the covenant promises through their efforts, or works, whereas Sarah, who corresponds to the heavenly Jerusalem, represents the reception of the covenant by grace through faith alone.[32] Contra Wright, Paul appeals to Abraham prior to the administration of the Torah. If the problem at Galatia were simply looking to the Torah as a boundary

---

28. Herman N. Ridderbos, *St. Paul's Epistle to the Churches of Galatia*, NICNT (Grand Rapids: Eerdmans, 1953), 173; also James D. G. Dunn, *The Epistle to the Galatians*, BNTC (Peabody, MA: Hendrickson, 1993), 243.

29. F. F. Bruce, *The Epistle to the Galatians*, NIGTC (Grand Rapids: Eerdmans, 1982), 217.

30. Ridderbos, *St. Paul's Epistle*, 175, 181–82.

31. Richard N. Longenecker, *Galatians*, WBC 41 (Dallas: Word, 1990), 219.

32. Ridderbos, *St. Paul's Epistle*, 181; also Seyoon Kim, *Paul and the New Perspective* (Grand Rapids: Eerdmans, 2002), 158–59 n. 113.

marker, then why does he appeal to Sarah and Abraham's sinful efforts to lay hold of the promises of the covenant, the gospel?[33] Why does he appeal to the sinful actions of two individuals when there are numerous examples of national sin throughout the Scriptures? What about Wright's appeal to the overall structure of Deuteronomy 27–30?

While Wright is correct to make the connections between national sin, exile, and restoration, at the same time one must recognize that national sin is rooted in the sin of the individual. For example, Deuteronomy 27:15 says: "'Cursed be the man who makes a carved or cast metal image, an abomination to the LORD, a thing made by the hands of a craftsman, and sets it up in secret.' And all the people shall answer and say, 'Amen.'" Contra Wright, there is no need to pit the individual against the nation. As this verse shows, it is the individual man who is cursed for idolatry, but the people must corporately respond in agreement.[34] Even if Wright's argument regarding the structure of Deuteronomy 27–30 is correct, one cannot divorce the *ordo* from the *historia salutis*. Assuming Wright's analysis is correct, for the moment, one must realize that the nation's exile is based upon the sins of individuals.[35] There is, as we have seen, however, good reason to doubt Wright's analysis of Deuteronomy 27–30. There is another element that one must consider in Wright's analysis of the relationship between Galatians 3:10 and Deuteronomy 27:26.

When Paul appeals to Deuteronomy 27:26, it is difficult to argue that he has only circumcision, food laws, and the Sabbath in mind when he uses the phrase "the works of the law," seeing that the people were to "keep all his commandments" (Deut. 26:18; 27:1), meaning the whole body of laws in chapters 12–26.[36] The verse comes at the end of a series of verses that go beyond Wright's covenant badges. Deuteronomy 27:15–25 deals with idolatry, honoring father and mother, moving boundary markers, theft, misleading the blind, perverting justice, incest, bestiality, and murder.

---

33. E.g., N. T. Wright, *Paul for Everyone: The Prison Letters, Ephesians, Philippians, Colossians, and Philemon* (London: SPCK, 2002), 59; similarly Dunn, *Galatians*, 246–47.

34. Patrick D. Miller, *Deuteronomy* (Louisville: Westminster John Knox, 1990), 195.

35. Ibid., 197–98.

36. J. G. McConville, *Deuteronomy*, AOTC (Downers Grove, IL: InterVarsity, 2002), 388, 394; Duane L. Christensen, *Deuteronomy 21:10–34:12*, WBC (Nashville: Thomas Nelson, 2002), 653, 663; Jeffery H. Tigay, *Deuteronomy*, JPSTC (Philadelphia: Jewish Publication Society, 1996), 248. Also see Elizabeth Bellefontaine, "The Curses of Deuteronomy 27: Their Relationship to the Prohibitives," in *A Song of Power and the Power of Song*, ed. Duane Christensen (Winona Lake, IN: Eisenbrauns, 1993), 256–68.

These verses pronounce a curse upon the one who violates the law at these points, and death would most likely come upon the individual who committed murder, incest, or bestiality.[37] As Andrew Das notes, "When Paul uses the phrase 'works of the law' in Gal. 3:10 and cites Deut. 27:26 (in a composite quote drawing on other statements in Deut. 27–30), the Deuteronomy context indicates that Paul has in mind the law in its *entirety*, including even actions done in private."[38] That Paul has the entirety of the law in view is especially evident, as we have noted before, in the difference between Deuteronomy 27:26 and Paul's quotation in Galatians 3:10. Paul adds a word not found in the MT: "Cursed be everyone who does not abide by *all* things written in the Book of the Law, and do them" (Gal. 3:10; cf. Gal. 5:3; Deut. 27:26, LXX).[39] Given this evidence, namely the emphasis upon both the corporate and individual responsibility, the need to maintain the unity of the *ordo* and *historia salutis*, and the appeal to the entirety of the law, it appears that Wright's analysis is incorrect. What about Wright's analysis of the contested phrase in Romans?

Romans

Paul's use of the contested phrase comes in chapter 3 where he explains the relationship of works of the law to justification. Wright argues similarly as he did regarding the occurrence of the phrase in Galatians. He makes reference to the only occurrence of the phrase in a pre-Christian text, namely the Dead Sea Scrolls' *Miqsat Ma'ase Ha-Torah* (4QMMT): "We have also written to you concerning some of the observances of the Law [lit. works of Torah], which we think are beneficial to you and your people" (4Q398–99).[40] Wright acknowledges that this occurrence of the phrase is somewhat different than Paul's usage in Romans and Galatians, but it does give the investigator an indication of how the phrase functioned in first-century Judaism. He states that the occurrence of the phrase in 4QMMT covers postbiblical rulings concerning temple purity aimed at defining one group of Jews over against others. On this evidence Wright contends that "works of the law" is a technical phrase

---

37. Miller, *Deuteronomy*, 195.

38. A. Andrew Das, *Paul, the Law, and the Covenant* (Peabody, MA: Hendrickson, 2001), 158; also Tigay, *Deuteronomy*, 253–54.

39. Longenecker, *Galatians*, 117–18.

40. Geza Vermes, ed., *The Complete Dead Sea Scrolls in English* (New York: Penguin, 1997).

that refers to those aspects of the law that define the Jews over and against the pagan nations.[41] Wright contends that "Paul's fellow Jews were not proto-Pelagians, attempting to pull themselves up by their moral shoe-laces. They were, rather, responding out of gratitude to the God who had chosen and called Israel to be the covenant people and who had given Israel the law both as the sign of that covenant membership and as the means of making it real."[42]

Once again, we see Wright's reliance upon Sanders's covenantal nomism. This leads Wright to draw the following conclusions regarding the nature of the problem of the works of the law:

> The "works" that were regarded in Paul's day as particularly demonstrating covenant membership were, of course, those things that marked out the Jews from their pagan neighbors, not least in the diaspora: the sabbath, the food laws, and circumcision. A strong case can therefore be made for seeing "works of the law," in Romans and Galatians, as highlighting these elements in particular. This case rests on the larger thrust of Paul's argument, in which "the Jew" is appealing not to perfect performance of every last commandment, but to possession of Torah as the badge of being God's special people.

The conflict is not over legalism but over Jewish identity badges.[43] There are, again, weaknesses in Wright's argument.

First, though Wright makes a nuanced appeal to 4QMMT, recognizing the differences between its use of the phrase and Paul's, he fails to explain other key phrases that mitigate his claim. Wright argues that 4QMMT puts forth the idea that

> the thing that marks them out in the present is precisely the specific "works of the Torah" that the text urges upon its readers—the detailed post-biblical regulations deemed necessary by the sect. These "works of Torah," then, were the sign that the future verdict (God's vindication of the sect) was anticipated in the present; the sect could be confident now of their

---

41. N. T. Wright, *Romans*, NIB (Nashville: Abingdon, 2003), 460–61; idem, "Paul and Qumran," *BRev* 14/5 (1998): 18, 54.

42. Wright, *Romans*, 460–61 n. 96.

43. Ibid., 461. Wright relies upon Dunn's analysis at this point (see James D. G. Dunn, *Romans 1–8*, WBC 38a [Dallas: Word, 1988], 153–60).

membership in the renewed covenant, the community of fresh blessing, the "returned-from-exile" people spoken of in Deuteronomy 30.[44]

Yet one must ask whether the Qumran community reduced the works of the law to a small subset of the law as Wright contends. There is evidence that demonstrates they did not limit the works of the law to a small subset.[45] In the Community Rule we find the following: "This is the rule for the men of the community who have freely pledged themselves to be converted from all evil and to cling to all his commandments according to his will" (1QS 5). Each member of the community had to "undertake by a binding oath to return with all his heart and soul to every commandment of the Law of Moses in accordance with all that has been revealed" (1QS 5:10).

Moreover, contra Wright, the Qumran community did not look at the law in terms of covenantal nomism, in other words as the means of staying in the covenant. Rather, the practice of all of the precepts of the law was the means of entrance to the community:

> But when a man enters the covenant to walk according to all these precepts that he may be joined to the holy congregation, they shall examine his spirit in community with respect to his understanding and practice of the Law, under the authority of the sons of Aaron who have freely pledged themselves in the Community to restore His Covenant and to heed all the precepts commanded by Him, and the multitude of Israel." (1QS 5:20)

One should note that this does not at all conform to Sanders's covenantal nomism.[46] Indeed, here the law is the means of entering the cov-

---

44. Wright, *Romans*, 460.

45. See Thomas Schreiner, *Romans*, BECNT (Grand Rapids: Baker, 1998), 153, for citations from the Dead Sea Scrolls showing that Qumran did not delimit the scope of the works of the law. Also see Carolyn J. Sharp, "Phinehan Zeal and Rhetorical Strategy in 4QMMT," *RevQ* 18/2 (1997): 215; Gary A. Anderson, "Intentional and Unintentional Sin in the Dead Sea Scrolls," in *Pomegranates and Golden Bells* (Winona Lake, IN: Eisenbrauns, 1995), 49–64.

46. See Sanders, *Paul*, 272. Others have shown that Sanders's thesis does not adequately explain all of the documentary evidence (see Chris VanLandingham, *Judgment and Justification in Early Judaism and the Apostle Paul* [Peabody, MA: Hendrickson, 2006], 106; Kim, *Paul and the New Perspective*, 147; D. A. Carson, *Divine Sovereignty and Human Responsibility* [Grand Rapids: Baker, 1981], 55–74). Mark Adam Elliott, for example, notes in his exhaustive survey of second-temple literature: "After recognizing and considering the importance of covenantal thought to an understanding of Judaism (ch. 6), we discovered that, far from evidencing an unconditional or unilateral covenantal theology, all indications pointed to a

enant community, and it is not merely the rite of circumcision or abiding by the kosher food laws, but the law in its entirety. There is therefore doubt concerning Wright's appeal to 4QMMT's use of the phrase "the works of the law." Moreover, 4QMMT supports the traditional perspective regarding the presence of legalism over and against Wright's interpretation. It appears that works-righteousness was a problem at Qumran.[47] If it was a problem at Qumran, then there is the possibility that legalism was a problem at Galatia and more specifically at Rome.[48]

Second, when one considers Paul's use of the contested phrase within the immediate context, one must strain to make Wright's interpretation fit. For example, in Romans 3:20 Paul states: "For by works of the law no human being will be justified in his sight, since through the law comes knowledge of sin." If one assumes Wright's interpretation, then he must read Paul's statement in this manner: "For by circumcision, kosher food laws, and the Sabbath, no human being will be identified as a member of the covenant, since through the covenant badges comes knowledge of sin." This makes little to no sense, though Wright might claim that his interpretation works quite well because circumcision reminds the Jew of his sinfulness and need for redemption.[49] Yet elsewhere when Paul writes of the knowledge of sin that comes through the law, he does not narrow the scope to Wright's Jewish identity badges: "Yet if it had not been for the law, I would not have known sin. I would not have known what it is to covet if the law had not said, 'You shall not covet'" (Rom. 7:7). Here in Paul's knowledge of sin through the law he refers to the tenth commandment.

Wright's interpretation confirms this analysis of Romans 7:7: "The law, in other words, was the channel not only for knowledge *about* sin but for knowledge *of* sin in the sense that, as a result of the process, 'I' knew, from the inside, what sin meant in practice."[50] Given Wright's interpretations

---

highly individualistic and conditional view of covenant" (*The Survivors of Israel* [Grand Rapids: Eerdmans, 2000], 639).

47. S. J. Gathercole, *Where Is Boasting?* (Grand Rapids: Eerdmans, 2002), 91–111.

48. See James D. G. Dunn, "4QMMT and Galatians," *NTS* 43 (1997): 153.

49. See, e.g., his treatment of Colossians 2:10–11 (N. T. Wright, *Colossians and Philemon*, TNTC [Grand Rapids: Eerdmans, 1986], 105; also idem, "Romans and the Theology of Paul," in *Pauline Theology*, ed. David M. Hay and E. Elizabeth Johnson [Minneapolis: Fortress, 1995], 3:37).

50. Wright, *Romans*, 562.

of Romans 3:20 and 7:7 one therefore has the following results: "For by circumcision, kosher food laws, and the Sabbath, no human being will be identified as a member of the covenant, since through the law [i.e., the Ten Commandments] comes knowledge of sin." This statement still makes little to no sense because verse 20b appears to be disconnected from the flow of thought. Why would the law refer only to the covenant badges in verse 20a, and then in 20b refer to the law in its entirety? It makes more sense that Paul refers to the entirety of the law, which also includes circumcision, food laws, and the Sabbath, in both 20a and b and that Paul is speaking about works-righteousness.[51] This conclusion is borne out when we explore the rest of Romans.

When one looks at the greater context of Romans, there is more evidence that undermines Wright's argument. When Paul, for example, rebukes the boasting Jew who lives by the law he states: "You call yourself a Jew and rely on the law and boast in God and know his will and approve what is excellent, because you are instructed from the law" (Rom. 2:17–18). As with his argument in Galatians, Wright argues that the ground of the boast is possession of the Torah and not obedience to its commands.[52] When Paul elaborates, however, upon the reason for boasting in the law, he does not refer to the covenant badges but to the law in general: "You then who teach others, do you not teach yourself? While you preach against stealing, do you steal? You who say that one must not commit adultery, do you commit adultery? You who abhor idols, do you rob temples? You who boast in the law dishonor God by breaking the law" (Rom. 2:21–23).[53]

Even though Paul connects the Jewish reliance upon the law to the commandments in general, Wright still tries to maintain the point that Paul speaks of the law as a covenant badge that distinguishes the Jew from the Gentile. As in Galatians, Wright argues that individual sin is not the subject under consideration, but the national sin of Israel. He argues that the subtext is the pattern of covenant, sin, exile, and restoration. The

51. Kim, *Paul and the New Perspective*, 67; C. E. B. Cranfield, *Romans*, 2 vols., ICC (Edinburgh: T & T Clark, 2001), 1:198; Schreiner, *Romans*, 171–72; Joseph A. Fitzmyer, *Romans*, AB (New York: Doubleday, 1993), 337–38; idem, "Justification by Faith in Pauline Thought," in *Rereading Paul Together*, ed. Aune, 88–89; cf. Dunn, *Romans 1–8*, 158–59.

52. N. T. Wright, "The Law in Romans 2," in *Paul and the Mosaic Law*, ed. James D. G. Dunn (Grand Rapids: Eerdmans, 2001), 139–40.

53. Schreiner, *Romans*, 132; Fitzmyer, *Romans*, 317–18; cf. Dunn, *Romans 1–8*, 117–18.

exile comes to an end, not through an intensification of Torah obedience, a use of the law in its boundary-marker function, but by faith in Christ. This and not legalism is what Paul has in view.[54] In other words the basis of the boasting is possession of the Torah, not obedience to it.

While it is true that possession of the Torah does distinguish the Jew from the Gentile, Wright ignores Paul's criticism that the Jews boast about possessing and keeping the law, but they keep it only with their lips and not with their hearts. This is the same type of legalism that Christ encountered (Matt. 5:27–32).[55] Moreover, if the pattern of continuing exile was in the forefront and the subject matter at hand was the national versus individual sin, why does Paul not cite any examples from the OT of Israel's national sin? Wright's reading does not fit the text; Paul deals with legalism. We find further confirmation of this when we see how Paul employs the term "works" elsewhere in Romans.

While Paul does speak of the works of the law, he also speaks of "works." When Paul, for example, explains who belongs to the covenant people, he makes his point with Jacob and Esau: "Though they were not yet born and had done nothing either good or bad—in order that God's purpose of election might continue, not because of works but because of his call—she [Rebecca] was told, 'The older will serve the younger'" (Rom. 9:11–12). It is important that one notes that Paul appeals to the patriarchal period prior to the revelation of the Torah, and therefore defines works, not in terms of the covenant badges as Wright might suggest, but in terms of "good or bad" to demonstrate that member-ship in the covenant does not depend on human effort, whether to enter or to maintain one's membership.[56] Wright, however, still tries to make the connection between works and the covenant badges: "In the present passage, though the emphasis is on 'works' as the doing of good rather than evil, the background in Paul's mind is most likely the regular rabbinic exegesis according to which the patriarchs were already obeying the Torah, even before it was given to Moses."[57] While Wright's suggestion is certainly possible, there is nothing in the text itself, or the

---

54. Wright, "Romans 2," 142–43.

55. Cranfield, *Romans*, 1:169.

56. Schreiner, *Romans*, 499; Fitzmyer, *Romans*, 562; cf. James D. G. Dunn, *Romans 9–16*, WBC 38b (Dallas: Word, 1988), 543–44.

57. Wright, *Romans*, 637.

surrounding context, that hints at this possibility. Paul's point is not that people are chosen apart from the use of the covenant badges, but that they are chosen apart from any consideration of any act they perform, whether good or evil.[58]

The evidence from Romans works against Wright's interpretation. Paul does not appear to narrow the scope of the works of the law to the covenant badges of membership, circumcision, food laws, and the Sabbath. On the contrary, it appears that he uses the contested phrase to describe those who attempt to perform and meet the requirements of the law.[59] The problem at Rome, and Galatia for that matter, is not boasting in the covenant badges but works-righteousness.[60] One can find corroboration of this conclusion in an examination of another occurrence of the broad use of the term "works" in the NT, namely the book of Ephesians.

Ephesians

At first glance some might protest the use of Ephesians as evidence for Paul's use of the term "works" as many scholars, including those of the New Perspective such as Dunn, deny its Pauline authorship.[61] Wright, however, is part of a "recalcitrant minority" that holds to the Pauline authorship of Ephesians.[62] At this point in Wright's writing, however, there is scant information available on his thoughts on Paul's use of the term "works."

"For by grace you have been saved through faith. And this is not your own doing; it is the gift of God, not a result of works, so that no one may boast" (Eph. 2:8–9). While Wright does not treat this passage in any of his scholarly works, he does briefly deal with it in his popular commentary on Paul's prison letters:

58. Das, *Paul*, 238.

59. Francis Watson, *Paul and the Hermeneutics of Faith* (Edinburgh: T & T Clark, 2004), 67–71.

60. Kim, *Paul and the New Perspective*, 151.

61. James D. G. Dunn, *The Theology of Paul the Apostle* (Grand Rapids: Eerdmans, 1998), 13 n. 39. There are some Reformed writers who, for the sake of debate, compromise with critical scholarship regarding the so-called undisputed Pauline epistles (see Cornelis P. Venema, *The Gospel of Free Acceptance in Christ* [Edinburgh: Banner of Truth, 2006], 148). This strategy, however, seems to concede too much, as Ephesians proves to be key in this debate. For a preferred methodology, see Guy P. Waters, *Justification and the New Perspectives on Paul* (Phillipsburg, NJ: P&R, 2004), 167.

62. N. T. Wright, *The Resurrection of the Son of God* (Minneapolis: Fortress, 2003), 236.

Paul speaks in Romans, Galatians and Philippians of being "justified" by faith; here, in verse 8, he speaks of being "saved" by grace. "Justification" and "salvation" are not the same thing. "Justification" has to do with people belonging to God's family. It answers the question as to how they are marked out as members of it. "Salvation" has to do with people being rescued from the fate they would otherwise have incurred. It answers the question as to how that rescue has taken place, and who is ultimately responsible for it.[63]

Wright's point, then, is that Paul addresses justification, or issues concerning covenant badges, in Romans and Galatians, and salvation, redemption from sin and death, here in Ephesians. However, can one successfully separate justification from salvation?

While one may try, as Wright does, to separate justification from salvation, it is quite difficult, if not impossible, to do (Rom. 10:10). Contradiction on this point even arises from Wright's own pen. For example, he states concerning Ephesians 2:8–9 that justification and salvation are separate issues, yet in his explanation of Romans 5:1–2 he states that those who have been justified by faith, marked as the people of God, are saved: "The point seems to be throughout, that what God has done in Jesus the Messiah, and what God is already doing through the Spirit, guarantees that all those who believe the gospel, and are thus 'justified by faith,' can be assured of their final hope. They will be delivered from wrath (5:9), in other words, 'saved.'"[64] Would Wright maintain that justification is not by grace? While it is certainly possible to distinguish justification from salvation, they cannot be separated. Contra Wright, whether one wants to speak of justification, an element within the broader picture of salvation, by works, or salvation by works, Paul rejects both. Moreover, in the overall flow of Paul's argument in Ephesians 2 he deals with the same issues as in Romans and Galatians, namely the salvation of both Jews and Gentiles by faith alone, not works.

In those contexts in which Paul must deal with Jews, he refers to the more specific error of "works of the law," and in the context of Ephesians where he deals primarily with Gentiles, he uses the more general "works," as he does in other Gentile-aimed epistles (see 2 Tim. 1:9; Titus

63. Wright, *Paul for Everyone*, 22.
64. Wright, *Romans*, 509.

3:5).[65] Beyond these points, even if Wright is correct in his analysis, Ephesians 2:8–9 represents a significant piece of evidence that Paul dealt with legalism of the Pelagian sort, a problem that Wright repeatedly denies existed in second-temple Judaism. Ephesians 2:8–9 represents the existence of works-righteousness, though Wright may contend that this was primarily directed to Gentiles and not the Jews of the first century.[66] It seems odd, though, that first-century Gentiles without the Torah would alone have the problem of works-righteousness, and the Jews who did have the Torah would be immune to this error. In other words, would the Gentiles with no revealed standard of conduct fall into works-righteousness, yet the Jews with the Torah who possess the standard never fall into legalism?

Given the subject matter of Ephesians 2:11–22, namely the incorporation of both Jew and Gentile into the covenant, and the question of circumcision, albeit indirectly, the danger of works-righteousness and legalism appears to be a problem for both the Jew and the Gentile. Though Andrew Lincoln denies Pauline authorship, commenting on Ephesians 2:8–10, he explains:

> The writer wishes to exclude any notion of earning salvation by human efforts which lead to self-congratulation. There has been a trend in recent Pauline interpretation either to play down his polemic against works of the law or to reinterpret it. On the one hand, it has been played down in the interests of stressing contemporary Judaism's witness to itself in terms of covenantal nomism as Paul's own starting-point for his criticism of the law in the exclusiveness of salvation by faith in Christ. On the other hand, it has been reinterpreted by arguing that Paul is attacking simply national righteousness not legal righteousness, the notion of pride in possessing the law and the badge of circumcision rather than the notion of keeping the law to gain God's approval. Could it be that Eph. 2:8–10, in taking up works and boasting as major Pauline themes and interpreting them in terms of human performance, has not totally distorted Paul's perspective but serves as a reminder of the centrality and significance of Paul's criticism of works of the law and the boasting

65. Douglas J. Moo, "'Law,' 'Works of the Law,' and Legalism in Paul," *WTJ* 45/1 (1983): 81.
66. Wright, *Paul for Everyone*, 23.

they involve in such passages as Rom. 3:27, 28; 4:1–5; 9:30–10:13; Gal. 3:10–14; Phil. 3:3–9?[67]

The presence of Ephesians 2:8–10, even if it is deutero-Pauline, represents a significant problem for Wright's argument. Again, Lincoln rightly argues:

Ephesians has already clearly interpreted Paul in this way by generalizing the discussion of Romans to make it one about salvation by grace as opposed to human effort in general rather than works of the law in particular. . . . Well before the time of Augustine, the generalization of justification and the focus on grace have an unmistakable precedent within the New Testament and within the Pauline corpus itself, as Ephesians sees works as human effort and performance which can obscure the gracious activity of God in providing a complete salvation.[68]

Even Dunn has acknowledged that Ephesians 2:8–10 deals with matters of works-righteousness, and for this reason rejects its Pauline authorship.[69] Ephesians, then, represents a problem for Wright's argument concerning Paul's use of the contested phrase.

Summary

Given our survey of Paul's use of the contested phrase and the more general term "works," Wright's case does not withstand close scrutiny. The

---

67. Andrew T. Lincoln, "Ephesians 2:8–10: A Summary of Paul's Gospel," *CBQ* 45/4 (1983), 628–29; idem, *Ephesians*, WBC 42 (Dallas: Word, 1990), 112–13.

68. Andrew T. Lincoln, "The Theology of Ephesians within the Pauline Corpus and the New Testament," in *New Testament Theology*, ed. Andrew T. Lincoln and A. J. M. Wedderburn (Cambridge: Cambridge University Press, 1993), 135–36. See also Fitzmyer, "Justification by Faith," 92.

69. Dunn, *Theology of Paul*, 370–71 n. 150. Dunn has recently tried to argue that, despite the question surrounding the authorship of the so-called deutero-Pauline epistles, the Pastorals add little if anything to the discussion and that Ephesians 2:8–10 does not call into question the New Perspective on Paul. Dunn writes, "The author could go on to insist that good works are expected of 'the saved,' without any fear that the works in view might be confused with the now passé demand of earlier Jewish believers that works of the law were still necessary for (final) salvation" (*New Perspective*, 53). Yet Dunn places his grid of initial and final justification upon this passage when Paul says nothing of the sort. Dunn still assumes a conditionality of the believer's salvation, a dependency upon the believer's works in a way foreign to Paul's explanation. Contra Dunn, Paul does not say that the believer's good works are the necessary condition for salvation, but rather the effect or fruit of that gracious redemption.

evidence from Galatians, and its use of Deuteronomy 27:26, Romans, and especially Ephesians, demonstrates that legalism was a problem within the early church. Even if one dismisses the Pauline authorship of Ephesians or appeals to the other so-called deutero-Pauline epistles, they still represent the existence of legalism within the first-century church (e.g., Titus 3:4–7). They represent first-century documents that deal with the problem of works-righteousness.

Summary and Conclusion

In our investigation we surveyed Wright's explanations of Paul's use of the phrase "the works of the law." If one adopts the view that the contested phrase refers only to a small subset of the Torah, circumcision, food laws, and Sabbath, it is difficult to make this explanation fit, which was evident in Romans 3:20. Elsewhere, for example, in Galatians, Paul uses more generic examples of human effort to obtain the blessings of the gospel, not the specific Jewish boundary markers. One of the strongest pieces of evidence that demonstrates the presence of legalism is Ephesians 2:8–9, because even Wright admits that Paul was highlighting the antithesis between grace and moral effort in salvation. Given these findings, it appears that the traditional understanding of the works of the law is the preferable interpretation; the phrase refers to the effort to obtain righteousness through obedience to the law as well as boasting about that obedience.[70] These conclusions yield important information concerning the historical context for understanding the doctrine of justification.

The exegetical data establish that legalism, or works-righteousness, was the primary error to which Paul responded with the doctrine of justification.[71] Paul faced groups of individuals who believed they could obtain righteousness through obedience to the law. What the Judaizers did not realize, however, was the incompatibility between the Mosaic covenant and eschatology.[72] In other words, the first Adam in the temple-garden had the ability to obtain his justification by his obedience to the

70. Das, *Paul*, 153; Waters, *Justification*, 170.

71. Similarly, Fitzmyer, "Justification by Faith," 89–90.

72. Similarly Albert Schweitzer, *The Mysticism of Paul the Apostle*, trans. William Montgomery (1931; Baltimore: Johns Hopkins University Press, 1998), 189.

command of God. Given the fall, however, and the introduction of the eschaton with the advent of the last Adam, and especially his resurrection from the dead, obtaining one's justification by obedience to the law was no longer possible.[73] One can be justified only by the work of the last Adam. It is to justification by faith alone, then, that we turn.

73. See Francis Turretin, *Institutes of Elenctic Theology*, trans. George Musgrave Giger, ed. James T. Dennison Jr., 3 vols. (Phillipsburg, NJ: P&R, 1992–97), 16.2.2.

7

JUSTIFICATION BY FAITH ALONE

In the previous chapters we have surveyed the work of the last Adam, particularly as it relates to Christ taking up the broken covenant of works. Where Adam failed, Christ succeeded. We have also seen how Christ's active and passive obedience constitutes his work. The connection between the failed work of the first Adam and the faithful work of the last Adam is quite clear in 1 Corinthians 15:45–49: "As was the man of dust, so also are those who are of the dust, and as is the man of heaven, so also are those who are of heaven" (v. 48). At this point in our study, the question we should ask is, How does one benefit from the work of the last Adam? In other words, now that our redemption has been accomplished, how is it applied to the believer? The short answer is, justification by faith alone. This short answer, however, requires that we examine the constituent elements of justification: that (1) it is by faith alone; (2) it is the remission of sins; and (3) it is the imputation of righteousness. These three elements, however, address only those aspects that touch upon the *ordo salutis*, or the application of redemption to the individual believer. While it is important to explore the *ordo salutis*, it is crucial that we do not divorce it from the *historia salutis*, or redemptive history. This is one area where, in some respects, some within the Reformed community have faltered. So, when we complete our exploration of justification by faith alone as it pertains to the *ordo salutis*, we will then locate this application of salvation within the *historia salutis*, or redemptive history. We may now turn to the first element, namely that justification is by faith alone.

By Faith Alone

As a result of the failed work of the first Adam, man is no longer holy or righteous. Paul makes this clear: "For all have sinned and fall short of the glory of God" (Rom. 3:23). Paul makes the connection between the sin of the first Adam and his offspring when he writes, "Sin came into the world through one man, and death through sin, and so death spread to all men because all sinned" (Rom. 5:12). The solidarity between Adam and his offspring is evident not only in the universal presence of death in the human race but also in the level of intimacy with God. On the heels of Adam's sin he and Eve were cast out from the garden-temple under a sentence of death with cherubim guarding the entrance to the garden-temple. Subsequently, only the high priest once a year could enter the Holy of Holies but only after following strict ritual cleansing and cultic sacrifice (Lev. 16). No amount of human effort can remove the guilt and corruption of sin: "By works of the law no human being will be justified in his sight, since through the law comes knowledge of sin" (Rom. 3:20; cf. Ps. 143:2). If the path of works is blocked and allows no one to reach justification by this means, then what avenue is available? Justification must come by faith alone. There are three key texts to which one must turn: Genesis 15:6, Romans 4:3–5, and 1:17.

Genesis 15:6

In this text we find important data concerning the role of faith in justification. Here we read that Abraham "believed the LORD, and he counted it to him as righteousness." In the surrounding context of Genesis 15:6 we find Abraham questioning God's initial promise to make him a great nation (Gen. 12:2). How can Abraham become a great nation if he does not have an heir? In Genesis 15:3, therefore, Abraham told God that Eliezer of Damascus would be his heir. God, however, countered Abraham's intentions with yet another promise, namely, Abraham would have an heir from his own body, a son (Gen. 15:4). God also took Abraham and showed him the stars of the sky and said, "Look toward heaven, and number the stars, if you are able to number them." God then renewed his promise of Genesis 12:2 and said, "So shall your offspring be." Now it is important that we understand the significance of this interchange between God and Abraham.

The significance of this interchange is that Abraham looks to the promise of God by faith, and through Abraham's faith, his trust in God's promise, God counted Abraham's faith as righteousness. This conclusion is evident from the vocabulary of Genesis 15:6. First, we read that Abraham *wehe'emin* the LORD, which means that he relied on, gave credence to, and trusted in God's promise.[1] This verb is often used of people in the OT who do not believe God or someone (Gen. 45:26; Ex. 4:8; 14:31; Num. 14:11; 20:12; Deut. 1:32; 9:23). But in this context Abraham's faith is the correct response; moreover, as we will see with Paul's explanation of this text, Abraham is set forth as a model for all of his descendants to follow.[2]

Second, we see that as a result of Abraham's faith in God's promise, God counted him (*hashab*) righteous. This term is important because it is used in a number of legal texts for counting (Lev. 7:18; 17:4; Num. 18:27, 30; Prov. 27:14; Ps. 106:31). This element is significant because the term is used in legal settings where priests would declare a sacrifice acceptable (Lev. 7:18), men clean or unclean (Lev. 13), or someone righteous (Ezek. 18:9).[3] God counted Abraham righteous, not for what he did, but because of his faith in the promise.[4]

Third, we see that as a result of Abraham's faith in God's promise that God counts Abraham's faith as *tsedaqah*, or righteousness. Within the broader context of the Pentateuch we see that *tsaddiq* is the term that in legal contexts is applied to those who should be acquitted by the judges

1. E. A. Speiser, *Genesis*, AB 1 (New York: Doubleday, 1962), 112.
2. Gordon J. Wenham, *Genesis 1–15*, WBC 1 (Dallas: Word, 1987), 329; Meredith G. Kline, "Abram's Amen," *WTJ* 31/1 (1968–69): 2, 9.
3. Wenham, *Genesis 1–15*, 330; Kline, "Abram's Amen," 3; Gerhard von Rad, *Genesis*, OTL (Philadelphia: Westminster, 1972), 184–85.
4. Bo Johnson, "*tzdq*," in *TDOT* 12:253–54; Nahum Sarna, *Genesis*, JPSTC (Philadelphia: Jewish Publication Society, 1989), 113; Lloyd Gaston, "Abraham and the Righteousness of God," *HBT* 2 (1980): 39–68; Bo Johnson, "Who Reckoned Righteousness to Whom?" *SEÅ* 51–52 (1986–87): 108–15.

(Deut. 25:1).[5] Within the narrower context of the early Genesis narratives Abraham intercedes for Sodom and Gomorrah on the basis that there would be at least ten righteous men, which would spare the cities from judgment. Here the contrast is between the righteous and the wicked. We see a similar bifurcation between the righteous and the wicked in the flood judgment; righteous Noah was spared whereas the wicked were judged (Gen. 6:9; 7:1; cf. Ezek. 18:5).[6]

These three elements of Genesis 15:6 give us important information regarding justification by faith alone, as Abraham receives his status of righteous through his faith in God's promise. The emphasis upon faith is key to Genesis 15:6, and for this reason Gerhard von Rad writes that Abraham's "righteousness is not the result of any accomplishments, whether of sacrifice or acts of obedience. Rather, it is stated programmatically that belief alone has brought Abraham into a proper relationship to God."[7] For this reason, Paul quotes Genesis 15:6 two times in his epistles, which brings us to our next passage.

Romans 4:3–5

In the overall context of Romans, Paul has cut off the path to justification by means of works: "For by works of the law no human being will be justified in his sight" (Rom. 3:20a). In the immediate context of chapter 4, Paul reiterates this same point: "What then shall we say was gained by Abraham, our forefather according to the flesh? For if Abraham was justified by works, he has something to boast about, but not before God" (Rom. 4:1–2). The only avenue of approach is through faith alone, which is why Paul quotes Genesis 15:6 in verse 3: "For what does the Scripture say? 'Abraham believed God, and it was counted to him as righteousness.'" Paul especially highlights the antithesis between faith and works in verses 4–5: "To the one who works, his wages are not counted as a gift but as his due. And to the one who does not work but trusts him who justifies the ungodly, his faith is counted as righteousness." The one who works does something, whereas the one who trusts receives.[8] The only way that a person, therefore, can be righteous is

---

5. Joseph A. Fitzmyer, "Justification by Faith in Pauline Thought," in *Rereading Paul Together*, ed. David E. Aune (Grand Rapids: Baker, 2006), 78–79.

6. Wenham, *Genesis 1–15*, 330; Kline, "Abram's Amen," 3; von Rad, *Genesis*, 185.

7. von Rad, *Genesis*, 185.

8. Thomas Schreiner, *Romans*, BECNT (Grand Rapids: Baker, 1998), 215.

through faith, not through works, not by doing. Now Paul's position stands in stark contrast to a common opinion of his day.[9]

When one surveys the literature of second-temple Judaism, a different picture emerges concerning the relationship between works and justification.[10] First Maccabees (c. 104 B.C.) 2:52 states: "Was not Abraham found faithful when tested, and it was reckoned to him as righteousness?"[11] This statement contradicts Paul's; Paul says that Abraham's righteousness came through faith, whereas the author of 1 Maccabees states that Abraham was accounted righteous based on his faithfulness.

This trend is present in other second-temple writings such as Sirach (c. 180 B.C.):

Abraham was the great father of a multitude of nations, and no one has been found like him in glory. He kept the law of the Most High, and entered into a covenant with him; he certified the covenant in his flesh, and when he was tested he proved faithful. Therefore the Lord assured him with an oath that the nations would be blessed through his offspring; that he would make him as numerous as the dust of the earth, and exalt his offspring like the stars, and give them an inheritance from sea to sea and from the Euphrates to the ends of the earth. (Sir. 44:19–21)

Notice in this quotation that Abraham's law-keeping precedes God's covenant with him.[12]

We find a similar idea in Jubilees (c. 160–40 B.C.) 23.10a: "For Abraham was perfect in all of his actions with the LORD and was pleasing

---

9. Contra Wright, who argues: "Paul develops the bookkeeping metaphor in the direction of employment and wage-earning. This is the only time he uses this metaphorical field in all his discussions of justification, and we should not allow this unique and brief sidelight to become the dominant note, as it has in most post-Reformation discussion" (N. T. Wright, *Romans*, NIB 10 [Nashville: Abingdon, 2003], 491).

10. See Chris VanLandingham, *Judgment and Justification in Early Judaism and the Apostle Paul* (Peabody, MA: Hendrickson, 2006), 15, 18; Paul A. Rainbow, *The Way of Salvation* (Carlisle: Paternoster, 2005), 15; Simon J. Gathercole, *Where Is Boasting? Early Jewish Soteriology and Paul's Response in Romans 1–5* (Grand Rapids: Eerdmans, 2002), 1–196; Mark Adam Elliot, *The Survivors of Israel* (Grand Rapids: Eerdmans, 2000), 245–308.

11. See D. A. Carson, "The Vindication of Imputation: On Fields of Discourse and Semantic Fields," in *Justification*, ed. Mark Husbands and Daniel J. Treier (Downers Grove, IL: InterVarsity, 2004), 56; Francis Watson, *Paul and the Hermeneutics of Faith* (Edinburgh: T & T Clark, 2004), 181–82.

12. So James D. G. Dunn, *Romans 1–8*, WBC 38a (Dallas: Word, 1988), 200; Watson, *Paul*, 10.

through righteousness all of the days of his life" (see also Jub. 16.28).[13] This statement runs contrary to what Paul writes, when he states that God "justifies the ungodly" (Rom. 4:5), which means that Paul calls Abraham ungodly.[14]

In Jubilees we also find the following interchange between God and Isaac, where God explains why he blessed Abraham: "All of the nations of the earth will bless themselves by your seed because your father obeyed me and observed my restrictions and my commandments and my laws and my ordinances and my covenant" (Jub. 24:10).[15] Again, this statement runs contrary to what Paul has written in Romans 3:20, but especially to what Paul states in Romans 4:13–14: "For the promise to Abraham and his offspring that he would be heir of the world did not come through the law but through the righteousness of faith. For if it is the adherents of the law who are to be the heirs, faith is null and the promise is void." If one pardons the anachronism, the author of 1 Maccabees makes Abraham's obedience to the law the basis of God's entering into a covenant with Abraham, which is Pelagian. This does not fit the so-called pattern of covenantal nomism, where God's grace precedes the faithful response.[16]

Some of the other statements which we have surveyed, which do fit the pattern of covenantal nomism, nonetheless introduce a synergism that is absent from Paul, which makes them semi-Pelagian in nature. Given the common opinions of Paul's day, the apostle was combating legalism, the notion that one somehow merited the status of being righteous by obedience to the law. Against these legalistic tendencies, Paul reiterates the import of Genesis 15:6, namely that Abraham is justified by faith alone, not his works.[17] This is the significance of Paul's use of the verb *logizomai*, "counted," or "reckoned" (NASB), an aorist passive (*elogisthē*), which again highlights that Abraham is the recipient of the action, not the

---

13. See S. J. Gathercole, "Justified by Faith, Justified by His Blood: The Evidence of Romans 3:21–4:25," in *Justification and Variegated Nomism*, 2 vols., ed. D. A. Carson et al. (Grand Rapids: Baker, 2004), 2:156.

14. C. E. B. Cranfield, *Romans*, 2 vols., ICC (1975; Edinburgh: T & T Clark, 2001), 1:232; see also Joseph A. Fitzmyer, *Romans*, AB 33 (New York: Doubleday, 1993), 375; VanLandingham, *Judgment*, 35–36.

15. For further references to rabbinic opinions regarding Abraham and works see Cranfield, *Romans*, 1:227–30; also VanLandingham, *Judgment*, 25.

16. VanLandingham, *Judgment*, 33.

17. Cranfield, *Romans*, 1:231.

subject of the verb; God is the subject of the verb.[18] Moreover, especially in light of Romans 4:4, Cranfield notes, "When once the significance of *episteusen* in Gen. 15:6 is brought out, it immediately becomes clear that the verb *logizesthai* (as used in that verse) must signify a counting which is not a rewarding of merit but a free and unmerited decision of divine grace."[19] This brings us to the third passage for investigation.

Romans 1:17

In this famous verse from Paul's epistle to Rome, we see once again the unique place of faith highlighted. Paul quotes the prophet Habakkuk: "For in it the righteousness of God is revealed from faith for faith, as it is written, 'The righteous shall live by faith.'" Paul explains that in the gospel one sees the "power of God for salvation to everyone who believes" (Rom. 1:16). In this gospel, writes Paul, "the righteousness of God is revealed," which has been variously interpreted throughout the history of the church. There are three major views concerning the interpretation of this phrase:[20]

1. An attribute of God (possessive genitive):
   a. It refers either to his *iustitia distributiva* (distributive justice), a view popular in the early church,[21]
   b. Or it refers to God's faithfulness, especially in relation to his covenant with Israel. This view has its origins in the early church as well, though it has gained much popularity in recent years.[22]
2. A status given by God (genitive of source): the righteousness by which believers are made righteous by God. In Protestant interpretation, this righteousness is forensic, not transformative.
3. An activity of God (subjective genitive): the saving action of God, his salvific intervention on behalf of his people.[23]

18. Schreiner, *Romans*, 219; Fitzmyer, *Romans*, 373.
19. Cranfield, *Romans*, 1:231; Watson, *Paul*, ix.
20. See Douglas Moo, *Epistles to the Romans*, NICNT (Grand Rapids: Eerdmans, 1996), 70–72.
21. Alister McGrath, *Iustitia Dei*, 2 vols. (Cambridge: Cambridge University Press, 1986), 1:51.
22. Ibid., 1:52; more recently Wright, *Romans*, 424–25.
23. So Dunn, *Romans 1–18*, 41–42, though Dunn would argue that God's saving activity is within the context of the covenant, which is similar to the view espoused by Wright.

We do not have the space to explore the merits of each of these exegetical possibilities; nevertheless, it appears that option (2) is the strongest for several reasons.

It does not appear that God's *iustitia distributiva* is in view, as Paul has broader issues in view, not simply God's justice but also salvation and justification. It also does not appear that God's covenant faithfulness is in view. Recent research has demonstrated that the concepts of righteousness and the covenant, while certainly connected, do not appear in the same context.[24] It is possible that the phrase could be a subjective genitive and therefore refer to God's saving action on behalf of his people, as this is a theme that one finds in the OT (Mic. 7:9; Isa. 46:13; 50:5–8). Yet nothing in the immediate context seems to point in this direction.[25]

It appears that the strongest option is that it is a genitive of source, the righteousness by which believers are made righteous by God. Evidence for this view is in the connection that Paul makes between righteousness and faith (Rom. 1:17; 3:21–22; 10:3–4). As Douglas Moo notes, "It is no exaggeration to call this a leitmotif of the letter." This conclusion is further strengthened when we consider that Paul also uses the term "righteousness" to denote the "gift of righteousness" (Rom. 5:17), which is a status that God bestows upon those who believe (Rom. 4).[26] This conclusion is evident, for example, in Paul's statement: "Not having a righteousness of my own that comes from the law, but that which comes through faith in Christ, the righteousness from God that depends on faith [*ek theou dikaiosynēn epi tē pistei*]" (Phil. 3:9). What, then, does Paul go on to say about the righteousness of God?

Paul explains that the righteousness of God comes through faith, though there is a question regarding the translation of the phrase *ek pisteōs eis pistin*, which the ESV renders, "from faith for faith." The phrase has been variously interpreted to refer to:

1. From faith in the law to faith in the gospel (Augustine)[27]

24. See Mark A. Seifrid, "Righteousness Language in the Hebrew Scriptures and Early Judaism," in *Justification and Variegated Nomism*, ed. Carson, et al., 1:415–42; also idem, "Paul's Use of Righteousness Language," in *Justification and Variegated Nomism*, 2:39–74.

25. Moo, *Romans*, 73.

26. Ibid.; Herman Ridderbos, *Paul: An Outline of His Theology*, trans. John Richard de Witt (1975; Grand Rapids: Eerdmans, 1992), 163.

27. Augustine, *The Spirit and the Letter* 11.18, in NPNF[1] 5:90.

2. The believer's growth in faith (Calvin)[28]
3. God's faithfulness and the believer's faith (Barth)[29]
4. God's faithfulness and the believer's faithfulness (Dunn, Wright)[30]
5. The instrumentality of faith in the reception of righteousness upon all who believe (Murray)[31]
6. A rhetorical combination that intends to emphasize the exclusivity of faith (Moo)[32]

Without going into a full-blown analysis of each option, it seems that the best position is a combination of options (5) and (6).[33] Option (1) seems the least likely, as Paul does not speak of faith in the law. Option (2) is a possibility, but there are other grammatical considerations, as we will see momentarily, that rule out this interpretation. Options (3) and (4) are very similar, though this is not to say that they are identical. Option (4), the position of Dunn and Wright, largely seems predicated upon their understanding of the "righteousness of God" (*dikaiosynē theou*), one that we have determined is incorrect. Moreover, they introduce the believer's good works at this point, which seems to be foreign both to the immediate and broader context of Romans.

Paul's emphasis throughout Romans is upon the importance of faith, which is extraspective in character—the believer looks to Christ by faith. Yet Wright and Dunn, for example, argue that the best translation is "from God's faithfulness to human faithfulness." This translation is certainly grammatically possible, but it goes against the grain of what Paul has written in the broader context of Romans (3:20–28) and especially in the immediate context of 1:17 and the quotation of Habakkuk 2:4, which we will explore momentarily.[34] Additionally, to introduce human faithfulness at the very threshold where Paul is about to introduce human

28. John Calvin, *Romans and Thessalonians*, trans. Ross Mackenzie, CNTC (Grand Rapids: Eerdmans, 1960), 28.
29. Karl Barth, *The Epistle to the Romans*, trans. Edwyn C. Hoskyns (1933; Oxford: Oxford University Press, 1968), 41.
30. Dunn, *Romans 1–8*, 43–44; Wright, *Romans*, 424–25.
31. John Murray, *The Epistle to the Romans*, NICNT (Grand Rapids: Eerdmans, 1968), 32.
32. Moo, *Romans*, 76.
33. Similarly, Watson, *Paul*, 51.
34. See Fitzmyer, *Romans*, 263.

unfaithfulness (Rom. 1:18–32), seems a bit out of place. What is it, then, that commends a combination of options (5) and (6)?

The answer comes from several other places in Paul. First, we turn to Romans 3:22 where Paul writes of "the righteousness of God through faith in Jesus Christ for all who believe" (cf. Gal. 3:22). John Murray explains that in Romans 3:22 the expression "for all who believe" (*eis pantas tous pisteuontas*) is unnecessary because Paul has already said that righteousness comes "through faith" (*dia pisteōs*). Why the double emphasis upon faith? Murray writes that the purpose of the repetition "is to accent the fact that not only does the righteousness of God bear savingly upon us *through faith* but also that it bears savingly upon *every one who believes*."[35] Hence we can gloss Romans 1:17 as "For in the gospel the righteousness of God is revealed through faith to those who believe."

Moo points out that we find a similar grammatical construction in another place in Paul's writings: "To one a fragrance from death to death, to the other a fragrance from life to life" (*hois men osmē ek thanatou eis thanaton, hois de osmē ek zōēs eis zōēn*) (2 Cor. 2:16). Here in 2 Corinthians 2:16 we find the same combination of prepositions that we find in Romans 1:17, and in the former the purpose is one of emphasis, whether of death or life. Hence the purpose in the latter, argues Moo, is clearly one of emphasis, in that "nothing but faith" can put us into a right relationship with God.[36] It seems, though, that the opinions of Murray and Moo are not at all mutually exclusive but are saying essentially the same thing, namely the centrality and importance of faith. This interpretation is confirmed by Paul's quotation of Habakkuk 2:4.

Paul quotes Habakkuk 2:4 to demonstrate his point, namely the centrality of faith in one's justification: "The righteous shall live by faith." Now, to be sure, the interpretation of Paul's quotation of Habakkuk 2:4 is debated. This is due to the textual variants involved with the verse in question. The MT states: *wetsaddiq be'emunato yihyeh* or "The righteous shall live by his faith." The MT has the pronoun "his," which emphasizes that the faith or faithfulness of the Israelite is in view. We must say faith or faithfulness because the latter typically defines the Hebrew term *'emunah*. The LXX, on the other hand, inserts the personal pronoun *mou*,

35. Murray, *Romans*, 32; similarly Moo, *Romans*, 76 (cf. 2 Cor. 2:16).
36. Moo, *Romans*, 76.

"my," after the word *pisteōs*: *ho de dikaios ek pisteōs mou zēsetai*, "But the just shall live by my faith." The LXX, therefore, translates Habakkuk 2:4 in such a way that it highlights God's faithfulness, not that of the Israelite. Now when Paul quotes Habakkuk 2:4, his quotation has the effect of bringing the verse closer to its original form because he does not include the personal pronoun: *ho de dikaios ek pisteōs zēsetai*, "The righteous shall live by faith."[37] So, then, how is one to understand Paul's use of Habakkuk 2:4 given these textual variants?

While there is difference of opinion regarding the route taken, it appears that Paul authoritatively interprets Habakkuk 2:4.[38] He uses the verse specifically against the notion that righteousness is obtained by one's works or faithfulness.[39] This certainly seems to be the import of his use of Habakkuk 2:4 in Galatians 3:11: "Now it is evident that no one is justified before God by the law, for 'The righteous shall live by faith.'" In other words, righteousness comes through faith, not through performing the works of the law. Once again, there is a stark contrast between Paul and a common opinion of his day. We read in the Dead Sea Scrolls' commentary on Habakkuk 2:4 that the verse "concerns all those who observe the Law in the House of Judah, whom God will deliver from the House of Judgment because of their suffering and because of their faith in the Teacher of Righteousness" (1QpHab 8.1–3).[40] There is an antithesis between the emphasis upon works in second-temple literature and Paul's emphasis upon faith. Murray explains this antithesis quite well:

We are required to ask how the principle of faith is so rigidly exclusive of and antithetical to works of the law in the matter of justification. The only answer is the specific quality of faith as opposed to that of works. Justification by works always finds its ground in that which the person is and does; it is always oriented to that consideration of the virtue attaching to the person justified. The specific quality of faith is trust and commitment to another; it is essentially extraspective and in that respect is the diametric opposite of works. Faith is self-renouncing; works are *self*-congratulatory. Faith looks to what God does; works have respect to what we are. It is

37. Schreiner, *Romans*, 71–75.
38. Watson, *Paul*, 154.
39. Ridderbos, *Paul*, 172.
40. Moisés Silva, *Interpreting Galatians* (Grand Rapids: Baker, 2001), 165–67; Watson, *Paul*, 112–26, 159–61.

this antithesis of principle that enables the apostle to base the complete exclusion of works upon the principle of faith.[41]

We must keep the extraspective character of faith in mind as we move forward. Faith looks without to the work of Christ and to his righteousness.

Summary

In all three texts, Paul highlights the centrality of the need for faith and its antithesis to works in justification. It is for this reason that historically the Reformed tradition has insisted upon *sola fide*: "Faith, thus receiving and resting on Christ and His righteousness, is the alone instrument of justification" (WCF 11.2a). We must therefore conclude that justification is by faith alone. We must continue, however, on to the next element involved in justification.

The Remission of Sins

The second component of justification that we must consider is the remission of sin. This element is evident in Romans 4:6–8: "David also speaks of the blessing of the one to whom God counts righteousness apart from works: 'Blessed are those whose lawless deeds are forgiven, and whose sins are covered; blessed is the man against whom the Lord will not count his sin.'" Here Paul quotes Psalm 32:1–2, which demonstrates once again that the doctrine of justification is firmly rooted in the OT. We also see in Paul's quotation that justification involves the forgiveness of sin. This is evident in the synonymous parallelism in verses 7–8. As Murray comments, "David's religion, therefore, was not one determined by the concept of good works but by that of the gracious remission of sin, and the blessedness regarded as the epitome of divine favor, had no affinity with that secured by works of merit."[42] We must understand, however, that justification is not merely the remission of sin. Indeed, "Justification embraces remission, and, in respect of the antithesis between works and faith, the specific character of justification is of that sort which remission exemplifies."[43] However, justification also involves the imputation

41. Murray, *Romans*, 123.
42. Ibid., 134.
43. Ibid., 135.

200

of righteousness.[44] We see interconnection between the imputation of righteousness and the remission of sin particularly in Romans 4:6–8.

Paul writes in Romans 4:6 that "David speaks of the blessing of the one to whom God counts righteousness apart from works" (*Dauid legei ton makarismon tou anthrōpou hō ho theos logizetai dikaiosynēn chōris ergōn*). It is important that we note Paul's use of the passive *logizetai*. God is the subject, not man; man cannot obtain righteousness by his works. Conversely, we also see in Romans 4:8 that "blessed is the man against whom the Lord will not count his sin" (*makarios anēr hou ou mē logisētai kyrios hamartian*). Again, notice Paul's use of *logizomai*; in this case we see the noncounting of sin in justification. Paul shows us that justification involves both the imputation of righteousness and the nonimputation of sin.[45] Hence, "justification must be forensic, as remission itself is."[46] The imputation of righteousness as part of one's justification naturally leads to the question, What is the source of righteousness in imputation? This question leads us to our third element.

The Imputation of Christ's Righteousness

We have thus far seen that justification (1) is by faith alone and (2) involves the remission of sins. It also entails (3) the imputation of righteousness. What is the source of righteousness? The source is Christ. There are two primary places where Paul elaborates upon the imputation of Christ's righteousness, 2 Corinthians 5:19–21 and Romans 5:19, though this is not to say that the doctrine is not found in other places in Scripture or in Paul (see, e.g., Lev. 16; 17:4; Ps. 32:2; Isa. 53:6–11; Zech. 3:1–5; Rom. 4:1–8, 22–24; James 2:23). We will briefly explore these two Pauline texts, though a fuller treatment will follow in the subsequent chapter on the doctrine of imputation.

2 Corinthians 5:19–21

Within the greater context of 2 Corinthians 5, Paul elaborates upon the ministry of reconciliation that has been given to him and the other apostles: "All this is from God, who through Christ reconciled us to

---

44. Contra Wright, *Romans*, 492–93; Dunn, *Romans 1–8*, 207.
45. Cranfield, *Romans*, 1:233; Carson, "Vindication of Imputation," 61; similarly Moo, *Romans*, 265–66; contra Wright, *Romans*, 492–93; cf. Dunn, *Romans 1–8*, 229–30.
46. Murray, *Romans*, 134.

himself and gave us the ministry of reconciliation" (2 Cor. 5:18). What is the specific nature of the reconciliation? Paul explains how God has reconciled the world to himself. The word order of verse 19 emphasizes that God was "in Christ" reconciling the world to himself. How did God accomplish this in Christ? Paul states that God was "not counting their trespasses against them" (*mē logizomenos autois ta paraptōmata*) (v. 19b). Once again we see the verb *logizomai* resurface, the idea that God was not counting the sins of the world. What happens to the sin that is not counted to the world? Though the text does not explicitly say it, Paul implies that the sin is imputed to Christ: "For our sake he made him to be sin who knew no sin" (2 Cor. 5:21a). Again, God does not write off the sin, but instead Christ bears the guilt and penalty for the sin of God's people. We do see the other side of the equation in verse 21b: "So that in him we might become the righteousness of God."

The dual nature of the imputation, the imputation of sin to Christ and his righteousness to believers, is evident in the parallel structure of the verse (fig. 6).[47]

Fig. 6. Structure of 2 Corinthians 5:21

a	b	c	d
ton mē gnonta hamartian	*hyper hēmōn*	*hamartian*	*epoiēsen*
Him who knew not sin	**on our behalf**	**sin**	**he made**

hina			
in order that			

a′	d′	c′	b′
hēmeis	*genōmetha*	*dikaiosynē theou*	*en autō*
we	**might become**	**the righteousness of God**	**in him**

Calvin succinctly explains the nature of this double imputation:

> How can we become righteous before God? In the same way as Christ became a sinner. For He took, as it were, our person, that He might be the offender in our name and thus might be reckoned a sinner, not because of His own offences but because of those of others, since He Himself was

47. C. K. Barrett, *The Second Epistle to the Corinthians*, BNTC (Peabody, MA: Hendrickson, 1983), 179; contra N. T. Wright, "On Becoming the Righteousness of God: 2 Corinthians 5:21," in *Pauline Theology*, ed. David M. Hay (Atlanta: SBL, 2002), 2:200–8.

pure and free from every fault and bore the penalty that was our due and not His own. Now in the same way we are righteous in Him, not because we have satisfied God's judgment by our own works, but because we are judged in relation to Christ's righteousness which we have put on by faith, that it may become our own.[48]

This passage, then, shows us in greater detail what Paul wrote in Romans 4:1–8 concerning the relationship between the remission of sins and the imputation of righteousness. The sin does not drift away into the night but is placed upon the shoulders of Christ on the cross. Yet this is not the only place where Paul explicates the concept of double imputation. We must also examine Romans 5:19.

Romans 5:19

To say the least, Romans 5:12–19 is a passage that is steeped in the doctrine of imputation. Paul elaborates upon the connections between the two federal heads, the first and last Adams. This is evident when Paul writes in Romans 5:14: "Yet death reigned from Adam to Moses, even over those whose sinning was not like the transgression of Adam, who was a type of the one who was to come." We must see that Adam is a *typos*, or type, of the one who was to come, namely Christ.[49] It is important, though, that we also see the connection between Adam and his sin and Christ and his obedience. First, note the connection that Paul makes between Adam and those after him: "Sin came into the world through one man, and death through sin, and so death spread to all men because all sinned" (Rom. 5:12). Paul makes the connection between the sin of Adam and the spread of death. All men die because of Adam's sin. Paul drives his point even harder when he writes: "For sin indeed was in the world before the law was given, but sin is not counted where there is no law. Yet death reigned from Adam to Moses, even over those whose sinning was not like the transgression of Adam" (Rom. 5:13–14c).

Notice that death reigned from the time of Adam's sin to Moses, who is a synecdoche for the Mosaic covenant and the administration of the law at Mount Sinai. Paul establishes a parallel between Adam and Israel

---

48. John Calvin, *2 Corinthians and Timothy, Titus and Philemon*, trans. T. A. Smail, ed. David W. Torrance and T. F. Torrance, CNTC 10 (Grand Rapids: Eerdmans, 1960), 78; see also Carson, "Vindication of Imputation," 69.

49. Moo, *Romans*, 333–34; Dunn, *Romans 1–8*, 277.

in terms of the directly revealed command(s), whether in the prohibition against eating from the tree of knowledge or in the revealed law (Torah) at Sinai. In this way, using the terms of systematic theology, we can see how Paul establishes a parallel between the covenant of works and the Mosaic covenant and the demand for perfect obedience (cf. Lev. 18:5; Rom. 10:5; Gal. 3:10). How is it possible that men die when their sin was unlike Adam's, namely they did not disobey a directly revealed command of God as Adam did?[50] The answer is back in verse 12; Adam's sin and guilt were imputed to his offspring, and for this reason all men die because "the wages of sin is death" (Rom. 6:23a).[51] The Adam-death connection is only one side of the equation, as Paul also elaborates upon the Christ-life connection.

Paul contrasts the death that comes through Adam with the life that comes through Christ: "But the free gift is not like the trespass. For if many died through one man's trespass, much more have the grace of God and the free gift by the grace of that one man Jesus Christ abounded for many" (v. 15). This parallel becomes more pronounced in verse 19: "For as by the one man's disobedience the many were made sinners, so by the one man's obedience the many will be made righteous." We see once again familiar language; recall that God made Christ to be sin. God imputed the sin of the believer to Christ. Here in verse 19 we see both sides of the equation quite clearly: By Adam's sin the many were made sinners, but by Christ's obedience many are made righteous. Murray succinctly explains that "the parallel to the imputation of Adam's sin is the imputation of Christ's righteousness. Or to use Paul's own terms, being 'constituted sinners' through the disobedience of Adam is parallel to being 'constituted righteous' through the obedience of Christ."[52]

Summary

In these two passages we see the inextricable link between justification and double imputation. God does not simply write off sin when he

---

50. Moo, *Romans*, 333.

51. Moo, *Romans*, 331–32; Fitzmyer, *Romans*, 416–17; contra Wright, *Romans*, 525–27, esp. 526; Dunn, *Romans 1–8*, 273–74; for different interpretive options see Fitzmyer, *Romans*, 413–17.

52. John Murray, *The Imputation of Adam's Sin* (Philadelphia: P&R, 1959), 76; see also Fitzmyer, *Romans*, 421–22; Moo, *Romans*, 344–46; Cranfield, *Romans*, 1:290–91; cf. Dunn, *Romans 1–8*, 297.

forgives the believer. Rather, God imputes the sin and guilt of the believer to Christ, who has borne the penalty for that sin and guilt upon the cross. At the same time God imputes the righteousness and perfect obedience of Christ to the believer. Sever either the remission of sins or the imputation of Christ's righteousness, and the sinner stands inextricably in a quandary, as the sinner requires not only the forgiveness of sins but also the righteousness and obedience of Christ. If the believer receives only the remission of sins, then justification would not be possible, as God would have to postpone his judgment to await the outcome, to wait and see whether the void of sin would be filled by obedience. This, however, is not the nature of our justification because when God eliminates our sin he fills the void with the perfect obedience of Jesus Christ, and right then and there the believer, like Abraham, is counted righteous, and indefectibly so because God has imputed the righteousness of Christ to the believer. This means that historic Reformed expressions of justification by faith alone are correct.

The Westminster divines, for example, correctly define justification in the following manner:

> Q. What is justification?
> A. Justification is an act of God's free grace unto sinners, in which he pardons all their sins, accepts and accounts their persons righteous in his sight; not for any thing wrought in them, or done by them, but only for the perfect obedience and full satisfaction of Christ, by God imputed to them, and received by faith alone. (LC 70)

The divines elaborate more thoroughly upon the forensic nature of justification when they write:

> Those whom God effectually calls He also freely justifies; not by infusing righteousness into them, but by pardoning their sins, and by accounting and accepting their persons as righteous: not for anything wrought in them, or done by them, but for Christ's sake alone: nor by imputing faith itself, the act of believing, or any other evangelical obedience, to them as their righteousness; but by imputing the obedience and satisfaction of Christ unto them, they receiving and resting on Him and His righteousness, by faith: which faith they have not of themselves; it is the gift of God. (WCF 11.1)

In both quotations we see that the divines emphasize the very points that Paul elaborates throughout Romans. They place emphasis upon the instrumental nature of faith and identify the material cause of justification as Christ's righteousness.[53] Now at this point in our investigation we have largely focused our attention upon issues that relate to the *ordo salutis* and justification. To be sure, we have inevitably dealt with matters that pertain to the *historia salutis*, particularly the inextricable link between the believer's justification and Christ's work in history. It is the connection between justification and the *historia salutis* that requires further expansion and exploration.

Justification and the *Historia Salutis*

As we have noted from the beginning of the study, we must constantly remember our place in redemptive history. One's justification is inextricably linked with the work of the last Adam, Jesus Christ. The connection is of course quite clear in the crucifixion of Christ as we have noted, but we must also recognize the connection of justification to the resurrection of Christ. The connection between justification and Christ's resurrection is most prominent in Romans 4:23–25. In exploring this text we will also examine the christological and eschatological connections to justification.

Romans 4:23–25

Within the broader context of Romans 4 Paul has explained the nature of justification, that it is by faith in Christ and that it results in the remission of sins and the imputation of righteousness. Paul then explains that the words of Genesis 15:6 were not written for Abraham's sake alone: "But the words 'it was counted to him' were not written for his sake alone, but for ours also. It will be counted to us who believe in him who raised from the dead Jesus our Lord, who was delivered up for our trespasses and raised for our justification" (Rom. 4:23–25). Paul states that those

53. This is a point that some seem to miss. One author, for example, confuses both Paul's and the Reformation position when he writes: "If the acquittal is based on faith, how can it also be based on works, which for Paul stand in direct opposition to faith?" (VanLandingham, *Judgment*, 10). The Reformers, or Paul for that matter, do not state that the acquittal is based *on* faith, but rather that the acquittal comes *by* faith, which looks to the works of Christ, the ground of the acquittal.

who believe in God the Father, who raised Jesus Christ from the dead, will receive the forensic declaration that they are righteous, like Abraham before them. Now there is a natural connection between the forgiveness of sins and the crucifixion of Christ—he was crucified "for our trespasses." Here we find a clear allusion to Isaiah 53:12 and the suffering servant, the one who suffers for the sins of Israel. There is, however, the curious and at first glance seemingly out-of-place connection to the resurrection of Christ. What is the connection between the resurrection and the justification of God's people?

Christology and Justification

Paul's curious statement has been variously explained, but the most convincing answer comes from the connections between Christology, eschatology, and soteriology. We must note the causal relationship between Christ's death and resurrection and the forgiveness of sins and justification. Notice that there is a parallel between Christ's crucifixion and resurrection: Christ was delivered *dia*, for or because of, our sins—this demonstrates a causal link. The same causal link exists between our justification and Christ's resurrection: Christ was raised *dia*, for or because of, our justification (Rom. 4:25). This means that Christ's resurrection confirms and authenticates that our justification has been secured.[54] In what way, though, does Christ's resurrection confirm and authenticate our justification?

Some have explained that Christ's resurrection is connected to our justification because it represents the vindication of Jesus.[55] While it is certainly true that in some sense Christ's resurrection was a vindication, we cannot look at the resurrection purely in terms of vindication. In more than several places Paul makes the resurrection of Christ the power of soteriological realities. Christ, writes Paul, "has been raised from the dead, in order that we may bear fruit for God" (Rom. 7:4). The resurrection is also linked to Christ's current priestly intercession (Rom. 8:34). We also see Paul explain, "If Christ has not been raised, your faith is futile and you are still in your sins" (1 Cor. 15:17).[56] In other words, one cannot receive the forgiveness of sins if Christ remains dead in the

---

54. Schreiner, *Romans*, 243–44; Cranfield, *Romans*, 1:252.
55. So Wright, *Romans*, 504.
56. Dunn, *Romans 1–8*, 225.

tomb. If Christ remains dead in the tomb, then the powers of sin and death have not been conquered and Christ's crucifixion was legitimate, for the wages of sin is death (Rom. 6:23). In this regard, then, we can say that the resurrection of Christ not only secures the victory over Satan, sin, and death, but it also authenticates the victory as well.

If Christ has been raised, Christ has conquered sin and death, and death had no claim over him, which means that his sacrifice was acceptable and that the sins of God's people have been atoned.[57] Vos explains the significance of Christ's resurrection as it pertains to justification:

> The resurrection thus comes out of justification, and justification comes, after a manner most carefully to be defined, out of the resurrection; not, be it noted, out of the spiritual resurrection of the believer himself, but out of the resurrection of Christ. On the basis of merit this is so. Christ's resurrection was the *de facto* declaration of God in regard to his being just. His quickening bears in itself the testimony of his justification. God, through suspending the forces of death operating on Him, declared that the ultimate, the supreme consequence of sin had reached its termination. In other words, resurrection had annulled the sentence of condemnation.[58]

There is, then, an inextricable link between Christology and justification in that the life, death, and resurrection of Christ are absolutely indispensable. Christ's death atones for the sins of God's people; his resurrection is the evidence that death had an illegitimate claim upon him, for he lived his life in perfect obedience to the law. Attempt to extract one of the three, life, death, or resurrection, from justification, and our redemption collapses. We should not, however, miss the eschatological connection to justification especially as it relates to the resurrection.

Eschatology and Justification

We must remember that justification is firmly rooted in the soil of eschatology. It is eschatological for several reasons. First, justification is connected to the resurrection of Christ, which is an eschatological event. This is especially evident when Paul links the resurrection of believers with Christ's resurrection in 1 Corinthians 15:45: "Thus it is written,

57. Cranfield, *Romans*, 1:252; Moo, *Romans*, 289–90.
58. Geerhardus Vos, *The Pauline Eschatology* (1930; Phillipsburg, NJ: P&R, 1994), 151.

'The first man Adam became a living being'; the last Adam became a life-giving Spirit."[59] Here Paul's two-age structure of history is clearly evident, the first and last Adams.[60] Moreover, it is the resurrection of Christ that inaugurates the eschatological age. The eschaton has dawned with the resurrection of Christ, who is the firstfruits of the eschatological harvest, and now we simply await the conclusion of this present evil age (1 Cor. 15:20–28; Gal. 1:4). There is, then, a clear connection between eschatology and justification—one cannot divorce justification from its redemptive historical context and inextricable link to Christ's resurrection. This, however, is not the only eschatological connection with justification.

If the resurrection signals the acceptance of Christ's sacrifice and the conquest of sin and death, then it also stands to reason that Christ's death brings forward the day of judgment, but God's wrath falls, not upon the believer, but upon Christ on the cross. Vos notes:

> Here lies precisely the point where eschatology and justification intersect. By making both the negative element of the forgiveness of sin and the positive element of bestowal of the benefits of salvation unqualified, the Apostle made the act of justification to all intents, so far as the believer is concerned, a last judgment anticipated. If the act dealt with present and past sins only, leaving the future product in uncertainty, it could not be regarded as possessing such absoluteness, and the comparison with the last judgment would break down at the decisive point.[61]

Justification, therefore, opens the eschatological world of the age to come to the one who places his faith in Jesus Christ. The final judgment is brought forward as well as the declaration of righteousness—Christ bears the eschatological wrath of God on the cross, the foundation of the remission of sins, and God imputes the perfect obedience of Christ to the believer.[62]

59. Modified ESV.

60. Vos, *Pauline Eschatology*, 10.

61. Ibid., 55.

62. The absence of acknowledging the eschatological nature of justification is a key difference between Reformed and Roman Catholic views that often goes unnoted. An exception is George Hunsinger, "*Fides Christo Formata*: Luther, Barth, and the Joint Declaration," in *The Gospel of Justification in Christ*, ed. Wayne C. Stumme (Grand Rapids: Eerdmans, 2006), 69–84; cf. VanLandingham, *Judgment*, 199.

Summary

When we examine the doctrine of justification, we must never sever it from the *historia salutis*. If we do so, we create an abstract system of doctrine divorced from history and can quickly lose sight of the concrete, historical, and hence christological cast of justification. Moreover, we also fail to recognize that justification is eschatological, which brings comfort for those believers who look to the day of judgment in fear. Quite literally, justification becomes the entry point to the eschatological age; this aspect must not be lost. The *ordo salutis* must not swallow up the *historia salutis*.

Conclusion

We have examined that justification is: (1) by faith alone; (2) the remission of sins; and (3) the imputation of righteousness. We have also seen that all three of these elements find their significance in the person and work of Christ, his life, death, and resurrection. For the believer must look to Christ in faith to receive the forgiveness of sins and the imputation of his righteousness. We have also seen how this aspect of soteriology is rooted in redemptive history and especially eschatology. Justification, however, is not the only doctrine in soteriology. To isolate justification from the rest of the *ordo salutis* would do violence to the teaching of Scripture. We will explore the key elements of the *ordo salutis*, then, and see the relationships to justification. We must first explore the conclusions raised thus far vis-à-vis the recent challenges of the New Perspective on Paul, primarily through dialogue with N. T. Wright. We will explore the claims of the New Perspective concerning justification and imputation.

8

JUSTIFICATION AND THE NEW PERSPECTIVE ON PAUL

With the rise of the New Perspective on Paul (NPP) there have been many modifications offered to the traditional Protestant view on many teachings within the Scriptures.[1] With Stendhal's ground-breaking essay, followed by the work of Sanders and Dunn, the NPP has challenged the typical reading of the Gospels and Paul, citing the need to read the New Testament (NT) within its first-century context, not in the context of the debates over justification, whether in fifth-century north Africa or sixteenth-century Europe.[2] In this recontextualized evaluation of the teaching of the NT, some scholars of the NPP claim that not works-righteousness and legalism, but the inclusion of the Gentiles into

1. This chapter is a revised and modified version of J. V. Fesko, "A Critical Examination of N. T. Wright's Doctrine of Justification," *Confessional Presbyterian* 1 (2005): 102–15.
2. Krister Stendhal, "The Apostle Paul and the Introspective Conscience of the West," in *Paul among Jews and Gentiles* (Minneapolis: Fortress, 1976), 78–96; E. P. Sanders, *Paul and Palestinian Judaism* (Minneapolis: Fortress, 1977), 1–29; James D. G. Dunn, *Jesus, Paul and the Law* (Louisville: Westminster John Knox, 1990), 183–241.

211

the covenant people of God was at the heart of Paul's teaching. Central to Paul's message, NPP proponents claim, is the proper understanding of the phrase "the works of the law." This phrase refers not to crass legalism but to the covenant badges, circumcision, food laws, and Sabbath observance. In other words, could Gentiles be admitted to the covenant apart from the covenant badges? It is within this matrix that one finds the traditional Protestant doctrine of justification by faith alone set on an entirely different trajectory.

We have already seen the improbability of the NPP interpretation of the phrase "works of the law." Nevertheless, it is still necessary to explore the specific claims of the NPP vis-à-vis the doctrine of justification. N. T. Wright, one of the most popular and prolific proponents of the NPP, contends that the doctrine of justification

> in the first century was not about how someone might establish a relationship with God. It was about God's eschatological definition, both future and present, of who was, in fact, a member of his people. In Sanders' terms, it was not so much about "getting in," or indeed about "staying in," as about "how you could tell who was in." In standard Christian theological language, it wasn't so much about soteriology as about ecclesiology; not so much about salvation as about the church.[3]

Central to Wright's claim is that justification is about ecclesiology, or sociology, not soteriology.[4] If Wright's claim about justification is true, then, needless to say, the NPP represents something of a Copernican revolution in the church's understanding of the Scriptures. This chapter will argue that the NPP, specifically Wright's doctrine of justification, represents an incorrect reading of the NT. The traditional Protestant reading as it comes from Reformed confessionalism, specifically the Westminster Standards, and what has been expounded in the previous chapter, is still correct. To demonstrate Wright's errors we will first examine his doctrine of justification as he has presented it in his popular and academic works. Second, we will critique his views on justification,

3. N. T. Wright, *What Saint Paul Really Said* (Grand Rapids: Eerdmans, 1997), 119.
4. N. T. Wright, "The Letter to the Galatians: Exegesis and Theology," in *Between Two Horizons*, ed. Joel B. Green and Max Turner (Grand Rapids: Eerdmans, 2002), 233–34.

demonstrating that Reformed confessionalism still represents the teaching of the Scriptures.

Wright on Justification by Faith

Central to Wright's understanding of justification are two key tenets: (1) a proper understanding of the term "righteousness," and (2) what a first-century Jew would have understood by the term "justification." One should also examine Wright's specific evidence in support of his views, namely his exegesis of Romans 4:1–8. How, then, does Wright define the term "righteousness"?

Righteousness

It is important, Wright argues, to understand properly the concept of righteousness. Righteousness is not something that is imputed to the Christian by faith, as argued in traditional Reformed explanations of justification, but rather is a demonstration of God's faithfulness to his covenant promises. Common exegesis of Paul, alleges Wright, has involved the imposition of doctrinal categories from the sixteenth, seventeenth, and eighteenth centuries, categories that are foreign to Paul's first-century Jewish worldview.[5] The first-century Jew was not concerned about how one might have a saving relationship with God. Rather, the first-century Jew was already a member of the covenant and possessed a relationship with his covenant Lord. What was perplexing for the first-century Jew was, how could the chosen people of God be under the Roman occupation? Had not God promised in his covenant to Abraham that Israel would rule over the nations? Yet Israel was under the thumb of Rome. Though Israel was in the promised land, they were essentially in exile. It is with these questions that God's righteousness, or covenant faithfulness, enters the picture.

Wright argues that "righteousness" refers to God's covenant faithfulness: "The question of the righteousness of god, as expressed by Jews in this period, can be stated as follows: when and how would Israel's god act to fulfill his covenant promises?"[6] In other words, when would God bring

---

5. N. T. Wright, *The Climax of the Covenant* (Minneapolis: Fortress, 1993), 17, 122.

6. N. T. Wright, *The New Testament and the People of God* (Minneapolis: Fortress, 1992), 271.

the Israelites out of exile, out from under Roman rule? Wright argues that God's covenant faithfulness, or righteousness, is the major theme of Paul's epistle to Rome and is the primary focus of Romans 3:21–4:25: "'God's righteousness'—that is, God's faithfulness to the covenant with Abraham—has been unveiled in the gospel events concerning Jesus."[7] Wright states that God's covenantal faithfulness, or righteousness, was manifest through Christ's ministry—Christ had dealt with the covenant curses due Israel, and began to lead her out of exile and inaugurate the eschaton, the age to come: "Israel's god had at last acted decisively, to demonstrate his covenant faithfulness, to deliver his people from their sins, and to usher in the inaugurated new covenant."[8] The righteousness of God, then, is primarily a demonstration of his covenantal faithfulness. Texts such as Romans 1:17, then, should be read as: "For in [the gospel] the righteousness [covenantal faithfulness] of God is revealed."[9] This primary significance of the term "righteousness" of course has implications for Wright's views on justification.

Wright argues that the divine righteousness, or covenant faithfulness, is not the same thing as the righteousness that humans possess when they are declared members of the covenant. Wright states:

In the Hebrew law court the judge does not give, bestow, impute, or impart *his own "righteousness"* to the defendant. That would imply that the *defendant* was deemed to have conducted the case impartially, in accordance with the law, to have punished sin and upheld the defense-less innocent ones. "Justification," of course, means nothing like that. "Righteousness" is not a quality or substance that can thus be passed or transferred from the judge to the defendant. The righteousness of the judge is the judge's own character, status, and activity, demonstrated in doing these various things. The "righteousness" of the defendants is the status they possess when the court has found in their favor. Nothing more, nothing less. When we translate these forensic categories back into their theological context, that of the covenant, the point remains

---

7. Wright, *People of God*, 458; also idem, *The Resurrection of the Son of God* (Minneapolis: Fortress, 2003), 246.

8. Wright, *People of God*, 458.

9. On Romans 1:17 see Wright, *Saint Paul*, 100–103; also idem, *Romans*, NIB (Nashville: Abingdon, 2003), 425–28.

fundamental: the divine covenant faithful is not the same as human covenant membership.[10]

This statement is an important element of Wright's view on justification. God's righteousness remains his own. God does not impute his righteousness to the member of the covenant. Wright stipulates that though the same word, "righteousness," is used for both God's covenant faithfulness and the human's status within the covenant, it demonstrates only their close reciprocal relationship, not their identity.[11] Wright argues that when the term "righteousness" is used in connection with human beings, it means "membership within the covenant."[12] In other words, the righteous God, one who is faithful to his covenant, declares those who place their faith in Christ to be righteous, members of the covenant, or recipients of God's covenantal faithfulness. This understanding of righteousness, both human and divine, informs Wright's understanding of justification.

Justification

Wright argues that there are three foundational presuppositions that one must understand before he can properly understand the doctrine of justification. First, Scripture speaks of justification in terms of covenant. One must not read justification in terms of the covenant theology of the sixteenth and seventeenth centuries, but in terms of second-temple Judaism and the covenant promises that God made to his people. Second, justification is spoken of in terms of law-court language. When God made his covenant promise to Abraham, patriarch of the people of God, it was God's way of correcting the sin of Adam and putting the world to rights. In the law court the people of God will be vindicated before the world and shown to be "in the right." Third, Scripture speaks of justification in terms of eschatology. Justification is not part of some abstract system of doctrine by which people are saved, but is rooted in the decisive action of God in Jesus Christ whereby he rescues the cosmos from sin through the Holy Spirit, bringing all things under the authority of Jesus.[13] From

10. N. T. Wright, "Romans and the Theology of Paul," in *Pauline Theology*, ed. David M. Hay and E. Elizabeth Johnson (Minneapolis: Fortress, 1995), 3:38–39.
11. Ibid., 3:39.
12. Wright, *Covenant*, 148; idem, *Romans*, 465, 491.
13. Wright, *Saint Paul*, 117–18.

these three premises, one can begin to see the nature of Wright's view of justification emerge.

Justification is not about the imputation of a communicable attribute of God to the one who professes faith in Christ. Rather, justification is the vindication of the covenant people of God before the world. Justification is about demonstrating that the people of God are "in the right" before the unbelieving world, those who refuse to place their faith in Jesus Christ and oppress the people of God. The people of God had placed their faith in the one true God who, through the covenant, would put the world to rights. What was difficult for the Israelites is that it appeared as though God was doing nothing to fulfil his unbreakable covenant—the Israelites were in exile under Roman rule. When and how would God vindicate, or justify, the people of God?[14] Wright summarizes the overall context in which one finds the Scripture's message of justification:

a. The creator god calls Israel to be his people;
b. Israel, currently in "exile," is to be redeemed, precisely because she is the covenant people of this god;
c. Present loyalty to the covenant is the sign of future redemption;
d. Loyalty to this covenant is being tested at this moment of crisis;
e. At this moment, what counts as loyalty, and hence what marks out those who will be saved/vindicated/raised to life, is . . .[15]

Though Wright ends his last summary point with an ellipsis, he eventually fills in the blank with "faith in Jesus Christ."

Jesus Christ was the ultimate fulfilment of the covenant promise that God made to Abraham. Loyalty to the covenant was no longer to be demonstrated by a commitment to Torah and its attendant badges of covenant membership, circumcision, food laws, and Sabbath observance, but by the new sign of covenant membership, faith in Christ. No longer were the covenant members to see the Torah as the rallying point of the covenant, but Jesus himself.[16] Moreover, if Torah no longer defined the covenant

14. N. T. Wright, *Jesus and the Victory of God* (Minneapolis: Fortress, 1996), 203.
15. Wright, *People of God*, 335.
16. Wright, *Victory of God*, 201.

people of God but faith in Christ was their membership badge, Gentiles could now be a part of the covenant people apart from the traditional Jewish identity badges. How one defines the people of God is the central issue of justification, argues Wright. Are the people of God, the recipients of the righteousness of God, covenant faithfulness, marked by the badges of membership, circumcision, food laws, and Sabbath, or by faith in Jesus Christ? This was the nature of the debate at Galatia and the substance of Paul's epistle to the Romans, not crass works-righteousness or legalism.[17] There is a twofold division of justification that Wright stresses: (1) present justification—namely the vindication that people possess presently, which is marked out by their faith in Christ and indicates who will be vindicated in the end; and (2) final or future justification—the actual declaration of being "in the right" before the world. The idea of justification as vindication, then, is the primary thrust of Wright's understanding of the doctrine. What specific evidence does Wright marshal in support of his view of justification?

Wright on Romans 4:1–8

Though not comprehensive in nature, examining Wright's understanding of Romans 4:1–8 will help the investigator see how he arrives at his conclusions regarding justification. Wright begins his analysis of Romans 4 by explaining that this chapter is about Abraham's family, not the traditional Reformed view of justification by faith. He contends that the chapter hinges on the question of whether Jews and Gentiles can point to Abraham as their father.[18] Wright then goes on to analyze verse 2: "For if Abraham was justified by works, he has something to boast about, but not before God." Wright states that Paul is not dealing with self-help legalism, but that Paul is saying that Abraham was not justified, vindicated, or reckoned within the covenant by the works of the Torah, circumcision, food laws, and Sabbath. The works of Torah were the identity markers of Jews, not Gentiles. In this verse, according to Wright, Paul is saying that Abraham is not reckoned as a member of the covenant by the Jewish identity markers. Paul's point is to deny the Jews grounds for boasting

17. Wright, *People of God*, 241.
18. Wright, *Romans*, 489.

because of their Jewish identity and possession of Torah (Rom. 2:17–20; 3:27–30).[19] Wright goes on to explain in the following verse.

Paul writes: "For what does the Scripture say? 'Abraham believed God, and it was counted to him as righteousness'" (4:3). Here Wright explains that the phrase "it was counted to him" (*elogisthē*) is a book-keeping metaphor, though the phrase is rare. He argues that the meaning of the phrase must therefore be sought in the Genesis account and the rest of Romans 4; the idea is also restated in Psalm 106:31 and in *Misqat ma'ase ha-torah* (MMT) C. Wright enters first upon the meaning of the phrase within its original context in Genesis 15. Genesis 15 opens with Abraham's puzzlement because God has made great promises to him, but has yet to fulfil them. God promised him children, yet Abraham has none. Wright identifies the promise as that Abraham would have a family as numerous as the stars in heaven. Because Abraham believed this promise, God reckoned his belief in the promise, argues Wright, as righteousness. Righteousness, one must remember, is not a moral quality but covenant membership. Wright paraphrases the quotation from Genesis 15 as "God counted Abraham's faith as constituting covenant membership," or "Abraham's believing the promise was seen by God as the sign that Abraham was 'in the right.'"[20]

Wright then explains that Paul briefly uses a bookkeeping metaphor in Romans 4:4–5 to explain the significance of verse 3: "Now to the one who works, his wages are not counted as a gift but as his due. And to the one who does not work but trusts him who justifies the ungodly, his faith is counted as righteousness." Wright argues that Paul uses verse 4 to suggest the hypothetical situation that had Abraham obtained his status by works, then his place within the covenant would not have been by God's grace. Wright stipulates that this is the only time that Paul "uses this metaphorical field in all his discussion of justification, and we should not allow this unique and brief sidelight to become the dominant note, as it has in much post-Reformation discussion."[21] The main point is:

> One who believes in this God, therefore, will discover that this "faith" will be regarded, not as a meritorious spiritual act (how could that be,

19. Ibid., 490.
20. Ibid., 490–91.
21. Ibid., 491.

for the "ungodly"?), but as the badge of covenant membership given by God in sheer grace. And already the answer to the opening question of v. 1 is starting to emerge: We (Jewish and Gentile Christians alike) have not found Abraham to be our father according to the flesh, but according to God's promise.[22]

In support of this conclusion, Wright explains that Paul calls upon a second witness beyond Abraham, King David.

In verse 6 Paul explains: "David also speaks of the blessing of the one to whom God counts righteousness apart from works." He then goes on to quote Psalm 32:1–2 (31:1–2 LXX): "Blessed are those whose lawless deeds are forgiven, and whose sins are covered; blessed is the man against whom the Lord will not count his sin" (vv. 7–8). Here Wright argues that Paul uses this quotation to show what it means to be counted as righteous, or as a member of the covenant. To be counted as righteous means to be forgiven of sin, not that one has moral perfection. This means, then, that according to Wright Romans 4:1–8 explains how Abraham's family can have both Jew and Gentile, that the sign of covenant membership is faith, not the works of Torah, and that those who are righteous, covenant members, receive the forgiveness of sins. This is what it means, according to Wright's understanding of Paul, to be justified by faith, or vindicated and reckoned as a member of the covenant. Before we proceed to a critical analysis of Wright's understanding of justification, it will be helpful to summarize his views.

Summary

To understand Wright's views on justification one must recognize that justification is rooted in redemptive history, the outworking of the covenant promise of God. Justification is a manifestation of the covenant faithfulness of God, his righteousness, in sending Jesus to put the world to rights. Those who place their faith in Christ, the new sign of the covenant, are vindicated in the present (present justification), and identified as those who will be vindicated in the future (final justification). Justification is covenantal, because Jesus is the one who brings about the vindication of the people of God, the fulfilment of God's covenant promises. Justification is a law-court metaphor, which manifests itself in the declaration

22. Ibid., 492.

JUSTIFICATION AND THE NEW PERSPECTIVE ON PAUL

of vindication for those who place their faith in Jesus. And justification is eschatological, in that it is the in-breaking of the age to come in the middle of history—the in-breaking of the lordship of Jesus, the one who will vindicate his people and put the world to rights.

Wright's overview statement of Romans 3:21–4:25 does well to summarize his beliefs concerning justification:

> Faith then becomes the badge that identifies, in the present time, the members of the people of God. This is the meaning of Paul's doctrine of "justification by faith." The verdict of the last day has been brought forward into the present in Jesus the Messiah; in raising him from the dead, God declared that in him had been constituted the true, forgiven worldwide family. Justification, in Paul, is not the process or event whereby someone becomes, or grows as, a Christian; it is the declaration that someone is, in the present, a member of the people of God. This is inevitably controversial, but is I believe borne out by careful study of the relevant texts. We may remind ourselves of the triple layer of meaning in Paul's "righteousness" language: The covenantal declaration, seen through the metaphorical and vital lens of the law-court, is put into operation eschatologically. The verdict to be announced in the future has been brought forward into the present. Those who believe the gospel are declared to be "in the right."[23]

With this summary of Wright's teaching on justification, we may now move forward to a critical examination of his doctrine.

A Critical Examination of Wright's Doctrine of Justification

Our critique will focus on two primary questions: (1) does the term "righteousness" mean "membership in the covenant"; and (2) does Scripture speak of justification in terms of vindication or being "in the right"?[24] Is the declaration of righteousness for one who enters the covenant a declaration of membership, as Wright contends, or is it that God "accepts us as righteous in his sight, only for the righteousness of Christ

---

23. Ibid., 468.
24. On the question of the nature of the righteousness of God, see Wright, *Saint Paul,* 97–111; idem, *People of God,* 271, 336–37, 458; cf. C. E. B. Cranfield, *Romans,* 2 vols., ICC (1975; Edinburgh: T & T Clark, 2001), 1:91–106; Mark A. Seifrid, "Righteousness Language in the Hebrew Scriptures and Early Judaism," in *Justification and Variegated Nomism,* ed. D. A. Carson et al., 2 vols. (Grand Rapids: Baker, 2001), 1:415–42.

imputed to us," as the Westminster Shorter Catechism states (q. 33)? Also, is Wright's explanation of Romans 4:1–8 accurate? We may turn to the first issue, namely, Is the term "righteousness" best understood as "covenant membership"?

Righteousness

As we saw above, a key element to Wright's understanding of justification is that when the Scriptures speak of a person's righteousness, they are referring to his status of covenant membership. We will examine several passages of Scripture to demonstrate that Wright's definition is wanting. There are places in Scripture where Wright's proposed understanding might be a possibility; however, upon closer scrutiny there are other passages that simply do not fit Wright's definition. One such passage is Job 29:11–17. In Job's speech he defends his life and character from the accusations of Eliphaz: "For you have exacted pledges of your brothers for nothing and stripped the naked of their clothing. You have given no water to the weary to drink, and you have withheld bread from the hungry. The man with power possessed the land, and the favored man lived in it. You have sent widows away empty, and the arms of the fatherless were crushed" (Job 22:6–9).

Note that Eliphaz's accusations describe Job as morally deficient. Job responds to these accusations: "I put on righteousness, and it clothed me; my justice was like a robe and a turban. I was eyes to the blind and feet to the lame. I was a father to the needy, and I searched out the cause of him whom I did not know. I broke the fangs of the unrighteous and made him drop his prey from his teeth" (Job 29:14–17). One must note that Job clothed himself in righteousness (*tsedeq*), and righteousness clothed him, what the second half of the synonymous parallelism in verse 14b explains as Job's justice (*mishpat*)(cf. Ps. 132:9; Isa. 6:5; 59:17; 61:10). Job's righteousness is not characterized as covenant membership, as Wright contends, but as justice: verses 15–17 describe Job as assisting the blind and the poor and opposing the unrighteous.[25] These verses, then, represent "a strong claim both to right behavior and right status, the assertion of which is the whole point of Job's closing speech."[26]

25. John E. Hartley, *The Book of Job*, NICOT (Grand Rapids: Eerdmans, 1988), 391.

26. David J. Reimer, "*tzdq*," in *NIDOTTE*, 3:760; Norman C. Habel, *The Book of Job*, OTL (Philadelphia: Westminster, 1985), 410.

There are other passages of Scripture that confirm that righteousness is not covenant membership but both right behavior and right status. For example, in Psalm 7 David asks whether he has repaid a friend with evil or plundered an enemy without cause (v. 4). To the possibility of being guilty of this wrongdoing, David responds, "Judge me, O LORD, according to my righteousness and according to the integrity that is in me" (v. 8).[27] David's plea to have God judge him according to his righteousness is not a claim of moral self-qualification, or self-righteousness, but a request that God declare him innocent of wrongdoing, rendering a "not guilty" verdict.[28] Again, covenant membership is not in view but legal status, namely David's righteousness.

This understanding of righteousness comes forth as well in Psalm 18:20: "The LORD dealt with me according to my righteousness; according to the cleanness of my hands he rewarded me." This verse is a declaration of status, or righteousness, clearly evident again by the second half of the synonymous parallelism.[29] In Psalm 18:20 righteousness is equivalent to having clean hands. But, in the following verses, the legal status of righteous is indexed by obedience to the Torah—the declaration of loyalty on the part of the one who worships: "For I have kept the ways of the LORD, and have not wickedly departed from my God. For all his rules were before me, and his statutes I did not put away from me" (Ps. 18:21–22; cf. Deut. 8:6; 10:12; 11:22; 19:9; 26:17; 28:9; 30:16; Josh. 22:5).[30]

One finds this same connection between righteousness and obedience to the Torah in the gate-liturgy psalms. With the pre-exilic temple those who sought admission would stand in the forecourt at what the psalmist calls the gates of righteousness (Ps. 118:19–20) and be met with the question: "Who shall ascend the hill of the LORD? And who shall stand in his holy place?" (Ps. 24:3). To this question the cultic officials would answer from within the inner court: "He who has clean hands and a pure heart, who does not lift up his soul to what is false and does not swear deceitfully" (Ps. 24:4). Von Rad explains the significance of this question and answer between the people and the cultic officials:

27. Derek Kidner, *Psalms 1–72*, TOTC (Downers Grove, IL: InterVarsity, 1973), 64; Charles A. Briggs, *Psalms*, vol. 1, ICC (1909; Edinburgh: T & T Clark, 1969), 55.
28. Hans-Joachim Kraus, *Psalms 1–59*, trans. Hilton C. Oswald (Minneapolis: Fortress, 1993), 172–73.
29. Briggs, *Psalms*, 146.
30. Kraus, *Psalms 1–59*, 262; Briggs, *Psalms*, 146.

This means that a selection of Jahweh's commandments was put before those who entered. Admittedly, we do not have to conclude from this that in ancient Israel the fulfilling of the commandments was in principle antecedent to the reception of salvation in the cult, since those seeking admission were certainly not coming before Jahweh for the first time—they had been members of the community of Jahweh from the beginning. But this much becomes clear: those who came to worship were asked for something like a declaration of loyalty to Jahweh's will for justice. These commandments were regarded as perfectly capable of being fulfilled, and indeed were easy to fulfill. The question whether those who sought entrance avowed themselves to be loyal to them now, and had been so in the past, was therefore nothing but the question of their *tsedaqah*. Hence, "the gates of righteousness" are spoken of, through which only "righteous people" enter.[31]

Once again, Wright's definition of righteousness as covenant membership does not fit the context of the gate-liturgy psalms. As von Rad points out, those who approach the gates were already members of the covenant. The covenant members are asked whether they are righteous, or have obeyed the law.[32] Can their behavior be categorized as loyal to the covenant, to the commandments of God?

Throughout the OT, righteousness is not a term that means covenant membership, contra Wright.[33] Rather, righteousness, when referring to people, is usually the status of righteousness demonstrated by obedience to Torah.[34] Those who are righteous will live; the unrighteous, those who disobey Torah, die: "When the righteous turns from his righteousness and does injustice, he shall die for it. And when the wicked turns from his wickedness and does what is just and right, he shall live by them" (Ezek. 33:18–19; see Dan. 4:27; Matt. 6:1; 1 John 3:7, 10, 12).[35] With this definition of righteousness we may move forward and examine Wright's exegesis of Romans 4:1–8.

31. Gerhard von Rad, *Old Testament Theology*, vol. 1 (1962; Louisville: Westminster John Knox, 2001), 377–78.
32. See also Peter C. Craigie, *Psalms 1–50*, WBC (Dallas: Word, 1983), 213.
33. There is no lexical evidence in either the OT or NT to support the claim that righteousness means "covenant membership." See BDB, 841–42; *TWOT*, 2:751–55; *TDOT*, 12:239–64; BAGD, 196–97; LSJ, 429; *TDNT*, 2:192–210.
34. So *TWOT*, 2:753. See also *TDOT*, 12:250; *TDNT*, 2:190–91, 198–99; Mark A. Seifrid, *Christ, Our Righteousness* (Downers Grove, IL: InterVarsity, 2000), 41.
35. Daniel I. Block, *The Book of Ezekiel: Chapters 25–48*, NICOT (Grand Rapids: Eerdmans, 1998), 252.

Romans 4:1–8

Romans 4:1–8 centers upon an important statement, one upon which a proper understanding of justification hinges. Paul quotes Genesis 15:6: "Abraham believed God, and it was counted to him as righteousness" (Rom. 4:3). Wright is correct to explain that "it was counted to him" is a bookkeeping metaphor. He is also correct that the meaning of this phrase must be sought in the original context and the rest of Romans 4. Yes, Genesis 15 opens with Abraham's puzzlement because God has made promises to him, but he has yet to see the fulfilment of these promises. God promised Abraham children, yet he has none. Wright is correct to identify the promise as having offspring as numerous as the stars of heaven.[36] Yet Wright is incorrect to say that God counted Abraham's belief in the promise as covenant membership. Rather, given the OT's use of righteousness as obedience to Torah, one must read Genesis 15:6 as, "Abraham believed God, and it was counted to him as covenant loyalty, or obedience." What Genesis 15:6 states, therefore, is that Abraham believed God's promise, and God counted that belief, or faith, in the stead of righteousness, or obedience.[37] Paul then goes on to clarify why he quotes Genesis 15:6.

Wright is correct to state that verses 4–5 are epexegetically related to verse 3: "Now to the one who works, his wages are not counted as a gift but as his due. And to the one who does not work but trusts him who justifies the ungodly, his faith is counted as righteousness." Contra Wright, these verses are not the only place where Paul juxtaposes faith against

36. One should stipulate that Wright identifies the formal nature of the promise, i.e., many offspring. He does not identify the substance of the promise, i.e., that it refers to Christ (Gal. 3:16; cf. John 8:56). Wright states: "We might suggest that the singularity of the 'seed' in v. 16 is not the singularity of an individual person contrasted with the plurality of many human beings, but the singularity of one *family* contrasted with the plurality of families which would result if the Torah were to be regarded the way Paul's opponents apparently regard it" (*Covenant*, 163; see also 164–65).

37. O. Palmer Robertson, "Genesis 15:6: New Covenant Expositions of an Old Covenant Text," *WTJ* 42 (1980), 264. Also see Victor P. Hamilton, *The Book of Genesis*, vol. 1, NICOT (Grand Rapids: Eerdmans, 1990), 423–27, 439; Brevard S. Childs, *Old Testament Theology in Its Canonical Context* (Philadelphia: Fortress, 1985), 219–20; Nahum M. Sarna, *Genesis*, JPSTC (New York: Jewish Publication Society, 1989), 113; Gordon J. Wenham, *Genesis 1–15* (Dallas: Word, 1987), 330. Cranfield notes: "That to Rabbinic Judaism Gen. 15:6 was no proof at all that Abraham was not justified on the ground of works is absolutely clear." For citations from rabbinic literature that saw Abraham meriting his righteous status see Cranfield, *Romans*, 1:229.

works.[38] A real problem within first-century Judaism was the idea that one could obey Torah. This attitude is certainly present in the rich young ruler who told Christ that he had obeyed the Torah (Matt. 19:16–22).[39] While there were certainly exceptions to the rule, second-temple Judaism had misread the OT, particularly the means by which a person obtained righteousness. Many thought that they could obtain their righteousness through obedience to the law. This is why Paul contrasts works and faith, or human effort with trust in Christ. This is why Paul uses the metaphor of wages earned. One does not obtain righteousness by human effort but by faith, trusting in the covenant promise of God: "And to the one who does not work but trusts him who justifies the ungodly, his faith is counted as righteousness" (Rom. 4:5).[40]

What about a person's sin? How does sin figure into the question of justification? Verses 6–8 answer the question of what God does with the sin of those whom he justifies: "Just as David also speaks of the blessing of the one to whom God counts righteousness apart from works: 'Blessed are those whose lawless deeds are forgiven, and whose sins are covered; blessed is the man against whom the Lord will not count his sin.'" Wright contends that being counted as righteous, or a covenant member, means that one's sins are forgiven. True enough, those whom God justifies certainly receive the forgiveness of sins, but one must not equate the forgiveness of sins with the status of being righteous, or obedient to the Torah. The forgiveness of sin is only one half of the justification equation. The one who is justified looks to Christ by faith, his faith is counted as obedience to the Torah, and his sins are also not counted against him. Who is the source of righteousness, or obedience to Torah? Paul explains that it is Christ (Rom. 5:12–19). As we saw in the previous chapter, there are

---

38. Brian Vickers notes that "in Romans 4 Paul uses *logizomai* twelve times (including OT quotes), 4:3, 4, 5, 6, 8, 9, 10, 11, 22, 23 (twice), 24. Although simply counting words does not necessarily prove that the bookkeeping metaphor is not merely 'a brief sidelight,' and while most of the occurrences are a matter of repetition, one might get the impression that Paul does intend to draw special attention to the metaphor" (Brian Vickers, *Jesus' Blood and Righteousness: Paul's Theology of Imputation* [Wheaton, IL: Crossway, 2006], 61, n. 138). One should note that Vickers's uncritical adoption of "metaphor" language in justification is undesirable.

39. Leon Morris, *The Gospel according to Matthew*, PNTC (Grand Rapids: Eerdmans, 1992), 489–91; W. D. Davies and Dale C. Allison, *The Gospel according to Matthew*, vol. 3, ICC (Edinburgh: T & T Clark, 1997), 45.

40. Cranfield, *Romans*, 1:231; Douglas J. Moo, *The Epistle to the Romans*, NICNT (Grand Rapids: Eerdmans, 1996), 265.

two parts of justification: the imputation of righteousness through faith and the forgiveness of sins. This interpretation is confirmed when we examine Psalm 106:31 and MMT C, the two places where Wright states that the matters Paul deals with in Romans 4:1–8 are restated.

Psalm 106:31

Psalm 106:31 comments upon the events of Numbers 25:1–3, when the Israelites "began to whore with the daughters of Moab," and the people yoked themselves to Baal Peor. Phinehas, a priest and grandson of Aaron, made a swift intervention against the Israelite idolatry and sin by spearing an Israelite man and Moabite woman while in the middle of an act of fornication. Why did Phinehas slay this couple? Phinehas offered a sacrifice to stop God's judgment from destroying the Israelites; this was his function as a Levite: "to make atonement for the people of Israel, that there may be no plague among the people of Israel when the people of Israel come near the sanctuary" (Num. 8:19). Sacrifices could stop a plague dead in its tracks.[41] This interpretation, thus far, is confirmed by Psalm 106:29–30: "They provoked the LORD to anger with their deeds, and a plague broke out among them. Then Phinehas stood up and intervened, and the plague was stayed." Phinehas made atonement and stood between the living and dead (Num. 25:13).[42] When Israel was heading toward idolatry, Phinehas acted faithfully and zealously for God's covenant and especially the Torah. Phinehas is therefore declared righteous: "And that was counted to him as righteousness from generation to generation forever" (Ps. 106:31).

At first glance, this event appears to contradict Paul's stated principle, namely that a person is reckoned righteous by faith alone.[43] In Psalm 106:31 it appears that Phinehas is counted as righteous because of his action, not his faith. Yet one must recognize the overall picture and all of the constituent elements at work: (1) the motivating source of Phinehas's action, (2) the contrast between the faithful and faithless, (3) the reward Phinehas receives, and (4) the typological connection to Christ. First,

---

41. Jacob Milgrom, *Numbers*, JPSTC (Philadelphia: Jewish Publication Society, 1990), 478–79.

42. Derek Kidner, *Psalms 73–150*, TOTC (Downers Grove, IL: InterVarsity, 1973), 381; Gordon J. Wenham, *Numbers*, TOTC (Downers Grove, IL: InterVarsity, 1981), 188.

43. So John Calvin, *Psalms 93–150*, trans. James Anderson, CTS (Grand Rapids: Baker, 1979), 232–33.

what motivates Phinehas's action is faith in his covenant Lord. What, for example, was the difference between those Israelites who wanted to enter the land of promise and those who did not? The author of Hebrews states that it was the presence or absence of faith: "For good news came to us just as to them, but the message they heard did not benefit them, because they were not united by faith with those who listened" (Heb. 4:2). Hence faith in God motivates Phinehas's actions.[44]

Second, the Israelites were acting unfaithfully, disobediently; they were unrighteous, whereas Phinehas was acting righteously, demonstrating obedience and loyalty to the Torah and ultimately to Yahweh. Third, one must not miss what reward Phinehas receives. He receives a perpetual priesthood, not justification: "Behold, I give to him my covenant of peace, and it shall be to him and to his descendants after him the covenant of a perpetual priesthood" (Num. 25:12–13).[45] Last, and fourth, is the typological connection to Christ: the priest acts righteously and his act of obedience is imputed to his offspring. This, of course, points to Christ, whose obedience is imputed to his offspring, the church. Ultimately, therefore, Phinehas's faith motivates his action, or obedience or righteousness, which secures a perpetual priesthood. So, while Wright is correct to say that Psalm 106:30–31 restates the problem of Romans 4:1–3, it actually works against his overall case. Psalm 106:30–31 is an instance where righteousness is imputed to others. One should note, however, that Paul does not appeal to Psalm 106:30–31 but to Genesis 15:6. The reason for his appeal to Genesis 15:6 will be evident in our examination of MMT C.

MMT C

Wright draws attention to the connection between Paul's arguments in Romans 4:1–8 and the literature of second-temple Judaism. MMT C, as in Romans 4:1–8, discusses the reckoning of righteousness, and like

---

44. Franz Delitzsch, *The Psalms*, trans. Francis Bolton, vol. 2 (Edinburgh: T & T Clark, 1901), 156; Vickers, *Jesus' Blood*, 82, 96; D. A. Carson, "The Vindication of Imputation: On Fields of Discourse and Semantic Fields," in *Justification*, ed. Mark Husbands and Daniel J. Treier (Downers Grove, IL: InterVarsity, 2004), 57; John Murray, *Epistles to the Romans*, NICNT (Grand Rapids: Eerdmans, 1968), 131–32.

45. Wenham, *Numbers*, 188; A. F. Kirkpatrick, *The Book of Psalms* (Cambridge: Cambridge University Press, 1902), 631; A. A. Anderson, *The Book of Psalms*, vol. 2 (London: Marshall, Morgan, and Scott, 1972), 745; Calvin, *Psalms 93–150*, 232.

Paul, also uses King David as an example: "Remember David, that he was a man of piety, and that he was also saved from many troubles and pardoned."[46] Wright argues beyond this parallel that Paul and Qumran have parallel understandings concerning eschatology:

> MMT expounds Deuteronomy 30 and 31 as a prophetic text envisaging future blessings and curses, culminating in the curse of exile, after which Israel will turn to God, and God will restore her "at the end of the days." This, says the writer of MMT, is now coming to pass, and the works of the law are the sign of the people to whom "it will be reckoned as righteousness" in the future. In other words, the works of the law function within an inaugurated eschatology—an understanding that the end time has already begun—to mark out those who will be restored, who will be the true Israel. At this point MMT's theology runs parallel to Paul's. He too has an inaugurated eschatology—in which the true Israel is marked out by faith.[47]

Wright is correct that there are some parallels between Paul and Qumran. Yet there are some significant differences.

The most significant difference comes in MMT's explanation of how a person is reckoned as righteous: "And it will be reckoned for you as righteousness when you perform what is right and good before Him, for your own good and for that of Israel."[48] This statement stands in stark contrast to what Paul writes in Romans 4:1–8. MMT C states that a person has righteousness reckoned to him for performing what is right and good, whereas Paul states that Abraham believed God, and his faith was reckoned as righteousness. In MMT C the person is counted righteous because of his right and good deeds whereas Abraham is counted righteous because of his faith. Wright maintains that this statement, however, is not contradictory to Paul and that, though similar, MMT speaks of types of requirements, or works, different from what Paul refutes in Romans and Galatians, namely the works of the law, or circumcision, food laws, and Sabbath observance.

Wright argues that one must understand the difference between the Jewish works of the law, circumcision, food laws, and Sabbath observance,

---

46. Wright sees other parallels between MMT and Paul, for example, in his instructions concerning children in a mixed marriage (see N. T. Wright, "Paul and Qumran," *BRev* 14/5 [1998]: 18).

47. Ibid.

48. Geza Vermes, ed., *The Complete Dead Sea Scrolls in English* (1962; New York: Penguin, 1997), 4Q398 14–17 ii with 4Q399, (p. 228).

and the requirements of the Qumran community. Qumran, according to Wright, was a sect within first-century Judaism and defined itself in relationship to the temple. Wright gives several reasons as to why MMT is not in Paul's crosshairs:

1) The laws that MMT commands are designed to mark out the scroll community against other groups within the wider Jewish world. The works that Paul opposes define all Jews and proselytes over against the gentile, pagan world.

2) MMT insists on postbiblical laws whereas Paul battles those who insist upon biblical laws. Qumran is concerned about codes regarding animal fetuses, banning the blind and lame from the temple, observing certain purity laws relating to streams of liquid, whereas Paul deals with the Jewish identity markers, circumcision, food laws, and Sabbath.

3) Qumran was concerned with the purity of the temple, whereas Paul mentions nothing regarding the temple.[49]

It is on the basis of these differences that Wright rejects the idea that Paul has MMT in mind when he opposes those who seek righteousness on the basis of the works of the law. What is problematic with Wright's position is that he focuses attention upon several particulars that appear to support his position without taking note of the general scope of MMT. In other words, Wright misses the forest for the trees. There are several reasons why Wright's dismissal of the Paul-MMT connection is wanting.

First, one must take into account the title of MMT. Wright translates the title *Misqat ma'ase ha-torah* as "selection of the works of the law."[50] The translation "selection," however, does not point to a random sampling but rather to those laws that are important to the author. Martin Abegg notes that the title should therefore be translated as "some important" or "pertinent" laws.[51]

49. Wright, "Paul and Qumran," 18.
50. Ibid.
51. Martin Abegg, "Paul, 'Works of the Law' and MMT," *BAR* 20/6 (1994): 52; idem, "4QMMT, Paul, and 'Works of the Law,'" in *The Bible at Qumran*, ed. Peter W. Flint (Grand Rapids: Eerdmans, 2001), 205.

Second, *ma'ase ha-torah* should be translated "the works of the law," as Wright correctly does. Abegg points out, however, that a few minutes with a concordance of the LXX leaves little doubt that the Greek equivalent of *ma'ase ha-torah* is likely *erga nomou*. It is this Greek phrase, of course, that Paul argues against (Rom. 3:20, 28; Gal. 2:16; 3:2, 5, 10). What is more interesting is that the phrase appears only in Paul and in MMT; it does not at all appear in rabbinic literature in the first or second century.[52]

Third, while Wright is correct to state that MMT is concerned with temple purity, one must remember that Qumran was a conservative reaction against lax views toward the law. In other words, it is not that Qumran observed only the minor aspects of the law but rather the law in its entirety, including what many first-century Jews might consider minor aspects of the law. As we saw in chapter 6, that Qumran observed the whole of Torah is evident from the Community Rule: "This is the rule for the men of the community who have freely pledged themselves to be converted from all evil and to cling to all his commandments according to his will"(1QS 5). Each member of the community had to "undertake by a binding oath to return with all his heart and soul to every commandment of the Law of Moses in accordance with all that has been revealed" (1QS 5.10).

Fourth, one must consider again the statement "And it will be reckoned for you as righteousness when you perform what is right and good before Him, for your own good and for that of Israel."[53] Abegg notes that this statement contradicts what Paul states in Romans 4:3.[54] He speculates as to the source of the contradiction and supposes that the author of MMT could have read Genesis 22:16, but believes that the more likely scenario is that the author relied upon Psalm 106:30–31.[55] Abegg writes:

> Upon examination of the Hebrew text of MMT, it becomes clear that MMT echoes this passage from Psalm 106. The same passive verb—"it was reckoned" in Psalm 106 and "you shall be reckoned" in MMT—is one clear reflection of this dependence. The only difference is that the past

52. Abegg, "Paul, 'Works of the Law,'" 53.

53. Vermes, *Dead Sea Scrolls in English*, 4Q398 14–17 ii with 4Q399 (p. 228).

54. See Robert Eisenman and Michael Wise, *The Dead Sea Scrolls Uncovered* (New York: Penguin, 1992), 183–84.

55. So Carolyn J. Sharp, "Phinehan Zeal and Rhetorical Strategy in 4QMMT," *RevQ* 18/2 (1997): 210.

tense of the verb in Psalm 106 is changed to the future tense in MMT to convert it into a promise for the addressee.[56]

There are other considerations in addition to the verbal parallels, namely the concern for holiness and the connection to the priesthood. Psalm 106 celebrates what Phinehas did, zealously pursuing the law. In this connection the Qumran community called themselves "sons of Zadok," who was the high priest during the reigns of David and Solomon, the direct descendant of Phinehas. It is a likely possibility that the author of MMT read Psalm 106:30–31 and drew the incorrect conclusion that the people of God are reckoned righteous because of their performance of the law, failing to see that Phinehas did not receive justification but only a perpetual priesthood. In this regard, it is telling that Paul appeals to Genesis 15:6 and not Psalm 106:30–31.

Fifth, Wright correctly states that MMT expounds Deuteronomy 30–31. Yet what is the subject under consideration in these two chapters? Chapters 30 and 31 largely explain the curses and blessings of the covenant. To receive the blessings Israel had to obey the law (Deut. 30:16). MMT C states: "We have written to you that you should understand the Book of Moses and the Books of the Prophets and David and all the events of every age."[57] Here reference is made to the importance of the entirety of the OT, not just some portions of it. Qumran had strictness toward the entirety of the law.[58] Indeed, Israel was to return to the commandments of Torah. The Qumran community certainly observed the Torah, as is evident from their entrance requirements—namely their pledge of loyalty to all the commandments. MMT, however, wrongly understood the purpose of the law—it was not to usher in the eschatological age but to bring death (Rom. 7:5; 1 Cor. 15:56).[59] The law was supposed to cause Israel to seek Christ, the source of righteousness (Gal. 3:24–26; cf. Lev. 26:1–39, 40–42).

56. Abegg, "Paul, 'Works of the Law,'" 55; idem, "4QMMT," 208; Eisenman and Wise, *Dead Sea Scrolls*, 184, 198.

57. Vermes, *Dead Sea Scrolls*, 227; also Eisenman and Wise, *Dead Sea Scrolls*, 199.

58. Sharp, "Phinehan Zeal," 215; also Gary A. Anderson, "Intentional and Unintentional Sin in the Dead Sea Scrolls," in *Pomegranates and Golden Bells*, ed. David P. Wright et al., (Winona Lake, IN: Eisenbrauns, 1995), 49–64.

59. See E. E. Ellis, *Gospel of Luke*, NCB (London: Thomas Nelson, 1966), 215–16.

For these five reasons, therefore, while one cannot be absolutely certain, Paul possibly included the work-wages metaphor to counter the ideas of MMT C, which caused Paul to write statements such as "For the promise to Abraham and his offspring that he would be heir of the world did not come through the law but through the righteousness of faith" (Rom. 4:13), and "Not having a righteousness of my own that comes from the law, but that which comes through faith in Christ, the righteousness from God that depends on faith" (Phil. 3:9).[60] The evidence examined thus far is not consonant with Wright's explanation of Romans 4:1–8. Verses 5–6 are not a one-time occurrence of the works-wages metaphor but a specific refutation of a common misconception, namely that one could be righteous by obedience to the Torah. Instead, Paul states that one is righteous, obedient to the Torah, by faith in Christ, not by human effort. With this data, we may move forward to a critical engagement of Wright's understanding of justification.

Justification

Wright is correct about his three presuppositions regarding justification: it is covenantal, law-court language, and eschatological. Though he correctly identifies these three key presuppositions, his use of these categories requires some redirection. First, Wright is correct, justification is covenantal. But he argues that one must not understand "covenantal" to mean the covenant theology of the sixteenth, seventeenth, and eighteenth centuries. The problem with this claim is that Wright does not explain how or in what way classic covenant Reformed theology is at odds with Scripture.[61] He cites no evidence to support his claim. The assertion of error is something that requires reexamination and the presentation of specific evidence on Wright's part. He moves on, however, to say that

---

60. Guy P. Waters, *Justification and the New Perspectives on Paul* (Phillipsburg, NJ: P&R, 2004), 154; Douglas Moo, "'Law,' 'Works of the Law,' and Legalism in Paul," *WTJ* 45 (1983): 92, 94.

61. It seems that Wright has no interest in investigating classic Reformed theology in that from his very first publication on the subject to one of his most recent, there is no evidence that he has sought to remedy this gap in his theology. He even goes as far as to say that he is ignorant of most other theological explanations, with the exception of a few of the Fathers and Reformers. Even then, his knowledge of the Reformers is suspect, as no reference to their works seems to appear in his writings (N. T. Wright, *Paul: In Fresh Perspective* [Minneapolis: Fortress, 2005], 13; idem, "The Paul of History and the Apostle of Faith," *TynBul* 29 [1978]: 61–88).

what one must understand by "covenantal" is that worldview and understanding of the OT embodied in second-temple Judaism. Wright claims that God made a covenant with Abraham, calling Israel to be his people, and that it is this covenant to which the Israelites look for their vindication, or justification, before the Gentile world. The Jews living in the first century under Roman rule were looking to be vindicated against their Roman oppressors.

Wright is correct in that one must be sensitive to the surrounding cultural and historical context of the NT; however, he gives his interpretation of second-temple Judaism too great a role in defining the covenantal nature of justification. At various points Wright invokes the literature of second-temple Judaism to explain what lies behind Paul's thought. What is problematic about this methodology is that Paul never directly cites the literature of the second temple.

In contradistinction to Wright, J. Gresham Machen explains, "It is significant that when, after the conversion, Paul seeks testimonies to the universal sinfulness of man, he looks not to contemporary Judaism, but to the Old Testament. At this point, as elsewhere, Paulinism is based not upon later developments but upon the religion of the Prophets and the Psalms."[62] Wright assumes that second-temple Judaism has authoritatively interpreted the OT and that Paul builds upon this understanding. Machen notes, however, the great divergence on a number of subjects concerning the doctrine of the Messiah as it is presented in the OT and in the literature of the second temple.[63]

While Wright may be correct in his sketch of the worldview of second-temple Judaism, though there is some doubt as to the accuracy of his explanation, he has not demonstrated that it is consonant with the view of the OT.[64] Is justification in Paul covenantal in the sense of the

---

62. J. Gresham Machen, *The Origin of Paul's Religion* (1925; Eugene, OR: Wipf & Stock, 2002), 180. Also see Cornelis P. Venema, *The Gospel of Free Acceptance in Christ* (Edinburgh: Banner of Truth, 2006), 147; Waters, *Justification*, 154–57; Guy P. Waters, *The End of the Law in Deuteronomy in the Epistles of Paul* (Tübingen: Mohr Siebeck, 2006), 243–45; Kent Yinger, *Paul, Judaism and Judgment according to Deeds* (Cambridge: Cambridge University Press, 1999), 1–4, 166, 288–89.

63. Machen, *Paul's Religion*, 182–200.

64. There has been criticism against the monolithic picture of first-century Judaism that Wright portrays. See Richard B. Hays, "Adam, Israel, Christ: The Question of Covenant in the Theology of Romans: A Response to Leander E. Keck and N. T. Wright," in *Pauline Theology*, ed. David M. Hay and E. Elizabeth Johnson (Minneapolis: Fortress, 1995), 3:79; Alister E.

vindication of the people of God over against their oppressors, as Wright maintains, informed by second-temple Judaism? Or is justification covenantal in the sense that God has provided deliverance from sin and death through his covenant dealings with his people in Adam, Noah, Abraham, and Israel?

The answer lies in Paul's explanation of justification in Romans 4. If Wright is correct, what is noticeably absent is any direct connection to the literature of second-temple Judaism and any of the themes Wright claims are connected to justification. In this regard Wright contends that "in the NT Israel's expectation is radically redefined." Wright states that in Christ's "welcome for outcasts and sinners, Jesus enacts God's vindication of (apparently) the wrong group in Israel—the poor, the humble. 'This man [the tax collector], rather than the other [the Pharisee], went home justified before God' (Luke 18:14)."[65] Wright, however, cannot posit a radical redefinition of Israel's expectation for two reasons. If the NT redefined Israel's expectation, then first-century Judaism has correctly interpreted the OT, but Christ and the apostles have redefined it. In other words, Christ and the apostles correct the view of the OT. Or first century Judaism has misinterpreted the OT, and it was first-century opinion that required correction. If it is the latter, then there has been no redefinition of Israel's hope.

Instead, as Machen argues, Paul appeals to the OT, to Abraham, not to the erroneous positions of first-century Judaism. And as classic Reformed covenant theology has argued, the Abrahamic covenant, which Paul calls the gospel (Gal. 3:8), is built ultimately upon the protoevangelium, not the hopes of first-century Jews of being delivered from their Roman overlords. Paul's concern is not the supposed exile under Rome as Wright contends, but the greater exile under the powers of Satan, sin, and death.[66] The protoevangelium, of course, was the promise to deliver Adam and Eve out from under the dominion of sin and death, and to conquer the serpent

---

McGrath, "Reality, Symbol and History: Theological Reflections on N. T. Wright's Portrayal of Jesus," in *Jesus and the Restoration of Israel*, ed. Carey C. Newman (Downers Grove, IL: InterVarsity, 1999), 170; Seifrid, *Christ*, 21–25.

65. N. T. Wright, "Justification," in *New Dictionary of Theology*, ed. Sinclair B. Ferguson, David F. Wright, and J. I. Packer (Downers Grove, IL: InterVarsity, 1988), 359.

66. Joseph Fitzmyer, "Justification in Pauline Thought," in *Rereading Paul Together*, ed. David E. Aune (Grand Rapids: Baker, 2006), 122. For a critique of Wright's exile thesis, see Brant Pitre, *Jesus, the Tribulation, and the End of Exile* (Grand Rapids: Baker, 2005).

and his seed, the failed covenant of works (Gen. 3:15). Justification, then, is covenantal in the sense that God has provided deliverance from sin and death through his covenant dealings with his people in Adam, Noah, Abraham, and Israel; the ultimate fulfilment of these covenant dealings comes through the life, death, and resurrection of Jesus Christ.

What about the law-court aspect of justification? Wright maintains, and correctly so, that justification is law-court language:

> The covenant was there to deal with the sin, and bring about the salvation, of the world. It was therefore utterly appropriate, as I said earlier, that this great event should be described in terms drawn from the setting in which evil was regularly dealt with, namely that of the law court. . . . God himself was seen as the judge; evildoers (i.e. the Gentiles, and renegade Jews) would finally be judged and punished; God's faithful people (i.e., Israel, or at least the true Israelites) would be vindicated.[67]

Wright correctly states that justification is explained in terms of a law court. What is problematic is the concept of metaphor and the orientation of the court. We saw in chapter 2 in setting forth the relationship to prolegomena, that justification is not a metaphor. There is nothing metaphorical about sin, condemnation, and standing before the throne of God, which means that justification is not a metaphor. Additionally, according to Wright the people of God look for vindication before the world. Yet, once again, while this may be the view of second-temple Judaism, it is not how Paul explains justification. In the context surrounding Romans 4, Paul's great concern is seeking justification before the tribunal of God, not the world, which is in no way metaphorical: "For by works of the law no human being will be justified in his sight, since through the law comes knowledge of sin" (Rom. 3:20). According to Paul the one who has been justified has peace with God: "Therefore, since we have been justified by faith, we have peace with God through our Lord Jesus Christ" (Rom. 5:1). Paul shows no concern for what the enemies of the people of God might or might not think; Paul shows concern only for what God will say concerning the one who stands before his throne.

Justification, therefore, is not about the vindication of the people of God before the world as Wright maintains. Rather it is about the ver-

67. Wright, *Saint Paul*, 118; idem, "Justification," 359.

dict that God passes upon the person who stands in his presence, the verdict of guilty or innocent. This theme of standing before the tribunal of God is found in the OT: "Keep far from a false charge, and do not kill the innocent and righteous, for I will not acquit the wicked" (Ex. 23:7; Deut. 25:1; Prov. 17:15).[68] God will not acquit the wicked, which is why Paul explains that Abraham receives his righteous status by faith alone. Moreover, God imputes the obedience, or righteousness, of Christ to Abraham. This interpretation is also confirmed by Christ's use of the term "justification."

Christ explains in the parable of the Pharisee and the tax collector the nature of justification and how it relates to righteousness:

> He also told this parable to some who trusted in themselves that they were righteous, and treated others with contempt: "Two men went up into the temple to pray, one a Pharisee and the other a tax collector. The Pharisee, standing by himself, prayed thus: 'God, I thank you that I am not like other men, extortioners, unjust, adulterers, or even like this tax collector. I fast twice a week; I give tithes of all that I get.' But the tax collector, standing far off, would not even lift up his eyes to heaven, but beat his breast, saying, 'God, be merciful to me, a sinner!' I tell you, this man went down to his house justified, rather than the other." (Luke 18:9–14)

Notice that Christ uses the parable against those who trusted in themselves, who thought they were righteous or innocent before God and loyal to the Torah.[69] In this parable Christ describes the Pharisee, not in Wright's terms of loyalty to the covenant badges, circumcision, food laws, and Sabbath observance, but in terms of the general commands of Torah: thievery, injustice, adultery, fasting, and tithing.[70] It is in these terms of Torah observance that some of the Jews thought they were righteous. Fitzmyer observes that this parable shows that Christ

> recognized that righteousness in God's sight was not to be achieved by boasting or even by self-confident activity (either the avoidance of evil or the striving for good in the observance of Mosaic and Pharisaic regulations).

68. Francis Turretin, *Institutes of Elenctic Theology*, trans. George Musgrave Giger, ed. James T. Dennison Jr., 3 vols. (Phillipsburg, NJ: P&R, 1992–97), 16.1.4.

69. So Joel B. Green, *The Gospel of Luke*, NICNT (Grand Rapids: Eerdmans, 1997), 646.

70. Ibid., 647–48.

This saying about justification is important for it may reveal that the NT teaching about the matter is somehow rooted in Jesus' own attitude and teaching: One achieves uprightness before God not by one's own activity but by a contrite recognition of one's own sinfulness before him. Hence, "the Pauline doctrine of justification has its roots in the teaching of Jesus."[71]

For these reasons Paul makes statements like "a person is not justified by works of the law but through faith in Jesus Christ" (Gal. 2:16), to counter the idea that a person is righteous by being obedient to the Torah. By contrast, the tax collector who sought the mercy of God and the forgiveness of sins was justified before the tribunal of God. Hence, justification is a law-court metaphor, but the court is oriented in a God-ward not world-ward direction.

What about the last of the presuppositions, namely that justification is eschatological? Again, Wright is correct in explaining that justification is eschatological. Wright argues that the justification, or vindication, of the people of God is a long-awaited hope. Hence, according to Wright, the fulfilment of this long-expected hope is eschatological. Wright explains:

> "Justification" in the first century was not about how someone might establish a relationship with God. It was about God's eschatological definition, both future and present, of who was, in fact, a member of his people. In Sanders' terms, it was not so much about "getting in." In standard Christian theological language, it wasn't so much about soteriology as about ecclesiology; not so much about salvation as about the church.[72]

So, then, according to Wright justification is eschatological in that it is the long-awaited fulfilment of the covenant promises as well as the final and ultimate definition of who belongs to the people of God.[73] While Wright is correct to say that justification is eschatological, he is incorrect to divorce justification from soteriology. As Richard Gaffin notes, "All soteric experience derives from solidarity in Christ's resurrection and involves existence in the new creation age, inaugurated by his res-

---

71. Joseph A. Fitzmyer, *The Gospel according to Luke*, AB 28a (Garden City, NY: Doubleday, 1985), 1184–85; Ellis, *Luke*, 215–16.
72. Wright, *Saint Paul*, 119; idem, *Victory of God*, 203, 288, 513.
73. Wright, "Justification," 359.

urrection."[74] In other words, all soteriology, including justification, is eschatological because of its connection to the resurrection of Christ, the in-breaking of the eschaton.

As we briefly saw in the last chapter, one finds the connection between justification, eschatology, and soteriology prominently in Romans 4:25 where Paul states that Christ was "delivered up for our trespasses and raised for our justification." Paul makes an explicit connection between the resurrection of Christ and the justification of the people of God. Now Wright correctly argues that the resurrection is an eschatological event.[75] He also correctly explains that the resurrection of Jesus was his vindication, though it is preferable to say that it was his justification, the Father's declaration of his Son's innocence and loyalty to the Torah.[76] Christ was innocent of the charges for which he was crucified. But Wright goes on to explain,

> Thus, if faithful Jesus is demonstrated to be Messiah by the resurrection, the resurrection also declares in principle that all those who belong to Jesus, all those who respond in faith to God's faithfulness revealed in him, are themselves part of the true covenant family promised to Abraham. In other words, the resurrection of Jesus can at this level be seen as the declaration of justification.[77]

Paul, however, does not draw the connection between the resurrection and ecclesiology as Wright contends, when Wright describes the resurrection as a declaration of those who belong to Jesus.

Rather, Paul connects the resurrection directly to soteriology: "If Christ has not been raised, your faith is futile and you are still in your sins" (1 Cor. 15:17).[78] Paul ties the resurrection to the conquest of sin and death: "To Paul's way of thinking, as long as Christ remains dead, Satan and sin are triumphant, or more broadly, the dominion of the old aeon remains unbroken."[79] If there is no resurrection, then the protoevangelium and the

---

74. Richard B. Gaffin Jr., *Resurrection and Redemption* (1978; Phillipsburg, NJ: P&R, 1987), 138.

75. Wright, *Saint Paul*, 36.

76. Wright, "Justification," 359.

77. Wright, *Romans*, 504.

78. A. C. Thiselton, *The First Epistle to the Corinthians*, NIGTC (Grand Rapids: Eerdmans, 2000), 1219–20.

79. Gaffin, *Resurrection*, 116.

covenant promises to Adam, the patriarchs, Israel, and the people of God are empty. If there is no resurrection, then those who look to Christ by faith cannot be counted as righteous. There is no deliverance from their sins; they can no longer say, "And such were some of you" (1 Cor. 6:11).[80] If there is no resurrection, then there has been no sacrifice to redeem the people of God from the curse of the law (Gal. 3:13).[81] So, yes, justification is eschatological, but not in the way that Wright explains.

Justification is not an eschatological definition of the people of God but the inbreaking of the eschatological age, the outpouring of the power of the age to come, the Holy Spirit, manifest in the resurrection of Christ, bringing about the victory over sin and death, ensuring the justification of the people of God by raising Christ from death. Christ has been raised and therefore his people are no longer in their sin because God the Father has accepted the sacrifice on their behalf. Like Phinehas, Christ has stood between the living and the dead, and his obedience, his righteousness, has been credited to those who place their faith in him and his work, and they receive a perpetual priesthood. Hence Wright is correct to say that justification is covenantal, law-court language, and eschatological. But these categories require reorientation because Paul does not discuss justification in the way that Wright does. Wright bases these categories in his understanding and construction of the worldview of second-temple Judaism and the longing for deliverance from Rome. Paul, on the other hand, bases these categories in the protoevangelium, the longing for deliverance from sin and death. We may now move forward to some concluding observations.

Conclusion

In this chapter we have examined key aspects of Wright's understanding of justification and found it wanting. While there are broad aspects with which one can agree, there is much in the specific details that is problematic. Wright argues that justification is about the vindication of the people of God before their enemies. Justification, according to Wright, is a declaration that a person is "in the right" and righteous, a member

---

80. Gordon D. Fee, *The First Epistle to the Corinthians*, NICNT (Grand Rapids: Eerdmans, 1987), 743–44.

81. Geerhardus Vos, *The Pauline Eschatology* (1930; Phillipsburg, NJ: P&R, 1994), 151.

of the covenant. Justification is about the fulfilment of God's covenant promises to give Abraham a family that includes both Jews and Gentiles and the ultimate eschatological fulfilment of that long-awaited hope.

While all of Wright's claims may be true, Paul presents an entirely different picture. For Paul justification is not vindication before the world but a declaration of righteousness before the tribunal of God. It is the long-awaited fulfilment of the covenantal promises of God, first promised to Adam and Eve, then Abraham, Isaac, and Jacob, and then Israel, to deliver the people of God out from under the dominion of sin and death. Justification is an eschatological reality, in that the new creation has burst forth in the middle of this present evil age, and through the resurrection of Christ has declared the victory of Christ over sin and death, which means that his people are justified, innocent before God because of the intercessory work of Christ. Moreover, for those who place their faith in Christ, in his work—life, death, and resurrection—God reckons, or credits them with righteousness, innocence, and loyalty to the Torah.

It appears, therefore, that the classic Reformed view of justification as it comes through the Westminster Standards is correct. Justification is indeed an act of God's free grace wherein he pardons all our sins, and accepts us as righteous in his sight, only for the righteousness of Christ imputed to us, and received by faith alone. This is not the only challenge, however, to the traditional Reformed understanding of the doctrine of justification. As explained before, justification hinges upon the doctrine of imputation. Yet the doctrine of imputation has come under fire. So, then, it is to an examination of Wright's rejection of imputation that we now turn.

9

JUSTIFICATION AND IMPUTATION

Before we can proceed to examine the connections between justification and other aspects of the *ordo salutis*, we must first stop to explore and then critique challenges to one of the key elements of the doctrine of justification: the concept of imputed righteousness.[1] The idea of imputation has been part and parcel of the historic Protestant understanding of justification but in recent years the doctrine has come under fire. Historically, Reformed theologians have maintained the doctrine of imputation over and against Roman Catholic views of infusion as it relates to the doctrine of justification.[2] Some advocates of the New Perspective on Paul (NPP), however, counter that imputation is unscriptural.

N. T. Wright's disdain for the idea is quite evident when he writes in his popular work *What Saint Paul Really Said*, "If we leave the notion of 'righteousness' as a law-court metaphor only, as so many have done in the past, this gives the impression of a legal transaction, a cold piece

---

1. This chapter is a modified version of J. V. Fesko, "N. T. Wright on Imputation," *RTR* 66/1 (2007): 2–22.
2. See WCF 11.1; LC 70, 73; SC 30. Cf. "The Canons and Dogmatic Decrees of the Council of Trent (1563)," session 6 (1547), in Philip Schaff, *The Creeds of Christendom*, 3 vols. (1931; Grand Rapids: Baker, 1990), 2.89–118.

of business, almost a trick of thought performed by a God who is logical and correct but hardly one we would want to worship."[3] Though Wright does not explicitly mention imputation, the allusion to the idea is clear. What remains only as an allusion to his rejection of imputation in this popular work is clearer in his other writings. Wright makes only a passing rejection of imputation in one of his most recent works, *The Resurrection of the Son of God*. Concerning 2 Corinthians 5:21 Wright states that the "phrase has routinely been understood in terms of the righteous status which the covenant god reckons or 'imputes' to believers, but this interpretation then regularly leaves the verse dangling off the edge of the argument."[4] Elsewhere in an interview Wright states that 2 Corinthians 5:21 is not at all about the imputation of the righteousness of Christ to the believer:

> The key text, which is 2 Corinthians 5:21, has been read for generations, ever since Luther at least, as an isolated, detached statement of the wondrous exchange. . . . I can see how frustrating it is for a preacher who has preached his favorite sermon all these years on the imputation of Christ's righteousness from 2 Corinthians 5:21 to hear that this is not the right way to understand it but I actually think that there's an even better sermon waiting to be preached.[5]

Wright is clear—2 Corinthians 5:21 does not teach anything about imputed righteousness. Is Wright correct? No, he is not. This chapter will argue that Wright's explanation of 2 Corinthians 5:21 is incorrect. We will first examine Wright's analysis of this key text. Second, we will broaden the scope of our examination of Wright on imputation to include two other key passages to which Reformed theologians commonly appeal to support the doctrine of imputation, 1 Corinthians 1:30 and Romans 5:12–21. Nevertheless, we will turn first to Wright's analysis of 2 Corinthians 5:21.

---

3. N. T. Wright, *What Saint Paul Really Said* (Grand Rapids: Eerdmans, 1997), 110. While we will focus primarily on Wright's rejection of imputation, there have been others who have registered similar opinions (see Robert H. Gundry, "The Nonimputation of Christ's Righteousness," in *Justification*, ed. Mark Husbands and Daniel J. Treier [Downers Grove, IL: InterVarsity, 2004], 17–45).

4. N. T. Wright, *The Resurrection of the Son of God* (Minneapolis: Fortress, 2003), 305.

5. Travis Tamerius, "An Interview with N. T. Wright," *RRJ* 11/1 (2002): 129–30.

Wright on 2 Corinthians 5:21

In the recent debate over imputation Wright argues that there are only two passages to which one might appeal: 1 Corinthians 1:30 and 2 Corinthians 5:21: "For our sake he made him to be sin who knew no sin, so that in him we might become the righteousness of God."[6] At first glance, however, one has to wonder why Wright would overlook Romans 4:5–6, 22–25, and 5:12–19, as these texts undoubtedly deal with imputation. We will first turn our attention to 2 Corinthians 5:21 and then treat Romans below. Wright gives his analysis of 2 Corinthians 5:21 in a brief essay entitled "On Becoming the Righteousness of God."[7] Wright identifies two key issues surrounding the interpretation of this verse: (1) the meaning of the phrase *dikaiosynē theou*, "the righteousness of God," and (2) the overall context of the verse.

The Meaning of the "Righteousness of God"

Wright argues that "Paul's other uses of the phrase (all in Romans) treat *theou* as referring to a *dikaiosynē* that is God's own, rather than a *dikaiosynē* that he gives, reckons, imparts, or imputes to human beings."[8] In contrast to reading the phrase as a genitive of origin, he understands it as a possessive or subjective genitive.[9] Wright argues that throughout Paul's writings, especially in Romans, the God of Israel has in Christ been faithful to the covenant that he made with Abraham. He therefore contends that *dikaiosynē theou* is a technical term that means "the covenant faithfulness of Israel's God."[10] Elsewhere Wright argues that while the Greek of this phrase can be rendered as a genitive of origin, that is, the status that Christians have as a result of God's justifying action, there is no warrant to translate it in this manner given Paul's Jewish background.[11] According to Wright, "righteousness" is a technical term that originates in postexilic and second-temple Judaism:

6. N. T. Wright, "New Perspectives on Paul," paper given at the 10th Edinburgh Dogmatics Conference, Rutherford House (25–28 August 2003), 7.

7. N. T. Wright, "On Becoming the Righteousness of God: 2 Corinthians 5:21," in *Pauline Theology*, ed. David M. Hay (Atlanta: SBL, 2002), 2:200–208.

8. Ibid., 200–201.

9. Wright, *Saint Paul*, 101, 104–5.

10. Wright, "Righteousness of God," 203.

11. N. T. Wright, *Romans*, NIB 10 (Nashville: Abingdon, 2003), 425.

This problem is often seen in the later biblical and second-temple literature in terms of the covenant faithfulness (*tsedaqah*, "righteousness") of Israel's god—a topic which becomes exceedingly important in the study of Pauline theology. The question of the righteousness of god, as expressed by Jews in this period, can be stated as follows: when and how would Israel's god act to fulfill his covenant promises?[12]

The reader, therefore, cannot ignore the historical context of the meaning of this term, especially as it occurs in Paul. This brings us to the second of Wright's points, namely the context of 2 Corinthians 5:21.

The Overall Context

Wright takes issue with the traditional reading of 2 Corinthians 5:21.[13] He argues that the verse "has traditionally been read as a somewhat detached statement of atonement theology: we are sinners; God is righteous, but in Christ what Luther called a 'wondrous exchange' takes place, in which Christ takes our sin and we his 'righteousness.'"[14] Wright then goes on to cite four reasons as to why this interpretation does not best explain the verse:

1. Paul never actually says this anywhere else (except perhaps 1 Cor. 1:30).
2. Here we become "God's righteousness," not Christ's.
3. The typical explanation does not fit the overall discussion—the paradoxical nature of the apostolic ministry in which Christ is portrayed in and through the humiliating work of the apostle (2 Cor. 4:7–6:13).

12. N. T. Wright, *The New Testament and the People of God* (Minneapolis: Fortress, 1992), 271.

13. See, e.g., John Calvin, *2 Corinthians and Timothy, Titus and Philemon*, trans. T. A. Smail, ed. David W. Torrance and T. F. Torrance, CNTC (Grand Rapids: Eerdmans, 1960), 81–82.

14. Wright, "Righteousness of God," 203. Though Wright invokes the name of Luther, he does not directly cite him. He instead cites Bultmann, Barrett, Hooker, and Furnish. See Rudolf Bultmann, *The Second Letter to the Corinthians* (Minneapolis: Fortress, 1985), 165; C. K. Barrett, *A Commentary on the Second Epistle to the Corinthians* (London: A & C Black, 1973), 180–81; M. D. Hooker, *From Adam to Christ* (Cambridge: Cambridge University Press, 1990), 17, 181; and Victor Paul Furnish, *II Corinthians*, AB 32a (New York: Doubleday, 1984), 351–53.

4. If we take the traditional reading, it falls off the end of the preceding argument to the point that commentators suggest that the break in thought occurs not between 5:21 and 6:1 but between 5:19 and 5:20.[15]

In contrast to the traditional interpretation, then, Wright offers an alternative.

Wright argues that from 2:14 on Paul addresses the issue of the question of his own apostleship, and especially in chapter 3 he does so in relation to the new covenant.[16] Paul's argument is that he is a minister of the new covenant (3:6) and that his ministry is not mitigated by his suffering but is instead enhanced (4:7–18). In his suffering Christ is revealed more clearly to those to whom he ministers. The argument continues into chapter 5, but 5:1–5 is not an isolated fragment about personal eschatology. Rather, Paul works all the more intensely in his ministerial labors in the knowledge that he will receive, as one who is in Christ, the further clothing of the glorious resurrection body. Wright contends that Paul's argument should be read in this manner because the *oun* ("therefore") in verse 11 indicates that verses 1–10 contribute to what follows. Throughout Paul's argument, then, he unpacks what it means to be a minister of the new covenant. This means that Paul's statements of 5:14–17 should not be isolated from the overall argument and read as gobbets of traditional soteriology. All of this contributes to what Paul says in verses 18–19: "All this is from God, who through Christ reconciled us to himself and gave us the ministry of reconciliation; that is, in Christ God was reconciling the world to himself, not counting their trespasses against them, and entrusting to us the message of reconciliation." This brings Paul, argues Wright, to the crux of his argument.

Paul, having been reconciled to God by the death of Christ, has now been given the task of ministering to others the same reconciliation that he has received. Hence, Paul states: "Therefore, we are ambassadors for Christ, God making his appeal through us. We implore you on behalf of Christ, be reconciled to God" (v. 20). Wright argues that it is in this trajectory that Paul brings 5:21 to the forefront. Wright states,

15. Wright, "Righteousness of God," 204.
16. See N. T. Wright, *The Climax of the Covenant* (Minneapolis: Fortress, 1993), 175–92.

The "earthen vessel" that Paul knows himself to be (4:7) has found the problem of his own earthiness dealt with, and has found itself filled, paradoxically, with treasure indeed: "for our sake God made Christ, who did not know sin, to be a sin-offering for us, *so that in him we might become God's covenant-faithfulness.*" The "righteousness of God" in this verse is not a human status in virtue of which the one who has "become" it stands "righteous" before God, as in Lutheran soteriology. It is the covenant faithfulness of the one true God, now active through the paradoxical Christ-shaped ministry of Paul, reaching out with the offer of reconciliation to all who hear his bold preaching.[17]

It is on the basis of this argumentation, then, that Wright rejects the traditional reading of 2 Corinthians 5:21.

Analysis of Wright's Exegesis of 2 Corinthians 5:21

Wright has rejected imputation for two main reasons: (1) the "righteousness of God" refers to his covenant faithfulness and not something that is communicated to the believer, and (2) the overall context of 2 Corinthians 5:21 mitigates the traditional interpretation. Let us first examine Wright's claim that the "righteousness of God" refers only to his covenant faithfulness.

The Meaning of "the Righteousness of God"

Wright argues on the basis of Paul's Jewish background that the *dikaiosynē theou* is a technical term in both postexilic and second-temple Judaism that refers to God's covenant faithfulness. In support of this claim Wright cites Ezra 9:6–15, Nehemiah 9:6–38, Daniel 9:3–19, Tobit 3:2, Isaiah 40–55, and Baruch 3:9–5:9.[18] In addition to this Wright is careful to distinguish between God's righteousness and the "righteousness" that humans possess when they enter the covenant:

The divine "righteousness" (covenant faithfulness) is emphatically not the same as the "righteousness" that humans have when they are declared to be covenant members. That idea, despite its often invoking the "forensic" setting of the language, fails to understand what that forensic setting means.

17. Wright, "Righteousness of God," 205–6.
18. Wright, *People of God*, 271, 109; idem, *Saint Paul*, 118–20.

In the Hebrew lawcourt the judge does not give, bestow, impute, or impart *his own "righteousness"* to the defendant. That would imply that the *defendant* was deemed to have conducted the case impartially, in accordance with the law, to have punished sin and upheld the defenseless innocent ones. "Justification," of course, means nothing like that. "Righteousness" is not a quality or substance that can thus be passed or transferred from the judge to the defendant. The righteousness of the judge is the judge's own character, status, and activity, demonstrated in doing these various things. The "righteousness" of the defendants is the status they possess when the court has found in their favor. Nothing more, nothing less. When we translate these forensic categories back into their theological context, that of the covenant, the point remains fundamental: the divine covenant faithful is not the same as human covenant membership. The fact that the same word (*dikaiosynē*) is used for both ideas indicates their close reciprocal relationship, not their identity.[19]

Righteousness, then, is a term for either God's covenant faithfulness or the Christian's covenant membership. Yet there is evidence that presents a problem for Wright's argument.

In the OT the psalmist asks the question, "Who shall ascend the hill of the LORD? And who shall stand in his holy place?" (Ps. 24:3). To this question the psalmist provides the following answer: "He who has clean hands and a pure heart, who does not lift up his soul to what is false and does not swear deceitfully. He will receive blessing from the LORD and righteousness from the God of his salvation" (Ps. 24:4–5). Now it is important that we take notice specifically of verse 5: the one with clean hands and a pure heart will receive blessing and righteousness from Yahweh, a conceptual equivalent to the *dikaiosynē theou*. What is the nature of the righteousness that is from God? Some modern translations offer "vindication" (so NIV, NRSV, RSV). Wright argues in various places that vindication is often the meaning behind the *tsdq* and *dikai-* word groups and that this is what it means to be righteous or justified.[20] Yet in this passage the one who has clean hands and a pure heart requires no vindication. At the same time, neither of Wright's explanations for the "righteousness of God" fits this context. The fact that blessing (*berakah*)

19. N. T. Wright, "Romans and the Theology of Paul," in *Pauline Theology*, ed. David M. Hay and E. Elizabeth Johnson (Minneapolis: Fortress, 1995), 3:38–39.

20. Wright, *People of God*, 334.

is synonymous with righteousness (*tsedaqah*) denies the possibility that it can refer to the covenant faithfulness of God or covenant membership, Wright's two main definitions for righteousness.[21] In contrast to Wright's common explanations for righteousness Hans-Joachim Kraus argues that from "Yahweh the *tsedaqah* in the form of a declaration of imputation goes out to the *tsaddiq*." He goes on to state,

> The declaratory act of imputation of righteousness must also have had an importance in connection with the Torah liturgy, that is, in reference to the list of characteristics in v. 4. But he who is declared "righteous" thereby receives the blessing, and that means the full enrichment and fulfillment of the life in the cultic area and in everyday life. The *tsaddiqim* are the blessed of God.[22]

Kraus is not alone in his observations. The LXX does not translate this verse using the standard equivalent *dikaiosynē* but instead *eleēmosynē*, or mercy. In other words, this righteousness is something that the one with clean hands and a pure heart receives from God, what the LXX renders as a genitive of source, *para theou*.[23] This is not God's covenant faithfulness, vindication, or covenant membership. There is further evidence from the NT to consider.

In the NT we find the following statement from Paul: "Not having a righteousness of my own that comes from the law, but that which comes through faith in Christ, the righteousness from God that depends on faith" (Phil. 3:9). Wright does not believe, however, that this verse demonstrates that there is a righteousness of God that he communicates to the believer. He states, "The case of Phil. 3:9, often cited as if it were an example of 'god's righteousness' seen as a human status, is not to the point; it is the status of covenant membership that is *ek theou, 'from God.'*"[24] In other words, God does not bestow an attribute but the status of covenant membership upon believers. If Wright's definition of righteousness, however, is faulty, then it seems from the grammar that Philippians 3:9 controverts Wright's point. This conclusion is indicated quite clearly by

21. David J. Reimer, "*tsdq*," in *NIDOTTE*, 3:760.
22. Hans-Joachim Kraus, *Psalms 1–59*, trans. Hilton C. Oswald (Minneapolis: Fortress, 1993), 314; James L. Mays, *Psalms* (Louisville: John Knox, 1994), 121–22.
23. Reimer, "*tsdq*," 3.760.
24. Wright, "Romans and the Theology of Paul," 39 n. 10; idem, *Saint Paul*, 124.

the preposition *ek*. There is little question surrounding the interpretation of this preposition compared to the ambiguous nature of translating the genitive of *dikaiosynē theou*. The phrase *ek theou* cannot refer to an attribute or quality of God.[25] This phrase means that God communicates righteousness to the believer.

At this point in our analysis thus far we have found sufficient grounds to question the first portion of Wright's argument. There is good reason to believe that the *dikaiosynē theou* is not exclusively an attribute or quality of God. In our brief examination of Psalm 24:5 "righteousness" does not appear to be God's faithfulness, vindication, or covenant membership of the believer. Moreover, given that God does communicate righteousness to the believer, such as in Paul's case (Phil. 3:9), there is good exegetical warrant to support the view that God does indeed impute his righteousness to the believer. Yet we must still investigate Wright's second point, namely the overall context of 2 Corinthians 5:21.

Wright's Third and Fourth Objections

In Wright's analysis of the context of 2 Corinthians 5:21 he gives four reasons why the traditional explanation of the verse does not fit. We will first examine Wright's third and fourth objections, namely that the typical explanation does not fit the overall discussion and that it affects the flow of the argument. First, Wright is correct regarding the thrust of Paul's overall argument—Christ is portrayed in the apostolic ministry of Paul (4:7–6:13). Wright is also correct in that Paul unpacks what it means to be a minister of the new covenant. Where one should take issue with Wright is in his analysis of 5:14–17 and his contention that the verses should not be read as gobbets of traditional soteriology. When Paul states that "if anyone is in Christ, he is a new creation" (v. 17a), he deals with, despite Wright's protestations, soteriology. To say that Paul does not expound upon soteriology is akin to saying that he simply appears on the stage of history as an incarnation of the suffering of Christ without a message of salvation (cf. 6:2). Wright pits the *ordo* and *historia salutis* against one another, as if a passage cannot speak to both. Rather, Paul explains, "The old has passed away; behold, the new has come. All this is from God, who through Christ reconciled us to himself and gave us the ministry of

25. M. J. Harris, "Prepositions and Theology in the Greek New Testament," in *NIDNTT*, 3:1188; and BAGD, 235, 3c.

reconciliation" (vv. 17b–18). Paul's statement involves both the *ordo* and *historia salutis*. The present evil age is passing away as the age to come dawns, the *historia salutis*, but this is inextricably linked with the soteric activity of God, the *ordo salutis* (cf. Isa. 43:18–19; 65:17; 66:22). At this point in Paul's argumentation it is important that we notice how Paul segues to the next verse. In verse 19 Paul explains how God reconciled the world to himself.[26]

Given the word order, Paul emphasizes that God was "in Christ" reconciling the world to himself. How did God accomplish this reconciliation in Christ? G. K. Beale notes that the subtext to 2 Corinthians 5–7 is Isaiah 40–66. Beale writes:

> Therefore the complex of ideas found in 2 Corinthians 5:14–21 can already be seen in Isaiah 40–66. In the light of the thematic overview of Isaiah 40–66 it is plausible to suggest that the "reconciliation" in Christ is Paul's way of explaining that Isaiah's promises of "restoration" from the alienation of exile have begun to be fulfilled by the atonement and forgiveness of sins in Christ.[27]

Hence God accomplishes the reconciliation through atonement, by not counting (*mē logizomenos*) the sins of the world against them (v. 19b). This is the first part of how God reconciles the world to himself. Again, we are clearly in the realm of soteriology at this point contra Wright's protestations. It is this message of "not counting their trespasses," or forgiveness, that God has entrusted to the apostles.[28]

There is, however, a second portion of the message of reconciliation of which Paul speaks in verses 20–21. In verse 20 Paul implores the Corinthians to heed the message of the apostles and to be reconciled to God. Paul then, for a second time, explains how God reconciles the world through Christ: "For our sake he made him to be sin who knew no sin, so that in him we might become the righteousness of God" (v. 21). Here we

---

26. C. K. Barrett, *The Second Epistle to the Corinthians*, BNTC (Peabody, MA: Hendrickson, 1983), 176. Cf. BAGD, 589; 2 Thess. 2:2; 2 Cor. 11:21; and Vul 2 Cor. 5:21.

27. G. K. Beale, "The Old Testament Background of Reconciliation in 2 Corinthians 5–7 and Its Bearing on the Literary Problem of 2 Corinthians 6:14–7:1," *NTS* 35 (1989): 556; Seyoon Kim, "2 Corinthians 5:11–21 and the Origin of Paul's Concept of 'Reconciliation,'" *NovT* 39 (1997): 364 n. 19; idem, *Paul and the New Perspective* (Grand Rapids: Eerdmans, 2002), 214–38.

28. M. D. Hooker, "Interchange in Christ," *JTS* 22 (1971): 353.

see that when God forgave sin, he did not simply write it off. Rather, he made Christ "to be sin who knew no sin." Now this is an important point in Paul's argumentation thus far—God placed the sin of the world upon Christ. Did Jesus actually commit sin? No. This would contradict Paul's statement that Christ "knew no sin." The impeccability of the Messiah is attested not only in the NT but also in the literature of second-temple Judaism (Heb. 4:15; Pss. Sol. 17.40; Test. Judah 24.1; Test. Levi 18.9). So, then, in what way did God make "him to be sin"? The answer lies in imputation, or Paul's use of *logizomenos* in verse 19.

God does not impute the sin and guilt of the world to those who are guilty, those who are actually sinful. He instead imputes the guilt and sin of the world to Christ, one who is sinless. There is a second half to this reconciliation equation, which is amply illustrated in the structure of verse 21 (fig. 7).[29]

Fig. 7. Structure of 2 Corinthians 5:21

a	b	c	d
ton mē gnonta hamartian	*hyper hēmōn*	*hamartian*	*epoiēsen*
Him who knew not sin	**on our behalf**	**sin**	**he made**

hina			
in order that			

a'	d'	c'	b'
hēmeis	*genōmetha*	*dikaiosynē theou*	*en autō*
we	**might become**	**the righteousness of God**	**in him**

The second half of the equation is the imputation of the righteousness of God, in Christ, to the world, made clear by the parallel structure of the verse. If one may use Wright's chief complaint regarding the traditional interpretation of this verse, if we merely say that Christ became sin by imputation and we only become God's covenantal faithfulness, it leaves the first half of the equation dangling. Christ would receive the sin of the world but does not impute righteousness to it. The parallelism loses its structure with Wright's interpretation.[30] Moreover, one should

---

29. Barrett, *Second Corinthians*, 179; also Hooker, "Interchange in Christ," 349.

30. Murray J. Harris, *The Second Epistle to the Corinthians*, NIGTC (Grand Rapids: Eerdmans, 2005), 455–56 n. 207.

press Wright at this point and ask the pointed question, If his offered interpretation regarding the covenant faithfulness of God is correct, in what way is God faithful to his covenant? What does his covenant faithfulness actually mean? Would it not entail the forgiveness of sins? Would not God's covenant faithfulness entail the atonement of Christ? Would it not involve soteriology, the salvation of sinners? Even if his contention regarding the proper understanding of the righteousness of God is correct, it is unclear how he can excise or underemphasize the soteriological aspects from this passage. Nevertheless, that Paul refers to imputed righteousness is further confirmed by the Isaianic subtext of 2 Corinthians 5–7.

Beale argues that recent NT scholarship, specifically the work of O. Hofius, places Isaiah 53 as the specific subtext behind 2 Corinthians 5:21.[31] Beale writes that "Hofius' proposal should be judged as plausible with respect to 2 Corinthians 5:21, since the combined ideas of a sinless penal substitute, the imputation of sin to a sinless figure to redeem a sinful people and the granting of righteousness are uniquely traceable to Isaiah 53:4–12."[32] We see the dual ideas of forgiveness and imputation, for example, when we read "the LORD has laid on him the iniquity of us all" (Isa. 53:6b) and "by his knowledge shall the righteous one, my servant, make many to be accounted righteous, and he shall bear their iniquities" (Isa. 53:11). Contra Wright, therefore, God imputes his righteousness in Christ, which means the righteousness of Christ to those who are saved.[33]

Moreover, this conclusion fits the overall thrust of Paul's argumentation. He and the other apostles share in the sufferings of Christ in their ministry and implore the Corinthians not to eschew their labor because God has entrusted to them the message of reconciliation. What is the message of reconciliation? That God imputes the sin of the world to Christ and imputes his own righteousness to them in Christ. Paul does not separate the *ordo* from the *historia salutis* as Wright is inclined to do.

---

31. Beale cites O. Hofius, "Erwägungen zur Gestalt und Hefkunft des paulinischen Versöhnungsgedankens," *ZTK* 77 (1980): 186–99, esp. 196–99.

32. Beale, "Old Testament Background of Reconciliation," 559–60; also Kim, "Reconciliation," 376, 380, 383.

33. D. A. Carson, "The Vindication of Imputation: On Fields of Discourse and Semantic Fields," in *Justification*, ed. Mark Husbands and Daniel J. Treier (Downers Grove, IL: InterVarsity, 2004), 69.

This addresses Wright's third and fourth criticisms. What about Wright's first and second criticisms?

Wright's First and Second Objections

We must recall that Wright claims that, first, Paul does not potentially refer to the idea of the communication of righteousness anywhere else except in 1 Corinthians 1:30. Second, according to Wright, Paul says that we become "God's righteousness," not Christ's. Let us first examine Wright's second objection. Wright's objection at this point borders on what can only be called a literalistic biblicism. Yes, he is correct to state that it is "God's righteousness" to which Paul refers. Nevertheless, Paul also emphasizes that God's righteousness comes *en autō* ("in him"), in Christ. It is not possible to separate the righteousness of God from the righteousness of Christ unless one wishes to posit a radical tritheism, a separation of the ontological Trinity. Contra Wright, we see an example of the unity of attributes of the Trinity in 1 Corinthians 1:3–4: "Grace to you and peace from God our Father and the Lord Jesus Christ. I give thanks to my God always for you because of the grace of God that was given you in Christ Jesus." We see that grace comes both from the Father and the Son, but that the grace of God comes *en Christō*. Can one truly separate the grace of God from the grace of Christ? No. Rather, the grace of God, which Paul can call the grace of Christ, comes *en Christō*. Likewise, the righteousness of God comes *en autō* (cf. 2 Peter 1:1). Let us turn our attention to Wright's first criticism.

Wright argues that the only other possible place that Paul uses imputation language concerning righteousness is in 1 Corinthians 1:30: "He is the source of your life in Christ Jesus, whom God made our wisdom and our righteousness and sanctification and redemption." Wright, however, objects to this verse as evidence of the imputation of Christ's righteousness:

> It is difficult to squeeze any precise dogma of justification out of this shorthand summary. It is the only passage I know where something called "the imputed righteousness of Christ," a phrase more often found in post-Reformation theology and piety than in the New Testament, finds any basis in the text. But if we are to claim it as such, we must also be prepared to talk of the imputed wisdom of Christ; the imputed sanctification of Christ; and the imputed redemption of Christ; and that, though no doubt they

are all true in some overall general sense, will certainly make nonsense of the very specialized and technical senses so frequently given to the phrase "the righteousness of Christ" in the history of theology.[34]

Wright assumes that if imputation governs the nature of the communication of righteousness, then it must also govern the communication of wisdom, sanctification, and redemption. There is nothing, however, stated in this verse that requires Wright's conclusion. What governs this verse is not the idea of imputation, as Wright presumes of those who appeal to this verse, but being *en Christō*, or in the terms of systematic theology, union with Christ. The four qualities, wisdom, righteousness, sanctification, and redemption, belong together and come through Christ.[35] But as the immediate context shows, wisdom, for example, comes not through imputation but through the preaching of the cross: "We preach Christ crucified . . . to those who are called, both Jews and Greeks, Christ the power of God and the wisdom of God" (vv. 23–24).[36] In the context of Paul's introduction, it is God's "called" (v. 24) or "chosen" (cf. v. 2) who are *en Christō* (v. 30).[37] In other words, preaching or calling God's chosen governs the way in which believers receive the wisdom of God.

By contrast, "redemption" is a term that usually has three components: (1) liberation from a state of bondage, (2) liberation by an act, and (3) liberation to a new situation of service. Throughout the NT when one sees the term "redemption" it often invokes allusions to Israel's deliverance from Egypt, in which they were: (1) liberated from Egypt, (2) by God's saving acts, which involved the shedding of blood, the firstborn of Egypt, and the Passover lamb, and (3) en route to the promised land. This is plausibly the background that Paul has in mind here at Corinth. The Corinthians were: (1) lowly "nothings," (2) freed by Christ's costly death on the cross, (3) to a new state of freedom and glory.[38] The Corinthian redemption, however, comes to them *en Christō*. Now it is important to note that if wisdom and redemption have different instrumental means by which they

---

34. Wright, *Saint Paul*, 122–23; idem, "Righteousness of God," 204 n. 7.

35. A. C. Thiselton, *The First Epistle to the Corinthians*, NIGTC (Grand Rapids: Eerdmans, 2000), 191; cf. Wright, "Righteousness of God," 204 n. 7.

36. James D. G. Dunn, *Christology in the Making* (1980; London: SCM Press, 1989), 178.

37. Victor P. Furnish, "Theology in 1 Corinthians," in *Pauline Theology*, ed. David M. Hay (Atlanta: SBL, 2002), 2:85.

38. Thiselton, *First Corinthians*, 194–95.

come to the believer, then it is entirely possible that righteousness and sanctification can also come through alternative instrumental means.[39] What unifies the four qualities is not their instrumental means of communication but the material means, namely being *en Christō*. When one is united to Christ he receives the wisdom of God through calling, righteousness through imputation, sanctification through the indwelling of the Holy Spirit, and redemption through the cross.

Summary

Thus far we have examined Wright's exegesis of 2 Corinthians 5:21 and 1 Corinthians 1:30 and found it wanting. Wright's claim that righteousness is always God's covenant faithfulness, vindication, or covenant membership does not fit all of the biblical evidence as Psalm 24:5 and Philippians 3:9 demonstrate. Moreover, the traditional interpretation of 2 Corinthians 5:21 is much more convincing than Wright's explanation due to the presence of the parallelism in the verse. We must proceed, however, to the second portion of our investigation, namely another passage of Scripture that deals with the subject of imputation, Romans 5:12–21.

Imputation and Romans 5:12–21

We must remember Wright's claim that there are only two passages of Scripture that possibly deal with the imputation of Christ's righteousness, which we have examined above.[40] There is, however, another passage that deserves our consideration; the Westminster Confession appeals to Romans 5:12–21, especially verses 17–19, on the matter of imputation.[41] Romans 5:17–19 contains important parallels to 2 Corinthians 5:21, particularly the themes of sin, righteousness, and being in Christ. Paul writes:

> If, because of one man's trespass, death reigned through that one man, much more will those who receive the abundance of grace and the free gift of righteousness reign in life through the one man Jesus Christ. Therefore,

---

39. Brian Vickers, *Jesus' Blood and Righteousness: Paul's Theology of Imputation* (Wheaton, IL: Crossway, 2006), 201.

40. Wright, "Righteousness of God," 204 n. 7.

41. See WCF 11.1; SC 33; LC 70.

as one trespass led to condemnation for all men, so one act of righteousness leads to justification and life for all men. For as by the one man's disobedience the many were made sinners, so by the one man's obedience the many will be made righteous.

Before we analyze these verses it is necessary to examine how Wright interprets them.

Wright on Romans 5:17–19

We must first understand what Wright believes is the overall theme of Romans before we can rightly expound his exegesis of Romans 5:17–19. Wright believes the main theme of Romans is God's righteousness, or covenant faithfulness. In Romans 1–4 Paul explains that God has been faithful to his covenant promise to Abraham and has done this through the Messiah, Jesus. Adam first failed to yield obedience so God replaced Adam with Abraham.[42] Israel arose from Abraham and was supposed to be the answer to the fall of Adam: "If Abraham and his family are understood as the creator's means of dealing with the sin of Adam, and hence with the evil in the world, Israel herself becomes the true Adamic humanity . . . in terms (for the moment) of Israel's own role . . . she is taking the place—under God and over the world—which according to the Genesis picture was the place of Adam."[43] As we know, however, Israel was disobedient and God therefore placed them in exile. God therefore sent Christ to fulfil the covenant that he had made with Abraham. Where Israel failed, Christ succeeded: "In the face of a world in rebellion and a chosen people unfaithful to their commission, God has, through the surrogate faithfulness of Jesus the Messiah, created a worldwide—that is, a Jewish and Gentile—family for Abraham, marked out by the covenant sign of faith."[44] Concerning Romans 5–8 Wright argues that Paul spells out the implications of chapters 1–4:

God has thereby done what the covenant was set up to do: to address and solve the problem expressed in biblical terms as the sin of Adam. In the Messiah, Jesus, God has done for this new people what was done for Israel

42. Wright, *People of God*, 262–63.
43. Ibid., 262, 264.
44. Wright, *Romans*, 405; also idem, *Jesus and the Victory of God* (Minneapolis: Fortress, 1996), 125–44.

of old in fulfillment of the promise to Abraham: Redeemed from the Egypt of enslavement to sin, they are led through the wilderness of the present life by the Spirit (not by the Torah), and they look forward to the inheritance, which will consist of the entire redeemed creation.[45]

Now it is in this overall trajectory that Wright gives his analysis of Romans 5:12–21, and more specifically verses 17–19.

Wright does not follow the typical Reformed exegesis of Romans 5:12–21.[46] Regarding verses 18–19 Wright argues that Paul explains the significance of Christ's obedience in contrast to Adam's disobedience. It is here that Wright takes issue with the traditional Reformed exegesis:

A long tradition within one strand of the Reformation thought has supposed that Paul was here referring to Jesus' perfect obedience to the law. In this view, Christ's "active obedience" and his "passive obedience" work together. His active obedience acquires "righteousness," which is then "reckoned" to those "in Christ"; his passive obedience, culminating in the cross, deals with his people's sins. Powerful though this thought is, and influential though it has been (even in liturgy, where "the merits and death of Christ" are sometimes mentioned in the double sense), it is almost certainly not what Paul has in mind here.[47]

What alternative does Wright offer in place of the traditional Reformed view? Wright argues that Romans 5 must be read in the light of the overarching narrative, namely the covenant faithfulness of God. God has sent Christ to fulfil the role that Israel failed to perform:

Israel's obedience/faithfulness should have been the means of undoing the problem of Adam, of humanity as a whole (2:17–24; 3:2f.); as we saw, the death of Christ (which is clearly the subject throughout this paragraph) functions as the true obedience/faithfulness of Israel through which this purpose is achieved. Rom. 5:12–21 thus restates, in multiple and overlapping ways, what had been argued in 3:21–26. Christ has offered not merely Adam's obedience, but Israel's, the "obedience" that was to begin where the "many trespasses" of Adam left off (5:16). Christ, in other words, did not start where Adam started, but where Adam (and Israel) finished.

45. Wright, *Romans*, 405.
46. E.g., Charles Hodge, *Romans* (1835; Edinburgh: Banner of Truth, 1989), 142–91.
47. Wright, *Romans*, 529.

Coming into the reign of death, he reinstated the divinely intended reign of human beings (5:17).[48]

What this means, then, is that we must read verses 18–19 in the following manner:

> Therefore, as one trespass [Adam and Israel's failure] led to condemnation for all men [presence of evil in the world], so one act of righteousness [Christ's obedience] leads to justification [vindication and being "in the right"] and life for all men. For as by the one man's disobedience [Adam and Israel's] the many were made sinners, so by the one man's obedience [Christ's death on the cross] the many will be made righteous [covenant members].[49]

We see that Wright's exegesis of Romans 5:12–21 is significantly different from the traditional Reformed interpretation. Moreover, we also see why Wright would therefore not appeal to Romans 5:12–21 as a possible text that deals with the imputation of Christ's righteousness. There are, however, significant problems with Wright's interpretation of Romans 5:12–21.

Analysis of Wright's Exegesis

First, presuppositions drive conclusions. Wright's presuppositions, namely that Romans 5–8, indeed Romans as a whole, deals with Adam and Israel's disobedience and how Christ embodies the covenant faithfulness of God in taking up Israel's failed responsibility, drive him in a direction away from anything that might yield information regarding imputation. According to Wright, the passage revolves more around narrative than it does theology, how Christ takes up Israel's place in redemptive history. Once again, he seems to pit the *ordo* against the *historia salutis*. Yet, one should ask, Where does Paul ever say that Israel's obedience should have remedied the problem of Adam, or that Christ has rendered obedience for Adam and Israel?[50] If Paul wanted to incorporate Israel at this juncture, why would he not do so explicitly?

---

48. Wright, "Romans and the Theology of Paul," 46; idem, *Romans*, 529.
49. Wright, *Romans*, 529.
50. Richard B. Hays, "Adam, Israel, Christ: The Question of Covenant in the Theology of Romans: A Response to Leander E. Keck and N. T. Wright," in *Pauline Theology*, ed. David M. Hay and E. Elizabeth Johnson (Minneapolis: Fortress, 1995), 3:81.

Second, at key points in Romans 5:12–21 Wright avoids important exegetical details to facilitate his interpretation. For example, concerning Romans 5:12, "Therefore, just as sin came into the world through one man, and death through sin, and so death spread to all men because all sinned," Wright acknowledges the deeply controversial nature of the interpretation of the phrase *eph' hō pantes hēmarton* ("because all sinned"). He asks, "Does the verb refer to actual sins committed by all people (as in the 'many sins' of v. 16), or to the primal act of Adam seen as the time when 'all sinned'?" Wright dissects the phrase and agrees with the NIV's translation ("because all sinned"), which recognizes the aorist tense, over and against the NRSV, which translates it as if it were in the perfect tense ("because all have sinned"). Wright then states that it is possible to see this as a reference to Adam, but then argues that too much weight should not be placed on the aorist since this verse can be summed up by the aorist of Romans 3:23: *pantes gar hēmarton* ("for all sinned"). Wright then argues that Paul's main point is thus: "What matters is that all human sin can now be lumped together into one. 'All sinned.'"[51] Nevertheless, we should ask, are not Romans 3:23 and 5:12 saying the same thing, in that would not Romans 3:23, despite the use of the aorist, also refer to Adam's sin?

What about the connection between the sin of Adam, "just as sin came into the world through one man," and the rest of mankind, "because all sinned"? Wright argues,

> Faced with this dilemma, some scholars emphasize the responsibility of each individual, while others, not least those anxious to maintain Paul's parallel between Adam and Christ, emphasize the primal sin as somehow involving all subsequent humanity (it is not necessary, to hold this view, to espouse along with it any particular theory of the mode by which sin is then transmitted).[52]

In other words, Wright tries to argue that Paul's main point is that mankind is guilty of sin and that it is not important whether it is the primal sin of Adam or actual sin; mankind is simply guilty of sin. Wright summarizes his exegesis at this point and states: "Paul's meaning must

51. Wright, *Romans*, 526.
52. Ibid.

in any case be both that an entail of sinfulness has spread throughout the human race from its first beginnings and that each individual has contributed their own share to it. Paul offers no further clue as to how the first of these actually works or how the two interrelate."[53] Wright's conclusions here at Romans 5:12, of course, support his overall exegesis of Romans 5:12–21. His conclusions are, however, problem-laden.

Wright has not given the reader a crucial piece of exegetical work that establishes his case for the overall interpretation of Romans 5:12–21. He has ineffectively sidestepped a critical element in Paul's argumentation, namely the parallel between Adam and Christ. If Paul is not concerned with the manner of the transmission of sin in verse 12, then of course verses 13–21 do not deal with the subject of imputation. The question, however, still stands, How can Paul say that when Adam sinned, all sinned? There is little trouble understanding how Adam is subject to death: he sinned. But why does death spread to mankind? Paul answers quite succinctly, "Because all sinned." Paul with unmistakable clarity asserts that the universal reign of death rests upon the one sin of the one man Adam. This is evident in verse 12 when we compare "sin came into the world through one man" and what verse 18 calls "one trespass," and verse 19 calls "one man's disobedience."[54] Paul is keenly aware of and interested in precisely the manner of transmission of the sin of Adam.

Contra Wright, there is no question that Paul has in mind the primal sin of Adam distinct from the sins of mankind. Neither does Paul have Israel's disobedience in view. Rather, as in 2 Corinthians 5:21, Paul sets up a parallel, this time between the sin of Adam and the obedience of Christ: "The parallel to the imputation of Adam's sin is the imputation of Christ's righteousness. Or to use Paul's own terms, being 'constituted sinners' through the disobedience of Adam is parallel to being 'constituted righteous' through the obedience of Christ."[55] Just as the world was not present in the garden to commit sin but is held accountable for Adam's rebellion, so too those who are in Christ, though they personally do not merit eternal life, receive it as a result of Christ's obedience and the imputation of his righteousness.[56]

---

53. Ibid., 527.
54. John Murray, *The Imputation of Adam's Sin* (Philadelphia: P&R, 1959), 19–20.
55. Ibid., 76.
56. So Thomas R. Schreiner, *Romans*, BECNT (Grand Rapids: Baker, 1998), 288–90; C. E. B. Cranfield, *Romans*, 2 vols., ICC (1975; Edinburgh: T & T Clark, 2001), 1:274–81. Fitzmyer also points out concerning Romans 5:19 that, once again, Paul may be alluding to Isaiah

Summary

Needless to say, there is a great divergence between the traditional Reformed reading of Romans 5:12–21 and Wright's interpretation. For Wright, the passage deals with God's covenant faithfulness in Christ, who takes up the failed work of Adam and Israel and puts the world to rights. God forgives the sin of those who are in Christ, but there is no communication of the righteousness of Christ, only the communication of status—covenant membership. Wright argues that there is no exchange of man's sin for Christ's righteousness. Our examination has shown, however, that Wright is able to make his case only by sidestepping Paul's point in Romans 5:12—when one sinned, all sinned. Saying that Paul merely wants to emphasize the sinfulness of all mankind avoids the clarity of Paul's parallel between Adam and Christ. Contra Wright, Romans 5:12–21 is an important text that deals with the subject of imputation.

Conclusion

We have examined Wright's claims regarding the supposed absence of imputation in Paul. Wright claims that there are only two potential passages that deal with the subject, 1 Corinthians 1:30 and 2 Corinthians 5:21. He arrives at this conclusion, though, by sidestepping important exegetical details in Romans 5:12–21. Contra Wright, there is solid exegetical evidence to support the idea that the righteousness of Christ is imputed to the believer in his justification. While Wright's exegesis and rejection of imputation have been found wanting, there are broader implications bound up in Wright's views on this matter for the Reformed community.

Wright believes that he brings a necessary *semper reformanda* to the church's understanding of Pauline theology, especially as it relates to the doctrine of justification, and as we have seen here, more specifically imputation. He also believes that his own exegetical proposals on, over, and against the doctrine of imputation render the same results as the traditional view:

The imputation of Christ's righteousness is one of the big sticking points for sure. I think I know exactly what the doctrine is about and I believe you

---

53:11–12 (Joseph A. Fitzmyer, *Romans*, AB 33 [New York: Doubleday, 1993], 421; see also Hooker, "Interchange in Christ," 355, 358.

don't lose anything by the route I propose. The force of what people have believed when they have used the idea of imputation is completely retained in what I have tried to do. Why? Because in Christ we have all the treasures, not only of wisdom and knowledge (Col. 1, and also 1 Cor. 1), but in whom we have the entire package, meaning sanctification and wisdom, as well as righteousness. So Paul's theology of being in Christ gives you all of that.[57]

Wright therefore proposes that while he denies the concept of imputation, the believer nonetheless receives the righteousness of Christ through union with him. Yet according to Wright's own exegesis this is a hollow statement because the believer never really receives the righteousness of Christ. As Wright is fond of reminding his readers, "When either the plaintiff or the defendant is declared 'righteous' at the end of the case, there is no sense that in either case the judge's *own* righteousness has been passed on to them, by imputation, impartation, or any other process."[58] In other words, because Wright's version of the believer's union with Christ is devoid of the imputation of his righteousness, it is incomplete. Calvin once commented regarding the inseparable nature of our union with Christ and the imputation of righteousness:

> Therefore, that joining together of Head and members, that indwelling of Christ in our hearts—in short, that *mystical union*—are accorded by us the highest degree of importance, so that Christ, having been made ours, makes us sharers with him in the gifts with which he has been endowed. We do not, therefore, contemplate him outside ourselves from afar in order that his righteousness may be imputed to us but because we put on Christ and are engrafted into his body—in short, because he deigns to make us one with him. For this reason, we glory that we have fellowship of righteousness with him.[59]

For those who embrace Wright's views on imputation, these words are just as timely and significant as when Calvin first penned them, especially in light of Wright's rejection of imputation.[60]

---

57. Tamerius, "Interview," 129.
58. Wright, "New Perspectives," 7; idem, "Romans," 38–39.
59. John Calvin, *Institutes of the Christian Religion*, ed. John T. McNeill, trans. Ford Lewis Battles, LCC 20–21 (Philadelphia: Westminster, 1960), 3.11.10.
60. Richard B. Gaffin Jr., "Biblical Theology and the Westminster Standards," *WTJ* 65/2 (2003): 178.

Do we truly have union with Christ if we do not share in his righteousness through imputation? Some will answer yes. But to deny imputation, at least as it comes from Wright's pen, lacks exegetical warrant. While we must always be willing to employ *semper reformanda* to the church's understanding of Scripture, we should first be willing to apply the principle to our own understanding of doctrine. Perhaps it is our own views that require correction. In this particular case, it does not appear that the Reformed appeal to 2 Corinthians 5:21, 1 Corinthians 1:30, or Romans 5:12–21 is unwarranted to support the doctrine of the imputed righteousness of Jesus Christ. We may now turn to the question of the relationship between justification and the believer's union with Christ.

10

JUSTIFICATION AND UNION WITH CHRIST

Over the last several chapters we examined the elements of justification by faith, that it is: (1) by faith alone, (2) the remission of sins, and (3) the imputation of the righteousness of Christ, as well as explored these elements vis-à-vis the challenges brought forward by the New Perspective on Paul, specifically from the writings of N. T. Wright. These elements pertain to the *ordo salutis* and the application of redemption to the individual believer. We also explored the connections between justification and the *historia salutis*, or redemptive history. We saw that justification is inextricably linked to the resurrection of Christ, which means that justification is eschatological. Justification is also eschatological because it brings forward into the present the judgment from the last day. This is nowhere more evident than in Paul's famous statement "There is therefore now no condemnation for those who are in Christ Jesus" (Rom. 8:1), which could be alternatively stated, "There is therefore now justification for those who are in Christ Jesus." At the same time this statement of Paul raises the question, What does it mean to be "in

Christ"? Paul's statement raises the question of what is the relationship between justification and union with Christ.

We have made some preliminary observations in the chapter on prolegomena on the broader issue of justification and the *ordo salutis*. However, we must expand upon these observations so we can set forth a full-orbed understanding of the relationship between the two doctrines. In the past, Reformed theologians saw no tension between the *ordo salutis* and union with Christ, or more specifically imputation and union with Christ. Yet in subsequent centuries, particularly in the nineteenth century, this recognition of the harmony between the two doctrines was questioned. And in recent years others within the Reformed community have questioned the relationship between the two, arguing that the doctrine of imputation is redundant in the light of the believer's union with Christ.

To address these challenges to the doctrine of justification and especially its relationship to union with Christ, we will first survey the claims of those who believe there is a tension between the so-called legal, imputation, and relational, union with Christ, categories. Second we will set forth the biblical data for the doctrine of union with Christ. Third, we will set forth a theological formulation based upon the biblical data. And, fourth, we will then explain the relationship between justification and the believer's union with Christ.

Disharmony between Justification and Union with Christ

Historically, there have been those who have pitted the forensic against the filial aspects of God's relationship with mankind and more specifically his people. Along similar lines, recently others have argued that in light of one's union with Christ, the forensic or legal aspects of justification are redundant or unnecessary. There are four main figures upon whom we should focus: Albert Schweitzer, Albrecht Ritschl, N. T. Wright, and Rich Lusk.[1]

Schweitzer and Ritschl

Albert Schweitzer famously once wrote, "The doctrine of righteousness by faith is therefore a subsidiary crater, which has formed within the rim

---

1. There are others whom we can group with these aforementioned authors, such as Karl Barth, T. F. Torrance, and Trevor Hart (see Andrew T. B. McGowan, "Justification and the *Ordo Salutis*," in *Justification in Perspective*, ed. Bruce L. McCormack [Grand Rapids: Baker, 2006], 158–60).

of the main crater—the mystical doctrine of redemption through the being-in-Christ."[2] Schweitzer tended to see the doctrines of justification and union with Christ as representing two competing strains within Paul's theology. One finds similar trends in the theology of Albrecht Ritschl. Ritschl's understanding of justification is important as we consider justification and union with Christ because he anticipates some of the current trends within the Reformed community.

First, Ritschl argues that justification is synonymous with the forgiveness of sins.[3]

Second, Ritschl argues that the concept of God as lawgiver and judge has no place in the doctrine of justification. Ritschl writes:

> We may at the outset concede to the orthodox theology that the imputation of the double obedience of Christ to the law, for the purpose of judging sinners as righteous, may be represented as a special instance of the application of law by the Judge. We cannot, however, represent this act as isolated from the antecedent gracious purpose of God, His purpose, namely, to bless sinners; nor must we lose sight of the fact that God has Himself brought into court the Righteous One, Whose obedience to the law, according to the presupposition, He judicially imputes to sinners. On these two accounts, God in executing the judicial act of imputing the righteousness of Christ to sinners, cannot be conceived as Lawgiver and Judge, but as the Dispenser of grace and love to men. The act of imputation, moreover, when placed in its true connection with the whole, is only the means to an end. The judicial quality in God, therefore, can be admitted only as a co-operating element in the act of justification, or as a subordinate trait in the conception of His character as the Author of justification.[4]

Ritschl argues against the idea of God as Judge, for example, because a judge always makes analytical, not synthetic, declarations. If justification is a synthetic judgment in the case of the believer, then, argues Ritschl, justification is an act of grace, not justice. Ritschl argues that "pardon, or the forgiveness of sins, is connected, not with God's special attribute as

2. Albert Schweitzer, *The Mysticism of Paul the Apostle*, trans. William Montgomery (1931; Baltimore: Johns Hopkins University Press, 1998), 223–26.

3. Albrecht Ritschl, *The Christian Doctrine of Justification and Reconciliation* (1902; Eugene, OR: Wipf & Stock, 2004), 38–40.

4. Ibid., 87.

Lawgiver, but with His general attribute as King and Lord of His Kingdom among men."[5]

Third, Ritschl observes that according to Scripture the proper way to view the relationship of the pardon of sin to God is that "Jesus explicitly connected this operation of God with His attribute as Father."[6] Ritschl, though, highlights the supposed contradiction between God as Judge and Father when he writes:

> The title of Judge as applied to God has therefore for Christians no real place alongside of, or over, the relation in which He stands to them as Father. It is only, therefore, when the love of God, regarded as Father, is conceived as the will which works toward the destined end, that the real equivalence of forgiveness and justification, which is represented in the religious conception of things, can be made good. If, however, God be preconceived as Judge in the forensic sense, the two ideas come into direct antagonism with one another, as was indeed explicitly maintained by the leading representatives of the older theology.[7]

Ritschl, therefore, posits an antithesis between the forensic, or legal, and the filial, or relational, understanding of justification as it is commonly represented.

Fourth, Ritschl believes that all men, because they are created in the image of God, are God's children. For believers, then, there is no need for an analytical judgment in their justification because parents make synthetic judgments in regard to their children.[8] Or, in other words, a father always judges his children on the basis of grace, not justice.

Fifth, upon the presupposition that all men are God's children, as his attribute as Father is determinative, justification and adoption are substantially equivalent ideas.[9]

We can summarize Ritschl's views: he presupposes that justification must be founded upon the idea of God as Father and mankind as his children. In such a context, the father has no problem making synthetic judgments as it concerns his children. Given that justification is predi-

5. Ibid., 92.
6. Ibid., 93.
7. Ibid., 94.
8. Ibid., 97–98.
9. Ibid., 97.

cated upon God as Father, Ritschl posits that justification, or the legal or forensic, is essentially equivalent to the doctrine of adoption, or the filial. Ritschl resolves the supposed tension between the forensic and filial by melding the doctrines of justification and adoption—the legal is swallowed up by the filial. This trend continues in our own day.

Wright and Lusk

Recently there have been those who have argued that in light of the believer's union with Christ the concept of the imputed righteousness of Christ is an unnecessary redundancy. This view has received much impetus from N. T. Wright and has been incorporated by some Reformed thinkers. In Wright's rejection of the imputed righteousness of Christ he argues:

> The force of what people have believed when they have used the idea of imputation is completely retained in what I have tried to do. Why? Because in Christ we have all the treasures, not only of wisdom and knowledge (Col. 1, and also 1 Cor. 1), but in whom we have the entire package, meaning sanctification and wisdom, as well as righteousness. So Paul's theology of being in Christ gives you all of that.[10]

Along these lines Rich Lusk argues that because Christ's resurrection was his justification, it also represents the justification of all of those who are in him. Christ's justified status belongs to the believer through union with him:

> This justification requires no transfer or imputation of anything. It does not force us to reify "righteousness" into something that can be shuffled around in heavenly accounting books. Rather because I am in the Righteous One and the Vindicated One, I am righteous and vindicated. My in-Christ-ness makes imputation redundant. I do not need the moral content of his life of righteousness transferred to me; what I need is a share in the forensic verdict passed over him at the resurrection. Union with Christ is therefore key.[11]

10. See Travis Tamerius, "An Interview with N. T. Wright," *RRJ* 11/1 (2002): 129; N. T. Wright, "On Becoming the Righteousness of God," in *Pauline Theology*, ed. David M. Hay (Atlanta: SBL, 2002), 2:200–208.

11. Rich Lusk, "A Response to 'The Biblical Plan of Salvation,'" in *The Auburn Avenue Theology*, ed. E. Calvin Beisner (Fort Lauderdale: Knox Theological Seminary, 2004), 142;

One should also note that, in parallel with Ritschl, Lusk often pits the forensic and filial against one another, that is, a child cannot be treated under legal categories: "The covenant of works construction strikes at the filial nature of covenant sonship. Adam was God's son, not his employee."[12] We may summarize this current trend in some portions of the Reformed community as a rejection of the imputed righteousness of Christ because the filial aspect of God's relationship to his people is primary. Justification of the believer, therefore, is reached, not through imputation, but through union with Christ. Let us turn to set forth a positive formulation of the doctrine of union with Christ. From this positive formulation we can then critique the idea that there is an antithesis between justification and union with Christ, or the supposed legal and filial, or relational categories.

Positive Formulation

A typical definition of union with Christ comes from Louis Berkhof: "That intimate, vital, and spiritual union between Christ and His people, in virtue of which He is the source of their life and strength, of their blessedness and salvation."[13] Union with Christ is also called "mystical," because as A. A. Hodge notes, "It so far transcends all the analogies of earthly relationships, in the intimacy of its communion, in the transforming power of its influence, and in the excellence of its consequences."[14] Union with Christ is an all-encompassing doctrine, as it embraces the full scope of one's redemption, from eternal election to glorification.[15] To substantiate these definitions and characterizations, let us survey some of the biblical data.

Biblical Data

When we come to the subject of the believer's union with Christ, we find a host of Scripture references that speak of the believer being *en*

Robert H. Gundry, "The Non-Imputation of Christ's Righteousness," in *Justification: What's at Stake in the Current Debates*, ed. Mark Husbands and Daniel J. Treier (Downers Grove, IL: InterVarsity, 2004), 17–45.

12. Rich Lusk, "Private Communication 27 May 2003," cited in James B. Jordan, "Merit vs. Maturity: What Did Jesus Do for Us?" in *The Federal Vision*, ed. Steve Wilkins and Duane Garner (Monroe, LA: Athanasius Press, 2004), 155.

13. Louis Berkhof, *Systematic Theology: New Combined Edition* (1932–38; Grand Rapids: Eerdmans, 1996), 449; Lewis B. Smedes, *Union with Christ* (Grand Rapids: Eerdmans, 1970), 25.

14. A. A. Hodge, *Outlines of Theology* (1860; Edinburgh: Banner of Truth, 1991), 483; John Murray, *Redemption Accomplished and Applied* (Grand Rapids: Eerdmans, 1955), 167.

15. Murray, *Redemption*, 161, 165.

Christō, or in Christ. There are some twenty-five occurrences of this phrase in Paul's epistles; the phrase signifies the intimate fellowship believers enjoy with Christ.[16] There are several passages that deserve our attention. As we have already seen, as a result of the believer's union, for those who are in Christ, there is "now no condemnation" (Rom. 8:1). This is, of course, because Christ has paid the penalty of sin, and God has imputed the righteousness of his Son to the believer (Gal. 3:10–13; Rom. 4:1–8; 5:12–21). At this point, though, as we have noted, the nature of the believer's justification is purely forensic—the believer's guilt is imputed to Christ, and his righteousness is imputed to the believer. To be "in Christ," however, is something more than a forensic declaration. We see the organic nature of the union especially in Paul's epistle to Ephesus.

Perhaps one of the most explicit passages that addresses the believer's union with Christ comes in Paul's epistle to the Ephesians. It is in the fifth chapter where Paul demonstrates the typological connection between Adam and Eve, the first husband and wife, and the last Adam and his bride, the church. Paul writes, "In the same way husbands should love their wives as their own bodies. He who loves his wife loves himself" (Eph. 5:28). Here we see that though the husband and wife are two separate human beings, through the lens of marriage they are considered one single entity. This is especially evident when Paul says that husbands must love their wives, and that the one who loves his wife loves himself.[17] Paul continues along these lines, stating that "no one ever hated his own flesh, but nourishes and cherishes it" (Eph. 5:29ab). So, then, the husband supplies his wife with all of her needs, "just as Christ does the church, because we are members of his body" (Eph. 5:29c–30). Paul amplifies the nature of the union between the husband and wife by quoting Genesis 2:24: "Therefore a man shall leave his father and mother and hold fast to his wife, and the two shall become one flesh" (Eph. 5:31). It is important that we note the emphasis upon the union of the husband and wife and their identity as "one flesh."

Paul takes this verse and typologically applies it to Christ and the church: "This mystery is profound, and I am saying that it refers to

---

16. Simon J. Kistemaker, *II Corinthians*, NTC (Grand Rapids: Baker, 1997), 193.
17. Andrew T. Lincoln, *Ephesians*, WBC 42 (Dallas: Word, 1990), 379.

Christ and the church" (Eph. 5:32). In other words, the church is joined to Christ and is considered one flesh with him.[18] Now, to be sure, there are certainly other scriptural images of Christ's union with the church beyond marriage: the vine and the branches (John 15:5); the foundation of the temple (1 Peter 2:4–5), head and body (Eph. 4:4–6), and putting on the armor of God (Eph. 6:10–18).[19] Nevertheless, in the same way that the husband provides for the needs of the wife, so Christ provides for the needs of his bride. The provision of needs is not simply providential care but also the grace of redemption: "He is the source of your life in Christ Jesus, whom God made our wisdom and our righteousness and sanctification and redemption" (1 Cor. 1:30).[20] This verse certainly speaks to the application of the *ordo salutis* through one's union with Christ. There is also, however, a redemptive-historical connection that we should consider.

We must always place the *ordo salutis* within the context of the *historia salutis*, or redemptive history. In this case, we should note that union with Christ involves the application of the *ordo salutis* but its application is an eschatological event. We see this, for example, in Paul's affirmation: "If anyone is in Christ, he is a new creation. The old has passed away; behold, the new has come" (2 Cor. 5:17; cf. Isa. 43:18–19).[21] Once again we know of the connections between the believer's salvation and the resurrection of Christ, an eschatological event: "We were buried therefore with him by baptism into death, in order that, just as Christ was raised from the dead by the glory of the Father, we too might walk in newness of life" (Rom. 6:4). It is Christ's work, but especially his resurrection, that inaugurates the eschatological age, the new creation. Paul's affirmation, then, that those who are "in Christ" are a new creation is not simply a statement of new beginnings or future possibilities. Rather, Paul invokes the language of Isaiah: "For behold, I create new heavens and a new earth,

18. Ibid., 382; Peter T. O'Brien, *The Letter to the Ephesians*, PNTC (Grand Rapids: Eerdmans, 1999), 432–35.

19. Murray, *Redemption*, 168; also Donna R. Reinhard, "Ephesians 6:10–18: A Call to Personal Piety or Another Way of Describing Union with Christ?" *JETS* 48/3 (2005): 521–32.

20. So Anthony C. Thiselton, *The First Epistle to the Corinthians*, NIGTC (Grand Rapids: Eerdmans, 2000), 191–92; also Simon J. Kistemaker, *I Corinthians*, NTC (Grand Rapids: Baker, 1993), 64.

21. Smedes, *Union*, 37.

and the former things shall not be remembered or come into mind" (Isa. 65:17; see also Isa. 43:16–21; 65:16–23; 66:22–23).[22]

So, then, the believer's union with Christ is part of the eschatological fabric of the new creation. Just as with the first creation, made by Christ by the power of the Holy Spirit, so too now Christ creates the new heavens and earth by the power of the Spirit, along with a new eschatological humanity, which comes about in the lives of believers through their union with Christ (Gen. 1:1–2; see also John 1:1–3; Col. 1:16; 1 Cor. 5:1–6:20; 2 Cor. 6:14–7:1).[23] Given this information, the connections between the *ordo* and *historia salutis*, how should we collate the biblical data so we can present a coherent picture of what we find in Scripture?

Theological Formulation

Understanding the relationship between justification and the believer's union with Christ hinges upon at least two factors: (1) a proper understanding of the phases of our union with Christ; and (2) understanding the relationship between the *ordo salutis* and union with Christ. First, one must recognize that there are three phases to the believer's union with Christ. The three phases are the predestinarian "in Christ"; the redemptive-historical (or *historia salutis*) "in Christ," the union involved in the once-for-all accomplishment of salvation; and the applicatory "in Christ," which is the union in the actual possession or application of salvation. These three phases refer not to different unions but rather different aspects of the same union.[24] This first observation leads to a second, namely the relationship between union with Christ and the *ordo salutis*.

Union with Christ is not merely one element of the *ordo salutis* but undergirds the entire *ordo*. We can see this, for example, in the predesti-

22. Scott J. Hafemann, *2 Corinthians*, NIVAC (Grand Rapids: Zondervan, 2000), 244; C. K. Barrett, *The Second Epistle to the Corinthians*, BNTC (Peabody, MA: Hendrickson, 1983), 173–74.

23. James D. G. Dunn, *Romans*, WBC 38a (Dallas: Word, 1988), 134; Leonhard Goppelt, *Theology of the New Testament*, trans. John Alsup, 2 vols. (Grand Rapids: Eerdmans, 1982), 2:105–6.

24. Richard B. Gaffin, "Union with Christ: Some Biblical and Theological Reflections," in *Always Reforming*, ed. A. T. B. McGowan (Leicester: Apollos, 2006), 275. For a similar division see Sinclair B. Ferguson, *The Holy Spirit* (Downers Grove, IL: InterVarsity, 1996), 106–11.

narian aspect of our union with Christ when Paul writes that God "chose us in him before the foundation of the world" (Eph. 1:4). In this regard we have already observed in the chapter on prolegomena the differences between the typical Lutheran and Reformed understandings of the *ordo salutis* (figs. 8 and 9).[25]

Fig. 8. Lutheran *ordo*
Election   Regeneration   Calling   Faith   Justification   Union   Adoption   Sanctification   Glorification

Fig. 9. Reformed *ordo*
Election   Regeneration   Calling   Faith   Justification   Adoption   Sanctification   Glorification
————————————————————— Union with Christ —————————

Given this difference between the Lutheran and Reformed understandings of union with Christ, it should be no surprise that Heinrich Heppe would comment that "at the root of the whole doctrine of the appropriation of salvation lies the doctrine of *insitio* or *insertio in Christum*, through which we live in him and he in us."[26] It is this view that characterizes the Westminster Larger Catechism, which states that justification, adoption, sanctification, and whatever other benefits flow from Christ to the believer manifest the believer's union with him (q. 69).[27] Given this understanding, we may now turn to explain the relationship between justification and union with Christ.

Justification and Union with Christ

There is not at all a conflict between the doctrine of justification, or more specifically imputation, and union with Christ. Rather, imputation is the legal-forensic aspect of our union with Christ. We must keep this conclusion in the foreground as we move forward to critique some of the ideas that have been put forth by Schweitzer, Ritschl, Wright, and Lusk. The ideas that we want to examine are: (1) the interconnected nature of

25. See Berkhof, *Systematic Theology*, 447.

26. Heinrich Heppe, *Reformed Dogmatics*, ed. Ernst Bizer, trans. G. T. Thomson (London: George Allen & Unwin, 1950), 511.

27. Others such as Herman Witsius, John Owen, and Thomas Boston understood the relationship between the *ordo salutis* and union with Christ in this manner (see McGowan, "Justification and the *Ordo Salutis*," 156–57). One can also find similar formulations in Samuel Rutherford, *The Covenant of Life Opened* (Edinburgh, 1655), 208; and Amandus Polanus, *The Substance of the Christian Religion* (London, 1595), 93.

the filial and legal categories, and (2) the foundational nature of the legal, or justification, for the transformative.

The Interconnected Nature of the Filial and Legal Categories

The rejection of the imputation of Christ's righteousness in light of one's union with Christ seems to be predicated upon the presupposition that there is an irreconcilable conflict between the forensic and filial categories. This is certainly evident in Ritschl's rejection—he cannot rectify the apparent contradiction between God as Father and Judge. So, in a Hegelian sleight of hand, he takes the thesis of God as Judge and the antithesis of God as Father, and subsumes the former into the latter, creating a synthesis—equating justification with adoption.[28] While such a methodology might resolve the tensions in Ritschl's understanding of justification, it does not rightly reflect the forensic and filial categories as they are set forth in Scripture. The same may be said of the current trend in some parts of the Reformed community to base justification on the believer's union with Christ at the expense of the imputation of Christ's righteousness.

We should begin by noting that the forensic and filial categories are not at all antithetical to one another but in fact are complementary and interconnected. This is especially evident when we see Paul's use of the language of adoption. Paul writes that we have received the "Spirit of adoption as sons" (Rom. 8:15; Gal. 4:5; Eph. 1:5). Adoption is unquestionably a legal concept.[29] Yet we also see that it is connected to the relational or filial concept of sonship. This is one clear example where the filial and legal are clearly inextricably conjoined. We can see this inextricable relationship between the legal and filial in Christ. Christ was God's Son but nevertheless was born under the law and fulfilled the obligations of the law (Gal. 4:4; Matt. 5:17). Given this evidence, we must therefore reject the presupposition that the legal-forensic is not relational. Clearly the status as an adopted son shows us that there are legal aspects to a relationship. This evidence goes against the tendency to characterize union with Christ exclusively as relational and the legal as something less. As Richard Gaffin explains: "The participatory or relational involves an inalienable

28. See Alister E. McGrath, *Iustitia Dei*, 2 vols. (1986; Cambridge: Cambridge University Press, 1995), 2:160, 164.
29. See James M. Scott, *Adoption as Sons of God* (Tübingen: Mohr Siebeck, 1992), 3–60.

legal, forensic aspect, and the forensic does not function apart from but always within the participatory." Gaffin goes on to write,

> Both the forensic and the transformative, justification and sanctification, are functions or manifestations of the relational. Concretely, both are manifestations or aspects of union with Christ. Christ "in us" continues to be, and is as such also Christ "for us." In union with us Christ has a significance that is decisively forensic as well as powerfully transforming.[30]

Another place where we see the inseparable wedding of the legal and filial, which are both relational, is in the person and work of Christ. Geerhardus Vos explains that in Christ we find the wedding of the legal and filial, which therefore creates the paradigm for God's treatment of his people. Vos points to Philippians 2:9: "Therefore God has highly exalted him and bestowed on him the name that is above every name":

> Paul here uses the verb *echarisato* to describe the bestowal by God upon Christ of the name above every name. *Echarisato* means that God bestowed it as a gracious gift, not, of course, in the specific sense of the word "grace," implying that there was any unworthiness in Christ which God had to overlook, but in the more general sense implying that this was an act in which the graciousness, the kindness of God manifested itself. Righteousness and love, therefore, as coordinated principles of the divine procedure, do not exclude each other.[31]

Vos's observation becomes clearer when we consider that Christ was God's Son, yet at the same time God, as Judge, poured out his wrath upon his Son on the cross on behalf of those whom he justifies. In the crucifixion of Christ, God is "just and the justifier of the one who has faith in Jesus" (Rom. 3:26b). If God is both Father and Judge, which is not antithetical as Paul holds both together, then it stands to reason that a forensic justification is not at odds with the believer's mystical union with Christ.[32] Historically, Reformed theologians have viewed union with Christ not only in relational terms but also legal. Hodge, for example, writes:

---

30. Richard B. Gaffin Jr., *By Faith, Not by Sight* (Carlisle: Paternoster, 2006), 40–41.

31. Geerhardus Vos, "The Alleged Legalism in Paul's Doctrine of Justification," in *Redemptive History and Biblical Interpretation*, ed. Richard B. Gaffin Jr. (Phillipsburg, NJ: P&R, 1980), 398–99.

32. Schweitzer, *Paul the Apostle*, 223–26.

The first aspect of this union is its federal and representative character, whereby Christ, as the second Adam (1 Cor. 15:22), assumes in the covenant of grace those broken obligations of the covenant of works which the first Adam failed to discharge, and fulfills them all in behalf of all his "sheep," "they whom the Father has given him." The consequences which arise from our union with Christ under this aspect of it are such as the imputation of our sins to him, and of his righteousness to us, and all of the forensic benefits of justification and adoption.[33]

To be more specific, then, imputation is the legal-forensic aspect of our union with Christ. Imputation is not at all antithetical to but inextricably linked to our union with Christ. However, we must see how the legal-forensic cannot be sidelined in favor of a misconstrued relational union-with-Christ model.

The Foundational Nature of the Legal

Vos long ago noted the trend to eliminate the forensic aspect of redemption in liberal expositions of justification. Vos writes that the center of Paul's teaching is justification by faith, but that

> recent attempts to dislodge it from this position, and to make the mystical aspect of the believer's relation to Christ, as mediated by the Spirit, entirely coordinated with it—so that each of the two covers the entire range of religious experience, and becomes in reality a duplicate of the other in a different sphere—we cannot recognize as correct from the apostle's own point of view. In our opinion Paul consciously and consistently subordinated the mystical aspect of the relation to Christ to the forensic one. Paul's mind was to such an extent forensically oriented that he regarded the entire complex of subjective spiritual changes that take place in the believer and of subjective spiritual blessings enjoyed by the believer as the direct outcome of the forensic work of Christ applied in justification. The mystical is based on the forensic, not the forensic on the mystical.[34]

33. Hodge, *Outlines of Theology*, 482; see also Edmund P. Clowney, "The Biblical Doctrine of Justification by Faith," in *Right with God*, ed. D. A. Carson (1992; Eugene, OR: Wipf & Stock, 2002), 46; Gaffin, *By Faith*, 38.

34. Vos, "Legalism in Paul's Doctrine of Justification," 384. See also Hodge, *Outlines of Theology*, 484.

Vos rightly observes that for Paul the forensic is the ground of the transformative.[35] The legal aspect of our union with Christ is the ground of the transformative aspect of our union with Christ—justification is the ground of our sanctification. This conclusion is evident in several places in the Pauline corpus.

For example, Ritschl's presupposition of the universal fatherhood of God seems difficult to square against statements such as "You were dead in the trespasses and sins in which you once walked, following the course of this world, following the prince of the power of the air, the spirit that is now at work in the sons of disobedience" (Eph. 2:1–2). Prior to one's justification by faith, Paul places the unbeliever squarely in the category of an enemy, not a child, of God (Rom. 5:10; cf. 1 John 3:10). After a person's justification, he is considered a son of God, not before. There is a time when a person stands outside of the kingdom and is God's enemy. After his justification by faith, the person stands within the kingdom and is God's child and is joined to Christ (Rom. 8:1–17; Gal. 3–4). What effects the transition from the kingdom of darkness into the kingdom of light is the forensic declaration of righteousness. The legal aspect of our union with Christ is the ground of the transformative aspect of our union.

The priority of the forensic is prominent when Paul states: "The free gift is not like the result of that one man's sin. For the judgment following one trespass brought condemnation, but the free gift following many trespasses brought justification" (Rom. 5:16). Here we see the priority of the forensic—both condemnation and justification are forensic in nature and flow from the actions, the disobedience and obedience, of the respective covenant-representatives to the legal demands of the law (Gal. 3:14). Commenting on the priority of the forensic aspect of our union with Christ, Berkhof observes:

> The mystical union in the sense in which we are now speaking of it is not the judicial ground, on the basis of which we become partakers of the riches that are in Christ. It is sometimes said that the merits of Christ cannot be imputed to us as long as we are not in Christ, since it is only on the basis of our oneness with Him that such an imputation could be reasonable.

---

35. One must read Vos's statement in the light of the rest of his work to understand what he means when he states that justification is at the center of Paul's theology (see Richard B. Gaffin Jr., *Resurrection and Redemption* [1978; Phillipsburg, NJ: P&R, 1987], 13–14).

But this view fails to distinguish between our legal unity with Christ and our spiritual oneness with Him, and is a falsification of the fundamental element in the doctrine of redemption, namely, of the doctrine of justification. Justification is always a declaration of God, not on the basis of an existing condition, but on that of a gracious imputation—a declaration which is not in harmony with the existing condition of the sinner. The judicial ground for all the special grace which we receive lies in the fact that the righteousness of Christ is freely imputed to us.[36]

Or, to put it in Pauline terms, the righteousness of Christ is a free gift, which means, as Berkhof notes, our justification is not on the basis of a preexisting condition.

We may alternatively state Berkhof's point in the following manner: the legal aspect of our union with Christ is foundational for the transformative aspect of our union with Christ.[37] Michael Horton develops this idea quite powerfully when he likens the declarative verdict of justification to the speech God uttered to bring forth the creation. Horton explains:

> While union with Christ and the sanctification that results from that union are more than forensic, they are the consequences of God's forensic declaration. Both justification ("Let there be . . . !") and inner renewal ("Let the earth bring forth . . . !") are speech-acts of the Triune God. . . . Like *ex nihilo* creation, justification is not a process of transforming an already existing state of affairs. In other words, it is a synthetic rather than an analytic verdict.[38]

Horton echoes the explanation of Berkhof and Vos in terms of the priority of the forensic over the mystical, though one should add that Calvin was of the same mind.

Horton points to the structure in Calvin's understanding of justification, evident in the Reformer's comments on Ephesians 3:17: "By faith we not only acknowledge that Christ suffered for us and rose from the dead for us, but we receive Him, possessing and enjoying Him as He offers Himself to us. This should be noted carefully. Most consider fellowship with

---

36. Berkhof, *Systematic Theology*, 452.

37. Lane G. Tipton, "Union with Christ and Justification," in *Justified in Christ*, ed. K. Scott Oliphint (Fearn, Scotland: Mentor, 2007), 24; Gaffin, "Union with Christ," 287.

38. Michael S. Horton, *Covenant and Salvation* (Louisville: Westminster John Knox, 2007), ch. 10, see also ch. 9.

Christ and believing in Christ to be the same thing; but the fellowship which we have with Christ is the effect of faith."[39] Calvin clearly places faith in a cause-and-effect relationship to union with Christ. This is why Calvin, for example, wrote that justification is the "main hinge" upon which religion turns. Moreover, justification, not union with Christ, is the foundation upon which the believer's salvation is established.[40] In Calvin's response to the proclamations of Trent, he highlights the priority of justification: "In short, I affirm, that not by our own merit but by faith alone, are both our persons and works justified; and that the justification of works depends on the justification of the person, as the effect on the cause. Therefore, it is necessary that the righteousness of faith alone so precede in order, and be so pre-eminent in degree, that nothing can go before it or obscure it."[41]

It is the verdict of justification, therefore, that "gives life to the dead and calls into existence the things that do not exist" (Rom. 4:17). Apart

---

39. John Calvin, *Galatians, Ephesians, Philippians, and Colossians*, ed. T. F. Torrance and David W. Torrance, trans. T. H. L. Parker, CNTC (1965; Grand Rapids: Eerdmans, 1996), 166–67; Horton, *Covenant and Salvation*, ch. 10.

40. John Calvin, *Institutes of the Christian Religion*, ed. John T. McNeill, trans. Ford Lewis Battles, LCC 20–21 (Philadelphia: Westminster, 1960), 3.11.1. One should note the attempts of Richard Gaffin and others, who maintain that union with Christ is the more foundational and central category for Calvin. Gaffin explains concerning Calvin's interaction with the decrees of Trent: "Calvin proceeds as he does, and is free to do so, because for him the relative 'ordo' or priority of justification and sanctification is indifferent theologically. Rather, what has controlling soteriological importance is the priority to both of (spiritual, 'existential,' faith-) union with Christ" (Richard B. Gaffin Jr., "Biblical Theology and the Westminster Standards," *WTJ* 65 [2003]: 176–77). One of the chief elements of Gaffin's contention for the priority of union with Christ is the order that one finds in the *Institutes*. Namely, Calvin supposedly treats union with Christ prior to justification (Gaffin, "Biblical Theology," 170, 177). Yet this thesis has weaknesses. First, Gaffin confuses the order of the *Institutes* with Calvin's understanding of the manner in which we receive Christ in redemption, what later Reformed theologians call the *ordo salutis*. In the technical terms of Calvin studies, Gaffin confuses the *ordo docendi* with the *ordo salutis*. Calvin wrote the *Institutes* in such a manner as to present the theological teaching of Scripture in the most pedagogically effective manner, one ultimately based upon the order of subjects in Paul's epistle to the Romans, not to answer a theological question of the order of the application of salvation, a doctrinal development anachronistic to Calvin's theology (see Calvin, *Institutes*, 1:3–5; Richard A. Muller, *The Unaccommodated Calvin* [Oxford: Oxford University Press, 2000], 118–32). Second, if union with Christ was as central to Calvin as Gaffin claims, then why did Calvin not devote a single chapter to the subject? For a fully argued case on these points and bibliography, see Thomas L. Wenger, "The New Perspective on Calvin: Responding to Recent Calvin Interpretations," *JETS* 50/2 (2007): 311–28.

41. John Calvin, "Acts of the Council of Trent with the Antidote," in *Selected Works of John Calvin*, ed. Henry Beveridge, 7 vols. (1851; Grand Rapids: Baker, 1983), 3:128.

from redemption accomplished, there can be no redemption applied. This conclusion is something that plays a key role in the differences between the Reformed and Roman Catholic understanding of justification and salvation. For the Reformers, salvation came about because of the declaration of righteousness in justification, whereas for the Roman Catholic Church, even to this day, it is inverse: transformation precedes the declaration, the transformative is the judicial ground for the forensic. We will explore these differences in the chapter on the Roman Catholic view of justification.

Conclusion

When we stop to consider the relationship between justification and union with Christ, it is important that we recognize the relational nature of the legal aspects of our redemption. Moreover, it is also important that we recognize that the entire *ordo salutis* is undergirded by union with Christ. One cannot help but observe that much of the recent literature in the confessional Reformed community that pits imputation against union with Christ has unwittingly imbibed from the theology of the historical-critical school. Some have embraced the presuppositions espoused by theologians such as Schweitzer and Ritschl and have placed antithesis where there is none.

While those within the confessional Reformed community undoubtedly hold to a strong commitment to the inspired nature of the Scriptures, only someone who does not hold such a commitment can conclude that there are competing models of redemption in Paul, the legal and the relational. If the Holy Spirit inspired Paul when he wrote his epistles, then it seems important that we follow the apostle in the construction of our own theology of justification. Namely, it is imperative that we hold together imputation and union with Christ, the priority of the legal-forensic over the transformative, all of which are relational. We may now proceed with our investigation and consider the relationship between justification and sanctification. What is the relationship between the believer's good works and his justification?

11

JUSTIFICATION AND SANCTIFICATION

We have thus far examined the nature of justification by faith and its relationship with the believer's union with Christ. This now brings us to the question, What is the relationship between justification and works? Are good works necessary for salvation? The answer to this question is, Yes. Good works are necessary for salvation. At the same time, it depends on how one relates justification to good works when answering this question. As we saw in the introduction, the history of the development of the doctrine of justification has been beset by the dual dangers of antinomianism and neonomianism. Some argue that *sola fide* invariably leads to a diminution of the doctrine of sanctification and to antinomianism.[1] An unacceptable response has been to argue that we are not justified by faith alone, but by faithfulness, which is neonomianism.[2]

1. See, e.g., Paul A. Rainbow, *The Way of Salvation* (Carlisle: Paternoster, 2005), xx–xxi.
2. So Norman Shepherd, *The Call of Grace* (Phillipsburg, NJ: P&R, 2000), 50; idem, "Justification by Faith in Pauline Theology," in *Backbone of the Bible*, ed. P. Andrew Sandlin (Nacogdoches, TX: Covenant Media Foundation, 2004), 101; see also idem, "Justification by Works in Reformed Theology," in *Backbone*, 103; N. T. Wright, *Paul for Everyone*, vol. 1, *Romans* (London: SPCK, 2004), 167.

A proper understanding of justification by faith alone, however, does not lead to antinomianism, nor should it lead to neonomianism. Rather, we must recognize that there is a close inextricable link between justification and sanctification. One cannot have the one without the other.

Therefore we will first examine what the Scriptures have to say on good works, particularly as they relate to the *historia salutis*. In other words, what place do good works have in the grand scope of redemptive history? We will answer this question by the examination of two primary OT texts: Jeremiah 31:31–34 and Ezekiel 36:16–37. Second, we will turn to the subject of good works and the *ordo salutis*. In other words, how do good works relate to justification in the application of redemption in the individual? We will primarily examine James 2 in this regard. In this chapter, we will demonstrate that good works are necessary for one's salvation. They are necessary in the sense that they are not the cause of one's justification but rather the effects of justification. The effect of one's justification by faith and union with Christ by the indwelling of the Holy Spirit is that he will produce good works. This is not a unique conclusion but is rather the historic understanding of the Reformed church.

When we consider the historic witness of the Reformed church on the matter of faith and works, there has always been the understanding that works are the fruit of a justifying faith. We see expression of this truth in Calvin:

> Whomever, therefore, God receives into grace, on them he at the same time bestows the spirit of adoption, by whose power he remakes them to his own image. But if the brightness of the sun cannot be separated from its heat, shall we therefore say that the earth is warmed by its light, or lighted by its heat? The sun, by its heat, quickens and fructifies the earth, by its beams brightens and illumines it. Here is a mutual and indivisible connection. Yet reason itself forbids us to transfer the peculiar qualities of the one to the other.[3]

Notice that Calvin compares faith and works to the relationship between the heat and light of the sun. Heat is not light and light is not heat; each has a unique and distinct function, but at the same time neither can heat

---

3. John Calvin, *Institutes of the Christian Religion*, ed. John T. McNeill, trans. Ford Lewis Battles, LCC 20–21 (Philadelphia: Westminster, 1960), 3.11.6.

and light be separated. We see a similar explanation of the role of faith and works from the Westminster Confession: "Faith, thus receiving and resting on Christ and His righteousness, is the alone instrument of justification; yet is it not alone in the person justified, but is ever accompanied with all other saving graces, and is no dead faith, but works by love" (11.2). Along the same lines we read in the Westminster Larger Catechism that "faith justifies a sinner in the sight of God, not because of those other graces which do always accompany it, or of good works that are the fruits of it, not as if the grace of faith, or any act thereof, were imputed to him for his justification; but only as it is an instrument by which he receives and applies Christ and his righteousness" (q. 73).

Francis Turretin in his usual perspicacious and precise manner explains how good works relate to the various stages of the *ordo salutis*:

> Works can be considered in three ways: either with reference to justification or sanctification or glorification. They are related to justification not antecedently, efficiently and meritoriously, but consequently and declaratively. They are related to sanctification constitutively because they constitute and promote it. They are related to glorification antecedently and ordinatively because they are related to it as the means to the end; yea, as the beginning to the complement because grace is glory begun, as glory is grace consummated.[4]

So, then, while the Reformed church has always affirmed that justification is by faith alone, the faith is not alone in the person that is justified, as good works always accompany saving faith and are its fruit. We should now proceed to examine good works in their redemptive historical context and substantiate that the historic witness of the Reformed tradition is correct in its understanding of the relationship between justification and sanctification, or more specifically good works.

Good Works in the *Historia Salutis*

Jeremiah 31:31–34

When we consider the subject of good works, we must return first to the OT and see an important aspect of prophecy regarding the eschato-

---

4. Francis Turretin, *Institutes of Elenctic Theology*, trans. George Musgrave Giger, ed. James T. Dennison Jr., 3 vols. (Phillipsburg, NJ: P&R, 1992–97), 17.3.14.

logical age. In Jeremiah's day, the seventh century B.C., Israel was far from obedient to the law of God. For their sin and rebellion God prophesied through Jeremiah that he would give Jerusalem over to the Chaldeans and the Babylonians; the Babylonians would conquer the southern kingdom of Judah and carry them into exile (Jer. 32:28).[5] The causal link between Israel's disobedience and exile is certainly evident in Jeremiah 32:30: "For the children of Israel and the children of Judah have done nothing but evil in my sight from their youth. The children of Israel have done nothing but provoke me to anger by the work of their hands, declares the LORD" (see also vv. 34–35).[6]

Yet at the same time, in the midst of Jeremiah's message of judgment and exile, God also sends a message of eschatological hope and restoration. We know that Jeremiah looks to the eschaton because he precedes his prophecy with the words, "Behold, the days are coming" (Jer. 31:31), which signals that the fulfilment will come in a future age.[7] Jeremiah prophesies of a time when God would gather the Israelites from the various countries in which they resided in exile and bring them back to Jerusalem, to the promised land; God would return them from exile (Jer. 32:37; cf. Deut. 30:1–5).[8] This return from exile, however, would be markedly different from Israel's previous inhabitance of the promised land.

God promised that Israel would return from exile to the promised land, but they would do so under the aegis of an everlasting covenant (Jer. 32:40; cf. Isa. 55:3; Ezek. 16:60; 37:26). Jeremiah prophesied and explained how the new covenant would be different from the old covenant. Israel broke the old covenant, that is, the Mosaic covenant, which God made with them when he brought them up out of Egypt (Jer. 31:31–32; cf. Ex. 19–20). God says through Jeremiah that in the new covenant "I will put my law within them, and I will write it on their hearts. And I will be their God, and they shall be my people" (Jer. 31:33). This declaration is a stark contrast to the Mosaic covenant, which was written in stone (Ex. 31:18; 34:28–29; Deut. 4:13; 5:22) or in a book (Ex. 24:7). As J. A. Thompson notes, "There could be no obedience and no recognition of Yahweh's

5. J. A. Thompson, *The Book of Jeremiah*, NICOT (Grand Rapids: Eerdmans, 1980), 594.
6. Meredith G. Kline, *Kingdom Prologue* (Overland Park, KS: Two Age Press, 2000), 345.
7. William J. Dumbrell, *The End of the Beginning* (1985; Eugene, OR: Wipf & Stock, 2001), 87.
8. Thompson, *Jeremiah*, 595.

sovereignty as long as the covenant was externalized. It needed to touch the life deeply and inwardly in mind and will."[9] Inscribing the law upon the heart, then, is significant, as it means that God's people would obey his law.[10] Remember, this prophecy comes in the midst of Israel's disobedience, a situation that God will remedy by this new covenant. We see similar themes emerge in the prophecies of Ezekiel.

Ezekiel 36:16–37

When we come to the prophecies of Ezekiel, Jeremiah's prophecy of exile had begun to be fulfilled. The southern kingdom was taken away into exile including the prophet Ezekiel (2 Kings 24:8–12). It is from Babylon that Ezekiel made his prophecies, prophecies of the restoration of Israel to the promised land. Ezekiel's prophecy begins in similar fashion to that of Jeremiah with God recounting the evil deeds of Israel: "Son of man, when the house of Israel lived in their own land, they defiled it by their ways and their deeds. Their ways before me were like the uncleanness of a woman in her menstrual impurity" (Ezek. 36:17). Israel was therefore taken into exile for their sins, and for their deeds God judged them (Ezek. 36:18–19; Deut. 9:4–5).[11] Yet even in the midst of exile Israel still profaned the name of the Lord. It was therefore out of the desire to vindicate his holy name that God promised yet again that he would act to remedy Israel's sinful ways.

God promised that he would return Israel from exile to the land of promise, cleanse them by sprinkling them with clean water, metaphorical language for cleansing them of their sin (Ezek. 36:25). The terminology used here for "uncleanness" (*tum'ah*) occurs in the plural only here and in reference to the day of atonement (Lev. 16:16, 19), which points out that the sin would be removed by atonement.[12] This is also confirmed by the use of the phrases "sprinkle clean water on you" and "cleanse you," which are phrases used in priestly cleansing and blood sprinkling-ceremonies (Ex. 19:10; 29:4; Num. 8:7; 19:11–19; see also v. 21; Lev. 16:4, 24, 26).[13]

9. Ibid., 581.
10. William L. Holladay, *Jeremiah 2* (Minneapolis: Fortress, 1989), 198.
11. Daniel I. Block, *The Book of Ezekiel: Chapters 25–48*, NICOT (Grand Rapids: Eerdmans, 1998), 345; Walther Zimmerli, *Ezekiel 2* (Minneapolis: Fortress, 1983), 246.
12. Zimmerli, *Ezekiel 2*, 249.
13. Block, *Ezekiel*, 354.

Like Jeremiah before him, Ezekiel also prophesied of how God would vindicate his name: "I will give you a new heart, and a new spirit I will put within you. And I will remove the heart of stone from your flesh and give you a heart of flesh. And I will put my Spirit within you, and cause you to walk in my statutes and be careful to obey my rules" (Ezek. 36:26–27).[14] Here we see another aspect of Jeremiah's earlier prophecy that was latent but that Ezekiel brings to the surface. Jeremiah prophesied that God would make a new covenant with his people and write his law upon their hearts. Ezekiel's prophecy explains the way in which God would write his law upon the hearts of his people and what the resulting effect would be. God would place his Spirit within his people, which would produce the effect that his people would obey his law. The net effect of this Spirit-produced obedience would be that God's name would be vindicated among the nations by the obedience of his people. As a result, God would restore the desolated cities throughout the promised land, and the people would say: "This land that was desolate has become like the garden of Eden, and the waste and desolate and ruined cities are now fortified and inhabited" (Ezek. 36:35; cf. Isa. 51:3). We see that God would return the land to its garden-temple status.[15] We will explore this aspect of the eschatological prophecy of Ezekiel below.

At this point it is important that we coordinate the following elements and take note of the trajectory set by the prophecies of Jeremiah and Ezekiel. Both prophets speak of an eschatological time when God would make a new covenant with his people; it would be by the agency of the Holy Spirit, would bring the forgiveness of sin, the inscription of the law upon the heart, and create an eschatological people that would produce good works that would bring glory to the name of their covenant Lord.[16] Keeping these points in mind, we can now look to the NT to see the fulfilment of these eschatological prophecies.

NT Fulfilment of Jeremiah's and Ezekiel's Prophecies

While there are certainly several places in the NT where one can find reference or allusion to the prophecies of Jeremiah and Ezekiel, one place

14. Zimmerli, *Ezekiel 2*, 249; also Geerhardus Vos, *Biblical Theology* (1948; Edinburgh: Banner of Truth, 1996), 299–300.

15. Dumbrell, *End of the Beginning*, 95–96.

16. Block, *Ezekiel*, 360–61.

where the fulfilment of these prophecies is clear is Romans 8:1–17. In this section of the epistle to Rome Paul begins with his well-known statement, "There is therefore now no condemnation for those who are in Christ Jesus" (Rom. 8:1). We see the redemptive historical and eschatological elements surface when Paul says "now" (*nyn*), which is a temporal indicator that a new age of redemptive history is present.[17] We also know that we are in the midst of the eschatological age because (1) we are now in the wake of the life, death, and resurrection of Christ, the eschatological Adam; and because (2) Paul coordinates the eschatological *nyn* with the person and work of the Spirit: "You, however, are not in the flesh but in the Spirit, if in fact the Spirit of God dwells in you. Anyone who does not have the Spirit of Christ does not belong to him" (Rom. 8:9). Paul identifies the Holy Spirit as the Spirit of Christ because, as a result of Christ's eschatological work, the Holy Spirit is virtually identified with Christ: "'The first man Adam became a living being'; the last Adam became a life-giving Spirit" (1 Cor. 15:45*). As Geerhardus Vos notes, "Being thus closely and subjectively identified with the Risen Christ, the Spirit imparts to Christ the life-giving power which is peculiarly the Spirit's own: the Second Adam became not only *Pneuma* but *pneuma zōopoioun*."[18] At the same time we should also note how the Spirit inhabits God's people.

The forensic element of our redemption is evident when Paul says that there is "now no condemnation for those who are in Christ Jesus" (Rom. 8:1). Once again we see the forensic declaration of righteousness but it is only for those who are "in Christ." Those who are justified by faith alone receive the imputed righteousness of Christ and are united to him, which also brings the indwelling of the Holy Spirit. The connection between the forensic and the resulting transformative indwelling power of the Spirit is evident when Paul writes: "God has done what the law, weakened by the flesh, could not do. By sending his own Son in the likeness of sinful flesh and for sin, he condemned sin in the flesh, in

---

17. Thomas R. Schreiner, *Romans*, BECNT (Grand Rapids: Baker, 1998), 397; Joseph A. Fitzmyer, *Romans*, AB 33 (New York: Doubleday, 1993), 481; C. E. B. Cranfield, *Romans*, 2 vols., ICC (1975; Edinburgh: T & T Clark, 2001), 1:373; James D. G. Dunn, *Romans*, WBC 38a (Dallas: Word, 1988), 415; Herman Ridderbos, *Paul: An Outline of His Theology*, trans. John Richard De Witt (1975; Grand Rapids: Eerdmans, 1992), 167.

18. Geerhardus Vos, *The Pauline Eschatology* (1930; Phillipsburg, NJ: P&R, 1994), 168–69; also see Dunn, *Romans*, 428–29; idem, *Christology in the Making* (1980; London: SCM Press, 1989), 141–48.

order that the righteous requirement of the law might be fulfilled in us, who walk not according to the flesh but according to the Spirit" (Rom. 8:3–4).[19] Notice that the purpose clause is predicated upon the judicial and forensic work of Christ—sin was condemned in Christ upon the cross, *hina* the righteous requirement of the law might be fulfilled in us (see Gal. 3:13–14; Acts 2:33). Jeremiah's and Ezekiel's prophecies that God would write his law upon the hearts of his people, fill them with his Spirit, and cause them to walk in his statutes, then, are being fulfilled at this very moment.[20]

At this point it is important that we recognize several factors regarding the nature of good works. First, the manifestation of good works by God's people is an eschatological event. God promised through the prophets that there would come a time when his people would walk in obedience to the law, and that time has dawned with the life, death, and resurrection of Christ and outpouring of the Spirit (Acts 2:33).[21]

Second, we must note that there is an already–not yet tension to the fulfilment of these eschatological promises. Yes, at the same time that God's people walk in the Spirit and "put to death the deeds of the body" (Rom. 8:13) we must realize that this redeemed eschatological humanity dwells torn between two major epochs in redemptive history. God's people straddle this present evil age (Gal. 1:4) and the age to come (Eph. 1:21; Heb. 6:5).[22] We see this already–not yet tension exhibited, for example, when Paul talks about the outer and inner man: "Though our outer man is wasting away, our inner man is being renewed day by day" (2 Cor. 4:16b*). Paul's inner man has been raised with Christ in his justification (Rom. 6:1–4); his outer man, however wastes away and for this reason he awaits the final day and the resurrection of the dead.[23]

We also see the tension of living between the two ages, or the tension between the inner and outer man when Paul writes: "I myself serve the

---

19. Geerhardus Vos, "The Eschatological Aspect of the Pauline Conception of the Spirit," in *Redemptive History and Biblical Interpretation*, ed. Richard B. Gaffin Jr. (Phillipsburg, NJ: P&R, 1980), 96.

20. Schreiner, *Romans*, 396.

21. Vos, "Eschatological Aspect," 98.

22. James D. G. Dunn, *The Theology of Paul the Apostle* (Grand Rapids: Eerdmans, 1998), 474–75.

23. Ridderbos, *Paul*, 227; also Simon J. Kistemaker, *II Corinthians*, NTC (Grand Rapids: Baker, 1997), 159.

law of God with my mind, but with my flesh I serve the law of sin" (Rom. 7:25). In this regard James Dunn observes that Romans 7:25b

> is a classic statement of the eschatological tension set up by the death and resurrection of Christ; through his death writing finis to the age of Adam and through his resurrection introducing the age of the last Adam. In Paul's understanding the tension is not one that is natural to man, or one that is consequent upon the fall of man. The fallenness of man is one side of it, but the tension is only set up by the introduction of the eschatological "now" in Christ. And it only becomes personal for Paul with conversion-initiation. The tension then is a tension not simply of redemption delayed, but precisely of a redemption already begun but not yet completed. The very fact that he can envisage a service of the law of God with the mind presupposes a renewed mind (cf. 12:2), a having died with Christ (6:2–11); while the continuing service of the law of sin with the flesh clearly indicates a dimension of the believer's existence not yet caught up in the risen life of Christ (cf. 8:11, 23), a having-not-yet-been-raised with Christ (6:5, 8). The assurance of future deliverance does not itself bring to an end the eschatological tension in which believers find themselves caught.[24]

This observation of the tension of the eschatological already–not yet leads to a third observation.

Third, the already–not yet has implications for the judicial value of the good works that believers produce. Because of this tension that exists in the believer, what we may call the struggle to obey the law, the ground of the believer's forensic status cannot and does not shift from the work of Christ to the Spirit-led works of the believer.[25] More will be said about this in the following chapter, but for now let us notice that the believer's forensic status does not depend upon his Spirit-led works, the transformative aspect of his union with Christ, but upon the imputed righteousness of Christ, the legal aspect of his union with Christ (Rom. 8:1). If there is a not-yet aspect of justification that awaits a judgment according to Spirit-produced work, it depreciates the eschatological "now" (*nyn*) of the forensic declaration for those who are in Christ. Shifting the ground of justification from the work of Christ, his life, death, and resurrection, which is where Paul places it in Romans 8:1, to the believer's Spirit-led

---

24. Dunn, *Romans*, 411.
25. Contra N. T. Wright, *Romans*, NIB 10 (Nashville: Abingdon, 2003), 580.

good works in Romans 8:4, is to rearrange what Paul has stated in a way contrary to his intention.

Fourth, when we consider the trajectory of redemptive history, we must remember that Romans 8:1–17 is predicated upon Jeremiah 31:31–34 and Ezekiel 36:16–37. The purpose of the Spirit-produced works in God's people is not their justification, or their forensic declaration of righteousness before the throne of God, but the vindication and honor of the holy name of God among the nations (Ezek. 36:23). Moreover, in both prophecies we see that God forgives the sin of his people: "For I will forgive their iniquity, and I will remember their sin no more" (Jer. 31:34). We see especially in Ezekiel's prophecy that the indwelling of the Spirit is predicated upon the forgiveness of sin:

> I will sprinkle clean water on you, and you shall be clean from all your uncleannesses, and from all your idols I will cleanse you. And I will give you a new heart, and a new spirit I will put within you. And I will remove the heart of stone from your flesh and give you a heart of flesh. And I will put my Spirit within you, and cause you to walk in my statutes and be careful to obey my rules. (36:25–27)

What the NT makes clear is that the ground constituted by the forgiveness of sin is the believer's justification by faith alone in Christ alone. The Spirit-led works follow, therefore, the believer's justification and are the cause of his justification neither in the present nor the future. Rather, these works are the fruit of faith. In the passages from Jeremiah and Ezekiel, neither do we see God's people first offering their good works and obedience, which then causes God to show mercy to them, nor do we see the pattern of covenantal nomism, where God makes a covenant with Israel, and then on the basis of God's antecedent grace Israel maintains their place in the covenant. Rather, in both prophecies we see a broken covenant, and then a new covenant initiated by God, the forgiveness of sins, which is the justification of sinners (Rom. 4:1–18), the outpouring of the Holy Spirit, and the consequent good works, or obedience, that follow. One must remember that the new covenant is not like the old. There is a cause-and-effect relationship, not between the person's obedience and justification, but rather God's antecedent fulfilment of the legal demands of the law and the outpouring of the Spirit and the believer's good works. This cause-and-effect relationship between faith and good works becomes clearer when we consider the epistle of James.

James 2:14–26: Faith and Works

Whenever we come to consider what James has to say regarding faith and works, we tread upon highly debated territory because of the apparent conflict between James and the apostle Paul on the relationship of works to one's redemption, or more specifically the application of the *ordo salutis*. Paul, for example, states, "For by grace you have been saved through faith. And this is not your own doing; it is the gift of God, not a result of works, so that no one may boast" (Eph. 2:8–9). On the other hand James writes, "A person is justified by works and not by faith alone" (James 2:24). This apparent contradiction has led some to conclude that the teachings of Paul and James are contradictory. Others have suggested that James was greatly influenced by the theology of his day, particularly the exegetical tradition surrounding the evaluation of Abraham and the means of his justification.[26] The best answer, however, comes in recognizing several things: (1) the problems that James and Paul address; (2) the use of the term "justified" in the context of each epistle; and (3) the nature of the *ordo* and *historia salutis* as it pertains to justification and sanctification, or justification and good works. Let us first turn to the matter of the problems Paul and James address.

The Problems

In the interpretation of any epistle not only must one identify the historical context but also the problems that are peculiar to it. In this case, it is important to identify what problems Paul and James were addressing in each of their epistles. First, in Paul's epistle to the Ephesians it is evident that Paul was addressing the problem of legalism, the idea that one's works contributed to his salvation; hence Paul places emphasis upon the exclusion of works: "For by grace you have been saved through faith. And this is not your own doing; it is the gift of God, not a result of works, so that no one may boast" (Eph. 2:8–9). This instruction against boasting especially as it concerns the subject of works echoes Paul's argument in

26. See Robert W. Wall, "The Intertextuality of Scripture: The Example of Rahab (James 2:25)," in *The Bible at Qumran*, ed. Peter W. Flint (Grand Rapids: Eerdmans, 2001), 217–36.

Romans: "For if Abraham was justified by works, he has something to boast about, but not before God" (Rom. 4:2). Paul's statement, then, is directed against legalism.

James, on the other hand, appears to be dealing with a problem of an entirely different nature: "But someone will say, 'You have faith and I have works.' Show me your faith apart from your works, and I will show you my faith by my works. You believe that God is one; you do well. Even the demons believe—and shudder!" (James 2:18–19). We see that James addresses the problem of a nominal faith, those who merely claim to believe. This interpretation is confirmed by James's appeal to the demons—they too believe that God is one, but this does not mean that their belief constitutes a faith in him. While it may be a broad application of the term, James, unlike Paul, addresses the problem of antinomianism, namely that one can claim to have faith but ignore or violate the claims of the law (see James 2:8–12). James and Paul, therefore, address different problems: "The faith that James is condemning is not the faith that Paul is commending."[27] Alternatively, the works that James commends are not the works that Paul condemns. This brings us to our second issue.

The Use of the Term "Justify"

Both James and Paul use the term "justify" (*dikaioō*), which naturally leads to the opinion that they are using the term in the same manner. From what we have seen thus far in Paul's use of the term, it is clear that Paul uses the term "justified" to denote the forensic declaration of righteousness before the throne of God: "For by works of the law no human being will be justified in his sight, since through the law comes knowledge of sin" (Rom. 3:20; also 3:28). Again, Paul states: "For what does the Scripture say? 'Abraham believed God, and it was counted to him as righteousness.' Now to the one who works, his wages are not counted as a gift but as his due. And to the one who does not work but trusts him who justifies the ungodly, his faith is counted as righteousness" (Rom. 4:3–5). We should

---

27. J. Gresham Machen, *Machen's Notes on Galatians*, ed. John H. Skilton (Nutley, NJ: P&R, 1972), 220; also Joachim Jeremias, "Paul and James," *ExpTim* 66 (1954–55): 368–71; Peter H. Davids, *The Epistle of James*, NIGTC (Grand Rapids: Eerdmans, 1982), 125; James B. Adamson, *The Epistle of James*, NICNT (Grand Rapids: Eerdmans, 1982), 125–27; contra Wall, "Example of Rahab," 222 n. 9, 233–36; Richard N. Longenecker, "The 'Faith of Abraham' Theme in Paul, James and Hebrews: A Study in the Circumstantial Nature of New Testament Teaching," *JETS* 20 (1977): 203–7.

note two things about Paul's statements: (1) the forensic declaration that one is righteous comes apart from works of the law; and (2) the only way a person can be justified in the sight of God is by faith. Here the legal character of Paul's use of the term "justify" is clear; Paul writes of sin, the ungodly, and righteousness, all forensic categories, categories of guilt or righteousness. Moreover, before we move forward we should also note that Paul appeals to Genesis 15:6 to argue his case for Abraham's justification by faith. How does James use the term "justified"?

It is fair to say that James uses the term "justified" in a different sense than Paul. This is evident on two counts: (1) the OT passages to which James appeals; and (2) the way he interprets the OT passages he uses. First, in contradistinction to Paul, who appeals to Genesis 15:6, James appeals first to Genesis 22: "Was not Abraham our father justified by works when he offered up his son Isaac on the altar?" (James 2:21). This is our first hint that James does not make the same argument as Paul.[28] James's argument becomes clear when we consider how he relates his appeal to Genesis 22 to his quotation of Genesis 15:6: "The Scripture was fulfilled that says, 'Abraham believed God, and it was counted to him as righteousness'—and he was called a friend of God" (James 2:23). This brings us to our second point, namely the way James interprets these two passages. Notice that in 2:23 James states, "the Scripture was fulfilled." James's use of this phrase is akin to the NT's appeal to the fulfilment of prophecy but seems out of place here in his explanation of the relationship between faith and works. This conclusion, however, would be hasty.

James's argument is as follows: Genesis 15:6 and the declaration of Abraham's righteousness are confirmed, or demonstrated to be true, by Genesis 22 and his willingness to sacrifice Isaac. Genesis 22 is a fulfilment of Genesis 15:6 in the sense of cause and effect. In this regard John Calvin notes that James "wants to show what kind of faith this was, that justified Abraham, not inactive, not fading, but capable of making him obedient to God." Calvin continues, "A man is not justified by faith alone—that is, only by a bare and empty awareness of God. He is justified by works—that is, his righteousness is known and approved by its fruits."[29]

---

28. Adamson, *James*, 129; also Brian Vickers, *Jesus' Blood and Righteousness* (Wheaton, IL: Crossway, 2006), 90.

29. John Calvin, *A Harmony of the Gospels: Matthew, Mark, and Luke & James & Jude*, trans. A. W. Morrison, ed. David W. Torrance and T. F. Torrance, CNTC (Grand Rapids:

This is the point that James makes: "You see that faith was active along with his works, and faith was completed by his works" (James 2:22). Or, as James Adamson explains, verse 22 is a statement that "a faith already perfect is revealed by its works."[30]

This conclusion is confirmed by James's appeal to Genesis 22, which is different than the typical appeals to this text in his day, as he predicates Abraham's justification upon Genesis 15:6 in parallel fashion with Paul (Rom. 4:1–4; cf. 1 Macc. 2:52; Jubilees 17:17; 19:8).[31] We read, for example, from the Apocrypha: "Was not Abraham found faithful when tested, and it was reckoned to him as righteousness?" (1 Macc 2:52). Paul and James placed the imputation (*logizomai*) of Abraham's righteousness in Genesis 15:6, not Genesis 22. James, then, is using the term "justified" in the same way that Christ used it: "Wisdom is justified by all her children" (Luke 7:35; cf. Matt. 11:19). Christ's point here is not that wisdom will be declared wicked or righteous, as with Paul's use of the term, but that wisdom will be proven true by its fruit.[32] James and Paul, then, are using the term "justified" in different senses. We can restate the differences between Paul and James in the following manner: Paul is interested in explaining how Abraham is justified, whereas James is interested in explaining how Abraham's *faith* is justified. Abraham is justified by faith alone whereas Abraham's faith is justified by works. This brings us to our next point, namely the nature of the *ordo* and *historia salutis*.

The Nature of the Ordo and Historia Salutis

We must remember that both Paul and James operate within the same realm of inaugurated eschatology. Both James and Paul have theological taproots that reach into the prophetic stream of the eschatological prophecies of Jeremiah and Ezekiel. As we saw above, when God promised to return his people from exile, he not only promised to forgive their sins, what we would now in the light of the advent of Christ call justification by faith alone, but he also promised that he would write his law upon the hearts of his people, fill them with his Holy Spirit, and cause them

---

Eerdmans, 1972), 286; Davids, *James*, 129–30; Adamson, *James*, 130–31; Cornelis P. Venema, *The Gospel of Free Acceptance in Christ* (Edinburgh: Banner of Truth, 2006), 78.

30. Adamson, *James*, 130; see Venema, *Gospel*, 76–77.

31. Davids, *James*, 127.

32. See Donald A. Hagner, *Matthew 1–13*, WBC, vol. 33a (Dallas: Word, 1993), 311.

to walk in his statutes.[33] We therefore see a bond between the *historia salutis*, the eschatological outpouring of the Holy Spirit, and the *ordo salutis*, the application of redemption to the individual. It is the unity of the *ordo* and *historia salutis* that causes James to say, "You see that a person is justified by works and not by faith alone" (James 2:24). In the context of dealing with the problem of antinomianism, to say that works are unnecessary for one's salvation is akin to saying that the eschatological age has not been inaugurated, the law has not been inscribed upon our hearts, and believers are not indwelt by the Holy Spirit. This, however, is an impossibility, which is why James says: "For as the body apart from the spirit is dead, so also faith apart from works is dead" (James 2:26).

One must wonder at this point if James has Ezekiel 36–37 as a subtext in addition to the oft-acknowledged allusion to Genesis 2:7, as it is God's Spirit that brings the valley of bones to life (Ezek. 37:1–14, esp. v. 5).[34] Some might at first object to such a proposition, as many do not connect the book of James with concerns for eschatology but rather see it as moral parenesis. Yet there are key points in James's epistle that demonstrate that James has the same redemptive-historical awareness of inaugurated eschatology. One should note that James 1:2–12 and 4:6–5:12 are largely drawn from the prophetic literature of the OT, which links it to the eschatological context.[35] We can briefly see four examples that demonstrate the eschatological awareness of James.

First, James addresses his letter "to the twelve tribes in the Dispersion" (1:1). There was the expectation in the OT that God would gather his people together from the nations at the end of time (Isa. 43:4–7). Dispersion was connected to the blessings and curses of the covenant; it was punishment for Israel's sin (Deut. 30:3–4). Hence the implied idea in addressing his letter to the dispersion is that James was awaiting the eschatological gathering of God's people, not simply Jews, but those who looked to Christ by faith.[36]

33. Vos, "Eschatological Aspect," 109–10.
34. Block, *Ezekiel*, 356; idem, "The Prophet of the Spirit: The Use of *rûaḥ* in the Book of Ezekiel," *JETS* 32/1 (1989): 34–38.
35. Todd C. Penner, *The Epistle of James and Eschatology* (Sheffield: Sheffield Academic Press, 1996), 158–59.
36. 182–83; Douglas Moo, *The Letter of James*, PNTC (Grand Rapids: Eerdmans, 2000), 50; Davids, *James*, 64.

Second, in the verses that immediately follow James's opening sentence we find James making very similar statements to those of the apostle Paul concerning the relationship between the present suffering of God's people and the blessings of the consummation:

> The Spirit himself bears witness with our spirit that we are children of God, and if children, then heirs—heirs of God and fellow heirs with Christ, provided we suffer with him in order that we may also be glorified with him. (Rom. 8:16–17)

> Count it all joy, my brothers, when you meet trials of various kinds, for you know that the testing of your faith produces steadfastness. And let steadfastness have its full effect, that you may be perfect and complete, lacking in nothing. . . . Blessed is the man who remains steadfast under trial, for when he has stood the test he will receive the crown of life, which God has promised to those who love him. (James 1:2–4, 12)[37]

In both James and Paul eschatological blessing will eclipse present suffering. There are still further connections to eschatology present in James.

Third, we read, "Let the lowly brother boast in his exaltation, and the rich in his humiliation, because like a flower of the grass he will pass away. For the sun rises with its scorching heat and withers the grass; its flower falls, and its beauty perishes. So also will the rich man fade away in the midst of his pursuits" (James 1:9–11). This language is drawn from Isaiah 40, especially verses 7–8, where the context is clearly eschatological—the coming of the Lord to lead his people on the eschatological exodus, to judge the wicked, and redeem his people (cf. Mark 1).[38]

Fourth, we see similar themes of coming judgment upon the wicked in James 5:6: "You have condemned; you have murdered the righteous person. He does not resist you. Be patient, therefore, brothers, until the coming of the Lord" (James 5:6–7). James's message is one against the wealthy who are wicked in that they have "laid up treasure in the last days [*eschatais hēmerais*]" (James 5:3). Given these four elements, one may safely conclude that James, like Paul, writes with acute awareness of his eschatological context, namely the already–not yet—the recognition of

37. Penner, *James and Eschatology*, 183; Davids, *James*, 70.
38. Penner, *James and Eschatology*, 204–6; Rikki E. Watts, *Isaiah's New Exodus in Mark* (Grand Rapids: Baker, 2001).

the dawn of the eschaton but at the same time the hope of its consummation with the return of Christ.[39]

In addition to redemptive-historical sensitivities in both Paul and James, one also finds further parallels in both authors especially as concerns antinomianism. One cannot sever the redemptive work of Christ from the outpouring of the Spirit, which is what antinomianism tries to do. This is why we find the same arguments that James makes in Paul's epistle to the Romans:

> Are we to continue in sin that grace may abound? By no means! How can we who died to sin still live in it? Do you not know that all of us who have been baptized into Christ Jesus were baptized into his death? We were buried therefore with him by baptism into death, in order that, just as Christ was raised from the dead by the glory of the Father, we too might walk in newness of life. (Rom. 6:1–4)

The coordination of the work of Christ and the outpouring of the Holy Spirit as it pertains to the prophecy of Jeremiah 31:31–34 is of course evident in Hebrews 8–10 (esp. 8:6–13). When we take, therefore, these three elements into consideration, the problems Paul and James address, their respective use of the term "justified," and the nature of the *ordo* and *historia salutis*, we see that James and Paul speak with one voice on justification by faith alone. Paul, of course, makes the same point as James when he states: "For we are his workmanship, created in Christ Jesus for good works, which God prepared beforehand, that we should walk in them" (Eph. 2:10; cf. Rom. 7:1–4; Isa. 65:17; 66:22; 2 Cor. 5:17).[40] It is in this way, then, that one can say that works are necessary for salvation. They are necessary, not as the cause of one's justification but as its fruit, the fruit of faith.[41]

Conclusion

When we consider the relationship of justification to good works, we must always do so in light of both the *ordo* and *historia salutis*. We must

---

39. Penner, *James and Eschatology*, 210; Moo, *James*, 29–30.

40. See Peter T. O'Brien, *The Letter to the Ephesians*, PNTC (Grand Rapids: Eerdmans, 1999), 178–81; also Sam K. Williams, "Justification and the Spirit in Galatians," *JSNT* 29 (1987): 98.

41. Chris VanLandingham, *Judgment and Justification in Early Judaism and the Apostle Paul* (Peabody, MA: Hendrickson, 2006), 205–7.

recognize that Ezekiel and Jeremiah prophesied of an eschatological day when God would pour out his Spirit upon his people, write his law upon their hearts, and cause them to walk in his statutes. With the advent of Christ and the outpouring of the Holy Spirit at Pentecost, we know that the eschaton has been inaugurated. As the Holy Spirit applies the work of redemption to the individual believers, they are justified by faith alone, but because of his indwelling presence, they also produce the fruit of the Spirit, that is, good works. This is not a picture that should seem odd, as it is one that appeared in preredemptive history.

If we acknowledge that the garden of Eden was the first temple and that the first Adam stood in the midst of a garden surrounded by fruit-bearing trees, then it should come as no surprise that the Scriptures show the conclusion of all history with the last Adam standing in the midst of the eschatological city-temple with an innumerable host of saints gathered from every tribe, tongue, and nation (Rev. 7:9). To what does Scripture compare the righteous but to fruit-bearing trees? It is the righteous man who is "like a tree planted by streams of water that yields its fruit in its season, and its leaf does not wither" (Ps. 1:3). Christ also tells us that a "tree is known by its fruit" (Matt. 12:33). Indeed, Ezekiel uses the creation imagery to characterize the results of God's outpouring of his Spirit upon his people: "This land that was desolate has become like the garden of Eden" (Ezek. 36:35a). It has been God's intention since the very beginning to create a people that glorifies his name by their good works, and so the last Adam will stand in the midst of a garden of fruit-bearing trees, the redeemed people of God, those who have been justified by faith alone but at the same time yield the fruit of good works. This brings us to the next subject for our consideration, namely the relationship between justification and the final judgment.

12

JUSTIFICATION
AND THE FINAL JUDGMENT

We have thus far surveyed the nature of justification by faith alone, the relationship to union with Christ, and sanctification. It is here that we will explore the relationship between justification and the final judgment. We must note, however, an important point regarding justification and eschatology. Given the structure of redemptive history, something we explored in chapter 3, we must recognize that justification is an eschatological event. Justification does not, therefore, touch upon eschatology only as it relates to the final judgment. This relationship between justification and eschatology will surface throughout this chapter. Another issue that arises is how to relate justification to the already–not yet structure of redemptive history. In what way is justification "already," and is there any element of it that is "not yet"? There are still yet other questions that surface when we consider justification and the final judgment. How does one harmonize Paul's statements that justification is by faith alone (Rom. 3:28) but that it is the doers of the law who will be justified (Rom. 2:13)?

Some who attempt to solve this puzzle pursue an answer through a well-worn path: Paul's understanding of the law.[1] While it is certainly important to establish Paul's theology of the law to obtain a correct understanding of how justification relates to the final judgment, it seems as though few take into account the nature of the final judgment itself. There appears to be an unchecked assumption regarding the final judgment, namely that the parousia, resurrection, and final judgment are separate events. Given this presupposition, it is only natural that interpreters would examine the final judgment in isolation from the other events of the last day.

It is the thesis of this chapter, however, that the way to find the relationship between justification and the final judgment lies not only in Paul's understanding of the law, but also in the nature of the final judgment. More specifically, this chapter will argue that the final judgment is not a separate event on the last day but is part of the single organic event of parousia–resurrection–final judgment. In other words, the final judgment is the resurrection. We will support this thesis by examining (1) the significance of Christ's resurrection, taking note of its paradigmatic and forensic nature; (2) the resurrection of the church, or of those who are in Christ, noting its forensic nature; (3) the resurrection–final judgment as one event in connection with the resurrection of the inner and outer man, the immediacy and extent of the resurrection, and the ground of the final judgment; (4) the relationship between justification and the resurrection–final judgment, looking at the crucifixion and how justification relates to the already–not yet; and (5) the reward of believers at the resurrection–final judgment.

The Resurrection of Christ

Paradigmatic for the Church

Whenever one considers the resurrection, it is important to begin with the resurrection of Christ, as it is paradigmatic for believers. Beginning with Paul and John we see that they call Christ "the firstborn from

1. For a cross-section of explanations, see, e.g., Paul A. Rainbow, *The Way of Salvation* (Carlisle: Paternoster, 2005), 17–18, 189–203; Chris VanLandingham, *Judgment and Justification in Early Judaism and the Apostle Paul* (Peabody, MA: Hendrickson, 2006), 200; Kent L. Yinger, *Paul, Judaism, and Judgment according to Deeds* (Cambridge: Cambridge University Press, 1999), 143–59; Cornelis P. Venema, *The Gospel of Free Acceptance in Christ* (Edinburgh: Banner of Truth, 2006), 257–92.

the dead" (Col. 1:18; Rev. 1:5). Louis Berkhof notes in this regard, "This implies that the resurrection of the people of God will be like that of their heavenly Lord."[2] Christ is, of course, the firstborn of many brothers (Rom. 8:29). The connection between the resurrection of Christ and the church is especially evident when Paul calls Christ "the firstfruits of those who have fallen asleep" (1 Cor. 15:20b). That Christ is the firstfruits, imagery based in the OT feast of weeks (Lev. 23:9–22), means that his resurrection is (1) prior in temporality; (2) a representation of the same quality or character; and (3) a promise or pledge of more of the same kind to come.[3] In this regard, Geerhardus Vos writes: "The resurrection of Christ is prophetic of that of all believers."[4] Given, then, the paradigmatic role of Christ's resurrection, we must explore its nature to understand our resurrection.

Resurrection as Forensic Declaration: Christ Is Righteous and God's Son

The first place we see the forensic emerge in connection with the resurrection of Christ is in the opening verses of Paul's epistle to Rome: "Concerning his Son, who was descended from David according to the flesh and was declared to be the Son of God in power according to the Spirit of holiness by his resurrection from the dead, Jesus Christ our Lord" (Rom. 1:3–4). Historically, Reformed interpreters have explained these verses in terms of Christ's ontological constitution: that Christ was descended from David according to the flesh refers to his humanity, and that he was raised from the dead refers to and is evidence of his deity. Charles Hodge argues that when Christ was declared to be the Son of God, "Son of God is not a title of office, but of nature, and therefore Christ cannot be said to have been constituted the Son of God." He goes on to state: "When Christ is said to be constituted the Son of God, we are not to understand that he became or was made Son, but was, in the view of men, thus determined."[5] This is essentially the view of John Calvin, and is

---

2. Louis Berkhof, *Systematic Theology: New Combined Edition* (1932–38; Grand Rapids: Eerdmans, 1996), 722; so also N. T. Wright, *The Resurrection of the Son of God* (Minneapolis: Fortress, 2003), 316.

3. Anthony C. Thiselton, *The First Epistle to the Corinthians*, NIGTC (Grand Rapids: Eerdmans, 2000), 1224.

4. Geerhardus Vos, *Grace and Glory* (1922; Edinburgh: Banner of Truth, 1994), 167.

5. Charles Hodge, *Romans* (1835; Edinburgh: Banner of Truth, 1989), 19.

also defended by B. B. Warfield.[6] In recent years, however, an alternative interpretation has been offered.

Vos has offered a different and more convincing exegesis of Romans 1:3–4. Vos takes into account the *sarx-pneuma* antithesis as representative terms of the two major epochs in redemptive history, the two-age structure dominated by Adam and Christ (1 Cor. 15:45; Rom. 5:12–21).[7] Vos notes the parallel structure of Romans 1:3–4 (fig. 10).

Fig. 10. The parallel structure of Romans 1:3–4

genomenou	*horisthentos*
descended	**declared**
kata sarka	*kata pneuma hagiōsynēs*
according to the flesh	**according to the Spirit of holiness**
ek spermatos David	*ex anastaseōs nekrōn*
from the seed of David	**by his resurrection from the dead**

Vos explains that by "the twofold *kata* the mode of each state of existence is contrasted, by the twofold *ek*, the origin of each. Thus the existence *kata sarka* originated 'from the seed of David,' the existence *kata pneuma* originated 'out of the resurrection from the dead.'" With this exegesis Vos concludes, and rightly so, that "the resurrection is to Paul the beginning of a new status of sonship: hence as Jesus derived His sonship, *kata sarka*, from the seed of David, He can be said to have derived His divine-sonship-in-power from the resurrection."[8] In other words, the

6. See John Calvin, *Romans and Thessalonians*, trans. Ross Mackenzie, ed. David W. Torrance and T. F. Torrance, CNTC (Grand Rapids: Eerdmans, 1960), 16–17; B. B. Warfield, "The Christ That Paul Preached," in *Works of B. B. Warfield*, ed. Ethelbert D. Warfield et al., 10 vols. (1930; Grand Rapids: Baker, 1981), 2:235–54; Richard B. Gaffin Jr., *Resurrection and Redemption* (1978; Phillipsburg, NJ: P&R, 1987), 100. For more recent advocates of this view see Joseph A. Fitzmyer, *Romans*, AB 33 (New York: Doubleday, 1993), 233–36; C. E. B. Cranfield, *Romans*, 2 vols., ICC, (1975; Edinburgh: T & T Clark, 2001), 1:57–62.

7. Geerhardus Vos, "The Eschatological Aspect of the Pauline Conception of the Spirit," in *Redemptive History and Biblical Interpretation*, ed. Richard B. Gaffin Jr. (Phillipsburg, NJ: P&R, 1980), 104; similarly James D. G. Dunn, *Romans 1–8*, WBC 38a (Dallas: Word, 1988), 13.

8. Vos, "Eschatological Aspect," 104; see also Gaffin, *Resurrection*, 98–112; Thomas Schreiner, *Romans*, BECNT (Grand Rapids: Baker, 1998), 41–45; Douglas Moo, *Epistle to the Romans*, NICNT (Grand Rapids: Eerdmans, 1996), 50–51. See also James D. G. Dunn, "Jesus—Flesh and Spirit: An Exposition of Romans 1:3–4," *JTS* 24 (1973), 40–68; idem, "Jesus—Flesh and Spirit: An Exposition of Romans 1:3–4," in *The Christ & the Spirit*, vol. 1

resurrection of Christ is not merely the acknowledgment of the divinity of Christ but rather the inauguration of the eschatological creation as well as the declaration of Christ's sonship, the royal enthronement of the Messiah (Ps. 2:7).[9] This means that the resurrection is not simply an event but is invested with forensic significance.

We find confirmation of this conclusion in Paul's first epistle to Timothy when he writes: "He was manifested in the flesh, justified in the Spirit, seen by angels, proclaimed among the nations, believed on in the world, taken up in glory" (1 Tim. 3:16*). Though Paul does not specifically mention the resurrection, when we compare this verse with Romans 1:3–4, we see that the resurrection is in view, especially with Paul's reference to Christ being "justified" (*edikaiōthē*) in the Spirit.[10] Hence we may say that Christ's resurrection constituted not merely his conquest of death but also his justification, the declaration that he was God's Son as well as righteous. The forensic element is also present in another text that deals with the resurrection of Christ.

In Romans 4:25 Paul states that Christ was "delivered up for our trespasses and raised for our justification." We have already explained the connection between our justification and Christ's resurrection, but it bears brief repetition. Recall that Paul elsewhere stated that "if Christ has not been raised, your faith is futile and you are still in your sins" (1 Cor. 15:17). In other words, if Christ remains dead in the tomb, then the powers of sin and death have not been conquered and Christ's crucifixion was legitimate, for the wages of sin is death (Rom. 6:23).[11] Concerning Christ's resurrection Vos explains: "Christ's resurrection was the *de facto* declaration of God in regard to his being just. His quickening bears in itself the testimony of his justification."[12]

(Grand Rapids: Eerdmans, 1998), 126–53; Dan G. McCartney, "*Ecce Homo*: The Coming of the Kingdom as the Restoration of Human Vicegerency," *WTJ* 56 (1994): 2; John Murray, *The Epistle to the Romans*, NICNT (Grand Rapids: Eerdmans, 1968), 10; Wright, *Resurrection*, 221 n. 29.

9. N. T. Wright, *Romans*, NIB 10 (Nashville: Abingdon, 2003), 416.

10. Wright, *Resurrection*, 270–71; also Lane G. Tipton, "Union with Christ and Justification," in *Justified in Christ*, ed. K. Scott Oliphint (Fearn, Scotland: Mentor, 2007), 30.

11. Gaffin, *Resurrection*, 116; G. C. Berkouwer, *The Work of Christ*, trans. Cornelius Lambregtse (Grand Rapids: Eerdmans, 1965), 190.

12. Geerhardus Vos, *Pauline Eschatology* (1930; Grand Rapids: Eerdmans, 1994), 151; similarly Murray, *Romans*, 156–57; Wright, *Romans*, 504; Moo, *Romans*, 289–90; Schreiner, *Romans*, 244; Cranfield, *Romans*, 1:252; Fitzmyer, *Romans*, 389–90.

Vos elsewhere expands upon the significance of Christ's resurrection when he writes:

> As the curse laid upon him had assumed the visible form of separation between body and soul, it was necessary that in the same physical sphere, in the same palpable form, the divine absolution should be solemnly pronounced and placed on record. By raising Christ from death, God as the supreme Judge set his seal to the absolute perfection and completeness of his atoning work. The resurrection is a public announcement to the world that the penalty of death has been borne by Christ to its bitter end and that in consequence the dominion of guilt has been broken, the curse annihilated forevermore.[13]

Once again we see the declarative, or forensic, connected to the resurrection of Christ. In fact, given Paul's statements in Romans 1:3–4, 4:25, and 1 Timothy 3:16, we may say that the resurrection of Christ is not only the laying of the cornerstone of the eschatological creation but at the same time the declaration of Christ's righteousness and sonship. We must keep this dual-forensic aspect of Christ's resurrection in the foreground as we move forward to consider the resurrection of the church, as Christ's resurrection is paradigmatic for the church.

The Resurrection of the Church

When we consider the resurrection of God's people, we must do so with an eye to the resurrection of Christ. In several places the very themes associated with Christ are brought to bear upon the church in its resurrection. We see connections between the church and Christ in the dual forensic aspects of sonship and righteousness. We begin first with sonship.

Sonship

In Romans 8:23 we read that we "who have the firstfruits of the Spirit, groan inwardly as we wait eagerly for adoption as sons, the redemption of our bodies." Here there is an explicit connection between the forensic,

---

13. Vos, *Grace and Glory*, 161; see also Brian McNeil, "Raised for Our Justification," *ITQ* 42 (1975): 97–105; W. Waite Willis Jr., "A Theology of Resurrection: Its Meaning for Jesus, Us, and God," in *Resurrection*, ed. James H. Charlesworth et al. (London: T & T Clark, 2006), 210. See the analysis of Wright who draws out the judicial aspect of the resurrection in the OT, second-temple literature, and the NT (Wright, *Resurrection*, 116, 149, 151, 156–59, 233).

adoption, and the redemption of the body, or the resurrection from the dead.[14] Christ brings out the connection between sonship and resurrection when he states that those who are raised "cannot die anymore, because they are equal to angels and are sons of God, being sons of the resurrection" (Luke 20:36).[15] It is also important that we note that believers have the "firstfruits of the Spirit," which is essentially synonymous with the word *arrabōn*, which Paul uses to describe the indwelling presence of the Holy Spirit as guarantee or pledge of the believer's future resurrection (2 Cor. 5:5; Eph. 1:13–14).[16] Romans 8:23 means that we will be declared sons of God by the resurrection of our bodies, when what is sown perishable is raised imperishable (1 Cor. 15:42–44).[17] Just as Christ was declared to be the Son of God by his resurrection, those who are in Christ will likewise be declared to be sons of God. Vos notes, "'Adoption' is by parentage a forensic concept; yet it fulfills itself in the bodily transforming change of the resurrection."[18] The forensic element of righteousness is also connected to both Christ's and the believer's resurrection.

Righteousness

When we consider that the wages of sin is death (Rom. 6:23), then those who are raised from the dead are quite obviously innocent of sin—they are righteous in the sight of God. One place where the righteousness-resurrection link surfaces is when Paul compares the resurrection to being clothed: "For in this tent we groan, longing to put on our heavenly dwelling, if indeed by putting it on we may not be found naked" (2 Cor. 5:2–3).

Paul does not want to be naked on the day of judgment: to be naked is to be in the state of shame and guilt. Scott Hafemann explains:

> Paul longs to "be clothed with" his heavenly dwelling because he can assume that he "will not be found naked" (like Adam after the Fall); that is, that he will not be condemned by God in the final judgment (5:3). Inasmuch as

14. Fitzmyer, *Romans*, 510–11; Wright, *Romans*, 597–98; Murray, *Romans*, 308.
15. Vos, "Eschatological Aspect," 104 n. 24.
16. Cranfield, *Romans*, 1:418; Moo, *Romans*, 519–20.
17. Schreiner, *Romans*, 438–39.
18. Vos, *Pauline Eschatology*, 152.

the image of "being clothed" in 5:2–3 refers primarily to the resurrection body, it is important to see that believers receive this body "in Christ."[19]

Hafemann's observations are not new, as Earle Ellis gave the same explanation almost fifty years ago:

> Nakedness, a term used of the abbreviated dress of slaves and war captives, came to have this connotation of guilt and judgment. Such attire might be adopted in symbolic proclamation of the coming calamity. Thus Isaiah (20:2–4) goes "naked" as a portent of God's verdict of destruction upon Egypt and Ethiopia; Micah (1:8) does the same regarding Judah. In the latter may be the additional thought of the prophet's participation in the guilt and judgment of his people. Sometimes the ethical symbolism emphasizes the sin-guiltiness of man in the presence of a holy God with the element of impending judgment less explicit or absent. Fallen Adam "heard the sound" of God and hid because he was "naked" (Gen. 3:10); Israel, "naked" of virtue, is clothed with God's covenant blessings (Ezek. 16:7f.); even Sheol is bared under God's discerning eye (Job 26:6).[20]

The resurrection of the believer, then, is akin to putting on clothing so that one is not found naked on the day of judgment. So, then, just like Christ, the believer's resurrection is his de facto declaration of righteousness because death has no claim upon those who are righteous (1 Cor. 15:55–57).

Summary

When we consider the evidence, we are led to the conclusion that the resurrection is not simply raising people from death but rather is an event wrapped in forensic significance: for those who are in Christ the resurrection is the declaration of their sonship and righteousness just as it was for Christ. This is not a unique conclusion as Vos has previously stated:

> In the resurrection there is already wrapped up a judging-process, at least for believers: the raising act in their case, together with the attending change, plainly involves a pronouncement of vindication. The resurrection does more than prepare its object for undergoing the judgment; it sets in motion

19. Scott J. Hafemann, *2 Corinthians*, NIVAC (Grand Rapids: Zondervan, 2000), 211–12; see also Murray J. Harris, *The Second Epistle to the Corinthians*, NIGTC (Grand Rapids: Eerdmans, 2005), 382.

20. E. Earle Ellis, "2 Corinthians 5:1–10 in Pauline Eschatology," *NTS* 6 (1959–60): 220.

and to a certain extent anticipates the issue of judgment for the Christian. And it were not incorrect to offset this by saying that the judgment places the seal on what the believer has received in the resurrection.[21]

Yet we might go one step further than Vos in this regard by concluding that the resurrection of the church is not the anticipation of the issue of judgment, or the de facto declaration of judgment, but is *de iure* the final judgment. As Herman Bavinck writes, "The resurrection of the dead in general, therefore, is primarily a judicial act of God."[22] Stated simply, the resurrection is not the penultimate event prior to the final judgment; the resurrection is the final judgment.[23] This proposition might cause some to recoil at first, as some conceive of the resurrection and final judgment as separate events, especially those coming from a premillennial (dispensational or historic) background.[24] Yet an exploration of the various texts concerning the nature of the final judgment will confirm the conclusion that the resurrection and the final judgment are one and the same.

Confirmation of the Resurrection–Final Judgment Thesis

There is confirmation of the thesis that the resurrection and final judgment are one and the same event when we consider: (1) being raised with Christ according to the inner and outer man; (2) the immediacy of the transformation of the body; (3) the extent of the resurrection; and (4) the ground of the final judgment.

21. Vos, *Pauline Eschatology*, 261; Tipton, "Union with Christ," 37. Wright similarly states concerning 2 Maccabees 7 that the righteous "are finally declared to be truly his children through the resurrection" (*Resurrection*, 175).

22. Herman Bavinck, *The Last Things*, trans. John Vriend, ed. John Bolt (Grand Rapids: Baker, 1996), 133.

23. One can find the resurrection-as-penultimate construction in some older Reformed theology. For example, in one catechism from the seventeenth century we find: "Q. What shall be the preparation to the judgment? A. The resurrection of the dead and change of the living" (Ezekiel Rogers, *The Grounds of Christian Religion* [London, 1642], in *Catechisms of the Second Reformation*, ed. Alexander F. Mitchell [London: James Nisbet & Co., 1886], 64).

24. See David J. MacLeod, "The Sixth 'Last Thing': The Last Judgment and the End of the World (Rev. 20:11–15)," *BSac* 157 (2000): 315–30, esp. 321; Millard J. Erickson, *Christian Theology* (Grand Rapids: Baker, 1985), 1209–12, 1223–24. One should note, though, that some older Reformed theologians have held the resurrection and final judgment as separate events (see Heinrich Heppe, *Reformed Dogmatics*, trans. G. T. Thomson, ed. Ernst Bizer [London: George Allen & Unwin, 1950], 703).

Raised with Christ: Inner and Outer Man

We must first correlate the resurrection with the fact that those who place their faith in Christ have already been raised and seated with him in the heavenly places (Rom. 6:4; Eph. 2:6). In other words, because of the believer's justification by faith alone, he is already ruling over the creation with Christ. Were a person guilty of sin and worthy of condemnation, he would neither be raised with Christ nor seated with him in the heavenly places. We have been raised, of course, according to our inner man. Our outer man is wasting away and awaits the redemption of the body, the resurrection (2 Cor. 4:16–5:5). The resurrection of believers, then, is simply the visible manifestation or revelation of those who are already raised with Christ. The resurrection is the raising of the outer man of those who have already been raised according to their inner man. To this end Paul writes: "For the creation waits with eager longing for the revealing of the sons of God" (Rom. 8:19). The revelation of the sons of God occurs, not after the final judgment, but at the resurrection (Rom. 8:23).[25] What about the immediacy of the resurrection?

Immediacy of the Resurrection Transformation

The apostle Paul is quite clear that the resurrection transformation of believers is something that occurs in an instant: "in a moment, in the twinkling of an eye, at the last trumpet. For the trumpet will sound, and the dead will be raised imperishable, and we shall be changed" (1 Cor. 15:52).[26] The immediacy of the resurrection transformation is in contrast to at least one idea that was extant in first-century Jewish literature. In the Syriac Apocalypse of Baruch (c. A.D. 100), there is the pattern of resurrection → judgment → glorification:

> For the earth will surely give back the dead at that time; it receives them now in order to keep them, not changing anything in their form. But as it has received them so it will give them back. And as I have delivered them to it so it will raise them. For then it will be necessary to show those who live that the dead are living again, and that those who went away have come back. And it will be that when they have recognized each other,

---

25. Moo, *Romans*, 515; Dunn, *Romans 1–8*, 470; Schreiner, *Romans*, 434–35.

26. Anthony C. Thiselton, *The First Epistle to the Corinthians*, NIGTC (Grand Rapids: Eerdmans, 2000), 1295–96; Gordon D. Fee, *The First Epistle to the Corinthians*, NICNT (Grand Rapids: Eerdmans, 1987), 801–2.

those who know each other at this moment, then my judgment will be strong, and those things which have been spoken of before will come. And it will happen after this day which he appointed is over that both the shape of those who are found to be guilty as also the glory of those who have proved to be righteous will be changed. For the shape of those who now act wickedly will be made more evil than it is (now) so that they shall suffer torment. Also, as for the glory of those who proved to be righteous on account of my law, those who possessed intelligence in their life, and those who planted the root of wisdom in their heart—their splendor will then be glorified by transformations, and the shape of their face will be changed into the light of their beauty so that they may acquire and receive the undying world which is promised to them. (2 Bar. 50:2–51:3)

The pattern is clear, glorification occurs after the final judgment according to this excerpt. Yet Paul clearly states that those who are in Christ are immediately transformed and receive their glorified bodies.[27] What about the extent of the resurrection?

The Extent of the Resurrection

The extent of the resurrection is another element that confirms its final judgment status. We see in several places in Scripture that the resurrection is for both the people of God and those outside the covenant. We read, for example, in the prophet Daniel: "But at that time your people shall be delivered, everyone whose name shall be found written in the book. And many of those who sleep in the dust of the earth shall awake, some to everlasting life, and some to shame and everlasting contempt" (Dan. 12:1b–2). It appears from this statement that the resurrection is a judgment unto itself, in that as the earth yields up the dead there is already a known separation between the righteous and the wicked.[28] It is not, as we saw above, resurrection → judgment → glorification, but rather even before the resurrection the status of those who rise from the dead is already known. Once again resurrection is coterminous with glorification for some, whereas judgment is coeval with resurrection for

---

27. See Murray J. Harris, "2 Corinthians 5:1–10: Watershed in Paul's Eschatology," *TynBul* 22 (1971): 40. For older historic Reformed expressions of this point, see Heppe, *Reformed Dogmatics*, 702–3.

28. Similarly C. D. Elledge, "Resurrection of the Dead: Exploring Our Earliest Evidence Today," in *Resurrection*, ed. Charlesworth et al., 28.

others. We find this same pattern in Christ's teaching on the resurrection: "Do not marvel at this, for an hour is coming when all who are in the tombs will hear his voice and come out, those who have done good to the resurrection of life, and those who have done evil to the resurrection of judgment" (John 5:28–29; see also Luke 14:14). Prior to the resurrection there is knowledge of the final outcome of history. This knowledge, however, is not simply rooted in the decree of election but rather in inaugurated eschatology.

It is true, God has foreknowledge of who will be raised to life and death based upon his sovereign decree of election (Eph. 1:11–12; Rom. 9:1–24). So when we consider the two-age structure of redemptive history and that the eschatological age has begun, we must recognize at the same time that not only have the blessings of the age to come been revealed but so have the curses. The propagation of the gospel has a twofold effect: salvation and judgment (2 Cor. 2:16–17). If the gospel is the in-breaking of the eschatological blessings of the age to come for those who believe, then for those who refuse to believe the gospel there is the in-breaking of the eschatological wrath of God: "Whoever believes in him is not condemned, but whoever does not believe is condemned already, because he has not believed in the name of the only Son of God" (John 3:18).[29] On the basis of the in-breaking of the eschaton with the first advent of Christ, Jesus can say: "Now is the judgment of this world; now will the ruler of this world be cast out" (John 12:31).[30]

Paul also attests to the revelation of God's eschatological wrath in the present when he writes: "For the wrath of God is revealed from heaven against all ungodliness and unrighteousness of men, who by their unrighteousness suppress the truth" (Rom. 1:18).[31] Given the in-breaking of the eschaton, the resurrection is not the penultimate step before the final judgment but instead is the final judgment in that it

29. D. A. Carson, *The Gospel according to John*, PNTC (Grand Rapids: Eerdmans, 1991), 207; Herman N. Ridderbos, *The Gospel of John*, trans. John Vriend (Grand Rapids: Eerdmans, 1997), 139–40; see also Bavinck, *Last Things*, 138.

30. Leon Morris, *The Gospel according to John*, NICNT (Grand Rapids: Eerdmans, 1971), 597; Ridderbos, *John*, 437–39; Carson, *John*, 442–43.

31. Wolfhart Pannenberg, *Systematic Theology*, trans. Geoffrey W. Bromiley, 3 vols. (Grand Rapids: Eerdmans, 1998), 3:612 n. 265; also Fitzmyer, *Romans*, 277–78; Moo, *Romans*, 101; Dunn, *Romans 1–8*, 54–55; Seyoon Kim, *The Origin of Paul's Gospel* (Grand Rapids: Eerdmans, 1981), 286.

visibly reveals what has come with the first advent of Christ. At the second advent of Christ, the righteous, those who have been justified by faith alone, are instantaneously clothed in immortality; they receive a *sōma pneumatikon*. The wicked are also raised but are naked; they still have a *sōma psychikon*; their condemned status is immediately evident. God need not utter a word, as the justified and condemned statuses of the righteous and the wicked are revealed through the resurrection, just as for Jesus.

The case for the resurrection as final judgment becomes stronger when we compare the teaching of Scripture concerning the extent of the resurrection with the common opinion of the Pharisees, who taught that only the righteous would be resurrected (1 Enoch 103:4; 108:11–12; Apocalypse of Baruch 30:1–5; 85:15). According to Josephus, the Pharisees "believe that souls have an immortal vigor in them, and that under the earth there will be rewards or punishments, according as they have lived virtuously or viciously in this life; and the latter are to be detained in an everlasting prison, but that the former shall have power to revive and live again" (*Antiquities* 18.1.3; *Wars* 2.8.14). Though the position of the Pharisees is erroneous in the light of Daniel 12:1–2 and the teaching of Christ in John 5:28–29, the point still stands that the Pharisees considered the resurrection itself to be the reward, not the penultimate step prior to reward.

One finds the same view that the resurrection is itself the reward in other second-temple literature such as 2 Maccabees, where seven brothers are martyred but are hopeful that they will be raised from the dead because of their righteousness: "The King of the universe will raise us up to an everlasting renewal of life, because we have died for his laws" (2 Maccabees 7:9). Similarly, at Qumran: "Surely the Lord shall seek the pious ones, and shall call the righteous by name. . . . For he shall heal the slain ones, and bring life to the dead ones" (4Q521).[32] In *Pseudo-Ezekiel*, we find the author putting the following words in the mouth of the prophet: "I have seen many in Israel who have loved your name and have walked on paths of justice. When will these things happen? And how will they be rewarded for their loyalty?" The prophet then receives a response echoing Ezekiel 37:

---

32. See J. H. Charlesworth, "Where Does the Concept of Resurrection Appear and How Do We Know That?" in *Resurrection*, 14–15.

"Son of man, prophesy over the bones and say: May a bone connect with its bone and a joint with its joint." And so it happened. And he said a second time: "Prophesy, and sinews will grow on them and they will be covered with skin all over." And so it happened. And again he said: "Prophesy over the four winds of the sky and the winds of the sky will blow upon them and they will live and a large crowd of men will rise and bless YHWH Sabaoth who caused them to live." (4Q385, frag. 2)[33]

These cited examples help us see that for many second-temple Jews, it is the resurrection that is the reward, which shows that there were some who saw the resurrection as a judicial act.[34] It appears that Paul shared this understanding of the resurrection with some of his contemporaries. The resurrection is not something that happens prior to the judgment but is itself the judgment. There is a difference, though, between Paul and his contemporaries, namely the judicial ground of the final judgment. For some of Paul's contemporaries, the ground of the final judgment was the believer's works, but this is not so for Paul.

The Ground of the Final Judgment

In the examination of the thesis that the resurrection is the final judgment the most challenging test comes from passages of Scripture that speak about a judgment according to works. Paul, for example, writes, "For it is not the hearers of the law who are righteous before God, but the doers of the law who will be justified" (Rom. 2:13; see also 14:10–12; 2 Cor. 5:10). Now, to be sure, the explanations of Paul's statement are legion, so there is insufficient space here to explore each of the possible interpretations.[35] Nevertheless, Douglas Moo has convincingly argued that at this point in Paul's epistle he explains how one is justified *if* one

33. See Florentino García Martínez, *The Dead Sea Scrolls Translated* (Grand Rapids: Eerdmans, 1996); Elledge, "Resurrection of the Dead," 29–35, esp. 33, 35.

34. Cf. Francis Watson, *Paul and the Hermeneutics of Faith* (Edinburgh: T & T Clark, 2004), 91.

35. See e.g. Dunn, *Romans 1–8*, 85–86, 97–98; Wright, *Romans*, 440; Schreiner, *Romans*, 115, 119, 137–45. For a survey of recent literature see Peter T. O'Brien, "Justification in Paul and Some Crucial Issues of the Last Two Decades," in *Right with God*, ed. D. A. Carson (1992; Eugene, OR: Wipf & Stock, 2002), 89–94; see also Russell Pregeant, "Grace and Recompense: Reflections on a Pauline Paradox," *JAAR* 47 (1979): 73–96; Karl Paul Donfried, "Justification and the Last Judgment in Paul," *ZNW* 67 (1976): 90–110; Nigel M. Watson, "Justified by Faith, Judged by Works—an Antinomy?" *NTS* 29 (1983), 209–21; Klyne R. Snodgrass, "Justification by Grace—to the Doers: An Analysis of the Place of Romans 2 in the Theology of Paul," *NTS* 32 (1986): 72–93; C. H. Cosgrove, "Justification in Paul: A Linguistic and Theological Reflec-

pursues justification by obedience to the law.[36] In other words, at this point in Paul's epistle, he lays out the demands of the law, whether those presented to Adam in the garden-temple or those republished to Israel at Sinai (Rom. 2:12–16; 5:12–21). Paul shows that apart from faith in Christ the standard one must meet is judgment according to works. Moo observes, "Like the bark of the dog in the Sherlock Holmes story 'Silver Blaze,' the word 'faith,' introduced in 1:17 as the way in which God's righteousness can be appropriated, is conspicuous in 2:1–3:8 by its absence."[37]

In terms of the broader scope of redemptive history, Paul is in effect saying, one can pursue justification in solidarity with either the first or last Adam. One can have either the federal representative disobedience of the first Adam, and hence a judgment according to works, or the federal representative obedience of the last Adam, and hence justification by faith alone. But note that there is a regression in arguing that we are justified by faith alone (Rom. 3:28) but that there is still a judgment according to works (Rom. 2:6–9). Moving from Romans 3:28 back to 2:6–9 negates the whole point of Romans 3:21–31.[38] We can confirm this conclusion from another famous passage of Scripture that deals with the final judgment.

One of the clearest pictures of the final judgment comes to us from John's apocalypse:

> Then I saw a great white throne and him who was seated on it. From his presence earth and sky fled away, and no place was found for them. And I saw the dead, great and small, standing before the throne, and books were opened. Then another book was opened, which is the book of life.

---

tion," *JBL* 106 (1987): 653–70; Thomas Schreiner, "Did Paul Believe in Justification by Works? Another Look at Romans 2," *BBR* 3 (1993): 131–58.

36. Moo, *Romans*, 125–77. See also Yinger, *Paul*, 143–59; VanLandingham, *Judgment*, 215–32; Venema, *Gospel*, 276–85; Guy P. Waters, *Justification and the New Perspectives on Paul* (Phillipsburg, NJ: P&R, 2004), 175–76; Hodge, *Romans*, 53–54.

37. Moo, *Romans*, 126.

38. See Waters, *Justification*, 175–77; Hodge, *Romans* (1864; Edinburgh: Banner of Truth, 1972), 49–57; Geerhardus Vos, "The Alleged Legalism in Paul's Doctrine of Justification," in *Redemptive History and Biblical Interpretation*, ed. Richard B. Gaffin Jr. (Phillipsburg, NJ: P&R, 1980), 393–94; also David VanDrunen, "Natural Law and the Works Principle under Adam and Moses," in *The Law Is Not of Faith*, ed. Bryan Estelle, J. V. Fesko, and David Van-Drunen (Phillipsburg, NJ: P&R, 2009).

And the dead were judged by what was written in the books, according to what they had done. (Rev. 20:11–12)

At first glance, this passage seems to controvert two important elements argued thus far, for (1) it appears that the final judgment is according to works, and not faith alone; and (2) it appears as though it is a separate event, one that follows the resurrection. Let us address these two issues.

What is the ground of the final judgment? Here in Revelation 20:11–12 it appears to be works. On the other hand, this is not the best interpretation when we consider all of the exegetical issues in this passage. We must note the Danielic OT background of Revelation 20:11–12. In Daniel 7 the books that are opened appear to deal exclusively with "the evil deeds of the end-time persecutor of God's people."[39] By contrast there is another book: "Your people shall be delivered, everyone whose name shall be found written in the book" (Dan. 12:1). Throughout the Scriptures there is mention of a book or record of those who belong to God and are worthy of life (Ex. 32:32–33; Ps. 69:28; Isa. 4:3; Mal. 3:16).[40] That there are two books present in the scene depicted in Revelation 20:11–12 is evident: the books of deeds and life. There is good reason, not only from the immediate text itself, but also from literature of the day, that each book represents the ground of judgment. The ground of judgment for the wicked is the book of deeds, and for the righteous, it is the book of life: "Now, you sinners, even if you say, 'All our sins shall not be investigated or written down,' nevertheless, all your sins are being written down every day"(1 En. 104:6–7). We also find the following: "And he will be wiped out of the book of the discipline of mankind, and he will not be written (on high) in the Book of Life for (he is written) in the one which will be destroyed" (Jub. 36:10).

---

39. G. K. Beale, *The Book of Revelation*, NIGTC (Grand Rapids: Eerdmans, 1999), 1032; also Robert H. Mounce, *The Book of Revelation*, NICNT (1977; Grand Rapids: Eerdmans, 1998), 374; Jan Lambrecht, "Final Judgments and Ultimate Blessings: The Climactic Visions of Revelation 20:11–21:8," *Bib* 83/3 (2000): 366; David E. Aune, *Revelation 17–22*, WBC 52 (Dallas: Word, 1998), 1102: "The plural in both Dan. 7:10 and here probably reflects the early Jewish tradition of *two* heavenly books, one for recording the deeds of the righteous and the other for recording the deeds of the wicked."

40. Ernest C. Lucas, *Daniel*, AOTC (Downers Grove, IL: InterVarsity, 2002), 182–83.

Given this evidence, Beale concludes that the basis "for judgment of the impious is the record of their evil deeds."[41] As Paul stated in Romans 2:6 and implied in Romans 2:13, the wicked are judged *kata ta erga autōn*, "according to their works" (Rev. 20:12e).[42] We can conclude that it is the wicked alone who are judged according to their works because it is "the dead" who stand before the throne to be judged (Rev. 20:12). The dead are contrasted with those who "came to life and reigned with Christ for a thousand years" (Rev. 20:4c), that is, those who participate in

41. Beale, *Revelation*, 1033; also Lambrecht, "Final Judgments," 369; Mounce, *Revelation*, 376–77. For differing historic views on this point see Heppe, *Reformed Dogmatics*, 705.

42. Richard Gaffin tries to argue, on the basis of the grammar involved in a similar Pauline statement, that works are not the ground of judgment: "It is not for nothing, I take it, and not to be dismissed as an overly fine exegesis to observe, that in Romans 2:6 Paul writes, 'according (*kata*) to works,' not 'on account of (*dia*),' expressing the ground, nor 'by (*ek*) works,' expressing the instrument" (*By Faith, Not by Sight* [Carlisle: Paternoster, 2006], 98–99; similarly, Venema, *Gospel*, 266). Though Gaffin's comment concerns Paul's statement in Romans 2:6, at the same time we find the same prepositional combination with the accusative in John's statement in Revelation 20:12e, the only difference being in the use of the singular and plural pronouns (cf. Rom. 2:6). Gaffin argues this point because he wants to preserve *sola fide* in the judgment of the works of the believer. Relying upon the analysis of Ridderbos and Murray, Gaffin's finer point is that the judgment *kata* works is "in accordance with" the works, and such works are synecdochical for faith in Christ (see Herman Ridderbos, *Paul: An Outline of His Theology*, trans. John Richard de Witt [1975; Grand Rapids: Eerdmans, 1992], 178–81; Murray, *Romans*, 78–79).

Yet can such a fine distinction be supported by the grammar alone? The use of *dia* with the accusative means "because of, on account of," and the use of *kata* with the accusative means "in accordance with, corresponding to" (Daniel B. Wallace, *Greek Grammar beyond the Basics* [Grand Rapids: Zondervan, 1996], 368–69, 376–77). One must ask, what difference exists between the two? In fact, when we delve more deeply into the significance of *kata* with the accusative, we find that "often the noun that follows *kata* specifies the criterion, standard or norm in the light of which a statement is made or is true, an action is performed, or a judgment is passed. The prep. will mean 'according to,' 'in conformity with,' 'corresponding to.' This use is common in reference to the precise and impartial standard of judgment that will be applied at the great Assize (Matt. 16:27; Rom. 2:6; 1 Cor. 3:8; 2 Tim. 4:14; 1 Peter 1:17; Rev. 2:23)" (Murray J. Harris, "Prepositions and Theology in the Greek New Testament," in *NIDNTT*, 3:1200). *Pace* Gaffin and Venema, their argument apparently fails to account for judgment *kata* works for the wicked. This point seems to be borne out by Paul's own use of *kata*, as he says, "He will render each one according to [*kata*] his works" (Rom. 2:6), but this rendering *kata* works is for both the righteous (v. 7) and the wicked (v. 8). According to Gaffin's interpretation, are the wicked judged according to their works, but are they not the ground of their condemnation (see 2 Cor. 11:15)? Again, note how Paul uses *kata*: "Now to the one who works, his wages are not counted as a gift but as his due [*tō de ergazomenō ho misthos ou logizetai kata charin alla kata opheilēma*]" (Rom. 4:4; see also Brian Vickers, *Jesus' Blood and Righteousness* [Wheaton, IL: Crossway, 2006], 95; Yinger, *Paul*, 21–26, 89–90, 135–36, 175, 182, 186). Judgment therefore is indeed *kata* (in accordance with, or on the basis of) works—the evil works of the unbeliever and the good works, or righteousness, of Christ.

the first resurrection (Rev. 20:5b).[43] These righteous are granted eternal life because their names are written in the book of life.

This separation between the wicked and righteous accords with what we have already seen from John's Gospel: "Those who have done good to the resurrection of life, and those who have done evil to the resurrection of judgment" (5:29; Rev. 11:18).[44] Notice that Christ says that only the wicked are raised to judgment. Those who are written in the book of life are spared judgment according to works because the book is "the book of the life of the Lamb that was slain" (Rev. 13:8). Beale explains, "They do not suffer judgment for their evil deeds because he has already suffered it for them: he was slain on their behalf (esp. 1:5; 5:9; 13:8). The Lamb acknowledges before God all who are written in the book (3:5) and are identified with his righteousness and death."[45] The ground of judgment is the book of deeds for the wicked and the book of life for those who are in Christ. We will explore the significance of the ground of judgment for believers when we explore the connection between justification and the resurrection–final judgment. What, however, about the apparent sequential nature of the events of Revelation 20:11–15, first resurrection (v. 13a) and then final judgment (v. 13b)?

Though the resurrection and final judgment appear as sequential and separate events in this passage, we must note several things about the book of Revelation. We must remember that the book of Revelation is highly symbolic, not literal, in nature.[46] The symbolic nature of the description of the final judgment in Revelation 20:11–15 is evident in the use of "books." Beale explains, "The record books are metaphorical for God's unfailing memory, which at the end provides the account of the misdeeds of the wicked to be presented before them."[47] Similarly, the book of life "is metaphorical for God's unfailing memory, and at the end God recognizes those who have taken refuge in the Lamb and have

43. Beale, *Revelation*, 999–1000, also 1002–7; see also Meredith G. Kline, "The First Resurrection," *WTJ* 37 (1975): 366–75; idem, "The First Resurrection: A Reaffirmation," *WTJ* 39 (1976): 110–19.

44. Beale notes that of the nine uses of the verb *krinō* in the book of Revelation, they "all refer to the judgment of the ungodly (6:10; 16:5; 18:8, 20; 19:2, 11; 20:12–13). Likewise, *krisis* always refers to 'judgment' of non-Christians (14:7; 16:7; 18:10; 19:2)" (*Revelation*, 618).

45. Beale, *Revelation*, 1037; Yinger, *Paul*, 134.

46. Beale, *Revelation*, 52.

47. Ibid., 1033.

been recorded in the book for an inheritance of eternal life."[48] Given the symbolic nature of the book as a whole, then, we must recognize that the scene depicted in Revelation 20:11–15 is not literal. This explanation is not to deny the reality of the final judgment, as it is a real event that will occur at the conclusion of history; rather, the way in which it is described in Revelation is not literal but symbolic. As Charles Hodge notes, "The descriptions of the judgment are designed to teach us moral truths, and not the physical phenomena by which the solemn adjudication on the destiny of men is to be attended."[49] In other words, the white throne judgment symbolically conveys the judicial aspect of the resurrection–final judgment.

Summary

We have examined the four elements that confirm the thesis that the resurrection is the final judgment. If believers are already raised with Christ according to their inner man, then they simply await the resurrection of their outer man. The resurrection transformation of the body is immediate, as Paul says it takes place in the twinkling of an eye. This immediacy therefore precludes a commonly assumed pattern of resurrection → final judgment → glorification but instead demands that we recognize that resurrection and glorification are simultaneous events. The resurrection transformation, however, is only for those who are in Christ. The wicked are also raised but they are not glorified. The resurrection reveals who is justified and who is condemned and in this way is the final judgment. Last, we have explained that the ground of the final judgment is different for the righteous and the wicked: the books of deeds and life.

The depiction of the final judgment, however, is not the description of a separate event following the resurrection but rather an aspect of the one organic event of resurrection–final judgment. This conclusion is not unique as others have argued that the events of the last day are one. Berkhof states, "All the great Confessions of the Church represent the general resurrection as simultaneous with the second coming of Christ,

---

48. Ibid., 1037.
49. Charles Hodge, *Systematic Theology*, 3 vols. (1881; Grand Rapids: Eerdmans, 1993), 3:849.

the final judgment and the end of the world."[50] Similarly, Hodge writes: "The general resurrection, the second advent, and the last judgment, are contemporaneous events."[51] Likewise Bavinck observes: "The resurrection and the last judgment are intimately associated as in a single act."[52] Given these conclusions, we may now proceed forward to explore the relationship between the resurrection–final judgment and the doctrine of justification.

Justification and the Resurrection–Final Judgment

We must explore the crucifixion and recognize its eschatological nature as well as the already–not yet and see how these two elements bear upon the doctrine of justification by faith alone.

The Crucifixion

We have noted from the outset of our study the structure of redemptive history, the two-age construction. As we have seen, soteriology, Christology, and eschatology are inextricably intertwined.[53] What this tightly bound relation means is that soteriology is inherently eschatological. The eschatological nature of justification emerges in the nature of the crucifixion and its relationship to the final judgment. When Christ was in the garden of Gethsemane, he asked the Father if it was possible to avoid the crucifixion: "My Father, if it be possible, let this cup pass from me; nevertheless, not as I will, but as you will" (Matt. 26:39). It is significant that Christ calls the crucifixion a "cup," as it is certainly a metaphor for suffering and death. The "cup" is, however, also a reference to God's eschatological wrath.

We see the connection to the eschatological wrath emerge in the punishment that God metes out upon those who receive the mark of the beast: "If anyone worships the beast and its image and receives a mark on his forehead or on his hand, he also will drink the wine of God's wrath, poured full strength into the cup of his anger, and he will be tormented with fire and sulfur" (Rev. 14:9–10). Elsewhere we see the cup filled with

---

50. Berkhof, *Systematic Theology*, 720–21.
51. Hodge, *Systematic Theology*, 3:847.
52. Bavinck, *Last Things*, 132.
53. Vos, *Pauline Eschatology*, 28–29.

"the wine of the fury of his wrath" (Rev. 16:19; cf. Isa. 51:17, 22).[54] That Christ, therefore, drinks the cup of God's wrath means that the eschatological wrath of God reserved for the wicked is brought forward into the present and poured out upon Christ. Christ, of course, bears the eschatological wrath of the day of judgment on behalf of those who are in him, on behalf of God's people.

Vos explains the significance and connection between the crucifixion and justification when he writes:

> Here lies precisely the point where eschatology and justification intersect. By making both the negative element of the forgiveness of sin and the positive element of bestowal of the benefits of salvation unqualified, the Apostle made the act of justification to all intents, so far as the believer is concerned, a last judgment anticipated. If the act dealt with present and past sins only, leaving the future product in uncertainty, it could not be regarded as possessing such absoluteness, and the comparison with the last judgment would break down at the decisive point.[55]

Through the believer's faith in Christ, he knows that his sins, past, present, and future, have been atoned. The believer's declaration of righteousness in justification, then, is also an eschatological reality. Just as the cross brings forward into the present the eschatological wrath and judgment of God upon Christ, so too the believer's justification brings forward into the present the declaration of righteousness from the day of judgment.

Beale encapsulates and summarizes the eschatological nature of justification when he explains:

> Justification too is a doctrine that pertains to the last judgment concomitant with the destruction of the cosmos. This doctrine can be viewed purely in legal terms, whereby Christ bore the eternal wrath of God as our penal substitute so that we could be declared righteous. When we see justification in the light of inaugurated eschatology, we see that the final judgment that unbelievers will face in the future has been pushed back for believers to the cross in the first century. Believers have already passed through

---

54. Donald A. Hagner, *Matthew 14–28*, WBC 33b (Dallas: Word, 1995), 783; see also Pss. 11:6; 75:7–8; Isa. 51:19; Jer. 25:15–16, 27–29; 49:12; 51:57; Lam. 4:21; Ezek. 23:31–34; Hab. 2:16; Zech. 12:2 (D. A. Carson, *Matthew 13–28*, EBC [Grand Rapids: Zondervan, 1995], 543–44). See also Beale, *Revelation*, 759–60.

55. Vos, *Pauline Eschatology*, 55.

the great last judgment when Christ suffered the eternal last judgment for them on the cross.[56]

The eschatological character of the believer's justification that Beale explains can be seen as well in Paul's statement, "There is therefore now no condemnation for those who are in Christ Jesus" (Rom. 8:1). Paul further expands upon the permanent righteousness of God's people, even in the day of judgment, when he writes: "Who shall bring any charge against God's elect? It is God who justifies. Who is to condemn? Christ Jesus is the one who died—more than that, who was raised—who is at the right hand of God, who indeed is interceding for us" (Rom. 8:33–34).[57] Now most commentators will agree with the above analysis, namely with the eschatological connection between the crucifixion and justification. Where disagreement lies, however, is precisely how justification relates to the already–not yet structure of redemptive history.

Justification and the Already–Not Yet

There are some, such as N. T. Wright, who straddle justification across the already–not yet structure of redemptive history. This straddling is evident when Wright states that justification "is not a matter of how someone enters the community of the true people of God, but of how you tell who belongs to that community, not least in the period of time before the eschatological event itself, when the matter will become public knowledge." Wright expands upon his explanation and formally defines justification in the following manner:

> "Justification" in the first century was not about how someone might establish a relationship with God. It was about God's eschatological definition, both future and present, of who was, in fact, a member of his people. In Sanders's terms, it was not so much about "getting in," or indeed about "staying in," as about "how you could tell who was in." In standard Chris-

---

56. G. K. Beale, "The New Testament and New Creation," in *Biblical Theology*, ed. Scott J. Hafemann (Downers Grove, IL: InterVarsity, 2002), 167.

57. There are some who all but strip the hope out of such a passage given their commitment to covenantal nomism and a future justification: "Thus, while Romans 8:1 may rightly be celebrated as Paul's great shout of victory and assurance for believers vis-à-vis condemnation, this may not be taken as an unqualified denial of all relevance of present and future condemnation for Christians, nor as contradicting Paul's expectation of judgment according to works in 2:6" (Yinger, *Paul*, 194).

tian theological language, it wasn't so much about soteriology as about ecclesiology; not so much about salvation as about the church.[58]

What is evident in Wright's description is that there are elements of justification that are "already," but there are also elements of justification that are "not yet." There is in Wright's formulation a "present justification," where the believer is declared to be one of God's people in the present. There is also a "final justification" where the believer is declared to be one of God's people on the last day at the final judgment before the world. We should note, though, that Wright believes that present justification is based upon the work of Christ, whereas final justification is based upon the Spirit-produced works of the believer, the life judged as a whole.[59] Commenting on Romans 8:3–4 Wright states: "As I pointed out earlier, this in no way compromises present justification by faith. What is spoken of here is the future verdict, that of the last day, the 'day' Paul described in 2:1–16. That verdict will correspond to the present one, and will follow from (though not, in that sense, be earned or merited by), the Spirit-led life of which Paul now speaks."[60]

There are others, such as Herman Ridderbos, who reject such a construction. Ridderbos argues that justification cannot be an initial judicial act of God that takes place in the present to be followed by a justification on the ground of works at the final judgment. Rather, Ridderbos argues that "faith is involved in justification by the grace of God and by nothing else, even so work emanates from this same faith; as faith it cannot remain empty and work-less, but becomes known as faith precisely in works."[61] In other words, for the believer faith and works are synecdochical; to refer to the believer's works is at the same time to refer to his faith, the root

---

58. N. T. Wright, *What Saint Paul Really Said* (Grand Rapids: Eerdmans, 1997), 119.

59. This is strikingly similar to the Roman Catholic understanding of a second justification, one that has historically come under criticism (see, e.g., John Owen, *The Doctrine of Justification by Faith*, in *Works of John Owen*, 16 vols. [1850–53; Edinburgh: Banner of Truth, 1993], 5:137–52).

60. Wright, *Romans*, 580; also 440. For similar views see Donfried, "Justification and the Last Judgment," 99–102; Snodgrass, "Justification by Grace," 85; Joachim Jeremias, "Paul and James," *ExpTim* 66 (1954–55): 370. Wright does make a connection between the resurrection and justification, but does not fully develop the significance of the resurrection as a judicial event, one inextricably linked to the resurrection of Christ, not the Spirit-led works of the believer (see Wright, *Resurrection*, 222, 245, 248, 259, 271, 442 n. 126). See also VanLandingham, *Judgment*, 66, 205–10, 335.

61. Ridderbos, *Paul*, 180.

of his good works. Ridderbos demonstrates the synecdochic relationship by appealing to Ephesians 2:8–10: "For by grace you have been saved through faith. And this is not your own doing; it is the gift of God, not a result of works, so that no one may boast. For we are his workmanship, created in Christ Jesus for good works, which God prepared beforehand, that we should walk in them." Ridderbos explains:

> The unity of grace, faith, and works cannot be elucidated more clearly than here. That is not to say that in every pronouncement, whether on justification by faith or on judgment according to works, this whole indissoluble unity is always transparent. But in the whole framework of Paul's unfolding of salvation as redemption in Christ, all this constitutes an integral unity.[62]

Now one can see that Ridderbos's explanation is superior to Wright's, as he preserves the ground of justification, both present and future, in the work of Christ.[63] Additionally, contra Wright, as we examined in the chapter on justification and sanctification, how can a believer, who is betwixt this age and the age to come, and who carries about the body of sin, have his good works withstand the scrutiny and absolute perfection that is required before the throne of God? Wright also appears to fail to take into account the redemptive-historical character of good works. According to the prophetic trajectories of Jeremiah and Ezekiel, the good works of the church serve a doxological, not judicial, end (Jer. 31:31–34; Ezek. 36:16–37). Nevertheless, despite the divergence between Ridderbos and Wright on the ground of one's future justification, both have something in common regarding their understanding of the final judgment.

Ridderbos and Wright appear to have this in common: they both conceive of the final judgment in the same way—as a separate event that follows the resurrection. That Ridderbos, like Wright, conceives of the final judgment as a separate event is evident when he writes:

> However true it may be in itself that in Romans 2 and 3:1–10 Paul is elucidating over against Judaism the impossibility of justification by faith as the only way of salvation, this does not mean that on this latter, "evangelical,"

---

62. Ridderbos, *Paul*, 180; see also O'Brien, "Justification in Paul," 94.
63. Guy P. Waters, "Introduction: Whatever Happened to *Sola Fide*?" in *By Faith Alone*, ed. Gary L. Johnson and Guy P. Waters (Wheaton, IL: Crossway, 2006), 28, 31.

standpoint the judgment to come has been abrogated for believers with the death and resurrection of Christ, nor either that in this judgment the criterion would lie only in the presence of faith and not also of works.[64]

Ridderbos's statement appears to have weight, namely the judgment according to works even for believers, until we broaden our scope of investigation to the Johannine portions of Scripture, John 5:28–29 and Revelation 20:11–15. The wicked are judged according to the book of deeds whereas the righteous are judged according to the book of the life of the Lamb who was slain. Moreover, given the evidence that we have surveyed thus far concerning the unity of the resurrection and final judgment, we must not separate the final judgment as if it were a separate event. In effect, both Ridderbos and Wright posit two separate verdicts: one in the present and the other in the future.[65] They both straddle justification over the already–not yet structure of redemptive history. If the resurrection and final judgment, however, are the same event, then there is a better way to conceive of justification as it relates to the already–not yet.

Positing two separate verdicts, one in the present and one in the future, inherently diminishes the eschatological "already" of the believer's justification.[66] Moreover, two separate verdicts does not seem to concur with Paul's pronouncements of the believer's righteousness in the present (Rom. 8:1, 33–34). Rather than straddling justification over the already–not yet, in light of the resurrection–final judgment unity, we must instead recognize that the one declaration of justification in the present is revealed in the future by means of the resurrection. In other words, it is not that justification has two parts, present and future, but rather that it has two levels of publication, the resurrection according to the inner and outer man, or in terms of the *ordo salutis*, justification and glorification. When the believer is justified by faith alone, he is immediately raised with Christ. As Edmund Clowney notes,

> Our justification does not await the last day when all shall appear before God's judgment. Since we are united to Christ, what is true of him is true

---

64. Ridderbos, *Paul*, 179.

65. In similar fashion see Richard B. Gaffin Jr., "Justification and Eschatology," in *Justified in Christ*, ed. K. Scott Oliphint (Fearn, Scotland: Mentor, 2007), 1–22; Rainbow, *Way of Salvation*, 155–74; Seyoon Kim, *Paul's Gospel*, 286–87.

66. See Donfried, "Justification and the Last Judgment," 99–103.

of us. When he died to sin, so did we; when he rose to eternal life, we rose with him. When he ascended to heaven, we entered the heavenly places with him. For that reason, our justification is not simply a future hope but a present reality, made ours through faith.[67]

Believers are therefore raised with Christ immediately upon their justification because Christ has offered total and perfect obedience to the law and borne the eschatological wrath of the final judgment on behalf of the believer. The condemnation of the final judgment is brought forward into the present in the crucifixion of Christ, and therefore believers can look to the last day with hope, knowing that Christ has secured their redemption.

The immediacy and finality of the believer's justification are evident in such passages as Luke 23:43: the thief joined Christ in paradise the very day of his death. What awaits the believer is not a second verdict at the final judgment but rather his bodily resurrection, the revelation of the verdict that has already been passed in his justification.[68] When the believer is justified, he is raised with Christ according to his inner man, which is based upon the life, death, and resurrection of Christ and is by grace alone through faith alone in Christ alone. The justified person awaits the revelation of his justification, which occurs through the resurrection–final judgment as only those who are in Christ are raised to eternal life and immediately transformed according to the outer man.[69] The believer is immediately clothed in immortality, whereas the unbeliever is raised but neither clothed in immortality nor raised to life but to death. In terms of the historic formulation, the believer is "openly acknowledged and acquitted" not by a judgment according to works, but through the resurrection of his outer man (LC 90; SC 38).

67. Edmund P. Clowney, "The Biblical Doctrine of Justification by Faith," in *Right with God*, ed. Carson, 47.

68. Historically, some have explained the relationship between justification and the final judgment in a similar manner. In a seventeenth-century catechism, we find the following questions and answers: "Q. What are the fruits of justification? A. Adoption, sanctification, Christian liberty, and glorification," and, "Q. What is the last fruit of justification? A. Our glorification" (Thomas Wyllie, *Another Catechism*, in *Catechisms of the Second Reformation*, ed. Mitchell, 258, 261). More recently, Michael Horton has argued along these same lines (see *Covenant and Salvation: Union with Christ* [Louisville: Westminster John Knox, 2007], ch. 12).

69. Yinger, for example, treats 2 Corinthians 5:10 without any reference to the surrounding context, specifically vv. 1–9 and the resurrection (*Paul*, 260–70).

In this regard Vos insightfully draws the connection between resurrection and justification when he writes: "Resurrection thus comes out of justification, and justification comes, after a manner most carefully to be defined, out of the resurrection." We should go a step beyond Vos's analysis of the connection between resurrection and justification. Yes, as Vos states, "Christ's resurrection was the *de facto* declaration of God in regard to his being just."[70] The resurrection of Christ, however, is also the *de iure* declaration, as Romans 4:25 and especially 1:3–4 make clear. The resurrection of Christ, as we have seen above, is paradigmatic for the church.

Vos draws out the connection between the resurrection and justification as it relates to Christ and the church when he writes:

> Much light falls on the forensic significance of the resurrection in believers from a comparison with the case of Christ's resurrection. The Spirit is in Christ the seal and fruit of his righteousness, and at the same time it is in Him through his exalted state, produced by the resurrection, the perpetual witness of the continuous status of righteousness in which He exists. In Him unintermittedly springs up that fountain of justification, from which all believers draw. To say that forgiveness of sin procured through the imputation of Christ's merit constitutes only the initial act in the Christian life, and that thereafter, the slate having been wiped clean, there is no further need for nor allowance of recourse to it, all being thenceforth staked on sanctification, is, apart from all other criticism, wrong, because it ignores the forensic righteousness as a vital factor in the exalted state of the Savior. If this were not so, it would remain unexplainable why, in the matter of justification, Paul directs the gaze of faith not merely to the cross retrospectively, but likewise upward to the glorified existence of Christ in heaven, wherein all the merit of the cross is laid up and made available forever.[71]

Vos's point is that in the doctrine of justification, one must always relate it to the resurrection of Christ. This pertains not only to the effectiveness of the justification, that is, that Christ was raised for our justification (Rom. 4:25), but also as it relates to the final judgment and justification. If the resurrection of Christ is any clue to the final judgment, then it stands

---

70. Vos, *Pauline Eschatology*, 151.
71. Ibid., 153–54 n. 9.

to reason that the resurrection and final judgment are one and the same event. This conception of the resurrection–final judgment preserves the eschatological nature of justification and eliminates the tension between justification and judgment by works. Unbelievers are judged according to works, and believers are judged according to the works of Christ. That believers are judged according to the works of Christ is evident not only from what we have previously seen, namely the presence of the book of life at the throne of judgment (Rev. 20:11–15), but also from how the book of Revelation describes the works of believers.

When we consider the works of believers as they pertain to the final judgment, we must take into account Revelation 19:7–8: "Let us rejoice and exult and give him the glory, for the marriage of the Lamb has come, and his Bride has made herself ready; it was granted her to clothe herself with fine linen, bright and pure—for the fine linen is the righteous deeds of the saints." We must connect Revelation 19:7–8 with 20:11–15, as this provides us with important exegetical data to support the contention that for believers, the ground of judgment is not their works but the works of Christ. First, structurally, we must recognize that the events of Revelation 19:7–8 are chronologically parallel to those of 20:11–15, not chronologically sequential. In other words, the structure of the book of Revelation is that of a progressive parallelism.[72]

Second, we must note the Isaianic (61:10) background to appreciate fully the significance of Revelation 19:7–8: "I will greatly rejoice in the LORD; my soul shall exult in my God, for he has clothed me with the garments of salvation; he has covered me with the robe of righteousness, as a bridegroom decks himself like a priest with a beautiful headdress, and as a bride adorns herself with her jewels." Within the immediate context, Isaiah prophesies of Israel's end-time restoration and likens it to a wedding with the bridegroom and bride adorning themselves with wedding garments.[73] God clothes Israel with the garment of salvation, which is called a robe of righteousness; the garment of salvation and robe of righteousness are synonymous expressions, as "salvation is a state of being right with God."[74] So, then, while Revelation 19:7b states, "his

---

72. See William Hendricksen, *More than Conquerors* (1939; Grand Rapids: Baker, 1960), 48; also Beale, *Revelation*, 972, 974–83.

73. Beale, *Revelation*, 938–39.

74. E. J. Young, *The Book of Isaiah*, vol. 3 (1972; Grand Rapids: Eerdmans, 1997), 466.

Bride has made herself ready," it is further explained in verse 8a that "it was granted [*edothē*] her to clothe herself with fine linen." So, then, God clothes the bride, the church, in the robe of righteousness, which verse 8b calls "the righteous deeds of the saints." What is the source of the robe of righteousness, the righteous deeds of the saints?

We must realize that the righteous deeds of the saints originate with God, not with the believer. Moreover, that the deeds are given to the saints is evident in both Isaiah 61:10 and Revelation 19:8. When we correlate these data with Revelation 20:11–15 and the book of life of the Lamb that was slain (Rev. 20:12; 13:8), what emerges is that it is the obedience, or righteousness, of Christ that is imputed that is the ground of judgment for the believer. We see the same wedding-garment imagery connected with the work of Christ in Paul: "Husbands, love your wives, as Christ loved the church and gave himself up for her, that he might sanctify her, having cleansed her by the washing of water with the word, so that he might present the church to himself in splendor, without spot or wrinkle or any such thing, that she might be holy and without blemish" (Eph. 5:25–27).[75] The bride of Christ, then, is clothed in righteousness, which by imputation is the righteous deeds of the saints. The picture that emerges concerning judgment according to the works of Christ is further confirmed when we consider the connections between justification and the resurrection–final judgment, specifically as it relates to the wedding garments.

In Revelation the saints are already clothed in white garments but at the same time await to be clothed in white garments: "Yet you have still a few names in Sardis, people who have not soiled their garments, and they will walk with me in white, for they are worthy. The one who conquers will be clothed thus in white garments, and I will never blot his name out of the book of life" (Rev. 3:4–5a). That believers are already clothed in white garments but await another enrobing corresponds, as we have already seen, to the resurrection of the inner and outer man (2 Cor. 4:16). Just as Paul did not want to be found naked on the day of judgment but clothed in his resurrection body (2 Cor. 5:2–3), so too Christ exhorts believers not to be "found naked" (Rev. 3:17–18; 16:15).

75. Beale, *Revelation*, 942.

We can correlate these exegetical data with Christ's parable of the wedding feast. Only those dressed in wedding garments are allowed to stay for the wedding feast (Matt. 22:11–13; cf. Zech. 3:1–5). Putting Christ's parable into the terms of systematic theology, we may say that only those who are clothed in the imputed righteousness of Christ will enjoy the wedding feast of the Lamb. And, at the resurrection–final judgment, those who are raised to life will be raised according to the outer man, revealing that they have been judged and justified, but that the ground of their justification was the work of Christ. The resurrection–final judgment simply reveals to the world what has already been known to God and accomplished in the believer's justification. There is one last question that we must answer, namely, How does the resurrection–final judgment relate to the rewarding of believers' good works?

The Final Judgment and Reward

We have thus far considered the nature of the final judgment and have concluded that it is one and the same with the resurrection. The image of a multitude of people standing before the throne of God to await judgment is a symbolic way to describe the judicial aspect of the resurrection. There are not literal books, for example, from which the wicked and righteous are judged. The books imagery is the way the Bible describes the omniscience of God in judging the sins of the wicked and his perfect knowledge of those who have sought refuge in the life, death, and resurrection of Christ. Now, if the final judgment is the resurrection, the question will undoubtedly arise, When and how will believers be rewarded for their good works? The question will most likely arise because, according to the typical scheme, mankind stands before the throne of God and is judged according to works. For the wicked, the result is their condemnation. For the righteous, judged on the basis of the works of Christ and granted eternal life, their good works are rewarded at this time. If, however, the final judgment is the resurrection, then when and how are believers rewarded?

We must first realize that the believer is raised because of the work of Christ, not because of one's own good works, which is in stark contrast to the evidence we have gathered from second-temple sources, which make the believer's works the cause of the resurrection glorification. The evaluation of the believer's good works stands logically after the resurrection, not before. The believer is already raised with Christ according to both the inner and outer man by his faith in Christ. Keeping this in mind, we may observe that the reward for good works is not within the scope of justification by faith. Or we may put this in terms of the *ordo salutis*: the reward of the believer's good works is part of his glorification, not his justification by faith alone. Moving forward, in 1 Corinthians 3:11–15 we receive a clue as to the nature of the way in which the reward of good works will transpire.

When we investigate 1 Corinthians 3:11–15, we must first note an important contextual element that helps us understand the passage. Namely, Paul does not deal directly with the nature of rewards for good works in this passage. Rather, he deals specifically with God's evaluation of the work of ministers as it pertains to building the church, the eschatological temple. This interpretation is evident from the context, where Christ is the foundation (v. 11) and Paul, an apostle, is "a skilled master builder" (v. 10).[76] Nevertheless, we see a paradigm emerge in verse 13 regarding how the works of ministers will be evaluated on the day of judgment: "Each one's work will become manifest, for the Day will disclose it, because it will be revealed by fire, and the fire will test what sort of work each one has done." It seems safe to assume that the manner by which the works of ministers will be evaluated is the same manner in which the works of believers will be evaluated, namely by fire on the day of judgment. The question is, of course, what is the nature of the fire?

Throughout the Scriptures, especially in the prophets, fire is the means by which God purifies and purges out everything that is incompatible with either his being and attributes or, as we see here, the new creation (Isa. 1:25; Mal. 3:2–3; Isa. 66:15–16; Heb. 10:27; Jude 7; Rev. 8:5–11; 19:12).[77] We must ask, Is the fire literal or is this a figure of speech used to refer to something else? Space does not permit an explanation, but the language is figurative and refers to the second coming of Christ. It is

76. See Robert L. Dabney, "An Exposition of 1 Corinthians 3:10–15," in *Discussions*, vol. 1 (1890; Edinburgh: Banner of Truth, 1967), 551–74; also Craig A. Evans, "How Are the Apostles Judged? A Note on 1 Cor. 3:10–15," *JETS* 27 (1984), 149–50; Harm W. Hollander, "The Testing by Fire of the Builders' Works: 1 Cor. 3:10–15," *NTS* 40 (1994), 89–104; Donfried, "Justification and the Last Judgment," 106.

77. Pannenberg, *Systematic Theology*, 3:611.

Jesus Christ who is the fire of purification at the final judgment.[78] There are hints of this, for example, when the author of Hebrews calls God "a consuming fire" (Heb. 12:29). There is, however, a more direct statement from Paul: "The Lord Jesus is revealed from heaven with his mighty angels in flaming fire, inflicting vengeance on those who do not know God and on those who do not obey the gospel of our Lord Jesus" (2 Thess. 1:7–8; also Rev. 1:14; 2:18; Mal. 3:1–3).[79] Once again, we must coordinate the resurrection, final judgment, and now, the return of Christ, as one event, not three separate events.

If we conceive of the one parousia–resurrection–final judgment event, then in light of Paul's statement in 1 Corinthians 3:13, believers' works will either survive and hence yield reward or be burned in judgment. What allows one's work to survive is whether he builds with gold, silver, precious stones, materials associated with the construction of the temple, in this case the eschatological temple, the church (1 Chron. 29:2; Ex. 25:3–7; 31:4–5; 1 Chron. 22:14–16).[80] In other words, one must build with eternal materials, materials associated with the age to come, that which is consistent with the foundation, Jesus Christ.[81] If the believer, however, builds with wood, hay, and straw (1 Cor. 3:12), namely those things that are transient in this present evil age, his works will be destroyed.

Again, as with justification, the parousia–resurrection–final judgment simply reveals what is known to God, in this case whether a person's works were the works of Christ, prepared beforehand for us to walk in them (Eph. 2:8–10), or whether they were the works of the flesh. Those works that survive the parousia of Christ will receive a reward (1 Cor. 3:14), which is perhaps that the work endures into eternity, brings eternal glory to the triune Lord, and receives the praise of the triune Lord, "Well done, good servant!" (Luke 19:17; Matt. 6:1–6; 1 Cor. 10:31). Moreover, we should not forget the redemptive-historical trajectory for the purpose of the good works of God's people that we saw in the last chapter. Namely, according to Ezekiel, the works of his people vindicate God, and therefore

---

78. Ibid., 3:611–17.

79. Dabney, "Exposition of 1 Corinthians 3:10–15," 556; F. F. Bruce, *1 and 2 Thessalonians*, WBC 45 (Dallas: Word, 1982), 150–51. Charles A. Wanamaker, *The Epistles to the Thessalonians*, NIGTC (Grand Rapids: Eerdmans, 1990), 226–27.

80. Hollander, "Testing by Fire," 93.

81. Simon J. Kistemaker, *I Corinthians*, NTC (Grand Rapids: Baker, 1993), 111; Thiselton, *First Epistle to the Corinthians*, 311.

we can say that they justify his name before the world (Ezek. 36:23). The answer to the question of the final judgment and reward, then, comes in seeing the return of Christ as coterminous with the resurrection and final judgment.

Conclusion

In our investigation of the relationship between justification and the final judgment, this chapter has set forth the thesis that the final judgment is part of the one parousia–resurrection–final judgment event. While one may distinguish elements of this one event, he must not separate any one aspect from the other two. To examine the final judgment apart from the resurrection fails to account for the forensic character of the resurrection, which has led to the creation of tension in the relationship between justification and the final judgment. If, however, one maintains the unity of the parousia–resurrection–final judgment, one preserves the eschatological nature of justification and that the believer's righteousness in the present is revealed by the resurrection on the last day. When one considers the subject of justification, especially as it relates to the final judgment, he must not simply look to the crucified Christ but to the resurrected and glorified Christ seated in the heavens at the right hand of the Father. For as Christ was justified and declared to be the Son of God in power according to the Holy Spirit by his resurrection, so believers will be raised in like manner. It is this knowledge that causes the apostle John to look forward to the return of Christ: "Beloved, we are God's children now, and what we will be has not yet appeared; but we know that when he appears we shall be like him, because we shall see him as he is" (1 John 3:2). We must now move forward and explore the connections between justification and the doctrine of the church.

13

JUSTIFICATION AND THE CHURCH

The doctrine of justification is an important element of the *ordo salutis*, which primarily deals with the salvation of the individual. That justification largely deals with the salvation of the individual does not mean, however, that the individual is therefore saved to the exclusion of the corporate body, namely the church. In the history of the doctrine of justification, there have certainly been those theologians who have developed the doctrine almost exclusively in terms of the individual at the expense of the church. The doctrine of justification, properly understood, builds up the church and does not tear it down. Other issues also arise concerning justification and the church, namely the question of whether "corporate justification" is a proper theological category. Some scholars with New Perspective concerns have argued that the chief issue at stake in the doctrine of justification is ecclesiology, not soteriology. To this end they argue that justification is not so much about the salvation of the individual but the corporate vindication of the church at the final judgment.

In addition to these two issues there are also matters concerning the church's mission as the herald of the gospel. And there are pastoral issues related to justification, such as the assurance of one's salvation. What implications does the doctrine of justification have in the face of pastoral questions of congregants who doubt their salvation or lose a loved one to suicide? There is also the question of the relationship between justification and the sacraments, particularly that of baptism. These are the issues that confront the investigator when he looks for the connections between justification and the church. Each one of these subjects invites a separate monograph, which is far beyond the scope of our survey. Nevertheless, it will prove helpful to outline how justification relates to each of these subjects, as they in some way relate to the doctrine of the church. To that end we will explore justification and: (1) the church, or corporate body; (2) corporate justification; (3) missions; (4) pastoral counseling; and (5) the sacrament of baptism.

The Church

Throughout the history of the development of the doctrine of justification one can see a trend of moving from incorporation in the covenant community to radical isolation from it. One finds that Rudolf Bultmann's understanding of justification was colored by his existentialist reading of the NT, in which "man's death has its cause in the fact that man in his striving to live out of his own resources loses his self," but on the other hand, "life arises out of surrendering one's self to God, thereby gaining one's self."[1] In such an affirmation, justification is oriented solely around the individual; there seems to be little concern for the corporate body, the church.[2]

Others, such as N. T. Wright, argue from the other side of the spectrum. Wright argues that Paul's epistle to Rome, for example, is "not a detached statement of how people get saved, how they enter a relationship with God as individuals, but an exposition of the covenant purposes of the creator God."[3] Wright goes on to state:

"Justification" in the first century was not about how someone might establish a relationship with God. It was about God's eschatological definition,

---

1. Rudolf Bultmann, *Theology of the New Testament: Complete in One Volume*, trans. Kendrick Grobel (New York: Charles Scribner's Sons, 1951–55), 1:270.
2. For a similar existentialist understanding of justification see Paul Tillich, *Systematic Theology*, 3 vols. (1957; Chicago: University of Chicago Press, 1977), 2:13–16.
3. N. T. Wright, *What Saint Paul Really Said* (Grand Rapids: Eerdmans, 1997), 131.

both future and present, of who was, in fact, a member of his people. ... In standard Christian theological language, it wasn't so much about soteriology as about ecclesiology; not so much about salvation as about the church.[4]

So, then, in contrast to Bultmann, who emphasizes the individual, Wright places emphasis upon the corporate body, the church.[5] What one must realize, however, is that both Bultmann's and Wright's understandings represent a skewed conception of the relationship between justification and the church.

One must recognize that, yes, justification deals first with the individual. Justification, as we have seen, is one element of the *ordo salutis*, which deals with the application of the redemptive work of Christ to the individual. That justification deals primarily with the individual is evident from the nature of Paul's explanation of the doctrine. Abraham's righteous status came through faith—in other words, Abraham exercised his personal faith, which was God-given, in the promises of God concerning the gospel (Gal. 3:16; Rom. 4:1–8; Eph. 2:8–10). We see the emphasis upon the individual in other places in the NT when individuals ask the question, "What must I do to be saved" (Acts 16:30; Luke 18:18)?

At the same time, the Scriptures also teach that the individual is not saved to an indefinite end but to the end of incorporation into the body of Christ, the church. Moreover, given that justification is at the core of the church's preaching of the gospel, the church continues to propagate the gospel so that other individuals may be incorporated into the body of Christ. As Karl Barth comments about the conduct of the justified sinner (Ps. 51:13–15): "The completion of justification cannot and will not be a private matter, but as such his commissioning for the service for God among men. It will attain its end in his calling. In the calling of the same man."[6] In other words, the justification of the individual has a *telos* in his role as a witness to other men about the saving grace of God, which has its goal in the edification of the church.

4. Ibid., 119.
5. See Richard B. Gaffin Jr., "Paul the Theologian," *WTJ* 62/1 (2000): 127–28.
6. Karl Barth, *Church Dogmatics*, trans. G. W. Bromiley, ed. G. W. Bromiley and T. F. Torrance, vol. 4.1 (1956; Edinburgh: T & T Clark, 1988), 580.

So often justification, a part of the *ordo salutis*, has been severed from its necessary connection to the church. To do so, however, is unscriptural. Stuart Robinson once observed concerning redemption vis-à-vis the church:

> It is set forth as a distinguishing feature of the purpose of redemption, that it is to save not merely myriads of men as *individual men*, but myriads of sinners, as composing a Mediatorial body, of which the Mediator shall be the head; a Mediatorial Kingdom, whose government shall be upon His shoulder forever; a Church, the Lamb's Bride, of which He shall be the Husband; a bride whose beautiful portrait was graven upon the palms of His hands, and whose walls were continually before Him, when in the counsels of eternity He undertook her redemption (Col. 1:18–20; Isa. 9:6–7; Eph. 5:25; Isa. 49:16).[7]

One finds both the individual and the corporate body in the Scriptures, neither one being eclipsed by the other. The both/and of the individual and the corporate body is aptly illustrated by the apostle Paul in his use of the individual members forming the one body, no one part more important than the other (1 Cor. 12). One finds this dual emphasis upon the individual and the church vis-à-vis the doctrine of justification in the historic Reformed faith.

John Calvin emphasized both the individual and the church body in his theology. We find evidence of this in Calvin's definition of the invisible church, which he defines as "all God's elect," that is, those who receive justification as individuals.[8] When we recall the radically individualistic age in which we now live, Calvin by contrast lived in a time that was marked by corporate solidarity.[9] Corporate solidarity was maintained by creeds, confessions, and catechisms. Calvin, for example, established the practice of requiring all the inhabitants of Geneva to subscribe to a common confession. This was done to maintain the corporate unity of

---

7. Stuart Robinson, *The Church of God as an Essential Element of the Gospel and the Idea, Structure, and Functions Thereof* (1858; Greenville, SC: GPTS, 1995), 38–39.

8. John Calvin, *Institutes of the Christian Religion*, trans. Ford Lewis Battles, ed. John T. McNeill, LCC 20–21 (Philadelphia: Westminster, 1960), 4.1.2.

9. Despite attempts to place emphasis upon community, a corporate faith is lacking in those who come from the Emerging Church (see, e.g., Brian D. McLaren, *A Generous Orthodoxy* [Grand Rapids: Zondervan, 2004]).

the city.[10] Calvin's *Instruction in Faith,* the city's catechism, for example, states the following regarding baptism: "Baptism . . . is a mark by which we publicly declare that we wish to be numbered among the people of God, to the end that we, together with all believers, may serve and honor, with one same religion, one God."[11] Calvin stresses the idea that the individual is baptized into a corporate body. So we see that Calvin does not miss the importance of the corporate nature of the church and its connection with justification. This has been the historic witness of the Reformed churches, evident in confessions and catechisms.[12]

Corporate Justification

Another issue that is related to the doctrine of justification and the church is the question of what some have called "corporate justification." This understanding of justification stems from those with New Perspective concerns, especially Wright. As we saw above, Wright argues that justification is not so much about soteriology but about ecclesiology. Moreover, the justification, or vindication, of the people of God is what Paul has in mind, according to Wright. Justification, according to Wright, and as we saw in our chapter on his view, is about the vindication of the people of God before the world—the demonstration that they are "in the right."[13] Some have therefore concluded that the doctrine of justification is more concerned with the corporate vindication of God's people, hence their corporate justification. Is there a corporate justification? We must answer, no, there is not, at least not in the sense in which Wright explains the doctrine.

We have seen above, as well as throughout our study, that the doctrine of justification is an element of the *ordo salutis,* which concerns the application of the work of Christ to the individual. The salvation, and justification, of the individual, however, is not only about the individual's relationship to God but ultimately his relationship to God as part of the corporate body, the

10. François Wendel, *Calvin,* trans. Philip Mairet (1950; Grand Rapids: Baker, 1997), 51.

11. John Calvin, *Instruction in Faith (1537),* trans. and ed. Paul T. Fuhrmann (1977; Louisville: Westminster John Knox, 1992), §28.

12. See Belgic Confession 27; Heidelberg Catechism 54; Second Helvetic Confession 17.1; Westminster Confession 25.1–2; cf. Ola Tjørhom, "The Church the Place of Salvation: On the Interrelation between Justification and Ecclesiology," *ProEccl* 9 (2000): 288–89.

13. N. T. Wright, *The New Testament and the People of God* (Minneapolis: Fortress, 1992), 335.

church. One may say, therefore, that justification, contra Wright, is primarily about soteriology, but that the soteriology yields an ecclesiology. Or that the doctrine of justification produces an ecclesiological epiphenomenon that rests upon a soteriological root or core.[14] In the strict definition of justification qua an element of the *ordo salutis*, there is consequently no doctrine of corporate justification. There is no corporate application of the *ordo salutis*. There is no regeneration or effectual calling of the corporate body at the exact same time, for example. This does not mean, however, that there is not a corporate justification of the body of Christ as it is more broadly understood, especially as it relates to the *historia salutis*. There are two places in redemptive history where we might set the corporate justification of the church, the already and the not yet.

First, there is the corporate justification of the church in the present that is tied to the complex of events in the resurrection and ascension of Christ and the outpouring of the Holy Spirit at Pentecost: "This Jesus God raised up, and of that we all are witnesses. Being therefore exalted at the right hand of God, and having received from the Father the promise of the Holy Spirit, he has poured out this that you yourselves are seeing and hearing" (Acts 2:32–33). That Jesus is raised from the dead is in effect his justification, the Father's declaration concerning the righteousness of his Son (Rom. 1:3–4; 4:25; 1 Tim. 3:16). That Christ, as the head of the body, the church, is justified, declared righteous, by his resurrection, is consequently to declare that the church as a corporate body has a righteous standing before God. The church's righteous standing before God, however, is also manifest in the outpouring of the Holy Spirit at Pentecost. Richard Gaffin writes:

> Pentecost is not only the efficacious empowering of the church for kingdom-service (it is that, to be sure), but is also the effective demonstration that the church is no longer subject to God's wrath. The eschatological life of the Spirit poured out on the church at Pentecost seals its acquittal and the definitive removal of its guilt. The baptism with the Holy Spirit openly attests that "there is now no condemnation for those who are in Christ Jesus" (Rom. 8:1). The Spirit of Pentecost is the Spirit of justification.[15]

14. I owe this aphorism to my colleague Richard B. Gaffin.
15. Richard B. Gaffin Jr., "Justification in Luke-Acts," in *Right with God*, ed. D. A. Carson (Eugene OR: Wipf & Stock, 1992), 112.

It is the Spirit's indwelling of the church, then, which occurs in the present, or is an inaugurated, or "already," aspect of eschatology.

The second place in which we can set the corporate justification of the church is in the not yet, or in the general resurrection of the church. As we saw in the chapter on the resurrection and final judgment, the resurrection is the final judgment in that it is the revelation of the verdict that has been passed upon not only the individual, as it is individuals who are raised, but also upon the corporate body, as it is the church that is raised from the dead and clothed in immortality. The church will be glorified by God and in his presence be revealed for what he has known her to be as a consequence of the work of his Son, a spotless bride (Eph. 5:25–27; Rev. 7:13–14; 19:7–8; Ps. 45; Isa. 61:10–11). God will reveal the righteous status of his people, which they have received by faith alone, through their resurrection, and in this sense they will be publicly declared righteous (see LC 90; SC 38). It is in this manner, in terms of the *historia salutis*, then, that we may speak of a corporate justification.

Missions and Evangelism

From the very outset of our study, we have seen that the doctrine of justification is at the heart of the church's proclamation of the gospel. The doctrine of justification encapsulates the direct and normative consequences of the revelation of Jesus Christ to the world. In its proclamation of the gospel, the church announces to the world that the saving work of Christ can be obtained only by faith in him.[16] The doctrine of justification, which is at the core of the proclamation of the gospel, therefore lies at the heart of missions. The doctrine of justification by faith alone stands in stark contrast to the soteriologies of the world religions. We can see this illustrated in two religions, Islam and Hinduism.

In Islam, for example, it is good works that save a person from the damnation of evil:

> It is not righteousness that you turn your face to the East and the West; but righteous is he who believes in Allah and the Last Day and the angels and the Scripture and the Prophets; and gives his wealth, for love of Him,

16. Alister E. McGrath, *Iustitia Dei*, 2 vols. (1986; Cambridge: Cambridge University Press, 1995), 1:1.

to kinsfolk and to orphans and the needy and the wayfarer, and to those who ask, and to set slaves free; and observes proper worship and pays the poor due. And those who keep their treaty when they make one, and the patient in tribulation and adversity and time of stress, such as they who are sincere, such as the God-fearing. (Surah 2.177)

We see in this quote from the Qur'an that one is saved by both his faith in Allah and his good works. The *Hadith*, the recorded sayings of the prophet Muhammad, and second in authority only to the Qur'an, states concerning martyrdom and jihad: "Allah guarantees (the person who carries out Jihad in His Cause and nothing compelled him to go out but Jihad in His Cause and the belief in His Word) that He will either admit him into Paradise (Martyrdom) or return him with reward or booty he has earned to his residence from where he went out."[17] In other words, one can be saved by his martyrdom in the cause of jihad.

One finds a similar understanding of salvation by works in Hinduism. In Hinduism there is the concept of the transmigration of the soul, which is based upon a caste system and the concept of karma. In the concept of karma, one reaps what one sows, and the reaping is ultimately experienced in a series of births: "Those who are of pleasant conduct here—the prospect is, indeed that they will enter a pleasant womb, either the womb of a Brahman, or the womb of a Kshatriya, or the womb of Vaishya. But those who are of stinking womb, either the womb of a dog, or the womb of a swine, or the womb of an outcast." This understanding of transmigration represents a system of justification by works.[18]

The two offered examples of Islam and Hinduism illustrate the stark antithesis that exists between the message of the gospel, which has at its heart justification by faith alone, and the messages of the world's religions—a person remedies his fallen human condition by his works, whether by achieving enlightenment in Buddhism, paradise by martyrdom or good works in Islam, higher existence by works in Hinduism, or salvation by works in the theology of the Jehovah's Witnesses or Mormons. In this regard, we may say that the world's religions are introspective, in that

17. See Chris Marantika, "Justification by Faith: Its Relevance in Islamic Context," in *Right with God*, ed. Carson, 228–42; see also Paul Marshall, Roberta Green, and Lela Gilbert, *Islam at the Crossroads* (Grand Rapids: Baker, 2002), 19–40.

18. Sunand Sumithra, "Justification by Faith: Its Relevance in Hindu Context," in *Right with God*, ed. Carson, 216–27.

a person must ultimately look to himself and his own labors. In contra-distinction, the Christian faith is extraspective, in that the believer looks to the works of another, Jesus Christ, the only one who was obedient to the Father's will, and has paid the penalty in the place of those who have violated it. In this regard, justification by faith alone stands at the heart of Christian missions, one of the chief callings of the church.

Pastoral Counseling

The doctrine of justification also has implications vis-à-vis the doctrine of the church as it concerns pastoral counseling.[19] So often the pastor of a local congregation is confronted with counseling issues that pertain to the issue of assurance of one's salvation. If a person rightly understands that his salvation is based upon the work of Christ and not his own, then he can be assured of his righteous status before the throne of God. The correct understanding of justification, especially as it is tied to the rest of the *ordo* and *historia salutis*, that is, that sanctification follows, and that the believer's justification is the in-breaking of the verdict of the final judgment in the present, should engender hope and assurance in the heart of a true believer. For God has condemned the believer's sin in Christ and declared the sinner righteous by faith alone and has poured out the Holy Spirit upon the believer that he might walk in the newness of life. Such a message is not only a clarion of hope when people lack assurance, but is also a hope-filled message in other pastoral counseling contexts.[20]

For those who have a prodigal child, no truth other than the justification of the ungodly (Rom. 4:5) gives parents hope. It imparts hope, not only because the parents can pray that their wayward child may still yet awaken to the hope that Christ is his righteousness by faith, no matter what he has done, but it is also the salve for the guilty consciences of parents who feel they have failed in their parenting.[21] Likewise, for the family and friends who have lost a loved one to suicide, so long as the

19. For a more thorough treatment of the subject, see Dennis E. Johnson, "*Simul iustus et peccator*: The Role of Justification in Pastoral Counseling," in *Covenant, Justification, and Pastoral Ministry*, ed. R. Scott Clark (Phillipsburg, NJ: P&R, 2007), 399–430.

20. See D. A. Carson, "Reflections on Christian Assurance," *WTJ* 54 (1992): 1–29; Joel R. Beeke, *The Quest for Full Assurance* (Edinburgh: Banner of Truth, 1999).

21. John Piper, *Counted Righteous in Christ* (Wheaton, IL: Crossway, 2002), 31.

person looked to Christ by faith, nothing can undo his justification. While it is sad and true that the one who commits suicide ends his life on an emphatic sin, it is not unpardonable. There is no sin that can overturn one's justification by faith alone. Often, however, the message of justification by faith alone is lost in the tragedy of suicide because people think that it is a sin greater than others, perhaps even the unpardonable sin. Suicide is not the unpardonable sin.[22]

Protestants would do well to recall that all Christians die struggling with sin. Christians are *simul iustus et peccator*, at the same time righteous and a sinner, because of the abiding presence of sin. Recall as we saw in the chapter on justification and sanctification that the believer lives betwixt this present evil age and the age to come, as he is raised according to his inner man and enters the age to come, but has still yet to depart the present evil age because his outer man has yet to have been raised, and for this reason the believer constantly struggles with sin (Rom. 7). Nevertheless, the struggle with sin, even if it ends in suicide, does not overturn the believer's justification. The believer's justification is based upon the work of Christ, not his own works.

This implication for justification vis-à-vis suicide is not necessarily so for those who hold to a Roman Catholic understanding of justification, as justification is based partly on the grace of God in Christ and partly upon the believer's good works.[23] Additionally, the believer can lose his justification.[24] For this reason, for Roman Catholicism, suicide can indeed represent the loss of the believer's justification.[25] In this regard, the sacrament of last rites, or extreme unction, is of the utmost importance, as it gives the believer an extra-added measure of grace as he is in the throes of death, to prevent him from apostasy in the final moments of his life.[26] While such a conception of justification is true of Roman

22. See, e.g., Mark 3:28–30 (Morna D. Hooker, *The Gospel according to St. Mark* [Peabody, MA: Hendrickson, 1991], 117–18; R. T. France, *The Gospel of Mark*, NIGTC [Grand Rapids: Eerdmans, 2002], 174–77).
23. See, e.g., "Canons and Decrees of the Council of Trent," session 6, ch. 10, in Philip Schaff, *Creeds of Christendom*, 3 vols. (1931; Grand Rapids: Baker, 1990), 2:99.
24. Ibid., session 6, ch. 15, in Schaff, *Creeds*, 2:106–7.
25. See, e.g., Karl Keating, *Catholicism and Fundamentalism* (San Francisco: Ignatius Press, 1988), 166; Joseph Cardinal Ratzinger, ed., *Catechism of the Catholic Church* (Ligouri: Ligouri Publications, 1994), § 2283, p. 550.
26. Ratzinger, *Catechism*, § 1523, p. 381.

Catholic theology, as we will see in the following chapter, it is not true of the scriptural doctrine of justification by faith alone.

Baptism

The last issue upon which we want to touch is the relationship between justification and the sacrament of baptism. Many Protestants see little connection between justification and baptism because baptism only represents the believer's pledge to serve his Savior. We see this pledge-element in one definition of baptism: "Baptism is, then, an act of faith and a testimony that one has been united with Christ in his death and resurrection, that one has experienced spiritual circumcision. It is a public indication of one's commitment to Christ."[27] In other words, baptism is merely a symbol. One finds this type of definition historically coming from Ulrich Zwingli, the first-generation Swiss Reformer. Zwingli explains:

> The word sacrament means a covenant sign or pledge. If a man sews on a white cross, he proclaims that he is a Confederate. And if he makes the pilgrimage to Nähenfels and gives God praise and thanksgiving for the victory vouchsafed to our forefathers, he testifies that he is a Confederate indeed. Similarly the man who receives the mark of baptism is the one who is resolved to hear what God says to him, to learn the divine precepts and to live his life in accordance with them.[28]

On the other side of the spectrum, there is the Roman Catholic Church (RCC), which views baptism as the instrumental means of justification. We see baptism described in this manner by the Council of Trent (1546): "The instrumental cause [of justification] is the sacrament of baptism, which is the sacrament of faith, without which no man was ever justified."[29] Which of these two positions is correct?

There are some, such as Wolfhart Pannenberg, a Protestant, who argue that the RCC was correct to place baptism at the heart of its justification decree. Pannenberg states, "If Reformation theology had done the same,

---

27. Millard J. Erickson, *Christian Theology* (Grand Rapids: Baker, 1985), 1101.

28. Ulrich Zwingli, "On Baptism," in G. W. Bromiley, ed., *Zwingli and Bullinger* (Philadelphia: Westminster, 1953), 131.

29. "Canons and Decrees of the Council of Trent," session 6, ch. 7, in Schaff, *Creeds of Christendom*, 2:95.

its teaching on justification by faith alone would have been less open to misunderstanding, for baptism was traditionally regarded as the sacrament of faith."[30] Pannenberg argues:

> Baptism is the basis for the adoption of believers as God's children (Gal. 3:26–27; cf. John 1:12–13). Baptism relates to hope of the inheritance of eternal life (1 Peter 1:3–4), which for Paul, too, is part of belonging to God's family (Gal. 4:7; Rom. 8:17). The word of the righteousness of faith also relates to baptism (Gal. 3:24–27; cf. Titus 3:7). Baptism is thus the common reference point for all these theological interpretations.[31]

Pannenberg has a valid observation, in that the sacrament of baptism is indeed connected to the various elements of our redemption. It means, yes, one should explicate the relationship between baptism and justification. In this regard, we may dismiss the common Protestant evangelical understanding of baptism—it is not merely a symbol of the believer's faith or pledge to serve Christ. On the other hand, this does not mean that we must agree with the RCC; baptism is not the instrumental means of our justification.

While it is true that baptism is coordinated with several different elements of our redemption, it is not the instrumental means of our justification. As Barth long ago noted concerning Trent's statements on baptism and justification,

> Where in Paul—not only the Paul of Galatians but Paul generally—do we find anything like the *gratia praeveniens* in virtue of which even before a man believes and is baptized he is set in motion *ad convertendum se ad suam iustificationem*, that is, to the "disposing" (*c.* 5 and *can.* 4–5) of himself for grace as his own *liberum arbitrium*, which has only been weakened (*c.* 1), assenting to it and co-operating with it (*assentiendo et cooperando*)? Does Paul know anything of a natural man who, by reason of this *gratia praeveniens*, is in a position to accept the revelations and promises of God, out of fear of Him to turn to His mercy, to trust in the goodness addressed to him *propter Christum*, to begin to love Him, to hate and despise his sins and to repent, and finally to ask for baptism and

---

30. Wolfhart Pannenberg, *Systematic Theology*, trans. G. W. Bromiley, 3 vols. (Grand Rapids: Eerdmans, 1998), 3:233.
31. Ibid., 3:235.

JUSTIFICATION AND THE CHURCH

a new life and obedience (*c.* 6)? And could Paul possibly have described baptism as the *causa instrumentalis* of what he called *dikaiosynē*, as the Council of Trent does (*c.* 7)?[32]

Though there are elements of Barth's doctrine of baptism that are objectionable, such as his rejection of infant baptism, nevertheless, his observations concerning the RCC are on point. As we will see in the following chapter on justification and the RCC, the Roman Catholic view has justification mediated through the priesthood and through the sacrament of baptism. Yet this is a sacramental construction of which the Scriptures know nothing. Given Pannenberg's statements, then, how is one to relate justification, and even the other elements of our redemption, to baptism? The answer comes from the historic Reformed faith.

It is in the historic Reformed confessions, such as the Westminster Standards, where one finds the proper relationship set forth between justification and the sacrament of baptism. The Westminster Standards take into account the scriptural nature of baptism, that it is a sacrament, a sign and seal of the covenant, and that it is a means of grace, all the while avoiding the Scylla of emptying the sacrament of its meaning, as in many evangelical constructions, and the Charybdis of giving baptism too much weight and falling into a Roman Catholic understanding.

First, we must understand that a "sacrament," a word that many evangelicals eschew because of its use by the RCC, is a visible sign that points to the invisible grace of God, dispensed within the context of a covenant: "A sacrament is an holy ordinance instituted by Christ, wherein, by sensible signs, Christ, and the benefits of the new covenant, are represented, sealed, and applied to believers" (SC 92).[33] That baptism is a sign and seal of the covenant is evident, for example, in Abraham's circumcision, where Paul calls circumcision, which was the sign of the covenant (Gen. 17:11), "a seal of the righteousness that he had by faith" (Rom. 4:11). Notice that Abraham already possessed righteousness by faith, prior to his circumcision (Gen. 15:6; 17:11; Rom. 4:1–3). In other words, circumcision was

---

32. Barth, *Church Dogmatics*, 4.1:625; idem, *The Teaching of the Church regarding Baptism* (1943; Eugene, OR: Wipf & Stock, 2006).

33. Louis Berkhof, *Systematic Theology: New Combined Edition* (1932–38; Grand Rapids: Eerdmans, 1996), 617; Calvin, *Institutes*, 4.14.1.

not the instrumental means of his justification; the instrumental means of justification was faith alone. Paul makes this point clear, as Abraham serves as the model for both OT and NT believers; he is justified by faith alone.[34] This excludes, therefore, the Roman Catholic conception of the relationship between justification and baptism. If circumcision serves as the sign and seal of the old covenant, then baptism serves as the sign and seal of the new.

Paul places circumcision and baptism in parallel, showing that baptism has superseded circumcision, when he writes that "in him also you were circumcised with a circumcision made without hands, by putting off the body of the flesh, by the circumcision of Christ" (Col. 2:11). Notice that Paul identifies the symbolic significance of circumcision as "putting off the body of the flesh." In other words, for the Israelite who joined faith to his circumcision, his circumcision signified the putting off of the body of the flesh, or the body of sin (Rom. 2:28). For the Israelite who never wedded faith to his circumcision, the cutting of the foreskin was symbolic of being cut off from the covenant community (Gen. 17:14). The same holds true for baptism.

In the following verse, Paul states: "Having been buried with him in baptism, in which you were also raised with him through faith in the powerful working of God, who raised him from the dead" (Col. 2:12). Notice that baptism points to the same spiritual reality as circumcision, removal of the body of sin, which here Paul characterizes as being buried with Christ, and elsewhere he again calls being "buried therefore with him by baptism into death" (Rom. 6:4); in baptism "our old self was crucified with him in order that the body of sin might be brought to nothing" (Rom. 6:6). Herein lies the parallel—circumcision symbolized cutting away the body of sin, and baptism symbolizes burial of the body of sin. In the same way that circumcision was the initiatory rite into the Israelite covenant community, so too baptism is the initiatory rite of entrance into the visible covenant community of the church.[35]

Whether the sign of circumcision or baptism, the initiatory sacrament is first and foremost the sign of God's covenant and second a seal of the

34. So Joseph A. Fitzmyer, *Romans*, AB 33 (New York: Doubleday, 1993), 373; C. E. B. Cranfield, *Romans*, 2 vols., ICC (1975; Edinburgh: T & T Clark, 2001), 1:231–32; Douglas Moo, *Epistle to the Romans*, NICNT (Grand Rapids: Eerdmans, 1996), 263–64.

35. See Calvin, *Institutes*, 4.14.24.

believer's righteousness. We see the Westminster Confession maintain this balance as it relates baptism to the other elements of our redemption, which would also include our justification, when it states: "Baptism is a sacrament of the new testament . . . not only for the solemn admission of the party baptized into the visible Church; but also, to be unto him a sign and seal of the covenant of grace, of his engrafting into Christ, of regeneration, of remission of sins, and of his giving up unto God, through Jesus Christ, to walk in newness of life" (28.1). It is indisputable that baptism is interconnected with our justification, but only as a sign and seal, not as an instrumental means thereof. At the same time, we should also note that while baptism is a sign and seal, it also functions as a means of grace.

The sacrament of baptism exhibits the grace of God in a visible form when accompanied by the preaching of the word.[36] For this reason, we see the Scriptures speak of baptism in redemptive terms: "For as many of you as were baptized into Christ have put on Christ" (Gal. 3:27).[37] Paul also writes, "Do you not know that all of us who have been baptized into Christ Jesus were baptized into his death?" (Rom. 6:3).[38] So, yes, Paul coordinates baptism and redemption, but is careful to stipulate that our justification comes, not because of works but according to the mercy of God, which is given by faith and visibly signified and sealed in baptism (see Rom. 3:28; 4:1–8; Gal. 2:16; Eph. 2:8–10; Titus 3:5–7). For this reason Calvin explains that "sacraments are truly named the testimonies of God's grace and are like seals of the good will that he feels toward us, which by the attesting that good will to us, sustain, nourish, confirm, and increase our faith."[39]

So while a person is justified by faith alone, at the same time his justification is visibly portrayed in his cleansing in the waters of baptism, from which he visibly arises as a new creation. Calvin explains the connection between baptism and the righteousness of justification in the following manner:

---

36. Ibid., 4.14.3.
37. Herman N. Ridderbos, *The Epistle of Paul to the Churches of Galatia*, NICNT (Grand Rapids: Eerdmans, 1953), 147–48; Richard N. Longenecker, *Galatians*, WBC 41 (Dallas: Word, 1990), 155–56.
38. See Moo, *Romans*, 359–60; similarly, Fitzmyer, *Romans*, 430–35.
39. Calvin, *Institutes*, 4.14.7.

Through baptism, believers are assured that this condemnation has been removed and withdrawn from them, since (as was said) the Lord promises us by this sign that full and complete remission has been made, both of the guilt that should have been imputed to us, and of the punishment that we ought to have undergone because of the guilt. They also lay hold on righteousness, but such righteousness as the people of God can obtain in this life, that is, by imputation only, since the Lord of his own mercy considers them righteous and innocent.[40]

That which has taken place within to the inner man by faith alone is made visible through the sacrament of baptism, accompanied by the word, and brings with it grace, which edifies the believer's faith.

Because the sacraments, specifically baptism, are means of grace, the Reformed tradition has recognized that the word, sacraments, and prayer "are effectual to the elect for their salvation" (LC 54, 161; SC 88, 91). In other words, the grace that accompanies the sacraments causes a person to grow in his faith; hence the Larger Catechism's use of the phrase "effectual . . . for their *salvation*" (emphasis added), which is the broader, more encompassing term; note the divines do not say the sacrament of baptism is effectual for one's justification. In the case of the baptism of infants, where faith is not necessarily present, the Westminster Confession explains:

> The efficacy of Baptism is not tied to that moment of time wherein it is administered; yet, not withstanding, by the right use of this ordinance, the grace promised is not only offered, but really exhibited, and conferred, by the Holy Ghost, to such (whether of age or infants) as that grace belongs unto, according to the counsel of God's own will, in His appointed time. (28.6)

This means that when an infant is baptized, the grace exhibited in baptism becomes effectual to his salvation after his justification by faith alone, and his faith is further strengthened as he witnesses others who are baptized. Once again, recognizing the individual-community relationship, baptism is ultimately not just a means of grace for the individual but for the corporate body.

40. Ibid., 4.15.10.

Conclusion

In this brief survey we have explored in outline the connections between justification and the doctrine of the church. There is undoubtedly a monograph that lies behind each subsection of this chapter. Nevertheless, we have seen how justification pertains to the individual as the application of redemption, but that the individual is saved to be part of the body, the church. The church has been corporately justified in the complex of events surrounding the resurrection and ascension of Christ and the outpouring of the Spirit at Pentecost, which will be consummated at the second advent with the resurrection of the church. We have also seen the implications of justification for missions and pastoral counseling—justification is at the heart of the proclamation of the gospel, which brings salvation to the nations and healing balm to the sin-affected life of the church. And, lastly, we have seen that justification is related to baptism, in that baptism is a sign and seal of our redemption, not a bare symbol, but a means of grace by which we visibly see our redemption. This does not exhaust the relationship between justification and the church, as there are many other connections that one could make. To this end, in the subsequent two and final chapters we will explore the relationship of justification to the doctrine of the church, particularly as it relates to ecumenism—the ecumenical efforts to reunify Protestants with the RCC and the Eastern Orthodox Church. It is to explore justification and the RCC that we now turn.

14

JUSTIFICATION AND THE ROMAN CATHOLIC CHURCH

Ever since the Reformation, theologians on both sides of the aisle, Roman Catholic and Protestant, have explored the possibility of reunification. Historically, the doctrine of justification has been an impediment to ecumenical efforts, especially in the wake of the Council of Trent and its famous anathemas against the battle cries of the Reformation, *sola fide* and *solus Christus*. Yet many argue that on the basis of changing conceptions of doctrine, as well as changing attitudes between the heirs of the Reformation and other communities of faith, ecumenical reconciliation is closer to becoming a reality than it has been in the previous four hundred plus years since the Reformation. This chapter will argue, however, that such an outlook is based upon a shallow reading of the doctrinal issues at stake, most notably key elements of the doctrine of justification. To substantiate this thesis, we will investigate the historical background leading up to the Council of Trent, the Tridentine pronouncements on justification, and recent ecumenical efforts between Roman Catholics and Protestants, and last, we will identify key issues concerning the doctrine of justification that must be addressed in future ecumenical dialogues.

Historical Background: Regensburg and Trent

Colloquy of Regensburg (1541)

Over the years there have been many different attempts to have representatives of the Protestant Reformation and the Roman Catholic Church (RCC) enter into dialogues to see if the breach between the two parties could be mended. One of the first attempts at reconciliation was at the Colloquy of Regensburg (1541). The Roman Catholic participants included Nicholas Granvella, Gasparo Contarini, and Johannes Eck. The Protestant participants included Martin Bucer, Wolfgang Capito, John Calvin, and Philip Melanchthon, though Bucer was largely the chief participant on the Protestant side. The final product of the colloquy was not a document with which the respective sides could mend the breach. The doctrine of justification was not the only matter of dispute as other doctrines also contributed to the divide, such as the Lord's Supper and the nature of church authority.[1]

Nevertheless, for the purpose of our investigation, it is primarily the fifth article of the Regensburg Agreement that is of interest to us. The fifth article states:

> Although the one who is justified receives the righteousness and through Christ as the inherent [righteousness], as the apostle says [1 Cor. 6:11]: "you are washed, you are sanctified, you are justified, etc." (which is why the holy fathers made use of [the term] "to be justified" even to mean "to receive inherent righteousness"), nevertheless, the faithful soul depends not on this, but only on the righteousness of Christ given to us as a gift, without which there is and can be no righteousness at all. And so by faith in Christ we are justified or reckoned to be righteous, that is, we are accepted through his merits and not on account of our own worthiness or works. And on account of the righteousness inherent in us we are said to be righteous, because the works which we perform are righteous, according to the saying of John [1 John 3:7]: "whoever does what is right is righteous."[2]

1. Anthony N. S. Lane, *Justification by Faith in Catholic-Protestant Dialogue* (Edinburgh: T & T Clark, 2002), 52.
2. Ibid., "Appendix 1," 235.

This article was an attempt to hammer out compromise between the two camps but in the end only juxtaposes the Protestant and Roman Catholic views against one another. Therefore, one may conclude that the fifth article does not represent a great ecumenical triumph for a Protestant–Roman Catholic rapprochement on the doctrine of justification. Nevertheless, there are several things we should note.

Alister McGrath identifies several important points regarding the colloquy and its article on justification. First, the parties present at the colloquy were not representatives of their respective institutions, so whatever agreement they achieved was somewhat limited. Second, the agreement that they achieved has been called a "scissors and paste job," as the Protestant and Roman Catholic views are merely juxtaposed without any serious interaction as to how the representative concerns relate. In other words, how does imputed righteousness relate to inherent righteousness?[3] McGrath's analysis is not an isolated one, as those who were involved were critical of Bucer's role. Martin Luther, Melanchthon, and Calvin were critical of Bucer's conciliatory attitude toward the Regensburg agreement.[4] Nevertheless, this did not mean that all believed that every aspect of the agreement was a total loss.

In a letter to his colleague Guillaume Farel, Calvin notably registered his guarded satisfaction with the fifth article and especially the concession on the part of the Roman Catholic participants on the matter of imputation:

> The debate in controversy was more keen upon the doctrine of justification. At length a formula was drawn up, which, on receiving certain corrections, was accepted on both sides. You will be astonished, I am sure, that our opponents have yielded so much, when you read the extracted copy, as it stood when the last correction was made upon it, which you will find enclosed in the letter. Our friends have thus retained also the substance of the true doctrine, so that nothing can be comprehended within it which is not to be found in our writings; you will desire, I know, a more distinct explication and statement of the doctrine, and, in that respect you shall find me in complete agreement with yourself. However, if you consider

---

3. Alister McGrath, *Iustitia Dei*, 2 vols. (Cambridge: Cambridge University Press, 1993), 2.60–61.

4. See Hastings Eells, *Martin Bucer* (New Haven: Yale University Press, 1931), 296.

with what kind of men we have to agree upon this doctrine, you will acknowledge that much has been accomplished.[5]

Calvin was likely surprised that the Roman Catholic theologians would agree to the idea of imputation, and it is in this regard that he acknowledged that much progress had been made.

However, given the "cut and paste" nature of the statement, Calvin knew that Farel would want a greater explanation of the fifth article.[6] Despite the progress that Calvin saw, he eventually saw that progress stall. Concerning the colloquy, Calvin, in a letter to Pierre Viret, later complained, "The Diet concluded very much as I had always foretold that it would; for the whole place of pacification passed off in smoke, while all has been referred to an Universal Council, or, at least, to a National one, if the former cannot be soon obtained."[7] The agreement was never officially remanded to a Roman Catholic council. Nevertheless, very shortly thereafter the Roman response to the Reformation was published in the decrees of the Council of Trent.

The Council of Trent (1546)

The official Roman Catholic response to the Reformation on a host of doctrines but especially the doctrine of justification came from the Council of Trent. While we do not want to engage in a full-blown analysis of Trent, as others have ably done this, at the same time we want to highlight several key points as they pertain to the doctrine of justification. First, we should note that Trent went to great lengths to distance itself from the heresies of Pelagius (c. 400), who had been condemned by the Synod of Orange (529): "If anyone asserts, that the sin of Adam injured himself alone, and not his posterity . . . let him be anathema."[8] Moreover, the council also affirmed the necessity of grace and faith for salvation: "We are therefore said to be *justified by faith*, because faith is the begin-

---

5. John Calvin, "Letter 67—To Farel, 11 May 1541," in *Selected Works of John Calvin*, ed. Henry Beveridge and Jule Bonnet, 7 vols. (Grand Rapids: Baker, 1983), 4:260.

6. There are those, however, who have a much more positive assessment of Regensburg; see A. N. S. Lane, "A Tale of Two Imperial Cities: Justification at Regensburg (1541) and Trent (1546–47)," in *Justification in Perspective*, ed. Bruce L. McCormack (Grand Rapids: Baker, 2006), 130.

7. Calvin, "Letter 72—To Viret, 3 August 1541," in *Selected Works*, 4:279.

8. "Canons and Decrees of the Council of Trent," session 5, ch. 2 in Philip Schaff, *Creeds of Christendom*, 3 vols. (1931; Grand Rapids: Baker, 1990), 2:85.

ning of human salvation, the foundation, and root of all justification . . . but we are therefore said to be justified *freely* [*gratis autem justificari ideo dicamur*], because that none of those things which precede justification—whether faith or works—merit the grace itself of justification."[9] So we see that Trent was insistent upon justification by grace through faith, though their definition and exposition of justification were significantly different from the fifth article of the Regensburg agreement.

While there are certainly other features to their distinct understanding of justification, Trent was insistent upon the rejection of the doctrine of imputation, something that the Roman Catholic theologians who participated at Regensburg were more willing to accept. We find Trent's rejection of imputation in several places. For example, they state that "justification itself, which is not the remission of sins merely," and the righteousness of justification are received, not through imputation, but through infusion, "Whence, man, through Jesus Christ, in whom he is engrafted, receives, in the said justification, together with the remission of sins, all these [gifts] infused at once, faith, hope, and charity."[10] The most explicit rejection of imputation comes in Canon 11: "If any one says, that men are justified, either by the sole imputation of the righteousness of Christ, or by the sole remission of sins, to the exclusion of the grace and the charity which is poured forth in their hearts by the Holy Spirit, and is inherent in them; or even that the grace, whereby we are justified, is only the favor of God: let him be anathema."[11] Indeed, whatever progress was made at Regensburg on imputation went up in smoke at Trent.

In addition, Trent set forth other distinctives to their understanding of justification. Trent argued that the believer's justification was something that would be declared only of one who was actually and inherently righteous. Therefore, the believer's justification was pronounced, not immediately upon a profession of faith in Christ, but at the conclusion of the believer's life, when he would be inherently righteous. To this end Trent stated that believers "through the observance of the commandments of God and of the Church, faith co-operating with good works, increase in that righteousness which they have received through the grace of Christ,

9. Ibid., session 6, ch. 8, in Schaff, *Creeds*, 2:97.
10. Ibid., session 6, ch. 7, in Schaff, *Creeds*, 2:94–97.
11. "On Justification," canon 11, in Schaff, *Creeds*, 2:112–13.

and are still further justified."[12] At the same time, the contrary was also true—if a believer could increase in the righteousness he received through the grace of Christ, then he could also, through sin, lose righteousness as well, which meant he could lose his state of justification:

> Before men, therefore, who have been justified in this manner,—whether they have persevered uninterruptedly in the grace received, or whether they have recovered it when lost,—are to be set the words of the Apostle: Abound in every good work, knowing that your labor is not in vain in the Lord; for God is not unjust, that he should forget your work, and the love which you have shown in his name; and, do not lose your confidence, which has a great reward (Heb. 10:35). And, for this cause, life eternal is to be proposed to those working well unto the end, and hoping in God, both as a grace mercifully promised to the sons of God through Jesus Christ, and as a reward which is according to the promise of God himself, to be faithfully rendered to their good works and merits.[13]

These conclusions should come as no surprise, as they are ultimately built upon the foundation of Augustine's realistic understanding of justification, which was carried into the Middle Ages and is found in the theology of Thomas Aquinas, as we saw in chapter 1.

Recall that Augustine's view confused what Reformed theologians would later call justification and sanctification, or the declarative and the transformative. If justification was based also upon the transformative, then it is only logical that justification ultimately required the total sanctification of the believer, or the presence of a complete and total inherent righteousness. It is for these reasons that Trent rejected the Reformation's *sola fide* and *solus Christus*: "If anyone says that by faith alone the impious is justified, in such wise to mean, that nothing else is required to cooperate in order to the obtaining the grace of justification, and that it is not in any way necessary, that he be prepared and disposed by the movement of his own will: let him be anathema."[14]

The difference between the Roman Catholic view and a typical Reformed view on justification is evident in figure 11, outlining the causes of justification.

---

12. Ibid., session 6, ch. 10 in Schaff, *Creeds*, 2:99.
13. Ibid., session 6, ch. 16, in Schaff, *Creeds*, 2.107.
14. *Canons and Decrees*, in Schaff, *Creeds*, 2:112.

Fig. 11. Causes of justification

Cause	Protestant (Calvin, *Institutes*, 3.14.17)	Council of Trent (Session 6, Ch. 7)
Material	"Surely the material cause is Christ, with his obedience, through which he acquired righteousness for us."	"The meritorious cause is his most beloved only-begotten, our Lord Jesus Christ, who, when we were enemies, *for the exceeding charity wherewith he loved us*, merited Justification for us by his most holy Passion on the wood of the cross, and made satisfaction for us unto God the Father."
Formal	"What shall we say is the formal or instrumental cause but faith?"	"The alone formal cause is the righteousness of God, not that whereby he himself is just, but that whereby he makes us just, that to wit, with which *we*, being endowed by him, *are renewed in the spirit of our mind*, and we are not only reputed, but are truly called, and are just, receiving righteousness within us, each one according to his measure, *which the Holy Spirit distributes to everyone as he wills*, and according to each one's proper disposition and co-operation."
Final	"As for the final cause, the apostle testifies that it consists both in the proof of divine justice and in the praise of God's goodness."	"The final cause indeed is the glory of God and of Jesus Christ, and life everlasting."
Efficient	"For Scripture everywhere proclaims that the efficient cause of our obtaining eternal life is the mercy of the Heavenly Father and his freely given love toward us."	"The efficient cause is a merciful God who *washes and sanctifies* gratuitously, *signing*, and anointing with the holy *Spirit of promise, who is the pledge of our inheritance*."
Instrumental	"What shall we say is the formal or instrumental cause but faith?"	"The instrumental cause is the sacrament of baptism, which is the sacrament of faith, without which no man was ever justified."

One can see that there are both areas of significant agreement but equally areas of significant disagreement. Most notably, there is formal agreement between Calvin and Trent on the material, or meritorious, cause, namely the obedience of Christ, though as we will shortly see, one must stipulate that this is formal agreement only. Likewise, in the final cause, one also sees basic agreement—the glory of God; also the efficient cause is the mercy of God. Where one finds antithetical propositions is in the formal-instrumental

355

cause, and as one delves deeper, the material cause. According to Calvin, and the Reformed, faith alone is the instrumental cause of justification, whereas for Trent, the instrumental cause is the sacrament of baptism, which they identify as a sacrament of faith. Moreover, according to Trent, the formal cause is not only the righteousness of God, but also the outpouring of the Holy Spirit in the grace of sanctification, that is, cooperating good works. Calvin therefore states, "They falsely represent the material and the formal cause, as if our works held half the place along with faith and Christ's righteousness. But Scripture cries out against this also, simply affirming that Christ is for us both righteousness and life, and that this benefit of righteousness is possessed by faith alone."[15]

It is these differences that have historically separated Protestants from the RCC. Most notably, Rome insists upon a realistic-ontological and confessional Protestants upon a legal-forensic understanding of justification. There have been those, however, who have recently made great effort to diminish the breach that exists between the two communions.

Recent Attempts at Ecumenical Reunion

A. N. S. Lane has recently identified eight separate documents that have tried to mend the breach between Protestants and the RCC, among them Hans Küng's *Justification*, Karl Lehmann and Wolfhart Pannenberg's *Condemnations of the Reformation Era*, and *The Joint Declaration on the Doctrine of Justification*.[16] While we do not want to explore each detail of these documents, as Lane has done this admirably, at the same time it will prove helpful to explore key claims, as these documents in one form or another make an attempt to bring a reunification between Protestants and the RCC. After exploring the basic claims of each document, we will critique the arguments set forth in each. What one must note, however, is that the critique is not directed at ecumenical efforts, as all concerned parties should be open and willing to conduct ecumenical dialogues to explore continually the possibility of reunification.

---

15. John Calvin, *Institutes of the Christian Religion*, ed. John T. McNeill, trans. Ford Lewis Battles, LCC 20–21 (Philadelphia: Westminster, 1960), 3.14.17.

16. Lane, *Justification*, v.

Hans Küng: Barthian-Catholic Rapprochement?

Claims

In *Justification*, Hans Küng wrote a landmark study on the doctrine of justification in the theology of Karl Barth and compared it to the Roman Catholic understanding of the doctrine. Küng made the claim that Barth's view of justification was compatible with the Roman Catholic understanding. To this claim, Barth responded, "If what you have presented in Part Two of this book is actually the teaching of the RCC, then I must certainly admit that my view of justification agrees with the Roman Catholic view."[17] Barth interpreted this apparent agreement in no small way and commented,

> So then, like Noah I look forth from the window of my ark and salute your book as another clear omen that the flood tide of those days when Catholic and Protestant theologians would talk only against one another polemically or with one another in a spirit of noncommittal pacifism, but preferably not at all—that flood tide is, if not entirely abated, at least definitely receding.[18]

Given Küng's understanding of justification as a Roman Catholic theologian, and his agreement with Barth's formulation, the two saw the floodwaters of conflict receding.

Critique

Though Küng's claims have received much attention over the years since their original publication in 1964, one must seriously doubt at least two chief elements of Küng's assessment: (1) that Barth is the best representative for a Protestant understanding of the doctrine of justification; and (2) that Küng's own theology represents the teaching of the RCC. While we do not have the space for a full exposition of Barth's doctrine of justification, it is possible nonetheless to highlight certain aspects that demonstrate Barth's dissonance with the classic Protestant understanding of justification. First, while Barth does affirm the importance of the covenant and argues that the creation is the external basis of the covenant, at the same time his mono-covenantalism, that is, his rejec-

---

17. Hans Küng, *Justification* (1964; Louisville: Westminster John Knox, 2004), lxviii.
18. Ibid., lxix.

tion of the covenant of works, proves problematic for maintaining the proper relationship between faith and works in justification, especially as it relates to the work of the first and last Adams.[19] It seems impossible, furthermore, to build a historical gospel upon the supposed unhistorical events of Genesis 1–3, as Barth denies the historicity of Adam.[20]

Second, Barth's dialectical theology is certainly different from that of the Protestant Reformation.[21] Küng notes, for example, that Barth does not accept the position of the Reformers on total depravity without qualification and, one might add, modification. Describing Barth's position, Küng notes: "Man is *not* totally corrupted, and yet he is *totally* corrupted."[22] Third, most are familiar with Barth's conception of election, namely that Jesus Christ is both the elected and rejected man. One can see not only Barth's understanding of election but also his dialecticism informing his understanding of justification in the following:

> We are dealing with the history in which man is both rejected and elected, both under the wrath of God and accepted by Him in grace, both put to death and alive: existing in a state of transition, not here only, but from here to *there*; not there only, but from *here* to there; the No of God behind and the Yes of God before, but the Yes of God only before as the No of God is behind. This history, the existence of man in this transition, and therefore in this twofold form, is the judgment of God in its positive character as the justification of man.[23]

That Christ is the one elected and rejected man, the one who is both chosen by God and at the same time reprobated by him, has an impact upon the doctrine of justification.

For in God's yes and no in Christ, his election and rejection, the yes of God is made manifest in justification. If all men are elected and justified in Jesus Christ, then one has to wonder why Paul would place such

---

19. Karl Barth, *Church Dogmatics*, ed. G. W. Bromiley and T. F. Torrance, 13 vols. (Edinburgh: T & T Clark, 1936–62), 3.1:94–329.

20. See Cornelius Van Til, *Christianity and Barthianism* (Philadelphia: P&R, 1962), 383.

21. There are those, however, who believe that Barth's doctrine, despite the differences, is fundamentally compatible with the historic Reformed view (Bruce L. McCormack, "*Justitia aliena*: Karl Barth in Conversation with the Evangelical Doctrine of Imputed Righteousness," in *Justification in Perspective*, ed. McCormack, 169).

22. Küng, *Justification*, 50; see Barth, *Church Dogmatics*, 4.1:492–95.

23. Barth, *Church Dogmatics*, 4.1:516.

an emphasis upon the necessity of justification by faith, faith in Christ. In Barth's construction faith is ultimately rendered superfluous; at least that is the logical implication of his doctrine of election vis-à-vis justification.[24] Given these few observations, it is difficult if not outright impossible to say that Barth is the best representative of the classic Protestant understanding of justification.[25] Barth's theology of justification, while bearing many similarities to the formulations of the Reformation and post-Reformation period, at many points is also significantly different. We may make a similar observation regarding the theological formulations of Küng.

Is Küng's understanding of justification representative of the RCC? To this question, one must reply no. Küng's views are somewhat different from classic Roman Catholic formulations. First, Küng fails to make the all-important distinction between the magisterium, the official teaching of the RCC, and the opinions of individual theologians. We have already seen this division materialize in the Colloquy of Regensburg. The Roman Catholic representatives, Eck, Contarini, and Granvella, were willing to agree to the idea of imputed righteousness, yet this agreement was totally eclipsed by the condemnations of Trent. It is encouraging to see that Küng affirms the forensic nature of justification: "According to the original biblical usage of the term, 'justification' must be defined as a *declaring just by court order*." Küng also cites other Roman Catholic theologians who agree with the forensic definition of justification, but what Küng does not do is cite the magisterium.[26] Individual theologians may hold to various opinions, but what is the official stance of the RCC?[27] In order for Küng to make his case, he would have to cite the teaching of the RCC.

Second, when Küng does interact with the magisterium vis-à-vis the Protestant Reformation, he completely razes genuine issues of debate in an effort to minimize the differences between the two groups. Küng writes, "Protestants speak of a declaration of justice and Catholics of a making just; and Catholics of a making just which supposes a declaring

---

24. Ibid., 4.1:550; cf. Van Til, *Christianity and Barthianism*, 361; Stanley J. Grenz and Roger E. Olson, *Twentieth-Century Theology* (Downers Grove, IL: InterVarsity, 1992), 74–77.

25. Van Til, *Christianity and Barthianism*, 382; Robert B. Strimple, "Roman Catholic Theology Today," in John Armstrong, ed., *Roman Catholicism* (Chicago: Moody, 1994), 90.

26. Küng, *Justification*, 209–10.

27. Alister McGrath, "Justification: Barth, Trent, and Küng," *SJT* 34/6 (1981): 521.

just. Is it not time to stop arguing about imaginary differences?"[28] Küng's observation is off point. No Reformed theologian has ever stated that the RCC does not acknowledge the doctrine of sanctification. The point of debate comes in where the doctrine of sanctification falls in the *ordo salutis* and how it relates to justification. Is justification based upon the imputed righteousness of Christ alone, or is it based upon the infused righteousness of Christ in the believer? Is justification an in-breaking of the eschatological verdict of the final judgment in the present, declaring the believer righteous on the basis of Christ suffering the eschatological wrath of God on the cross? Or is justification merely something that might anticipate a verdict at the final judgment depending on whether the person perseveres and is further justified, to use the language of Trent, by his faith cooperating with good works?

To this end we see Karl Keating, a Roman Catholic apologist, acknowledge this very point: "For Catholics, salvation depends on the state of the soul at death."[29] Elsewhere he writes, "The Bible is quite clear that we are saved by faith. The Reformers were quite right in saying this, and to this extent they merely repeated the constant teaching of the Church. Where they erred was in saying that we are saved by faith alone."[30] It is one thing to have a disagreement over these points, and entirely another to say that both sides have no idea what they are talking about and are arguing over nothing. In this regard, one must recognize that Trent is a reaffirmation of the teaching of Augustine on justification, who mixed justification and sanctification, something that the Reformation universally rejected, though at the same time appreciating many other aspects of the great African theologian's teaching.[31] We may therefore say that Küng has fallen far short of his stated goal, and in the end, as McGrath observes, he has demonstrated only that "Barth and the Roman Catholic *magisterium* share a common anti-Pelagian, Christocentric theology of justification."[32] Küng is not alone in his efforts to see the reunion between Protestants and the RCC.

28. Küng, *Justification*, 221.

29. Karl Keating, *Catholicism and Fundamentalism* (San Francisco: Ignatius Press, 1988), 166.

30. Ibid., 175.

31. McGrath, "Barth, Trent, and Küng," 518. See also Theodore W. Casteel, "Calvin and Trent: Calvin's Reaction to the Council of Trent in the Context of His Conciliar Thought," *HTR* 63 (1970): 91–117.

32. McGrath, "Barth, Trent, and Küng," 517.

Condemnations of the Reformation Era

Claims

Karl Lehmann and Wolfhart Pannenberg argue that the condemnations of the Reformation era are no longer relevant. They are no longer relevant, first, because given the development of doctrinal interpretations, the positions of the sixteenth century are no longer held.[33] The authors explain:

> Neither the Protestant Confessions, nor even the decrees and canons of the Council of Trent, may be read primarily as texts directed against the genuine doctrine of the other side, for which that other church was prepared to answer. In the condemnations relating to the doctrines of justification and the sacraments especially, it is evident that the Protestant Confessions were mainly directed against late scholastic positions; and conversely, the Council of Trent had as its target Protestant positions as they had been presented to the conciliar fathers from the lists of errors laid before the Council—lists that had often been drawn up at second or third hand.[34]

In other words, the confessions and decrees on both sides of the debate represent old opinions for which there are no contemporary advocates.

Second, many of the statements in the documents of both parties were based upon misunderstandings of one another's positions.[35] Third, the authors argue that the Protestant insistence upon the *extra nos* of righteousness has a proper biblical foundation (1 Cor. 1:30). But, at the same time, so does the idea of inherent grace, grace that is "poured into" the soul and "adheres" to it (Rom. 5:5). So, then, there are valid biblical bases for the concerns of both camps.[36] Fourth, each party is concerned for the very same things; it is simply that each communion speaks of the concerns in a different manner:

> If we translate from one language to another, the Protestant talk about justification through faith corresponds to Catholic talk about justification through grace; and on the other hand, Protestant doctrine understands

33. Karl Lehmann and Wolfhart Pannenberg, eds., *The Condemnations of the Reformation Era*, trans. Margaret Kohl (Minneapolis: Fortress, 1990), 19.
34. Ibid., 20.
35. Ibid., 27.
36. Ibid., 47–48.

substantially under the one word "faith" what Catholic doctrine (following 1 Cor. 13:13) sums up in the triad of "faith, hope, and love."[37]

In other words, both sides, Protestant and Roman Catholic, are concerned about justification and sanctification and that these realities occur by God's grace through faith. For Protestants, however, justification and sanctification are distinct acts of the *applicatio salutis*, whereas for Roman Catholics, the declarative and transformative both fall under the category of justification. The authors conclude, "Catholic doctrine does not overlook what Protestant faith finds so important, and vice versa; and Catholic doctrine does not maintain what Protestant doctrine is afraid of, and vice versa."[38]

Critique

Lehmann and Pannenberg's claim that the condemnations of the Reformation era no longer apply to the contemporary theological landscape is built upon a foundation of thin air. The authors make this claim but ignore the Reformed and Lutheran confessional communities that still exist and hold to the reformational understanding of justification, especially as it concerns the doctrine of imputation. To be sure, there is likely a majority within contemporary evangelical circles that would no longer consider imputed versus infused righteousness a doctrinal debate.[39] Nevertheless, contrary to the claims of some who see the confessional Reformed and Lutheran communities insisting upon the doctrine of imputation because it is part of their theological tradition, there is a failure to do justice to the claim that it is important, not because it was important for Luther or Calvin, but because it is the teaching of Scripture.[40] It is Paul, not Luther or Calvin, who says that Abraham was righteous by imputation through faith (Rom. 4:3, 22–24). Furthermore, it is an error to say that the RCC does not hold to the doctrinal positions of Trent.

If there are churches that still hold to the positions of the Reformation, indeed those of Paul, then without question the condemnations of the Council of Trent do have a contemporary target. On the Roman

---

37. Ibid., 52.
38. Ibid., 53.
39. So Mark A. Noll and Carolyn Nystrom, *Is the Reformation Over?* (Grand Rapids: Baker, 2005), 179.
40. Contra Noll and Nystrom, *Is the Reformation Over?* 188–89.

Catholic side of the equation Pope John Paul II, for example, stated concerning Trent's pronouncements on the doctrine of justification that it was "one of the most valuable achievements for the formulation of Catholic doctrine" and that "the council intended to safeguard the role assigned by Christ to the Church and her sacraments in the process of sinful man's justification."[41] Furthermore, the pope believed that "the dogmatic statements of the Council of Trent naturally retain all their value."[42] That Trent is still binding and influential is evident in the pope's statement asserting that justification comes through the sacraments and that it is a process, two points that reflect Trent's insistence that justification is based on the believer's sanctification and that baptism is the instrument by which one is justified. The other element of Lehmann and Pannenberg's arguments echoes Küng, namely that Protestants and Catholics are concerned about both justification and sanctification. We have dealt with this point above. No one has ever denied that both groups affirm justification and sanctification. The debate has always been about the proper relationship between the two, between the declarative and the transformative.

Joint Declaration

Claims

In 1999 the Lutheran World Federation and the RCC met in Augsburg, Germany. They recognize that the doctrinal condemnations found in the Lutheran Confessions and in the Council of Trent "are still valid today and thus have a church-dividing effect."[43] Nevertheless, in this ecumenical dialogue both sides attempted to set forth a common statement on justification, recognizing that it was not full-orbed, but that it encompassed a "consensus on basic truths of the doctrine of justification and shows that the remaining differences in its explication are no longer the occasion for doctrinal condemnations."[44]

41. John Paul II, "Trent: A Great Event in Church History," *The Pope Speaks* 40/5 (1995): 291.
42. Ibid., 293.
43. *Joint Declaration on the Doctrine of Justification: The Lutheran World Federation and the Roman Catholic Church* (Grand Rapids: Eerdmans, 2000), 9.
44. Ibid., 10; Michael Root, "Continuing the Conversation: Deeper Agreement on Justification as Criterion and on the Christian as *simul iustus et peccator*," in *The Gospel of Justification in Christ*, ed. Wayne C. Stumme (Grand Rapids: Eerdmans, 2006), 42.

First, the *Declaration* defines justification as the forgiveness of sins and the liberation from the dominating power of sin and death and from the curse of the law.[45] Second, on the basis of this definition both parties confess: "By grace alone, in faith in Christ's saving work and not because of any merit on our part, we are accepted by God and receive the Holy Spirit, who renews our hearts while equipping and calling us to good works."[46] Third, as far as the reception of the righteousness of Christ, the *Declaration* states that Lutherans intend "above all to insist that the sinner is granted righteousness before God in Christ through the declaration of forgiveness and that only in union with Christ is one's life renewed."[47] Fourth, both sides confess: "In baptism the Holy Spirit unites one with Christ, justifies, and truly renews the person."[48] And, fifth, when people voluntarily separate themselves from God, it is not enough to return to observing the commandments, "for they must receive pardon and peace in the Sacrament of Reconciliation through the word of forgiveness imparted to them in virtue of God's reconciling work in Christ."[49]

On the basis of these areas of broad agreement, the *Declaration* closes with the following statement:

> The doctrinal condemnations of the sixteenth century, insofar as they relate to the doctrine of justification, appear in a new light: The teaching of the Lutheran churches presented in this *Declaration* does not fall under the condemnations of the Council of Trent. The condemnations in the Lutheran Confessions do not apply to the teaching of the RCC presented in this *Declaration*. Nothing is thereby taken away from the seriousness of the condemnations related to the doctrine of justification. Some were not simply pointless. They remain for us "salutary warnings" to which we must attend in our teaching and practice.[50]

So, though the *Declaration* begins and ends with the affirmation of the importance and abiding validity of the condemnations of the Reformation era, at the same time, based upon the current teaching of both the

---

45. *Joint Declaration*, 13.
46. Ibid., 15.
47. Ibid., 18.
48. Ibid., 20.
49. Ibid., 22.
50. Ibid., 26; see also David E. Aune, ed., *Rereading Paul Together* (Grand Rapids: Baker, 2006), 11.

Lutheran Church and RCC, what they have jointly presented in the *Declaration* does not fall under the condemnation of either communion.

Critique

The *Declaration* suffers from the same maladies as other similar ecumenical documents—a lack of theological precision. Apart from precise formulations, one can easily house a number of views on justification. For example, it is true that Lutherans, Reformed, and Roman Catholics all believe that justification involves the forgiveness of sin. That aspect of the doctrine of justification has never been an issue of contention. What has been a subject of debate is the nature of the forgiveness. Is the forgiveness only the nonimputation of sin, or is there the positive imputation of righteousness? Therein lies the debate, something that the following statement from the declaration ignores: "Justification is the forgiveness of sins (cf. Rom. 3:23–25; Acts 13:38–39; Luke 18:13–14), liberation from the dominating power of sin and death (Rom. 5:12–21) and from the curse of the law (Gal. 3:10–14)."[51] This statement appeals to Romans 5:12–21, in which very passage Paul speaks of "the gift of righteousness" (Rom. 5:17), which Reformed and Lutherans have historically understood as coming through imputation (Rom. 4:3, 22–24). The Heidelberg Catechism, for example, states that in the forgiveness of sins God "imparts to me the righteousness of Christ so that I may never come into condemnation" (q. 56). Moreover, it is odd that in the *Declaration's* statement that defines justification, there is no appeal to Romans 4:1–5, 22–24, the locus classicus for the doctrine of justification.[52]

One finds further imprecision regarding the place and function of faith. The *Declaration* states, "By grace alone, *in faith* in Christ's saving work and not because of any merit on our part, we are accepted by God and receive the Holy Spirit, who renews our hearts while equipping and calling us to good works."[53] The statement uses the preposition "in" rather than the traditional Protestant use of "by" or "through," which reflects the instrumental nature of faith in the believer's justification. If one uses such language to preserve the instrumental nature of faith, then baptism

---

51. *Joint Declaration*, 13.

52. See, e.g., Formula of Concord (1577), "Epitome" 3; Heidelberg Catechism (1563) 61–62; Second Helvetic Confession (1566) 15.3; WCF 11.1.

53. *Joint Declaration*, 15, emphasis added.

can no longer function as the instrumental cause of justification, as it is understood by Rome, and defined by Trent. That the *Declaration* preserves the role of the sacraments in justification is evident when it states, "Believers are totally righteous, in that God forgives their sins through Word and Sacrament and grants the righteousness of Christ, which they appropriate in faith."[54] The place of the sacraments in justification is even more clearly pronounced later in the *Declaration*, where it reflects the idea that penance is the "second plank" of justification: "But when individuals voluntarily separate themselves from God, it is not enough to return to observing the commandments, for they must receive pardon and peace in the Sacrament of Reconciliation through the word of forgiveness imparted to them in virtue of God's reconciling work in Christ."[55]

Moreover, to say that we are justified "in faith" leaves open the possibility of allowing justification to be a lifelong process as it is in the Roman Catholic understanding, rather than a definitive once-for-all declaration as Protestants have historically understood it. The use of the phrase "in faith" to preserve the understanding of justification as a process rather than a definitive declaration is evident in the following statement: "God justifies sinners in faith alone (*sola fide*). In faith they place their trust wholly in their Creator and Redeemer and thus live in communion with him."[56] Notice that living "in communion" with Christ is part of the definition of faith according to the *Declaration*, whereas, historically, faith has been defined solely in terms of trusting Christ: "Q. What is faith in Jesus Christ? A. Faith in Jesus Christ is a saving grace, whereby we receive and rest upon him alone for salvation, as he is offered to us in the gospel" (SC 86).

Given these theologically imprecise statements, it is difficult to agree with the authors of the *Declaration* when they state: "The teaching of the Lutheran churches presented in this *Declaration* does not fall under the condemnations of the Council of Trent. The condemnations in the Lutheran Confessions do not apply to the teaching of the RCC presented in this *Declaration*."[57] It may be true that Trent and historic confessional

---

54. Ibid., 21; see Henri A. Blocher, "The Lutheran-Catholic Declaration on Justification," in *Justification in Perspective*, ed. McCormack, 209.

55. *Joint Declaration*, 22.

56. Ibid., 19.

57. Ibid., 26.

Lutheranism do not have in view the statements of the *Declaration*. However, does the *Declaration* articulate the historic Lutheran, or Protestant, understanding of justification?[58] Clearly, we have seen that this document does not reflect the historic formulations of the Reformation on justification. In places, the *Declaration* affirms what all Christians would and should affirm, salvation is by grace, faith is important, and justification involves the forgiveness of sins. However, the document leaves out key elements such as imputation and the instrumental nature of faith, as well as includes problematic statements concerning the role of baptism and penance in justification. The document leaves key elements of the historic Reformation understanding of justification out in the margins in order to accomplish doctrinal "peace."

Furthermore, that the *Declaration* does not fall under the condemnations of Trent is nothing all that significant, as the *Declaration* echoes Trent regarding the nature of faith and especially the place of the sacraments in justification. That the *Declaration* does not come under the condemnation of the Lutheran confessions is highly dubious, especially in the darkness of ill-defined terms. It is probably safer to say that the Lutheran World Federation has abandoned its theological heritage and no longer is concerned with the theology of its historic confessions and catechisms. The words of Luther appear to echo no longer in the ears of the Lutheran World Federation, which has signed a document on justification where not one syllable regarding imputed righteousness appears: "Nothing in this article can be conceded or given up, even if heaven and earth or whatever is transitory passed away."[59]

58. See Root, "Continuing the Conversation," 60–61; Blocher, "The Lutheran-Catholic Declaration on Justification," 198; David G. Truemper, "Introduction to the Joint Declaration on the Doctrine of Justification," in *Rereading Paul Together*, ed. Aune, 42. There are some, however, who do believe that the *Joint Declaration* has endorsed the traditional Lutheran doctrine of justification (see Chris VanLandingham, *Judgment and Justification in Early Judaism and the Apostle Paul* [Peabody, MA: Hendrickson, 2006], 244).

59. Martin Luther, "Smalcald Articles" 1.2, in Robert Kolb and Timothy J. Wengert, eds., *The Book of Concord* (Minneapolis: Fortress, 2000), 301. One should note, though, that not all Lutherans have accepted the *Joint Declaration*, as Missouri Synod Lutherans did not participate (Truemper, "Introduction to the Joint Declaration," 32). For the importance and centrality of imputation for Luther's doctrine of justification, see R. Scott Clark, "*Iustitia Imputata Aliena*: Alien or Proper to Luther's Doctrine of Justification?" *CTQ* 71 (2007): 269–310.

Summary

In the ecumenical documents we have explored, we find several significant flaws. First, there is the quest for peace at the expense of truth. Ecumenists, at least those represented by the above documents, are more concerned with unity and therefore sacrifice the truth. This is especially evident in the methodology that many ecumenists employ. There is little exegesis of Scripture; instead, one finds an exegesis and eisegesis of theological tradition. The typical argument one finds is that each side in the debate misunderstood the other. It seems that contemporary ecumenists condescendingly chastise their theological forefathers, and accuse them of stupidity, when they argue that the Reformation was simply a misunderstanding. When someone makes an argument of this nature, one has to wonder how familiar with the primary sources, or perhaps unfamiliar is more precise, is the one who makes such a claim. One commentator writes: "It is time for ecumenists to come out of the clouds of the 'meta-level,' where they act as if they stood in a monarchical position from which to censor church history and confessional assertions as applying or not, and reinterpreting where necessary."[60]

Second, to base ecumenism upon broad and imprecise statements, as has been the practice with many recent documents, such as the *Joint Declaration* or "Evangelicals and Catholics Together" (ECT) (1996), is a hollow and empty victory for unity. ECT states, for example, "We affirm together that we are justified by grace through faith because of Christ."[61] Yes, this statement is true in what it says, yet it is what it does not state that is of key importance for the Protestant–Roman Catholic debate over justification. The Reformation has historically understood that justification was by faith *alone*; it is the "alone" that is absent from the statement.[62] This point has not gone unnoticed, as William Shea, a Roman Catholic theologian, states, "Can it be said by consistent evangelicals that consistent Roman Catholics are Christians? The answer from the evangelical perspective must rest on some version of the *sola fide, sola*

---

60. Steven D. Paulson, "The Augustinian Imperfection: Faith, Christ, and Imputation and Its Role in the Ecumenical Discussion of Justification," in *Gospel of Justification in Christ*, ed. Stumme, 105.

61. See "Evangelicals and Catholics Together: The Christian Mission in the Third Millennium" (1992), n.p.

62. For analysis of ECT on this point see R. C. Sproul, *Faith Alone* (Grand Rapids: Baker, 1995), 35–50.

gratia, and *sola scriptura,* else the Reformation and Protestantism has lost its point."[63]

The truth, by definition, is narrow and precise. As G. K. Chesterton once observed, "It is always simple to fall; there are an infinity of angles at which one falls, only one at which one stands."[64] One finds true ecumenism, for example, in the assembly of the Westminster divines, where one hundred theologians over a period of several years hammered out a precise statement of common Reformed doctrinal beliefs. The Synod of Dort (1618–19), likewise, represents true ecumenism as a body of international Reformed scholars and pastors wrote a common statement of belief concerning the doctrine of election and related doctrines despite differences of opinion. Such labor is what must undergird true ecumenism. One should be doubtful when representatives of two traditions that have historically been bitter enemies hammer out an agreement in relatively quick order on the chief issue that has divided them for over four hundred years and emerge declaring "Peace!"

Third, there will be those who are critical of an emphasis upon doctrinal precision and truth in the quest for ecumenical peace. This certainly seems to be the trend in evangelical circles, especially among those who are associated with the Emerging Church movement. For example, Brian McLaren, a leading spokesman for the movement, writes,

> A generous orthodoxy, in contrast to the tense, narrow, controlling, or critical orthodoxies of so much of Christian history, doesn't take itself too seriously. It is humble; it doesn't claim too much; it admits it walks with a limp. It doesn't consider orthodoxy the exclusive domain of prose scholars (theologians) alone but, like Chesterton, welcomes the poets, the mystics, and even those who choose to say very little or to remain silent, including the disillusioned and the doubters.[65]

Those like McLaren accuse those who affirm the importance of theological precision as being narrow-minded or arrogant. It seems, though, that it is the likes of McLaren who are arrogant. Oddly enough, it was

---

63. William M. Shea, *The Lion and the Lamb* (Oxford: Oxford University Press, 2004), 184.

64. G. K. Chesterton, *Orthodoxy* (1959; New York: Doubleday, 1990), 101.

65. Brian D. McLaren, *A Generous Orthodoxy* (Grand Rapids: Zondervan, 2004), 155.

Chesterton, one to whom McLaren often appeals, who explained that people suffer from humility in the wrong place:

> But what we suffer from today is humility in the wrong place. Modesty has moved from the organ of ambition. Modesty has settled upon the organ of conviction; where it was never meant to be. A man was meant to be doubtful about himself, but undoubting about the truth; this has been exactly reversed. Nowadays the part of a man that a man does assert is exactly the part he ought not to assert—himself. The part he doubts is exactly the part he ought not to doubt—the Divine Reason.[66]

This is precisely the type of modesty from which McLaren suffers.

McLaren is "modest and humble" about knowing the truth. Yet his book is not ultimately about the truth, but about himself, which is evident in its subtitle: *Why I am a missional + evangelical + post/protestant + liberal/ conservative + mystical/poetic + biblical + charismatic/contemplative + fundamentalist/calvinist + anabaptist/anglican + methodist + catholic + green + incarnational + depressed-yet-hopeful + emergent + unfinished Christian.* In a book supposedly dedicated to the subject of generous orthodoxy, it appears that it is less about defining orthodoxy and more about McLaren. This seems light years away from Paul's warnings of damnation for those who had abandoned the gospel (Gal. 1:8–9) or his statement "If anyone has no love for the Lord, let him be accursed" (1 Cor. 16:22). It seems much more profitable to have committed Roman Catholics and Protestants come to the table with strong convictions about the truth, and in love and humility share those convictions. Ecumenism founded upon the truth as it is revealed in Christ, is true unity, not the hollow cry of unity founded upon empty affirmations. One author writes, "Let the condemnations fly rather than consider it epoch-making to reach agreements that only condemn the straw man Pelagius."[67] Therefore, what issues should be addressed by those who are interested in ecumenical relations with the RCC?

Moving Forward

To see real progress on the ecumenical front in relation to the RCC, there are several key areas of doctrine that must be addressed as they

---

66. Chesterton, *Orthodoxy*, 31.
67. Paulson, "Augustinian Imperfection," 106–7.

pertain especially to the doctrine of justification. The five areas are, the doctrine of imputation, the nature of justification, justification by faith alone, justification on the basis of the work of Christ alone, and the nature of the church, particularly as it pertains to the magisterium and the role of the sacraments in justification.[68]

Imputation

In the early history of the debates between Protestants and the RCC, the doctrine of imputation has featured prominently. Since the Colloquy of Regensburg, Reformed and Lutheran theologians have insisted upon the idea of imputed righteousness. As we have seen in our study thus far, this is not simply an issue of theological tradition, or one that will be resolved by searching for alternative metaphors, or one that can be swallowed by the doctrine of the *unio mystica*. Rather, imputation is a Pauline doctrine, one with which the RCC must come to terms. While individual Roman Catholic theologians have acknowledged the forensic nature of justification and hence the foundational nature of imputation, it is the magisterium that must acknowledge this doctrine.[69] The whole debate, however, over the question of imputed versus infused righteousness is not one that will be solved only by exegeting the relevant NT texts (e.g., Rom. 4:1–8; 5:12–19; 1 Cor. 15:20–28; 2 Cor. 5:20–21). The question of Adam's original state in the initial creation must also figure in the debate.

It seems as though much of the debate over infused versus imputed righteousness hinges upon the presuppositions of each party. The typical Reformed understanding is that Adam was created upright, or righteous, and that God justified, or declared righteous, the initial creation as well as man in his declaration that everything was "very good" (Gen. 1:31). We see the Westminster Larger Catechism echo this point when it states that God created man in "righteousness, and holiness, having the law of God written in their hearts, and power to fulfill it" (q. 17). By way of contrast, the typical Roman Catholic understanding of Adam's original state holds to the necessity of infused righteousness. Roman

---

68. These points of difference are noted by others (see Avery Cardinal Dulles, S.J., "Justification and the Unity of the Church," in *Gospel of Justification in Christ*, ed. Stumme, 126–27).

69. See Küng, *Justification*, 208–21; Joseph A. Fitzmyer, *Romans*, AB 33 (New York: Doubleday, 1993), 373.

Catholic theologians typically hold to the idea of the *donum superadditum* ("superadded gift"). Medieval Roman Catholic theologians, for example, argue that the *donum superadditum* was a part of the original constitution of man, that it represented his original capacity for righteousness. We see, then, from the outset, that man in his unfallen state required infused righteousness in the form of the *donum superadditum*. If man requires infused righteousness in the prefall state, then he would most assuredly require it in his sin-fallen but redeemed state.[70] The original state of man, then, is an issue that must feature in any dialogues over the question of imputation.

Justification: Confusing the Declarative and Transformative

We have seen throughout this study that the RCC typically confuses the categories of justification and sanctification. This confusion is due to several factors, such as Augustine's initial formulation of justification, namely that it included both the declarative and transformative, a formulation which was later reiterated in the Council of Trent, as we saw above. Once again, this issue does not hinge solely upon the definition of categories of systematic theology and terms in the NT. Yes, some Roman Catholic theologians have acknowledged that when Paul uses the *dikai-* word group that he has its forensic or declarative meaning in mind. Hence justification cannot be a transformative process; it cannot include sanctification but is a once-for-all declaration of the sinner's righteousness. However, though individual theologians may affirm this important point, the magisterium will not do so until it exposes one of its fundamental presuppositions as unbiblical.

At the radix of the Roman Catholic understanding of justification is not simply the teaching of the early church, but ultimately, and once again, its conception of man's original created state. Aquinas, for example, begins his discussion on the being and existence of God, not in terms of what Scripture has revealed concerning God, but in terms of ontology, particularly Aristotelian ontology.[71] While the apologetic use of Aristotelian categories as a point of contact with the unbeliever is one issue,

---

70. Richard A. Muller, *Dictionary of Latin and Greek Theological Terms* (Grand Rapids: Baker, 1987), 96–97, s.v. "*donum superadditum.*" See also Thomas Aquinas, *Summa Theologica*, 5 vols. (1948; Westminster, MD: Christian Classics, 1981), Ia q. 95.

71. See Aquinas, *Summa Theologica*, Ia IIae q. 113 a. 8.

debatable at that, the use of Aristotelian ontology as the starting point for unpacking God's being and attributes and one's anthropology is a beast of an entirely different stripe.[72] Recall from the chapter on prolegomena that Francis Turretin rejected Aquinas's ontologically framed discussion of the being and attributes of God and instead opted for the twin foci of covenant and Christology as the means by which God has revealed himself. Turretin writes,

> Nor is he to be considered exclusively under the relation of deity (according to the opinion of Thomas Aquinas and many scholastics after him, for in his manner the knowledge of him could not be saving but deadly to sinners), but as he is our God (i.e., covenanted in Christ as he has revealed himself to us in his word not only as the object of knowledge but of worship).[73]

Turretin's point is that theology is not revealed to us in terms of ontology but in the Word of God, which comes to us through Christ and covenant. Turretin is not alone in this criticism.

In Aquinas's understanding of the *donum superadditum* the lower powers of man, the powers of the intellect, were subject to reason. When man fell he lost the *donum superadditum*, or his inherent righteousness, but his lower powers, governed by reason, were not affected. Cornelius Van Til notes in this regard, "Romanism makes the effort to attach a Christian faith principle to a non-Christian principle of reason. The result is a compromise with the non-Christian principle of the autonomous man."[74] Inherent in Aquinas's understanding of man's original state, namely the pristine condition of his reason both before and after the fall, is reliance upon Aristotle. For the historic Reformed faith, however, there are only two kinds of people in the world, covenant-breakers and covenant-keepers. Van Til explains that covenant-keepers make man in God's image, whereas covenant-breakers make God in man's image.[75]

72. See J. V. Fesko and Guy M. Richard, "Natural Theology and the Westminster Confession," in J. Ligon Duncan, ed., *The Westminster Confession into the Twenty-first Century*, vol. 3 (Fearn, Scotland: Mentor, forthcoming).

73. Francis Turretin, *Institutes of Elenctic Theology*, trans. George Musgrave Giger, ed. James T. Dennison Jr., 3 vols. (Phillipsburg, NJ: P&R, 1992–97), 1.5.4.

74. Cornelius Van Til, "Introduction," in B. B. Warfield, *The Inspiration and Authority of the Bible*, ed. Samuel G. Craig (Philadelphia: P&R, 1948), 26.

75. Cornelius Van Til, "St. Thomas and Calvin," address at Calvin College, n.d., 6.

Now this might not seem all that significant, but William Shea notes that Aristotle conceives of ontology in terms of form and matter and actuality and potentiality. By trying to wed the ontology of Aristotle and anthropology of Scripture, one tries to join scriptural revelation with a commitment to autonomous reason.[76]

According to Roman Catholic theology, then, one does not find man in covenant confronted with the revelation of God, and bound either to obey or disobey. It was Calvin, for example, who taught that man cannot know himself without knowing himself as a creature of God. Instead, Aquinas and Roman Catholic theology begin first with the concept of being and then only later introduce the Creator-creature distinction.[77] Van Til amplifies the nature of the antithesis between faith and reason as Roman Catholic theology understands it:

> Frequently, and in particular in the case of the Romanist, it may then be added that God will not require man to believe on faith something that is contrary to what he has already learned by his God-given reason. In doing so men virtually assert that the faith principle that is to be accepted must be adjusted to the principle of reason that is already at work in the so-called lower dimensions of life.[78]

If this is the case, namely that faith cannot contradict God-given reason, which supposedly remained unaffected by the fall, then, as Van Til explains:

> There can therefore be no such thing as a finished Bible. All reality is process and revelation too is in process. There can be no incarnation once for all in the past. The meaning of a finished incarnation as an individual fact in history could never be made reasonable. The incarnation is a process continued in the church as the whole of human personality is in process of divinization. There could be no one fact at the beginning of history by which all men are influenced to the extent of being guilty as well as polluted. So there cannot be one finished fact in history by virtue of which men are made righteous and holy in principle. The distinction between justification and sanctification is practically wiped out. Or rather justifica-

76. Shea, *Lion and the Lamb*, 152.
77. Van Til, "Thomas and Calvin," 20.
78. Van Til, "Introduction," 26.

tion is virtually reduced to the process of sanctification and sanctification is virtually so to be elevation in the scale of being.

Van Til concludes his observations by stating, "The idea of redemption is woven deep into the pattern of metaphysical being. How else could it be made acceptable to natural man?"[79]

Shea comments concerning Van Til's criticism that the RCC "was originally constituted by a compromise between the scripture and Greek culture. Although abstract (necessarily so, since it is theoretic), the criticism should make a Catholic thinker uncomfortable. Van Til struck home cleanly, and did so without insult."[80] It seems, then, that the confusion over the correct understanding of justification will not be resolved until the starting point of Roman Catholic theology is reexamined and modified. Either man is conceived of in terms of potentiality and actuality, which is a constant process, and hence justification is a process, or as a covenant-breaker, one in need of redemption, which has been definitively and decisively accomplished once and for all by Jesus Christ and is received by faith alone.[81]

Sola fide?

One of the key points of debate is over the Reformation slogan *sola fide*, which has historically been misrepresented by the RCC that one can

79. Van Til, "Thomas and Calvin," 22–23.

80. Shea, *Lion and the Lamb*, 153. For similar observations and trenchant analysis of the mutually exclusive soteriologies of Luther and the RCC see Daphne Hampson, *Christian Contradictions: The Structures of Lutheran and Catholic Thought* (Cambridge: Cambridge University Press, 2001), esp. 9–142; also see on this point, George Hunsinger, "*Fides Christo Formata*: Luther, Barth, and the Joint Declaration," in *Gospel of Justification in Christ*, ed. Stumme, 70–71.

81. Cf. Van Til, *Christianity and Barthianism*, 383. This point is thoroughly investigated in Michael S. Horton, *Covenant and Salvation: Union with Christ* (Louisville: Westminster John Knox, 2007), ch. 9. Horton explains that the ontologies of Roman Catholic and Protestant theology are different, though this was a point that the Reformers did not fully explore or reform, especially as it relates to the doctrine of sanctification. Sanctification, he argues, is often construed along Roman Catholic lines, in terms of an infused habit of grace. For example, Samuel Rutherford states: "It is most unsound to affirm, that justification and regeneration are all one; for this must confound all acts flowing from justification, with those that flow from regeneration, or the infused habit of sanctification" (*Christ Dying and Drawing Sinners to Himself* [Edinburgh, 1727], 313; see more recently, e.g., Paul A. Rainbow, *The Way of Salvation* [Carlisle: Paternoster, 2005], 228). This seems to be the way in which some in the Reformed community who see union with Christ as the central category conceive of justification, especially the so-called future justification.

be saved to the exclusion of the transformative. We have seen, however, that this criticism fails, as the historic Reformed position has never been one that advocates salvation apart from sanctification. First, justification is by faith alone, which is the sole instrumental means in the believer's justification. As the aphorism goes, a person is justified by faith alone but not a faith that is alone. One must recall Calvin's illustration of the light and heat of the sun; one cannot separate the light and heat but can distinguish them. Likewise, one can distinguish between justification and sanctification but cannot separate them, as they are a part of the holistic redemption, or the *applicatio salutis*.[82]

Second, the Roman Catholic understanding of justification is couched almost entirely in questions of ontology, or the *ordo salutis*, and is not at all concerned with questions of the *historia salutis*, or redemptive history. In other words, if all soteriology is eschatology, and the eschaton is inaugurated with the first advent of Christ and the outpouring of the Holy Spirit, the power of the age to come (Heb. 6:4–5), then one cannot say that a person is justified but not sanctified. One cannot divorce the declarative from the transformative given the context of the *ordo salutis* within the *historia salutis*. In other words, if a believer is justified, the verdict of the final judgment is brought forward into the present in both the crucifixion and resurrection of Christ and the believer's declaration of righteousness in the presence of God. Hence Paul affirms, "There is therefore *now* no condemnation for those who are in Christ Jesus" (Rom. 8:1, emphasis added).[83]

Correlatively, the believer enters by faith the eschatological age to come and is indwelt by the Holy Spirit, who causes the believer to walk in the newness of life, to use Paul's language (Rom. 6:1–4), or the Spirit causes the believer to walk in God's statutes, to use the language of Ezekiel (36:27; cf. Jer. 31:31–34). In other words, the age of the eschaton is the age of the Spirit of Christ, righteousness, and holiness. Because those who dwell in the inaugurated age to come have been raised according to the inner man (2 Cor. 4:16–17), they will produce the fruit of the Spirit (Gal. 5:22–23). Roman Catholic views of justification fail to take into account the eschatological nature of salvation, especially as it relates to

---

82. See Calvin, *Institutes*, 3.11.6.
83. See Geerhardus Vos, *The Pauline Eschatology* (1930; Phillipsburg, NJ: P&R, 1994), 38 n. 45.

justification.[84] Not only does the RCC fail to account for the eschatological nature of justification, but they also ignore the connection between justification and the *unio mystica*.

While the Protestant Reformers were intent on insisting that the believer is justified by a *iustitia aliena*, at the same time they also saw justification intimately connected to the believer's union with Christ. In light of the believer's union with Christ, the righteousness is no longer alien but belongs to the believer; it is anything but alien. As Calvin explains,

> Therefore, that joining together of Head and members, that indwelling of Christ in our hearts—in short, that mystical union—are accorded by us the highest degree of importance, so that Christ, having been made ours, makes us sharers with him in the gifts with which he has been endowed. We do not, therefore, contemplate him outside ourselves from afar in order that his righteousness may be imputed to us but because we put on Christ and are engrafted into his body—in short, because he deigns to make us one with him. For this reason we glory that we have fellowship of righteousness with him.[85]

While union with Christ, therefore, holds an important connection to justification, especially as it relates to sanctification, the RCC has failed to take this important theological datum into account. Instead of making progress with the doctrine of justification in accounting for its eschatological nature and the connections to the *unio mystica*, the magisterium has taken great steps backward.

Some have recently argued that with the watershed of Vatican II a new age has dawned in Protestant-Catholic relations and that much of the Protestant analysis of Roman Catholic theology has been rendered obsolete.[86] Yet one has to wonder whether Vatican II actually moves the discussion forward. Instead, Vatican II more clearly reveals the Roman Catholic doctrine of justification. Trent affirmed the idea that justification is based on both the forensic and transformative. Moreover, given that one can be even further justified by his faith cooperating with good

---

84. See Wolfhart Pannenberg, *Systematic Theology*, trans. Geoffrey W. Bromiley, 3 vols. (Grand Rapids: Eerdmans, 1998), 3:223.

85. Calvin, *Institutes*, 3.11.10.

86. So Noll and Nystrom, *Is the Reformation Over?* 35, 55, 60.

works, then it does not seem like that far of a stretch to argue that even unbelievers can be justified on the basis of their own works apart from the work of Christ.

Such is the teaching of Vatican II's *Lumen Gentium*, which states that Muslims are part of the plan of salvation: "The plan of salvation also includes those who acknowledge the Creator, first among whom are the Muslims: they profess to hold the faith of Abraham, and together with us they adore the one, merciful God, who will judge humanity on the last day."[87] To say the least, this statement is completely at odds with the historic understanding of Christianity vis-à-vis Islam. It is one thing to say that Muslims are theists, and entirely another to say that Allah and Yahweh are one and the same and that Muslims hold to the faith of Abraham, which Paul calls the gospel (Gal. 3:8–9). Furthermore, if Muslims worship the same God, then is the Bible or the Qur'an God's authoritative revelation? According to the Qur'an, one is justified both by his faith in Allah and his good works:

> It is not righteousness that you turn your face to the East and the West; but righteous is he who believes in Allah and the Last Day and the angels and the Scripture and the Prophets; and gives his wealth, for love of Him, to kinsfolk and to orphans and the needy and the wayfarer, and to those who ask, and to set slaves free; and observes proper worship and pays the poor due. And those who keep their treaty when they make one, and the patient in tribulation and adversity and time of stress, such as they who are sincere, such as the God-fearing. (Surah 2.177)

This is a complete contradiction of the Bible's message of justification by faith alone, which Paul states is by faith in Christ apart from works (Rom. 3:28; 4:1–8; Gal. 2:16).

From this passage in the Qur'an Chris Marantika explains that there are six main tenets of the Muslim faith that all Muslims must believe:

1. Belief in one absolute and sovereign God (Allah)
2. Belief in an angel who is next to Allah and who intercedes for men

---

87. "Lumen Gentium" 16, in Austin Flannery, O.P., ed., *The Basic Sixteen Documents of Vatican Council II: Constitutions, Decrees, Declarations* (Northpoint: Costello, 1996), 221–22.

3. Belief in the Holy Qur'an as a direct revelation from Allah to the Prophet Muhammad, and henceforth as the basis of all Muslim teaching
4. Belief in the Prophets of Allah
5. Belief in judgment, paradise, and hell, where Allah will give all men their eternal reward or punishment
6. Belief in the divine decrees

Another thing that Muslims must do is called Din, the practice of faith, consisting in the five pillars of Islam:

1. The recitation of confession of faith (*Shahadat*)
2. The observance of prayers (*Salat*)
3. The obligatory contribution (*Zakat*)
4. An obligatory fasting for adults during the month of Ramadan (*Saum*)
5. A pilgrimage to Mecca at least once in a lifetime (*Hajj*)

These are the things that Muslims must do to enter paradise.[88] It is fair to say that the Christian and Muslim doctrines of justification are antithetical to one another. Even so, one can argue that according to Vatican II, the RCC has embraced the Muslim understanding of justification, or justification by works.

Lumen Gentium essentially affirms a doctrine of justification by works when it states:

> Nor is God remote from those who in shadows and images seek the unknown God, since he gives to everyone life and breath and all things (see Acts 17:25–28) and since the Savior wills everyone to be saved (see 1 Tim. 2:4). Those who, through no fault of their own, do not know the Gospel of Christ or his church, but who nevertheless seek God with a sincere heart, and, moved by grace, try in their actions to do his will as they know it through the dictates of their conscience—these too may attain eternal salvation. Nor will divine providence deny the assistance necessary for salvation to those who, without any fault of theirs, have not yet arrived at an explicit knowledge of God, and who, not without

88. Chris Marantika, "Justification by Faith: Its Relevance in Islamic Context," in D. A. Carson, ed., *Right with God* (1992; Eugene, OR: Wipf & Stock, 2002), 228–29.

grace, strive to lead a good life. Whatever of good or truth is found amongst them is considered by the church to be a preparation for the Gospel and given by him who enlightens all men and women that they may at length have life.[89]

To say that a person can be saved, which entails his justification, by his good works, or his "good life," even if it is founded in the grace of God, represents a Pelagian understanding of salvation and one compatible with a Muslim understanding of justification. To argue that Vatican II renders all previous Protestant assessments obsolete seems to ignore the RCC's total abandonment of the gospel. In Vatican II, then, we see that the RCC not only continues to affirm its previous statements concerning justification in its reaffirmation of the Council of Trent, but it also goes beyond Trent and advocates justification by works.[90] This understanding of justification also has, as one can well imagine, implications for the *solus Christus* of justification.

Solus Christus?

Can the RCC really and truly maintain the *solus Christus* of justification if they confuse justification and sanctification, thus placing the believer's works on the same plane as those of Christ, and if they affirm a justification by works for well-intentioned unbelievers who never hear the gospel? The answer to this question is an unqualified no. At the same time, the sole place of Christ in justification is obscured not only by the believer's good works and the unbeliever's good intentions, but also by the cult of Mary and the doctrine of purgatory, and with it the doctrine of indulgences.

First, the RCC officially recognizes the "cult of the blessed virgin," though it is quick to claim that this cult "differs essentially from the cult of adoration which is offered equally to the Incarnate Word and to the Father and the Holy Spirit, and is most favorable to this adoration."[91] The RCC believes that because Mary

89. "Lumen Gentium" 16, in Flannery, *Vatican Council II*, 222.

90. See "Lumen Gentium" 51, in Flannery, *Vatican Council II*, 77; and "Sacrosanctum Concilium" 55 in Flannery, *Vatican Council II*, 137. See also Karl Rahner, *Foundations of Christian Faith*, trans. William V. Dych (New York: Crossroad, 1990), 228.

91. "Lumen Gentium" 66, in Flannery, *Vatican Council II*, 88.

conceived, gave birth to, and nourished Christ, she presented him to the Father in the temple, shared his sufferings as he died on the cross. Thus, in a very special way she cooperated by her obedience, faith, hope and burning charity in the work of the Savior in restoring supernatural life to souls. For this reason she is a mother to us in the order of grace.

Furthermore, the RCC teaches that when Mary was "taken up to heaven, she did not lay aside this saving office but by her manifold intercession continues to procure for us the gifts of eternal salvation."[92] For these reasons "the blessed Virgin is invoked in the church under the titles of advocate, helper, benefactress, and mediatrix."[93] This is an element that is completely and totally foreign to the Scriptures, the NT, and Paul.[94] Whether with Trent or now especially with Vatican II, the RCC cannot in any way maintain the *solus Christus* of justification.

Second, concerning purgatory and the related issue of indulgences, the RCC still affirms the necessary existence of purgatory, at least to remain consistent with its understanding of justification. If a person dies before he is actually righteous, then purgatory is necessary to purge the sin from the believer.[95] Related to the doctrine of purgatory is the matter of indulgences. Some may think that indulgences are antiquated notions of a bygone era, yet the teaching on indulgences has been clarified in three recent documents: the *Indulgentiarum doctrina* of Paul VI (1967), the new *Enchiridion of Indulgences*, (1968), and the new *Code of Canon Law of the Roman Catholic Church* (1983). In the last document one finds the following concerning indulgences:

> An indulgence is the remission before God of the temporal punishment due for sins already forgiven as far as their guilt is concerned. This remission the faithful, with the proper dispositions and under certain determined conditions, acquire through the intervention of the church which, as minister of the redemption, authoritatively dispenses and applies the treasury of the satisfaction won by Christ and the saints. The faithful can

92. Ibid., 61–62, in Flannery, *Vatican Council II*, 85.
93. Ibid., 62, in Flannery, *Vatican Council II*, 86.
94. Noll and Nystrom, *Is the Reformation Over?* 133–37.
95. See Joseph Cardinal Ratzinger, ed., *Catechism of the Catholic Church* (Vatican City: Libreria Editrice Vaticana, 1994), §§ 1030–32, pp. 268–69.

gain partial or plenary indulgences for themselves or apply them for the dead by way of suffrage.[96]

In the light of such a statement is it really possible to argue for the sole sufficiency of the life, death, and resurrection of Christ or for his place as the sole mediator between God and man if Mary and the saints also assist in the essential atonement for sins and temporal punishment, a point not granted by Protestant theology?

The Doctrine of the Church

One of the core issues at the heart of the debates over justification is the doctrine of the church. There are some analysts who recognize this important element but only do so with the question of the abiding validity of the decrees, and especially the condemnations, of the Council of Trent. Anthony Lane, for example, in his effort to claim that the RCC is no longer interested in condemning Protestants, states, "The *Catechism* does not go back on the Tridentine doctrine of justification, but it qualifies that doctrine and does not repeat the condemnation of the Protestant doctrine."[97] To be sure, the conciliar pronouncements of the RCC must be taken into account as part of the discussion concerning the relationship between justification and the doctrine of the church. However, what few take into account is the very nature of the RCC. The RCC has historically been very clear concerning the relationship between the church, justification, the sacraments, and the priesthood. Let us address briefly these two issues, the abiding validity of the conciliar decisions of the RCC and the relationship between the church, justification, and the sacraments.

First, despite the attempts of several, such as Lane, Pannenberg and Lehmann, and Noll, who argue that the pronouncements and condemnations of Trent are no longer relevant, one must dismiss such claims, as they fail to account for the Roman Catholic understanding of church councils. Many are familiar with the Roman Catholic doctrine of papal infallibility, that when the pope speaks ex cathedra he does so infallibly.

---

96. As cited in Alister McGrath, "What Shall We Make of Ecumenism?" in Armstrong, ed. *Roman Catholicism*, 211; see also Susan K. Wood, "Catholic Reception of the Joint Declaration on the Doctrine of Justification," in *Rereading Paul Together*, ed. Aune, 50–51.

97. Lane, *Justification by Faith*, 220.

Many analysts fail to take into account, however, the functional infallibility of church councils. Once again *Lumen Gentium* states:

> Although individual bishops do not enjoy the prerogative of infallibility, they do, however, proclaim infallibly the doctrine of Christ when, even though dispersed throughout the world but maintaining among themselves and with Peter's successor the bond of communion, in authoritatively teaching matters to do with faith and morals, they are in agreement that a particular teaching is to be held definitively. This is still more clearly the case when, assembled in an ecumenical council, they are, for the universal church, teachers and judges in matters of faith and morals, whose definitions must be adhered to with the obedience of faith.[98]

This statement means, then, that the decrees of previous ecumenical councils, which would include the Council of Trent, are infallible in their pronouncements and condemnations, and are therefore irreformable.[99] That the RCC still adheres to the pronouncements and condemnations of Trent is evident when *Lumen Gentium* states, "This sacred council accepts loyally the venerable faith of our ancestors . . . and it reiterates the decrees of the Second Council of Nicea, the Council of Florence, and the Council of Trent."[100] Any attempt, therefore, to reconcile the RCC with Protestant churches must deal with the doctrine of conciliar infallibility. One cannot simply ignore the doctrine of conciliar infallibility and try to argue that Trent is no longer relevant when the RCC still recognizes Trent's validity and infallibility.

Second, there are the definition and nature of the church itself. The Reformed church has historically placed the doctrine of justification by faith alone at the foundation of its understanding of ecclesiology. The Westminster divines, for example, state: "The visible Church . . . consists of all those throughout the world that *profess the true religion*" (WCF 25.2, emphasis added; see also LC 62).[101] In other words, the church is founded upon the gospel of Jesus Christ, which is bound up with one's profession of faith, his justification by faith alone. The RCC, by way of

---

98. "Lumen Gentium" 25, in Flannery, *Vatican Council II*, 35.
99. Barth, *Church Dogmatics*, 4.1:626.
100. "Lumen Gentium" 51, in Flannery, *Vatican Council II*, 77.
101. See also Heidelberg Catechism 55; Second Helvetic Confession 17.1; Augsburg Confession 7–8.

contrast, argues that justification is inextricably linked with the sacrament of baptism, which, rather than faith alone, is according to the Council of Trent, the instrumental means of justification.[102] In this regard Barth asks, "Could Paul possibly have described baptism as the *causa instrumentalis* of what he called *dikaiosynē*, as the Council of Trent does?"[103] Reformed theology rejects the sacrament of baptism as the instrumental cause of one's justification; it is instead a "sign and seal of the covenant of grace" and a means of grace, what the Westminster Larger Catechism calls an "effectual means of salvation" (WCF 28.1, 4–6; LC 161). Within Roman Catholic ecclesiology, it is only the priesthood that can administer the sacrament of baptism. Moreover, in the event that a person commits mortal sin and requires penance, the second plank of justification, a priest must administer this sacrament. It is the church, then, that administers justification through the sacraments. This conclusion is borne out once again by the conciliar pronouncements of Vatican II.

In *Unitatis Redintegratio* Vatican II is willing to confer the title of "Christian" upon those who have been justified by faith in baptism: "It remains true that all who have been justified by faith in baptism are incorporated into Christ; they therefore have a right to be called Christians, and with good reason are accepted as sisters and brothers in the Lord by the children of the Catholic Church."[104] This is a telling statement that illustrates the differences between Protestant and Roman Catholic understandings of the church. We see that the RCC is willing to call anyone a Christian who has "been justified by faith in baptism," which echoes the pronouncements of the Council of Trent. Yet given that Protestants do not agree with such a formulation but instead see the sacraments, such as baptism, as signs and seals of the covenant of grace, not as an instrumental means of justification, it appears that they would not have a right to the title of "Christian." Looking past this issue for the sake of discussion and assuming that the RCC would accept Protestants as Christians, and therefore as brothers and sisters in the Lord, we note that what is absent from the Vatican statement is that these separated brothers and sisters constitute a church. The RCC

---

102. "Decrees of the Council of Trent," session 5, ch. 7, in Schaff, *Creeds*, 2:94–95; see also Ratzinger, *Catechism*, § 1992, p. 482; Pannenberg, *Systematic Theology*, 2:233.

103. Barth, *Church Dogmatics*, 4.1:625.

104. "Unitatis Redintegratio" 3, in Flannery, *Vatican Council II*, 502–3.

is ready to acknowledge that as individuals, those who are justified by faith in baptism are Christians, but not that they corporately constitute the church.

We see the insistence upon the sole legitimacy of the RCC when *Unitatis Redintegratio* states,

> It is through Christ's Catholic church alone, which is the universal help toward salvation, that the fullness of the means of salvation can be obtained. It was to the apostolic college alone, of which Peter is the head, that we believe our Lord entrusted all the blessings of the New Covenant, in order to establish on earth the one Body of Christ into which all those should be fully incorporated who belong in any way to the people of God.[105]

This statement means that though Protestants may be part of Protestant churches, they are separated from the one true church, which is the RCC. Shea has enlightening comments in this regard when he writes:

> To my knowledge, Rome has never publicly admitted that Protestant churches represent permanent and valid organizations of the Christian community; nor has it admitted that biblical Christianity represents an entirely valid and adequate witness to Jesus. It cannot do so, I believe, without changing its criteria of authenticity, the chief among which are communion of faith and worship with the bishops and the bishop of Rome.[106]

It is no exaggeration to say that if the RCC accepted the Protestant understanding of justification by faith alone, then by necessity it would also require the dissolution of the Roman Catholic understanding of the doctrine of the church, as justification would no longer come through the sacraments of baptism and penance, and be supported by indulgences, but through the proclamation of the gospel appropriated by faith alone.[107]

---

105. Ibid., 503–4.

106. Shea, *Lion and the Lamb*, 305; see the similar comments by Michael S. Horton, "What Still Keeps Us Apart?" in Armstrong, ed., *Roman Catholicism*, 247.

107. This is not to deny the importance of the sacraments of baptism and the Lord's Supper administered by ordained ministers, nor to deny the role of the sacraments as means of grace (see WCF 27.4; D. G. Hart, *Recovering Mother Kirk* [Grand Rapids: Baker, 2003], 21–40; idem and John R. Muether, *With Reverence and Awe* [Phillipsburg, NJ: P&R, 2002], 131–44).

Given this fundamental difference regarding the relationship of justification to ecclesiology, it seems that the two understandings of the church are incompatible.[108] The only way ecumenical reunion between the RCC and Protestant churches will occur is if one side surrenders its doctrines of the church and justification. Indeed, the doctrine of justification by faith alone lies at the foundation of the idea of the universal priesthood of all believers, which is central to the Protestant and Reformed doctrine of the church.[109] Anyone committed to a biblical understanding of justification must reject the Roman Catholic understanding. This is not a unique conclusion, and has agreement from a broad spectrum of Protestant theologians, not simply those committed to confessional Reformed theology. Jacob Arminius, famous for his opposition to Reformed theology, nevertheless concluded on the basis of the Roman Catholic understanding of good works, the sacrifice of the mass, and indulgences, "The Church of Rome, we declare that her doctrine stands directly opposed to that of the apostle."[110]

Similarly Barth, one not shy of parting with historic orthodoxy, nonetheless concluded: "It is difficult to see in the Tridentine doctrine of justification anything better than what Paul meant by another gospel. It has no light from above."[111] In this regard, we can conclude that the RCC is not a true church, seeing that it does not have at least two of the three key marks of the church, namely the right preaching of the gospel and the proper administration of the sacraments.[112] There is still a church amidst the RCC; in other words, those who look to Christ by faith alone are part of the one invisible church, but the RCC as an institution is not a church. If the RCC were to reverse the decisions of Trent, or at least express the willingness to do so, then we might be able to witness true progress on the ecumenical front.[113] Until then, consistent Protestants and Catholics must remain divided, as their understandings of justification and the church are mutually exclusive.

---

108. Shea, *Lion and the Lamb*, 305.

109. Eberhard Jüngel, *Justification*, trans. Jeffrey F. Cayzer (Edinburgh: T & T Clark, 2001), 251.

110. Jacob Arminius, *The Works of Jacob Arminius*, trans. James Nichols and William Nichols, vol. 2 (1828; Grand Rapids: Baker, 1996), disp. 19.11, p. 258; Carl Bangs, *Arminius: A Study in the Dutch Reformation* (Eugene, OR: Wipf and Stock, 1998), 344–45.

111. Barth, *Church Dogmatics*, 4.1:626.

112. Calvin, *Institutes*, 4.1.9; Augsburg Confession 7; Belgic Confession 29; WCF 21.5.

113. Horton, "What Still Keeps Us Apart?" 260.

Conclusion

In our survey of the history of justification vis-à-vis the RCC, the Council of Trent, Vatican II, and recent ecumenical dialogues, we have seen that there is still a chasm that separates the RCC from confessional Protestant churches of the Reformation. Recent ecumenical dialogues either ignore exegesis and dwell upon theological formulations, or ignore the Roman Catholic condemnations of the past in their effort to bridge the chasm. Such efforts, while undoubtedly well intended, will always fall short, and whatever progress they make will ultimately be insignificant because they are based upon shallow definitions and doctrinal imprecision. Documents such as the *Joint Declaration on Justification* and "Evangelicals and Catholics Together," while attempting to affirm much, in the end say very little. They affirm only that grace, faith, and Christ are important elements in one's understanding of the doctrine of justification, which Pelagius and Augustine would both affirm.

If true ecumenical progress is to be made, then significant dialogues on matters such as philosophical presuppositions concerning faith and reason, man's abilities and state at the initial creation, imputation, justification by faith alone, and the nature of the church must be undertaken. Until that is done, ecumenical dialogues will continue, discussions will abound, and unity will be achieved at the expense of the truth. Such a peace is empty. As James Buchanan long ago observed:

> The attempts which have been made to minimize the difference, on this subject, between the Popish and Protestant Churches, on the one hand, and between the different sections of Protestants, on the other, by those who have assumed the name of "reconcilers," have often resulted in the sacrifice of some portion of God's revealed truth, and have seldom, if ever, been conducive to the real peace, and spiritual edification, of His Church.[114]

Though Buchanan's comments are over one hundred years old, they are still relevant. It is not possible to declare, therefore, that the Reformation is over as some have done.[115]

---

114. James Buchanan, *The Doctrine of Justification* (1867; Edinburgh: Banner of Truth, 1991), 411.
115. Noll and Nystrom, *Is the Reformation Over?* 232.

15

JUSTIFICATION AND THE EASTERN ORTHODOX CHURCH

E ver since the split between the Eastern and Western churches, relatively few have interacted with the theology of the Eastern Orthodox Church (EOC).[1] Most of the theological literature in the West has
originated from among the various fractured pieces of the church since
the Reformation, whether Reformed-Lutheran or Protestant–Roman
Catholic. In recent years, however, more theologians of the West have
been interacting with theologians of the EOC. There have been some,
for example, who argue that the EOC doctrine of theosis, or deification,
is compatible with the Western church's doctrine of justification. Others have claimed that theosis is more compatible with the Reformation
doctrine of the *unio mystica*, or the believer's mystical union with Christ.
Roman Catholic theologian Avery Dulles, for example, argues that the
Eastern Orthodox doctrine of theosis is an important contribution that
"can help to offset the distortions introduced by the excessive preoccupa-

1. A notable recent exception is Robert Letham, *The Holy Trinity* (Phillipsburg, NJ: P&R,
2004), 201–51, 322–55.

tion of Protestants with sin and guilt and of Catholics with the mechanics of created grace."[2] If such claims are true, that the Eastern Orthodox doctrine of theosis is compatible with some aspect of the Western, and more specifically Protestant, understanding of the *ordo salutis*, then perhaps ecumenical reunification between the Eastern and Western churches is not as impossible as once thought.[3]

It is the thesis of this chapter that, contrary to recent claims, the Eastern Orthodox doctrine of theosis is not compatible with either the doctrine of justification or union with Christ. To substantiate this thesis we will explore the claims of those who argue for compatibility. We will then evaluate those claims by exploring, first, historical theological claims, second, hermeneutics, third, the nature of theosis, and fourth, the problematic absence of a doctrine of justification in Eastern Orthodox soteriology.

Claims of Compatibility

Recently Tuomo Mannermaa, professor at the University of Helsinki, has led a new school of thought in Luther studies, arguing that the sixteenth-century Reformer's doctrine of justification has been misunderstood and misinterpreted by later Lutheranism. Basing his case on Martin Luther's early writings on justification and union with Christ, Mannermaa argues: "The Lutheran understanding of the indwelling of Christ implies a real participation in God and is analogous to the Orthodox doctrine of participation in God, or *theosis*."[4] Mannermaa argues that later Lutheranism latched on to Luther's lesser-emphasized forensic expression of justification and marginalized his greater-emphasized doctrine of union with Christ. Mannermaa therefore claims:

> The notion of the presence of Christ as favor and gift in faith is the essence of Luther's concept of justification. At least on the level of terminology, the distinction, drawn in later Lutheranism, between justification as forgiveness and sanctification as divine indwelling, is alien to the Reformer.

2. Avery Cardinal Dulles, "Justification and Unity in the Church," in *The Gospel of Justification in Christ*, ed. Wayne C. Stumme (Grand Rapids: Eerdmans, 2006), 140.

3. See Gabriel Fackre, "Affirmations and Admonitions: Lutheran and Reformed," in *Gospel of Justification in Christ*, ed. Stumme, 7.

4. Tuomo Mannermaa, "Justification and Theosis in Lutheran-Orthodox Perspective," in Carl E. Braaten and Robert W. Jenson, eds., *Union with Christ* (Grand Rapids: Eerdmans, 1998), 35.

Forgiveness and indwelling of God are inseparable in the person of Christ, who is present in faith. In that sense, in Luther's theology, justification and *theosis* as participation in God are also inseparable.[5]

On the basis of these claims, Mannermaa believes that the "true" Lutheran understanding of justification, which is linked with union with Christ, is compatible with the Eastern Orthodox doctrine of theosis. In fact, in Mannermaa's most recent work, he makes the claim that "the analysis of Luther's theology in his *Lectures on Galatians* shows that his doctrine of justification involves a way of thinking that can be described by using the technical term 'divinization' or 'deification.' The idea of divinization is present in Luther's theology not only as a term but also in concept."[6]

There are others who have made similar claims concerning justification and theosis. Also originating from the University of Helsinki, Veli-Matti Kärkkäinen, who studied under Mannermaa, and is now professor of systematic theology at Fuller Seminary, approvingly cites Mannermaa's definition of theosis: "Divine life has manifested itself in Christ. In the church as the body of Christ, man has a share in this life. Man partakes thereby of 'the divine nature' (2 Peter 1:4). This 'nature,' or divine life, permeates the being of man like a leaven in order to restore it to its original condition as *imago Dei*."[7] Kärkkäinen explains that the concept of theosis is most popularly expressed by two patristic texts authored by Irenaeus (c. 150–90) and Athanasius (c. 296–377). Irenaeus writes of "the Word of God, our Lord Jesus Christ, who did, through His transcendent love, become what we are, that He might bring us to be even what He is Himself."[8] Likewise, Athanasius writes, "For He was made man that we might be made God; and He manifested Himself by a body that we might receive the idea of the unseen Father."[9] Kärkkäinen creates a formula that includes the combination of the Eastern patristics, such as Irenaeus and

5. Ibid., 38.

6. Tuomo Mannermaa, *Christ Present in Faith: Luther's View of Justification* (Minneapolis: Fortress, 2005), 87.

7. Tuomo Mannermaa, "Theosis as a Subject of Finnish Luther Research," *ProEccl* 4/1 (1995): 42; Veli-Matti Kärkkäinen, *One with God: Salvation as Deification and Justification* (Collegeville, MN: Liturgical Press, 2004), 25.

8. Irenaeus, *Against Heresies* 5, preface, in ANF 1:526.

9. Athanasius, *On the Incarnation* 54.3, in NPNF[2] 4:65.

Athanasius, with the recent historical theological labors of Mannermaa in the new interpretation of Luther, which yields the result that justification and theosis are compatible concepts.

Relying upon Mannermaa, Kärkkäinen rejects the distinction between justification and sanctification in Luther's theology, arguing that it is a post-Luther innovation, and therefore that what is "traditionally called 'justification,' can also be called *theosis* according to the ancient doctrine of the fathers with whom Luther agreed. Justification and deification, then, mean the 'participation' of the believer in Christ which, because Christ is God, is also a participation in God himself."[10]

Other evangelicals have made claims similar to those of Kärkkäinen. Clark Pinnock, arguing along similar lines, claims that Protestant theology has overly emphasized the legal-forensic metaphor in Scripture. Pinnock argues that union with Christ was not the central category for the Reformers but needs to be emphasized as such. Pinnock believes that union with Christ is the more central metaphor and that this was the trend of the church fathers, such as Irenaeus and Athanasius. He argues, "God invites creatures to participate in this divine dance of loving communion. God has not left us outside the circle of his life. We are invited inside the Trinity as joint heirs together with Christ." He stipulates, however, that "what we call union (theosis or divinization) is not pantheism—there is no absorption of the person in God." The believer's union with God, argues Pinnock, "is a personal union, not an ontological union."[11] Taking note of these claims, we must now evaluate them and demonstrate why they fall short.

Evaluating the Claims

One can challenge the claim that justification is compatible with theosis and prove their incompatibility by exploring the claims of the aforementioned authors on several fronts: (1) the historical theological; (2) the hermeneutical; (3) the definition of theosis; and (4) the nature of Eastern Orthodox soteriology. Let us therefore proceed to our first issue, that of historical theology.

10. Kärkkäinen, *One with God*, 37, 46.
11. Clark H. Pinnock, *Flame of Love* (Downers Grove, IL: InterVarsity, 1996), 153–55.

Historical theological

The first area of weakness in the claims of the aforementioned authors is their historical theological research. The new Finnish interpretation of Luther is a skewed revisionist understanding of the Reformer. Mannermaa and Kärkkäinen, for example, base their interpretation of Luther almost exclusively upon the Reformer's pre-Reformation and early Reformation works. One sees this selective reading of Luther most clearly in Kärkkäinen's monograph. Relying upon the work of the Mannermaa school, Kärkkäinen quotes two passages from sermons that Luther preached in 1519 and 1514 respectively, to substantiate the claim that Luther made no distinction between justification and sanctification, and that union with Christ was more central, which is compatible with theosis:

> For it is true that a man helped by grace is more than a man; indeed, the grace of God gives him the form of God and deifies him, so that even the Scriptures call him "God" and "God's son."
>
> Just as the word of God became flesh, so it is certainly also necessary that the flesh became word. For the word becomes flesh precisely so that the flesh may become word. In other words: God becomes man so that man may become God. Thus power becomes powerless so that weakness may become powerful. The logos puts on our form and manner.[12]

While it is indisputable that Luther made these statements, one must seriously question such a selective reading of the German Reformer.

Luther scholars have long recognized that in the early phase of Luther's career, 1515–19, the Reformer understood justification as a process of becoming, in which the sinner was gradually conformed to the likeness and image of Jesus Christ through a process of inner renewal. In Luther's later writings, however, dating from the mid-1530s, he began to see justification as a forensic act rather than a process.[13] In fact, Carl Trueman points out that there was "huge intellectual development between 1516

---

12. Kärkkäinen, *One with God*, 47 n. 41.

13. Alister McGrath, *Christian Theology* (1994; Oxford: Blackwell, 1998), 444; Paul Althaus, *The Theology of Martin Luther*, trans. Robert C. Schultz (Philadelphia: Fortress, 1975), 226–27; Bernard Lohse, *Martin Luther's Theology*, trans. Roy A. Harrisville (Minneapolis: Fortress, 1999), 258–66; R. Scott Clark, "*Iustitia Imputata Aliena*: Alien or Proper to Luther's Doctrine of Justification?" *CTQ* 71 (2007): 269–310.

and 1520, let alone 1535, when the great commentary on Galatians is published."[14] Therefore we may fault the Finnish interpretation of Luther on at least two points. First, they produce questionable historical theological results because they rely on too small a cross-section of the Reformer's works rather than evaluating his entire corpus of thought. Second, can one truly base ecumenical efforts on the exegesis of theological tradition rather than the Scriptures? One may grant, for the sake of argument, that the new Finnish interpretation of Luther is accurate; this does not mean, however, that the results are scriptural, that the Finns have uncovered Paul's understanding of justification and union with Christ. This brings us to our second issue, namely that of hermeneutics.

Hermeneutics

One of the elements that few of the aforementioned authors take into account is that of theological presuppositions, namely hermeneutics. In the Western church, for example, especially in the churches of the Reformation, there was a break from the medieval quadriga and an emphasis upon the literal reading of Scripture (see WCF 1.9). That is, a passage of Scripture had to be understood according to its literary genre, was it poetry, historical narrative, or didactic in nature? Other elements that had to be taken into consideration were the original intent of the author, the historical setting in which the passage was written, and the redemptive historical context of the passage.

Eastern Orthodox theologians, on the other hand, have not felt constrained by the literal reading of the Scriptures. Jaroslav Pelikan, for example, explains the idea of theosis from the theology of Eastern Orthodox theologian Maximos the Confessor (c. 580–c. 662):

> The purpose of the Lord's Prayer was to point to the mystery of deification. Baptism was "in the name of the life-giving and deifying Trinity." When guests at the wedding in Cana of Galilee, as described in the Gospel of John, said that their host had "kept the good wine until now," they were referring to the word of God, saved for the last, by which men were made divine. When, in the epistles of the same apostle John, "the Theologian," it was said that "it does not yet appear what we shall be," this was a reference to "the future deification of those who have now been made children of

14. Carl R. Trueman, "Is the Finnish Line a New Beginning?" *WTJ* 65/2 (2002): 236.

God." When the apostle Paul spoke of "the riches" of the saints, this, too, meant deification.[15]

One can immediately begin to see problems with such a description of the Confessor's hermeneutics.

In the above paragraph we see that the texts to which the Confessor appeals make no mention of deification (Matt. 6:9–13; 28:18–19; John 2:1–11; 1 John 3:2; Rom. 10:12; Eph. 1:7, 18, etc.). Rather, the Confessor assumes these passages teach deification. In fact, when one delves deeper into Eastern Orthodox hermeneutics, he finds that they are not as concerned with the literal meaning of the text as they are open to its spiritual interpretation. Eastern Orthodox hermeneutics bears some similarities to that of the Roman Catholic Church, in that both hold that the church produced the Scriptures rather than, as in the Protestant understanding, that the Scriptures produced the church.[16] As one scholar explains, "Tradition is the matrix in which the Scriptures are conceived and from which they are brought forth. Tradition, however, is the 'living memory of the Church' (Fr. Sergius Bulgakov). It is the Church, in other words, that produces the canonical Scriptures. . . . Viewed in this light, we can affirm that both the Old and New Testaments are 'books of the Church' and constituent elements of Holy Tradition."[17] This understanding of hermeneutics, as one can imagine, has a direct impact upon one's understanding of the doctrine of justification.

Kärkkäinen attempts to counter the argument that Eastern Orthodox theologians take passages of Scripture out of context in their efforts to expound the doctrine of theosis. He argues that, on the basis of their hermeneutics, which is rooted in church tradition, that Eastern Orthodox theologians are comfortable with the spiritual interpretation of a text.[18] Kärkkäinen explains:

15. Jaroslav Pelikan, *The Christian Tradition*, 5 vols. (Chicago: University of Chicago Press, 1971), 2:10.
16. See Herman N. Ridderbos, *Redemptive History and the New Testament Scriptures* (1963; Phillipsburg, NJ: P&R, 1988), 25.
17. John Breck, "Orthodox Principles of Biblical Interpretation," *SVTQ* 40/1–2 (1996): 77–78.
18. Kärkkäinen, *One with God*, 19.

Orthodox theology is lived theology rather than analytical speculation. In fact, definite limits are set on human inquiry into things divine by *apophatic* theology, characteristic of Orthodoxy, that proceeds mainly by negation. What theology is able to say about God and God's dealings with humanity are mainly what these things are *not* rather than what they are.[19]

This statement seems to be directed at those interested in theological and exegetical precision. Precision in theology and exegesis is important, and contra Kärkkäinen, is not synonymous with speculation. In fact, Reformed theology has historically eschewed ontological speculation, such as that found in the theology of Thomas Aquinas, instead embracing the idea that God reveals himself, not in terms of ontology, but in terms of the divine condescension in Christ through covenant.[20] That Christ through covenant reveals who God is and what he has done echoes the categories of archetypal and ectypal theology, not that of rationalistic speculation.[21] In this regard, it hardly seems like speculation to dismiss an interpretation of a text if it fails to account for the author's original intent and historical and redemptive historical settings. One can see this point in a short examination of the texts to which Eastern Orthodox theologians appeal to substantiate their doctrine of theosis.

Kärkkäinen explains that there are two cardinal texts to which Eastern Orthodox theologians appeal:[22]

By which he has granted to us his precious and very great promises, so that through them you may become partakers of the divine nature, having escaped from the corruption that is in the world because of sinful desire. (2 Peter 1:4)

I said, "You are gods, sons of the Most High, all of you." (Ps. 82:6; cf. John 10:34–36a)

19. Ibid.
20. See Francis Turretin, *Institutes of Elenctic Theology*, trans. George Musgrave Giger, ed. James T. Dennison Jr., 3 vols. (Phillipsburg, NJ: P&R, 1992–97), 1.5.4; cf. Thomas Aquinas, *Summa Theologica*, 5 vols. (Westminster, MD: Christian Classics, 1946–47), 1a qq. 12–13.
21. See Richard A. Muller, *Dictionary of Latin and Greek Theological Terms* (Grand Rapids: Baker, 1987), 299–300, s.v. "*theologia archetypa*" and "*theologia ectypa*"; Michael S. Horton, *Lord and Servant* (Philadelphia: Westminster John Knox, 2005), 17.
22. Kärkkäinen, *One with God*, 18; also see Georgios I. Mantzaridis, *The Deification of Man* (Crestwood, NY: St. Vladimir's Seminary Press, 1984), 7.

While at first glance, these texts may appear possibly to confirm the doctrine of theosis, upon further examination this is not the case. First, concerning Psalm 82:6, the psalmist does not state that man is created to be redeemed to become a god, which appears to be the import of earlier statements made by Athanasius and Irenaeus, "God became man that man might be God." While there is significant debate surrounding the interpretation of this verse, that is, whether it refers to the Israelite judges, angelic powers, or even perhaps a relic of polytheism, a good case can be made that it is a reference to the Israelite judges, not a detached statement regarding the ontological goal of man's redemption.[23]

When one takes into account the historical setting of Israel's reception of the Mosaic law, we see that masters were called 'elohim, which is also the word used for "God," and "gods," and was also a title given to judges (Ex. 21:6; 22:8–9, NASB).[24] Taking this historical-contextual information and broadening the scope to the redemptive historical context, we can see that Psalm 82:6 is therefore not a statement concerning soteriology and man's deification, but rather typology that finds fulfilment in Christ. The line of thought is that judges, or 'elohim, were representative of God's authority. We see this in that Adam, the first prophet, priest, and king, was called God's son (Luke 3:38), Israel is called God's "firstborn son" (Ex. 4:22) and was a kingdom of priests (Ex. 19:6), which finds its fulfilment in Christ, the true son of God and ultimate prophet, priest, and king, and ultimately the one true 'elohim, or Yahweh in the flesh.[25] This interpretation finds confirmation from two sources.

First, there is confirmation from the immediate context in the very next verse: "I said, 'You are gods, sons of the Most High, all of you; nevertheless, like men you shall die, and fall like any prince'" (Ps. 82:6–7). Notice that the "gods" will fall like "any prince," that is, any other ruler; this says nothing of the deity or deification of man in his redemption. Second, we find confirmation in Christ's use of Psalm 82:6: "Jesus answered them, 'Is it not written in your Law, "I said, you are gods"? If he called them gods

23. Derek Kidner, *Psalms 73–150*, TOTC (Downers Grove, IL: InterVarsity, 1981), 296–97; Hans-Joachim Kraus, *Psalms 60–150*, trans. Hilton C. Oswald (Minneapolis: Fortress, 1993), 157.

24. Exodus 21:6; 22:8–9, LXX; John I. Durham, *Exodus*, WBC 3 (Dallas: Word, 1987), 321, 326.

25. Meredith G. Kline, *Treaty of the Great King* (Grand Rapids: Eerdmans 1963), 97; idem, *Images of the Spirit* (1980; Eugene, OR: Wipf & Stock, 1998), 26–28.

to whom the word of God came—and Scripture cannot be broken—do you say of him whom the Father consecrated and sent into the world, "You are blaspheming," because I said, "I am the Son of God"?'" (John 10:34–36). Here Jesus refutes the Pharisees charge of blasphemy when he identified himself as the Son of God by reminding them that the Pentateuch called the judges of Israel, those who received the law and were supposed to sit in judgment of others, "gods." The OT judges were mere mortals. One might also add, however, that the ultimate thrust is that Jesus is the antitype to which the OT "gods," or judges, pointed.[26]

Moving on to 2 Peter 1:4 it is doubtful that this text means what its Eastern Orthodox interpreters claim it means. Richard Bauckham points out that there are parallels to the famous phrase, "partakers of the divine nature" (*theias koinōnoi physeōs*), in the literature of the time: "to share in a divine inheritance" (*theias meridos katēxiōthēsan*) (4 Macc. 18:3); "For God created us for incorruption (*aphtharsia*), and made us in the image of his own eternity" (*eikona tēs idias aidiotētos*) (Wis. 2:23).[27] In these parallels from Hellenistic Judaism, we do not see affirmations of deification but rather that in man's redemption he becomes like God, in that he becomes in a derivative sense immortal and incorruptible; only God has aseity; man's immortality is contingent. Given this historical contextual information, when we pull back for the larger redemptive historical picture, we must recognize that in the age to come, it is the Holy Spirit who raises man from death to life, who clothes him in immortality (Rom. 8:11; 1 Cor. 15:42–53).[28] It is in this sense that redeemed man partakes "of the divine nature."

We see confirmation of this interpretation within the verse itself, which states, "partakers of the divine nature, having escaped from the corruption that is in the world because of sinful desire." To escape corruption is to become incorruptible, to be redeemed, not to become a "god," or to be deified. John Calvin explains how some in his own day read 2 Peter 1:4 along the lines of Eastern Orthodoxy, and then contrasts the Reformed understanding, which is grounded in the goodness of the original creation, not speculative ontology:

26. D. A. Carson, *The Gospel according to John* (Grand Rapids: Eerdmans, 1991), 396–99.

27. Richard J. Bauckham, *Jude, 2 Peter*, WBC 50 (Dallas: Word, 1983), 180.

28. Ibid., 181.

The word *nature* does not denote essence but kind. The Manicheans used to dream that we took our roots from the stem of God and that when we have finished the course of our life we shall revert to our original state. Likewise today there are fanatics who imagine that we cross over into God's nature so that His nature absorbs ours. This is how they explain Paul's words in 1 Corinthians 15:28—"that God may be all in all." They take this passage in the same sense. This kind of madness never occurred to the minds of the holy apostles. They were simply concerned to say that when we have put off all the vices of the flesh we shall be partakers of the divine immortality and the glory of blessedness, and thus we shall be in a way one with God so far as our capacity allows.

Calvin goes on to explain how the melding of man with God originates not in Scripture, but in the philosophy of Plato:

This teaching was not unfamiliar to Plato, because he defines the highest human good in various passages as being completely conformed to God. But he was wrapped up in the fog of errors, and afterwards he slid away into his own invented ideas. We, however, must leave aside these empty speculations and be content with this one thing, that the image of God in holiness and righteousness is reborn in us on the condition of our sharing in eternal life and glory, so far as is necessary for complete blessedness.[29]

There are some, however, who might claim that when Eastern Orthodox theologians use the term "deification" or "theosis," they do not mean this in the strict sense, that is, that redeemed man becomes a god.[30] A closer examination of the definition of theosis, however, will reveal that this is indeed what some Eastern Orthodox theologians intend.

Defining Theosis

Some theologians who have defined theosis have argued that a true deification of man is not intended by the term. As we saw above, Pinnock is careful to stipulate, "What we call union (theosis or divinization) is not

29. John Calvin, *Hebrews and 1 & 2 Peter*, CNTC (1963; Grand Rapids: Eerdmans, 1994), 330–31. I am grateful to Mike Horton for drawing my attention to this passage in Calvin, which he cites in his own work *Covenant and Salvation: Union with Christ* (Louisville: Westminster John Knox, 2007), ch. 12.

30. John Meyendorff and Robert Tobias, eds., *Salvation in Christ* (Minneapolis: Augsburg Fortress, 1992), 19–20.

pantheism—there is no absorption of the person in God." The believer's union with God, argues Pinnock, "is a personal union, not an ontological union."[31] And again, Pinnock writes, "Let me reiterate: union with God is not pantheism—creatures never cease to be creatures. This is not ontological unification."[32] While there are some, like Pinnock, who are careful in their use of the term "theosis," this does not necessarily mean that they are using the term as it has been historically understood in Eastern Orthodox theology.

One can substantiate this claim by looking at how Eastern Orthodox theologians define theosis. Vladimir Lossky explains:

> The descent (*katabasis*) of the divine person of Christ makes human persons capable of an ascent (*anabasis*) in the Holy Spirit. It was necessary that the voluntary humiliation, the redemptive *kenosis*, of the Son of God should take place, so that fallen men might accomplish their vocation of *theosis*, the deification of created beings by uncreated grace. Thus the redeeming work of Christ—or rather, more generally speaking, the Incarnation of the Word—is seen as directly related to the ultimate goal of creatures: to know union with God. If this union has been accomplished in the divine person of the Son, who is God become man, it is necessary that each human person should in turn become god by grace, or become "a partaker in the divine nature," according to St. Peter's expression (2 Peter 1:4).[33]

It appears that in this quote Lossky defines theosis in terms of a true deification. His understanding of deification appears to rest upon the presupposition of a kenotic Christology, in which God sheds his divine attributes to become man; hence, if God can shed his attributes to become man, then man, by grace, can acquire God's attributes to become god. One finds further confirmation of this interpretation in the writings of another Eastern Orthodox theologian.

John Meyendorff argues that the best way to understand theosis is to explore the statements of Irenaeus, who as we saw above spoke about, "the Word of God, our Lord Jesus Christ, who did, through His transcendent love, become what we are, that He might bring us to be even what

---

31. Pinnock, *Flame of Love*, 153–55.

32. Ibid., 181.

33. Vladimir Lossky, "Redemption and Deification," in *In the Image and Likeness of God* (Crestwood, NY: St. Vladimir's Seminary Press, 1974), 97–98.

He is Himself."[34] Meyendorff explains that according to Irenaeus, man is tripartite: "The complete man is composed—flesh, soul, and spirit."[35] It is man's tripartite composition, explains Meyendorff, that is key to understanding theosis. Concerning the body, soul, and spirit of man, Irenaeus explains: "One of these does indeed preserve and fashion the man—this is the spirit; while as to another it is united and formed—that is the flesh; then comes that which is between these two—that is the soul, which sometimes indeed, when it follows the spirit, is raised up by it, but sometimes it sympathizes with the flesh, and falls into carnal lusts."[36]

One can immediately see from this quote the inherent Platonic philosophical categories—the need of the spirit to balance the flesh, or body, evident in the soul's oscillation between the spirit and body, or immaterial good and material evil.[37] Now, according to Irenaeus, as Meyendorff points out, the spirit in man is actually part "Spirit."[38] Note how Irenaeus defines man as he was created: "Man, and not merely a part of man, was made in the likeness of God. Now the soul and the spirit are certainly a *part* of the man, but certainly not *the* man; for the perfect man consists in the commingling and the union of the soul receiving the spirit of the Father, and the admixture of that fleshly nature which was molded after the image of God."[39] Irenaeus is clear: to be created in the image of God means to have man's spirit mixed, or commingled, with the Holy Spirit. Contrary to the protestations of those like Pinnock, theosis, at least as it comes from the pens of Irenaeus and Meyendorff, is indeed ontological unification. This means that there is a good case to be made that Eastern Orthodox theologians read 2 Peter 1:4 literally—there is a literal sharing, a literal deification, of man in his redemption because his redemption restores him to his created state in which his spirit was commingled with the Holy Spirit.[40]

34. Irenaeus, *Against Heresies* 5, preface, in ANF, 1:526.

35. Irenaeus, *Against Heresies*, 5.9.1, p. 534.

36. Ibid.

37. See David M. Rylaarsdam, "Interpretations of Paul in the Early Church," in *Rereading Paul Together*, ed. David E. Aune (Grand Rapids: Baker, 2006), 151; Dulles, "Justification and Unity in the Church," 139.

38. John Meyendorff, "Humanity: 'Old' and 'New'—Anthropological Considerations," in Meyendorff and Tobias, eds., *Salvation in Christ*, 60.

39. Irenaeus, *Against Heresies*, 5.6.1, p. 531.

40. McGrath is careful to observe that in the theology of Eastern patristics, one must be careful to distinguish between defining deification as "becoming God" (*theōsis*) and as

Theosis as it has been defined, whether by Lossky, Meyendorff, or Irenaeus, is something that is quite different from the Reformed and Protestant doctrine of union with Christ. Historically union with Christ has been understood as an "intimate, vital, and spiritual union between Christ and his people," and not as a commingling of the deity of Christ and his people.[41] As we saw, for example, in Calvin's explanation of 2 Peter 1:4, he rejected the idea of an ontological union. This is precisely the type of construction Calvin rejected, as did confessional Lutheranism, in his debate with Andreas Osiander. Calvin writes, "He says that we are one with Christ. We agree. But we deny that Christ's essence is mixed with our own."[42] Hence, those who argue that justification, as the legal aspect of the believer's union with Christ, is compatible with the Eastern Orthodox doctrine of theosis, fail to define properly how theosis has historically been explained. Once again, as with the ecumenical efforts between Protestants and Roman Catholics, we find theological imprecision at this point. Moreover, as we have seen throughout our study, one's soteriology must begin with a consideration of protology. Failure to develop a proper anthropology and to account for the covenant of works will affect one's soteriology. In this regard we must explore the impact of the Eastern Orthodox anthropology and theosis upon its soteriology, especially its doctrine of justification.

Eastern Orthodox Soteriology and Justification

When it comes to Eastern Orthodox soteriology, the understanding of man at his initial creation has an impact upon the understanding of justification. Eastern Orthodoxy does not conceive of the fall in terms of imputed sin and guilt, let alone even inherited guilt. Meyendorff acknowl-

---

"becoming like God" (*homoiōsis theōi*). He explains that the former is associated with the Alexandrian school, which conceived of deification as union with the substance of God; and the latter, which was associated with the Antiochene school, which saw redemption in terms of sharing in that which was divine, conceived of deification in terms of ethical perfection (see McGrath, *Christian Theology*, 414). See also Robert W. Jenson, *Christian Theology*, 2 vols. (Oxford: Oxford University Press, 1999), 2:341.

41. Louis Berkhof, *Systematic Theology: New Combined Edition* (1932–38; Grand Rapids: Eerdmans, 1996), 449.

42. John Calvin, *Institutes of the Christian Religion*, ed. John T. McNeill, trans. Ford Lewis Battles, LCC 20–21 (Philadelphia: Westminster, 1960), 3.11.5–6. For confessional Lutheranism's rejection, see Formula of Concord 3, Rejection of Contrary Teaching 4, in *The Book of Concord*, ed. Robert Kolb and Timothy J. Wengert (Minneapolis: Fortress, 2000), 497.

edges that there is no place for the concept of inherited guilt, though he admits that man incurs the consequences of Adam's sin. In fact, "There is indeed a consensus in Greek patristic and Byzantine traditions in identifying the inheritance of the Fall as an inheritance essentially of mortality rather than of sinfulness, sinfulness being merely the consequence of mortality."[43] Elsewhere Meyendorff explains,

> The fall consisted of the human rejection of the Spirit which was a part of humanity itself. This was a rejection of God's image and therefore freedom, reducing human life to an "animal" condition determined by fleshly needs and to inevitable mortality. Thus, fallen humanity is no longer "complete" humanity because it has lost participation in divine life.[44]

This is a telling statement, as it characterizes man's estrangement from God, not in moral-ethical terms, that is, covenantal terms, but virtually purely in ontological terms. If there is no moral-ethical estrangement between God and man in Eastern Orthodox theology, then it should come as no surprise that there is no concept of justification in that theology, or at least that justification is not a legal-forensic declaration.

Maximos Aghiorgoussis in explaining the nature of justification according to Paul in Romans 8:28–30 states: "God predestines and calls all people to salvation in Christ and conformity with his glorious humanity. Then he justifies and glorifies them in a sole redemptive act, in the Holy Spirit, who is the 'perfecting cause' and source of sanctification." Aghiorgoussis further elaborates upon the nature of justification when he writes that "justification is not a separate act of God but the negative aspect of salvation in Christ, which is freedom from sin, death, and the devil; whereas sanctification is the positive aspect of God's saving act, that of spiritual growth in new life in Christ communicated by God's Holy Spirit."[45] One can see from this explanation that for Eastern Orthodoxy, justification is a process; in its conception

---

43. John Meyendorff, *Byzantine Theology* (New York: Fordham University Press, 1974), 145.

44. Meyendorff, "Humanity: 'Old' and 'New,'" 60–61.

45. Maximos Aghiorgoussis, "Orthodox Soteriology," in Meyendorff and Tobias, eds., *Salvation in Christ*, 48–49.

of justification, there is no forensic aspect—there is no declaration of righteousness.[46]

Justification is not a once-for-all declaration of the sinner's righteousness before the tribunal of God, but is instead a process, a process of reacquiring the lost ontological union he once had with God through the Holy Spirit in the initial creation. Note, for example, how Dumitru Staniloae characterizes the ontological separation from the Holy Spirit: "Christianity links decrease of spiritual life, or the death of the soul, and consequently sickness, corruption, and physical death also to sin and separation from the Spirit of God."[47] Death results, not because it is the wages of sin, but because man has lost his fellowship with the Spirit in his fall. The process of justification, therefore, begins first with the negative, that is, the forgiveness of sins, and then the positive aspect, that is, faith cooperating with good works, or sanctification, to regain the lost fellowship with God.[48] Hence salvation is viewed in affective terms rather than in terms of guilt and sin, as in historic Reformed Protestantism.[49] This is not to say, however, that Eastern Orthodox theology has maintained a uniform monolithic understanding of justification.

A survey of the historic Eastern Orthodox creeds shows some oscillation between the views we have seen here, that is, from a total absence of a concept of justification to an orthodox affirmation of justification by faith alone. The third question of the Longer Catechism of the EOC (1839), for example, states: "What is necessary in order to please God and to save one's own soul? In the first place, a knowledge of the true God, and a right faith in him; in the second place, a life according to faith, and good works."[50] Earlier, in the sixteenth century, Philip Melanchthon translated the Augsburg Confession into Greek and sent it to the bishop of Constantinople. It was not until 1576 that the bishop, Jeremias II, responded, and quite negatively at that: "We request that from henceforth

---

46. Don Fairbairn, "Salvation as *Theosis*: The Teaching of Eastern Orthodoxy," *Them* 23/3 (1996): 46.

47. Dumitru Staniloae, *The Experience of God*, trans. and ed. Ioan Ionita and Robert Barringer, vol. 2 (Brookline, MA: Holy Cross Orthodox Press, 2005), 191.

48. Emil Bartos, *Deification in Eastern Orthodox Theology* (Carlisle: Paternoster, 1999), 292.

49. There are some evangelicals who have adopted this approach in their soteriology (see Kärkkäinen, *One with God*, 83–84; Pinnock, *Flame of Love*, 150).

50. Longer Catechism, in Philip Schaff, *Creeds of Christendom*, 3 vols. (1931; Grand Rapids: Baker, 1990), 2:445.

you do not cause us more grief, nor write to us on the same subject."[51] In his response, Jeremias rejected the Lutheran understanding of justification by faith alone: "You contend that, as you believe, the remission of sins is granted mainly by faith alone. But the catholic church demands a living faith, which is made evident by good works."[52] On the other hand, the Eastern Confession of the Christian Faith (1633) contains an understanding of justification that is very similar to that of the Protestant Reformation.

Jaroslav Pelikan notes that the Eastern Confession of 1633 is "significantly closer to the tradition of Geneva than to that of Constantinople."[53] As one can imagine, for this reason the EOC has historically repudiated this confession.[54] For example, Cyril Lucar, the author of the confession, states concerning predestination: "We believe the most good God to have, before the foundation of the world, predestined those whom he has chosen without any regard for their works and having no motivating cause for this election except his good pleasure and his divine mercy."[55] Concerning justification he writes: "We believe that without faith no one can be saved. And we call faith that which justifies in Christ Jesus, which the life and death of our Lord Jesus procured, and the gospel proclaims."[56]

Now one might claim that such a statement is rather vague, and any number of Reformed, Roman Catholic, or Eastern Orthodox understandings of justification could be accommodated in such a formulation. Whatever ambiguity might exist, however, is completely removed when Lucar further explains:

> We believe that a man is justified by faith and not by works. But when we say by faith, we mean the correlative or object of faith, which is the righteousness of Christ, which, functioning as a hand, faith grasps and applies to us for our salvation. This we declare in order to sustain and not deter works. Truth itself teaches us that works are not to be neglected, for they are necessary means for a witness to faith and confirmation of our calling. But human frailty witnesses it to be false that works are sufficient

---

51. As quoted in *Creeds and Confessions of Faith in the Christian Tradition*, ed. Jaroslav Pelikan and Valerie Hotchkiss (New Haven: Yale University Press, 2003), 1:392.
52. Reply to Augsburg 4, in *Creeds*, ed. Pelikan and Hotchkiss, 1:401.
53. *Creeds*, ed. Pelikan and Hotchkiss, 1:549.
54. See Georgios A. Hadjiantoniou, *Protestant Patriarch* (Richmond: John Knox, 1961).
55. Confession 3, in *Creeds*, ed. Pelikan and Hotchkiss, 1:551.
56. Confession 9, in *Creeds*, ed. Pelikan and Hotchkiss, 1:553.

for our salvation, that they can enable one to appear boldly at the tribunal of Christ, and that of their own merit they can confer salvation. But the righteousness of Christ alone, applied to those who repent and imputed to them, justifies and saves the believer.[57]

We can see in Lucar's explanation all of the elements of the biblical doctrine of justification by faith alone: the instrumental nature of faith, the exclusion of works for justification but their necessity for sanctification, and the sole sufficiency of the imputed righteousness of Christ. So while the EOC as a whole has quite a different soteriology and lacks the doctrine of justification, there have been Eastern Orthodox theologians who have taught a correct doctrine of justification by faith alone.

Conclusion

The Eastern and Western conceptions of justification are significantly different if not outright incompatible. For Western theology, especially that of the Protestant Reformation, justification is a legal-forensic declaration based upon the imputed righteousness of Christ, which is received by grace alone through faith alone. In the East, justification is a process that is marked by faith, but good works are also necessary to reacquire the lost ontological fellowship between God and man in which man becomes deified through theosis. While Eastern Orthodoxy has a doctrine of justification, it is one in name only, and is more properly understood as sanctification or a version of mystical union.[58] Or we may say that the Protestant Reformation understands redemption to consist of the application of the *ordo salutis* where the doctrine of justification is the entry point, whereas the EOC sees redemption as theosis, which has faith, works, and the sacraments as the means by which one is deified.

In fact, it seems fair to say that for the most part, the EOC does not truly have a doctrine of justification. This conclusion is confirmed by the statements of Meyendorff: "Communion in the risen body of Christ; participation in divine life; sanctification through the energy of God, which penetrates true humanity and restores it to its 'natural' state, rather

57. Confession 13, in *Creeds*, ed. Pelikan and Hotchkiss, 1:553–54.
58. Fairbairn, "Salvation as *Theosis*," 49; Michael S. Horton, "Are Eastern Orthodoxy and Evangelicalism Compatible? No: An Evangelical Perspective," in James Stamoolis, ed., *Three Views on Eastern Orthodoxy and Evangelicalism* (Grand Rapids: Zondervan, 2004), 136–37.

than justification, or remission of inherited guilt—these are the center of Byzantine understanding of the Christian gospel."[59] In this regard, Meyendorff's statement concerning the development of Eastern Orthodox theology on this point is telling, "Byzantine theology did not produce any significant elaboration of the Pauline doctrine of justification expressed in Romans and Galatians."[60] Given these conclusions and observations, we may say that the doctrine of justification is incompatible with the Eastern Orthodox doctrine of theosis. Moreover, while it is true that the EOC affirms a version of the believer's union with Christ, and therefore some will argue that theosis is compatible with justification, any view of the *unio mystica* that does not have the sole basis for divine acceptance of sinners as the righteousness of Christ, which is imputed through faith alone apart from works, is a denial of the gospel.[61]

59. Meyendorff, *Byzantine Theology*, 146; see also 143.
60. Ibid., 160.
61. Horton, "Eastern Orthodoxy," 137.

CONCLUSION

The doctrine of justification by grace alone through faith alone in Christ alone, will always be assailed on both the left and the right, from either antinomianism or neonomianism, the ideas that justification is a license to sin or that man must in some way contribute to his justification by his obedience. However, such errors are inherently shortsighted in that they fail to see the grand scope of redemptive history and the nature of the proton and the eschaton. The first Adam was given two commands, not to eat of the tree of knowledge and to be fruitful, multiply, and fill all the earth. Upon the conclusion of his covenant labors, undergirded by his obedience to these two commands, the first Adam would have been declared righteous and would have entered the eternal rest of the seventh day. The first Adam failed; he rebelled and forfeited his right to the tree of life.

The last Adam came into the world to redeem a people for himself, and through his obedience and suffering, he not only secured freedom from the penalty of the law for God's people, but he also secured eternal rest for them. He secured the eschatological rest that was set before the first Adam, which he failed to enter. In this way we can say that the entirety of the Scriptures is about the probation of God's sons. We see the failure of God's sons Adam and Israel, and the successful probation of God's Son, Jesus. The Bible sets forth the representative disobedience and obedience of the protological and eschatological Adams respectively, and it is by faith alone in the life, death, and resurrection of the eschatological Adam that one can be justified in the sight of God. It is by faith alone that the sinner receives the imputed righteousness of the last Adam and stands in the presence of God and is declared righteous.

When antinomians hear in the doctrine of justification that their sins, past, present, and future, are forgiven, and then go away thinking they are free to sin, they fail to see the incongruity of such a response to the message of the gospel. They fail to see the incompatibility of sin with the righteousness that is supposed to mark the age to come and the kingdom of the eschatological Adam. They fail to see that the Spirit of righteousness is the air that the eschatological adamic humanity breathes, which yields the fruit of righteousness. Antinomians fail to recognize that those who have been justified by faith alone have entered the age to come according to their inner man. On the other hand, neonomians fail to see the two towering figures of the first and last Adams. They fail to see how all others have failed to offer God the obedience he has required, save one. It is the representative obedience of the last Adam that is all-sufficient and brings life. It is his obedience, his indefectible righteousness, that secures the eschatological declaration of righteousness before the throne of God. It is these points that the historic Reformed faith has set forth in its propagation of *sola gratia*, *sola fide*, and *solus Christus*. It is also these points that lead us to make several concluding observations.

Final Observations

We can organize these observations under the following headings: the necessity of maintaining the unity of the *ordo* and *historia salutis*; the necessity of the *ordo salutis*; the importance of the covenant of works; and the failure of recent challenges to the historic Reformed doctrine of justification by faith alone.

The Unity of the Ordo *and* Historia Salutis

One of the recurring themes throughout this essay has been the necessity of maintaining the unity of the *ordo* and *historia salutis*. This is one of the necessary elements for setting forth a solidly biblical doctrine of justification by faith alone. One must not only ask in what way the declaration of justification is applied to the individual and how it relates to the other elements of his redemption, but one must also take note of what time it is. In other words, how does the verdict of justification relate to the course of preredemptive or redemptive history? If Christ is the last Adam, and he is the fountainhead of the age to come, of the eschaton, then the justification pronounced over those who place their faith in him is eschatological, final, and irreversible. This means that the verdict from the final judgment on the last day has been declared in the present. Justification does not merely restore the sinner to the potentially defectible state of the first Adam only to face probation once again. Or, in simpler terms, justification does not merely return us to the garden. Rather, noting the inherently eschatological nature of justification tells us that Christ has performed the work for us and that we enter the eternal state by faith alone in him; by faith, we are propelled into the indefectible state of the last Adam.

Too many explanations of justification by faith alone fail to account for the all-important connections to redemptive history, and therefore justly fall under the criticism of creating a system of individual salvation, a system of getting into heaven. If, however, we note that justification is connected to the work of the eschatological Adam, to Christ, then we must always recognize that as individuals we are joined to him by faith, and that we are a part of his body, the eschatological adamic humanity, the bride of Christ, the eschatological Eve, the church. However, that we must emphasize the importance of the *historia salutis* does not in any way mean that we should diminish the importance and necessity of the *ordo salutis*.

The Necessity of the Ordo Salutis

One of the trends that we have seen is the overemphasis upon the *historia salutis*, almost to the point that the *ordo salutis* is eclipsed. There are those with ecumenical interests who want to collapse the *applicatio salutis* into an undifferentiated mass so that communions with different and antithetical doctrines of redemption can reunite, or those who claim that such doctrinal precision is foreign to the Scriptures, or there are even those within the Reformed community who argue that union with Christ renders the distinction between justification and sanctification, at minimum, an issue of indifference, or at maximum, superfluous. There have also been those, especially associated with biblical studies, who have little understanding of the concept, and therefore dismiss it.

Yet one thing we have seen is that apart from the *ordo salutis*, the gospel is lost. This is not to say that a foreign doctrinal construct cradles the gospel of Christ. Rather, one must recognize the priorities that Scripture itself places upon the aspects of our redemption. Yes, union with Christ underlies the whole *ordo salutis*, but it is not union with Christ that Paul brings to the fore at Galatia to confront the Judaizers, but justification by faith alone. It does matter how the believer's good works relate to his justification, whether they are the foundation and ground or the fruits and effects of his justification. It does make a difference whether justification is based upon the prior moral transformation of the sinner or the imputed righteousness of Jesus Christ. The point that all exegetes and theologians must acknowledge is that everyone has an *ordo salutis*. It is not a question of whether to have or have not, but rather that one's *ordo salutis* reflects the logical priorities in our redemption set forth in Scripture.

The Covenant of Works

Another issue that we have seen resurface in different ways has been the covenant of works. Some automatically reject this theological doctrine because they argue that the Scriptures do not speak of such a concept, whether it is biblical exegetes who say they want to use the language of Scripture or of Paul, or biblical positivists who claim the term does not occur, therefore the doctrine does not exist. However, all theologians and exegetes use theological constructs, terms that describe biblical phenomena. The term "Trinity" is such a construct.

So when Reformed theologians speak of the covenants of works and grace, they are the constructs that address the works and epochs of the first and last Adams. In this respect, then, we can quickly see the relevance and foundational nature of the covenant of works for the doctrine of justification. Too many come to the doctrine of justification as if it were a first-century answer to a first-century question. Adam is merely the one who created the mess in which we find ourselves. Others import foreign philosophical commitments into the Genesis narrative and think man was created in terms of potentiality and actuality. Still yet others think that by man's fall he merely estranged the human race from its full ontological potential and that man can rise above his creaturely status to be more than man, to be god.

All of these views fail to account for the goodness of man at his creation, his righteousness. Moreover, they fail to account for the fact that his righteousness needed to be tested. Adam was to stand before the throne of God and be declared righteous subsequent to his successful probation, which would have elevated him to a higher state, that of indefectible righteousness and eternal rest. The doctrine of justification therefore appears in the Scriptures long before first-century Jews wondered whether they would be vindicated before their Roman overlords. In addition to this, had Adam successfully passed his probation, he would not have become a god, but rather would have remained man, a good creature, one who bore the perfect and unsullied image of his Creator.

Lastly, it is the nature of Adam's probation in the garden that causes many to see the importance of the law-gospel hermeneutic in Scripture. The law is not, contrary to popular opinion, an evangelical aid given to man after his sins are forgiven to assist him in his journey of moral transformation that culminates in his declaration of righteousness at the final judgment. Rather, the law represents the requirement of perfect obedience, the requirement that God demanded of Adam, and later of Israel at Sinai. It was the requirement that all failed to meet, save the last Adam. Therefore, the law brings those same demands that God placed upon Adam, his disobedient son, in the garden-temple; upon Israel his stiff-necked firstborn son at the foot of Sinai; and upon Jesus, the Son of man, God's only begotten Son in whom he was well pleased, who was born under the law to redeem us from its curse. The demands of the law therefore drive sinners to look outside of themselves to the perfect obedience of another, to the righteousness of Jesus Christ. Our faith is extraspective, not introspective. It is the covenant of works that enables us to see that if Adam could not be justified by his works though he was sinless and righteous, we cannot be justified by our works in any sense. Only the perfect obedience of the last Adam justifies us.

The Failure of Recent Challenges

This brings us to our last observation, namely the recent challenges from the New Perspective on Paul. In many respects, the NPP is a theological movement that will one day fade away. It will be spoken of in the same breath as the history of religions school and Bultmann's demythologization program. One can come to these conclusions for the following reasons. First, though some will claim that the NPP is an exegetical movement in the field of biblical studies, one must note it is inherently theological in nature. Those from the NPP have a system of theology; their exegesis produces a way they understand the Scripture and its teaching. This has been one of the ironies, in that some from the NPP sweep away theological positions because of their flawed presuppositions, yet they fail to account for their own flawed presuppositions. In many respects, the NPP is the child of Enlightenment-influenced biblical studies, most notably evident in the truncated view of the Pauline corpus—the ineffective sidelining of the Pastoral Epistles, for example.

Second, it is a movement that is historically and theologically naive, in that it has made little to no effort to understand the history of the doctrine of justification. Their historical study consists of a few caricatures of the views of the sixteenth-century Reformers, and some well-placed criticism of nineteenth- and twentieth-century exegetes. Yet in their failure to study the history of the doctrine, they nevertheless superciliously come to the table and say that Roman Catholics and Protestants should listen to them because they have properly exegeted Paul. They argue that justification is the doctrine that should unite rather than divide the church. Scholars of the NPP are simply ignorant of both Roman Catholic and Protestant doctrines of justification and have yet to articulate convincingly the differences between the two.

The NPP therefore will one day die out because they have failed to establish their doctrine of justification on the authority of the Scriptures, rather than on simply a truncated Pauline corpus. And they have not studied and truly listened to what others have said on the subject throughout church history. The movement will expire as every other historical-critical movement has—a new generation of scholars will turn on their theological forefathers in an effort to establish a newer New Perspective on Paul. And this newer perspective will not thrive unless it is in some way superior to the New Perspective. The child will devour its parent.

Yet for those who seek to maintain the doctrine of justification by faith alone, there is nothing to improve. Instead, one must seek to preserve *sola fide*, not because one is afraid of progress, or because one wants to safeguard tradition, but because it is the doctrine that gave Adam hope on the heels of his rebellion and caused him to change his wife's name from woman to Eve—giver of life. Adam knew that as he stood naked in the presence of his Creator, only by faith in the promise of the seed of the woman would he be able to stand once again in the presence of his covenant Lord without guilt, shame, and fear.

Conclusion

In the end, the doctrine of justification by faith alone turns on the question of whether sinful man will take shelter in the righteousness of Christ. It is the glorious exchange where man's sin and guilt are imputed to Christ, and Christ's obedience is imputed to his people. *Sola fide* is indeed the main hinge on which all religion turns, the only foundation for our salvation. It is the article upon which the church stands or falls.

BIBLIOGRAPHY

Books

Adamson, James B. *The Epistle of James.* NICNT. Grand Rapids: Eerdmans, 1982.

Alexander, Donald L., ed. *Five Views of Sanctification.* Downers Grove, IL: InterVarsity, 1988.

Alison, C. Fitzsimons. *The Rise of Moralism: The Proclamation of the Gospel from Hooker to Baxter.* 1966; Vancouver: Regent College Publishing, 2003.

Althaus, Paul. *The Theology of Martin Luther.* Translated by Robert C. Schultz. Philadelphia: Fortress, 1975.

Ames, William. *The Marrow of Theology.* Translated by John Dykstra Eusden. 1968; Grand Rapids: Baker, 1997.

Anderson, A. A. *The Book of Psalms.* Vol. 2. London: Marshall, Morgan, and Scott, 1972.

Anderson, Francis I., and David Noel Freedman. *Hosea.* AB 24. New York: Doubleday, 1980.

Anselm. *Anselm of Canterbury: The Major Works.* Edited by Brian Davies and G. R. Evans. Oxford: Oxford University Press, 1998.

Aquinas, Thomas. *Summa contra Gentiles.* Translated by Charles J. O'Neil. 4 vols. 1957; London: University of Notre Dame Press, 1975.

———. *Summa Theologica.* 5 vols. Westminster, MD: Christian Classics, 1946–47.

Arminius, Jacob. *The Works of Jacob Arminius.* Translated by James Nichols and William Nichols. Vol. 2, 1828; Grand Rapids: Baker, 1996.

Armstrong, John, ed. *Roman Catholicism: Evangelicals Analyze What Divides and Unites Us*. Chicago: Moody, 1994.

Augustine. *Augustine: Earlier Writings*. Edited by John Baillie et al. Translated by John H. S. Burleigh. LCC 6. London: SCM Press, 1953.

———. *Epistolae quas scripsit reliquo tempore (ab anno 411 ad 430)*. *Patrologia Latina* 33. Edited by J.-P. Migne. Paris: 1841.

———. *Four Anti-Pelagian Writings*. Edited by Thomas P. Halton et al. Translated by John A. Mourant and William J. Collinge. Fathers of the Church 86. Washington: Catholic University of America Press, 1992.

Aune, David E., ed. *Rereading Paul Together: Protestant and Catholic Perspectives on Justification*. Grand Rapids: Baker, 2006.

———. *Revelation 17–22*. WBC 52. Dallas: Word, 1998.

Baker, J. Wayne. *Heinrich Bullinger and the Covenant: The Other Reformed Tradition*. Athens: Ohio University Press, 1980.

Bangs, Carl. *Arminius: A Study in the Dutch Reformation*. Eugene, OR: Wipf & Stock, 1998.

Barrett, C. K. *The First Epistle to the Corinthians*. BNTC. 1968; Peabody, MA: Hendrickson, 1996.

———. *Romans*. BNTC. 1957; Peabody, MA: Hendrickson, 1991.

———. *The Second Epistle to the Corinthians*. BNTC. Peabody, MA: Hendrickson, 1983.

Barth, Karl. *Church Dogmatics*. 13 vols. Edinburgh: T & T Clark, 1998.

———. *Community, State, and Church*. Gloucester, MA: Peter Smith, 1968.

———. *Epistle to the Philippians*. 1947; Louisville: Westminster John Knox, 2002.

———. *Epistle to the Romans*. Translated by Edwyn C. Hoskyns. 1933; Oxford: Oxford University Press, 1968.

———. *The Teaching of the Church regarding Baptism*. 1943; Eugene, OR: Wipf & Stock, 2006.

Barth, Markus. *Acquittal by Resurrection: Freedom, Law and Justice in the Light of the Resurrection of Jesus Christ*. New York: Holt, Rinehart, and Winston, 1964.

Bartos, Emil. *Deification in Eastern Orthodox Theology: An Evaluation and Critique of the Theology of Dumitru Staniloae*. Carlisle: Paternoster, 1999.

Bauckham, Richard J. *Jude, 2 Peter*. WBC 50. Dallas: Word, 1983.

Baur, F. C. *Paul the Apostle of Jesus Christ: His Life and Works, His Epistles and Teachings*. 1873; Peabody, MA: Hendrickson, 2003.

Bavinck, Herman. *In the Beginning: Foundations of Creation Theology*. Translated by John Vriend. Edited by John Bolt. Grand Rapids: Baker, 1999.

———. *The Last Things.* Translated by John Vriend. Edited by John Bolt. Grand Rapids: Baker, 1996.

———. *Reformed Dogmatics.* Translated by John Vriend. Edited by John Bolt. 3 vols. Grand Rapids: Baker, 2003–6.

Bayer, Oswald. *Living by Faith: Justification and Sanctification.* Translated by Geoffrey Bromiley. Grand Rapids: Eerdmans, 2003.

Beale, G. K. *The Book of Revelation.* NIGTC. Grand Rapids: Eerdmans, 1999.

Beeke, Joel R. *The Quest for Full Assurance: The Legacy of Calvin and His Successors.* Edinburgh: Banner of Truth, 1999.

Beisner, E. Calvin, ed. *The Auburn Avenue Theology: Pros and Cons. Debating the Federal Vision.* Fort Lauderdale: Knox Theological Seminary, 2004.

Berkhof, Louis. *The History of Christian Doctrines.* 1937; Edinburgh: Banner of Truth, 1991.

———. *Systematic Theology: New Combined Edition.* 1932–38; Grand Rapids: Eerdmans, 1996.

Berkouwer, G. C. *Faith and Justification.* Translated by Lewis B. Smedes. Grand Rapids: Eerdmans, 1954.

———. *The Work of Christ.* Translated by Cornelius Lambregste. Grand Rapids: Eerdmans, 1965.

Beza, Theodore. *A Brief Declaration of the Chief Points of Christian Religion Set Forth in a Table.* London, n.d.

Bierma, Lyle D. *An Introduction to the Heidelberg Catechism: Sources, History, and Theology.* Edited and translated by Lyle D. Bierma et al. Grand Rapids: Baker, 2005.

Black, David Alan. *It's Still Greek to Me: An Easy-to-Understand Guide to Intermediate Greek.* Grand Rapids: Baker, 1998.

Block, Daniel I. *The Book of Ezekiel: Chapters 25–48.* NICOT. Grand Rapids: Eerdmans, 1998.

Boersma, Hans. *A Hot Peppercorn: Richard Baxter's Doctrine of Justification in Its Seventeenth-century Context of Controversy.* 1993; Vancouver: Regent College Publishing, 2004.

Bousset, Wilhelm. *Kyrios Christos: A History of the Belief in Christ from the Beginnings of Christianity to Irenaeus.* Translated by John E. Steely. Nashville: Abingdon, 1970.

Braaten, Carl. *Justification: The Article by Which the Church Stands or Falls.* Minneapolis: Fortress, 1990.

Braaten, Carl, and Robert W. Jenson, eds. *Union with Christ: The New Finnish Interpretation of Luther.* Grand Rapids: Eerdmans, 1998.

Bradwardine, Thomas. *De Causa Dei, Contra Pelagium et De Virtute Causarum, ad suos Mertonenses.* London, 1618.

Brakel, Wilhelmus à. *The Christian's Reasonable Service.* Translated by Bartel Elshout. Vol. 1. Ligonier, PA: Soli Deo Gloria, 1992.

Briggs, Charles A. *Psalms.* Volume 1. ICC. 1909; Edinburgh: T & T Clark, 1969.

Bromiley, G. W., ed. *Zwingli and Bullinger.* Philadelphia: Westminster, 1953.

Bruce, F. F. *1 and 2 Thessalonians.* WBC 45. Dallas: Word, 1982.

Brunner, Emil. *The Christian Doctrine of Creation and Redemption.* Translated by Olive Wyon. Philadelphia: Westminster, 1952.

Buchanan, James. *The Doctrine of Justification.* 1867; Edinburgh: Banner of Truth, 1991.

Bultmann, Rudolf. *The Second Letter to the Corinthians.* Minneapolis: Fortress, 1985.

———. *Theology of the New Testament: Complete in One Volume.* Translated by Kendrick Grobel. New York: Charles Scribner's Sons, 1951–55.

Calvin, John. *Galatians, Ephesians, Philippians, and Colossians.* Translated by T. H. L. Parker. Edited by David W. Torrance and T. F. Torrance. CNTC. Grand Rapids: Eerdmans, 1960.

———. *A Harmony of the Gospels: Matthew, Mark, and Luke & James & Jude.* Translated by A. W. Morrison. Edited by David W. Torrance and T. F. Torrance. CNTC. Grand Rapids: Eerdmans, 1972.

———. *Hosea.* CTS 13. Grand Rapids: Baker, 1993.

———. *Institutes of the Christian Religion.* Translated by Ford Lewis Battles. Edited by John T. McNeill. LCC 20–21. Philadelphia: Westminster, 1960.

———. *Instruction in Faith (1537).* Translated and edited by Paul T. Furhmann. 1977; Louisville: Westminster John Knox, 1992.

———. *Psalms 93–150.* Translated by James Anderson. CTS. Grand Rapids: Baker, 1979.

———. *Romans and Thessalonians.* Translated by Ross Mackenzie. Edited by David W. Torrance and T. F. Torrance. CNTC. Grand Rapids: Eerdmans, 1960.

———. *2 Corinthians and Timothy, Titus and Philemon.* Translated by T. A. Smail. Edited by David W. Torrance and T. F. Torrance. CNTC. Grand Rapids: Eerdmans, 1960.

———. *Selected Works of John Calvin.* Edited by Henry Beveridge and Jule Bonnet. 7 vols. Grand Rapids: Baker, 1983.

Carson, D. A. *Divine Sovereignty and Human Responsibility: Biblical Perspectives in Tension.* London: Marshall Pickering, 1994.

———. *Exegetical Fallacies.* 1984; Grand Rapids: Baker, 1993.

———. *The Gospel according to John.* PNTC. Grand Rapids: Eerdmans, 1991.

———. *Matthew 13–28.* EBC. Grand Rapids: Zondervan, 1995.

Carson, D. A., ed. *Right with God: Justification in the Bible and the World.* Eugene, OR: Wipf & Stock, 2002.

Carson, D. A., Peter T. O'Brien, and Mark A. Seifrid, eds. *Justification and Variegated Nomism.* 2 vols. Grand Rapids: Baker, 2004.

Cassuto, Umberto. *A Commentary on the Book of Genesis.* Part One. *From Adam to Noah.* Translated by Israel Abrahams. Jerusalem: Magnes Press, 1998.

Charlesworth, James H., et al., eds. *Resurrection: The Origin and Future of a Biblical Doctrine.* Edinburgh: T & T Clark, 2006.

Chemnitz, Martin. *Loci Theologici.* Translated by J. A. O. Preus. 2 vols. St. Louis: Concordia Publishing House, 1989.

Chesterton, G. K. *Orthodoxy: The Romance of Faith.* 1959; New York: Doubleday, 1990.

Childs, Brevard S. *Old Testament Theology in Its Canonical Context.* Philadelphia: Fortress, 1985.

Christensen, Duane L. *Deuteronomy 21:10–34:12.* WBC. Nashville: Thomas Nelson, 2002.

Clark, R. Scott, ed. *Covenant, Justification, and Pastoral Ministry: Essays by the Faculty of Westminster Seminary California.* Phillipsburg, NJ: P&R, 2007.

———. *Recovering the Reformed Confession.* Phillipsburg, NJ: P&R, 2008.

Confession of Faith and Catechisms of the Orthodox Presbyterian Church with Proof Texts. Willow Grove, PA: The Committee on Christian Education of the OPC, 2005.

Craigie, Peter C. *Psalms 1–50.* WBC. Dallas: Word, 1983.

Cranfield, C. E. B. *On Romans and Other New Testament Essays.* Edinburgh: T & T Clark, 1998.

———. *Romans.* 2 vols. ICC. 1975; Edinburgh: T & T Clark, 2001.

Dabney, R. L. *Discussions: Evangelical and Theological.* Vol. 1. 1890; Edinburgh: Banner of Truth, 1967.

Dana, H. E., and Julius R. Mantey. *A Manual Grammar of the Greek New Testament.* 1927; New York: Macmillan, 1955.

Das, A. Andrew. *Paul, the Law, and the Covenant.* Peabody, MA: Hendrickson, 2001.

Davies, W. D. *Paul and Rabbinic Judaism.* London: SPCK, 1948.

Davies, W. D., and Dale C. Allison. *The Gospel according to Matthew.* Vol. 3. ICC. Edinburgh: T & T Clark, 1997.

Delitzsch, Frans. *The Psalms.* Translated by Francis Bolton. Vol. 2. Edinburgh: T & T Clark, 1901.

Doctrinal Testimony regarding Recent Errors. Dyer, IN: Mid-America Reformed Seminary, 2007.

Dumbrell, W. J. *Covenant and Creation: A Theology of the Old Testament Covenants.* Carlisle: Paternoster, 1984.

———. *The End of the Beginning: Revelation 21–22 and the Old Testament.* 1985; Eugene, OR: Wipf & Stock, 2001.

Dunn, James D. *The Christ and the Spirit.* Vol. 1. Grand Rapids: Eerdmans, 1998.

———. *Christology in the Making: A New Testament Inquiry into the Origins of the Doctrine of the Incarnation.* 1980; London: SCM Press, 1989.

———. *Jesus, Paul, and the Law: Studies in Mark and Galatians.* Louisville: Westminster John Knox, 1990.

———. *The New Perspective on Paul: Collected Essays.* Tübingen: Mohr Siebeck, 2005.

———. *Romans.* WBC 38a-b. Dallas: Word, 1988.

———. *The Theology of Paul the Apostle.* Grand Rapids: Eerdmans, 1998.

Durham, James I. *Exodus.* WBC 3. Dallas: Word, 1987.

Ebeling, Gerhard. *Word and Faith.* London: SCM Press, 1963.

Edwards, Jonathan. *The Works of Jonathan Edwards.* Edited by Edward Hickman. 2 vols. 1834; Edinburgh: Banner of Truth, 1992.

———. *The Works of Jonathan Edwards On-line.* Edited by Harry S. Stout, Kenneth P. Minkema, and Caleb J. D. Maskell. At www.edwards.yale.edu.

Eells, Hastings. *Martin Bucer.* New Haven: Yale University Press, 1931.

Eisenman, Robert, and Michael Wise. *The Dead Sea Scrolls Uncovered.* New York: Penguin, 1992.

Elliot, Mark Adam. *Survivors of Israel: A Reconsideration of the Theology of Pre-Christian Judaism.* Grand Rapids: Eerdmans, 2000.

Ellis, E. Earle. *Gospel of Luke.* NCB. London: Thomas Nelson, 1966.

Erickson, Millard J. *Concise Dictionary of Christian Theology.* Grand Rapids: Baker, 1994.

———. *Christian Theology.* Grand Rapids: Baker, 1985.

Fee, Gordon D. *The First Epistle to the Corinthians.* NICNT. Grand Rapids: Eerdmans, 1987.

———. *God's Empowering Presence.* Peabody, MA: Hendrickson, 1994.

Ferguson, Sinclair. *The Holy Spirit.* Downers Grove, IL: InterVarsity, 1996.

Fesko, J. V. *Diversity within the Reformed Tradition: Supra- and Infralapsarianism in Calvin, Dort, and Westminster.* Greenville, SC: Reformed Academic Press, 2003.

Fesko, J. V., et al. *Justification: A Report from the Orthodox Presbyterian Church.* Willow Grove, PA: The Committee on Christian Education for the OPC, 2007.

———. *Last Things First: Unlocking Genesis 1–3 with the Christ of Eschatology.* Fearn, Scotland: Mentor, 2007.

Fisher, Edward. *The Marrow of Modern Divinity.* 1645–49; New York: Westminster, n.d.

Fitzmyer, Joseph A. *The Gospel according to Luke: 10–24.* AB 28a. Garden City, NY: Doubleday, 1985.

———. *Romans.* AB 33. New York: Doubleday, 1993.

Flannery, Austin, ed. *The Basic Sixteen Documents of Vatican Council II: Constitutions, Decrees, Declarations. A Completely Revised Translation in Inclusive Language.* Northpoint: Costello, 1996.

France, R. T. *The Gospel of Mark.* NIGTC. Grand Rapids: Eerdmans, 2002.

Franke, John R. *The Character of Theology: A Postconservative Evangelical Approach.* Grand Rapids: Baker, 2005.

Furnish, Victor Paul. *II Corinthians.* AB 32a. New York: Doubleday, 1984.

Gaffin, Richard B., Jr. *By Faith, Not by Sight: Paul and the Order of Salvation.* Carlisle: Paternoster, 2006.

———. *Resurrection and Redemption: A Study in Paul's Soteriology.* 1978; Phillipsburg, NJ: P&R, 1987.

Gage, Warren Austin. *The Gospel of Genesis: Studies in Protology and Eschatology.* 1984; Eugene, OR: Wipf & Stock, 2001.

Gathercole, S. J. *Where Is Boasting? Early Jewish Soteriology and Paul's Response in Romans 1–5.* Grand Rapids: Eerdmans, 2002.

Gerstner, John H. *The Rational Biblical Theology of Jonathan Edwards.* 3 vols. Powhatan, VA: Berea Publications, 1991.

Goppelt, Leonhard. *Theology of the New Testament.* Translated by John Alsup. 2 vols. Grand Rapids: Eerdmans, 1981.

———. *Typos: The Typological Interpretation of the Old Testament in the New.* Translated by Donald H. Madvig. 1939; Grand Rapids: Eerdmans, 1982.

Green, Joel B. *The Gospel of Luke.* NICNT. Grand Rapids: Eerdmans, 1997.

Green, Roberta, and Lela Gilbert. *Islam at the Crossroads: Understanding Its Beliefs, History, and Conflicts.* Grand Rapids: Baker, 2002.

Gregory of Rimini. *Super Primum et Secundum Sententiae.* 1522; St. Bonaventure, NY: Franciscan Institute, 1955.

Grenz, Stanley J. *Theology for the Community of God.* Nashville: Broadman & Holman, 1994.

Grenz, Stanley J., and Roger E. Olson. *Twentieth-Century Theology: God and the World in a Transitional Age.* Downers Grove, IL: InterVarsity, 1992.

Gunkel, Herman. *Genesis.* Translated by Mark E. Biddle. Macon, GA: Mercer University Press, 1997.

Habel, Norman C. *The Book of Job*. OTL. Philadelphia: Westminster, 1985.

Hadjiantoniou, Georgios. *Protestant Patriarch: The Life of Cyril Lucaris, 1572–1638*. Richmond: John Knox, 1961.

Hafemann, Scott J. *2 Corinthians*. NIVAC. Grand Rapids: Zondervan, 2000.

Hagner, Donald A. *Matthew 1–13*. WBC 33a-b. Dallas: Word, 1993.

Hamilton, Victor P. *The Book of Genesis: Chapters 1–17*. NICOT. Grand Rapids: Eerdmans, 1990.

Hampson, Daphne. *Christian Contradictions: The Structures of Lutheran and Catholic Thought*. Cambridge: Cambridge University Press, 2001.

Harink, Douglas. *Paul among the Postliberals: Pauline Theology beyond Christendom and Modernity*. Grand Rapids: Brazos, 2003.

Harnack, Adolf von. *The History of Dogma*. Edited by T. K. Cheyne and A. B. Bruce. Translated by James Millar. 5 vols. London: Williams and Norgate, 1898.

Harris, Murray J. *The Second Epistle to the Corinthians*. NIGTC. Grand Rapids: Eerdmans, 2005.

Hart, D. G. *Recovering Mother Kirk: The Case for Liturgy in the Reformed Tradition*. Grand Rapids: Baker, 2003.

Hart, D. G., and John R. Muether. *Seeking a Better Country: 300 Years of American Presbyterianism*. Phillipsburg, NJ: P&R, 2007.

———. *With Reverence and Awe: Returning to the Basics of Reformed Worship*. Phillipsburg, NJ: P&R, 2002.

Hartley, John E. *The Book of Job*. NICOT. Grand Rapids: Eerdmans, 1988.

Hawthorne, Gerald F., Ralph P. Martin, and Daniel G. Reid, eds. *Dictionary of Paul and His Letters*. Downers Grove, IL: InterVarsity, 1993.

Hays, Richard B. *The Faith of Jesus Christ: The Narrative Substructure of Galatians 3:1–4:11*. 1983; Grand Rapids: Eerdmans, 2002.

Hendricksen, William. *More than Conquerors*. 1939; Grand Rapids: Baker, 1960.

Heppe, Heinrich. *Reformed Dogmatics: Set Out and Illustrated from the Sources*. Edited by Ernst Bizer. Translated by G. T. Thomson. London: George Allen & Unwin, 1950.

Hodge, A. A. *Outlines of Theology*. 1860; Edinburgh: Banner of Truth, 1991.

Hodge, Charles. *Romans*. 1835; Edinburgh: Banner of Truth, 1989.

———. *Systematic Theology*. 3 vols. Grand Rapids: Eerdmans, 1993.

Hoeksema, Herman. *Reformed Dogmatics*. Grand Rapids: Reformed Free Publishing Association, 1966.

Holladay, William L. *Jeremiah 2*. Minneapolis: Fortress, 1989.

Hooker, M. D. *From Adam to Christ: Essays on Paul.* Cambridge: Cambridge University Press, 1990.

———. *The Gospel according to St. Mark.* BNTC. Peabody, MA: Hendrickson, 1991.

Horton, Michael S. *Covenant and Eschatology: The Divine Drama.* Louisville: Westminster John Knox, 2002.

———. *Covenant and Salvation: Union with Christ.* Louisville: Westminster John Knox, 2007.

———. *God of Promise: Introducing Covenant Theology.* Grand Rapids: Baker, 2006.

———. *Lord and Servant: A Covenant Christology.* Louisville: Westminster John Knox, 2005.

Huey, F. B., Jr., and Bruce Corley. *A Student's Dictionary for Biblical and Theological Studies: A Handbook of Special and Technical Terms.* Grand Rapids: Zondervan, 1983.

Husbands, Mark, and Daniel J. Treier, eds. *Justification: What's at Stake in the Current Debates.* Downers Grove, IL: InterVarsity, 2004.

Jenson, Robert W. *Systematic Theology.* 2 vols. Oxford: Oxford University Press, 1997.

Jeon, Jeong Koo. *Covenant Theology: John Murray's and Meredith G. Kline's Response to the Historical Development of Federal Theology in Reformed Thought.* New York: University Press of America, 1999.

Joint Declaration on the Doctrine of Justification: The Lutheran World Federation and the Roman Catholic Church. Grand Rapids: Eerdmans, 2000.

Josephus. *The Works of Josephus.* Translated by William Whiston. Peabody, MA: Hendrickson, 1987.

Jüngel, Eberhard. *Justification: The Heart of the Christian Faith.* Translated by Jeffrey F. Cayzer. Edinburgh: T & T Clark, 2001.

Kärkkäinen, Veli-Matti. *One with God: Salvation as Deification and Justification.* Collegeville, Liturgical Press, 2004.

Käsemann, Ernst. *New Testament Questions of Today.* Minneapolis: Fortress, 1969.

Keating, Karl. *Catholicism and Fundamentalism: The Attack on "Romanism" by "Bible Christians."* San Francisco: Ignatius Press, 1988.

Keil, C. F., and Franz Delitzsch. *Commentary on the Old Testament.* 10 vols. 1866–91; Peabody, MA: Hendrickson, 1996.

Kidner, Derek. *Genesis.* TOTC. Downers Grove, IL: InterVarsity, 1967.

———. *Psalms.* 2 vols. TOTC. Downers Grove, IL: InterVarsity, 1973, 1981.

Kim, Jaegwon, and Ernest Sosa. *A Companion to Metaphysics.* Oxford: Blackwell, 1995.

Kim, Seyoon. *The Origin of Paul's Gospel*. Grand Rapids: Eerdmans, 1981.

———. *Paul and the New Perspective: Second Thoughts on the Origin of Paul's Gospel*. Grand Rapids: Eerdmans, 2002.

Kirkpatrick, A. F. *The Book of Psalms*. Cambridge: Cambridge University Press, 1902.

Kistemaker, Simon J. *I Corinthians*. NTC. Grand Rapids: Baker, 1993.

———. *II Corinthians*. NTC. Grand Rapids: Baker, 1997.

Kline, Meredith G. *Images of the Spirit*. 1980; Eugene, OR: Wipf & Stock, 1998.

———. *Kingdom Prologue: Genesis Foundations for a Covenantal Worldview*. Overland Park, KS: Two Age Press, 2000.

———. *The Structure of Biblical Authority*. Eugene, OR: Wipf & Stock, 1989.

———. *Treaty of the Great King: The Covenant Structure of Deuteronomy*. Grand Rapids: Eerdmans, 1963.

Kolb, Robert, and Timothy J. Wengert, eds. *The Book of Concord: The Confessions of the Evangelical Lutheran Church*. Minneapolis: Fortress, 2000.

Kraus, Hans-Joachim. *Psalms*. Translated by Hilton C. Oswald. 2 vols. Minneapolis: Fortress, 1993.

Küng, Hans. *Justification: The Doctrine of Karl Barth and a Catholic Reflection*. 1964; Louisville: Westminster John Knox, 2004.

Lane, Anthony N. S. *John Calvin: Student of the Church Fathers*. Grand Rapids: Baker, 1999.

———. *Justification by Faith in Catholic-Protestant Dialogue: An Evangelical Assessment*. Edinburgh: T & T Clark, 2002.

Leff, Gordon. *Gregory of Rimini: Tradition and Innovation in Fourteenth Century Thought*. Manchester: Manchester University Press, 1961.

Lehman, Karl, and Wolfhart Pannenberg, eds. *The Condemnations of the Reformation Era: Do They Still Divide?* Translated by Margaret Kohl. Minneapolis: Fortress, 1990.

Letham, Robert. *The Holy Trinity: In Scripture, History, and Worship*. Phillipsburg, NJ: P&R, 2004.

———. *The Work of Christ*. Downers Grove, IL: InterVarsity, 1993.

Lightfoot, J. B. *Paul's Epistle to the Galatians: A Revised Text with Introduction, Notes and Dissertations*. Peabody, MA: Hendrickson, 1999.

Lincoln, Andrew T. *Ephesians*. WBC 42. Dallas: Word, 1990.

Lincoln, Andrew T., and A. J. M. Wedderburn, eds. *New Testament Theology: The Theology of the Later Pauline Letters*. Cambridge: Cambridge University Press, 1993.

Lohse, Bernard. *Martin Luther's Theology: Its Historical Development.* Translated by Roy A. Harrisville. Minneapolis: Fortress, 1999.

Longenecker, Richard N. *Acts.* EBC. Grand Rapids: Zondervan, 1995.

———. *Galatians.* WBC 41. Dallas: Word, 1990.

Lossky, Vladimir, et al. *In the Image and Likeness of God.* Crestwood, NY: St. Vladimir's Seminary Press, 1974.

Lucas, Ernest C. *Daniel.* AOTC. Downers Grove, IL: InterVarsity, 2002.

Luther, Martin. *Lectures on Galatians.* LW 26. St. Louis: Concordia, 1963.

———. *Lectures on Genesis.* Edited by Jaroslav Pelikan. LW 1. St. Louis: Concordia, 1958.

———. *Lectures on Romans.* LW 25. St. Louis: Concordia, 1974.

Machen, J. Gresham. *God Transcendent.* 1949; Edinburgh: Banner of Truth, 1982.

———. *Machen's Notes on Galatians.* Edited by John H. Skilton. Nutley, NJ: P&R, 1972.

———. *The Origin of Paul's Religion.* 1925; Eugene, OR: Wipf & Stock, 2002.

Mannermaa, Tuomo. *Christ Present in Faith: Luther's View of Justification.* Minneapolis: Fortress, 2005.

Mantzaridis, Georgios S. *The Deification of Man.* Crestwood, NY: St. Vladimir's Seminary Press, 1984.

Martínez, Florentino Garcia. *The Dead Sea Scrolls Translated: The Qumran Texts in English.* Grand Rapids: Eerdmans, 1996.

McComiskey, Thomas. *Hosea.* The Minor Prophet 1. Edited by Thomas McComiskey. Grand Rapids: Baker, 1992.

McConville, J. G. *Deuteronomy.* AOTC. Downers Grove, IL: InterVarsity, 2002.

McCormack, Bruce L., ed. *Justification in Perspective: Historical Development and Contemporary Challenges.* Grand Rapids: Baker, 2006.

McFague, Sallie. *Metaphorical Theology: Models of God in Religious Language.* Philadelphia: Fortress, 1984.

McGowan, A. T. B. *The Federal Theology of Thomas Boston.* Carlisle: Paternoster, 1997.

McGrath, Alister E. *Christian Theology.* 1994; Oxford: Blackwell, 1998.

———. *The Intellectual Origins of the European Reformation.* Grand Rapids: Baker, 1987.

———. *Iustitia Dei: A History of the Christian Doctrine of Justification.* 2 vols. 1986; Cambridge: Cambridge University Press, 1995.

McLaren, Brian D. *A Generous Orthodoxy.* Grand Rapids: Zondervan, 2004.

Melanchthon, Philip. *Loci Communes (1543)*. Translated by J. A. O. Preus. St. Louis: Concordia, 1992.

Meyendorff, John. *Byzantine Theology: Historical Trends and Doctrinal Themes.* New York: Fordham University Press, 1974.

Meyendorff, John, and Robert Tobias, eds. *Salvation in Christ: A Lutheran-Orthodox Dialogue.* Minneapolis: Augsburg Fortress, 1992.

Milgrom, Jacob. *Numbers.* JPSTC. Philadelphia: Jewish Publication Society, 1990.

Miller, Patrick D. *Deuteronomy.* Louisville: Westminster John Knox, 1990.

Mitchell, Alexander F. *Catechisms of the Second Reformation.* London: James Nisbet & Co., 1886.

Moltmann, Jürgen. *The Spirit of Life: A Universal Affirmation.* Translated by Margaret Kohl. Minneapolis: Fortress, 1992.

———. *Trinity and Kingdom.* Translated by Margaret Kohl. Minneapolis: Fortress, 1993.

———. *The Way of Jesus Christ.* Translated by Margaret Kohl. Minneapolis: Fortress, 1993.

Moo, Douglas. *Epistle to the Romans.* NICNT. Grand Rapids: Eerdmans, 1996.

———. *The Letter of James.* PNTC. Grand Rapids: Eerdmans, 2000.

Morris, Leon. *The Gospel according to Matthew.* PNTC. Grand Rapids: Eerdmans, 1992.

Mounce, Robert H. *The Book of Revelation.* NICNT. 1977; Grand Rapids: Eerdmans, 1998.

Mueller, J. T. *Christian Dogmatics.* 1934; St. Louis: Concordia, 1955.

Muller, Richard A. *After Calvin: Studies in the Development of a Theological Tradition.* Oxford: Oxford University Press, 2003.

———. *Dictionary of Latin and Greek Theological Terms: Drawn Principally from Protestant Scholastic Theology.* Grand Rapids: Baker, 1987.

———. *Post-Reformation Reformed Dogmatics.* 4 vols. Grand Rapids: Baker, 2003.

———. *The Unaccommodated Calvin: Studies in the Foundation of a Theological Tradition.* Oxford: Oxford University Press, 2000.

Murray, John. *Collected Writings of John Murray.* 4 vols. 1977; Edinburgh: Banner of Truth, 1996.

———. *The Covenant of Grace: Biblical & Theological Studies.* London: Tyndale, 1954.

———. *The Epistle to the Romans.* NICNT. Grand Rapids: Eerdmans, 1968.

———. *The Imputation of Adam's Sin.* Philadelphia: P&R, 1959.

———. *Redemption Accomplished and Applied*. Grand Rapids: Eerdmans, 1955.

Newport, John P. *Paul Tillich*. Peabody, MA: Hendrickson, 1984.

Noll, Mark A., and Carolyn Nystrom. *Is the Reformation Over? An Evangelical Assessment of Contemporary Roman Catholicism*. Grand Rapids: Baker, 2005.

Oberman, Heiko A. *Archbishop Thomas Bradwardine, a Fourteenth Century Augustinian: A Study of His Theology in Its Historical Context*. Utrecht: Kemink & Zoon, 1957.

Oberman, Heiko A., ed. *Forerunners of the Reformation: The Shape of Late Medieval Thought*. London: Lutterworth, 1967.

———. *The Harvest of Medieval Theology: Gabriel Biel and Late Medieval Nominalism*. 1963; Grand Rapids: Baker, 2000.

———. *The Reformation: Roots and Ramifications*. Grand Rapids: Eerdmans, 1994.

O'Brien, Peter T. *The Letter to the Ephesians*. PNTC. Grand Rapids: Eerdmans, 1999.

Oden, Thomas. *The Justification Reader*. Grand Rapids: Eerdmans, 2002.

Oliphint, K. Scott, ed. *Justified in Christ: God's Plan for Us in Justification*. Fearn, Scotland: Mentor, 2007.

Olson, Roger E. *Arminian Theology: Myths and Realities*. Downers Grove, IL: InterVarsity, 2006.

Osbourne, Grant R. *The Hermeneutical Spiral: A Comprehensive Introduction to Biblical Interpretation*. Downers Grove, IL: InterVarsity, 1991.

Owen, John. *Works of John Owen*. 16 vols. Edited by William H. Goold. 1850–53; Edinburgh: Banner of Truth, 1993.

Packer, J. I. *The Redemption and Restoration of Man in the Thought of Richard Baxter*. 1954; Vancouver: Regent College Publishing, 2003.

Pannenberg, Wolfhart. *Systematic Theology*. Translated by Geoffrey Bromiley. 3 vols. Grand Rapids: Eerdmans, 1998.

Pelagius. *Pelagius's Commentary on St Paul's Epistle to the Romans*. Translated by Theodore de Bruyn. Oxford: Oxford University Press, 1993.

Pelikan, Jaroslav. *The Christian Tradition: A History of the Development of Doctrine*. 5 vols. Chicago: University of Chicago Press, 1971.

Pelikan, Jaroslav, and Valerie Hotchkiss, eds. *Creeds and Confessions of Faith in the Christian Tradition*. 3 vols. New Haven: Yale University Press, 2003.

Penner, Todd C. *The Epistle of James and Eschatology: Re-reading an Ancient Christian Letter*. Sheffield: Sheffield Academic Press, 1996.

Perkins, William. *The Art of Prophesying*. 1606; Edinburgh: Banner of Truth, 1996.

———. *The Works of That Famous and Worthy Minister of Christ W. Perkins.* Vol. 1. London, 1612.

Pieper, Francis. *Christian Dogmatics.* 4 vols. St. Louis: Concordia, 1951.

Pinnock, Clark. *Flame of Love: A Theology of the Holy Spirit.* Downers Grove, IL: InterVarsity, 1996.

Piper, John. *Counted Righteous in Christ: Should We Abandon the Imputation of Christ's Righteousness?* Wheaton, IL: Crossway, 2002.

Piscator, Johannes. *A Learned and Profitable Treatise on Man's Justification.* London, 1599.

Pitre, Brant. *Jesus, the Tribulation and the End of Exile: Restoration Eschatology and the Origin of the Atonement.* Grand Rapids: Baker, 2005.

Polanus, Amandus. *The Substance of the Christian Religion.* London, 1595.

Rad, Gerhard von. *Genesis.* OTL. Philadelphia: Westminster, 1972.

———. *Old Testament Theology.* Vol. 1. 1962; Louisville: Westminster John Knox, 2001.

Rahner, Karl. *Foundations of Christian Faith.* Translated by William V. Dych. New York: Crossroad, 1990.

Rainbow, Paul A. *The Way of Salvation: The Role of Christian Obedience in Justification.* Carlisle: Paternoster, 2005.

Räisänen, Heikki. *Paul and the Law.* Minneapolis: Fortress, 1983.

Ratzinger, Joseph Cardinal, ed. *Catechism of the Catholic Church.* Ligouri: Ligouri Publications, 1994.

Reitsenstein, Richard. *Hellenistic Mystery-Religions: Their Basic Ideas and Significance.* Translated by John E. Steely. Pittsburgh: Pickwick Press, 1978.

Report of Ad Interim Study Committee on Federal Vision, New Perspective, and Auburn Avenue Theology. Atlanta: Presbyterian Church of America, 2007.

Reymond, Robert L. *A New Systematic Theology of the Christian Faith.* Nashville: Thomas Nelson, 1998.

Ridderbos, Herman. *The St. Paul's Epistle to the Churches of Galatia.* NICNT. Grand Rapids: Eerdmans, 1953.

———. *The Gospel according to John: A Theological Commentary.* NICNT. Grand Rapids: Eerdmans, 1981.

———. *Paul: An Outline of His Theology.* Translated by John Richard De Witt. 1975; Grand Rapids: Eerdmans, 1992.

———. *Redemptive History and the New Testament Scriptures.* 1963; Phillipsburg, NJ: P&R, 1988.

Ritschl, Albrecht. *The Christian Doctrine of Justification and Reconciliation: The Positive Development of the Doctrine.* 1902; Eugene, OR: Wipf & Stock, 2004.

———. *A Critical History of the Christian Doctrine of Justification and Reconciliation.* Translated by John S. Black. Edinburgh: Edmonston and Douglas, 1872.

Robinson, Stuart. *The Church of God as an Essential Element of the Gospel and the Idea, Structure, and Functions Thereof.* 1858; Greenville, SC: GPTS, 1995.

Rutherford, Samuel. *Christ Dying and Drawing Sinners to Himself.* Edinburgh, 1727.

———. *The Covenant of Life Opened.* Edinburgh, 1655.

Ryrie, Charles C. *Dispensationalism Today.* Chicago: Moody, 1965.

Sanders, E. P. *Paul and Palestinian Judaism.* Minneapolis: Fortress, 1977.

Sandlin, P. Andrew, ed. *Backbone of the Bible: Covenant in Contemporary Perspective.* Nacogdoches, TX: Covenant Media Foundation, 2004.

Sarna, Nahum. *Genesis.* JPSTC. Philadelphia: Jewish Publication Press, 1989.

Schaff-Herzog Encyclopedia of Religious Knowledge. Edited by Samuel Macauley Jackson. 13 vols. New York: Funk and Wagnalls, 1910.

Schaff, Philip. *The Creeds of Christendom.* 3 vols. 1931; Grand Rapids: Baker, 1990.

Schleiermacher, Friedrich. *The Christian Faith.* Translated by H. R. Mackintosh and J. S. Stewart. 1830; London: T & T Clark, 2006.

———. *On Religion: Speeches to Its Cultured Despisers.* Translated by Richard Crouter. Cambridge: Cambridge University Press, 1988.

Schmid, Heinrich. *The Doctrinal Theology of the Evangelical Lutheran Church.* Translated by Charles A. Hay and Henry E. Jacobs. Philadelphia: Lutheran Publication Society, 1899.

Schreiner, Thomas. *Paul: Apostle of God's Glory in Christ.* Downers Grove, IL: InterVarsity, 2001.

———. *Romans.* BECNT. Grand Rapids: Baker, 1998.

Schweitzer, Albert. *The Mysticism of Paul the Apostle.* Translated by William Montgomery. 1931; Baltimore: Johns Hopkins University Press, 1998.

Scott, James M. *Adoption as Sons of God.* Tübingen: Mohr Siebeck, 1992.

Seifrid, Mark A. *Christ, Our Righteousness: Paul's Theology of Justification.* Downers Grove, IL: InterVarsity, 2000.

———. *Justification by Faith: The Origin and Development of a Central Pauline Theme.* Leiden: Brill, 1992.

Shea, William M. *The Lion and the Lamb: Evangelicals and Catholics in America.* Oxford: Oxford University Press, 2004.

Shepherd, Norman. *The Call of Grace: How the Covenant Illuminates Salvation and Evangelism.* Phillipsburg, NJ: P&R, 2000.

Silva, Moisés. *Interpreting Galatians: Explorations in Exegetical Method.* Grand Rapids: Baker, 2001.

———. *Philippians.* BECNT. 1992; Grand Rapids: Baker, 2005.

Smedes, Louis B. *Union with Christ: A Biblical View of New Life in Jesus Christ.* Grand Rapids: Eerdmans, 1970.

Speiser, E. A. *Genesis.* AB 1. New York: Doubleday, 1962.

Sproul, R. C. *Faith Alone: The Evangelical Doctrine of Justification.* Grand Rapids: Baker, 1995.

Spykman, Gordon J. *Reformational Theology: A New Paradigm for Doing Dogmatics.* Grand Rapids: Eerdmans, 1992.

Stamoolis, James. *Three Views on Eastern Orthodoxy and Evangelicalism.* Grand Rapids: Zondervan, 2004.

Staniloae, Dumitru. *The Experience of God: Orthodox Dogmatic Theology.* Vol. 2. *The World: Creation and Deification.* Translated and edited by Ioan Ionita and Robert Barringer. Brookline, MA: Holy Cross Orthodox Press, 2005.

Stelten, Leo F. *Dictionary of Ecclesiastical Latin.* Peabody, MA: Hendrickson, 1995.

Stendahl, Krister. *Paul among Jews and Gentiles.* Minneapolis: Fortress, 1976.

Stuart, Douglas. *Hosea-Jonah.* WBC 31. Dallas: Word, 1987.

Stumme, Wayne C., ed. *The Gospel of Justification in Christ: Where Does the Church Stand Today?* Grand Rapids: Eerdmans, 2006.

Tamburello, Dennis E. *Union with Christ: John Calvin and the Mysticism of St. Bernard.* Louisville: Westminster John Knox, 1994.

Thiselton, A. C. *The First Epistle to the Corinthians.* NIGTC. Grand Rapids: Eerdmans, 2000.

Thompson, J. A. *The Book of Jeremiah.* NICOT. Grand Rapids: Eerdmans, 1980.

Tigay, Jeffery H. *Deuteronomy.* JPSTC. Philadelphia: Jewish Publication Society, 1996.

Tillich, Paul. *A History of Christian Thought.* Edited by Carl E. Braaten. New York: Simon & Schuster, n.d.

———. *Systematic Theology.* 3 vols. 1957; Chicago: University of Chicago Press, 1977.

Torrance, T. F. *The Doctrine of Grace in the Apostolic Fathers.* Grand Rapids: Eerdmans, 1959.

Traill, Robert. *Justification Vindicated.* 1692; Edinburgh: Banner of Truth, 2002.

Triglot Concordia: The Symbolical Books of the Evangelical Lutheran Church. Translated by F. Bente and W. H. T. Dau. St. Louis: Concordia, 1921.

Trueman, Carl R. *The Claims of Truth: John Owen's Trinitarian Theology*. Carlisle: Paternoster, 1998.

Turretin, Francis. *Institutes of Elenctic Theology*. Edited by James T. Dennison. Translated by George Musgrave Giger. 3 vols. Phillipsburg, NJ: P&R, 1992–97.

Ursinus, Zacharias. *The Commentary of Zacharias Ursinus on the Heidelberg Catechism*. Translated by G. W. Williard. 1852; Phillipsburg, NJ: P&R, n.d.

VanLandingham, Chris. *Judgment and Justification in Early Judaism and the Apostle Paul*. Peabody, MA: Hendrickson, 2006.

Van Til, Cornelius. *Christianity and Barthianism*. Philadelphia: P&R, 1962.

Venema, Cornelis P. *The Gospel of Free Acceptance in Christ: An Assessment of the Reformation and New Perspective on Paul*. Edinburgh: Banner of Truth, 2006.

Vermes, Geza, ed. *The Complete Dead Sea Scrolls in English*. New York: Penguin, 1997.

Vickers, Brian. *Jesus' Blood and Righteousness: Paul's Theology of Imputation*. Wheaton, IL: Crossway, 2006.

Vos, Geerhardus. *Biblical Theology*. 1948; Edinburgh: Banner of Truth, 1996.

———. *The Eschatology of the Old Testament*. Edited by James T. Dennison Jr. Phillipsburg, NJ: P&R, 2001.

———. *The Pauline Eschatology*. 1930; Phillipsburg, NJ: P&R, 1994.

———. *Grace and Glory*. 1922; Edinburgh: Banner of Truth, 1994.

———. *Redemptive History and Biblical Interpretation: The Shorter Writings of Geerhardus Vos*. Edited by Richard B. Gaffin Jr. Phillipsburg, NJ: P&R, 1980.

Wallace, Daniel B. *Greek Grammar beyond the Basics: An Exegetical Syntax of the New Testament*. Grand Rapids: Zondervan, 1996.

Waltke, Bruce K. *Genesis: A Commentary*. Grand Rapids: Zondervan, 2001.

Walton, John H. *Genesis*. NIVAC. Grand Rapids: Zondervan, 2001.

Wanamaker, Charles A. *The Epistles to the Thessalonians*. NIGTC. Grand Rapids: Eerdmans, 1990.

Ward, Rowland S. *God & Adam: Reformed Theology and the Creation Covenant*. Wantirna: New Melbourne Press, 2003.

Warfield, B. B. *Collected Shorter Writings*. Edited by John E. Meeter. 2 vols. 1970; Phillipsburg, NJ: P&R, 2001.

———. *The Works of B. B. Warfield*. Edited by Ethelbert D. Warfield et al. 10 vols. 1930; Grand Rapids: Baker, 1981.

Waters, Guy P. *The Federal Vision and Covenant Theology: A Comparative Analysis*. Phillipsburg, NJ: P&R, 2006.

———. *Justification and the New Perspectives on Paul: A Review and Response.* Phillipsburg, NJ: P&R, 2004.

Waters, Guy P., and Gary L. W. Johnson, eds. *By Faith Alone: Answering the Challenges to the Doctrine of Justification.* Wheaton, IL: Crossway, 2006.

Watson, Francis. *Paul and the Hermeneutics of Faith.* Edinburgh: T & T Clark, 2004.

Watts, Rikki E. *Isaiah's New Exodus in Mark.* Grand Rapids: Baker, 2001.

Weber, Otto. *Foundations of Dogmatics.* Translated by Darrell L. Guder. 2 vols. Grand Rapids: Eerdmans, 1981.

Wendel, François. *Calvin: Origins and Developments of His Religious Thought.* Translated by Philip Mairet. 1950; Grand Rapids: Baker, 1997.

Wenham, Gordon J. *Genesis.* WBC 1–2. Dallas: Word, 1987, 1994.

———. *Numbers.* TOTC. Downers Grove, IL: InterVarsity, 1981.

Westermann, Claus. *Genesis 1–11.* Translated by John J. Scullion. Minneapolis: Fortress, 1994.

Wilkins, Steve, and Duane Garner. *The Federal Vision.* Monroe, LA: St. Athanasius, 2004.

Witsius, Herman. *Economy of the Covenants between God and Man.* Translated by William Crookshank. 2 vols. 1822; Phillipsburg, NJ: P&R, 1990.

Wrede, Wilhelm. *Paul.* Translated by Edwards Lummis. Boston: American Unitarian Association, 1908.

Wright, N. T. *The Climax of the Covenant: Christ and the Law in Pauline Theology.* Minneapolis: Fortress, 1993.

———. *Colossians and Philemon.* TNTC. Grand Rapids: Eerdmans, 1986.

———. *Jesus and the Victory of God.* Minneapolis: Fortress, 1996.

———. *The New Testament and the People of God.* Minneapolis: Fortress, 1992.

———. *Paul: In Fresh Perspective.* Minneapolis: Fortress, 2005.

———. *Paul for Everyone: The Prison Letters, Ephesians, Philippians, Colossians, and Philemon.* London: SPCK, 2002.

———. *The Resurrection of the Son of God.* Minneapolis: Fortress, 2003.

———. *Romans.* NIB 10. Nashville: Abingdon, 2003.

———. *What Saint Paul Really Said: Was Paul of Tarsus the Real Founder of Christianity?* Grand Rapids: Eerdmans, 1997.

Yinger, Kent L. *Paul, Judaism, and Judgment according to Deeds.* Cambridge: Cambridge University Press, 1999.

Young, E. J. *The Book of Isaiah.* Vol. 3. 1972; Grand Rapids: Eerdmans, 1997.

Zimmerli, Walther. *Ezekiel 2.* Minneapolis: Fortress, 1983.

Articles

Abegg, Martin. "4QMMT, Paul, and 'Works of the Law.'" In *The Bible at Qumran: Text, Shape, and Interpretation*, edited by Peter W. Flint, 203–16. Grand Rapids: Eerdmans, 2001.

———. "Paul, 'Works of the Law' and MMT." *BAR* 20/6 (1994): 52–55.

Anderson, Gary A. "Intentional and Unintentional Sin in the Dead Sea Scrolls." In *Pomegranates and Golden Bells: Studies in Biblical, Jewish, and Near Eastern Ritual, Law, and Literature in Honor of Jacob Milgrom*, 49–64. Winona Lake, IN: Eisenbrauns, 1995.

Babcock, W. S. "Augustine and Paul: The Case of Romans 9." *StPatr* 16/2 (1985): 474–79.

Baur, F. C. "The Christ-Party in the Corinthian Church, the Conflict between Petrine and Pauline Christianity in the Early Church, the Apostle Peter in Rome." *Tübinger Zeitschrift für Theologie* 4 (1831): 61–206.

Bayer, Oswald. "Justification as the Basis and Boundary of Theology." *LQ* 15 (2001): 273–92.

Beale, G. K. "Garden-Temple." *Kerux* 18/2 (2003): 3–50.

———. "The New Testament and New Creation." In *Biblical Theology: Retrospect & Prospect*, edited by Scott J. Hafemann, 159–73. Downers Grove, IL: InterVarsity, 2002.

———. "The Old Testament Background of Reconciliation in 2 Corinthians 5–7 and Its Bearing on the Literary Problem of 2 Corinthians 6:14–7:1." *NTS* 35 (1989): 550–81.

Bellefontaine, Elizabeth. "The Curses of Deuteronomy 27: Their Relationship to the Prohibitives." In *A Song of Power and the Power of Song: Essays on the Book of Deuteronomy*, edited by Duane Christensen, 256–68. Winona Lake, IN: Eisenbrauns, 1993.

Bierma, Lyle D. "Federal Theology in the Sixteenth Century: Two Traditions?" *WTJ* 45 (1983): 304–21.

Block, Daniel I. "The Prophet of the Spirit: The Use of *rûᵃh* in the Book of Ezekiel." *JETS* 32/1 (1989): 27–49.

Bonner, Gerald. "Les origines africaines de la doctrine augustinienne sur la chute et le péché original." In *God's Decree and Destiny: Studies on the Thought of Augustine of Hippo*, 97–116. London: Variorum Reprints, 1987.

Breck, John. "Orthodox Principles of Biblical Interpretation." *SVTQ* 40/1–2 (1996): 77–93.

Bultmann, Rudolf. "New Testament and Mythology: The Problem of Demythologizing the New Testament Proclamation." In *New Testament & Mythology and Other Basic Writings*, edited by Schubert M. Ogden, 1–44. Minneapolis: Fortress, 1984.

Carson, D. A. "Atonement in Romans 3:21–26: God Presented Him as a Propitiation." In *The Glory of the Atonement*, edited by Charles E. Hill and Frank A. James, 119–39. Downers, Grove, IL: InterVarsity, 2004.

———. "Reflections on Christian Assurance." *WTJ* 54 (1992): 1–29.

———. "Reflections on Salvation and Justification in the New Testament." *JETS* 40/4 (1997): 581–608.

Casteel, Theodore W. "Calvin and Trent: Calvin's Reaction to the Council of Trent in the Context of His Conciliar Thought." *HTR* 63 (1970): 91–117.

Clark, R. Scott. "*Iustitia Imputata Aliena:* Alien or Proper to Luther's Doctrine of Justification?" *CTQ* 71 (2007): 269–310.

Coates, Thomas. "The Barthian Inversion: Gospel and Law." *Concordia Theological Monthly* 26 (1955): 481–91.

Cosgrove, C. H. "Justification in Paul: A Linguistic and Theological Reflection." *JBL* 106 (1987): 653–70.

Couenhoven, Jesse. "Law and Gospel, or the Law of the Gospel? Karl Barth's Political Theology Compared with Luther and Calvin." *JRE* 30 (2002): 181–205.

Donfried, Karl Paul. "Justification and the Last Judgment in Paul." *ZNW* 67 (1976): 90–110.

Dunn, James D. G. "4QMMT and Galatians." *NTS* 43 (1997): 147–53.

———. "Jesus—Flesh and Spirit: An Exposition of Romans 1:3–4." *JTS* 24 (1973): 40–68.

———. "Once More, *Pistis Christou.*" In *Pauline Theology*, edited by E. Elizabeth Johnson and David M. Hay, 4:61–81. Atlanta: Scholars Press, 1997.

———. "The New Perspective on Paul." *BJRL* 65 (1983): 95–122.

Ellis, E. Earle. "2 Corinthians 5:1–10 in Pauline Eschatology." *NTS* 6 (1959–60): 211–24.

Evans, Craig A. "How Are the Apostles Judged? A Note on 1 Corinthians 3:10–15." *JETS* 27 (1984): 149–50.

Fairbairn, Don. "Salvation as *Theosis:* The Teaching of Eastern Orthodoxy." *Them* 23/3 (1996): 42–54.

Fesko, J. V. "Calvin on Justification and Recent Misinterpretations of His View." *MAJT* 16 (2005): 83–114.

———. "A Critical Examination of N. T. Wright's Doctrine of Justification." *Confessional Presbyterian* 1 (2005): 102–16.

———. "N. T. Wright and the Works of the Law." *Faith & Mission* 22/1 (2004): 64–83.

———. "The Legacy of Old School Confession Subscription in the OPC." *JETS* 46/4 (2003): 673–98.

———. "N. T. Wright on Imputation." *RTR* 66/1 (2007): 2–22.

Fesko, J. V., and Guy M. Richard. "Natural Theology and the Westminster Confession." In *The Westminster Confession into the Twenty-first Century: Essays in Remembrance of the 250th Anniversary of the Westminster Assembly*. Vol. 3, edited by J. Ligon Duncan. Fearn, Scotland: Mentor, forthcoming.

Furnish, Victor P. "Theology in 1 Corinthians." In *Pauline Theology*, edited by David M. Hay, 2:59–89. Atlanta: SBL, 2002.

Futato, Mark D. "Because It Had Rained." *WTJ* 60/1 (1998): 1–21.

Gabler, Johann P. "An Oration on the Proper Distinction between Biblical and Dogmatic Theology and the Specific Objectives of Each." In *The Flowering of Old Testament Theology: A Reader in Twentieth-Century Old Testament Theology, 1930–90*, edited by Ben C. Ollenburger, Elmer A. Martens, and Gerhard F. Hasel, 492–502. Winona Lake, IN: Eisenbrauns, 1992.

Gaffin, Richard B., Jr. "Biblical Theology and the Westminster Standards." *WTJ* 65/2 (2003): 165–80.

———. "Paul the Theologian." *WTJ* 62/1 (2000): 121–41.

———. "Union with Christ: Biblical and Theological Reflections." In *Always Reforming: Explorations in Systematic Theology*, edited by A. T. B. McGowan, 271–88. Leicester: Apollos, 2006.

Gaston, L. "Abraham and the Righteousness of God." *HBT* 2 (1980): 39–68.

Harris, Murray J. "2 Corinthians 5:1–10: Watershed in Paul's Eschatology." *TynBul* 22 (1971): 32–57.

Hays, Richard B. "Adam, Israel, Christ: The Question of Covenant in the Theology of Romans: A Response to Leander E. Keck and N. T. Wright." In *Pauline Theology*, edited by David M. Hay and E. Elizabeth Johnson, 3:68–86. Minneapolis: Fortress, 1995.

Hodge, A. A. "The Ordo Salutis: Or, Relation in the Order of Nature of Holy Character and Divine Favor." *PR* 54 (1878): 304–21.

Hollander, Harm. "The Testing by Fire of the Builders' Works: 1 Cor. 3:10–15." *NTS* 40 (1994): 89–104.

Hooker, M. D. "Interchange in Christ." *JTS* 22 (1971): 349–61.

Horton, Michael. "Law, Gospel, and Covenant: Reassessing Some Emerging Antitheses." *WTJ* 64/2 (2002): 279–88.

Hunsinger, George. "An American Tragedy: Jonathan Edwards on Justification." *Modern Reformation* 13/4 (2004): 18–21.

———. "Dispositional Soteriology: Jonathan Edwards on Justification by Faith Alone." *WTJ* 66/1 (2004): 107–20.

Irons, Lee. "Redefining Merit: An Examination of Medieval Presuppositions in Covenant Theology." In *Creator, Redeemer, Consummator: A Festschrift for Meredith G. Kline*, edited by Howard Griffith and John R. Muether, 253–69. Greenville, SC: Reformed Academic Press, 2000.

Jeremias, Joachim. "Paul and James." *ExpTim* 66 (1954–55): 368–71.

John Paul II. "Trent: A Great Event in Church History." *The Pope Speaks* 40/5 (1995): 289–94.

Johnson, B. "Who Reckoned Righteousness to Whom?" *SEÅ* 51–52 (1986–87): 108–15.

Jüngel, Eberhard. "On the Doctrine of Justification." *IJST* 1/1 (1999): 24–52.

Käsemann, Ernst. "The Righteousness of God in Paul." *ZTK* 58 (1961): 367–78.

Kim, Seyoon. "2 Corinthians 5:11–21 and the Origin of Paul's Concept of 'Reconciliation.'" *NovT* 39 (1997): 360–84.

Kline, Meredith G. "Abram's Amen." *WTJ* 31/1 (1968–69): 1–11.

———. "Because It Had Not Rained." *WTJ* 20/2 (1958): 146–57.

———. "The First Resurrection." *WTJ* 37 (1975): 366–75.

———. "The First Resurrection: A Reaffirmation." *WTJ* 39 (1976): 110–19.

———. "Gospel until the Law: Rom. 5:13–14 and the Old Covenant." *JETS* 34/4 (1991): 433–46.

Lambrecht, Jan. "Final Judgments and Ultimate Blessings: The Climactic Visions of Revelation 20:11–21:8." *Bib* 83/3 (2000): 362–85.

Lincoln, Andrew T. "Ephesians 2:8–10: A Summary of Paul's Gospel." *CBQ* 45/4 (1983): 617–30.

Logan, Samuel T., Jr. "The Doctrine of Justification in the Theology of Jonathan Edwards." *WTJ* 46 (1984): 26–52.

Longenecker, Richard N. "The 'Faith of Abraham' Theme in Paul, James, and Hebrews: A Study in the Circumstantial Nature of New Testament Teaching." *JETS* 20 (1977): 53–61.

MacLeod, David J. "The Sixth 'Last Thing': The Last Judgment and the End of the World (Rev. 20:11–15)." *BSac* 157 (2000): 315–30.

McCartney, Dan G. "*Ecce Homo:* The Coming of the Kingdom as the Restoration of Human Viceregency." *WTJ* 56 (1994): 1–21.

McClymond, Michael J. "Salvation as Divinization: Jonathan Edwards, Gregory Palamas and the Theological Uses of Neoplatonism." In *Jonathan Edwards: Philosophical Theologian*, edited by Paul Helm and Oliver D. Crisp, 139–60. Aldershot: Ashgate, 2003.

McGrath, Alister. "Justification: Barth, Trent, and Küng." *SJT* 34/6 (1981): 517–29.

———. "Reality, Symbol and History: Theological Reflections on N. T. Wright's Portrayal of Jesus." In *Jesus and the Restoration of Israel: A Critical Reassessment of N. T. Wright's Jesus and the Victory of God*, edited by Carey C. Newman, 159–79. Downers Grove, IL: InterVarsity, 1999.

McNeil, Brian. "Raised for Our Justification." *ITQ* 43 (1975): 97–105.

Montefiore, Claude G. "Rabbinic Judaism and the Epistles of St. Paul." *JQR* 13/2 (1900–1901): 161–217.

Moo, Douglas J. "'Law,' 'Works of the Law,' and Legalism in Paul." *WTJ* 45/1 (1983): 73–100.

Moore, George Foot. "Christian Writers on Judaism." *HTR* 14/3 (1921): 197–254.

Packer, J. I. "The Doctrine of Justification among the Puritans." In *Puritan Papers*, edited by J. I. Packer, 5:147–62. Phillipsburg, NJ: P&R, 2005.

Pregeant, Russell. "Grace and Recompense: Reflections on a Pauline Paradox." *JAAR* 47 (1979): 73–96.

Reinhard, Donna R. "Ephesians 6:10–18: A Call to Personal Piety or Another Way of Describing Union with Christ?" *JETS* 48/3 (2005): 521–32.

Robertson, O. Palmer. "Genesis 15:6: New Covenant Expositions of an Old Covenant Text." *WTJ* 42 (1980): 259–89.

Schafer, Thomas A. "Jonathan Edwards and Justification by Faith." *CH* 20 (1951): 55–67.

Schreiner, Thomas. "Did Paul Believe in Justification by Works? Another Look at Romans 2." *BBR* 3 (1993): 131–58.

Sharp, Carolyn J. "Phinehan Zeal and Rhetorical Strategy in 4QMMT." *RevQ* 18/2 (1997): 207–22.

Snodgrass, Klyne R. "Justification by Grace—to the Doers: An Analysis of the Place of Romans 2 in the Theology of Paul." *NTS* 32 (1986): 72–93.

Stendahl, Krister. "The Apostle Paul and the Introspective Conscience of the West." *HTR* 56 (1963): 199–215.

Tamerius, Travis. "An Interview with N. T. Wright." *RRJ* 11/1 (2002): 117–40.

Tjørhom, Ola. "The Church the Place of Salvation: On the Interrelation between Justification and Ecclesiology." *ProEccl* 9 (2000): 285–96.

Trueman, Carl R. "Is the Finnish Line a New Beginning?" *WTJ* 65/2 (2002): 231–44.

———. "John Owen's *Dissertation on Divine Justice*: An Exercise in Christocentric Scholasticism." *CTJ* 33/1 (1998): 87–103.

———. "A Small Step towards Rationalism: The Impact of the Metaphysics of Tommaso Campanella on the Theology of Richard Baxter." In *Protestant Scholasticism: Essays in Reassessment*, edited by Carl Trueman and R. Scott Clark, 181–95. Carlisle: Paternoster, 1998.

Trumper, Tim J. R. "Covenant Theology and Constructive Calvinism." *WTJ* 64/2 (2002): 387–404.

———. Review of *The Federal Theology of Thomas Boston*, by A. T. B. McGowan. *WTJ* 62/1 (2000): 153–57.

VanDrunen, David. "A System of Theology? The Centrality of Covenant for Westminster Systematics." In *The Pattern of Sound Doctrine: Systematic Theology at the Westminster Seminaries. Essays in Honor of Robert B. Strimple*, edited by David VanDrunen, 195–222. Phillipsburg, NJ: P&R, 2004.

Van Til, Cornelius. "Introduction." In B. B. Warfield, *The Inspiration and Authority of the Bible*, edited by Samuel G. Craig, 3–70. Philadelphia: P&R, 1948.

Waddington, Jeffrey C. "Jonathan Edwards's 'Ambiguous and Somewhat Precarious' Doctrine of Justification?" *WTJ* 66/2 (2004): 357–72.

Wall, Robert W. "The Intertextuality of Scripture: The Example of Rahab (James 2:25)." In *The Bible at Qumran: Text, Shape, and Interpretation*, edited by Peter W. Flint, 217–36. Grand Rapids: Eerdmans, 2001.

Watson, Nigel. "Justified by Faith, Judged by Works—an Antinomy?" *NTS* 29 (1983): 209–21.

Wenger, Thomas L. "The New Perspective on Calvin: Responding to Recent Calvin Interpretations." *JETS* 50/2 (2007): 311–28.

Wenham, Gordon J. "Sanctuary Symbolism in the Garden of Eden Story." In *I Studied Inscriptions from Before the Flood: Ancient Near Eastern, Literary, and Linguistic Approaches to Genesis 1–11*, edited by Richard S. Hess and David Toshio Tsumura, 19–25. Sources for Biblical and Theological Study 4. Winona Lake, IN: Eisenbrauns, 1994.

Williams, Sam K. "Justification and the Spirit in Galatians." *JSNT* 29 (1987): 91–100.

Wisse, Maarten. "*Habitus Fidei*: An Essay on the History of a Concept." *SJT* 56 (2003): 172–89.

Wright, N. T. "Justification." In *New Dictionary of Theology*, edited by Sinclair B. Ferguson, David F. Wright, and J. I. Packer, 359–61. Downers Grove, IL: InterVarsity, 1988.

———. "The Law in Romans 2." In *Paul and the Mosaic Law*, edited by James D. G. Dunn, 131–50. Grand Rapids: Eerdmans, 2001.

———. "The Letter to the Galatians: Exegesis and Theology." In *Between Two Horizons: Spanning New Testament Studies and Systematic Theology*, edited by Joel B. Green and Max Turner, 205–36. Grand Rapids: Eerdmans, 2002.

———. "On Becoming the Righteousness of God: 2 Corinthians 5:21." In *Pauline Theology*, edited by David M. Hay, 2:200–8. Atlanta: SBL, 2002.

———. "Paul and Qumran." *BRev* 14/5 (1998): 18–22, 54.

———. "The Paul of History and the Apostle of Faith." *TynBul* 29 (1978): 61–88.

———. "Romans and the Theology of Paul." In *Pauline Theology*, edited by David M. Hay and E. Elizabeth Johnson, 3:30–67. Minneapolis: Fortress, 1995.

Unpublished Sources

Van Til, Cornelius. "St. Thomas and Calvin." At Calvin College, n.d.

Wright, N. T. "New Perspectives on Paul." 10th Edinburgh Dogmatics Conference, Rutherford House, 25–28 August 2003.

INDEX OF SCRIPTURE

439

INDEX OF SUBJECTS AND NAMES

J. V. Fesko (MA, theology, Southwestern Baptist Theological Seminary, Fort Worth, Texas; Ph.D., theology, the University of Aberdeen, Scotland) is an adjunct professor of theology at Reformed Theological Seminary in Atlanta. He is also the pastor at Geneva Orthodox Presbyterian Church in Woodstock, Georgia.

Dr. Fesko has written numerous theological articles, has contributed to *Justification: A Report from the Orthodox Presbyterian Church*, and is a volume editor (with Bryan Estelle and David VanDrunen) of *The Law Is Not of Faith*. He is also the author of *Last Things First* and *Diversity within the Reformed Tradition*.